CHARLES DARWIN

Voyaging

Charles Darwin, around 1857

CHARLES DARWIN

VOYAGING

VOLUME I OF A BIOGRAPHY

JANET BROWNE

 Alfred A. Knopf   New York   1995

THIS IS A BORZOI BOOK
PUBLISHED BY ALFRED A. KNOPF, INC.

Copyright © 1995 by Janet Browne
All rights reserved under International and Pan-American
Copyright Conventions. Published in the United States by
Alfred A. Knopf, Inc., New York, and simultaneously in Canada
by Random House of Canada Limited, Toronto.
Distributed by Random House, Inc., New York. Published
in Great Britain by Jonathan Cape, Ltd., London.

Library of Congress Cataloging-in-Publication Data
Browne, E. J. (E. Janet).
Charles Darwin / by Janet Browne.—1st American ed.
p. cm.
Includes bibliographical references and index.
Contents: v. 1. Voyaging.
ISBN 0-394-57942-9 (v. 1)
1. Darwin, Charles, 1809–1882. 2. Naturalists—England—
Biography. I. Title.
QH31.D2B84 1995
575'.0092—dc20
[B]   94-6598   CIP

Manufactured in the United States of America

FIRST EDITION

"Never mind about his genius, Mr. Pesca. We don't want genius in this country, unless it is accompanied by respectability."

—Wilkie Collins, *The Woman in White*

Introduction

Some people called him an evil genius. Others just said he was a genius. Still, they unanimously saluted his brainpower. No other thinker shook Victorian England as deeply as Charles Darwin with his theory of evolution by natural selection. But Darwin was the most unspectacular person of all time, a man known to his contemporaries as a quiet, methodical worker, devoted to his family, hard to prise out of his house in the country, averse to ostentation, utterly conventional in his behaviour, modest and unassuming about his results. His personality did not seem to match the incisive brilliance other people saw in his writings.

Even Darwin sometimes wondered how he had done it. How had he, apparently one of the most ordinary of men, produced one of the most radical books of the nineteenth century and turned the society of his day upside down? The personal qualities he spelled out in his autobiography seemed to him insufficient for the changes his theories had introduced. "I have no great quickness of apprehension or wit," he confessed at the end of his life. "My power to follow a long abstract train of thought is very limited . . . my memory is extensive but hazy." He was too gullible to be a real scientist, he thought ruefully. No one else spent his old age investigating whether plants could hear a bassoon.

Looking back, he was equally surprised by the amount of work he had carried out over the years, bemused by the prominence his *Origin of Species* had brought. Other men, including Alfred Russel Wallace, Herbert Spencer, Robert Chambers, Jean Baptiste Lamarck, and his own grandfather Erasmus Darwin, had all proposed theories of evolution. A handful more claimed to have thought of natural selection before him. So why did Cardinal Manning denounce him alone for relieving God of the "labour of creation," or his friend William Whewell deny his book a place on the shelves of Trinity College library? Why did Carlyle quip that his ideas were rather a humiliating discovery and the less said about them the better? Darwin could understand Oxford students dangling a monkey from the roof of the Senate House when he went to receive an honorary degree: it was the same response to his work that led Edward Bulwer Lytton, in *What Will He Do With It?*, to lampoon him as Professor Long, the author of two huge volumes on limpets; and Charles Kingsley to put the moral question of animal ancestry at the satirical heart of the *Water Babies* ("If you have a hippopotamus major in your brain, you are no ape"). He was amused enough by the caricatures appearing in *Punch* and elsewhere to collect some of them at home.

He was far more perplexed about the adulation and abuse raining down in equal portions. Vicars thundered against him from pulpits all over Britain, while American theologians wrestled with the contradictions between his words and the Bible. Elizabeth Gaskell made him the romantic hero of *Wives and Daughters* at the same time as Madame Blavatsky contemptuously put a copy of the *Origin* under the arm of a stuffed baboon to signify the anti-Darwinian route theosophy would take, and the *Daily Telegraph* urged the electors of Southwark not to return Henry Fawcett to Parliament because he had reviewed the *Origin* favourably. Darwin's book certainly made him a scientific star. Yet he felt uncomfortable about this celebrity, about the endless unsolicited letters from stonemasons and schoolboys, from Gladstone, Marx, and "A Gorilla"; and was baffled by people's wanting to name their sons after him. Tourists—some of them just as famous as he was—called at his house hoping to catch a glimpse of him. Later on, Leslie Stephen dubbed him "a noble old hero of science." And in the end, an unknown admirer (appropriately called Mr. Rich) left him a handsome fortune in his will as a mark of his esteem.

All this for a man who did not use the word "evolution" in the modern sense until the last edition of the *Origin* published in his lifetime. Not even the phrase "survival of the fittest" was coined by him. "With such moderate abilities as I possess, it is truly surprising that thus I should have influenced to a considerable extent the beliefs of scientific men on some important points." How had it become Darwin's century?

The question still remains a puzzle today. Although more has been said or written about Charles Darwin than about any other scientist, and great libraries of his books and papers have been established in England and America, his house turned into a museum, and collections of his manu-scripts brought together at considerable cost, the individual behind the fuss remains elusive. Clearly he was not nearly as dull as he maintained, nor was he quite the burnished icon that Victorians and subsequent writers created.

His autobiography and the path of history itself have thrown up a smoke screen almost as effective as if no records had been left behind at all.[1]

One answer surely lies in the intricate relations between a man, his ideas, and the public. Darwinism was made by Darwin *and* Victorian society. Yet for all the continuing interest in Darwin's work and personality, remarkably little attention has been paid to the way he lived out his life on this interface: to his life as a gentleman-naturalist in an age when science first became prominent in British society, as a friend of eminent men, a traveller, husband, and father, a best-selling author, a dedicated experimenter, and a shawl-clad Victorian invalid. Many modern books, in fact, portray him as a relatively uncomplicated person, taking him as he liked to see himself. Others tend to search out a sense of purpose, an intellectual consistency, that did not always exist; or detect an inner torment that similarly seems exaggerated. Few attempt to paint a picture his wife or friends might recognise.

And all of them cover the last twenty years of his existence in a few short chapters, as if, after the account of the writing of the *Origin,* there were nothing more to say.[2] But like most people, Darwin was more complicated than he thought and changed in several significant ways as he grew older. What kind of man could write the *Origin of Species* and the *Descent of Man,* then start watching worms?

Darwin's own opinion of himself was characteristically mild. "I was born a naturalist," he stated in his reminiscences, as if that explained everything. "My love of natural science has been steady and ardent."[3]

In some sense there was little else he could have said. Darwin's love affair with nature dominated his life, as he freely acknowledged, always drawing him on to look further and more intently than other men at the world around him. He was "all eyes," as his medical friend Edward Lane once said, so alert to the intricacies of living beings and their relationships with their surroundings that explaining nature's ways became the self-imposed task of a lifetime— his despair and delight. The effort to understand nature was the thread that held his existence together.

Yet none of the influential thinkers, scientists, and philosophers of any historical period were "born" in this simple sense. Because Darwin believed in the Victorian ethos of character—in the inbuilt advantages of mind—and unconsciously endorsed the cult of great men and public heroes that was so much a part of nineteenth-century life, he did not—could not—see that figures like himself were the product of a complex interweaving of personality and opportunity with the movements of the times. Scientific ideas and scientific fame did not come automatically to people who worked hard and collected insects, as Darwin seems to have half hoped they would. A love of natural history could not, on its own, take a governess or a mill-worker to the top of the nineteenth-century intellectual tree. Nor can it, on its own, explain Darwin.

Darwin's self-assessment, too, was unavoidably subject to the literary and scientific conventions of the time. His autobiographical recollections, written for his family in 1876, six years before he died, tell us hardly anything about the issues that tantalise modern readers. He shrank from analysing motives and found it hard to give "the true key to my whole life," as John Henry Newman did. "I have never tried looking into my own mind," he told his cousin Francis Galton bleakly in answer to a questionnaire sent to him at roughly the same time.[4] He did not write his autobiography to settle old scores or to find personal insight for the future; nor did he try to justify the natural-history passions that ruled his mental world, not even to his wife, Emma, who spent most of her own life excluded from those innermost affairs. For all Darwin's well-known and likable transparency, his heart remained resolutely private. His autobiography was just as much an exercise in camouflage—a disguise—as it was a methodical laying out of the bare bones of his existence.

Inevitably, the things he left unsaid in this autobiography are the most revealing. Behind Darwin lay the vast unacknowledged support system of the Victorian gentry, and beyond that the farflung network of imperial, colonial Britain. He was born a wealthy child in a socially secure, well-connected family. His father was a rich physician and his mother a daughter of Josiah Wedgwood, the potter; his grandfathers on both sides were noted for their contributions to science, philosophy, and technology. He possessed many advantages in life, including an education at the best institutions Britain had to offer. The friends he made at Cambridge University proved influential figures over the years, especially in the way they generated an invitation for him to join the *Beagle*'s expedition round the world and then eased his entrance into London's scientific circles after his return. Soon after that return, Darwin married one of his Wedgwood cousins, who provided all the secure comforts of a sedately upper-class, countrified existence. Darwin was not an easy person to live with from a wife's point of view, and Emma Wedgwood, like the respectable Victorian woman she was, sacrificed many of her personal expectations so that he could devote his thoughts to science.

It is also clear that an extraordinary number of people were drawn one way or another into Darwin's scientific projects. His *Beagle* contemporaries, his wife, friends, and neighbours, a wide variety of colonial correspondents, pigeon fanciers, cousins, aunts, and nephews, local gardeners, country squires, the family butler, Darwin's children, other people's children, the village vicar, university professors, botanical and physiological experts, medical men, and unsuspecting household pets—all these were vital accessories in furthering the progress of his evolutionary researches. Darwin's work was entirely a social process in this sense, and the "facts" he collected represented a collaborative endeavour fully documented in his extensive correspondence.[5] Darwin did not simply sit in the middle of Victorian society soaking up the overriding themes of the age. On the contrary, Victorian society made him. He built his theories out of information physically extracted from others. He knew how to charm, how to make people help him. And the collaboration was always hierarchical, with Darwin acting as a greedy spider, throwing out a thread here, pulling in a fly there. He was a "miser with facts," he gloated in middle age, accumulating them like treasure trove. By no means can the *Origin* be seen as an individual triumph.

Furthermore, when the *Origin* was published, it was not Darwin but his scientific friends who took the brunt of defending the idea of evolution in public. Without Thomas Henry Huxley acting as a pugnacious bulldog to his stay-at-home Labrador, Darwin would have been lost in the ensuing conflict; and prominent figures like Joseph Hooker, Alfred Russel Wallace, Charles Lyell, and the Harvard botanist Asa Gray, who each had serious misgivings about some part of Darwin's theory or other, willingly picked up their cudgels on his behalf. Even Darwin's notorious illnesses were excused and glamorised by his contemporaries as the penalty of intellect: characteristic, it was believed, of the deeply thoughtful group of eminent men to which he belonged. As Darwin sheepishly admitted, continuous ill health "saved me from the distractions of society and amusement."

Darwin's real life, in short, belies the common view of him as an isolated recluse. There was a sliver of ice inside enabling him to make the most of all the advantages he possessed and the circumstances in which he found himself. Though he was often alone with his theories, morbidly turning over the ideas of death and struggle on which the concept of natural selection was based, frequently unable to cope with the pressures of publication and fearful of the controversies that were bound to follow, deliberately avoiding the demands of social engagements, almost bored with fame towards the end, and only too keen to close the study door safely behind him or to retreat to his greenhouse, he was also, in another sense, propped up by British society. His story is the story of the era—of the different ways in which a man could emerge as a profound thinker in Victorian Britain, of the way that someone could take up and turn around the assumptions of the age and become a hero for doing so. It is the story of the transformation, in a particular time and place, of an amiable but rather aimless young man into a scientific giant whose intellectual heights have scarcely ever been rivalled.

He was no more "born a naturalist" than he was a sailor or politician.

DARWIN

William Alvey = Jane Brown
Darwin | 1746–1835
1726–1783

John
1730–1805

Elizabeth Collier = Erasmus Darwin = Mary How
Pole | 1731–1802 | 1740–177
1747–1832

Charles
1758–177

Robert Waring
1724–1816

Edward
1782–1829

Erasmus
1759–179

Samuel Fox = Ann
1765–1851 | 1777–1859

Samuel Tertius = Frances Violetta
Galton | 1783–1874
1783–1844

Mary Ann
1802–1829

Elizabeth
1808–1906

Emma
1784–1818

William A
b. 1767

Eliza
1801–1886

Lucy
1809–1848

Francis
Sacheveral
1786–1859

Elizabeth
1763–176

Emma
1803–1885

Millicent
1810–1883

John
1787–1818

Henry Parker = Marianne
1788–1856 | 1798–185

William Darwin
1805–1880

Harriot
1790–1825

Robert
b. 1825

Frances
b. 1806

Emma
1811–1904

Henry
1827–1892

Julia
b. 1809

Darwin
1814–1903

Francis
1829–1871

Charles
b. 1831

Erasmus
1815–1909

Mary Susan
1836–1893

Louisa Jane Butler = Francis
1822–1911

William
Erasmus
1839–1914

Anne Elizabeth
1841–1851

Mary Eleanor
b. 1842

Henrietta
Emma (Etty)
1843–1930

George
Howar
1845–▶

WEDGWOOD

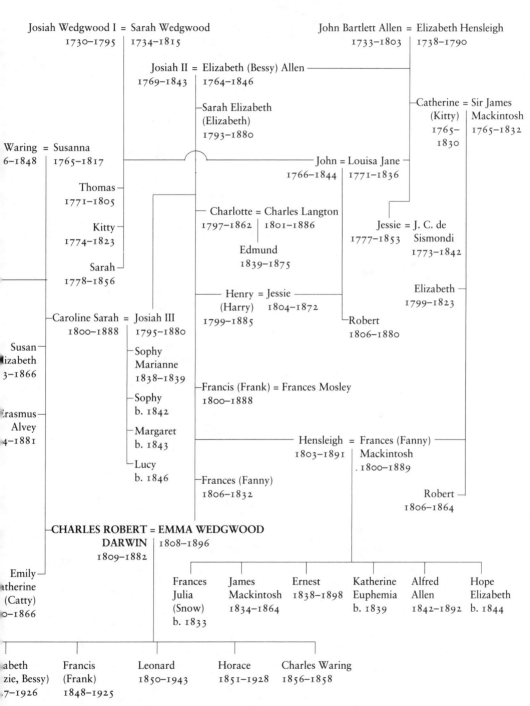

Josiah Wedgwood I = Sarah Wedgwood
1730–1795 | 1734–1815

John Bartlett Allen = Elizabeth Hensleigh
1733–1803 | 1738–1790

Josiah II = Elizabeth (Bessy) Allen
1769–1843 | 1764–1846

Sarah Elizabeth (Elizabeth)
1793–1880

Catherine = Sir James
(Kitty) | Mackintosh
1765– | 1765–1832
1830

Waring = Susanna
6–1848 | 1765–1817

Thomas
1771–1805

Kitty
1774–1823

Sarah
1778–1856

John = Louisa Jane
1766–1844 | 1771–1836

Charlotte = Charles Langton
1797–1862 | 1801–1886

Edmund
1839–1875

Jessie = J. C. de
1777–1853 | Sismondi
1773–1842

Henry = Jessie
(Harry) 1804–1872
1799–1885

Robert
1806–1880

Elizabeth
1799–1823

Caroline Sarah = Josiah III
1800–1888 | 1795–1880

Susan
lizabeth
3–1866

Sophy
Marianne
1838–1839

Sophy
b. 1842

Margaret
b. 1843

Lucy
b. 1846

rasmus
Alvey
4–1881

Francis (Frank) = Frances Mosley
1800–1888

Hensleigh = Frances (Fanny)
1803–1891 | Mackintosh
. 1800–1889

Frances (Fanny)
1806–1832

Robert
1806–1864

CHARLES ROBERT = EMMA WEDGWOOD
DARWIN | 1808–1896
1809–1882

Emily
atherine
(Catty)
0–1866

Frances
Julia
(Snow)
b. 1833

James
Mackintosh
1834–1864

Ernest 1838–1898

Katherine
Euphemia
b. 1839

Alfred
Allen
1842–1892

Hope
Elizabeth
b. 1844

abeth
zie, Bessy)
7–1926

Francis
(Frank)
1848–1925

Leonard
1850–1943

Horace
1851–1928

Charles Waring
1856–1858

COLLECTOR

BOBBY

E was born into Jane Austen's England. Indeed, the Darwins could have stepped straight out of the pages of *Emma,* the four girls sharply intelligent about the foibles of others, their father as perceptive as Mr. Knightley. The boys had several equally distinctive qualities. Charles Darwin and his older brother, Erasmus, were obliging and sympathetic young men full of the gentle humour, domestic attachments, and modest tastes that made Austen's characters stand out in the drawing rooms of local notables, with a good range of idiosyncratic failings to match. These natural attributes were enhanced by a substantial family fortune. Like sensible Mr. Weston with his warm heart and easy financial circumstances, the two were general favourites: "always acceptable," as Emma Woodhouse said of Weston. Behind the scenes presided Mrs. Darwin, a clever, well-educated woman, at one time a friend of the novelist Maria Edgeworth, who now led a retired life, the female counterpart to Mr. Woodhouse, "never quite well & never very ill," according to her sister Kitty.

The Darwins, like Austen's fictional families, lived in a sleepy market town in the countryside, in their case in Shrewsbury, the county capital of Shropshire, standing on the River Severn halfway between the manufacturing Midlands and Wales. Further downstream in the Severn Gorge smouldered William Hazledine's ironworks, the driving force of the Industrial Revolution. Upstream sat the smoking chimneys of the Potteries. But Shrewsbury itself was untouched by any signs of industrial change. The big black-and-white houses of Tudor wool merchants lined the narrow streets leading up to an old marketplace, eventually giving way to a castle and well-established "public" school for boys, while all around the bottom of the hill curved the river and its meadows, enclosing the town, as Daniel Defoe said, in the form of a horseshoe. It was a fine place to live, thought Defoe: a "large, pleasant, populous, and rich town; full of gentry and yet full of trade too."

This quiet provincial capital enclosed the Darwin family and others like them in a genteel, self-contained world defined in social terms by the landed gentlemen of neighbouring estates and wealthy manufacturers. Books and letters, newspapers, country walks, sewing, riding, painting, proper English talk about the weather, and debates about current affairs with like-minded friends were punctuated by regular visits to cousins and music festivals in nearby towns. "We are going on much in our usual hum drum style," wrote one of these friends: "a little hunting, a little shooting & now and then a little argument about the Reform Bill." Science—or natural philosophy, as it was then called—was very much a part of this culture. The Darwins kept abreast of all the latest improvements in factory technology and—the women included—were familiar with many of the leading scientific concepts of the age from their varied reading. Fireside discussions were as likely to range over recent changes in interpreting chemical phenomena, pottery glazes, or the classification of plants as they were to dissect *Rob Roy* or consider a collection of scenic prints. When talk on these subjects was exhausted, one or another of the sisters would read novels or improving literature aloud.

Their entertainments were just as sedate. "Balls, suppers, oyster-feasts, meets of hounds, an occasional visit from a party of strolling players," made up the winter's festivities, complained Eliza Meteyard, who spent her early years in Shrewsbury before escaping to London. The Darwins avidly followed the course of local elections, charitable movements, and parliamentary reform, attended dances, and speculated endlessly about marriages forged between branches of the Shropshire gentry. They went to dine at the great houses of the county during the season and gave their own parties in return. Still, "it is not the custom in this town," wrote Mrs. Darwin in surprise to her brother in Staffordshire, "to give dinners in summer." As consolation, they saw plays on tour from London, rode out to picturesque Welsh castles, and, on one memorable occasion, watched the militia performing exercises on the field opposite their house during the victory celebrations for Waterloo. The Darwin children were far too level-headed to think of running away to join them.

So, although Charles Darwin eventually became an archetypal Victorian, giving his name to a revolution in nineteenth-century thought and emerging as a figure as fully representative of the new age as Gladstone, Tennyson, or Dickens, his roots were embedded in a notably different context. The distinctive aura of late Georgian times left an indelible mark. Darwin's first and most formative experiences of life were politely Regency in spirit, seasoned with the vigorous intellectual activity of the early years of the Industrial Revolution.

These experiences, as for Austen and others of similarly high social standing, were of course far more rumbustious than the miniaturised lives of three or four families in a country village. The Darwins may have been sedate, but they lived through a period of extraordinary vitality and change in Britain—in politics, in social relations, in art and literature, in science, agriculture, trade, and manufacture. From the time of the American Revolution to the trial of Queen Caroline and the dramatic Cato Street conspiracy in 1820, there were hardly any other years in British history so full of contrasts, political uncertainties, and booming commercial expansion. Revolution and terror in Paris, the long-drawn-out wars with Napoleonic France, ardent radicalism at home, grain riots, crippling taxes, "gagging bills" in Parliament, and unparalleled antagonisms within English society suddenly made the prospect of civil strife—even bloody revolt—possible. It seemed as if the country was as close to internal rebellion as when Oliver Cromwell challenged the crown.

At the same time, new technology was transforming the national economy and landscape: factories and mills sprouted deep in the backbones of England and Scotland; iron, coal, textile, and pottery works inched through the Midlands; canals and bridges sliced the land; close-packed houses in terraced streets began altering the faces of towns like Birmingham, Derby, and Newcastle. Not yet fully encompassing either Blake's satanic visions or the belch of Coketown, and markedly regional in nature, these early industrial concerns stood witness to a new kind of machine- and goods-based future.

With them came extraordinary riches for the privileged few. Nothing the frame-breakers could do would alter the rapid acceleration towards modern capitalism and consumer culture characterising high society in late Georgian times. Despite the fact that Napoleon was actively gathering up Europe, the success of Trafalgar still rang in complacent British ears. Despite also the fact that the rolling northern landscape revealed the dramatic effects of enclosure and the beginnings of industrial expansion, the social repercussions of these fundamental changes barely impinged on the world the affluent landed classes knew. Regency London was the brightest, most opulent city in Europe: Edmund Kean was acting at Drury Lane; Lord Byron reading *Childe Harold* to swooning society ladies; Keats walking from Hampstead across the fields to Lisson Grove to visit the painter Benjamin Haydon; great commercial magnates like Josiah Wedgwood, Richard Arkwright, and Jedediah Strutt enjoying prodigious incomes from the sale of their fancy goods and turning themselves into landed gentlemen; the Prince Regent himself endlessly busy devising grandiose rebuilding schemes or seeking emotional release from the sobriety of his father's court.

Britain was becoming the first industrial nation: a nation of shopkeepers, according to Napoleon; of manufacturers and customers; of culture, taste, and elegance at one level; of fistfights and seditious literature at another. Its people were restlessly innovative, a Prometheus unbound.[1]

Few families were so well poised to take advantage of this changing world as the Darwins of Shrewsbury.

II

Charles Robert Darwin was born on 12 February 1809, the fifth child of Susanna and Robert Waring Darwin of The Mount, a large Georgian house overlooking the bend in the river with gardens running down to water meadows and the town beyond.[2] In one of those odd coincidences of history, Abraham Lincoln was born on the same day; Tennyson and Gladstone were born a few months later. His father was a prosperous physician, one of three practising in Shrewsbury, his mother a daughter of Josiah Wedgwood, the founder of the china company and an influential Staffordshire entrepreneur. They called their infant son "Bobby."

Darwin's parents typified everything that is known about the emergent entrepreneurial society of early industrial England, a classic example of the way wealthy members of the professional and manufacturing classes created a significant niche for themselves in a changing world.[3] But it is important to emphasise how far this social movement had already advanced by the time Darwin was born. His parents—grandparents even—considered themselves an integral part of the landed gentry: a readily recognisable upper stratum peculiar to British society firmly based on the ownership of land, usually through many generations, and accompanied by political and local commitments which counted for a great deal in the corridors of power. Not quite aristocrats, although frequently intermarrying with the aristocracy, the landed gentry of Britain considered themselves several notches higher than most industrialists or country doctors or lawyers, although, again, frequently intermarrying with them. They belonged to the ruling classes, even if they did not necessarily rule.[4] In a culture where finely nuanced distinctions between classes governed social behaviour, these notches meant everything. Dr. Darwin was solidly respectable, with brothers, cousins, a father, and an uncle well established in the gentlemanly upper reaches of medicine and the law. His family, furthermore, owned estates in Lincolnshire and Nottinghamshire and had been members of the English provincial gentry for generations. He carried heraldic arms dating from the sixteenth century. *Cave et aude* ran the motto: "Watch and listen."

The Wedgwood family was altogether richer, more fashionable, more part of the intellectual *beau monde,* or as the Darwin girls sometimes put it, the "rising *ton.*" The first Josiah Wedgwood moved in high society, courting aristocratic clients for his chinaware, running stylish showrooms in London, and creating sensational dinner services for the queen: one of the first leaders of public taste to emerge in the eighteenth century and one quick to invest his profits in the traditional finery of a large house and grounds in the countryside. Wedgwood's unerring commercial eye, as well as his support for philanthropic, scientific, and artistic causes, ensured that his daughter Susanna grew up more or less in the centre of British intellectual life. She knew Coleridge through her brother Tom Wedgwood, and Southey and Edgeworth, as well as Priestley, Flaxman, and Reynolds. George Stubbs painted her portrait just before her marriage: an equestrian family group, in which the horses, grumbled old Josiah, were better likenesses than the children. This Wedgwood connection, long-standing social respectability, and Dr. Darwin's medical success gave an indisputable upper-class gloss to the couple's position in Shrewsbury society.

Dr. Darwin was also an astute financier, a new kind of private investor appearing in response to commercial expansion and changing forms of financial opportunity brought about by manufacturing and technological developments in Britain.[5] Carefree young "Bobby"—the precursor to the shrewd economist of the natural world who became Charles Darwin—grew up in an atmosphere imbued with the principles of financial adaptation to circumstances, of investment, returns, and profit.

The doctor, in fact, was one of the first capitalists of the modern era; yet, unlike Josiah Wedgwood or any other better-documented figure, he was neither a manufacturer nor a proprietor.[6] Dr. Darwin specialised in private money-broking. At a time when factory and mill owners were rarely themselves men of capital and Britain's banking structure was only rudimentary, individual proprietors or business partners often found it difficult to raise the circulating capital needed for large-scale works like canals and roads. They depended on investors from the professional sector, on men normally hidden from history like Dr. Darwin who were prepared to move money from fixed reserves, such as land, into the fluid stock of manufacturing companies.[7] Dr. Darwin went further than most in the way he also acted as a financial middle man, arranging loans and raising cash for other local gentlemen who themselves wished to join the investors' market. Medicine and money in this sense went well together. He particularly favoured mortgages, a straightforward device for people to borrow large sums on the security of land or housing. Returns took the form of quarterly interest payments or a percentage of the profit. Within a few short years, the existence of this kind of flexible paper wealth—as distinct from the fields and stately country houses of squires and aristocrats—became a crucial element in supporting the new industrial society.

The risks, however, were as great as the profits were enticing. Dr. Darwin was careful: ruthless. He did not spread himself too widely. Arriving in Shrewsbury in 1787 with medical degrees from Edinburgh and Leiden and two small inheritances from his mother and an aunt, he first put his capital into housing, buying the freehold of several buildings in the town. The story much repeated among the family that there was only £20 in his pocket was apocryphal, though apt in its implied tribute to his ability to make money. Then, using the income from high rents, he moved into some of the big commercial ventures of the age, particularly the construction of new roads and canals. He was, for example, a major stockholder in the Trent and Mersey Canal running past the Wedgwood china factory, and an investor in the Holyhead Road, built by Thomas Telford, both of which opened up the manufacturing areas of Britain for increasing trade. Telford, who lived in Shrewsbury for a while, undoubtedly knew his backer by repute, if not personally, and may have provided him with other investment opportunities. Dr. Darwin certainly went on to support the Ellesmere Canal, linking the major river systems of the northwest, and the cast-iron bridges spanning the Severn and the Menai Straits that marked the culmination of Telford's career.[8]

His close connection with the Wedgwood pottery company provided further income: Mrs. Darwin's share of the family assets included a fifth of the Etruria Works and an inheritance of £25,000 on the death of Josiah Wedgwood in 1795. Some of this extra capital went into agricultural land: the doctor bought two large farms in Lincolnshire and rented them out to tenants at a healthy profit. More canal companies were added to the portfolio. But at this point avarice took over. Not content with personal investments, old farmland and new farmland, and a long list of local gentlemen contracted to pay interest on loans, Dr. Darwin took legal action against his stepmother and stepbrothers after his father's death in 1802 for full rights to another farm in the same area. Only partly successful, the case ran in and out of his financial papers for years, aggravating his temper fully as much as the gout he also began complaining about. He spent several hours a week contacting elderly spinster aunts and crossly poring over genealogical charts sent up from Lincolnshire to prove his argument. In the process he became expert in Darwin family history. Bloodlines and their monetary counterpart of family inheritance preoccupied his later days.

Only a third of his annual income, therefore, ever came from medical fees: about £3,000 in a good year. The greater part, as his account books show, was grounded in dividends on securities, in stocks and bonds, in rents and the interest on mortgages raised on local property.[9] He had a remarkable head for business.

Robert Waring Darwin's obvious commitment to the progress and profits of a new kind of Britain reflected politics that were equally entrepreneurial, and philosophical views tending to materialism. He was a Whig by upbringing and inclination, vehemently anti-Tory and critical of aristocrats whose fortunes were rooted in hereditary privilege, at heart probably an atheist. With views such as these he sometimes seemed ill placed in Shrewsbury, which by custom favoured "king and country" and was for centuries an enclave of Tory royalists. Writing to his brother-in-law Josiah Wedgwood, the second in the family of that name, he had nothing kind to say about the "indigent aristocracy" who worried about increases in the poor rate; he, by contrast, hoped "to change this proud idle town into a busy manufactory."[10] The Mount was a house full of strong liberal sentiment.

Nevertheless, beliefs like these did not brand him an English Jacobin or make him a political revolutionary scheming to overthrow the aristocracy. Dr. Darwin was as nimble-footed politically as he was financially. He put his faith in the idea of reform through legislation, and strong private opinions did not stop him encouraging professional relations with local Tory peers and churchgoing squires. There were plenty such among his medical practice.

Nor did he have any qualms about propping them up financially. Shropshire gentlemen queued up to consult Dr. Darwin for nonmedical reasons. Discretion was always assured. For fifty years he was the most significant financier in the region, finding sufficient capital in 1837 to lend Lord Berwick the sum of £10,200 outright and provide Viscount Clive with a mortgage for £15,000 on the Llewyn estate. Others on his financial list during the same year included Richard Corfield, whom he lent £1,000; Mr. Pinney, at £2,432; and Mr. Corbett, at £2,000. The Shrewsbury Infant School borrowed a few hundred. Financial support also went into public buildings like the town hall, the waterworks, the county gaol, and the infirmary; and it is likely he provided the capital for a new lunatic asylum, even though a rival medical man was the consulting physician in charge.

By the time the doctor died in 1848, he was worth a great deal, excluding his wife's private trust fund—on a level with the merchant princes of the era. The estate of his brother-in-law, the second Josiah Wedgwood, came to £150,000; Richard Arkwright's property ran to £500,000; and Robert Owen's share of the profits on New Lanark amounted to £128,000. Dr. Darwin left £223,759.[11] It was not said lightly that he owned three-quarters of Shrewsbury and knew the medical secrets of the rest.

In 1798 he decided to have his own house built in a style appropriate to this social prominence. The Mount was finished in 1800, and there Susanna and Robert Waring Darwin lived for the rest of their lives.

III

Into this affluent, forward-looking household came Charles Darwin, a dreamy, grey-eyed, thickset child, intent on his own thoughts behind a shock of brown hair, but warm-hearted and loving for all that. He was not good-looking in the conventional sense, for the square boyish face was blighted by a nose inherited from the doctor, almost too adult—"like a farmer," someone said— for a young boy. Darwin did not grow into this nose until he was much older and was always slightly embarrassed about it, his later jokes revealing a shaky self-image and a lack of confidence in the outer man that made his manners particularly retiring. It was a nose "as big as your fist," he plaintively wrote to a schoolfriend. Few portraits show him in profile for that reason.

Like his father, and Grandfather Darwin as well, he tended to stammer, having special difficulties with the letter *w*. There was a prize of sixpence waiting for the day he could manage to say "white wine": an odd requirement in a teetotal household.

He was so quiet that relatives found it difficult to say anything about his character beyond an appreciative nod towards an exceedingly placid temperament. To them he was a self-sufficient youngster, content to wander the country paths around Shrewsbury searching for birds, watching a fishing-float for hours from the banks of the Severn, or trailing helpfully after Abberley, the elderly gardener at The Mount, in his well-regulated cycle of horticultural duties.

Both the boy and his childhood appear to have been unremarkable, a point often commented on by friends and relations after he became famous. William Allport Leighton, an early schoolfriend, thought the nine-year-old Darwin entirely ordinary: no obvious candidate for subsequent achievement.

> In figure he was bulky and heavy-looking, and did not then manifest any particular powers of mind. He was reserved in manner, & we thought him proud inasmuch as he did not join in any play with the other boys but went directly home from school. . . . Though reserved in manner he was of a kind disposition & seemed pleased to do little acts to gratify his fellows— one instance of which was his bringing plants from his father's garden for our little gardens.[12]

His occupations at home consisted of such things as lying underneath the dining-room table reading *Robinson Crusoe*.[13] Even Darwin agreed that "I must have been a very simple little fellow."

Right from the start, this tranquil child was surrounded by lavish family affection. Three sisters and a brother preceded him, all of whom were a number of years older and well prepared to indulge the latest baby. Marianne, the eldest, was nearly eleven years his senior, an inhabitant of another world for a small child, but she enjoyed a close relationship with him despite the age gap. Caroline and Susan, nine and six years older respectively, doted on him. Darwin returned their affection ardently, the way much younger children normally do. The "sisterhood," as he dubbed them, were central to his early life and filled the greater part of his heart.

The rest of his heart was dedicated to Erasmus Alvey Darwin, almost five years older than he, of whom a schoolfriend wrote that "a more thoroughly honourable and excellent a man never lived."[14] Charles Darwin idolised his older brother, and for a long time afterwards Erasmus remained one of the most important figures in his personal and intellectual life. Their relationship was marked by close bonds of mutual regard, ties far stronger than mere brotherly concern. As children they shared boyish enthusiasms, finding each other's company congenial. As adults they were alike in many ways, both in their powerful intellects and retentive memories and in their delicate, hypochondriacal constitutions; they came to enjoy the same circle of London acquaintants, the literary side mingling freely with the scientific, and the same extended family of intermarrying cousins, once or twice finding their romantic interest kindled by the same girl, but more often agreeing on the failings of others. Moreover, they leaned in the same metaphysical direction, sharing similarly acerbic views on science, politics, and theology.

Where Erasmus differed from Darwin was in determination and physical energy. Erasmus eventually idled away his bachelor existence on a private income in London, much admired for his sweet nature and humorous disposition, thoroughly indulged by his father and sisters, his lazy charm sought out by other men's wives, Jane Carlyle and Fanny Mackintosh Wedgwood chief among them, as well as delighting Harriet Martineau when he felt energetic enough to escort her: quite the opposite of his brother, who came to do nothing but work. A great deal of Charles Darwin's later dogged persistence can be attributed to the struggle of a younger brother to match what he believed were the natural gifts of the older. And Erasmus was as close to him as only an older brother can be, closer perhaps than a wife. The two spoke freely in each other's company about the things they felt were disturbing—or boring—to the women they knew well. Curiously few studies of Darwin's life have done justice to his feelings for Erasmus and the comfortably open relations between them.

A year after Darwin was born, another sister arrived, the last child in the family. By virtue of their closeness in age, Catherine and Charles were perceived as a natural pair, the babies of the Darwin-Wedgwood circle. They played together—sitting in the arms of an old Spanish chestnut tree down by the river at the end of a broad promenade known as "the Doctor's Walk" —and ate together. They were taught their elementary lessons in the school-room under the eaves, where the window looked out over the Severn curling round the garden and the Shrewsbury streets behind, and they posed together— clutching choice plants from Dr. Darwin's hothouse—for their portrait when it was painted in 1816.

During these cossetted years, Caroline acted as governess to the two youngest children. Then, at the age of eight, Darwin was sent to be tutored by the Reverend George Case, a Unitarian minister in Shrewsbury whose chapel meetings were attended by Mrs. Darwin. As well as ministering to the faith in which Susanna Darwin had been raised, Case carried something of a reputation in the family as a serious and respected man. It was in Case's parsonage that Samuel Taylor Coleridge received an offer from the Wedg-wood brothers of financial assistance if he would refrain from sermonising and devote himself entirely to poetry. Case, they said privately, thought the plan a good one: he was no religious fanatic. Nor was Mrs. Darwin, if the truth were told. Unitarians were so low-church they seemed almost to belong to no church at all. As Dr. Darwin was fond of saying, Unitarianism was merely a featherbed to catch a falling Christian, gleefully repeating the words used by his own father about the first Josiah Wedgwood's gradual drift away from the orthodox church towards secularism.

Young Charles found Case's small school much more enjoyable than Caroline's home-based system, which was not completely successful. "I have been told that I was much slower in learning than my younger sister Catherine, and I believe that I was in many ways a naughty boy. Caroline was extremely kind, clever and zealous; but she was too zealous in trying to improve me, for I clearly remember after this long interval of years, saying to myself when about to enter a room where she was—'What will she blame me for now?' and I made myself dogged so as not to care what she might say."[15] He openly preferred old Nancy, the family nursemaid who used to bathe and dress them, because she spoiled him.

As was true of countless other boys in similarly patrician situations, Darwin's earliest interests were almost entirely based on outdoor activities. Woods and fields came right up to the edge of Shrewsbury, and in his family milieu it was only natural to encourage any inclinations he might show towards the traditional pursuits of English country gentlemen. He learned to ride ponies, to shoot and fish, indulged the family dog with tidbits, collected pebbles and plants, threw stones at sparrows, and helped himself to apples from the orchard when no one was looking. His aim was good enough, he remembered with horrified pride, to kill a hare in the flower garden with a marble. That same flower garden was obediently watered by him on other occasions with pans drawn from the well at Caroline's and Susan's command: neither of the older girls possessed the patience for this routine job, nor was pert, rebellious Catherine nearly so biddable. In his *Autobiography,* Darwin remembered this period as idyllic: a happy time, he thought, that provided a lasting image of what family life should be like.

Yet Darwin's own assessment of his simple tastes misses the strange intensity of his childhood amusements. He pursued natural history in its widest possible sense with total absorption. He was an avid collector from a very early age, giving undivided attention to accumulating any kind of natural or antiquarian object, ranging from birds' eggs and pebbles to the wax seals that came on letters. Mostly this concern emerged as an acquisitive desire to own things, the fierce urge to possess everything so common among children. "The passion for collecting which leads a man to be a systematic naturalist, a virtuoso or a miser, was very strong in me." Different-patterned biscuits would have done, he joked afterwards. "I had thus young formed a strong taste for collecting, chiefly seals, franks &c but also pebbles & minerals,—one which was given me by some boy, decided this taste.—I believe shortly after this or before I had smattered in botany, & certainly when at Mr Case's school I was very fond of gardening. . . . It was soon after I began collecting stones, ie when about 9 or 10 I distinctly recollect the desire I had of being able to know something about every pebble in front of the Hall door—it was my earliest—only geological aspiration at that time."[16] In a laborious nine-year-old hand he wrote his own labels: "A piece of tile found in Wenlock Abi. C. Darwin, January 23, 1819."[17]

Interests like these totally eclipsed the mundane operations of daily life. The high points of his visit to the Welsh seaside were seeing a snake, and the red beetles on the sand in front of their rented villa—probably *Cimex,* he proudly recalled.

IV

Real passion went into these natural history pursuits, to the extent of creating entirely imaginary achievements to impress his family or schoolboy friends—"for the pure pleasure of exciting attention & surprise." He often told lies about seeing rare birds. Other times, more complicated stories emerged, involving some preliminary scene-setting. Once he claimed to have discovered a pile of "stolen" fruit on a solitary ramble, which he had hidden himself just an hour or two beforehand. He rushed home breathless to break the news of his lucky discovery. He ring-barked trees for the same purpose. One day at Mr. Case's school, poor gullible Leighton was persuaded that Darwin could change the colours of polyanthuses and primroses by dosing them with special water: "a monstrous fable," stated the unrepentant pupil.

The lies were not connected with any sense of shame, Darwin later thought, but served instead as inspiring stories producing a great effect on his mind, "like a tragedy," he decided self-indulgently. More accurately, they mirrored a search for attention. He wanted to be admired. When stealing fruit to give to some boys in a cottage nearby, he would not hand it over until they watched how fast he could run—"I well remember that I was delighted at them declaring that they had never seen a boy run so fast!"

The inventions were, however, connected in important ways to the real world. He did not claim to see tigers in the Shropshire undergrowth, although Erasmus once taunted him with just such a suggestion. His youthful fictions mostly modified the run of ordinary events to make them more exciting. Exaggeration and intensification of experience were in this sense an imaginative rethinking of daily life, where unreal events were almost as real, and just as plausible, as the occurrences of bald reality. Lies—and the thrills derived from lies—were for him indistinguishable from the delights of natural history or the joy of finding a long-sought specimen.

Hand in hand with his exaggerations came an equivalent enthusiasm for secrets. He scrawled out pages of complicated codes for private messages and for disguising the date. Hidden in the old chestnut tree, he made Catherine pass these messages up into the branches across an ingenious system of ropes, weights, coloured rags, and pulleys.

"Our language and signs," he instructed her:

> Whistle—come
> Trumpet—lie still
> One pull—come
> Two pulls—lie still

His special words and phrases were similarly cryptic, showing something of his later deftness in decoding much more complicated natural history problems as well as the limited verbal imagination of children. "The secret place" was christened "Lorum":

> The crooked tree, Borum
> The tree which the owl is in, Owlo
> Some hole, Lacaho
> Strings, Dello
> Odd things, ab zorum, or any other place, Ly rachilo
> Pea spitter, Nanny
> Cross road, by zorum quello

Dr. Darwin was "Squirt."[18]

Here, undoubtedly, were the seeds of Darwin's fertile imagination, the ability when adult to visualise a world teeming with unseen phenomena, to speculate freely, often wildly, about the ways in which nature or nature's beings might behave. To lie, and to make secret places and languages, was to construct a new world order. The pleasure he so evidently derived from it must have been greatly influential in his developing enthusiasm for nature. Natural history, even at such an early age, was for him inseparably linked with the heady power of games and creative speculation.[19]

Dr. Darwin ignored these passing games with benign affection, and in old age Charles himself recognised that he stopped lying because no one paid any attention. Many of the boy's activities struck a chord with Dr. Darwin's own wide-ranging interest in nature. He particularly liked sharing his pleasure in gardening with his son, explaining the names of plants, perhaps reading them out of the botanical textbook composed by a great-uncle of Charles's also named Robert Waring Darwin, or reciting lines from a scientific poem *The Botanic Garden,* published in 1791 by Grandfather Erasmus.[20] Charles responded eagerly to this information. The garden at The Mount was full of horticultural rarities, some of which had originated in his grandfather's collections and were likely to be the actual plants described in his jaunty verses: the white-flowered "fly-catcher" that he used to sit and watch by the garden door was one, the ornamental opium poppy another.

Dr. Darwin was rich enough to indulge his hobby with tender shrubs and a hothouse for scented plants and bulbs. Nine large orange trees in pots, azaleas, camellias, ferns, and specimen primulas were all listed when the contents of The Mount were dispersed by auction in 1866. The doctor, moreover, had an intelligent, scientific concern in the turning of the seasons directly modelled on Gilbert White's account of Selborne (1789), and kept an elaborate "garden book" in which the first flowering or leafing of each plant was recorded on a daily basis in tandem with the temperature and weather.[21] Young Darwin and old Abberley, companionably walking round the vegetable beds together or looking out for the return of last year's swallow, were closely involved with observing and recording these details. "Papa asked me to do this," he recorded in a childish script. "Ther was in year 1819, 160 flower on the Poenies [Peonies]. In the year 1820, 384 flower. In the year 1821, 363 flower."

Dr. Darwin enjoyed the lad's company in other ways as well and sometimes took him out with him in his carriage—a tight fit, for it was a single-seater and the doctor was of ample proportions—to while away the time spent travelling between medical calls. "Nowhere," said Eliza Meteyard, "was Dr. Darwin seen to such advantage as in the invariable yellow chaise. This, and his burly form and countenance within, were known to every man, woman, and child over a wide extent of country." The doctor, according to his son, knew an extraordinary number of stories which he liked to tell, since he was a great talker, and convivially proposed "a theory for almost everything which occurred." With his prodigious memory prompting anecdotes on every road leading out of Shrewsbury, a gift for expansive talk and speculation, his "aerial-castle-building talents," and acute powers of observation, he was an impressive figure in the boy's eyes. Charles Darwin would fill in any conversational gaps by "telling him of my lessons, & seeing game & other wild birds, which was a great delight to me."[22]

Round about this time, Dr. Darwin felt it appropriate to give Darwin two elementary books on natural history from his own library, items of great sentimental value as the only remaining property of his oldest brother, who had died as a medical student and after whom the boy had been formally named. Of a size to slip easily into a pocket and well illustrated with engravings, one volume dealt with the "natural history of waters, earths, stones, fossils, and minerals, with their virtues, properties, and medical uses," the other with insects.[23] These were Darwin's first natural history textbooks.

Nothing in this period suggests that Dr. Darwin was in any way an oppressive father—some overbearing figure trampling on his son's nascent individuality or coming indirectly to represent all the diverse forms of Victorian authority that evolutionary theories later contested.[24] He was stern, certainly, with a firm patriarchal character, uncomprehending at times, frequently too busy with his patients and business ledgers to draw out his children, and intermittently frightening to younger visitors to The Mount with his immense bulk and insistence on dominating the conversation. "There was a want of liberty at Shrewsbury whenever the Doctor was in the room," said Emma Wedgwood, one of his many nieces. "He was genial and sympathetic, only nobody must go on about their own talk."[25]

It was all the more obvious to Emma in relation to the easy atmosphere at her own home in Staffordshire: she recoiled from what she interpreted as unbending formality. Her cousins, she thought dramatically, were not "free to do just what they liked." Still, her assertion that the doctor did not understand Darwin, "or sympathise with him as a boy," should be taken as the recollection of a young girl forced to be polite to her uncle. Emma did not care to be restricted and was "extremely glad when the Dr went off on a long journey, and sorry to see him come back again."

Another niece of the same age was rather more charitable. "My uncle, Dr Robert Darwin, was a tall, very large man, weighing more than 20 stone, but wonderfully active for his size and very fond of his garden. He was extremely cheerful and agreeable, full of amusing anecdotes and considered a very clever doctor."[26] Her view was echoed by one of Dr. Darwin's contemporaries in Shropshire, William Owen of Woodhouse. "There is something about him," he said, "so liberal, so high minded & yet so unassuming that it is quite impossible to know him well without respecting & loving him."[27]

The forceful side of Dr. Darwin's personality was nevertheless brought out and intensified by money. He was frugal to a fault, deliberately adopting the lifestyle of a modest country squire, furnishing The Mount with austerely practical items, and personally quite content with plain-cooked beef and a glass of hot water, just like "a careful statesman or ambassador who fears the loss of his dispatches," said his brother in despair. There was plenty of silver plate and fine china in the house, including a unique Wedgwood dinner service specially made as a wedding gift from Susanna's father, a good collection of furniture to accompany some Turkish carpets, and fashionable flowered chintzes on the easy chairs and ottomans. Yet these were hardly more than any of the Darwins' neighbours would possess. The Mount's interior was substantial but not showy.

It is not difficult to understand why. Dr. Darwin did not want either medical or financial clients thinking he was making large profits out of their mutual transactions: sober prosperity was an idealised image pursued by every provincial physician. Also, a lifelong horror of being poor, which he expressed more than once to his father and then to his brother and sons, generated caution. The doctor was compulsive about household accounts. Nothing went unrecorded in his ledgers, right down to the smallest portion of tea—an extraordinary attention to detail ultimately bequeathed to Darwin. Emma Wedgwood was appalled to find her cousin Caroline grateful for the luxury of a fire one December afternoon, and other stories of Shrewsbury thrift circulated with abandon in free-spending Wedgwood circles.

Naturally enough, Charles and Erasmus Darwin spent every penny of their allowance once they got out from under this shadow, and were for a time gleefully extravagant. Later on, they both became much more like their father. Charles through to his seventies stubbornly refused to buy any new china. He took grim satisfaction in using the same old Wedgwood teacup, the gilt trimmings rubbed off, and minus the saucer, for breakfast every day of his adult life.

Even so, Dr. Darwin's patients spoke of his kindly, sympathetic nature and munificence of spirit, "always scheming to give pleasure to others, and, though hating extravagance, to perform many generous actions." Cheeses were given, small debts were paid, strangers were trusted with delicate errands, charity patients were carefully attended to.

Accordingly, Charles Darwin was quite sincere, if overly sentimental, when he described his father as the "kindest man I ever knew." Dr. Darwin's chief characteristics, he remembered warmly, were his powers of observation and his sympathy, "neither of which have I ever seen exceeded or even equalled." Up until the very end, whenever he began a sentence with the words "My father thought" or "My father said," his wife and children knew that whatever followed was incontrovertible. It was mostly admiration, not antagonism, that linked father and son together throughout life, a particular cordiality between two very different men.

Caroline remembered the early rapport between them. "Instead of being 'a naughty boy' he was particularly affectionate, tractable & sweet tempered, & my father had the highest opinion of his understanding & intelligence. My father was very fond of him & even when he was a little boy of 6 or 7, however bustled & overtired, often had C. with him when dressing to teach him some little thing such as the Almanack—& C. used to be so eager to be down in time. C. does not seem to have known half how much my father loved him."[28] The point worried her long after Darwin's death. "I wish some years ago," she wrote in 1887, "I had known that Charles thought my Father did not understand or know what ability & power of mind he had—really he was so proud as well as fond of him that I often felt afraid that Erasmus might feel mortified & feel undervalued."[29]

Looked after, petted, and indulged wherever he turned, Darwin had little justification for complaint about being misunderstood in childhood. His early family background was comfortably secure.

V

This steady boyhood existence did not go completely unmarked by dramatic events. The even tenor of Shrewsbury life was violently overturned in 1817 when tragedy came in the form of Susanna Darwin's death, seven years after Catherine was born.

Chronic ill health was endemic to the Wedgwood family, and Susanna, aged fifty-two, was no exception, suffering from various intestinal upsets, a nasty bout of rheumatic fever when a bride, and headaches for years after her marriage, some of them abjectly chronicled in letters to her sisters. She often travelled to Bath and other spas to take the waters and for a period tried sea-bathing as a remedy. Like her own mother—also a Wedgwood by birth, a cousin of the first Josiah Wedgwood, whom she married in 1764—and her brother Tom, who was renowned for his scientific and literary friendships with Coleridge, Davy, and Southey and who died in 1805 after prolonged suffering from intestinal maladies and opium addiction, she was always ill. "Everyone seems young but me," she complained in 1815.

This time, however, it was different. In July she was suddenly taken ill with violent stomach pains, emphatically distinct from those that had come and gone before. Two days into the attack it seemed clear to Dr. Darwin that she could not survive. "It is impossible to have a worse account than I have to give you. . . . her suffering is terrible," wrote Susanna's unmarried sister Kitty, summoned to Shrewsbury at short notice.

> The Dr has not the slightest hope. . . . The pain indeed is gone that was her first illness, but she has such severe vomittings, & sickness that he says he does not think her sufferings much lessened. She was today for a few hours easier, & the Dr could not help feeling some little doubt whether it was not possible she might recover. This evening she is worse, & he is very wretched. Still though so exceedingly feeble, she has such a tenaciousness of life, that he fears she may suffer for some time. . . . Her senses are as perfect as ever. From feebleness she can hardly speak. She has not seen any of the children but Marianne & Caroline since Friday.

Later in the evening, a moment or two before sealing the letter, she added: "The Dr has just been to tell us he does not think she will pass this night."[30]

But Susanna Darwin struggled on. "After a wretched night my poor Sister yet lives, but the mortification is far advanced & must very soon be fatal." She died of what was probably peritonitis about twenty-four hours later. There was at that time no requirement for a certificate stating the immediate medical cause.

Darwin remembered very little about her death, writing candidly that "I recollect my mother's gown & scarcely anything of her appearance. Except one or two walks with her I have no distinct remembrance of any conversations, & those only of a very trivial nature.—I remember her saying 'if she did ask me to do something, which I said she had, it was solely for my good.' "[31]

It must have been heartbreakingly confusing for an eight-year-old, impossible to understand and for that reason pushed back into the corners of an unformed mind. He was not allowed into the sickroom during the entire course of Susanna's attack, and, as far as is known, was called to see her only after she died. There can have been no easy way for a child to connect the living mother of four days before with a corpse: "I can remember hardly anything about her except her death-bed, her black velvet gown, and her curiously constructed work-table."[32] Did he stand uncomfortably toying with the table not knowing what to do next?

The older girls, busy attending the doctor during the last gruelling days and alternately sitting with Susanna throughout, were more able to make the connection. They were all deeply affected, and "owing to their great grief" were apparently never able to speak of her again (although this remark, made gratuitously by Charles himself, was not strictly true, as Catherine certainly managed to discuss the death with him in later life). Robert Waring Darwin felt the loss intensely. He had known Susanna since they were children; she was the first and only woman he loved. The pain did not lighten as the years went by. He had no inclination to find another wife, either for his own sake or for the children's benefit. Corrosive depressions haunted his remaining years.

Marianne and Caroline bravely stepped into the gap and subsequently ran the household. Susan and Catherine joined them when old enough. None of the girls, nor Erasmus, left any written indication of their feelings about these changes. Charles Darwin was the only one who wrote about their mother's death, and that only briefly and retrospectively some thirty years afterwards. He was puzzled to hear that Catherine recollected almost all the circumstances, although when they were told to him he failed to record them for his own edification. "When my mother died, I was 8 & 1/2 old,—& she [Catherine] one year less, yet she remembers all particular & events of each day, whilst I scarcely recollect anything, except being sent for—memory of going into her room, my Father meeting us crying afterwards.—"[33]

Actually he found it hard to remember anything concrete from his very early life. More than once he wrote that "my memory here is an obscure picture." Only the very strongest internal impressions remained vivid for him later on, such as the fear of a particular dog, of a coach overturning, or of crossing a foaming river, and he remembered being frightened by a story of people pushed into a canal by the horse's towing ropes. Even so, he failed to remember the most fearful and dramatic emotion of all: a mother's death. Insects at Plas Edwards came to mind more clearly.

Nor did he remember her funeral. He easily recalled the burial of a total stranger—a soldier brought to St. Chad's in his coffin followed by a horse bearing a pair of military boots reversed in the stirrups: "This scene deeply stirred whatever poetic fancy there was in me."[34] Darwin must have suppressed all memory of his mother's death and its aftermath, the first compelling occasion in a life spent struggling with the desire to push all unpleasant things to one side.

Yet such an early introduction to death was not quite as disruptive or devastating as might be supposed. It would be misleading to project modern ideas about parent-child relations onto this particular family, or to suggest that Darwin failed properly to grieve.[35] Of course, many intimate ties were harshly and prematurely broken. He probably regretted the fact that his sisters found it hard to speak about their mother again. Nevertheless, Susanna Darwin had never been very prominent in the younger children's day-to-day existence: she was often ill and in her room, the obligations of social calls and outside visits filling much of the remaining time when she was well. Darwin's elementary lessons were learned at his sister Caroline's knee rather than from his mother, who would have been the more usual figure in conventional circumstances, and his entertainments were generally provided, not by his mother, but by any combination of sisters and brother, or by the family servants' allowing him to wander around behind them. Very young children in the gentlemanly classes of Britain, children like Darwin and his sister Catherine, took their meals in a nursery, perhaps only meeting their parents formally for an hour or two at the end of the day. Indeed, the only record of Susanna's relationship with her smallest son was inadvertently provided by the schoolboy Leighton, who remembered Darwin bringing a flower to school and saying his mother had taught him how, by looking at the blossom, the name of the plant could be discovered. The two boys stood peering inside for some time before giving up in bewilderment.[36] For his own part, Darwin could not recall this initiation into the mysteries of Linnaean nomenclature. Even his first memories, which he excavated for a concise autobiographical study composed in 1838 and which might be expected to include anecdotes featuring his mother, centred on Caroline alone. Darwin's earliest recollection was of sitting on his sister's lap while she peeled an orange out of the hothouse for him. His mother's voice, her touch, were nowhere present.

And when Susanna Darwin died, her place in Darwin's life was quickly filled by the three loving older sisters, all of them nearly full-grown women, easily representing maternal adults in the eyes of a child. Marianne was nineteen, tentatively being courted by the man who was to become her husband in 1824 and capable of looking after her younger brothers and sisters. Caroline, sixteen, was already something of a mother-substitute, if only intermittently. Affectionate and intellectual by nature, she was the one most like Susanna Darwin in character and looks: medallion portraits of mother and daughter show a strong physical resemblance. She was also exceedingly tender, a trait noticed approvingly by her aunt Bessy Wedgwood, who thought that "she deserves the name of a sweet girl more than anyone I know." It was Caroline who ensured Darwin's continuing education and that he knew his Bible; who took him to church—moving away from the Unitarian chapel run by Mr. Case in the High Street to favour St. Chad's, the parish church where the children had been christened and where Susanna Darwin was brought to be buried; Caroline who fondly called him "my dear Bobby" or "dearest Charley" and gave him news about the dogs, the one to whom he wrote when temporarily at a loss about his age. Susan, at that time only thirteen, became a sterner, more critical figure, relishing the nickname "Granny," never able to resist correcting Darwin's spelling and extracting promises of good handwriting through to middle age. Her sense of humour was anarchic, and she fussed less than Caroline. The three, whatever their sisterly faults, were much loved by Darwin.

In sum, his mother's death does not seem to have precipitated any discernible or long-lasting crisis in Darwin's emotional life. To all intents and purposes, he had merely lost one member of a larger group of attentive female relatives—and perhaps one who because of constant ill health exercised only a fleeting presence anyway. No second marriage or unfamiliar governess in the house came to interrupt the process of rehabilitation. No dramatic reduction in care or attention deflated his ego. No underlying swell of tenderness seems to have pierced his adult heart, nor does the existing historical record suggest any uncontrollable feelings of grief bursting out periodically to overwhelm him. The children and their father grieved deeply, as Darwin's note about Dr. Darwin's weeping suggests. A letter from Kitty Wedgwood who stayed on at The Mount to help the family over the first few weeks emphasised that the girls "have wept very much and expressed their sorrow fully since her death which gives me hope that they will be pretty well soon."[37] The weeping included Charles, as a letter of his written in old age to Caroline makes clear: he remembered "our crying so much."[38]

There is little evidence of maternal deprivation in the usual sense—not with older sisters so willing to provide emotional support for each other and for the two youngest children, and their everyday life continuing in its well-established pattern. The family clung together and found that they could cope. Darwin emerged much the same imperturbable, dreamy boy as before. Perhaps only his great pleasure in natural history, which in later days verged on the obsessive, can be seen as a first step in a general retreat from the frightening intensity of emotions in the real world.

The legacy of this death was manifested in other ways. Eventually, it determined the kind of woman that Darwin sought out as a wife, though it seems very likely that his choice was as much influenced by fondness for his sisters as by fading memories of a dead mother. Much more significant in the end, Darwin also came to fear that his continual ill health and the constitutional weaknesses of his children were inherited from his mother's side of the family. Marriage to his cousin Emma Wedgwood intensified these fears; and the possibility of hereditary disease became in his mind a terrifying threat that could bring a fatal attack to any of his loved ones—an attack just as sudden as Susanna Darwin's and just as unwelcome. Constant preoccupation with the state of his "accursed stomach" through the long decades of middle life carried with it the unspoken but understandable anxiety that he, or one of his children, might die from the same inexplicable complaint as had his own mother. With all the increased sensibilities of an adult, and then the passionate absorption of a husband and father, he came to dread the minutest sign of internal disorder for the destruction it might herald. Barely hidden fears came to the fore at these moments. It was the way in which his mother died that was the blow from which Darwin never quite recovered.

VI

A few months afterwards, at the age of nine, Darwin was sent away from home to board at Shrewsbury School in the centre of town. The plan had been formulated well before Susanna Darwin died, and Dr. Darwin saw no reason for changing it. Erasmus had made the move three years earlier at close to the same age.

Still, the impact of this formal divorce from home can hardly be over-estimated. Though the school was a mere fifteen minutes away from home, it might as well have been in another country. Going away to boarding school was bad enough for any small boy, even worse for one who had just lost his mother, and may well have been harder to negotiate than any unexpected death in the family—a critical personal turning point ignored by generations of Darwin scholars. School brutally separated Darwin from his supportive home environment at the very time he needed it most. Furthermore, the school was unpleasant in itself. For these reasons Darwin never displayed any of the affectionate regard 'that many grown Englishmen retain for their schooldays. On the contrary, the experience was every bit as ghastly as tradition dictated. He relied on Erasmus, a senior boy, as never before; and in the space of a few weeks he withdrew into an isolated protective shell.

Shrewsbury School catered for the sons of local gentlemen, both Whig and Tory, and trained them up for entrance to Oxford or Cambridge University, mostly the latter, after which they usually joined one of the established professions. Those who did not go to university were, it was hoped, provided with sufficient learning to live a cultivated life on family estates.

Such elevated ideals were rarely realised in raucous Regency England. The headmaster was Samuel Butler (grandfather of the novelist and writer and cynically portrayed by him as Dr. Skinner of Roughborough School in *The Way of All Flesh*), whose glittering mathematical career at Cambridge hardly prepared him for the rigours of running a boarding school, however small and select. Internally, his premises were woefully inadequate, the chapel doubling as a schoolroom and the dormitories hopelessly crowded: boys had to sleep in other houses nearby and also in a long attic gallery above the library. Individual beds were first introduced by Butler's successor in 1836. The sanitary arrangements, as Darwin described them, left a lot to be desired. "There was one particular long dormitory in which 20 or 30 boys slept in which there was only a single window at the end." After sixty years the thought of the "atrocious smell of that room in the morning" could still turn his stomach.[39] It is possible that that same revolting smell—of stagnant air, of chamber pots, faeces, urine-stained sheets—reminded him of his mother's sickroom, itself probably foul after a death by peritonitis. School food, moreover, was so unpleasant that parents supplied their children with baskets of meat, fruit, and pies: a "very pernicious indulgence," complained Butler, which encouraged a hidden market in goods and favours. Liquor was also much in evidence. Older pupils sometimes threatened each other with loaded pistols and often fought with factory boys down by the river. During the parliamentary election campaign of 1819, Butler was obliged to bribe the factory overseer to keep local youths—no supporters of the sons of Tory politicians or their landowning constituents—out of the way in the evenings.

These upper-class schoolboys were not just unruly, they were violent. In 1818, the year that Darwin arrived, some senior boys went on the rampage, intimidating farmers in the market, killing pigs, and breaking the library's ancient stained-glass windows. No stranger to firm action, Butler expelled the ringleaders and issued a circular to parents. Thereafter, a strict system of surveillance was instituted, with the lower boys made to present themselves every half-hour, the upper boys every two hours. There was a call-over at locking-up time, and boarders were visited in their bedrooms. Disciplinary beatings were common, though not quite as common as reported to parents. "I have never flogged the same boy twice [in] a week more than three times in twenty-six years," protested the headmaster in 1826.[40]

Darwin hated it:

> Nothing could have been worse for the development of my mind than Dr. Butler's school, as it was strictly classical, nothing else being taught except a little ancient geography and history. The school as a means of education to me was simply a blank. During my whole life I have been singularly incapable of mastering any language. Especial attention was paid to verse-making, and this I could never do well. I had many friends, and got together a grand collection of old verses, which by patching together, sometimes aided by other boys, I could work into any subject. Much attention was paid to learning by heart the lessons of the previous day; this I could effect with great facility learning forty or fifty lines of Virgil or Homer, whilst I was in morning chapel; but this exercise was utterly useless, for every verse was forgotten in forty-eight hours. I was not idle, and with the exception of versification, generally worked conscientiously at my classics, not using cribs. The sole pleasure I ever received from such studies, was from some of the odes of Horace, which I admired greatly. When I left the school I was for my age neither high nor low in it; and I believe that I was considered by all my masters and by my Father as a very ordinary boy, rather below the common standard in intellect.[41]

One of his tedious efforts comprised page after page of notes on Roman history. Hours were spent idly scribbling in textbooks, including an atlas and a copy of the headmaster's book *Ancient Geography,* relieved only by the occasional flourish of a signature, tried several different ways and upside down for variety.[42] The text confirms that Butler was by no means a lively teacher. Darwin did not enjoy dormitory life either, finding his bed "as damp as muck" and getting Erasmus to complain to their father on his behalf. The only response to Dr. Darwin's medical thunder was a letter full of headmasterly evasion. If the Darwin boys were to have new, or better, or more blankets, wrote Butler, why so would all the other boys have to have them, at an increased cost to parents.[43]

Darwin's dislike for school was expressed in other ways as well. He played an active part in a game known as "raising the Doctor" which "consisted of a dozen boys going into the room over the Doctor in the middle of the night & dancing a tattoo & then rushing back to bed & pretending to be asleep."[44] The game lost its popularity when one boy who really was asleep was woken up by an avenging Butler and thoroughly beaten.

Such a stultifying atmosphere and the lack of any kind of homely warmth obliged him to rely on his own mental resources. Bolstered by Erasmus, who had entered the school in 1815 and remained until 1822, Charles sought out other similarly minded boys and joined a circle of quiet intellectualism leavened by the carefree moments of most schoolboys' lives. Erasmus's friends became Charles's friends, among them Richard Henry Corfield and his brother (their father, unknown to them, being one of Dr. Darwin's nonmedical clients), John Price (another with a father financially obliged to Dr. Darwin), and Charles Thomas Whitley. Except for Charles Corfield, who died at the age of eighteen, all these friends went on to win scholarships to the universities. Of the fifty-four boys who entered school in Darwin's year, twelve eventually went to Cambridge and four to Oxford. Six of these attained college scholarships, indicating that their classical and mathematical education, despite Darwin's disparagement, was excellent. The cleverest went up to St. John's, a Cambridge college with special connections to the school, including the right to elect the head teacher; because of this there was much interchanging of fellowships and masterships back and forth between the two institutions.

Few of the remainder stayed any longer than necessary. Of Darwin's contemporaries, four left during the first year and nineteen during the three years after that. Only six of the intake of 1818, besides Darwin, were still there in 1825. Several made their own decisions to go. Catherine excitedly wrote a few months after Darwin left saying that seven pupils had run away that quarter.

Despite this lack of continuity, the Darwin brothers found a congenial set of friends stretching over the school. Darwin stated that he "had many friends amongst the schoolboys, whom I loved dearly, and I think that my disposition was then very affectionate." John Price, essentially a friend of Erasmus's and, in the terminology of the school, one of the "big fellows," obviously liked the younger boy's company, although he "looked down on him in every sense." Price gently patronised the shy, introverted nine-year-old. "I could point out the very spot in Jeudwine's school upstairs where he brought me a shell of Purpura lapillus and said 'Price what's this?' I believe I translated the Welsh name Gwichiad y cwn into Dog Periwinkle which satisfied the little man for the time, and caused him thenceforward to look up to Old Price (as I was even then called) as an oracle to be consulted."

Moving up through the school in his turn, Darwin dispensed the same kind of support to juniors, accompanying a boy called Edward Edwards along the banks of the Severn with a "botanical box in hand to collect specimens of wild flowers." Edwards remembered this small scientific kindness in an otherwise unhappy time at school with gratitude.[46] Frederick Hildyard, John Mort Wakefield, and Edward John Wingfield were similarly cultivated soulmates of Erasmus's; in 1826, Hildyard and Wakefield became assistant masters at the school. John Wood Warter, another of Erasmus's friends, coached Darwin in classics during the holidays, warning him, only half facetiously, "against the encouragement of idleness, to which I know you are ever fully inclined."[47] Frederick Watkins, nearer Darwin's own age, was unconcerned by this evident laziness. He liked the serene good nature his friend brought to bear: to Watkins, Darwin was a "genial yet thoughtful fellow, full of conversation interspersed with long silences, with his wits not wandering, but always following some bird or insect or reptile."[48]

Geniality was what was most often remembered by Darwin's schoolfriends: the good-humoured acquiescence of an inward-looking boy who did not appear much to mind whatever happened in life; this, and his ever-increasing interest in natural history and science. "At Shrewsbury we slept in the same room for some years & often beguiled the night with pleasant conversation," said John Lovett Cameron, who later coincided with him at Cambridge University. "He was always cheerful & good tempered & much beloved by his school-fellows. He was not a great proficient in the school studies, but was always busy collecting beetles, butterflies &c." He and Cameron read Shakespeare together, hunched up on the stone window seats next to the trees.

Several boys, including Cameron, struck up lasting friendships with him. Others who lived locally, though not particular friends, were always ready to join his holiday collecting expeditions, hunting for insects under stones on the hill or sifting through the sludge of a pond. Thomas Butler, the headmaster's pedantically unadventurous son, noticed how fast Darwin's natural history tastes were developing. "On one or two occasions during a winter holiday time I went out with him trying to shoot small birds which he was anxious to examine but was never present at the post-mortem investigation of them."[49] Most of these outdoor interests were easily shared with country-based friends.

On the other hand, some could barely remember Darwin when asked for anecdotes at the close of his life. Drifting aimlessly through his schooldays, he was not particularly concerned to cut any great figure among the other boys, nor was he academically noteworthy in the eyes of his masters. The only qualities he felt he possessed at the time were "strong and diversified tastes, much zeal for whatever interested me, and a keen pleasure in understanding any complex subject or thing. I was taught Euclid by a private tutor, and I distinctly remember the intense satisfaction which the clear geometrical proofs gave me. I remember with equal distinctness the delight which my uncle gave me (the father of Francis Galton) by explaining the principle of the vernier of a barometer."[50]

Forced into a straitjacket of classical learning and mentally far away from the security of family surroundings, Darwin was plainly unhappy at school. His growing dependence on natural history may well have begun as a defence mechanism bringing some sort of consolation in its wake. Other forms of escape took a more obvious line. Eating—the traditional route to solace—was a boyish comfort. He developed a taste for sticky cakes that far outran his pocket money, and a family reputation for undiscriminating appetite. Even the dogs came a poor second to breakfast, teased Catherine and Susan.

Another means of escape was literally going home. Since the distance from school to The Mount was little more than a mile, he sometimes played truant and ran there after call-over and before locking up at night. The sense of freedom was very real on these occasions. The familiar aura of The Mount, with his sisters looking up from their books and Spark the black-and-white mongrel ("dear little black nose") welcoming him noisily in the yard, reflected a world achingly apart from boarding school. Both at the time and much later on, Darwin believed these brief connections with home helped him come to terms with long periods away from the family. "This I think was in many ways advantageous to me by keeping up home affections and interests."

Great fear necessarily went hand in hand with the pleasure. He needed to run fast to get back before Butler's final lock-up, since expulsion loomed if he failed. When in doubt, he panted out earnest requests to God to help him. "I well remember that I attributed my success to the prayers and not to my quick running, and marvelled how generally I was aided."

VII

Erasmus was by far the most important figure in Darwin's expanding cognitive horizons during this period, both in school and out of it—far more significant than any youthful rejection of the unstimulating intellectual environment created by Butler.

Erasmus's interests coincided to a large degree with those of his younger brother, ranging from insect-collecting to mineralogy and amateur botanising. "My brother Erasmus possessed a remarkably clear mind, with extensive and diversified tastes and knowledge in literature, art, and even in science.... He was extremely agreeable, and his wit often reminded me of that in the letters and works of Charles Lamb. He was very kind-hearted; but his health from his boyhood had been weak, and as a consequence he failed in energy.... He read much, even whilst a boy, and at school encouraged me to read, lending me books."[51] He was "very sociable and pleasant," already a gifted though weakly young man. Darwin intensely admired him.

Erasmus, moreover, was a colleague in arms at home. The two of them often felt besieged by a phalanx of overeager sisters: "I think it a most abomnable thing, the minute Erasmus went out of the room, they began abusing him for being out of temper," Darwin wrote to a schoolboy friend, possibly Price, in the Christmas holidays of 1822; "you must know that he is not very well, that he hath got the rheumatism." A more serious problem was broached a day or two afterwards:

My Dear friend
You must know that after my Georgraphy she [Caroline] said I should go down to ask for Richards poney, just as I was going, she said she must ask me not a very decent question, that was whether I wash all over every morning. No. then she said it was quite disgusting, then she asked me if I did every other morning, and I said no, then she said how often I did, and I said once a week, then she said of course you wash your feet every day, and I said no, then she began saying how very disgusting and went on that way a good while, then she said I ought to do it. I said I would wash my neck and shoulders, then she said you had better do it all over, then I said upon my word I would not, then she told me [off], and made me promise I would not tell. then I said, why I only wash my feet once a month at school, which I confess is nasty, but I cannot help it, for we have nothing to do it with. So then Caroline pretended to be quite sick, and left the room, so then I went and told Erasmus, and he burst out laughing and said I had better tell her to come and wash them herself, besides that she said she did not like sitting by me or Erasmus for we smelt of not washing all over.[52]

Late in his schooldays, Erasmus devoted himself to chemistry, a subject running in his combined Wedgwood and Darwin blood. Under his supervision,

Charles came to love the subject just as fervently. Together they planned and equipped what they were pleased to call their "Laboratory," in their imagination the finest of experimental centres, but really little more than an old scullery or washing-room located in the back garden of The Mount.

The Lab possessed a range of chemical apparatus restricted only by the boys' ability to "milk the Cow," a way of referring to their father's tightly fastened pockets; and expensive glassware was the subject of endless discussions between them as to the advantages of this or that shape of jar or a particular kind of stopper which they would buy as soon as finances permitted. They invested in an Argand lamp, the main means at that time for supplying a flame for heating chemicals or gases. Uncle Josiah Wedgwood sent some fireproof china dishes—a Wedgwood patent—and an impressive industrial thermometer. The Lab also boasted a blowpipe of primitive specifications and equipment for measuring liquids.

Their ambitions far exceeded their ability to pay. "There is a shop here," Erasmus wrote awestruck from a visit to Cambridge, "with every sort of thing, it quite made my mouth water to see all the jars & stopcocks & all sorts of things, graduated tubes, blow pipes, cubic inch measures, test tubes, & ye Lord knows what besides." He could not bring himself to leave without buying something, in this case a handsome thermometer with a hinged scale to expose the bulb. Guiltily he bought a handful of minerals for his brother at a more agreeable price of one shilling, which soothed his conscience somewhat.

As their interests developed to include the chemical analysis of minerals and crystallography, Erasmus managed to buy a goniometer (an instrument to measure angles). When a windfall of £10 from an aunt appeared, he could hardly decide between a plethora of conflicting desires: it was too much to hope for an air-pump, although he longed to perform experiments in the vacuum that this could produce, his mind dancing with images derived from the early experiments of Robert Boyle and spread through a wider audience by Joseph Wright's 1768 painting of "An experiment on a bird in an air-pump." There was a family story that the people crowded round the lecturer's table in the painting included the first Erasmus Darwin, the boys' grandfather, who moved in the same literary and philosophical circles as Wright, and who would, like his namesake, have been interested in any such theatrical scientific investigation.[53]

But Erasmus opted instead for the construction of a separate cubicle to keep their instruments dry and "a shelf before the window, which would be an excellent place for weighing &c. and being South would do very well for any experiments with the Sun's rays, which is also a desideratum in our Lab."[54] As soon as he was master of his own financial account with Dr. Darwin, he lavished £8 10 shillings on chemical items: a huge sum for the time, which Dr. Darwin solemnly warned should not happen again. There were no further scientific extravagances until Erasmus left home for Cambridge University in 1822.

The subject was not at all unusual for a pair of schoolboys to take up in the 1820s. The great practical and theoretical changes brought about by the chemical revolution late in the eighteenth century had captured the imagination of many educated people, those of their paternal and maternal grandfathers among them. Both the first Erasmus Darwin, the doctor, scientific poet, and friend of the painter Wright, and Josiah Wedgwood, the Staffordshire potter, were deeply interested in the new chemistry, the one writing appreciatively of the social progress that chemical advances would bring and the other eagerly applying chemical technology in his quest for a perfect glaze and suitable combinations of clays for chinaware. As well as making his own experiments, Wedgwood organised a subscription fund to support Joseph Priestley's chemical research, supplying him with equipment from the family manufactory.[55] More than this, chemistry seemed to them the most awe-inspiring, the most visionary of the sciences, a science in which practitioners delved into a world of unseen elements in search of the composition of matter. To study it was to catch at the ultimate forces of nature itself.

If anything, the intellectual appeal of chemistry intensified during the first decades of the nineteenth century as the concepts of classical physics—the idea that matter was composed of myriads of basic corpuscles—expanded to include a more generalised interest in the immaterial powers or forces that acted in different ways on those particles, and evanescent phenomena like electricity, heat, and light came to be considered as keys to the inner nature of things. In particular, the development of gas chemistry after John Dalton's explanation of chemical activity in terms of atoms and atomic weights lent itself to repetition in home laboratories. Simple experiments performed in sheds like the Shrewsbury Lab became enormously popular among the gentry, with a large literature and range of apparatus being rapidly produced to suit.

The Darwin boys' activities can be placed firmly in this popular movement. They were primarily interested in determining the composition, in Daltonian terms, of commonplace chemical substances, mostly by producing "calxes," or oxides. The procedure was laid out in William Henry's *Elements of Experimental Chemistry* (1819), a textbook famous for its exposition of Dalton's work and mentioned by the boys on several occasions as being in their possession.[56] They had not, however, the apparatus to follow in Humphry Davy's heroic footsteps and electrolyse water into its constituent gases.

Instead, they contented themselves with analysing interesting minerals or the metallic residues in coins and various domestic materials like tea leaves, interspersed with several small financial outlays on compounds that could be purified by crystallisation into their constituent elements. Some of these raw materials were given to them by friends and relatives once their hobby became known. Mostly it was Thomas Blunt, the local chemist and dispensing apothecary, who supplied small samples of different substances for their researches, as well as filling the more conventional requests for distilled water and yet more glassware. Blunt, already well known to the boys through Dr. Darwin's medical practice, was thought by them to be the best chemist in the world.

They also, like many others at the time, found the symmetry of natural crystals extremely interesting. Erasmus used his goniometer for measuring the angles where the flat sides meet, and worked out the numerical formulae on which classification schemes were based. Soon they tried making their own specimens out of various chemicals and began building up a collection of the rocks and minerals in which crystals naturally occurred. This was the only time their studies at Shrewsbury School seemed useful, for the brothers were, if nothing else, well tutored in mathematics and geometry. Erasmus showed considerable aptitude for complicated mathematical calculations of all kinds. But Charles Darwin's aspirations far outstripped his limited talent in this area. However, with all the measurements, careful geometric diagrams, relatively easy experiments, and a satisfying diversity of different rocks and stones to collect, crystallography became his favoured occupation for a while. He read fairly widely in the subject and collected samples for his "cabinet." In this way a generalised enthusiasm for stones and minerals joined his other interests in natural history.

The significance of these first chemical experiences can easily be overlooked when considering the whole sweep of Darwin's remarkably powerful intellectual trajectory. Yet he was here establishing the footing for a lifetime of experimental science. To some extent the two brothers were participating in a wider research movement that aimed at discovering the ultimate fabric of matter, paring compounds down to their elemental bones. For Darwin, the vivid imaginings involved in delicately teasing apart complex materials were a natural continuation of the innocent fabrications of childhood. His imagination was channelled by the busy activity of experimentation into a search for the mysterious attributes of nature and the way they materialised in various substances. Of course the Shrewsbury Lab was tiny and poorly equipped, and chemistry was no more than a passing enthusiasm. He was unlikely to isolate new elements, as Davy had, or reveal new lines of chemical research like Dalton. He had no access to electrical devices or powerful oxy-hydrogen burners, much to his chagrin.

But the romance was there. Chemistry carried with it all the intensity of experience characteristic of the late Georgian period: intensity in discerning the activities and symmetries inherent in solid bodies, of bringing about transformations from gas to solid to liquid, of revealing the primary forces of nature. To Coleridge, chemistry was one of the highest forms of philosophical endeavour, representing a "striving after unity of principle, through all the diversity of forms ... poetry, as it were, substantiated and realised." Though the Darwin brothers hardly knew enough to identify themselves as members of any philosophical movement, let alone one as diverse in its features as Romanticism, they felt themselves part of a larger cultural concern with the fundamental powers of matter that gripped Europe in the first decades of the nineteenth century. For the rest of his life, Darwin believed natural science was concerned with all-pervasive unseen forces and visionary hypotheses. Lies and the excitement of possessing specimens merged indistinguishably with the imaginative engagement demanded by his chemical researches. His juvenile soul opened out like a flower to the creative wonder of speculative natural philosophy.

VIII

When Erasmus finished school in 1822 and left for Cambridge University to study medicine, Darwin dutifully carried on the affairs of the Lab, performing experiments and analyses at his brother's long-distance instruction, and following up his own interests in mineralogy and other aspects of the new chemistry.

The niceties of experimental work were very appealing to him. He usually heated substances over an open flame until they fused or dissolved, always an attractive part of the chemical armoury. The samples probably exploded sometimes too. Work with acids was just as gratifying in its visual effects. He loved the gadgets of chemistry, the delicate measurements, the delight of new equipment; and he thoroughly enjoyed the deft manipulations that were required to make an investigation come right. He was always on the lookout for bits and pieces for additional experiments, forever borrowing things from the kitchen or garden storerooms or persuading Susan to give up sewing needles for some essential project. One sorry entry in the doctor's account book shows how he was obliged to pay Nancy, the nursery nurse, the sum of ten shillings "on account of the loss of her brother's tools." These homemade improvisations were regarded as more than equal to any shop-bought item; and he was never as content as when fiddling about trying to make ends meet in an appropriate instrument for his youthful researches.

His chemical activities were not just confined to the Lab, either. John

Cameron ruefully recorded that at school Darwin "spent some time, most evenings, with a blow-pipe at the gas-light in our bedroom." Since this meant puffing air by mouth through a brass tube into the raw flame and balancing chemicals in his free hand, ready to stick them into the gas at a suitable moment, Cameron, under the circumstances, was remarkably casual about the possible dangers. While Erasmus was called "Bones" because of the medicines prescribed by Dr. Darwin to strengthen his lanky frame, Charles was for a long time "Gas" to the other boys. He only stopped these bedtime researches after receiving a public rebuke from the headmaster accompanied by a pull on his ears. "He called me very unjustly a 'poco curante,' and as I did not understand what he meant it seemed to me a fearful reproach."[57] Butler was not entirely wrong, however. *Pococurantism,* in his day, meant someone who was only interested in trifles.

Separated from his Lab while up at Cambridge, Erasmus wrote long letters about it to Darwin:

> You give me a very good account of our Lab: it is quite wonderful how perverse the glass house people are, for I particularly told them to make the test tubes round at the bottom & they must needs grind them flat. If the cow is not utterly consumed the next milking, it would be a very good thing to buy as many of the large green, stoppered bottles as possible, & have them all filled with distilled water, & then I shall not be obliged to *persuade* you quite so often to run down to Blunt for some water.
>
> Professor Cumming shewed us some of the most beautiful crystalls you can imagine, in fact they were artificial diamonds. The way he made them was, by putting a few drops of Sulphuret of Carbon at the bottom of a well stopped bottle, & the liquid, being the most volatile of any, crystallized against the sides of the vessel. They were far more brilliant than any diamonds I ever saw, but if air was admitted they melted away.
>
> I shall not bring you any minerals down this time as they would stand a very good chance of being knocked about, rather more than their constitution can bear.—I will bring you some wavellite, & uranite & likewise a petrifaction from a well near here, as I have bought them already.—
>
> What I shall buy in London will be principally stop cocks, & jars with stop cocks, for that is what we are principally deficient in, & we shall then be able to get over the ground rather quicker in our gas experiments. —The Lab will look very insignificant after all the grand things I see here.—[58]

Professor Cumming was most remarkable, Erasmus reported appreciatively, for his displays of scientific experiments. Most of these were designed to introduce students to the chemical and physical discoveries of the age. But Cumming was also familiar with party tricks like the manufacture of artificial diamonds. On one occasion he made for the class's amusement a batch of nitrous oxide—the "laughing gas" discovered by Priestley and investigated by Davy. After this lecture, Erasmus excitedly proposed to Darwin that they manufacture it themselves. "I hope you practise making gases, and have learnt to manage the argand lamp, quite beautifully.—In lecture the other day, 3 or 4 men got perfectly tipsy with the nitrous oxide or laughing gas (that one made from nitrate of ammonia) and made themselves utterly ridiculous. They all recovered in about a minute—one man said he felt just as if he could fly, & when he was drinking the gas, he began to jump, & twiddle his fingers, & made a kind of half laughing & screaming noise, & ye Professor gave a good tug before he would let the bladder be taken out of his mouth.—"

Though friends and sisters laughed at their esoteric enthusiasms, Dr. Darwin secretly empathised. He had more than a passing knowledge of the subject; he had attended Joseph Black's chemical lectures during his days as a medical student in Edinburgh and for a long time afterwards monitored the affairs of the Wedgwood manufactories. As a young man he had briefly lodged with Black for private tuition. Black was the most eminent professor of medicine and chemistry of the era, and the young doctor's graduation thesis on the physiology of colour perception was partly taken up with his teaching in mind.[59]

Dr. Darwin consequently reacted with equanimity to the news from Shrewsbury School that his younger son was not much of a classical scholar. From his own scientific interests and the pleasant hours shared with his son in the garden and carriage he could see it was only Butler's emphasis on traditional learning that generated indifference.

The idea that he should remove the boy from Shrewsbury began to take root. He tended to the view that Charles was best suited to become a doctor rather than any other kind of learned gentleman: a doctor like himself, and his father before him, and as Erasmus was intending to be. As a physician, Charles could direct his mind to useful ends; he could carry on collecting natural history specimens or start investigating the world in a more erudite way, just as many medical men had done in the past and continued to do throughout the nineteenth century; and he would be perpetuating a family tradition. He could never qualify as a lawyer, for example, with his dislike for Latin and Greek, and he was far too poor at mathematics to attempt natural philosophy at one of the universities. Dr. Darwin probably felt that his son had inherited his own practical tastes and would correspondingly enjoy the same kind of adult life, surrounded by the plants, books, children, and animals of a cultured medical man well situated in provincial English society.

None of these thoughts, however, would necessarily have led to action had not Erasmus been about to step out into a career. Erasmus was due to leave Cambridge in 1825 and needed to attend courses at an authorised medical school to fulfil the requirements for an M.B. degree.

It was this, more than anything, that brought Dr. Darwin to a firm decision: he would take Charles away from school rather earlier than usual and send him with his brother to Edinburgh. He could attend lecture courses in medicine, at first merely keeping Erasmus company and then staying on until he was old enough to sit for a medical degree. The two would lodge and work together, helping each other up to the mark.

And so, on 17 June 1825, at the age of sixteen, Darwin left Shrewsbury School: "for ever," as he gratefully put it. The Edinburgh scheme sounded a wonderful improvement. Erasmus was equally pleased. "Are you making any plans with regard to Edinbororough [*sic*]?" he asked his brother during the last weeks of his final term at Cambridge; "any nice little stony excursions? We'll have rare fun in planning if we dont have any in performing them. I've made five hundred for my share. How shall you fancy going there by sea? it is a 14 hour's passage from Liverpool to Glasgow. We can stay a day or two at ye Ile of Man if either of us feel inclined to give up the ghost [i.e., to be seasick], which wont be very unlikely I think. I shall be down in about 3 weeks & then Gracious Heavens! how *you* will chatter but."[60]

The only cloud on the horizon as far as Charles could see was that if they both went away, Spark the dog might go to Marianne now that she was married.

FROM MEDICINE ...

ENDING a son to become a doctor in Edinburgh was far more momentous an affair than redistributing the family pets. Although Dr. Darwin could not see it, the whole weight of ancestry was poised in the wings.

The two boys knew a certain amount, of course, about their personal connections with Scottish medicine, particularly in relation to their paternal grandfather, the first Erasmus Darwin, who lived from 1731 to 1802. That Erasmus had been one of a wave of eighteenth-century Englishmen taking advantage of Edinburgh's eminence as an alternative to the medical schools of Leiden and Padua. He held a scholarship at St. John's College, Cambridge, before deciding to read medicine in the north, and though he spent only a year in Edinburgh, as was customary for Oxford and Cambridge graduates, and returned to Cambridge to obtain his medical degree in 1755, again as was usual, much of his intellectual life took its expansive tone from the work of the men he met there. In Edinburgh he imbibed the ideology of social improvement and "progress" permeating Scottish literary culture at that time, where scepticism and a relative indifference to religion went hand in hand with the encouragement of wide-ranging political reform, and he became familiar with a much greater variety of nonconformist and freethinking philosophies of nature than was ever possible at the stiff Anglican colleges of Cambridge. The stars of the Scottish enlightenment, David Hume, Adam Smith, Adam Ferguson, Joseph Black, and James Hutton, were in place and in their prime; and the professors who constituted the core of the medical school, especially the first and second Alexander Monro, the father-and-son team responsible for anatomy teaching, were then of world-wide repute. Medical teaching was as innovative and as reform-based as teaching in the humanities.[1]

With a hedonistic gusto for the pleasurable side of life, an impressively large physique (he looked like a butcher, said Anna Seward, who wrote a book about him in 1804), and a flamboyant medical philosophy that emphasised the power of the mind, this Erasmus Darwin used his Edinburgh training to become a physician in Lichfield, later moving to Derby, where he ran a successful practice till his death in 1802.[2] Just like any country squire in *Tom Jones,* the doctor believed in the hearty joys of women, food, a little gardening and agricultural improvement, some practical inventions to discuss with friends, and agreeable company in the evenings, with good books and plenty of children for his old age. Like any red-cheeked farmer, he held level-headed and forcibly expressed opinions, which often spilled over into his medical diagnoses: he believed—along with many Edinburgh-trained physicians of the period—in the restoration of "balance" to the body by treatments that would either "excite" or "reduce" the afflicted temperaments. As a doctor, he attached great importance to the nervous system, emerging as one of the better-known medical men of the era to pay attention to mental conditions, and considering many diseases to be of nervous rather than strictly physical origin.[3] His skill in dealing with such cases apparently reached the ears of George III. The king asked him to come from Lichfield to be his doctor, no doubt hoping for more sympathetic treatment than that offered by Francis Willis, the royal "mad-doctor."[4] Erasmus Darwin, never favourably inclined towards kings and Tories, declined. The family thereafter took a sturdy pride in the way he had thus forfeited an almost certain elevation to the peerage.

He was, nevertheless, altogether more prominent as a scientific poet and radical evolutionary thinker than as a doctor—as prominent in the late-eighteenth-century and early-nineteenth-century intellectual world as his contemporary Jean Baptiste Lamarck was with theories of evolution that roughly matched his own. While Erasmus Darwin was often called the English Lamarck, it was equally the case that Lamarck appeared to contemporaries like a pale Parisian Darwin. The two were commonly linked together as the most influential proponents of transmutation of their period.

Where, however, the Frenchman described his evolutionary theories in heavily academic tomes with little public appeal,[5] Erasmus Darwin plunged into popular scientific poetry. Cantering along in the style—if not with the elegance—of Alexander Pope, he never aspired to greatness. His verses, however, were remarkable for their vivid pictures of evolution interlaced with stirring accounts of the advancement of science, technology, and human culture during the late eighteenth century, the very epitome of optimistic entrepreneurial thought applied to the natural world in the bright glow of the prerevolutionary era.

It is hard to recapture the full extent of the fame these writings, virtually forgotten today, brought him.[6] Yet for many readers of the 1790s, Darwin was *the* poet for the age of liberty and social advance: an advocate of industrialisation and cultural improvement; an avid admirer of the power of steam; a disciple of the French *philosophes,* revealing his Jacobin-like fervour for change and transformation at every turn, and deliberately provocative in taking as his publisher the radical Joseph Johnson, the Londoner who printed William Godwin and friends; at all times a poet of progress, with such an obvious sense of humour that his zest for life could not fail to amuse.[7] This exuberant synthesis led to his appearance in a satirical Tory poem by George Canning and in one of Gillray's caricatures. Among a throng of freethinking contemporaries pictured by Gillray, including Tom Paine, Fox, Erskine, Priestley, Lord Derby, Godwin, Wollstonecraft, Coleridge, and Southey, stood a street vendor with a basket labelled "Zoonomia, or Jacobin plants." Inside were the flowers of Erasmus Darwin's writings—sporting *bonnets rouges* and tricolour cockades instead of petals.[8] As he cried to James Watt in January 1790: "Do you not congratulate your grandchildren on the dawn of universal liberty? I feel myself becoming all French both in chemistry and politics."[9]

More than a touch of atheism coloured these scientific poems, for Erasmus Darwin teetered on the brink of claiming that nothing exists except matter and its movements and modifications; that even consciousness and the human will are caused by material—physical—agencies rather than taking their origin or shape from God. He did not publicly deny the existence of a Creator, and never quite abolished the idea of a final cause in his writings in the way La Mettrie, Baron d'Holbach, and others boldly did. But like many intellectuals in France, Holland, and Scotland, he certainly pushed divine agency into the background. What he described instead was a world in which life began with the spontaneous appearance of primeval filaments at an early stage in the earth's history. These advanced by self-generated variation and diversification to populate the world with all its modern species. His proposed mechanism for change was simple enough, depending on living beings developing useful characteristics that were passed on intact to the next generation—the idea of the inheritance of acquired characteristics. Such ideas were widespread in his era and similarly taken up by Lamarck and other enlightenment philosophers. Plants, animals, and people therefore owed their origin to a process of advancement through geological time that was not in any sense due to divine intervention or the continuing creative powers of God. He saw existence as governed by the "laws of nature," rather than by divine authority.

Organic Life beneath the shoreless waves
Was born and nurs'd in Ocean's pearly caves;
First forms minute, unseen by spheric glass,
Move on the mud, or pierce the watery mass;
These as successive generations bloom,
New powers acquire, and larger limbs assume;
Whence countless groups of vegetation spring,
And breathing realms of fin, and feet, and wing.
Thus the tall Oak, the giant of the wood,
Which bears Britannia's thunders on the flood;
The Whale, unmeasured monster of the main,
The lordly Lion, monarch of the plain,
The Eagle soaring in the realms of air,
Whose eye undazzled drinks the solar glare,
Imperious man, who rules the bestial crowd,
Of language, reason, and reflection proud,
With brow erect who scorns this earthy sod,
And styles himself the image of his God;
Arose from rudiments of form and sense,
An embryon point, or microscopic ens![10]

Three long poems in this buoyant Augustan style under the titles *The Economy of Vegetation*, *The Loves of the Plants* (these two reissued under a single title as *The Botanic Garden*), and *The Temple of Nature*, provided a full explanation of his evolutionary scheme and made clearer the mechanisms he thought were involved. Two further prose works directed to a professional medical audience—*Zoonomia* (1794–96) and *Phytologia* (1800)—reiterated the same theory in more technical detail. Through them his name became synonymous with unbridled speculation about a self-generated, godless universe—so much so that Mary Shelley's *Frankenstein* (1818) was directly inspired by her husband's talk of Erasmus Darwin's preserving "a piece of vermicelli in a glass case till by some extraordinary means it began to move with voluntary motion."[11]

Well aware of the public abominations he might generate, Erasmus Darwin for a time considered *Zoonomia* dangerous enough to warrant delaying its publication until after his death, although during the first few years of French revolutionary fervour he changed his mind. The book was placed on the Index Expurgatorius a few years after he died.[12]

Yet his gusts of breezy optimism, an insistence on the importance of **sex** and sexuality, and outrageous hyperbole—managing to impress Wordsworth at the same time as it "frankly nauseated" Coleridge—made his works irresistible to a wide section of the educated public. *The Loves of the Plants* was "the most delicious poem upon earth," said Horace Walpole. "How strange it is that a man should have been inspired with such an enthusiasm of poetry by poring through a microscope, and peeping through the keyholes of all the seraglios of all the flowers in the universe!"[13]

More soberly, as became the dour Scots, Thomas Thomson in the *Edinburgh Review* of 1803 identified Erasmus Darwin's basic heresy as undermining the distinction between mind and matter, thereby endowing matter with inherent vitality. Or, as Dr. Fellowes said, he dwelt so much and so exclusively on secondary causes he forgot "that there is a first."[14]

II

Such a naturalistic and progress-based view of the world brought the first Erasmus Darwin into contact with many of the most distinguished figures of his age, including Matthew Boulton, James Watt, William Withering (of digitalis fame), Samuel Galton, Josiah Wedgwood, Thomas Day, Richard Lovell Edgeworth, Fuseli, Walpole, Blake, and Coleridge. Coleridge found him "the most inventive of philosophical men ... the everything except the Christian!"[15]

During Erasmus Darwin's early years in Lichfield, some of these figures met on a monthly basis for philosophical and technological discussions—the carriage journeys to and from one another's houses taking place in the moonlight and inspiring him to dub the circle of friends the "lunar society." The group brought together some of the sharpest minds in the Midlands, uniting technological entrepreneurs, philosophers, social theorists, and wealthy manufacturers, all with a common enthusiasm for the "rational" and "improving" ethos of the age: the promoters of industrial society and of capitalist visions of progress based on heroic, competitive endeavour. It was one of the most active and successful of several similar provincial scientific societies, despite its lack of any institutional footing.[16]

Erasmus Darwin's private life, however, was not nearly as cheerful as his verses. His first wife, the frail and talented Mary Howard, died in 1770, aged thirty-one, of alcoholic poisoning exacerbated by "great doses of opium" administered by her husband.[17] He thought her illness was in some degree inherited from an alcoholic father, and never afterwards allowed himself, the family, or patients to touch any kind of liquor—a heavy injunction that lasted undiminished through the generations to his grandchild Charles, who as an adult more than eighty years later confessed he never took a glass of wine without feeling guilty. Erasmus Darwin rationalised the rule by explaining how it helped his gout: a good medical reason with which no one in the family was inclined to argue. Of the five children Mary Howard had borne, three small sons survived her.

Still, as an unidentified obituarist remarked of him, it proved easier to give up Bacchus than the charms of Venus. Erasmus Darwin had a passionate and earthy nature, at one with the liberal sexual views of eighteenth-century Paris. After the death of his wife he flung himself into the Rousseauvian world of natural love and fathered two daughters by a Mrs. Parker of Lichfield (the "Mrs." was apparently a courtesy title, since she was only eighteen) before marrying a handsome widow, Elizabeth Pole of Radbourne Hall, herself an illegitimate child, the half-sister of Lady Curzon.

No great catch at fifty, fat, gouty, pockmarked from an early bout of smallpox, "subject to piles and gravel," and a pronounced stammerer, Erasmus Darwin was more than happy with his second marriage. The new alliance— which included the motherless Darwin boys, three Pole children, and the two Parker girls, who continued to live with their father—moved to Derby, where seven more children were born in rapid succession (one baby died). The proud patriarch of this enormous tribe hardly needed anything more to convince him that sexual reproduction was the key to everything—the essential link in the great evolutionary chain of living beings, the "masterpiece of nature," as he wrote in his poems, the solace of human existence. "Hail the Deities of Sexual Love!" he trumpeted; "and sex to sex the willing world unite."[18]

Assertive and opinionated, this powerful personality completely dominated the next two generations of Darwins. Even grandchildren born years after his death felt his grip in a multitude of different ways. He was a tyrant, said Anna Seward, with some justification.

The Edinburgh medical connection, for one, was vigorously kept up.[19] Charles, the eldest son from Erasmus Darwin's marriage to Mary Howard, went north like his father to read medicine but died as a student in 1778, of septicaemia or possibly inflammation of the brain contracted through performing a postmortem on a child with "hydrocephalus internus." He was only nineteen years old. By all accounts a gifted young man, he was singled out as a favourite pupil by Andrew Duncan, a former contemporary of Erasmus Darwin's, and further showed promise by being elected to the new and exclusive Aesculapian Society of Edinburgh University, in which fifteen of the brightest medical students gathered to discuss scientific topics. Just before he died, the Aesculapiads awarded him their first annual medal for an article distinguishing "matter from mucus." Andrew Duncan arranged for the boy to be buried in the Duncan family vault in St. Cuthbert's Church, Edinburgh, while Erasmus Darwin published his son's unfinished medical thesis with a brief commemorative life attached to it in 1780. An anonymous elegy in his inimitable style followed soon after.[20] "Fame's boastful chisel, fortune's silver plume," the churchyard monument read: "Mark but the mouldering urn, or deck the tomb!"

III

Encouraging his second son to go into the law, Erasmus Darwin turned the full force of his medical aspirations onto the third, much younger son, Robert Waring Darwin. This son was forced, more or less against his will, into replacing his lost elder brother. As soon as he was old enough—barely old enough, at fifteen—he was sent to learn medical anatomy at William Hunter's school in London. From there after Hunter's death in 1783, he was dispatched to study medicine in Edinburgh, attending courses for three successive years from 1784 to 1787.[21] If he had had any choice in the matter, he used to say, nothing would have induced him to take up doctoring as a profession. Prim, difficult, and sensitive, he was so unlike his father or medical brother that it was a triumph of self-discipline for him to continue the training. To the end of his life an operation sickened him and he could scarcely endure the sight of blood.

Erasmus Darwin refused to notice these faint-hearted signs of rebellion. He wanted at least one of the family to be a great physician. To that end, he shamelessly solicited favours on the young doctor's behalf: he asked Edinburgh professors to promote his son's studies, and he published Robert's early researches post-haste at the back of new editions of his poems and other works. Robert's interests in plants and chemistry were pushed forward more than necessary, although he did, in the event, appreciate being close to several of Edinburgh's most notable experts in those subjects, especially the chemist Joseph Black, and John Hope, the professor of materia medica (drugs and natural remedies) and botany, from whom he acquired a long-lasting admiration for Linnaeus. He was also fortunate in being taught clinical medicine by William Cullen just before the latter's death in 1790.

Low-key achievements like these were not quite enough for the first Erasmus Darwin. The relentless programme included making a trip to Leiden, where he graduated as M.D. in 1785, plus a visit to the Paris hospitals to learn clinical technique, followed by an approach to Sir Joseph Banks, the president of the Royal Society of London, who was favourably disposed towards the older Darwin's botanical verses, to get him a fellowship to increase his standing in medical affairs. Robert was duly elected in 1788.

Relations were barely improved when Erasmus Darwin at last stopped interfering in his son's career and began to ignore him. After pushing the young man so far, he unaccountably refused to finance the move to Shrewsbury, clearly expecting him to start medical practice with nothing but his wits to rely on. Anguished letters from Robert conveying surprise, money worries, and resentment in turn were answered by exhortations to think cheerfully and work hard, and he would soon feel all right. Money, said the remorseless father, would come in due course if he was a good physician.

It was probably at this time that young Dr. Darwin decided to join the Freemasons—a fall-back position he did not use to full professional advantage but a step which must have reflected the feeling that he was cast out on his own without any of the introductions needed for establishing a strong medical constituency among local gentlemen. He went through a preliminary initiation ceremony which he believed involved drawing blood. He could feel it trickling down his arm, he said, though there was not a mark on him.[22]

Nor was that entirely all, for Erasmus Darwin then leaped into a bitter pamphlet war with William Withering, a reputable doctor from nearby Birmingham, about the correct diagnosis of one of Robert's first patients. The case nearly went to court; and the pamphlet in which the younger Darwin replayed the gist of the controversy was such a bitter attempt at self-vindication that he spent the rest of his life tracking down copies in order to burn them.[23] Robert Waring Darwin was, at the end of it, exasperated by his father's complete lack of understanding: a man, in his eyes, capable of withholding help when it was desperately needed and of giving quite the wrong kind when best avoided. That he eventually did achieve an independent success never made those first paternal jolts any easier to forget. The doctor's rancour ran long and deep. He vowed never to treat his own children in similar fashion.

Ten years later, Robert's last remaining brother committed suicide. One can only guess at the family pressures that lay behind the act. Neither of the two men had fully emerged from under the first Erasmus Darwin's shadow, for instance; and the death of their mother and older brother, taken in conjunction with their father's apparent indifference after his remarriage and obvious delight in a large second family, drew them closely together in what they undoubtedly saw as a generally hostile world.

But at least Robert Waring Darwin had a wife and children in Shrewsbury to take comfort in. His brother Erasmus had no one. Trained as a solicitor, he was a solitary, anxious person who over the years became progressively unable to handle his cases in Lichfield and sank into debilitating depressions. There was "a want of energy in his character, and too extreme a delicacy of feeling on the occurrence of every thing which was in the slightest degree repulsive," wrote Seward.[24] She thought it had been a mistake not to let him enter the church, as he had once wished. His energetic father was frequently "vexed at his retiring nature, and at his not more fully displaying his great talents."[25] Eventually, bills began to prey on his mind. Buying a new house at Breadsall with interesting monastic ruins in the grounds provided something of an answer, and he relayed plans for excavations and rebuilding works to

Robert in Shrewsbury. But financial problems finally engulfed him, and on 29 December 1799 he threw himself into the river at the bottom of his garden during what was called a temporary fit of insanity. A week before his death he sent Dr. Darwin a small cross of plaited grass taken from the tomb of their elder brother, Charles.[26]

This second death was almost more than Robert Waring Darwin could handle. By then married to Susanna Wedgwood with a rapidly increasing family of his own, he sadly commemorated his two dead brothers by naming his own small sons after them. The first little boy, Erasmus, was born five years to the day after his uncle killed himself, on 29 December 1804. The next one, Charles, was named for the brilliant medical student that Dr. Darwin never was nor wanted to be. If that was not enough, the doctor nicknamed them Ras and Bobby—the names he and his brother had called each other in letters. The two newest members of the family, he imagined, would recreate the history of the older generation under much happier circumstances.

With such heavy emotional underpinnings to a life in medicine, it was not altogether certain how the two of them would cope.

IV

Arriving in Edinburgh at the beginning of October 1825, Charles and Erasmus Darwin were earnestly committed to the idea of becoming doctors. Their father had spent much of the summer talking over his medical cases with them, filling their heads with the past and present complaints of Shropshire families and introducing them to the psychology of local practice. The doctor's advice was practical, if brusque: white lies and sympathy were usually all that was needed. Like the first Erasmus Darwin, Dr. Darwin had developed an almost intuitive sense of the mental state of patients: he often remarked how many miserable husbands and wives he had known. The best remedy, he told the boys, was to let people talk.

Whenever possible, he also took them out on his rounds. Erasmus accompanied Dr. Darwin on weekly visits to the clinical wards in the county infirmary (soon rebuilt at a cost of more than £18,000, with the business-minded doctor, as usual, a major shareholder), and on three or four occasions Charles Darwin was allowed to attend his father's charity outpatients, chiefly women and children with complaints too minor for admittance to hospital. Darwin liked what he experienced. "I wrote down as full an account as I could of the cases with all the symptoms, and read them aloud to my father, who suggested further enquiries, and advised me what medicines to give, which I made up myself. At one time I had at least a dozen patients, and I felt a keen interest in the work." Much later on, Darwin's son Francis remembered him saying he only made "a lot of unhappy children sick with tartar emetic" when they probably should have been treated for pneumonia.

Dr. Darwin was pleased. In his view, his son Charles would make a good physician, better perhaps than Erasmus, who already showed some of the sickly lassitude that dogged his later life. He had worried greatly about Erasmus's health all through school and university, and letters written from The Mount during that period recommended increasingly complicated precautions for him against the cold, the wind, the internal weaknesses: flannel waistcoats worn next to the skin gave way to strengthening medicines for the bones, which in turn were replaced by opiates and belladonna concoctions for rubbing onto his chest.[27] Since the doctor rarely wrote letters, it was a sign of his mounting concern that so many prescriptions were sent. Despite these fatherly instructions, Erasmus's health deteriorated during the summer of 1825, forcing Dr. Darwin to contemplate the possibility that Erasmus might be too much of an invalid to follow him into medical practice.

Private hopes were focussed on Charles, his younger son, to all appearances a strong, outdoors sort of fellow with the quietly sympathetic nature that characterised the best country physicians. Even at the tender age of sixteen, this son showed the potential, Dr. Darwin thought. "My father, who was by far the best judge of character whom I ever knew, declared that I should make a successful physician,—meaning by this, one who got many patients. He maintained that the chief element of success was exciting confidence; but what he saw in me which convinced him that I should create confidence I know not."[28]

For themselves, the two young men were more than happy to find their independent feet in the Scottish capital—the modern Athens, as Enlightenment anecdote had it, but to them as full of potential excitement as if the circus of ancient Rome had been reopened. City life and the thrill of starting out on new adventures were incomparably stimulating, far better than being at school or seeing docile charity patients in provincial Shrewsbury. Political and religious controversy ran intoxicatingly high as Calvinists and Covenanters, Jacobites and Tory Anglicans fought over the distribution of power within Scotland and between Scotland and England, few caring to distinguish sharply between them. Nationalism rode just as fast, brought to a crescendo with the first Waverley novels published anonymously by Sir Walter Scott and other stories based on Highland and border history like the gothic fable of demonic possession *Confessions of a Justified Sinner* by James Hogg, the "Ettrick shepherd": nationalism intensified one way or the other by hard-hitting writers in *Blackwood's Magazine* and the *Edinburgh Review,* celebrated literary periodicals established in the first decades of the century, and by the pomp of George IV's tartan-clad visit to the capital in 1822. Any relatively easy-going pragmatic English mind could easily believe itself in a foreign country.

Certainly, Charles Darwin found it an eye-opening experience. For a boy who had only been to Liverpool, the combination of Georgian elegance, urban squalor, and memorable natural scenery was full of dramatic effect. The castle perched on its mountainous eyrie, the New Town, Calton Hill, Holyrood Palace, and Salisbury Crags were very imposing: the outstanding features of one of the most visually striking cities in the world, "stately Edinburgh throned on crags," in Wordsworth's phrase. Down the High Street, equally imposing in its own way, sprawled the Old Town—a deep pool of jostling humanity where the infamous stacks of "flats" or tenements peculiar to Scottish city living were held up by the surrounding hills and one another. The poor here were unlike any poor Darwin had seen before. Drawn to the city by rural devastation, their numbers increased by swarms of Irish navigators ("navvies") who came to find work on the Grand Union Canal and stayed on to become the labour force of the Industrial Revolution, this sector of the Edinburgh populace had seen only the underside of Scotland's golden era. In Darwin's time they were already experiencing the slums that accompanied the beginnings of the factory age.

Over on the southern horizon, the bumpy lines of the Pentland Hills beckoned invitingly. To the north was the sea. Darwin could hardly wait to unpack his small library of natural history books, one of which, *A Naturalist's Companion* by George Graves, was specially bought in August with future seaside walks in mind. For the moment, however, the technological achievement of the North Bridge was the most remarkable thing he thought he had ever encountered: "when we first looked over the sides we could hardly believe our eyes, when, instead of seeing a fine river we saw a stream of people." He revelled in fresh impressions of all kinds. "We spend all our mornings in promenading about the town, which we know pretty well," he told his father, "and in the Evenings we go to the play to hear Miss Stephens, which is quite delightful." Eager to see all the sights, the brothers also went to church to experience at first hand the tub-thumping sermons traditional to Scottish kirk services. To Darwin's disappointment, the address lasted only twenty minutes: "I expected from Sir Walter Scott's account a soul-cutting discourse of 2 hours & a half."[29]

Romantic enthusiasm for Edinburgh's cultural heritage surged unabated for a while, intensified by the Shrewsbury girls' wistful letters about the castles and plays they might find time to visit. "Shrewsbury is going to make an attempt at gayety this week," Caroline lamely reported.

When they came to the university itself, the brothers were less impressed. The new university buildings begun in Robert Waring Darwin's day were still only half built, since wartime restrictions on building had brought work virtually to a halt in 1793. The site had been reactivated in more recent years by the architect William Playfair, and a palatial anatomy theatre with a classroom and museum underneath and the renowned natural history museum were more or less complete. The rest left a great deal to be done: the library, haphazardly balanced on the upper floor of a wooden building originally constructed in 1616, was propped up with buttresses to a neighbouring wall; messy construction works disfigured the precincts; and the crash of stones constantly accompanied lectures. Wooden scaffolding was everywhere. "Stony-hearted Edinburgh," lamented William Hazlitt a year or two before Darwin arrived; "a quarry, rather than the habitation of men!"[30] Darwin had not expected to find this ancient seat of learning a building site.

Widespread rapaciousness, a half-built university, and a rapidly deteriorating urban environment all contributed to an atmosphere completely at variance with anything the Darwin brothers had previously known. Jane Austen would never have felt at home there. Still, they found themselves a landlady in Lothian Street rather better than most: a Mrs. Mackay, who specialised in medical students, "a nice clean old body, and exceedingly civil & attentive."[31] She rented them two bedrooms and a sitting room much larger than the poky holes Charles saw elsewhere, "very nice & *light,*" he emphasised, sure that Dr. Darwin would understand how important this was. The rooms were on the fourth floor, another unexpected aspect of Edinburgh life; some of the lodgings they looked at were seven or eight flights of stairs above ground level. In places which were unsuitable to visit alone, tenements could be thirteen stories high.

V

Their first duty was to call on Richard Maddock Hawley, a medical acquaintance of Dr. Darwin's, bearing his good wishes and a request that he look after the boys during their first days in the city. This they did civilly enough and were quietly grateful for his attentions. Again, old Dr. Duncan remembered their dead uncle Charles and was equally obliging with his Friday-evening invitations—though the parties were "the very specimen of stupidity."

But independence from these careful precautions soon burst out. Within a couple of weeks, Erasmus insisted he would not countenance any more introductions on his and Charles's behalf. He dreaded the thought of finding himself forever obliged to dine with elderly cronies of his father's.

Understandably, he wanted to be responsible for his own social life. Even so, the rebellion represented something more personal, only touched on in letters. Erasmus rapidly found Edinburgh undergraduates very different from his previous contemporaries at Cambridge University. The majority of students were neither rich nor from the kind of cultured landed family he was most familiar with. They were sometimes extremely young, some as young as fourteen, as Thomas Carlyle was when he matriculated in 1809, or much older and more experienced, returning from the European wars. Many were ill prepared for university, and some did not seek a degree.

Moreover, they were rough, bold, and turbulent. Rowdy classes were normal in the medical school, because the audience sang, shouted, stamped, and scraped their benches as signs of approval or disapproval in lectures—making a "ruff," it was called. Trumpets and peashooters were common. One story still running in student circles when the Darwins arrived was that pistols had been discharged in the anatomy classroom.[32] "Never come into the class till after the hour," advised a student magazine of 1825; "and when you do come, make as great a noise as you can in opening the door and going to your seat, for it shows you are there, and it lets your acquaintance know where to find you when the class is over."

There were, Erasmus thought, scarcely any clever well-read soul-mates like those he had known at Christ's College, Cambridge, no literary society like the Cambridge "Apostles," which he had joined in 1823, almost at its foundation, for gentlemanly debate on philosophical affairs.[33] The student societies in Edinburgh were mostly either large, semiformal professional groups, such as the Royal Medical Society, founded in 1737 and incorporated by royal charter in 1778, which their father joined during his time in the city, or odd little cliques like the "Six-feet club," set up by Scott in 1826 for men of that height wishing to promote "the national games of Scotland." Having spent the greater part of his youth avoiding all forms of sports, Erasmus—though easily qualifying on the grounds of size—was unlikely to join forces with this or any similarly idiosyncratic group.

Retiring, frail in health, bookish, and finicky, he shrank from what he considered vulgar behaviour and plaintively withdrew into an ivory tower of his own. The only congenial company was his brother's.

"It is a great pity that Eras thought he should dislike his having acquaintances in Edinbourgh & so refused to take introductions," complained Caroline to Charles. "I want to know how you both like Edinburgh," echoed Marianne: "I suppose you like it better than the Drs [Dr. Butler's school] Eras not so well as his dear C.C.C."[34]

Sedately concurring with Erasmus's snobberies, the younger Darwin had no complaints about keeping his idolised elder brother company. During their first year in Edinburgh, neither of them bothered to find any new friends. Darwin socialised exclusively with Erasmus, and occasionally with a contemporary from Shrewsbury School called Henry Johnston who was also taking medical courses, while Erasmus poured out his fastidious heart in letters to Cambridge acquaintances. He nearly broke down when his friend Eyre died of a fever before he could travel south to see him.

The two did everything together. They attended the same lecture courses, dined out and in, walked to Newhaven and Port Leith on joint natural history expeditions, read the same political weeklies (try *The Age,* recommended Erasmus: it was even worse than *John Bull,* whose Tory hysteria the pair were relishing), and went to the theatre, always inseparable: the same two lanky figures earnestly striding out towards the classroom, the library, or cold, windy beach, defying the Scottish winter with stout flannel vests under their shirts as advised by their father, English upper-class reserve written all over their faces, needing no one else apart from each other, unapproachable and self-sufficient.

One feature of this mutually inward-looking satisfaction was that they did not join any of the local scientific societies, not even the student society for chemistry, which encouraged practical experimentation along the lines they had previously enjoyed at home in Shrewsbury. Nor did they make any attempt at recapturing the atmosphere of the Shrewsbury Lab or gas-lit dormitory in the privacy of their lodgings. Perhaps they felt they knew more about the subject than the others or that they had in some sense grown out of those interests.

Instead, as the borrowing list of the university library indicated, they filled their available free time with reading books. Erasmus had the distinction of borrowing more books (forty-one) than any other undergraduate in the five months that constituted the medical session of 1825–26, at least five or six of which were complex literary and philosophical works, including David Hume and Voltaire; Charles was not far behind, spending several uneventful evenings in lodgings working through Boswell's life of Johnson, which he carried off one volume at a time. He borrowed books on natural history and zoology throughout the rest of the session.[35]

Just as soon as Erasmus completed his medical coursework in April 1826, he returned to Shrewsbury, grateful not to have to continue living through the uncomfortable cultural contrasts of the north. Charles Darwin only really emerged out of this brotherly cocoon during a second year in Edinburgh after Erasmus had left.

VI

To create a cocoon was at least a useful way to cope with the harsh realities of academic life in Scotland. The university at that time was characterised by nothing less than uproar. Conflict swept through every unfinished building and through every argumentative heart; feuds were rife, expanding in acrimonious circles from the professors to the students, and then to the city worthies, the baileys on the town council, and the Edinburgh populace at large; ancient privileges were constantly disputed, schemes were hatched, reforms were proposed and aborted; and the style and content of the curriculum were brought under the fiercest attack until then experienced. Politics and religion were not far behind. By the time Darwin left, only the external authority of an English-based Royal Commission of Inquiry was capable of providing any form of resolution for the university's more generalised problems. Beginning in 1826 and eventually including all the Scottish universities, this commission introduced wide-ranging changes in the way higher education was run in the north.

Most of the troubles originated in the way the university was organised, for a student had no obligation to attend any course or courses in any order whatsoever, being free to pick and choose at will, and simply purchased a ticket for whichever set of subjects took his fancy, only bearing in mind that attendance at some specified courses was required for the award of a degree.[36] Professors, too, operated a similarly open market. They received scarcely any salary other than the fees taken directly from students who registered for their lectures, and they regarded their chairs as personal fiefdoms—or, more accurately, as profit-making business concerns. A great deal of academic effort went into maximising the spread and attraction of lectures while retaining a monopoly over the topics taught: more effort, it was often said, than went into the actual teaching.

A market-led system such as this naturally generated intense competition, leading to quarrels among the professors. Many classes were characterised by verbal abuse aimed at one lecturer by another, and apparently straightforward issues like access to the anatomical collections or the natural history museum—each under the sole control of the relevant professor—were whipped up into arguments over intellectual property rights and entrance fees that extended way beyond the college walls. Some controversies bit deep enough to end up in the courtroom, although not before personal revenge was exacted. James Gregory, a former professor of the practice of physic, once took to beating Alexander Hamilton, the then professor of midwifery, in the street with his walking-stick. Undergraduate magazines were crammed with these and other scurrilous stories that took advantage of the freedom of speech conferred by the financial hold students exerted over their teachers' income.[37] Nepotism of the most flagrant kind ran equally unchecked. The Rutherfords, Monros, Gregorys, Hopes, Duncans, and Hamiltons carved up the university's eleven professorial chairs exclusively among themselves in the period 1780 to 1830.

By far the most influential quarrel featured James Hamilton, the son and academic successor of the professor on the wrong end of Gregory's walking-stick. This Hamilton caused such a fracas in getting midwifery added to the list of compulsory degree topics from 1824 onwards that the British prime minister, Sir Robert Peel, was at last asked to intervene. Peel smartly set up the Royal Commission of 1826, which, while failing to soothe every frayed temper, provided a basis for major academic reform. Evidence was taken from all the teaching staff during Darwin's time at Edinburgh.

The angry atmosphere also spread far beyond the college into the city itself. One particularly sore point among university medical men was the existence of freelance medical courses, made available to students through the transformation of medical teaching outside the university system during the Napoleonic period by the rapid development of independent schools. These schools were run by private lecturers—invariably themselves Edinburgh graduates of great ability—who offered a wide variety of tuition in subjects like surgical anatomy, physiology, general and special pathology, and clinical medicine. The extramural schools also encouraged much more practical experience in anatomical dissection and surgery than the professors could muster. Since a university degree was not at that time a necessary qualification for medical practice, and the city of Edinburgh possessed its own influential licensing bodies, not to mention the point that both sets of lecturers depended on student fees for their income, rivalry was intense.

Yet it was not in anyone's interest to force a conclusive victory: nothing was so simple in medical Edinburgh.[38] The two forms of education ran side by side, each busying itself with complaints about the proper forms of demarcation between them, ever watchful of student numbers, quick to criticise their rivals, and always feeding off and into each other in a fluid, interdependent situation. Alexander Monro, for example, the third professor of anatomy to carry that name, saw his class—and his income—decline from a peak of around five hundred students to a mere two hundred in 1825, at the same time as John Barclay's extracurricular school expanded from two hundred to five hundred. Nevertheless, any student wishing to go home with a university medical degree was obliged to register for Monro's course, and the professor retained sufficient territorial power to block Barclay's appointment to a proposed new chair of comparative anatomy. A contemporary cartoon captioned "The craft in danger" showed Professors Monro, Jameson, and Hope—all of whom would lose students to a new anatomical professor—preventing Barclay's entry (on an elephant) through the college gates. The cartoon expressed their uneasy relationship exactly.

The information in these freelance courses was also very different from the traditional bodies of knowledge over which university men presided. For many of the university professors, the most important aspect of their work was the way in which higher learning reinforced and justified the system of natural theology popular in the upper reaches of British society and the academic context in general: a natural theology that sought to use the characteristics of the external world to establish the existence of a divine creator, and to provide proofs of his benevolence, wisdom, and power. Natural theology provided the rationale for most of the scientific work of the first half of the nineteenth century in Britain, explicitly fusing the domains of nature and religion and supporting a stable moral and social order by its marked emphasis on "natural law."[39] In a society where science was not an autonomous profession, where fears of a homegrown political revolution pervaded establishment thinking and were exacerbated by the long years of war with France, financial stringency, and continual threats of rebellion by subversive radicals, philosophical and professional men were under considerable pressure to show that their chosen field of endeavour enhanced—rather than undermined—the prevailing system. With this in view, a figure like Alexander Monro, who was appointed to a university chair in 1800, expressly stated that he taught anatomy "to get a view of the animal creation, which affords such striking illustrations of the wisdom and power of its Author."

The conservative backlash to the outcome of the French Revolution, moreover, extended to freewheeling philosophies of nature like those adopted by the first Erasmus Darwin, who was considered dangerously seditious in the early years of the nineteenth century. His transmutationary views, together with those of Lamarck and some of Lamarck's Parisian followers, were seen as extremist doctrines that many leading members of the intelligentsia felt should be suppressed in Britain, particularly in the medical domain with its close interest in questions about the life and death of human beings. As a result, the most violent, lasting attack on Erasmus Darwin's philosophy of nature came from the acid pen of Thomas Brown, a twenty-year-old Scot who dominated Edinburgh thinking on metaphysics after his appointment in 1810 as Dugald Stewart's successor in the university chair of moral philosophy.

Extramural lecturers did not see things in anything like the same way. Through their frequent visits to France and Germany during the Napoleonic period and their friendly relations with the major figures in European science, private teachers brought important new biological and medical theories direct to Scotland. The improved surgical and clinical techniques of French hospitals, fundamentally different since the reorganisations made during the Revolution; the exciting new work of Georges Cuvier in anatomy and palaeontology, of Francois-Xavier Bichat in physiology and pathology, of Franz Joseph Gall and Johann Caspar Spurzheim in neurology and mental science, of Lamarck in biology and evolutionary theory, and of Johann Friedrich Blumenbach, ceaselessly studying comparative anatomy and physiology in Göttingen: all these were made available to extramural students at the highest level from around 1825 onwards. Many of the brightest and best of these students went to Paris to learn for themselves in the decades following. It was one of the less fortunate coincidences of Darwin's early life that he missed this general exodus by a few years.

In particular, the extramurals taught a new form of comparative anatomy, or "philosophical anatomy," as it was sometimes called, which endeavoured to understand the structure and function of living beings without reference to any obvious divine causes. Parisian doctors went "inside" the living body, so to speak, to inquire into the ultimate nature of matter and provide definitions of life. Ideas of "organisation" and "function" became paramount in their theories, especially as they could be related to the minute structure of the body, and were expressed through the activity of the nervous system, which, with the brain, was expected to hold the key to organisation.[40] In this sense, life was thought to emerge out of organisation alone rather than being superadded to an inert framework by God or as the workings of an immaterial principle like the soul. The vital property was inherent to matter itself—a philosophy of "vital materialism."[41] "A French anatomist," stated the *Edinburgh Medical Journal* approvingly in 1825, "sticks closely to his subject, gives nothing but anatomy pure and unsophisticated,—and without conspicuous attempts either at exposition of final causes or practical application of anatomical facts, describes systematically and regularly the shape, situation, different parts, and component tissues of each organ."[42]

At the same time, accomplished Parisian naturalists such as Etienne Geoffroy Saint-Hilaire and Henri de Blainville, who were familiar with German philosophical movements of the period, reinterpreted animal form as a repetition of similar units which deviated from a common "plan," taking their researches into embryology to find a hierarchical developmental sequence, frequently linking animals and plants into a single evolutionary scale from the simplest to the most complex, and encouraging anatomists to search for analogies and homologies between different structures like the limbs of birds, bats, and men. Contrasts and complementarities between the two sciences of "form" and of "function" were for these medical and anatomical men the primary topics of the age, represented in their most extreme and versatile positions by the controversy between Cuvier and Geoffroy, even then rumbling behind the doors of the Paris Académie des Sciences and Muséum d'Histoire Naturelle and soon to erupt into a wider arena in 1830.[43]

Such philosophical anatomy appealed to many post-Revolutionary thinkers, both French and Scottish, because of the intellectual challenge of searching for the functional or "idealised" connections between species, and because of the daring quasi-materialistic—or at least naturalistic—tendency of its central themes. Not many philosophical anatomists were outright atheists or subversive revolutionaries, it should be said, nor were many of the extramu-ral lecturers in Edinburgh professed "evolutionists"—perhaps only Robert Knox and his friend Robert Grant secretly adopted this view of nature during the 1820s.[44] The great majority, by all accounts, were believers in God in one form or another, as evidenced by the writings of John Barclay, John Bell, John Lizars, and James Syme, one of the founders of the Edinburgh Medical Missionary Society.

Barclay apart, their anatomical and physiological science was nonetheless mostly unshackled from theist or deist explanations: free from the kind of natural theology which emphasised the "design" invoked in university lectures. Sceptical of traditional authority and often shocking to establishment figures in their reliance on idealist "plans" or on the operation of essentially vitalistic powers to explain the unique properties of living beings, these men were walking a sure road to atheism and materialism, spluttered John Abernethy from St. Bartholomew's Hospital in London.

One or two extramural lecturers and their students, in common with a large number of respectable Edinburgh gentlemen, also looked favourably on the new doctrine of phrenology—the system first advocated by Gall and Spurzheim in which mental attributes like love, fear, or jealousy were regarded as self-contained entities, each one possessing a special location in the brain specifically connected to the shape of the skull, and in which the human mind was considered no less a physical phenomenon than, say, the secretion of digestive juices: the brain was the "organ of mind," as popular maxim put it.

Here, too, there was intense controversy, part of the larger socio-political debate about phrenological systems of various denominations sweeping through Europe and America during the first half of the nineteenth century. Phrenology gathered extraordinary momentum as a science for the general public which promised self-improvement through self-knowledge, as well as stimulating important new perspectives in understanding the workings of the brain.[45] Although ultimately transformed in the 1860s by the American "phrenological Fowlers" into an all-embracing blend of medical and social prescriptions based on "bumps," the subject for a time offered enormous explanatory and reformist possibilities to a wide cross-section of society.

And it was in Edinburgh that phrenology roused the first and greatest civic emotion. As put forward by George Combe, the Edinburgh lawyer, and his medical brother Andrew from 1820 onwards, and then by other more outspoken reformist groupings within the city, phrenology stood for much more than bold anatomical pronouncements. In the same breath, it represented an entirely naturalistic understanding of mental activity that plainly contradicted the philosophy of a single, indivisible mind generally favoured by the Scots since Dugald Stewart's day, and it challenged the nature of the "facts" on which conventional theories of mental function were based. It raised doubts about the traditional view of the relations between God and mankind. What of the soul, if human minds were merely the mechanical workings of the brain? Most important, it promised fundamental social change for the middling classes through opposing the bastions of privilege enjoyed by the Scottish intellectual aristocracy and conveying some of the growing urban unrest found in the city. This kind of scientific naturalism shaded imperceptibly into evolutionism and exhortations to self-generated progress of the kind broadly espoused by Lamarck and the first Erasmus Darwin: into agitation for political and social reform, and threats of atheism. In some hands, the academics thought, phrenology could be political dynamite.

Across these factions, furthermore, ran the age-old divisions between Whig and Tory, between surgeon and physician. No wonder Robert Christison characterised Edinburgh medical men as being involved in one "deadly life-long feud with many estimable brethren, both in and beyond the University."[46]

VII

When Darwin came to sign up for courses, he took no chances and followed the conservative route taken earlier by his father and grandfather. He did not attend any extramural classes, whether radical or no. Rather, he paid for tickets for nine university courses over two years, covering the traditional areas of anatomy, surgery, the practice of physic, materia medica, and their ancillary topics, plus chemistry delivered by Thomas Charles Hope and, during his second year, natural history by Robert Jameson.[47] The last two were the jewels in the crown of formal Edinburgh University teaching. Erasmus took most of the same subjects, including chemistry, and also attended an extracurricular anatomy school run by John Lizars.

By January 1826, Darwin was certain he had made at least two mistakes. He wrote to Caroline dejectedly:

Many thanks for your very entertaining letter, which was a great relief after hearing a long stupid lecture from Duncan on Materia Medica—But as you know nothing either of the Lectures or Lecturers, I will give you a short account of them.— Dr Duncan is so very learned that his wisdom has left no room for his sense, & he lectures, as I have already said, on the Materia Medica, which cannot be translated into any word expressive enough of its stupidity. These few last mornings, however, he has shown signs of improvement & I hope he will "go on as well as can be expected." His lectures begin at eight in the morning.— Dr Hope begins at ten o'clock, & I like both him & his lectures *very* much. (After which Erasmus goes to Mr Lizars on Anatomy, who is a charming lecturer) At 12, the Hospital, after which I attend Munro on Anatomy— I dislike him & his Lectures so much that I cannot speak with decency about them. He is so dirty in person & actions— Thrice a week we have what is called Clinical Lectures, which means lectures on the sick people in the Hospitals—these I like *very* much.—I said this account should be short, but I am afraid it has been too long like the Lectures themselves.—[48]

A few weeks later his dissatisfaction crystallised around Monro's anatomy course.

There seems little doubt that Alexander Monro taught the subject with considerably less aplomb than his father and grandfather, both of whom were gifted long-term incumbents of the anatomical chair before him. His lectures were confused, prolix, and illogical, jibed the *Lancet:* Monro's voice was "the very murmur of ennui." On occasion, he even read out his grandfather's notes rather than drawing up a new lecture relevant to the anatomical developments of the era—to the point of reciting, "When I was a student in Leiden in 1719 . . . "[49]

Darwin had hardly gone to Edinburgh to hear the very same lessons his grandfather had heard. "Dr. Munro made his lectures on human anatomy as dull as he was himself," he complained.[50] Standing in front of the class in his fingerless gloves, a rusty scalpel in one hand, bloody forceps in the other, and a checked cotton apron tied with string to complete his anatomical costume, Monro was an unattractive figure all round. Darwin's notes for the course (now very incomplete) show that the professor failed to teach him the most elementary aspects of bones. "This is all general & useless anatomy," Darwin scribbled in despair on one piece of paper; "this bone . . . is unintelligible to me."[51]

The practical part of Monro's class was equally fusty. Anatomical demonstrations at that time were always performed by a "Prosector," a paid demonstrator, in the huge new amphitheatre in front of a steeply tiered audience of students. During the session one or two cadavers were displayed in turn, ostensibly matching the lecture course. But in Monro's case the dissection weaved about at random: legs one week, skin the next, as a student journal vociferously protested. Everything was stupefyingly boring:

> *Found dead a mouse,—the reason is, you know*
> *That she had lived a week with old Monro.*[52]

Using only one body at a time, and one which, at that, was displayed by someone else, was a practice long outmoded in the more forward-looking external schools. John Barclay and his successor, Robert Knox, the proprietors of the leading extracurricular school in Edinburgh, had for several years been providing students with their own material for first-hand experience of dissection. To watch from afar, they argued, was no way to teach would-be surgeons and physicians. Clattering up the circular stairs to their seats in the university theatre day after day, Monro's students probably agreed. At such a distance they could barely distinguish the fine structures under discussion: all they saw was the same pickled body slowly and grossly dismembered over the long weeks before term ended. Although some of the keener students practised dissection after the formal teaching periods, Darwin was not urged in any way to do so and never managed to overcome his initial dislike of the idea. He stayed as far away from a corpse as he possibly could. The lack of such practice was "an irremediable evil," he later thought. At the time, it felt much more like exquisite relief.

Darwin's dislike of dissection was intensified by other, more repugnant aspects of the anatomical theatre. This was the period notorious for the traffic in corpses, a trade etched into the memory by Robert Louis Stevenson's *Body-Snatchers* (set in an atmospheric Edinburgh during the late 1820s) and culminating in the machinations of the immigrant Irishman William Burke and his accomplice William Hare, who, in 1828, the year after Darwin left the university, murdered at least sixteen people in the Old Town for the cash paid on delivery of a body to the medical school's back door: £8 in summer, £10 in winter, said Burke at his trial, seasonal prices taking advantage of the subsequent difficulties of preservation, but more than twice the cost of a year's lodgings for an Irish labourer.

The body trade had a long history and wide geographical spread, yet was at its height in Edinburgh during the first three decades of the century and was closely tied up with the fortunes of medical teaching in the city.[53] By law, only the corpses of convicted murderers or paupers who died in the care of the authorities were released under licence for teaching purposes, maybe three or four a year if the anatomist was lucky. These always went to established departments of medicine. Even so, the benefit was hard to discern. "In Dr Monro's class," reported John Bell, with a satisfied sneer from his anatomy school outside the university system, "unless there be a fortunate succession of bloody murders, not three subjects are dissected in the year. On the remains of a subject fished up from the bottom of a tub of spirits, are demonstrated those delicate nerves, which are to be avoided or divided in our operations; and these are demonstrated once at the distance of one hundred feet."

Bell's school boasted far more cadavers: sometimes as many as twenty at a time for students to work on. Barclay and Knox, who accommodated four or five hundred students a year, had still higher numbers passing through their hands. Some bodies were brought in, shipped over from Dublin in kegs of

Irish whiskey or sent up from the London slums with neither the middleman nor the recipient asking too many questions. The great majority were otherwise illegally supplied by grave-robbers.

The shadowy figure of the resurrectionist therefore became a crucial, though unacknowledged, member of the Edinburgh medical fraternity, an entrepreneur of some ingenuity emerging out of the poverty-stricken Edinburgh underworld. He did not, to be sure, carry out his work completely on his own: university beadles, church sextons, and grave-diggers were relied on for essential assistance, as were medical students on intermittent occasions.

Horror stories abounded. When Robert Liston, a prominent surgeon in later life whom Darwin saw at work in the Edinburgh operating theatre, was an anatomical assistant to Barclay, he was known as a useful man for corpses, his name appearing in magazines of the time, "always turning up something new, one way or another." Three medical students just before Darwin's time were nearly caught manhandling a body from the graveyard of Rosyth—then a lonely seaside site on the edge of the Firth—and were saved only by their quick wits and speedy flight back to Edinburgh. The Monro family, too, were not averse to an extra body on the side, for the second Alexander Monro allowed his students to engage in a fight with William Cullen's pupils over the final resting place of Sandy M'Nab, a street singer who unwisely died in the infirmary. In scenes worthy of a Scottish farce, the corpse was winched back and forth from upper to lower windows until anatomy rather than clinical medicine captured the prize. Resurrectionists and body-buyers—the "sack 'em up men"—were consequently identifiable by name in Surgeon's Square. Merryless, Spune, and Mowatt, who worked together, were one well-known group in Edinburgh, usually the first at the door of tenements arranging to buy the bodies of the recently deceased; Geordie Mill, a gravedigger in Dundee, was another.

So commonplace was the business that in attempting to dispose of his first murdered body early in 1828, William Burke wheeled a laden cart into the infirmary yard in the middle of the day and asked a student where to take it. According to Burke's deposition, the unnamed student directed him without a second thought to Robert Knox, the charismatic new owner of Barclay's school.

Professor Monro, to his scarcely concealed delight, was never embroiled in the ensuing shock that engulfed the nation in 1828 and led to the trial and execution of Burke in 1829—his body appropriately enough going to the university anatomy school for dissection during the next winter session in front of a huge, primarily sightseeing audience—and the sorry decline of Knox into professional oblivion.

In reality, Knox was doing no more nor less than other extramural doctors attempting to teach anatomy properly.[54] Erasmus Darwin, busy learning the structure of the human body in the winter of 1825–26 at John Lizars's private school, probably worked with recently exhumed corpses. Indeed, a contemporary writer crossly recorded that a cadaver illegally delivered one evening to Lizars found its way—at someone else's profit—onto the dissecting table in Knox's school by the following morning. Erasmus would have been remarkably phlegmatic or inattentive to the world about him if doubts about the source of his material did not flicker at one time or another. Few medical students liked to be out and about in the countryside or in the Old Town late at night unless they had some dirty business in hand; and walks along the seashore in certain places were just as suspect. More than this, a simple tourist trip to the site of their Uncle Charles's grave indicated the scale of the problem. The Duncan family tomb was a sturdy affair, buttressed with walls, gates, and railings of a size suitable for tight security rather than medical honour. Just across the road at Greyfriars' Church there was the disturbing sight of a watchtower; and the stories of dogs guarding their masters' graves probably stirred Charles Darwin's sentimental heart. The whole context of medical student life was shot through and through with resurrection, not least with the jokes in undergraduate magazines, which in traditional bad taste made the most of the situation.

The brothers found the entire proceedings—the flayed and dismembered corpses in anatomical classes, the stench of preservative, the locked church-yards, the armed guards sullenly protecting graves, the newspaper reports of open tombs and disappearing bodies followed by innuendo and whispers in the seedy corners of Edinburgh, even the innocuous sight of a porter wheeling a trolley through the narrow wynds—creepily distasteful. It did not take much to imagine their uncle or even their mother under the cloth. Darwin hated it. Dead humans were not for him.

VIII

Monro's classes were macabre in another respect not usually alluded to by historians. Though boring and stodgy on most subjects, the professor was a noted opponent of phrenology. Body-snatching was one thing—secret, nasty, and unconfirmed during Darwin's time at Edinburgh—but this dispute about brains and skulls was just as distasteful in its way and thoroughly public. Darwin, like every other medical student in the city, was obliged to give it his attention.

In fact, anatomy students had to pay it more attention than most. In a bizarre episode of Edinburgh university life, Monro helped Sir William Hamilton, holder of the Regius Chair of Civil History and the most vigorous anti-phrenologist of the age, to perform experiments on domestic animals in an attempt to refute phrenology on anatomical grounds: the idea being that physical interference with the living brain must, if phrenology was to be believed, result in observable distortions of behaviour. The long summer vacations for Monro and Hamilton were spent pushing sewing needles and skeins of silk through the brains of ducks, rabbits, and chickens, which were then closely watched as they wandered around in Hamilton's large city garden. There was no change in behaviour, the two men triumphantly asserted. Monro overcame his academic stupor to document these anti-phrenological findings in footnotes to Hamilton's books and papers from 1825 onwards.

Monro and Hamilton also spent feverish hours amid the skulls in the university's medical museum, measuring internal capacity with sand, comparing the relative size of brains according to age, sex, and race, and contrasting the external proportions with those of animals. In all, they examined sixty pickled human brains and over three hundred human and seven hundred animal skulls. Oddly enough, Monro, who happened to be on friendly terms with the Combe family, was given access to George Combe's collection of skulls brought together for phrenological purposes.[56] Yet there was no measurable correlation, the professors claimed in 1825, between skull size and shape and any known mental features.

Furthermore, and probably pushed on by Hamilton, Monro performed his own researches into the supposed existence of frontal sinuses: spaces between the brain and the skull which would, under phrenological rules, make it impossible for there to be an accurate match between brain shape and exterior bumps. Not an easy anatomical point to prove either way, the question was a central issue in the Edinburgh phrenology debate.[57] Monro took a firm line and told his students sinuses existed. "Above these notches [for the ophthalmic nerves]," dutifully recorded Darwin in his lecture notes for the year, "are the small elevation of the frontal sinuses."[58] The human skulls Darwin examined in the anatomical museum as part of his coursework were sliced in the appropriate places to display the "disposition of the sinuses."[59]

Monro similarly studied cases of hydrocephalus (water on the brain) to show that the fluid—which usually distorted the skull—did not necessarily disturb brain function. Quite the reverse, he insisted. There were many cases of extreme hydrocephalus in which patients showed no trace of mental disturbance.[60]

Phrenology, Monro confidently asserted after these researches, was based on what he considered entirely false anatomical "facts." Hamilton subsequently relayed the findings in high-decibel attacks delivered in a university lecture hall early in 1827 and to the Royal Society of Edinburgh later in the year.

Monro published them himself in his *Anatomy of the Brain* in 1831.

The spectacle of his anatomy professor entering so forcefully into general debate with the Edinburgh populace and so clearly driven from behind by a more combative and stronger partner was not edifying for Darwin. Though he did not believe in phrenology any more than Hamilton and Monro, and went to the trouble of discussing it in the holidays with the mental and moral philosopher Sir James Mackintosh, a friend of his uncle Josiah Wedgwood, there was little in this academic behaviour to inspire youthful enthusiasm for the venerable ideals of the world of learning. It seemed to him as if university lecturers and extramurals alike were primarily interested in polemics, too absorbed in professional skirmishes to be illuminating on anything else.

Taking Monro's ghoulish interest in the size and distortion of brains together with his experiments on living animals, the work on the museum skull collection, the dismembered corpses in the anatomy theatre, and the seemingly unabashed collusion of medical men with grave-robbers, Darwin came to think Edinburgh doctors relished a taste for the abnormal as well as for controversy. An uncomfortable all-round anatomical nastiness depressed him. "The subject disgusted me."[61]

IX

Day by day the ordinary practical routine of a medical education began to seem more and more objectionable. Darwin started missing classes. But it was a mistake to let slip in a letter that he was reading two novels at once, in preference to attending lectures.

"I have a message from Papa to give you," wrote Susan, "which I am afraid you won't like."

> He desires me to say that he thinks your plan of picking & chusing what lectures you attend, not at all a good one; and as you cannot have enough information to know what may be of use to you, it is quite necessary for you to bear with a good deal of stupid & dry work: but if you do not discontinue your present indulgent way, your course of study will be utterly useless.—Papa was sorry to hear that you thought of coming home before the course of Lectures were finished, but hopes you will not do so.[62]

There was no more talk of novel-reading that term. As directed, Darwin plodded on with his chosen courses. Most of these admittedly did not turn his stomach in quite the same way as Monro's. William Pulteney Alison's and Robert Graham's clinical lectures were interesting, as he had already told Caroline, encouraging him to use some of the elementary experience he had acquired in Shrewsbury. His rudimentary notes listing cases and treatments drawn from the first Erasmus Darwin's medical tract, *Zoonomia,* with added comments from "My Father" and a supplementary sheet of Shrewsbury-based "Treatments for various conditions," suggest Darwin took this part of his training seriously.[63] He diligently studied John Mason Good's voluminous medical textbook and learned to appreciate the subtle art of diagnosis. Despite this, he did not find hospital visits particularly congenial. "Some of the cases distressed me a good deal, and I still have vivid pictures before me of some of them; but I was not so foolish as to allow this to lessen my attendance."

At the same time he regularly attended the weekly lecture on materia medica delivered by the younger Andrew Duncan. This left nothing but the memory of "cold breakfastless hours on the properties of rhubarb." At eight o'clock on a winter's morning, they were "something fearful to remember."[64]

After Alison's benevolence and Duncan's rhubarb it was all the more devastating when Darwin saw his first operation.

> I also attended on two occasions the operating theatre in the hospital at Edinburgh, and saw two very bad operations, one on a child, but I rushed away before they were completed. Nor did I ever attend again, for hardly any inducement would have been strong enough to make me do so; this being long before the blessed days of chloroform. The two cases fairly haunted me for many a long year.

Recoiling from the graphic emotional shock, Darwin was aghast. He probably saw an amputation, a brutal procedure at any time, especially before the introduction of anaesthetics. Screams, blood, and violence tumbled about in his mind afterwards, followed by the inevitable sleepless nights in which the whole question of medical intervention danced insistently and unanswered. How could his father, grandfather, uncle, and brother—each in his own way alert to affliction, responsive to distress—steel themselves against sights like these, the still-conscious patient writhing in agony, the gore? How could they come to terms with a child's pain? Erasmus managed. Why could he not do the same?

Rushing away from these two operations marked the turning point in Darwin's relations with medicine, just as similar trials must have done for many other potential physicians. Where watching work on dead bodies was just about bearable, perhaps because of the enforced distance, and in Darwin's case helped along by not actually touching a corpse, this was horrific—too close, too immediate, too real. How could a child be made to suffer so?

He shrank from blood ever afterwards. To the end of his life he feared the sight of it, becoming almost hysterical if one of his own children accidentally grazed his or her skin, and quite unable to locate or apply a "plaister" in his panic. Though the children laughed at him, it was a very real revulsion. The same morbid sensitivity welled up with the prospect of any medical condition involving blood and pain, some as routine as childbirth, which he always found alarming, others requiring more unexpected action, like an operation. He could not stand the idea of medicinal leeches and refused to be treated by doctors who still used them. He was similarly terrified by dentists and the spectre of a tooth extraction: it took all his resolution to make a feeble joke to friends about his "Robinsonophobia"; and he privately regarded Thomas Bell, the London dentist and naturalist who became a close professional colleague after the *Beagle* voyage, with apprehensive caution.

If this was medicine, he wanted nothing more to do with it. He was sure he could never send people—children—under the surgeon's knife. In his first tentative step towards independence from the family heritage, he recognised that this mode of life was not for him. His sympathetic, affectionate heart was stretched to the utmost.

X

Gradually, from that time onwards, Darwin began to disengage himself from the subject as taught in Edinburgh. A doctor's direct confrontation with death, blood, and disease and the way medical men grappled with fear and carried the hopes of patients through the drastic remedies available to them were nothing but a nightmare. He was too retiring, too easily disgusted, almost too scrupulous, too young, and certainly too squeamish to cope with the brawny side of medicine. Nothing in his life had equipped him to deal with suffering on a day-to-day basis. He had no ability to call up the brusque disassociations that his grandfather and father brought into play: the larger-than-life force of personality that submerged and occasionally denied the existence of illness. He did not possess the same silky capacity to withdraw that helped Erasmus sidestep any discomforting intellectual disturbances. He did not find sustenance in the higher realms of social duty or religion, for his experience of faith was not sufficiently intense to explain away these horrors as necessary evils, nor was there enough of a tradition of religious belief on the male, medical, side of the family to support the idea that unpleasant things were ultimately for the best. The liberal, sceptical, easy-going blend of provincial Anglicanism and Unitarianism that characterised the family's devotions was too informal to offer him much in the way of spiritual answers, let alone physical resolve.

Almost instinctively he knew he preferred the quiet pleasures of the natural history sciences. By the time the summer recess of 1826 came around, he was privately certain about needing to give up medicine. The catch was how to tell his father.

Well-developed avoidance techniques provided a temporary answer. Back home at The Mount for the summer holidays, Darwin invented all sorts of pressing occupations that required long absences from Shrewsbury, out of reach of his father's questions. There was a walking tour in Wales to take, trips to the Wedgwoods' house in Staffordshire to meet visiting politicians and liberal thinkers, a riding excursion with Caroline, essential week-long residencies with old family friends. He spent any remaining time safely out of the house in a paroxysm of sporting activity—the customary refuge for country gentlemen hoping to avoid thinking about a problem or admitting a difficult secret.

In Darwin's case, his sporting refuge also served as a kind of absolution, or resolution, in paradox. He took up shooting in earnest. The resulting bloodbath of animals—partridges, pigeons, rabbits, rats—which he killed with violent pleasure certainly put medicine into perspective. The uncontrollable could in this sense be controlled. He could wield his own kind of power over life and death with a smoking gun.

All summer long he avoided telling his father how patients screamed. He could not even bring himself to explain when it was time to return to Edinburgh for another year's training; so off he went, still keeping his convictions buried where his father could not find them. He knew that snails, birds, guns, and crystals were altogether less emotionally demanding. His life of gentle procrastination had begun.

...TO SEAWEEDS

ATURAL history became Darwin's safety valve after this, and what was formerly only a boyhood enthusiasm took on a different kind of emotional depth. Retreating into the study of the natural world provided a way of avoiding the ugliness he encountered in dealing with ordinary life.

Not surprisingly, Darwin's habitual activities in the natural history line had been pushed a little to one side during his first university session while he came to grips with the medical curriculum. But the warm Shrewsbury appreciation never waned. He and Erasmus spent several contented hours on the Sunday walks traditional to Scottish university students, tramping out to one of the nearby fishing villages on the edge of the Firth of Forth. Nothing was nicer, they found, than wandering about in the fresh seaside air looking for shells and interesting curiosities among the stones.

These long walks were necessary interludes for both of them from the demands of medical training. Darwin's diary described regular visits to the beach at Leith. "Caught a sea mouse, Aphrodita aculeata of Linnaeus," he recorded on 9 February 1826; "Turton states it has only two feelers. does not Linnaeus say 4? I thought I perceived them.—found also 3 Patella vulgaris." Four days later, "Erasmus caught a cuttle fish." There were "a great many sea mice on the shore. When thrown into the sea, rolled themselves up like hedgehogs."[1]

In the same diary Darwin wrote occasional ornithological observations like those shared with his father at Shrewsbury ("where do most birds roost in winter?") and once or twice lapsed into the easy format of Dr. Darwin's garden book. On 25 April, "no swallows, or rather the genus Hirundo, have appeared in or near Edinburgh." By this date, he knew they would be swooping over The Mount ready to nest again in the stables. Perhaps Abberley, leaning on his spade, had seen them.

At about this time Darwin also told Susan that he was going to learn to stuff birds "from a blackamoor, I believe an old servant of Dr Duncan." For an hour every day for two months, at a cost of one guinea, he was shown how to skin and dry birds for scientific purposes by John Edmonstone, a freed slave who had been taught taxidermy by the traveller Charles Waterton and now worked on a freelance basis mounting specimens for the university's natural history museum.[2] He "gained his livelihood by stuffing birds, which he did excellently: he gave me lessons for payment, and I often used to sit with him, for he was a very pleasant and intelligent man."[3] These old loves were reassuring in their familiarity: soothing, if a little submerged.

Lectures on chemistry delivered by the university's great showman Thomas Charles Hope served much the same function. They were the only ones Darwin exempted from the general condemnation that classes at Edinburgh were "intolerably dull." Hope had long ago abandoned all pretence of conducting original research and devoted himself entirely to making his course as popular as possible: gathering guineas not laurels, as Leonard Horner perceptively remarked.[4] His spectacular experimental demonstrations drew audiences of over five hundred people, easily the largest in the university. Hope also covered several natural history topics, including rival geological theories of the earth, as well as mineralogy, crystallography, some botanical chemistry, the physics of the atmosphere, and meteorology, all explained in flamboyant style and accompanied by exciting visual effects. "The experiments were prepared on a liberal scale," said Benjamin Silliman, an American student in Hope's early classes. "They were apposite and beautiful, and so neatly and skillfully performed, that rarely was even a drop spilled on the table."[5] For the two Darwins, the demonstrations embodied on a much grander scale something of the all-inclusive philosophical ideals of the Lab at Shrewsbury, then gradually reverting back to a toolshed.[6]

Hope's chemical and philosophical apparatus—the machinery of his scientific demonstrations—was equally inspiring. Legend had it that he spent more than £1,000 in providing the biggest and best of everything, a huge sum for a self-supporting professor, around three years' income from student fees. Such equipment, however, was not for the students to use. Despite Hope's emphasis on display and on a practical understanding of chemical effects, only his paid demonstrator was trusted with operating these substantial investments. "He did not encourage experimental inquiry among his students. His laboratory was open to no one but his class assistant," complained Robert Christison—which was why, he added, that Dr. Hope, with all his ability as a teacher, never produced any proper chemists. The students' chemistry society was consequently set up by Christison and others to provide the lab experience denied by Hope—although their activities were hampered by their having to supply all the apparatus and materials themselves. "Sulphuretted hydrogen and his janitor taught chemistry in the university," jeered one disillusioned (and anonymous) student writer in 1832; "the former was a man remarkable for his pride, covetousness, shocking bad legs, and two old coach horses; the latter was the prototype—a kind of duplicate—of his master."[7]

Darwin's lecture notes from Hope's class (now incomplete) nevertheless include careful drawings of some of the apparatus used in class and descriptions of the experimental technique involved, especially thermometers for measuring conduction and radiation and equipment relating to latent heat, a concept first disclosed by Hope's predecessor in the chemistry chair, Joseph Black, and afterwards considered Hope's particular forte. Darwin may have meant to repeat some of these at home.[8] The brothers found the lectures glamorous and informative, and were agog with pleasure when asked to dine at Hope's house. "I like both him & his lectures *very* much," reported Darwin in a letter. Disliking everything else, he had stayed on in Edinburgh after the end of the medical session of 1825–26 to catch the showpiece conclusion of Hope's classes.

II

Medicine looked even less attractive when Darwin returned to Scotland in October 1826 to begin his second year as a student. Most obviously, Erasmus was not there, having been sent off to London by Dr. Darwin to further his medical studies at the Windmill Street anatomical school—a tacit acknowledgement that the practical side of his Edinburgh training was none too successful for him either.

There was a sad gap where his brother had so comfortably been, both in Darwin's lodgings (now changed to a single set of rooms further down Lothian Street) and in scholarly companionship: no one to sit next to in class or join in idly leaning against the library wall in the weekly queue for books; no one with whom to crack jokes about professors and berate the rainy Edinburgh weekends. A complete absence of collegiate life intensified the unwelcome isolation of student lodgings.

This time Darwin was forced to make friends. Symbolically, and rather artlessly, he arrived back at university after the summer holidays aged seventeen with a pocketful of shiny new visiting cards engraved "Mr C. Darwin." The only one he kept for posterity was marked up on the reverse with his shooting tally for the summer: a total of 177 hares, pheasants, and partridges killed in the two months or so available to him when the season was open;

about three dead animals a day. It was unlikely, he thought with bloodthirsty relish, that he would be able to enjoy himself quite so much once lectures started.

At the same time he started taking snuff—a craze among the students for a couple of years previously and a sign of his intention to forge an adult identity of his own. "Snortalamus!" shrieked the Shrewsbury girls, oblivious to any developing masculine feelings. Deep into a pipe himself, Erasmus found it equally laughable. "I was reminded of you," he wrote from London, "by a snuffy old gentleman who in the most interesting part of the play unfortunately dropt all his snuff and was obliged to leave instantly."[9]

There was more. Integral to Darwin's new sense of independence was a belated recognition that his father was a wealthy man, an attractive idea enhanced by the scientific prestige of the family name and personal connections to the Wedgwood manufacturing fortune. With all the clarity of late adolescence, Darwin realised that he carried a famous surname—a useful asset for someone wishing to make his own way in a diffuse academic community like Edinburgh University—and that he was, or was about to become, rich. Sleekly brought up in the moneyed classes with hardly a passing thought about where the money might come from, he was suddenly conscious of being cushioned from the traditional privations of a younger son, and recognised he would lead a future life at least as handsome as the one already experienced in his father's house.

Dr. Darwin had not given him this information: on the contrary, the doctor cautiously downplayed any prospects of future wealth among his children and grandchildren. Darwin picked it up for himself through talk at home during the summer, especially in relation to Erasmus, the eldest son who was just coming into his majority and was due to inherit his portion of Susanna Wedgwood's dowry, and from Dr. Darwin's settlements on Marianne's two baby sons. These conversations gave Darwin the hint. Moreover, visits to his Wedgwood cousins at Maer that summer were thick with tension over the china company's finances. At the last moment, Dr. Darwin stepped in to prop up the family shares. It was like being saved from certain death, cried the doctor's sister-in-law Kitty.[10]

There was, as young Darwin privately came to see it, no financial necessity for him to become a doctor: no real need to practice medicine at all. "I became convinced from various small circumstances that my father would leave me property enough to subsist on with some comfort, though I never imagined that I should be so rich a man as I am; but my belief was sufficient to check any strenuous effort to learn medicine."[11]

He was indisputably in a better position than most to give way to the inclinations of the previous year. No stringent economic pressures or stern parental voice forced him to overcome his medical revulsion. No one made him work. The structure of the academic system fostered indolence just as much as industry, and he intended to make the most of it.

III

Left to his own devices in Edinburgh with only two more courses to take to fulfill the preliminary requirements for a degree (midwifery—the first year that this was compulsory—and the practice of physic), Darwin enrolled for Robert Jameson's natural history class and began to socialise with some of the other young men who registered.[12]

For someone with Darwin's interests, Jameson's natural history course was without doubt the best, as well as the only one like it, in the country. It advertised itself as covering zoology, botany, palaeontology, geology, mineralogy, and, as the syllabus stated, "the philosophy of zoology," and promised firsthand experience with museum specimens and occasional field trips led by the professor to local sites of natural history interest. Though Jameson had his foibles, including, most notoriously, his efforts to prevent students seeing any geological specimens that might contradict his own well-developed views, his natural history museum on the university site was the finest institution of its kind in Britain, rivalling the collection of the British Museum and far exceeding it in the display and relative accessibility of the material.[13]

Jameson's lectures and publications were similarly well thought of, to the extent that John James Audubon, the American ornithologist, came specially to Scotland to see him during a European trip made in the winter of 1826–27. He was the "first professor of the place," claimed Audubon.[14] Such fame rested partly on his long-standing concern with geographical exploration and a commitment to advancing the nation's scientific domain overseas that brought him into close contact with influential politicians like the foreign secretary, Lord Castlereagh, and with the British Admiralty, and enabled him to place Edinburgh-trained doctors on government ships and in numerous far-flung colonial positions. Encouraged by his Admiralty booklet entitled *Instructions for Naturalists,* these men and other members of his extensive network regularly sent material back to Edinburgh. Thanks to these contributions, the museum was quite remarkable, as was Jameson's stature at home and abroad.

Jameson also took an active role in promoting natural history in Scotland, first by founding a new learned society and then by co-editing the *Edinburgh Philosophical Journal*—and later taking on the whole journal after an argument with his joint editor David Brewster. In this way he established the Wernerian Natural History Society in 1808, providing a forum for expounding Abraham Gottlob Werner's geological system—a system which Jameson unceasingly advocated in lectures—and helped it become the major venue for research papers on natural history topics delivered by Scotland's foremost scholars; and he made the *Edinburgh Philosophical Journal* one of the most respected periodicals in the field.

Yet Darwin was terribly disappointed by "that old brown dry stick Jameson." The professor's outlook on life was almost Hogarthian in its caricature of a museum-based intellectual whose thoughts ran only to parched specimens, endless lists, and pointless classification schemes. Stylish expositions were not his métier, and the two or three metaphors he used to illustrate particular points were well known to students and eagerly awaited; when produced, these were welcomed with annual rounds of applause. Lectures, said one disgruntled student, were like the table of contents of a book being read out for an hour. "A chaos of facts," complained Thomas Carlyle. The man was "strange and uncouth," said Audubon; a "baked mummy," claimed another disillusioned visitor; a fossilised bore "said to be preserved in some cabinet in Germany."[15] "Gentlemen," Darwin would later mimic in derision, "the apex of a mountain is the top and the base of a mountain is the bottom."[16]

Jameson did not go out of his way to be boring or disagreeable. Several former students remembered their time with him with affection and appreciation; and one set of undergraduate notes, taken in 1830 by Robert McCormick, a naval surgeon whose subsequent career interweaved closely with Darwin's, suggests that the lectures were both comprehensive and useful, although failing to cover anything like so complete a syllabus as promised.[17] What seems more likely is that Darwin was predisposed to find everyone dull after Hope's exciting performances. Moreover, his own youthful pursuits at home at Shrewsbury, as well as Hope's wide-ranging lectures, gave him a fair background knowledge of some of the material addressed by Jameson and probably made him disinclined to pay attention after the first two or three classes. Hope, in short, spoiled him for anyone else.

This would not be anything more than a footnote to history if it were not for the way the contrast between the two professors influenced Darwin's first impressions of geology as a science. Hope and Jameson famously disagreed on their understanding of the history of the earth, an internecine geological controversy much enjoyed by the students, who went from course to course waiting for the moment when one professor would rudely dismiss the views of the other. United as the professors may have been in condemning Barclay's potential chair of comparative anatomy, which might take fee-paying students away from their individual courses, they otherwise preferred to differ. "It would be a misfortune if we all had the same way of thinking," admitted Jameson to the Royal Commission in 1827; "Dr Hope is decidedly opposed to me, and I am opposed to Dr Hope, and between us we make the subject interesting."[18]

Where Hope described the earth's geological structure in terms of the activity of a supposed internal heat, a physico-chemical theory worked out in 1785 by his Edinburgh friend the philosopher James Hutton, and afterwards endorsed by another friend and scientific populariser, John Playfair, Jameson advanced an alternative doctrine originating in the work of Werner, the most influential continental geologist of the age, in which water, not heat, took the primary role. Jameson had studied under Werner in Freiberg, becoming an intimate friend as he learned about his comprehensive system, and was almost single-handedly responsible for making Werner's views better known to British thinkers. These rival theories of fire and water (labelled "Vulcanist" and "Neptunist" by classically inclined Edinburgh commentators) stipulated such different interpretations of the origin of primary rocks like granite and basalt—were they aboriginal primitives, spewed up as molten rock from the centre of the earth, or had they crystallised out of a watery chemical soup?—and rested on such divergent philosophies of nature that they were to all intents and purposes irreconcilable opposites.[19] Students usually chose one side or the other while conceding, like the main university protagonists themselves, some limited serviceability in particular aspects of either alternative.

One of the most controversial points in the debate as it took shape in the 1820s was the formation of veins of granite and basalt—primary rocks in Werner's scheme—in rocks thought to be of a later date. It was a problem touched on by Hope in his chemistry class and regularly rebutted by Jameson in natural history lectures. Jameson believed these veins were once fissures that filled up with crystallised sediment from the waters above. Hope took the Huttonian line that they were injections of igneous melt from below. Darwin recalled in his *Autobiography* how Jameson demonstrated his interpretation on an excursion to Salisbury Crags. The professor pointed out one of these trap-dykes to the class, "adding with a sneer that there were men who maintained that it had been injected from beneath in a molten condition."

Soon Darwin rejected Jameson's teachings outright: his Neptunism, his dry analytic manner, his pedantic mineralogical diagnosis, and his dead, museum-based zoology. But he purchased Jameson's textbook for the course, *Manual of Mineralogy* (1821), and annotated it in a desultory way during classes. "The walls of Babylon were cemented by melted Mineral pitch," went one of his pencil notes next to the printed description of asphalt.[20] Though he may well have first learned the definition of a fossil from these pages, it was not nearly so much fun as drawing a mouse on the inside cover or passing his book over to an unidentified colleague who added his own thoughts beside Darwin's ownership inscription. Darwin's classmate was bored enough to dub him "M.D., F.R.S., ASS, Member of the Royal Medical Society of Edinburgh, Honorary Member of the Royal Plinian Society."

Darwin further bought and read Jameson's translation of Georges Cuvier's discourse on geology, *Essay on the Theory of the Earth* (1827), by then in its fifth edition.[21] In this text Cuvier's important views on the successive "revolutions" in the earth's history and his discussion of what both he and Jameson called the deluge were set out in comprehensive fashion. Darwin familiarised himself with Cuvier's information about fossils and extinction and became aware of disputes about "fossil human skulls."

He also had access to the collections in the natural history museum, as evidenced by his class ticket and as insisted on by Jameson. Students were expected to appear in the museum three times a week for practical work, although it is not known exactly how much or what was examined by Darwin or any other aspiring naturalist. One contemporary called William Ainsworth complained to the royal commissioners of his unsuccessful application to Jameson in 1827 to see "skulls, marble specimens and insects." Darwin, too, claimed he learned much more from talking with the museum's curator, William Macgillivray, a rough-hewn Scot who later became professor of natural history at Aberdeen University, than he ever did from consulting the museum specimens directly. Macgillivray gave him some rare shells and information about birds as well as his time.

Lectures were curtly dismissed. "The sole effect they produced on me was the determination never as long as I lived to read a book on geology or in any way to study the science."[22]

IV

Far more interesting and important was the independent natural history work he did at this time. Yet like all Darwin's work it was not nearly so independent as might at first be supposed. This second year in Edinburgh was entirely dominated by the medical men and the surprising intellectual currents he found swirling through a small student society which he joined in November 1826.

This was the Plinian Society, a small group of undergraduates who liked natural history and antiquarian researches and who met regularly during term time and occasionally went out on collecting expeditions together. The society's name evoked the encyclopaedic interests of Pliny the Elder, the Roman naturalist. Keen to fill the social gap left by Erasmus—and the intellectual gap left by Jameson's lectures—Darwin also joined the undergraduates' Royal Medical Society, almost essential for medical students at the university, and took up an introduction (made available to him by a Darwin cousin) to Leonard Horner, the reforming educationalist in Edinburgh, who came to figure prominently in Darwin's later scientific life. Horner fulfilled his obligations by taking the young man to see Sir Walter Scott, as president, open the 1826–27 season of meetings at the Royal Society of Edinburgh. This was Darwin's first introduction to the arcane rituals of the inner circles of high science, with their lengthy elections for the incoming council and the formal readings of papers and addresses, and a wonderful excuse for gaping at Scott, by then akin to royalty in the public mind: "I looked at him and at the whole scene with some awe and reverence." Much later on, when he was elected an honorary fellow of this prestigious society, the tribute tickled his vanity far more than anything granted by other similarly learned associations.

Shyly Darwin began to emerge from the self-imposed confinement of the previous year. "During the second year I was left to my own resources: and this was an advantage, for I became well acquainted with several young men fond of natural science."

The Plinian Society had an impact on Darwin quite out of proportion to the limited size and amateurish aura of the group. It had been founded in 1823 by a group of undergraduates (not by Professor Jameson, as is popularly supposed), and like many student enterprises eventually collapsed, in 1841, killed by its complicated administrative structure.[23] Members were under no illusions about its minor nature, a mere club rather than the grander apparatus of the Wernerian Society, for example, whose members were required to be graduates and whose papers were published in a series of scholarly transactions, or of the Royal Society of Medicine with its handsome premises, club room, and library.[24] The Plinian, as Darwin described it, "consisted of students and met in an underground room in the university for the sake of reading papers on natural science and discussing them." Little was published at that early stage in the society's life, and not much archival material accumulated.

Professors never attended—not even Jameson, the "Senior Honorary Member," as the students called him. Indeed, the Regius Professor of Natural History proved less than helpful when the Plinians tried to get a room set aside in the natural history museum building as a permanent venue for their meetings and for housing their own miniature "museum." Though Jameson put their case, as requested, before the governing body of the university, all that happened was that the rent payable on their old room went up. Eventually the society's officers grudgingly agreed to rent the Speculative Society's room on alternate Tuesdays—a sequence of events all indicative of the marginal role the club played in university affairs.

Professors did not exercise any control over meetings, either. When Andrew Duncan (the younger) came one evening in December 1826 intending to donate a copy of his latest book to the society's collection of reference works, there was such indignation that the incident was reported—with heavy satire—in an undergraduate magazine, itself edited by a Plinian called Edward Binns. "This is the first time, says our correspondent, we remember to have seen one of our Professors in the Plinian Society."[25]

Though the secretary claimed to have 150 past and present members on the books, only about twenty-five actually attended meetings in Darwin's time, and of these, five were joint presidents, three were other office-holders (secretary, treasurer, and "museum curator"), and five were members of the council. The remainder were invariably former presidents or something similar.[26] Everyone had strong ideas about how the society should be run, and the fortnightly business creaked under an absurd load of motions and resolutions, rotations of chairmen (sometimes four an evening), votes and counter-votes, which peaked every May with an elaborate reassessment of the rules.

Something of the society's ad hoc character can be gleaned from the fact that the week after Darwin joined (proposed by three of the incoming presidents—William A. F. Browne, John Coldstream, and George Fife), he was elected to the council. Barely four weeks had passed since term began, so it would be an exaggeration to claim that the students who nominated him had any special insight into his abilities or that he was already favourably known for his natural history interests.[27] They could not even be called his particular friends, although he did come to know one or two of them quite well, since it was commonplace for the presidents—all five of them—to take turns in proposing likely-looking new members. They saw only a keen classmate looking for company. These were quite sufficient grounds for a warm reception.

Most members, like Coldstream and Browne, and William Ainsworth, the temporary secretary, were medical students of Darwin's age who ultimately passed their M.D. examinations in 1827 or 1828, just as Darwin might have done had he persevered with the plans laid down by his father. Many were simultaneously members of the university's Royal Medical Society or Royal Physical Society, some later becoming student presidents of those groups as well. Of these promising young men, a striking proportion went on to become fellows of the Royal Society of Edinburgh or Wernerian Society, ending up as respectable provincial physicians, just as Darwin once expected to do, or joining the navy or the East India Company's medical services, or becoming attached to county infirmaries and asylums. Some three or four were already graduates—and were deferentially referred to as "Dr" in the written minutes. A fair number of members were legal students or from the humanities faculty, including two future Writers to the Signet (an ancient

Scottish legal adjunct to the Crown). About a dozen or so were English, reflecting the high proportion of English students in the university generally. Of the four members Darwin considered his friends during this year, two were English, three graduated with an M.D. in 1827, and all four became sufficiently well known as physicians to appear in Victorian history books.

By far the most notable figure in the Plinian Society in Darwin's time was Robert Grant, who graduated as a doctor from Edinburgh in 1814. Coming from a prosperous legal family, Grant had employed his patrimony in travelling around Europe's museums and mountains after taking his degree. During that period he studied anatomy and embryology in Paris with Cuvier and Etienne Geoffroy Saint-Hilaire respectively, and on returning to Edinburgh in 1824 he was appointed a lecturer on invertebrate animals at the extramural anatomy school established by John Barclay and subsequently run by Robert Knox. When Darwin knew him, he was thirty-three years old: a gifted linguist, cultivated, and interestingly thoughtful about a wide range of philosophical topics. He had just retired as the Plinian's secretary to take up a more demanding role on the council of the Wernerian Natural History Society. Darwin sometimes accompanied him as a guest to meetings of the Wernerian Society (Darwin was not a member, and could not be, because he was only an undergraduate), particularly if visitors like Audubon were scheduled to speak. According to an account of his life published in the *Lancet,* Grant sat in on Jameson's lectures from 1820 to 1827, interspersing these with his teaching and annual autumnal expeditions zoologising around the coasts of Scotland and Ireland.

Grant was a very different kind of person from any Darwin had met before. Excessively reserved and formal on the outside, a trait emphasised by his wearing full evening dress when lecturing at Knox's extramural school, he unbent in the company of friends into an inspired proponent of French philosophical anatomy. "He was a dry, melancholic, disappointed, humorous man, devoted to his subject with a burning zeal, a *perfervidum ingenium* much commoner north than south of the Tweed," said one contemporary. "Most retiring in his manners," said another.[28] Everyone agreed about his talent and engaging inner personality. There is a possibility that Grant was also homosexual, given to performing his dissections late into the night, alone but for his books and instruments and the company of a Mr. M'Donald (the "zealous and intelligent resident apothecary of the Royal Infirmary") or of some undergraduate acolyte from the Plinian Society or Knox's anatomy school such as John Coldstream. In later years, he liked to take strenuous Alpine tours with a succession of young pupils. He never married, being "single and much alone through life," as the *Lancet* put it.[29]

Underneath the outward austerity, Grant was warmly radical in his scientific, religious, and social views, later campaigning for medical reform with fiery Thomas Wakley of the *Lancet* and promoting secular comparative anatomy when he moved to London as a professor in 1827. He was, furthermore, a thoroughgoing transmutationist, basing his ideas on those of the French naturalist Lamarck and of the first Erasmus Darwin.[30] Most of his more startling opinions about evolution, admittedly, were expressed only some years after he became professor of comparative anatomy and zoology at the University of London (afterwards University College), itself founded in 1826 as a reformist "joint-stock" challenge to the aristocratic landed colleges of Oxford and Cambridge. Views like these would probably not have enhanced his early career, however forward-looking the institution, nor would they have been particularly welcome to the conservative and God-fearing individuals who provided his testimonials for this new job in London. Backed by a powerful array of Edinburgh expertise in the shape of Jameson, John Fleming, David Brewster, and Barclay, Grant's election to the London professorship—the very first chair in zoology and comparative anatomy in the very first department established for that subject in England—was instead heralded as a great triumph for scientific knowledge. Grant was destined to be the English Cuvier, boomed his friend Wakley in the *Lancet*.

Grant's evolutionary opinions may have been only half formed before he made that transition. Still, he was sufficiently open about his views in Edinburgh medical circles to represent at least some of the materialist dangers brought into focus by the emphasis on philosophical anatomy in the extracurricular schools and the phrenology debate, particularly as arguments for reform at all levels pressed hard on Edinburgh's administrative classes. Like his friend Robert Knox, Grant was an important figure in the academic counter-world of radical dissent.[31] Darwin came into his sparkling orbit just as fame and fortune seemed about to fall on him in the most gratifying way.

V

Though the ambiance of the Plinian was informal, the work produced by members for their own amusement was often of a high quality, much of it emerging out of Jameson's lectures or inspired by Grant and Robert Knox. Knox had been proposed, but not elected, as an honorary member of the society in 1826, an action that rated him, in the eyes of the nominating students, with Cuvier, Barclay, and the maverick Scottish fundamentalist scientist David Brewster, and demonstrated the respect many of them felt for him after attending his anatomical classes. Yet like so many of the society's undertakings, the motion was rejected as invalid on a technicality. Knox's name never appears in the record as attending any of the meetings either before or after this debacle. Grant, however, as a close colleague of Knox's and occasional visitor to Plinian meetings, was well able to represent the views of his friend and employer.

In time-honoured fashion, members usually sharpened their wits by criticising the opinions of established experts and brought their own thoughts together in brief papers that were for the main part their first independent scientific undertaking. Mostly these offerings were entirely conventional in focus: they dealt with the circulation of sea currents, the identity of new plants around Edinburgh, or the anatomy of marine animals found in the Firth of Forth.

A handful of members presented more radical thoughts to their friends. At one meeting, William Browne attacked Charles Bell's theory of the nervous system and human emotion, ridiculing his dependence on natural theology as a means of explanation. A few weeks later, Browne delivered a paper on "organization as connected with life" in which he proposed that life itself was just a function of the way the body was organised and—to the society's consternation—that "mind, as far as one individual's senses and consciousness are concerned, is material."

As these statements suggested, Browne was a keen phrenologist. He was intimate with George and Andrew Combe, and soon became popular as a public lecturer in Scotland on phrenological and mental and moral topics. In years to come, he learned a good deal about French psychiatric medicine under Pinel and Esquirol, and he became the first director of the Crichton Royal lunatic asylum, where he made many important changes in the treatment of madness, including the introduction of amateur theatricals. Browne was never afterwards quite as much of a hot-blooded radical as he appeared during these student days, though he remained a phrenologist. He married into one of the most notably devout Scottish Episcopalian families—the botanical Balfours—and matured into a solidly respectable citizen with conservative leanings who eventually became Commissioner in Lunacy for Scotland.[32] And only a few of his Plinian Society papers—not all—were characterised by the reductionist philosophy of mind that phrenologists often supported. Studies relating to the habits of cuckoos, to ghosts (he believed in them), and to plants collected around Edinburgh were just as prominent in his repertoire as risky speculations about the ultimate purpose and arrangements of nature.

Yet in one of the most exciting episodes of the society's existence, Browne's dangerous remarks on organisation were deliberately erased from the minute book (not completely enough to prevent them being read by anyone persistent enough to do so).[33] The arguments, resolutions, votes, and counter-votes that must have preceded this exorcism went unrecorded; and Browne's paper was never mentioned again. Stung, and probably retiring hurt, he

confined his subsequent offerings to much safer topics like the aurora borealis
and a new sighting of *Primula eliator* near Roslyn. Silently watching in the
audience, Darwin surely learned from this episode that even in the most
informal of settings, it was unwise to stray too far from the established path.

At other meetings, William Ainsworth discoursed on the principles of
natural classification, describing a hierarchical scheme amalgamating Cuvier's
emphasis on the functional systems of animals with the theories of structural
homology advanced by his rival Geoffroy, the latter supported by Grant in
particular. Darwin contributed to the discussion of the paper afterwards, but
the minutes do not record what was said. At another, William Rathbone
Greg attempted to prove that "the lower animals possess every faculty &
propensity of the human mind." In between, there were minerals and archaeological remains to talk about.

Several of these speakers became Darwin's companions. In the months
that followed, he and Ainsworth went out on a few collecting expeditions
together. Some of their excursions lured them quite far away from Edinburgh,
and once they were trapped overnight at Inch Keith, an island in the Firth of
Forth. According to Ainsworth, they took refuge in the lighthouse.[34] The
experience did not pull them any closer. "He was a Wernerian geologist,"
said Darwin afterwards, "and knew a little about many subjects, but was
superficial and glib with his tongue."

During that outing and others, Darwin mostly concentrated on shooting
birds. His kind of ornithology involved active participation with a gun, and
presumably he stuffed his victims afterwards, in the way John Edmonstone
had taught him. One of the few manuscripts remaining from this period is
a brief list of northern species copied out by Darwin from Brisson's *Ornithologie*
(1826), dirty and deeply creased from use in the field. He kept similar lists of
sea invertebrates ("Vermes") and fishes, copied from papers by Jameson and
Patrick Neill.[35] He also went out collecting on the beaches with John
Coldstream, the only Plinian with whom he maintained a correspondence of
sorts after leaving Edinburgh. Compared to Ainsworth, Coldstream "was a
very different young man, prim, formal, highly religious and most kind-
hearted: he afterwards published some good zoological articles."

VI

Darwin relaxed sufficiently in the company of these new colleagues to take a
step that now seems completely uncharacteristic. An English student named
William Kay, one of the presidents and then the secretary of the Plinian
Society after Ainsworth stepped down, persuaded him to join him in writing
a humorous article—or one that was meant to be humorous, in the usual
tradition of heavy-handed medical wit—which revealed no trace of an affec-

tionate relationship with either Scotland or their Scottish medical education. Never read before an audience, never published, never noticed as such by historians, this article sank virtually without trace. It represents a résumé of sorts of Darwin's feelings at a critical turn in his life.

Together Kay and Darwin produced an account of a "Zoological walk" to the nearby beach of Portobello—possibly completely fictitious, although it seems more likely that a real expedition served as a basis for their humour. Everything that could have gone wrong, they implied facetiously, went wrong.

Neither student believed himself a great satirist: they hoped only to puncture the pomposity of a Mr. Ritchie (one of three members with that name), who had delivered an interminable "journal of a walk from the source to the mouth of the Water of Fail in Ayrshire" with some "patriotic encomiums on Robert Burns and William Wallace." To describe a walk like this was a common literary device at weekly meetings, and one that also appeared regularly in the undergraduate and literary journals of the day. Darwin and Kay produced their own version of a similar excursion, including some English remarks on Scotland. They intended reading this out loud in alternate voices, with Darwin speaking of the driving rain and the sights they would have seen if it had not been so wet ("How could the event turn out but unsuccessful?"), and Kay delivering remarks from Samuel Johnson about the joy of seeing the "high-road to England."

The morning proved, as it usually does in such cases, most particularly unfavourable, quite characteristic of the Scottish climate. We had indeed flattered ourselves with the hope of one of those clear and shining mornings, so peculiar, in winter, to the more Southern parts of this Island. In this we were miserably disappointed, even near objects being rendered totally invisible by the dense and impenetrable mist. . . .

Leaving the busy hum of men and threading our way through dirty streets and cercuitous [*sic*] wynds, we at last reached Holyrood House. Who can see this remarkable pile without, at the same time, connecting in his mind the various scenes and changes it has witnessed? Who can behold it without thinking of the unfortunate Mary? But alas the time will soon arrive that this ancient building, so favoured in the chronicles of olden times, will by the ill taste of the Scotch Nation, be only recognised, as a newly decked out villa. . . .

If the day had been more favourable, we might have seen on our right hand, the far-famed Salisbury Craigs, another striking specimen of Scotch taste.—Not of picturesque beauty, but of money. At one time this belted hill was perchance an ornament of Edinburgh—now it merely stands, a monument [to] what gunpowder and ye Wedge [i.e., quarrying] can perform. Our only view was a broad dirty road, that cried out for Macadam at every step. Along such a road however, we steadily persisted, until at length, we gained the Portobello shore. We looked in vain for Inch Keith, the Bas rock, the distant hills in Fifeshire. All these indeed were hidden in an impenetrable cloud of obscurity. . . . [36]

The walk ended with a few paltry shells picked up on the shore (the tide was in, complained Darwin) and an excellent dinner, which they "discussed in a most scientific manner"—not of local country fare like haggis or Scotch collops, but of "substantial Beef-steak." The final Anglophile allusion would not have been lost on an audience steeped in the roast-beef chauvinism of the Napoleonic period.

This brave attempt at humour never got any further than the handwritten page. Had Browne's public squelching generated second thoughts? Or did Darwin's stutter turn the prospect of continued references to a walk in the rain into an impossibility?

VII

It was Robert Grant, not Kay, Ainsworth, or Coldstream, who took Erasmus's place in Darwin's life during these five winter months alone in Edinburgh. Grant walked him back down to Leith harbour, where the two brothers used to go, to look through the rock pools or to buy oysters, encrusted with other living beings for dissection, directly from the docks. Once or twice they went out on the choppy waters of the Firth with fishermen from Newhaven, taking a rare chance to collect spongy, gelatinous organisms from the seabed. These unformed creatures Grant made peculiarly his own, teasing out of their amorphous masses fascinating—almost unbelievable—stories of reproduction, generation, and change. Only the previous year he had similarly introduced Coldstream to these "little ocean beauties."

Indeed, Grant seemed warmly friendly towards Darwin, and Darwin gratefully responded in kind. "I knew him well," the younger man wrote afterwards; "he was dry and formal in manner, but with much enthusiasm beneath this outer crust." Under his tutelage, Darwin became enthralled by marine zoology. Back at Grant's house by the seashore after their collecting trips, Grant showed him how to dissect under seawater with a single-lens microscope and what to look for. From him Darwin learned things he had never learned before—and could hardly have learned anywhere else in Britain at that time. Grant gave him the early understanding of developmental studies among invertebrates that eventually formed the cornerstone of his evolutionary theories, and propelled him into becoming a "lifelong generation theorist."[36] Darwin never afterwards lost his zest for working on these and other insignificant organisms that acted out their great sagas of life, death, and metamorphosis unnoticed on the bottom of the sea.

Ideas of change and development among marine organisms were running high in Grant's mind at that time. He had already written two articles about the anatomy of sponges in which he demonstrated the sponge's animal nature by showing how it released mobile, free-swimming reproductive "gemmules" like the larvae of many other marine animals, and identified its simple in-and-out, water-based system of digestion. His other papers around this time described the sponge's calcareous and siliceous framework. Grant coined the family name "Porifera" and was recognised as a rising expert on this group by having his name bestowed on a new genus (*Grantia*) by John Fleming.

Most revealing from the point of view of Grant's developing evolutionary opinions was a study he published in 1826 on the spongilla, a principal component of the grey-green slime on stagnant lakes and inland pools. Grant announced that this too was an animal that reproduced by motile eggs and asserted that such simple forms must be more ancient than ordinary marine sponges, "most probably their original parent." He went on to propose that this natural ordering from simple to complex represented the historical order of the appearance of sponges in general. They changed their bodily form to match corresponding changes in the surroundings, he suggested: an inheritance of acquired characteristics that adapted organisms to new conditions as Lamarck proposed in his *Philosophie zoologique* of 1808.

In the same year, Grant seems to have gone even further in producing an anonymous essay boldly advocating a similar kind of evolutionary progress in living beings generally, more or less an extension of Lamarck's scheme of transmutation. The article carried the distinction of being the first significant statement linking Lamarck's scheme with the geological history of living beings. It was published in the October 1826 issue of Robert Jameson's *Edinburgh New Philosophical Journal*.[37] Even if the article was not Grant's (and the point is still hotly debated), its tilt towards blending the story of fossils with a probable capacity of living beings to adapt to circumstances would have been broadly acceptable to this particular naturalist at such a point in his career.

Most of Grant's research subsequently probed the connections between animals and plants with a general view to establishing that polyps—defined as plants until Lamarck insisted they were animals—were actually genuine intermediaries: animal-plants, or "zoo-phytes" as Grant called them. Like plants, they reproduced by buds; like animals, they also released free-swimming "ova" (actually larvae). In their simplicity and intermediate nature, they provided the key, Grant thought, to all the more complex phenomena of life and organisation. Even the intricate structure of human beings could be understood by examining such unsophisticated organisms. From "man to the monads," ran the bold argument of Grant's first course of lectures at University College in 1828.[38]

Darwin, eager to learn and obviously dissatisfied with his medical work, was willingly drawn into such a wide-ranging research programme. Before long, Grant gave him specimens of the zoophytes currently under his investigation and started treating him as a disciple—with which Darwin slavishly concurred. In a notebook begun at that time, Darwin recorded examining many different species of marine slugs, molluscs, and sea-worms for some of Grant's ciliated "ova," which were capable of "self-motion": animals on which Grant was working and later published his findings.

These zoological researches provided the occasion of Darwin's first properly scientific paper, delivered to the Plinian Society on 27 March 1827 (not "at the beginning of the year 1826" as stated in his *Autobiography*). Grant gave Darwin some small problems to resolve in relation to the genus *Flustra*, a highly anomalous colonial animal that creeps over tidal rocks rather like a seaweed, in which the minute polyps, though arranged in branches, are to all intents and purposes unconnected with one another. Part of the individual polyp's life cycle involved collapsing into a withered ball that subsequently regenerated apparently without sexual intervention. Did these too reproduce by eggs that swim?

Darwin, poring over a "wretched microscope" lent by Grant one evening, thought that they did. In one of the most intense moments of his early life, he witnessed the uninhibited fertilization dance of seaweeds and other simple organisms, where iridescent molecules (the spermatozoa and ova of modern science) shimmer and pulse around each other. The tiny reproductive gemmules "glided to & fro with so rapid a motion, as at some distance to be distinctly visible to the naked eye." Glowing with his first zoological discovery, and deeply excited by seeing life in all its marvellous activity going on under the microscope, he proudly recited a litany of famous zoologists who had missed seeing the same wonderful dance: "That such ova had organs of motion does not appear to have been hitherto observed either by Lamarck Cuvier Lamouroux or any other author."[39]

The point was announced by Darwin at the next meeting of the Plinian in tandem with a longer paper by Grant on the broader natural history of all the Scottish species of *Flustra*. At the same meeting, Darwin noted another small discovery that the "sea peppercorns" commonly attached to oysters and old shells were not buttons of seaweed as usually thought, but the eggs of a marine leech, *Pontobdella muricata*.

VIII

Grant did much more than provide Darwin with this promising professional start. He introduced him to the acute excitement of evolutionary thought. "He, one day, when we were walking together burst forth in high admiration of Lamarck and his views on evolution. I listened in silent astonishment." But, Darwin added, "as far as I can judge, without any effect on my mind."[40]

Grant had long appreciated not only Lamarck but also Darwin's grandfather Erasmus Darwin. It was Erasmus Darwin's work, Grant later claimed, that "first opened my mind to some of the laws of organic life."[41] Grant was probably delighted by the idea that his young disciple was a direct descendant of this famous English evolutionist. He probably expected Darwin to be equally unorthodox, predisposed to discuss transmutation with the same airy directness of his grandfather. In fact, Darwin may well have been the first man to hear of Grant's evolutionary beliefs. There are scarcely any other recorded occasions when Grant treated colleagues to similarly open-minded speculations, and he did not publicly reveal the full extent of his views until he delivered the Swiney lectures in London in the 1850s.[42] Moreover, Darwin was only a student, insignificant in the Edinburgh academic hierarchy. If Grant praised transmutation to a passing pupil, one who seemed agreeably predisposed to listen to all his zoological theories, a Darwin to boot, his career would not end up in shreds.

But Charles Darwin's phlegmatic response was puzzling. Far too disingenuous in his *Autobiography,* he was in truth well prepared to understand the importance both of Lamarck and of his grandfather. At the time Grant spoke to him, Darwin had already read Lamarck's technical guide to the classification of invertebrates, the *Système des animaux sans vertèbres* (1801), which included the text of a lecture in which Lamarck clearly proposed that species change through time.[43] From this lecture he would quickly have grasped the essentials of Lamarck's theory.

And he had by then studied Erasmus Darwin's evolutionary works, particularly the *Zoonomia.* A previously unknown list made by Darwin of the books he read during his second year at Edinburgh makes it plain that he studied his grandfather's volumes closely—closely enough to continue the interest by reading Anna Seward's biography of him (published in 1804) and following up crucial questions about the nature of life and organisation as raised in the *Zoonomia* and by contemporary debates in Edinburgh in other medical texts of the period.[44] Young Darwin, it now turns out, was well aware of evolutionary views and perfectly capable of grasping the full implications of what Grant had to say.

There can be no doubt that he was impressed by his grandfather and his ideas. Erasmus Darwin's theory of the generation of living "filaments" from which all animals and plants evolved fitted neatly with everything he was learning from Grant about "the simplest organised bodies, as *Monads* and *Globulinae,* [that] originate spontaneously from matter in a fluid state."[45] Erasmus Darwin additionally proposed that the sexual reproduction of organisms, particularly simple marine invertebrates, was the *raison d'être* of their existence. The eggs produced by sexual reproduction were fundamental to understanding the structure and classification of the lower, more gelatinous reaches of the animal kingdom. Peering through his microscope, Darwin agreed.

Moreover, there was less direct atheism in his grandfather's work than Darwin perhaps expected. The first Erasmus Darwin called on divine agency several times to account for the ultimate origin of living matter, though hardly giving enough detail to persuade alert readers that he truly meant it. It was hard to see his grandfather as a dangerous revolutionary.

> Would it be too bold to imagine, that in the great length of time, since the earth began to exist, perhaps millions of ages before the commencement of the history of mankind, would it be too bold to imagine, that all warm-blooded animals have arisen from one living filament, which the first great cause endowed with animality, with the power of acquiring new parts, attended with new propensities, directed by irritations, sensations, volitions, and associations; and thus possessing the faculty of continuing to improve by its own inherent activity, and of delivering down those improvements by generation to its posterity, world without end![46]

On the contrary, Erasmus Darwin's appeal lay in the emphasis on natural laws, on sexuality and sexual reproduction, and on progressive change— altogether pleasing for a young man eager to learn about nature's secrets. "At this time," Darwin said, "I admired greatly the *Zoonomia.*"

Anna Seward's biography gave Darwin a different, though no less fascinating, perspective. She wrote about "the person, the mind, the temper of Dr Darwin; his powers as a physician, philosopher, and poet; the peculiar traits of his manners; his excellencies and faults" and was not afraid to judge his scientific theories. Though laughed at by the *Edinburgh Review* for her salacious gush (Seward was a poetess, the reviewer patronisingly informed his readers), hers was the only available account, full of information impossible to get elsewhere, particularly from his reticent father. Robert Waring Darwin of Shrewsbury had tried hard to suppress the most racy parts of the biography after publication and was never fully appeased by Seward's subsequent apologies.[47]

Darwin therefore had the opportunity to think long and hard about his grandfather's philosophy of nature, the bohemian lifestyle, the personality of his unknown grandmother Mary Howard, the precipitate courtship with

Mrs. Pole, the characters and untimely deaths of his two Darwin uncles—cruelly described by Seward—and the dire consequences Miss Seward envisaged if evolutionary views were accepted. Seward briskly dismissed any links between animals and mankind, claiming Erasmus Darwin was all wrong in his understanding of instinct.

Darwin's reading provided a chance for him to come to terms with the fears evolution inspired in his own day. As well as reading the *Zoonomia*—in which, incidentally, he discovered his father's graduation thesis on ocular spectra printed at the back—he consulted John Abernethy's works on physiology, which dealt with the question of animal function and organisation, and those of John Barclay and John Fleming. Abernethy held no truck with what he called modern scepticism—shorthand for the "vital materialism" of Edinburgh men; nor could he accept doctrines such as the brain's ability to secrete thoughts. "Life," he sternly emphasised in the two books Darwin read, "does not depend on organization."[48]

The same message was reiterated by John Fleming in his *Philosophy of Zoology,* which Darwin had studied the previous year: the "different operations of living beings, which we have thus briefly enumerated, can never be regarded as the effect of their peculiar organization." Instead, there was a "living or vital principle" that was superadded to the basic matter of bodies.[49]

Barclay, in his influential *Treatise on Life and Organization* (1822), came to similar conclusions. Though it is not known if Darwin read this important text at that time, he did buy it during his two years in Edinburgh: the copy in his collection is bound in the same distinctive format as the other works bought there. His notes in the margins, however, all date from a later period. Considering the close professional relationship between Grant and Barclay despite their metaphysical differences, and the high esteem with which Barclay was regarded in Edinburgh's intellectual circles generally and in the Plinian Society specifically, it would be surprising if Darwin did not look at it at some stage. He gave a copy of another work by Barclay—on the human skeleton—to the Plinian Society as his parting gift in April. If nothing else, readers of Fleming's book were told that Barclay's *Treatise* "should be perused with care by every student of anatomy and natural history, as an effectual preservative against the doctrines of materialism."[50]

Barclay, in short, explained the main positions taken in Edinburgh and elsewhere in the medical-materialist debates.[51] In his opinion, there were "no animals like automatons"; and he attacked Erasmus Darwin, among other seditious philosophers, for his "wild eccentricities of fancy."[52]

Almost as if collecting all possible points of view about transmutation and secular science in general, Darwin went on to read the papers that Grant gave to him "with best wishes from his friend the author." He read articles in the

Edinburgh New Philosophical Journal, probably including the anonymous evolutionary essay of 1826. When Grant then unburdened his transmutationary heart, Darwin held a full range of contemporary opinion well in focus.

IX

His stony-faced reaction to Grant's Lamarckian fervour was therefore unexpected. Since this was his first direct exposure to evolutionary thought, immediately relevant to the researches he was then performing at Grant's behest, and expounded by a man he liked and admired, it is curious that he rejected—or, as he said, was unaffected by—the ideas so favourably promoted at that crucial juncture.

By then, however, Darwin had lost his respect for Grant. Professional rivalry had already created a barrier between them. Darwin's dancing *Flustra* eggs were the immediate cause, perhaps his enthusiasm too. Some forty years later, Henrietta Darwin told the story:

> When he was at Edinburgh he found out that the spermatozoa [ova] of things that grow on seaweed move. He rushed instantly to Prof. Grant who was working on the same subject to tell him, thinking, he wd be delighted with so curious a fact. But was confounded on being told that it was very unfair of him to work at Prof. G's subject and in fact that he shd take it ill if my Father published it. This made a deep impression on my Father and he has always expressed the strongest contempt for all such little feelings—unworthy of searchers after truth.[53]

His first scientific discovery, he told Henrietta, was marred by being also his first introduction to "the jealousy of scientific men."

What happened was that three days before Darwin's big moment at the Plinian Society when he intended announcing his observations on the moving eggs of *Flustra,* Grant fulfilled his threat and read to the Wernerian Natural History Society a long memoir detailing his own researches into *Flustra,* not only appropriating Darwin's observations as confirmation of moving "eggs" but including those relating to *Pontobdella muricata* as well. The printed report of the proceedings stated that "Dr Grant read a memoir regarding the anatomy and mode of generation of *Flustrae.* . . . The Doctor likewise read a notice on the existence of ciliae in the young of *Buccinum undatum, Purpura lapillus,* and some other molluscous animals; and also on the mode of generation of the *Pontobdella muricata* of Lamarck."[54] There was no acknowledgement of Darwin in the published version appearing in Jameson's *Edinburgh New Philosophical Journal* for 1827; and only the briefest reference to Grant's "zealous young friend Mr Charles Darwin of Shrewsbury" when the *Pontobdella* material was printed in David Brewster's

Edinburgh Journal of Science.[55] Not quite enough, thought Darwin, with some justification. Grant had destroyed the gratification he would have felt in describing his first scientific discovery. All the shine was blasted away from Darwin's public pronouncement.

Still, although Darwin believed he had made two original observations, it is clear that his efforts were derivative enough to create problems over attribution. Without Grant's ministrations and directions he could not have known what to look for or how to interpret his findings; and without Grant's theoretical programme he would have been incapable of evaluating his own researches. Moreover, as Robert Jameson later pointed out, the breeding habits of *Pontobdella muricata* were previously known to science, although not widely.

Nonetheless, Darwin felt his work had been commandeered by the older man. Had he but known it, John Coldstream, Grant's protégé of the previous season, had suffered much the same treatment in relation to his work on the "talking snail," *Tritonia arborescens,* which was able to make sounds that humans could hear. Grant had encouraged Coldstream to study these molluscs before using the student's findings with others of his own in a paper read before the Wernerian in 1825. Perhaps he endorsed the continental style of joint research programmes, according to which senior figures put forward their assistants' findings, or saw no reason for individual possessiveness in science; or he may have felt negotiations for the London professorship would be hurried along by several interesting new discoveries for which he alone was responsible. Or perhaps both young men proved unresponsive to late-night suggestions of a different nature. That summer, after graduating, Coldstream certainly experienced a nervous breakdown in Paris, wrestling with what he called "the foul mass of corruption within my own bosom," the "corroding desires" and "lustful imaginations" holding him captive to his body. He was greatly troubled with "doubts arising from certain materialist views, which are, alas!, too common among medical students."[56] His solemn, repressed Scottish Presbyterian soul evidently could not cope with the advanced ideas of Grant and others like him.

Scientific rivalry and disappointment were almost as painful for his Plinian friend. Darwin was mortified by Grant's treatment of him and some weeks later retrospectively wrote out his discovery in full in a private notebook, no doubt feeling he might as well describe his work properly if it was otherwise to be suppressed.[57] Through the rest of April he doggedly carried on with his investigations, possibly in deliberate defiance of Grant's proprietorial rulings. Three of the species he selected to examine were in fact molluscs omitted by Grant in his *Flustra* paper which listed other organisms with ciliated "ova." In each one, Darwin found motile eggs—a source of small but smug retaliation.

Grant was inspiring, maybe brilliant, as others acknowledged, but he had not a generous scientific character. If Grant wanted to talk evolution with him after all this, Darwin must have thought, he ought to try elsewhere. Their close zoological contact lasted four months at most.

One other detail may have been significant in Darwin's relative indifference to Grant's advocacy of transmutation. Grant's wish to link plants with animals through the existence of "zoo-phytes" at the bottom of the evolutionary scale was a proposal Darwin might well have considered doubtful. Both his grandfather Erasmus Darwin and the naturalist Lamarck claimed there was no possibility of uniting the two great natural kingdoms in this way: plants and animals were separate right from the start, they insisted, without any common root in the most primitive or simplest organisms.

A less widely known fact is that Thomas Charles Hope, Darwin's favoured professor of chemistry at Edinburgh, similarly propounded the absolute distinctness of plants from animals—although avoiding any evolutionary hints in his discussion of the question. The simplest chemical test, Hope believed, revealed that the basic constituents of animals and plants were fundamentally different. Given this practical demonstration, which struck at the core of Grant's researches, and was supported by his natural history reading during his second academic session, there were apparently reasonable grounds for Darwin's ignoring at least some of Grant's vivid speculations.

Darwin's year consequently closed on a sour note. There was nothing he liked about medicine or the men who pursued it, no qualities in the professors or other teachers to generate long-lasting respect. Even Robert Grant, so much admired, so much a replacement for Erasmus, disappointed him. Everything to do with medicine was disconsolately rejected: corpses, operations, blood, Jameson, Grant, social and individual controversy, the family connection with medicine, his father's opinion that he would make a worthy physician. He contemplated theories of transmutation, of scientific materialism, and reductionism, and, for the most part, put them aside. He did not want to be labelled a radical materialist—to be squashed like Browne or have his work suppressed by the jealousy of a philosophical anatomist. He did not want to be thought of as a repeat edition of his grandfather, another evolutionary Darwin who believed in "spontaneous generation and transmutation of species, with all their train of monstrous consequences."

Temporary as some of these decisions were, Darwin was at last firm in his own mind that this unlovely, faltering career would have to be abandoned. He would become himself only by leaving medicine behind.

"AN IDLE SPORTING MAN"

T was the first time Dr. Darwin was really angry with him. "You care for nothing but shooting, dogs, and rat-catching, and you will be a disgrace to yourself and all your family," he exploded. Humbled, Darwin had to agree. "He was very properly vehement against my turning an idle sporting man, which then seemed my probable destination."[1]

In the doctor's exasperated view, his son would have to buckle down quickly. If medicine was out of the running, what else was left? The law looked as unlikely as it had two years before. The armed forces or government service seemed equally unpromising. Could he go into the church? Darwin needed a profession of some kind: one reflecting the family's position in county society and making him relatively independent should his private inheritance suddenly fail. The Anglican establishment usually treated its gentleman-ministers well, providing them with rambling country parsonages, a comprehensive system of tithes, and an important niche in local affairs. Dr. Darwin's doctrinal misgivings were not so great that they outweighed such obvious advantages. And Darwin was unlikely to turn sanctimoniously Tory once dressed in his vestments. Like his cousins John Allen Wedgwood and Robert Wedgwood, he could depend on a certain form of landed Whig patronage when the question of an ecclesiastical living came around.

He told Darwin to examine his conscience and prepare for a clerical vocation.

I asked for some time to consider, as from what little I had heard and thought on the subject I had scruples about declaring my belief in all the dogmas of the Church of England; though otherwise I liked the thought of being a country clergyman. Accordingly I read with care Pearson on the Creed and a few other books on divinity; and as I did not then in the least doubt the strict and literal truth of every word in the Bible, I soon persuaded myself that our Creed must be fully accepted. It never struck me how illogical it was to say that I believed in what I could not understand and what is in fact unintelligible. I might have said with entire truth that I had no wish to dispute any dogma; but I never was such a fool as to feel and say "credo quia incredibile."[2]

There was not much room for manoeuvre, however. Whatever his son might think about the creed, Dr. Darwin had already decided to send him to Cambridge for an ordinary Arts degree—the first step in the formal process towards Holy Orders. He would follow Erasmus's footsteps by joining Christ's College as an undergraduate.

But he would have to start at the beginning again. In fact, a lot of preparatory work was needed beforehand, for it soon turned out that Darwin had forgotten almost all the Greek and Latin he had learned at school. Irritated, his father postponed the departure for Cambridge until the new year and engaged a private tutor to cram him during the rest of 1827.

Darwin's next nine months were spent in an uncomfortable, reproachful academic limbo. The only high spots were when he managed to slip away from his classical grind to the shooting and other pleasant diversions at his uncle Josiah Wedgwood's house in Staffordshire. Sensing a family atmosphere, Uncle Jos diplomatically encouraged these visits. He also took him on a short trip to Paris to collect the youngest Wedgwood girls, the first time Darwin travelled abroad and the only time he ever went to France. Darwin did not record whether he toured Cuvier's Muséum d'Histoire Naturelle or paid a call on John Coldstream, struggling with metaphysical problems in the academic *quartier*. Perhaps he did. He welcomed the breathing space more than anything—the feeling of being appreciated despite his failings. He burst into a "chorus of admiration" for Uncle Jos, Caroline Darwin reported from their French hotel, "whenever he leaves the room."

II

Arriving in Cambridge in January 1828 after this edgy start was a positive relief. Dr. Darwin was forced to stop grilling him to see if any of his expensive tutoring was sticking. Erasmus promised to visit as soon as possible from London. He had a handsome allowance of £300 a year to spend more or less as he wished.

To go to Cambridge was also to enter a world much more congenial to his tastes than either Shrewsbury or Edinburgh. There Darwin came to feel at home, relaxed and confident among people mostly from the same kind of background as himself—people with similar professional aspirations and familiar, if conventional, social graces. The church he could think about later. For the time being, he was back among the sons of the English gentry. The majority of his contemporaries sprang from families with sturdy country pedigrees reaching far back into history and, as often as not, some kind of long-standing connection with their college. There were noblemen and bishops' sons in residence, as well as fellow commoners and pensioners (Darwin was one of the latter), and scholarship boys, known as sizars: a subdivision of college life reflecting the hierarchy of society in general.

Elitism, moreover, extended further than this select student body. Senior members of the university played a leading role in the upper reaches of the British establishment, and the individual masters and fellows making up the core of the academic body were influential in national affairs, holding with Oxford the right of patronage for more than half the available ecclesiastical preferments, which ranged from small country parishes to politically significant appointments like bishoprics. The colleges owned great swaths of the British countryside, were primary landlords in the town of Cambridge, operated an independent legal system over their domains, elected their own member of Parliament, and, through an all-pervasive network of personal and political contacts, enjoyed ready access to government ministers, the aristocracy, churchmen, and royalty as required. Young men with money, ability, or good breeding, or any combination of the three, could expect to join a powerful web linking the people in Britain who really mattered: first as beneficiaries and then as patrons themselves. To attend this kind of university was to step purposefully into the English ruling classes.

Unlike the Scottish universities, Oxford and Cambridge were also theological training houses, literally wings of the Church of England. Ever since Henry VIII had seceded from the Roman Catholic Church and placed himself at the head of a new Anglican Communion, both institutions had been an integral part of the state and its official church. Theology, in this national context, blended indistinguishably into politics, especially in the House of Lords, where bishops took their seats alongside hereditary peers. Further than this, degrees were granted only to assenting members of the Anglican faith, and a declaration of belief in the Thirty-nine Articles was required on graduation. University regulations included compulsory reading in theology and moral philosophy and daily attendance at chapel services. College fellows were obliged to take Holy Orders after a number of years, some of them staying inside the "house" for the rest of their lives and assuming the institutional positions or professorships that were exclusively the preserve of unmarried Anglican divines, while others became eligible for a college benefice—a country parsonage, perhaps, like that of George Eliot's Mr. Cadwallader, or a prebendary stall or cathedral appointment for more senior figures. Either way, the Church of England was central to the life of the teachers and the taught, the officers and the recipients. "No thought can find place," sighed John Stuart Mill about Cambridge, "except that which can reconcile itself with orthodoxy."

Reactionary though the university undoubtedly was, it simultaneously quivered on the brink of a major upheaval. The spirit of reform sweeping the country did not stop politely at the great college gates to knock for admittance. It was becoming imperative in the eyes of many London thinkers that Oxford and Cambridge should forfeit at least some of their ancient privileges as other areas of the constitution and the economic structure of the nation were deliberately reframed. Attacks from outside had mounted through the 1820s as liberalising members of Parliament sought to limit the wilder excesses of college patronage, at the same time as the Whig-run *Edinburgh Review* conducted an acerbic campaign against the universities' mediaeval straitjacket and influential religious dissenters railed against restrictive practices in awarding degrees. Prominent nonconformists like Leonard Horner, whom Darwin met briefly in Edinburgh, began setting up their own teaching bodies, significantly including the new University College in London—the "godless institution" in Gower Street—to which Robert Grant moved in 1827 and which took its first students in 1828. Edinburgh University was repeatedly praised in the reformist press for its open doors, religious tolerance, and excellent tuition—not strictly true characterizations in the light of Darwin's experiences and the wide-ranging changes that Robert Peel needed to initiate after the Royal Commission, but useful propaganda all the same. To modernise and improve became the concerned Englishman's refrain.

The fresh air of criticism similarly blew inside some of Cambridge's panelled halls. A small band of fellows and younger professors, mostly based at Trinity College, worked hard during that same decade to restructure parts of the syllabus and revoke some of the more arcane freaks of administration relating to academic appointments. Being devout Anglican divines, few of these internal reformers urged any major changes in the religious exclusion acts. The upheaval that was sure to follow must, they felt certain, weaken the university's ties with the established church.

But they were anxious to pull the Cambridge educational system up to a standard appropriate for what they saw as the opening of an era of intellectual progress. "It would scarcely be believed," wrote George Pryme, who came up to Trinity as a freshman in 1799, "how very little knowledge was required for a mere degree when I first knew Cambridge. Two books of

Euclid's geometry, simple and quadratic equations, and the early parts of Paley's *Moral Philosophy* were deemed amply sufficient."[3]

Most important, political change was mooted: up until then, Cambridge University's public voice had been almost always Tory. Now, thought restless young college liberals, was the moment to campaign for a Whig member of Parliament.

The whole place consequently contrasted greatly with Edinburgh. Stepping off the coach after a long, cold jolt from Shrewsbury—a tall, well-built young man, according to James Heaviside at Sidney Sussex College, "rather thick set in physical frame & of the most placid, unpretending, & amiable nature"[4] —Darwin found Cambridge a sleepy backwater out on the windy edge of East Anglia. Enclosed, almost stifled, by its antiquity and social limitations, it offered little chance of meeting a Negro bird-stuffer or Lamarckian philosopher.

Reality, of course, in the shape of drink, sharp trading practices, street brawls, horse fairs, billiards, mud, and poverty, was never far away. Yet the Cambridge that Darwin ultimately knew best was not the Cambridge of prostitutes and taverns, of drunks in ditches, or riots ending in rick-burning; not the Cambridge that William Makepeace Thackeray had to leave without a degree after spending every day fencing, drinking, and gambling; not the Cambridge that Alfred Tennyson wandered through in the same tobacco-stained shirt for six weeks on end, "the slovenly one" of the three brothers educated there; nor yet the intellectualised Cambridge of the "Apostles," the exclusive philosophical group which his brother Erasmus joined and to which James Spedding, Frederick Denison Maurice, Arthur Hallam, and Edward Fitzgerald once belonged, full of politics and the "male routs" that Charles Lyell deplored during a visit in 1827.

Darwin had no natural tendency to dissipation, metaphysics, or political activity. His Cambridge was an easy-going affair, for the most part happily engaged with the internal world of his college in preference to any of the wider issues that might rampage outside. He dissociated himself almost completely from the town in which the university was located.

Because of his late arrival halfway through the academic year, no vacant rooms were available in Christ's College, where Darwin was supposed to live and be taught. So he took lodgings above a tobacconist in Sidney Street, just across the road, until "pleasant rooms on the south side of the first court of Christ's" became free the following October. These rooms had once been occupied by the eighteenth-century natural theologian William Paley, whose works were a significant part of the syllabus and for whom Darwin expressed youthful admiration. Down below, the poet John Milton had once walked and talked in the same courtyard. Awe-inspiring antecedents like these, coupled with his sitting room's "time-darkened panelling and its great

window seats," made Christ's very different from homely Mrs. Mackay's.[5]
Thereafter, he lived in the same set of rooms up to graduation in June 1831,
with a "gyp" called Impey, an otherwise faceless college servant, looking
after him and all the other students residing on the same staircase.

But the cultivation of "mind" at Christ's had yielded to lesser objects
since Milton's day; and academic reform had barely made headway. The
impression formed by one of Darwin's contemporaries was that the college
was fairly quiet, with a pronounced tendency to "horsiness." Many of the
"men" went to Newmarket during the racing season, following their senior
tutor's example. Discipline was attractively loose, and chapel services
conducted by the college dean, Edward John Ash, scarcely more than a
routine observed before dinner.[6] Such a casual, predominantly sporting
atmosphere certainly suited the new undergraduate better than that of intellectually demanding colleges like St. John's and Trinity.

Memories of the isolation of Edinburgh lodgings and much easier social
circumstances than before encouraged Darwin to make friends straight away.
True, it was not hard: Hensleigh Wedgwood, a cousin from Staffordshire
who was one of Erasmus's closest friends during his Cambridge days, was a
fellow at Christ's and more than willing to help Darwin find his feet. John
Price, another of Erasmus's friends from Shrewsbury School, was a graduate
scholar at St. John's studying for Holy Orders. William Allport Leighton, an
almost forgotten colleague from Mr. Case's primary school, was also at St.
John's, and former acquaintances from Shrewsbury School, including John
Cameron, Frederick Watkins, Thomas Butler, and James Turner, were scattered
through various colleges. Darwin found instant companionship with these
former schoolmates. One or two Shropshire people previously unknown to
him proved similarly congenial.

Most enjoyable, however, was his discovery of another cousin, this time
from the Darwin side of the family. William Darwin Fox was the only son of
Robert Waring Darwin's cousin Samuel, four years older than Darwin, and in
his final year studying for an ordinary Arts degree at Christ's. Gentle,
gossipy, unambitious, and sweet-natured, like a more tranquil version of
Erasmus, he hoped to become a clergyman after graduation. He was "a
clever and most pleasant man . . . with whom I became extremely intimate."
Darwin considered Fox's friendship one of the most satisfying things that
happened to him at Cambridge. The two became the closest and dearest of
friends.

Fox's overriding passion was collecting natural history curiosities, and
almost anything, it seems, was welcome for the eccentric "museum" haphazardly lying around his student rooms: stuffed swans, rare pine martens,
day-old chicks, the pupae of moths to incubate through the summer, the

corpse of a female goosander shot by Darwin one February, or some "Waxen Chatterers" bought from a freelance natural history supplier catering precisely for this kind of gentlemanly trade. Every available surface was draped with things that had once flown or grown, to the despair of the gyp who kept them clean and a Mr. Aiken who looked after the excess in bulging hampers in his cellar.

Fox similarly enjoyed rural sports such as shooting and riding. Most of all, he loved dogs. According to a series of letters exchanged between the cousins in 1828 and 1829, Fox kept two dogs in turn at university, which Darwin called "poor little Fan" and "Sappho, the best of bitches." Fox returned the compliment with style, offering lengthy tributes to Darwin's "Mr Dash," then living at Shrewsbury. Only Fox, Darwin said, knew the full significance of his holiday report that Dash's game-pointing technique was shaping up well. Only Darwin, said Fox, understood how important it was that Fan was "in very good keep & a very great favourite" some months after she was sold. Darwin was less open, though, about confessing that his schoolboy power of stealing away the love of someone else's dog continued unabated. After Fox graduated, Sappho brazenly transferred her affections to Darwin: she used to creep down inside his college bed and sleep at its foot every night.[7] Eventually he gave her to a Cambridge townsman named Markham.

Forged in this way amid strong family resemblances and a liking for what they called the same inherited tastes, the cousins' relationship was a real marriage of minds. Whenever Darwin nostalgically recalled his time at Cambridge he always thought first of Fox and the fun they had together. Indeed, although the two coincided for only six months or so before Fox went home to Osmaston in Derbyshire to ponder his next steps towards a curacy, the experience lent a happy glow to Darwin's remaining years at the university. Fox's friends were his friends, and Fox's enthusiasms were his continuing delight. "How I wish you had been able to have stayed up here. We should have suited so well, each of us reading all morning & being idle all evening.—But it is not only when I am solitary that I regret your absence. Many many times do I think of our cozy breakfasts & even wish for you to give me a good scolding for swearing, & being out of temper or any other of my hundred faults."[8]

But Darwin was rarely prone to moping. Long letters took the place of the breakfast table, and a constant flow of high-spirited chatter freely larded with demands for natural history information and more letters than his friend could ever hope to supply issued from Darwin's college rooms at regular intervals. "Recollect, that Deo Volente whether your Parsonage boast of a roof or not I shall pay you a visit this summer."

Back at home on the receiving end, Fox considered his cousin one of nature's impossible charmers. "Of all the blackguards" he had ever met with, Darwin was "the greatest," he cried after some preposterous request. "What deuced goodnatured fellows your friends must be."

Actually it was Fox—himself the most good-natured of men—who brought out the best in Darwin. During those Cambridge terms and for some years afterwards, the two of them were very alike in their ideals and aspirations, mutually supportive in their intention to take Holy Orders, each comfortable with the idea of becoming a country parson, vastly amused by their largely imaginary search for prospective parsonage wives, and united in groaning about the hard book-work they needed to do when so many alluring natural history exploits were calling over the fens. They shared their lives with unfeigned pleasure, right down to the complicated system of loans and back-payments which were offset against natural history expenses and bills from Cambridge grocers that they devised in 1828 and that taxed their nonmathematical minds with a vengeance for several years afterwards. Luckily for the local shopkeepers, Fox could add up a shade more efficiently than Darwin.

In many ways the similarities continued through to the end of their lives. Fox, in effect, became the man that Darwin never was, for if Darwin, instead of seizing the chance of joining the *Beagle* expedition, had stuck to his father's new plan of entering the church, he would have become just like his cousin, both in his future responsibilities as a country-loving gentleman-parson and in the same open-hearted, inquiring personality that found fulfilment in hosts of children, relatives, and animals, keeping abreast with scientific journals, making a few experiments in the garden and poultry yard, and reminiscing about gallops through the Cambridgeshire countryside. Fox too, though neither of them suspected it at the time, became a mild hypochondriac of the Darwinian kind; there was a long and increasingly contented run of letters in their middle age about the poor state of their health. When not ill enough themselves, there were always the children's problems to talk about. When we look at Fox, it is possible to see what Darwin could have been, what he at first intended for himself. The mirror image never fully faded.

III

Apart from his meeting Fox, the most striking aspect of Darwin's career at Cambridge University was the total lack of any engagement with academic work. His time was wasted as far as conventional studies were concerned, he said, as completely as at Edinburgh and at school. This was not altogether unusual. The university was then so lax that spending three years fishing or at Newmarket races was unremarkable, though not always acceptable to tutors and parents. Regency swells came up to colleges to pass their days pleasantly enough between a grand tour on the Continent and attending the London season; prospective clergymen tasted some of the sins they would later castigate in a parish; country boys acquired a social sheen; and young aristocrats squandered their allowances on claret. Darwin, somewhat more sedate than these, nevertheless abandoned any pretence of working until obliged by the examinations.

Officially, he was registered for an ordinary Bachelor of Arts degree, the usual preliminary for theological training, of the kind criticised by Pryme and the focus of much reformist attention during the 1820s. Only capable mathematicians went in for the honours ("Tripos") examinations. Darwin's syllabus included elementary mathematics, geometry, and algebra, the *Natural theology, or evidences of the existence and attributes of the Deity* of William Paley, and one or two classical texts in Latin and Greek. Working on Euclid gave him pleasure, as it had at school, and he liked the clear logic of Paley's arguments, the written equivalent of geometric demonstrations. "The careful study of these works, without attempting to learn any part by rote," he said, "was the only part of the academical course which, as I then felt, and as I still believe, was of the least use to me in the education of my mind."[9]

When the moment came, Darwin managed to rise to the limited mental requirements asked of him. In 1829, during his second year at Christ's, and after several weeks of hard work, he passed the "Previous" examination (the "Little-Go," in popular jargon) that was the product of reformist activity earlier in the decade: before then, students were not examined at all until their finals. Still, John Graham, Darwin's tutor, had to scare him badly before he would take the exam seriously enough. "Graham smiled & bowed so very civilly," Darwin muttered disconsolately to Fox in July, "when he told me that he was one of the six appointed to make the examination stricter, & that they were determined they would make it a very different thing from any previous examination. . . . I am sure it will be the very devil to pay amongst all idle men."[10]

Similarly scared by the "plucking" of one or two friends in their finals in 1830, he threw himself into learning the set texts during his last few months at Cambridge, concentrated furiously on extra tuition in mathematics, and came through the concluding examination quite well. It was an unexpected surprise to discover his final position was tenth out of the 178 candidates who did not go in for honours. "I must say," wrote a fox-hunting friend, George Simpson, "I should have been disappointed had you not been a leading man, knowing your predilection for Mathematicks."[11]

The main focus of Darwin's undergraduate life definitely lay elsewhere.

He was already armed with several well-developed natural history interests and sporting enthusiasms that ran to fox-hunting, riding, and shooting, and undiluted enjoyment was uppermost in his mind. To this he gave his whole-hearted attention.

"I live almost entirely with Fox," he told Erasmus in his first term. Mornings began with lectures and tutorials up to ten o'clock, after which the two invariably met for a late breakfast in Fox's rooms. The meal was a substantial mutton-chop-and-pudding affair involving a good deal of friendly gossip interrupted every now and then by dogs under the table or the arrival of hungry friends and animated discussions about stuffed birds or grocer's bills needing to be paid. From then until evening chapel (which was routinely followed by a formal dinner in hall and the traditional locking of the college gates), they were free to pursue their own inclinations.

Their days were accordingly filled with that special blend of lazy activity peculiar to students. "Cambridge, I find, is one of the few places, where if you anticipate a great deal of pleasure you do not find yourself disappointed," Darwin mused. He and Fox walked for miles in the countryside, browsed in the Cambridge print-shops, and visited the Fitzwilliam Gallery, the university's private art museum, where Darwin rhapsodised over Titian's *Venus,* no doubt teasing Fox that parsonage wives were never quite so voluptuous. The smell of the varnish and the way the nudes were hung behind curtains gave the two of them a quietly salacious thrill.

Fox encouraged Darwin to think seriously about music, particularly choral works, which they diligently sought out in Cambridge chapels: "I have at last got a very decided taste for music," he boasted one June. "When Roper was here we had a concert from morning to night: his visit here was very pleasant as it is quite delightful to hear anyone sing with such spirit, & excellent good taste."[12] Following up this new interest, Darwin went to hear Malibran sing in Birmingham in 1829. "Words cannot praise her enough," Fox read afterwards, "a person's heart must have been made of stone not to have lost it to her."

At other times Fox joked about Dash's tail, exchanged snuff-boxes with him, laid bets on the outcome of the final examinations, and scolded him for outlandish "humbug" and his tendency for "making speeches." They were both thoroughly idle. "I am leading a quiet everyday sort of a life; a little of Gibbon's history in the morning & a good deal of Van John [*vingt-et-un,* blackjack] in the evening. This with an occasional ride with Simcox & constitutional with Whitley, makes up the regular routine of my days."[13]

Fox also introduced Darwin to the one subject that fired his imagination through the long, carefree university days: not Latin or Greek, to be sure, for Darwin shamefacedly admitted that he did nothing in these subjects "except attend a few compulsory lectures"; nor mathematics, the other branch of the syllabus, which he avoided whenever possible.

He introduced him to beetles.

No pursuit at Cambridge was followed with nearly so much eagerness or gave me so much pleasure as collecting beetles. It was the mere passion for collecting, for I did not dissect them and rarely compared their external characters with published descriptions, but got them named anyhow. . . . No poet ever felt more delight at seeing his first poem published than I did at seeing in Stephens' *Illustrations of British Insects* the magic words, "captured by C. Darwin, Esq."

Entomology united all the pleasures the two held dear. They spent hours walking together over the watery college "backs" and further south to Trumpington and Grantchester, poking around in the leaves under the willows, dogs at their heels, occasionally letting out a murmur of delight as some odd insect was spotted and carried off in triumph to Fox's rooms; or riding out to local beauty spots searching for different kinds of terrain that might hide rare specimens, able to admire the scenery or jump a ditch or two as they went, and stopping in a country inn on their return to look over the booty.

Several other similar-minded students were drawn by the evident amusement involved and joined their breakfast deliberations in Christ's, although apparently not always as fervently as Darwin, who was ready to ride out at a moment's notice to scour some suggested new locality. Albert Way of Trinity College, later an archaeologist of some repute, and William Strong Hore, of Queens', were two such insect-chasing enthusiasts. Way captured the jolly combination of sport and science in scratchy pen sketches made at the time. "Go it Charlie!" a top-hatted young naturalist was exhorted, astride his beetle.

Intellectual stimulation ran just as high. The cousins took their collections very seriously, industriously pinning out specimens on boards and consulting textbooks and other entomologists about names—two or three of their investigations rising to standards as high as any museum might expect. "I am dying by inches," cried Darwin to Fox during the holidays, "from not having any body to talk to about insects." He went on to list all the possible identities of beetles caught near Shrewsbury. "I was not *fully* aware of your extreme value before I left Cambridge. I am constantly saying 'I do wish Fox was here.' . . . I have taken 3 species of Coccinellae, one the same as Hoar took in the Fens, which you said was rare, & another with 7 *white!* marks on each elytron. . . . Do you want any of the Byrrhus Pillula? I can get any number. . . . I should not send this very shamefully stupid letter, only I am very anxious to get some *crumbs* of information about yourself & the insects."[14]

Two weeks later he was asking, "is this a Cychrus? I make it so by Lamarck."

> Talking of *the science* I must tell tell you, that since beginning this letter, I think, sir, upon my soul sir, I will take my oath sir, (as Way would say), that I have discovered, that I possess a valuable insect, viz. Melasis Flabellicornis, as the description & habits in Samouelle & Lamarck *perfectly* agree. —look and see what Samouelle says, "once taken in Norfolk by J. C. Curtis" &c &c.; also I have taken 2 new Elaters; one with reddish brown elytra, the other with yellow elytra, red thorax & black head.—Also, have taken Tritoma Bipustulatum, vide Samouell. Pl. II; also a small black Byrrhus, with brownish band across the back; also a small Silpha, with a red spot on each elytron; also have twice !SEEN! the Bombylius Minor, but curses on my clumsiness missed catching them.[15]

All the reference books cited—Lamarck, Curtis, and Samouelle—were the most authoritative entomological texts available: the budding entomologist must have worked his way carefully along Dr. Darwin's library shelves while visiting Shrewsbury. His autobiographical protestations notwithstanding, he cared greatly about the accuracy of his beetle names. "It is quite absurd how interested I am getting about the science."

IV

For university students, the two were remarkably knowledgeable and active in pursuing their hobby. Very little was known at that time about local insect populations in Britain, for there were few standard collections in public hands, and only piecemeal descriptions of particular groups or localities appeared in natural history journals and books. In fact, the exotic entomology of the tropics was better documented than any regional beetles from Shropshire or Cambridge. Identifications were also necessarily shaky before the standardisation of species names was attempted in 1842 and the advent of inexpensive steel engravings in illustrated books and magazines around 1840, and even then they were always open to revision by other naturalists. There was plenty of scope for persistent young men to find new species among the willows or to amend expert opinion.

The problem was how to know when they reached that point. Many of the new natural history periodicals that began to appear in the 1820s and 1830s, as printing technology became more sophisticated, drew their material from enthusiasts just like Darwin and Fox, specialising in reporting British animals and plants recently identified or located. The journals frequently printed lists of species as a guide for other collectors. Darwin began subscribing to one such entomological work published in irregular parts by James Stephens, an employee of the Admiralty in London and a keen naturalist who assisted in classifying the insect collection of the British Museum.

As his knowledge and confidence increased, Darwin established personal contact with Stephens, eventually sending him thirty-four beetles and one moth captured in Cambridge. Although the species were well known to London experts, none had previously been recorded in Cambridge: quite a coup for a beginner. "You will see my name in Stephens' last number," he gloated in a letter to Fox.

At the same time he started comparing and exchanging specimens with other collectors, fully aware of the gentlemanly ethos of a free interchange of scientific information but secretly possessive and competitive about building up his own collection. One minor capture, he conceded to Fox, was not strictly necessary, but "I am glad of it if it is merely to spite Mr Jenyns." Scoring a victory over Leonard Jenyns—a Cambridge graduate living locally as a curate and much respected in university natural history circles—was all part of the excitement. These private collections and Stephens's publication became the sources against which the cousins evaluated their own—and their rivals'—rapidly accumulating specimen boxes.

Darwin's competitive thrust made him particularly successful in devising ways for trapping little-known insects. Looking under the bark of trees, as he often did, or examining the soft areas of old river posts or dead logs was not particularly unusual. Something else drove him on further. "I employed a labourer to scrape during the winter, moss off old trees and place [it] in a large bag, and likewise to collect the rubbish at the bottom of the barges in which reeds are brought from the fens, and thus I got some very rare species."[16]

The same craving for rarities characterised his own endeavours. "One day on tearing off some old bark, I saw two rare beetles and seized one in each hand; then I saw a third and new kind, which I could not bear to lose, so that I popped the one that I held in my right hand into my mouth. Alas it ejected some intensely acrid fluid, which burnt my tongue so that I was forced to spit the beetle out, which was lost, as well as the third one."[17] That beetle did not want to be caught, he laughed afterwards: insects could never be relied on to do what was expected. Strong nerves and determination, he discovered eagerly, were an integral part of the collecting process.

Darwin's preoccupations were not entirely idiosyncratic or isolated. He and his entomological friends stood on the threshold of the great explosion of interest in popular natural history that characterised the early Victorian period: the period when seashells, ferns, minerals, insects, flowering plants, seaweeds, fossils, birds, and all conceivable natural curiosities were collected for pleasure and lovingly arranged in private cabinets or used for decorating an astonishing range of household objects, and when amateurs and experts operated on a single scale as yet barely subdivided by professional qualifications.[18] It was as feasible for Mary Anning, the daughter of a shopkeeper in Lyme Regis, to collect and recognise an entirely new fossilised creature (eventually named *Ichthyosaurus*) in 1811 as it was for George Eliot, Philip Henry Gosse, Charles Kingsley, and the Duchess of Portland to seek out attractive sea anemones and shells, or for trained university personnel like Grant and Jameson to sail round the Firth of Forth gathering sponges to dissect. Despite rigid social divisions which created insurmountable barriers to movement between the classes based on these hobbies alone, the subject matter was not irrevocably compartmentalised into what could be called "high" and "low" science—the esoteric and the strictly popular. Collecting techniques and the underlying zest for accumulating specimens were much the same throughout.

Even so, Darwin did not rest until he had thoroughly mastered the subject. Insects were notoriously difficult to catch before the practice of sugaring trees came into common use, and other implements like candle traps and nets were rudimentary.[19] Ambitious naturalists had to develop a sixth sense about where to surprise the rarest quarry, to the point of shaking putrid autumn fungi to spill out their occupants or searching for the fresh sawdust in the bole of a hollow tree that might indicate a bees' nest. "I can remember the exact appearance of certain posts, old trees and banks where I made a good capture," said Darwin, who relished these practical challenges.

One rare Fenland beetle called *Panagaeus crux major* gave him a "famous chace" out by Whittlesea Mere, and several of the university's naturalists, Leonard Jenyns among them, were quick to pay a call to see it pinned out on a board in his rooms. Another time he buried a snake in order to dig it up again a few weeks later for the chance of finding some flesh-eating insects.

Much to Jenyns's surprise, Darwin produced a bag-net one summer in Cambridge. "He occasionally came over to me at my Vicarage, & we entomologised together in the woods of Bottisham Hall—he sweeping the long grass & weeds with a great canvas bag net in a most vigorous way—an implement I had not been in the habit of using myself."[20]

Along with the nets came tin cases and pasteboard boxes for getting the catch safely home (glass bottles still carried a prohibitive tax after the Napoleonic Wars as well as being breakable) and, for some, a cork-lined top hat to pin insects into direct from the field. Darwin's enthusiasm for gadgets and interesting equipment would have been enough to guarantee buying one of these hats if they were available in 1828, but this particular entomological aid was not marketed until a little later in the century; and by then he was a married man with all collecting urges sated by the voyage of the *Beagle*. His mouth and tin box would have to do. Anyway, explained Thomas Butler of St. John's, Darwin liked to keep specimens alive until he got home, although his partiality for collecting carnivorous beetles usually ended in the demolition of the rest of his catch.

The overall effect of this eccentric behaviour and curious paraphernalia was a strain of upper-class theatricality running through British entomology. "With all your implements about you," Kirby and Spence warned the beginner in 1826, "you will at first be stared and grinned at by the vulgar."[21] To avoid some of the probable embarrassment, William Swainson, another popular natural history author, recommended employing small boys or a labourer to carry the equipment (presumably walking a few steps behind) and take on some of the drudgery.

This, Fox and Darwin regularly did. "Marco Polo," as he was nicknamed in their letters, was hired many times in the space of several months to accompany the two college gentlemen as guide and bagman. He was "a sporting sort of guide who went by the name of Marco Polo, because he carried a leaping pole with a flat board fastened at the bottom for leaping the ditches."[22] Once he was familiar with their needs, he was paid to collect alone when the students were otherwise engaged. Mr. Baker, Mr. Aiken, Mr. Harbour, and a street-trader known only as the Pieman were other Cambridge figures who supplied their entomological services to undergraduates for money. This out-work system was so acceptable to rich young collectors like Darwin that they grumbled when their labour force failed in its duties. "Polo has not brought me many insects lately," Darwin complained in April 1829, "but the Pieman has brought me a great many, inter alia Chalaenius holoriseus." The Pieman helped fill three of his collector's specimen boxes. Soon afterwards, Polo rebelled. "I told Polo to collect," Darwin informed Fox plaintively, "but I am afraid he will never do much more as an Entomologist, he is grown far too idle. You had better try your hand at him, for I despair."[23]

In this peremptory way, steeped within the traditional master-and-servant relationships of the world of manners occupied by university gentlemen of the time, Darwin came to establish the foundation of his later collecting routines. The convenience of having an attendant so near at hand, he found, was difficult to give up once experienced. Ever afterwards he liked to have—and was prepared to pay for—someone to carry out the menial aspects of a collector's duties, a reflection of his social position that lasted right through the *Beagle* experience to his subsequent occupations at Down House, where a whole series of helpers, including Darwin's butler, the village children, and numerous contacts established for the purpose among the lowly shopkeepers, zoo attendants, gardeners, and laboratory assistants of Victorian natural history were paid to collect or do things for him. His researches were almost always a collective—hierarchical—enterprise in this sense. There were always other people hidden behind Darwin's immediate achievements.

Sitting on the edge of a cliff in Wales he inadvertently revealed this particular aspect of his life to come. During the university holidays, a friend said, Darwin "shot any bird on wing below him, which he wished to secure, and the guide who was at the foot of the Cliff had to pick it up, and carry it home for preserving."[24]

These Cambridge collecting days showed his fierce desire to outshine others in scope and ingenuity, and the beginnings of a methodical system of making full use of every available avenue of support.

V

Most of Darwin's university contemporaries were indulgent allies in his scientific researches and entertainments alike. "Have you bottled any more beetles, or impaled any butterflies?" inquired Henry Matthew from a garret in London, where he was trying to make his name as a literary figure after graduation. A witty, profligate individual already sent down from Oxford who survived only a year at Trinity before transferring to Sidney Sussex, Cambridge, Matthew acquired an illegitimate child and an unwanted wife in the process. Darwin was "rather fascinated" by him in the same way as Thackeray fell under his spell. Matthew recited Shelley's poems to Darwin in his rooms and was delighted by the sympathetic response he received from this "most humanised of Insect killers." For his part, Darwin loyally gave Matthew money under the disguise of a loan.

Other college friends spoke warmly of Darwin's genial temper and appetite for a whole host of subjects, the scientific ardour jostling noisily with his sporting and artistic fervour. He was fond of strong expressions like "by the Lord Harry" and "beyond belief," prided himself on his good horsemanship (keeping a hunting horse at Cambridge as well as Fox's dog during his final year), wondered briefly if he had got into a "dissipated low-minded" set, and liked a drink or two with a competitive game of *vingt-et-un* to follow. He spent his father's money freely.

Of these friends, Darwin was closest to quiet, clever, mathematical Whitley, formerly of Shrewsbury School and afterwards top of the Cambridge honours examination list, with whom he walked and talked in the same intimate manner as he once had with Fox. "I see a good deal of him," he told Erasmus, "and like him very much." More often than not, however, the wish to see his brother swamped any further admission of rival affections. "When is there any prospect of your coming back again? I long very much to see the Bachelor of Medicine again." Erasmus, he heard from John Price, was enviably ensconced in London lodgings while attending the private medical school in Windmill Street. His rooms were turned into a makeshift laboratory where he dissected animals that came his way—a codfish, said Price, and a greyhound. "Frogs were killed and as conscientiously fricasséed à la mode de Paris when we had learnt all other lessons from them." Darwin never joined in any of these ad hoc anatomical researches: "he had, I am pretty sure, that innate aversion to cutting up which has disqualified many for a profession to which they were otherwise inclined."[25] But Erasmus was making his own life far away from Cambridge. Darwin wrote to Fox about his growing respect for Whitley's excellent understanding and disposition. "Old Whitley has begun to take your place, & we have just commenced a regular series of constitutionals."[26]

With Whitley he shared an interest in fine art, going again to the Fitzwilliam collections located in Free School Lane. Judging from Darwin's developing tastes, Whitley was a much better artistic guide than Fox, and Darwin was sufficiently encouraged by him to start reading books about art, including those on style by Joshua Reynolds, and studying prints. He bought some "first class line engravings" for his rooms, including studies after Raphael by Rafaello Morghen, professor of engraving in Florence in 1793, one of which was a portrait of Leonardo; and one by Johann Mueller, whose chief engraved work was the *Sistine Madonna*. Though the choice may have been a little obvious in nineteenth-century terms, there was no denying Darwin's appreciation of the standards that served generations of enthusiasts, scholarly and untutored alike.

Ultimately more significant, Whitley seems to have taught Darwin how to look—how to search out the meaning behind the artist's composition and patiently to follow through the layers of technique and allusion. Though he learned a good deal about how to look at nature from Robert Grant, this cultural experience of "looking" gained through aesthetics was equally important in the development of his sensibilities. Darwin's early artistic values have long gone unremarked. "This taste, though not natural to me, lasted for several years and many of the pictures in the National Gallery in London gave me much pleasure; that of Sebastian del Piombo exciting in me a sense of sublimity."[27]

The heroic grandeur of Sebastiano's *Raising of Lazarus* was not wasted on Darwin after Whitley's coaching: the giant altarpiece, which was designed to match Raphael's *Transfiguration* and in which Michaelangelo had an influential hand, was Sebastiano's greatest work, casting Christ in the role of healer, the divine physician, to raise Lazarus from the dead. The outstretched arm calling up life, the vivid colour, and Lazarus's animal energy as he pushes away from his tomb suggest that Darwin's feelings were not cramped by scientific aridity; on the contrary, he leaned towards grandiose emotional experiences that swept him away on a tide of powerful sentiment. Furthermore, the religious theme did not impede his enjoyment. Sebastiano's text from St. John's Gospel went straight to the heart of Christianity, encompassing creation, resurrection, faith, and disbelief: "I am the resurrection, and the life." For the impressionable young Darwin, the sense of intense wonder was as readily inspired in an artistic and theological context as in exploring nature.

His most interesting acquaintance in several ways was Whitley's cousin John Maurice Herbert. Herbert displayed exaggerated respect for Darwin's scientific prowess and quickly took on the role of an admiring acolyte. Even in those early days he was dazzled by his friend's apparent gifts, and he later looked back at their time at Cambridge with satisfaction that he was among the first to recognise in Darwin something out of the ordinary.[28] Darwin liked him and was amused by the adulation. Yet once or twice he gave way to a shabby negligence, seen most obviously in his occasionally forgetting Herbert's first name. Herbert's lameness was something else Darwin forgot when it was convenient.

Herbert was very musical, and the two often went to King's College chapel to hear the anthem sung in weekday services. Encouraged by him, Darwin occasionally hired the choristers to perform in his rooms. On one of those afternoons at King's he turned to Herbert at the end of an anthem, saying with a deep sigh, "How's your backbone?" Darwin, said Herbert, would sometimes shiver with pleasure.[29]

It did not take long for Herbert to discover that for all his friend's delight in singing, he was a musical fraud, and he pushed Darwin into admitting, "I am so utterly destitute of an ear, that I cannot perceive a discord, or keep time and hum a tune correctly." Herbert enjoyed himself after that by asking Darwin to identify common tunes played more quickly or slowly than usual or on an unaccustomed instrument. "*God Save the King* when thus played was a sore puzzle," Darwin confessed. "There was another man with almost as bad an ear as I had, and strange to say he played a little on the flute. Once I had the triumph of beating him in one of our musical examinations."[30]

The contradictions continued. The same man with whom John Cameron spent pleasant evenings reading Shakespeare could not resist a sporting bet with Turner or Simpson. His Sunday church services were invariably followed by energetic beetle-hunts, his mathematics coaching by a long ride and hearty supper. "Good-eating and good-talking make a most harmonious whole (I hope you are disgusted)," he joked with Caroline. "I will excuse anybody till they have been to a Cam. dinner, & if they are there, and if they cry out 'what a disgusting thing a good dinner is' I must give them up."

One outcome of these diverse activities was the creation of the "Glutton" or "Gourmet" club, in which a group of students, comprising Darwin, Frederick Watkins, Whitley, Heaviside, Cameron, and Herbert, arranged to take supper together on the days when they did not dine in hall. The scheme was distinguished from a proliferation of similar supper clubs by the aim of eating "birds & beasts which were before unknown to human palate." The name "Glutton" was chosen "to show their contempt for another set of men who called themselves by a long Greek title meaning 'fond of dainties.' "

The club's menus, remarked Watkins, were frequently bizarre, for at different stages they made "devouring raids" on many kinds of animals, including a hawk and a bittern. "But the appetite for strange flesh did not last very long," he stated. The end came after tackling an old brown owl which was, in Watkins's word, "indescribable."[31]

VI

Herbert was willingly drawn into Darwin's entomological hobbies and helped serve "the science," as Darwin loved to call it. His tendency to do whatever Darwin wanted soon emerged. During a visit to Barmouth in the summer of 1828, in the course of which a party of Cambridge students were meant to repair their mathematics, despite his lameness Herbert tagged along behind Darwin—even on a ten-mile walk across the hills.

On these occasions Darwin entomologised most industriously, picking up creatures as he walked along, and bagging everything which seemed worthy of being pursued, or of further examination. And very soon he armed me with a bottle of alcohol, in which I had to drop any beetle which struck me as not of a common kind. I performed this duty with some diligence in my constitutional walks; but alas! my powers of discrimination seldom enabled me to secure a prize—the usual result, on his examining the contents of my bottle, being an exclamation, "Well old Cherbury" (the nickname he gave me, and by which he usually addressed me), "none of these will do."[32]

With such an eager friend, Darwin found it difficult not to take advantage. A few weeks after returning to Shrewsbury from this reading party, he fulfilled a promise to write to Herbert—who was still grappling with algebra and sailing round Barmouth bay—only to ask if he would catch him additional insects. "You cannot imagine how much you will oblige me by procuring some more specimens of insects which I dare say I can describe," he wrote, and confidently annexed a list of requests that involved Herbert's retracing their steps to the top of a nearby mountain followed by taking the ferry to a marshy headland where he would find under the stones "a very small pinkish insect, with black spots... also small yellowish transparent beetle, with 2 or 4 blackish marks on back.... These last 2 insects are *excessively rare:* & you really will extremely oblige me by taking all this trouble pretty soon."[33] Nowhere did Darwin acknowledge Herbert's deformed foot, which once required Darwin and Butler to carry him six miles home.

Perhaps it was only Herbert's ignorance of natural history that made Darwin's activities appear in such a glamorous light. Yet he saw enough in his friend's expertise to give Darwin the greatest scientific surprise of his life that far. In May 1831 an unsigned letter and parcel arrived at Christ's:

> If Mr Darwin will accept the accompanying Coddington's Microscope, it will give peculiar gratification to one who has long doubted whether Mr Darwin's talents or his sincerity be the more worthy of admiration, and who hopes that the instrument may in some measure facilitate those researches which he has hitherto so fondly and so successfully prosecuted.[34]

Herbert's gift was not anonymous for long, but the sense of amazement and intense pleasure that Darwin felt lasted for many, many years. "Do you remember giving me anonymously a microscope?" he wrote in 1872 to Herbert, by then a grey-haired judge. "I can hardly call to mind any event in my life which surprised & gratified me more."[35] The feeling was almost too great to convey adequately to Fox. "Some goodnatured Cambridge man has made me a most magnificent anonymous present of a Microscope: did you ever hear of such a delightful piece of luck? one would like to know who it was, just to feel obliged to him."[36]

This was Darwin's first proper scientific instrument, way beyond the bits of string and sealing wax called into use in the Shrewsbury Lab. Previously, under Robert Grant's tutelage in Edinburgh, he had worked with a simple dissecting microscope of the Ellis or Cuff type, undoubtedly borrowed from Grant. More complicated compound microscopes were rarely favoured for dissection at that time because of the distortions brought about by looking through two lenses: even the great microscopist Robert Brown made his observations on plant fertilisation and the vibrations of molecular bodies inside cells with a powerful single lens.[37] These technical problems were not resolved until J. J. Lister's work on achromatic lenses in the 1830s, which transformed the applications of compound instruments.[38]

Herbert's "Coddington" microscope nevertheless looked like a lorgnette for the opera: a folding hand-held device incorporating one of the most advanced optical systems possible to buy on a gentleman's university allowance. Its magnifying power was strong enough to make visible the internal details of cell structure.

Herbert had perhaps heard Henry Coddington, a mathematics tutor at Trinity, speak of his suggested improvements to microscope lenses in a paper delivered at the Cambridge Philosophical Society the previous March, or he may have taken the advice of the botany professor, John Stevens Henslow, who was secretary of the society and well prepared to note any advances in microscopy techniques.[39] In either event, Coddington's recommendation was taken up by George and John Cary, London instrument makers, who produced the new lenses to Coddington's specifications. As Coddington pointed out, "Mr Brown's active molecules may be pleasantly observed with this microscope with a power of about 360 . . . at an expense not more than five or six guineas."

The present was the most useful scientific gift Darwin could have hoped to handle. Every free moment was now filled with exploring the miniature delights of a natural history world formerly denied to him. His last two months at university were spent studiously gazing through the new instrument.

VII

The only object that could possibly have matched a microscope in Darwin's affections at that time was a gun; and a gun he already had. Shooting completely dominated those thoughts not given over to beetles. "I do not believe that anyone could have shown more zeal for the most holy cause than I did for shooting birds."

He had first learned to handle a gun at the end of his schooldays, but it did not become a passion until the summer of 1826, in the long vacation between medical sessions at Edinburgh University. Bessy Galton, a cousin from Fox's side of the family and for some months the unknowing focus of Fox's romantic daydreams, remembered the metamorphosis. "When about 15, he was staying with us and went out with my Father to practise shooting. On his return we asked if he had been successful. 'O,' said my Father, 'the birds sat upon the tree and laughed at him.' Some time after my Father and brothers went to Shrewsbury. My Father had hardly sat down, when Charles begged him to come out on the lawn, where he threw up a glove and hit it shooting, without missing, two or three times."[40]

What Bessy omitted to say was that her father, Samuel Tertius Galton, and his father before him, owned the leading firm of gunsmiths in Birmingham, a firm only recently closed down in order to establish a bank with the proceeds. To impress the Galtons was quite an undertaking. In this, as in everything, Darwin was determined to succeed.

"How I did enjoy shooting," he wrote in his *Autobiography*. "If there is bliss on earth, that is it." Every summer and autumn was dedicated to killing birds. "My zeal was so great," he sheepishly recalled, "that I used to place my shooting boots open by my bed-side when I went to bed, so as not to lose half-a-minute in putting them on in the morning." Dull nonshooting months were passed in studying handbooks about guns and in writing down useful information about the diameter of shot needed for different animals, the financial penalties for killing game out of season, and the fact that "no common person or gamekeeper can demand your certificate without producing his own."[41] Other books such as *Instructions for Young Sportsmen by an Old Sportsman* were thoroughly gleaned for their practical advice.

By 1828, his ambitions had well overrun his elderly equipment. He yearned for a more powerful double-barrelled gun with percussion caps—and cheekily petitioned his father and sisters in the formal style of a printed charitable bequest to which they were invited to add their subscriptions. Dire consequences were threatened if he continued using the old one, which was liable at any moment "to destroy the aforesaid Charles Darwin's legs arms body & brains."

He got his new gun: Dr. Darwin and the sisters each gave him five pounds. It was just as well they never heard how he used it at university. "When at Cambridge I used to practise throwing up my gun to my shoulder before a looking glass to see that I threw it up straight. Another and better plan was to get a friend to wave about a lighted candle, and then to fire at it with a cap on the nipple, and if the aim was accurate the little puff of air would blow out the candle. The explosion of the cap caused a sharp crack, and I was told that the Tutor of the College remarked, 'What an extraordinary thing it is, Mr Darwin seems to spend hours in cracking a horse-whip in his rooms, for I often hear the crack when I pass under his windows.' "[42]

The same eagerness flowed into compiling an elaborate game book—a record system subdivided into partridges, hares, and pheasants, in which Darwin kept a running total of everything he killed through the season. This sporting ledger was as emotionally important to him as shooting itself: the only time at Cambridge that he kept any kind of careful catalogue, barely listing his beetles or keeping a note of his financial outgoings for Dr. Darwin to look over in the holidays.[43] His accounts with Fox were in a mess for the same negligent reason. The game book, however, had the beginnings of an obsession about it. There was little point in shooting, he thought, if the tally was not taken.

One day when shooting at Woodhouse with Captain Owen, the eldest son, and Major Hill, his cousin, afterwards Lord Berwick, both of whom I liked very much, I thought myself shamefully used, for every time after I had fired and thought that I had killed a bird, one of the two acted as if loading his gun and cried out, "You must not count that bird, for I fired at the same time," and the gamekeeper perceiving the joke backed them up.

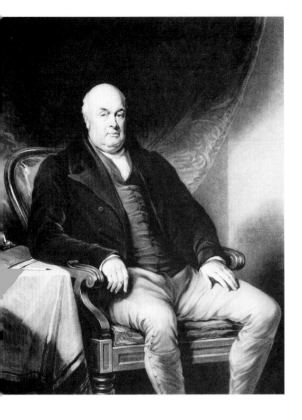

Charles's grandfather, Erasmus Darwin, a doctor in Lichfield and Derby, was famous for his evolutionary poetry.
(Wellcome Institute Library, London)

Charles's father, Dr. Robert Waring Darwin, the largest man Charles ever knew. His financial activities made the family rich.
(Wellcome Institite Library, London)

The Mount, Shrewsbury, with the River Severn running along the edge of the grounds.
(*Transactions of the Shropshire Archaeological and Natural History Society* 1884)

The Wedgwood family by George Stubbs, showing Darwin's mother,
Susanna, on horseback in the centre and his Uncle Jos next right.
Darwin's maternal grandfather, the potter Josiah Wedgwood, and
Mrs. Sarah Wedgwood are seated under the tree.

Charles and his younger sister, Catherine, drawn in 181

(H. Litchfield, *Emma Darwin* 1904)

Portraits of Darwin's mother, Susanna Darwin
(left), née Wedgwood, and his older sister
Caroline. Caroline looked after Charles after
their mother died.

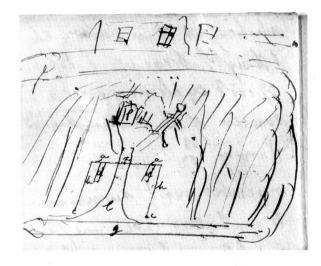

A piece of a tile found in Wenlock Abr C Darwin January 23 1819

The earliest scrap of Darwin's handwriting still extant. At age eight and nine, he was keen on collecting almost anything.

(Courtesy of Mrs. Ursula Mommens)

One of Darwin's childhood drawings showing him in a tree house, with ropes and pulleys for sending up messages.

(Courtesy of Mrs. Ursula Mommens)

Shrewsbury from the Welsh Bridge. The castle and Shrewsbury School can be seen.

(Castle Gates Library, Shrewsbury)

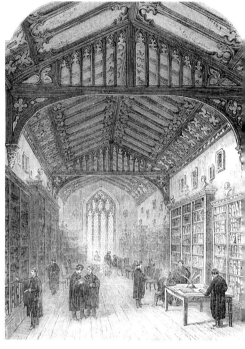

The schoolroom (above) and the library of
Shrewsbury School. Darwin did not do well at
the school, and his father took him away early.
(*Illustrated London News*)

Edinburgh University, where Charles and his
brother, Erasmus, studied medicine.
(J. Storer, *Views in Edinburgh* 1820. Wellcome
Institute Library, London)

Darwin was disgusted by anatomy lessons with Alexander Monro (left). Robert Jameson (right) was "incredibly dull."

Bodies for anatomy classes were supplied by resurrection men. This caricature was produced in 1829 when Robert Knox, owner of a private anatomy school in Ediburgh, was implicated in the Burke and Hare scandal.

Jameson's natural history museum was the pride of Edinburgh University. A puma (bottom left) was reputed to roam there at night.

Robert Grant told Darwin about
Lamarck's theories of transmutation.

(Wellcome Institute Library, London)

William Darwin Fox, Darwin's cousin
and best friend.

(Courtesy of Gerard J. Crombie)

Christ's College, Cambridge. Darwin went there intending to
become a clergyman.

(J. Le Keux, *Memorials of Cambridge* 1837. Wellcome Institute Library, London)

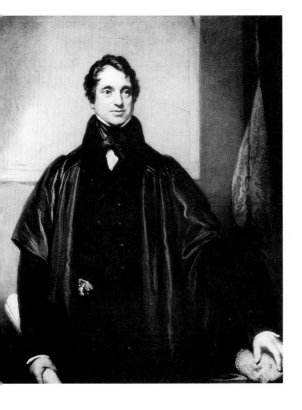

John Stevens Henslow, Cambridge
professor of botany, and Darwin's friend
and mentor.

(Lithograph by T. H. Maguire, 1849)

Adam Sedgwick, the professor of geology,
took Darwin on a field trip in Wales. It was
during this trip that the invitation to travel
on the *Beagle* arrived at Shrewsbury.

(Wellcome Institute Library, London)

The interior of Darwin's college rooms,
photographed in 1909. William Paley once
lived in the same set.

(*Christ's College Magazine* 1909)

Darwin spent most of his time collecting beetles and shooting. These sketches were made by Albert Way, an undergraduate who went out beetling with him.

(Darwin collection, courtesy of the Syndics of Cambridge University Library)

The geological map used by Darwin on the Welsh expedition, showing St. Asaph and Great Orme's Head.

(G. B. Greenough, 1820. Courtesy of the Syndics of Cambridge University Library)

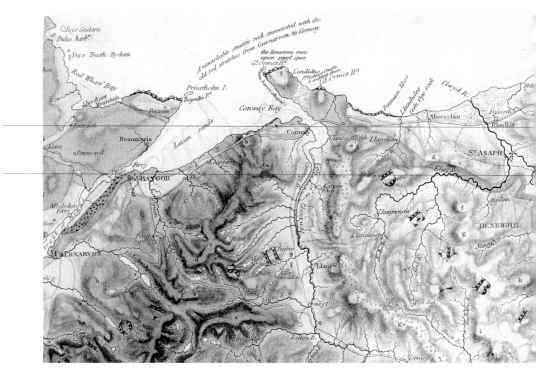

After some hours they told me the joke, but it was no joke to me for I had shot a large number of birds, but did not know how many, and could not add them to my list, which I used to do by making a knot in a piece of string tied to a button-hole. This my wicked friends had perceived.[44]

It was not hard for Darwin to find kindred sporting spirits among his Cambridge friends, his relatives, and the neighbouring Shropshire gentry. In his social circle, country estates were frequently given over to intensive game-rearing and residential shooting parties were an integral part of gentlemanly life. According to William Cobbett, after one of his rural rides in 1825, talk among the landed gentry was almost entirely about shooting unless it happened to be about hunting: between them, he said, the two topics accounted for more than 90 percent of the words exchanged in the English provinces.

Such an unabashed desire to shoot was a welcome trait in the eyes of his uncle Josiah Wedgwood. Uncle Jos had used most of his inheritance to get away from the business side of the family china company, buying a large estate which he carefully managed for sporting purposes; and like many members of the second and third generations of wealthy manufacturing families, he gradually disassociated himself from his mercantile, nonconformist roots to take on the trappings and most of the social opinions of the upper classes. But his four sons generally preferred the indoor life. Invitations for Darwin to join him at Maer Hall during the partridge or pheasant seasons, or to squeeze in a few days' rough shooting over the heath, were willingly offered and just as willingly accepted.

On these occasions uncle and nephew lived only for the game and each other's company, building up a mutual regard between generations. "I was ... attached to and greatly revered my Uncle Jos: he was silent and reserved so as to be a rather awful man; but he sometimes talked openly with me. He was the very type of an upright man with the clearest judgment. I do not believe that any power on earth could have made him swerve an inch from what he considered the right course. I used to apply to him in my mind, the well-known ode of Horace, now forgotten by me, in which the words nec vultus tyranni, etc. ["Nothing could shake him from his purpose"], come in."[45]

Year in and year out, Uncle Jos made sure that Darwin was at Maer at the appropriate time. "Bliss Castle," his appreciative nephew called it.

VIII

Closer to home, there was Woodhouse, the estate of William Mostyn Owen. The Owen family possessed several attractions for Darwin, not least two pretty daughters, friends of his sisters', and one of them soon the romantic idol of his heart. Mr. Owen, as Darwin always respectfully referred to him, was as partial to shooting as Uncle Jos. He too enjoyed Darwin's ardour, often asking him over for a day or two in university vacations, especially when the Owen boys, themselves capable sportsmen, were away from home and the girls off with their mother or their much-ridiculed chaperone "Ma'am Burton" in search of urban society.

Mr. Owen was the most convivial man in the world, thought Darwin. Pacing over the stubble in search of hares, guns bent over their elbows, they talked in comfortable fashion about all kinds of rural topics, mostly politics and reform, since Owen was a stout country liberal at heart, but also ranging over Darwin's university amusements, useful improvements in gun design, horses and dogs, and a fair amount about the comings and goings of the two families' many mutual friends. Like Sterne's Uncle Toby, Mr. Owen told Darwin of his military campaigns in Flanders, several times over according to the family jokes, and gave him well-meaning advice about leading a steady life. The infamous Jack Mytton, a wild and dissipated sportsman, was Mr. Owen's cousin: a man "worn out by debauchery of every kind ... & rarely sober enough to say that he was in his right senses"; a solemn warning for Darwin, he said, of the "miserable remains of an ill spent Life."

Darwin would have been forgiven for thinking that life at Woodhouse was similarly hedonistic. The household was large and rowdy, full of the "racket" missed by visitors to The Mount. After one exhausting week at Woodhouse, where "we never talked a word of common sense all day," and twenty-nine guests sat down to dinner, Catherine Darwin felt that "it is hardly possible for common mortals in my opinion to wind up their spirits to the Woodhouse pitch; more than half the gentlemen indeed were a little too stimulated." No wonder Darwin and his socially secluded sisters relished invitations to stay at "The Forest," as the Owen girls brightly called it.

Not far beneath the surface of both men's minds was the thought that they might at some stage become more closely related, a possibility quietly pleasing to each of them. Mr. Owen recognised in Darwin's behaviour at Woodhouse all the symptoms of unspoken infatuation with his second daughter, Fanny—the prettier and more engaging of the two oldest girls, in the Darwin family's opinion. Mr. Owen was well prepared to play the indulgent parent: in his view, Darwin was far the most suitable suitor who had appeared. With four girls among his nine children, marriage was beginning to prey on his mind, and he could think of no one he would rather welcome into the family than this likable shooting companion. He also owed Dr. Darwin a great deal of money.

Darwin's heart had not perhaps run as far into the future as the thoughts of a father might do. But he was intoxicated by the tumult of feelings that sweep in with first love.

At first he found it difficult to choose. The two Owen sisters were the "idols of my adoration," he told Fox, and Woodhouse "is to me a paradise, about which, like any good Musselman I am always thinking; the black-eyed Houris however, do not merely exist in Mahomet's noddle, but are real substantial flesh & blood."

Soon there could be no doubt about the extent of his enchantment with Fanny's girlishly exuberant froth.[47] She was one year older than Darwin and, as he put it in another letter to Fox, "the prettiest, plumpest charming Personage that Shropshire possesses."[48] She was quite the match for any of Fox's Bessy Galtons, or even of the "incomparable" Charlotte Wedgwood, whose serious mind and long blond hair struck Fox forcibly during a brief visit to Shrewsbury and Staffordshire. Blessed with the sort of strong personality that young men find exhilarating but must have made her parents despair, Fanny was an impetuous, forthright woman used to having her own way within the limits of polite society. She flirted incessantly, in letters if not in actual practice. She revelled in gossip, archly finding "black mysteries" at every turn. She fretted against Mr. Owen's ineffective family discipline, and her mind ran almost entirely on horses, marriages, and dances. Her chief charms were an irrepressible good nature and high spirits. She was always the belle wherever she went, said Catherine enviously: "I do not wonder, for I never saw such a charming girl altogether as she is."[49]

Both the Owen girls were old enough to attend the social season, the period of the year when the British squirearchy resolutely took their daughters out into the world of fashion to find spouses. Fanny and Sarah accompanied their mother and elderly female chaperone on a social round that included Bath in 1827, Exeter in 1828, and Buxton in 1829, as well as making frequent visits to the country houses of friends and relatives in the Shropshire area. During this time the two sisters corresponded freely with Darwin. But Sarah ("a most prodigious friend of Susan's") was rapidly approaching an understanding with someone in the neighbourhood called Edward Williams. She married her "hero Ted" in 1830 after a lengthy engagement, the delay owing to an understandable family caution after she was jilted by a former suitor named Robert Biddulph.

Nor was Fanny unambiguously free to reciprocate Darwin's affection. She was engaged, or virtually engaged, to her cousin John Hill in 1826 or 1827, with the arrangement seemingly broken off by Hill, since Susan Darwin at one point referred to a proposal followed by Hill's "cold-hearted behaviour." It is not clear exactly what Fanny may have felt for Darwin, especially as she went on to marry someone else in 1831, soon after Darwin joined the

Beagle. There certainly seems a case for thinking that the relationship was much warmer on his side than on hers. She may well have found him dull, gauche, or lacking in the romantic allure that country girls of the period fantasised about. Darwin, for example, made no bones about how much he hated dancing.

Yet it was quite a correspondence. Letters from Fanny regaled Darwin with her horse-riding and hunting exploits, and were full of anecdotes about the perils of social engagements during her first months in society, when every dance or game of cards was blighted by a clumsy partner. The "shootables" (as she and Sarah carelessly referred to eligible young men) were alternately derided and pitied by these sparky young ladies: "they are most of them remarkably frightful," complained Sarah, "& the *scarlet shootables* [soldiers] & scorpions [younger brothers] are also *remarkably useless* as very few of them go out & dance." Fanny tormented him with the thought of "plenty of *red coats* & *Moustachio's* which *you say must* be pleasant. I like Blue & silver better." Apart from what can only be a reference to one of Darwin's coats, the prospect of home was thoroughly boring:

> I never was so horror struck as to receive your leetle note the other day. My conscience upbraided me so much as really to prevent my eating any *breakfast* altho' a plate of *hot toast* was smoking before me. I reproach myself bitterly with ingratitude for your entertaining budgets, in having delayed so long sending you an effusion. pray forgive the *penitent* House-maid. She is truly sorry for her crime—I hope you had good sport at the Forest I hear you are become an *undeniable* shot.... We are very dissipated here, at a Ball or Party almost every night, which as you may suppose I find not *bad sport* in *its way,* but all must come to an end and I *fear* we shall be dragg'd away to the shades of the Forest and leave Brighton in the higths of its gaiety—no time is yet fix'd however. Poor Caddy tells me she is very triste at home having to *fight it out* with all the Boys who are very impudent—Pray tell me some Shrewsbury scandal.... I hope you will not be gone from Home when I return. I shall expect *cart loads* of *black mysteries* after so long an absence so pray collect all you can—How is Maam Burton, & who could have invented the report that her dear little Eliza was going to be *dragg'd* to the *Halter* by a Splendid *Shootable*—Is Mr Upper still as brilliant & *elegant* as when I left him—I must conclude this horride scrawl but I have a horride pen and am in a *horride* hurry—but will send you another effusion soon. I am too stupid & sleepy tonight to do any thing but sleep in the arm chair—I am sure you will say what a *stupid prosy* creature the Housemaid is become, but remember it is 1828 *& she is a year older*—Adieu my dr Postillion, believe me ever yrs sinly Fanny O.[50]

Nicknames abounded. Renegade John Hill was transmuted into Mr. Upper, male visitors to Woodhouse were "broadcloths," female visitors "muslin," the bedroom corridor was called "paradise row," invitations were "insinivations," and the black riding horse variously the Andalusian or Spaniard. Fanny's name for Darwin's entomological friend Frederick Hope—Forlorn Hope—spoke volumes. Everything was magnified and exaggerated to droll proportions. One small joke about bad handwriting—or perhaps being caught one day busy using the coal scuttle—escalated joyfully into an imaginary history of her being as unlettered as a housemaid, with Darwin taking the part of a postillion. His blue coat with the silver buttons looked like the livery coachmen usually wore.

Fanny rolled joyously in these quirky appellations. She used them all the time in letters. What would university men say, she shrieked, "of a *Housemaid* writing to Mr Charles Darwin—Ma'm Burton *would die of it* I *think.*" She never could, "and never *shall* write like a *lady.*" Apologies for her "horride pen" mounted up; "I have *such a Pen* and besides never could write like any thing but what *I am,* a *Housemaid.*"

Not surprisingly, the roles of housemaid and postillion invite speculation, particularly when these servants were the ones customarily involved in the first or illicit sexual liaisons of gentlefolk. There is no evidence, however, that Darwin and Fanny's relationship was anything other than wholly innocent and considerable alternative evidence suggesting her correspondence was merely flirtatious wordplay. The freedom with which Fanny lit on these and other expressions gives the lie to any hidden lover's code that could be sought out by Darwin, and her frequent orders to "Burn this as soon as read—or tremble at my fury and revenge" were attached as indiscriminately to unsensational family news as to frisky references to housemaids.[51] Her sister Sarah issued the same demands that Darwin should throw her "scrawl" straight into the fire.

Still, artless though they were, these letters from Fanny reflected physical and emotional awakenings noticeably different in scale from Sarah's seamless talk of weddings and flirtations. "Why did you not come home this Xmas?" Fanny protested one winter. "I fully expected to have seen you—but I suppose some *dear little Beetles,* in Cambridge or London kept you away—I know when a *Beetle is in the case* every other *paltry* object *gives way*—if I could have sent to tell you I had found a *Scrofulum morturorum* perhaps you might have been induced to come down!" Hardly knowing she was jealous, she laboriously searched out and (incorrectly) copied the name of the most dramatic beetle she could find in the Woodhouse library.

Pique easily extended to include her elder sister. "I was very much surprised to hear from Sarah that you have decided to become a *DD* instead of an *MD.* You never let *me* into the secret," she complained in 1828. "I *cannot & will not* play *second* fiddle."

And once or twice when Darwin showed mild interest in other young women in their Shrewsbury circle she quickly took her opportunity to criticise the new "lovee." Clare Leighton ("your Favorite," according to Sarah in 1828) ruined a perfectly good party, she told Darwin triumphantly from Woodhouse, when "with her *usual goodnature* she sang to the *admiring* and *awestruck multitude* almost all night."

Fanny was moreover determined to shine in Darwin's sporting eyes. Women at that time rarely went shooting, for reasons of social convention as well as because of the powerful recoil from firing. When she boldly picked up a gun one day, she captivated her speechless suitor. Even in old age Darwin could still see the toss of her head, the impetuous courage: "how charming she looked when she insisted on firing off one of their guns, and though the kick made her shoulder black and blue gave no sign." It was then, suspected Darwin's daughter Henrietta, who saw the expression on his face while he told the story, that he first knew he was in love.[52]

In similar possessive vein, Fanny was not averse to reminding Darwin of the time, probably in June 1827, that they lay in the sunshine at Woodhouse idly grazing in the strawberry beds.[53] The moment captured the essence of their relationship, combining uninhibited greed with the particular freedom of spirit characteristic of the Owen family. Lying on the ground eating strawberries was a whole world away from the demure strolls in Regency shrubberies popularised by the novelists Fanny read, although emotions surely ran high in both.

There was a lack of formality at Woodhouse—a lack of discipline or propriety, others might have called it—that made such behaviour outwardly acceptable despite the elaborate social obligations of the time. The gentle air of favoritism bestowed on Darwin by Mr. Owen allowed what might be called courting privileges. The strawberry beds were not a secret or even private rendezvous, since Caroline Owen, the next-youngest sister, and Susan Darwin independently recalled watching the pair gorging on berries, and in later days Fanny spoke of it to Susan with pleasure, no trace of innuendo in her words. Susan was similarly familiar with the rise and fall of Fanny's "*housemaid* spirits." These friends and sisters were not shocked.

But for Darwin the thought of Fanny making "a *beast of myself* in the *strawberry beds*" was full of unimaginable prospects. Simple enthusiasm for living surged through his unsophisticated soul. "The three years which I spent at Cambridge were the most joyful in my happy life."[54]

chapter

5

THE PROFESSORS

OMETHING of the same vitality caught John Stevens Hens-low's eye.

Henslow was professor of botany at Cambridge, a position he had held since 1825, and had been professor of mineral-ogy for three years before that, but was not nearly as old or conservative as these titles might suggest. One of the adventurous young reformers of the university, he was twenty-six when his election to the chair of mineralogy created uproar among the college masters and first highlighted the need for internal change. Uproar also surrounded his move to botany and forced the university to take an early step on the path to wider reform.[1] By 1828 or so, Henslow was influential in academic circles and politically active: altogether a lively figure in Cambridge affairs, some thirteen years older than Darwin. There was no sign of the venerable grey hair familiar from the well-known portrait made twenty years later, in 1849.[2]

Meeting this professor was rightly considered by Darwin as the one circumstance "which influenced my career more than any other." No other man had so immediate an impact on his developing personality, nor did any other figure have so important a role in directing the course of his early scientific experiences. Darwin became Henslow's devoted disciple and friend. Henslow, in turn, opened the door to Darwin's future.

And the meeting, if not the consequences, was more or less inevitable. Before arriving at Cambridge, Darwin heard much from Erasmus about the man "who knew every branch of science." Erasmus had attended Henslow's "very entertaining" mineralogy lectures and shared with him an interest in James Cumming's chemistry course: Henslow was Cumming's assistant in chemical demonstrations before moving to the chair of mineralogy. Erasmus apparently praised Henslow so fervently that Darwin was well "prepared to reverence him."

Less often remarked is Henslow's liking for gentle, cultivated Erasmus, one of the earliest Cambridge "Apostles," full of intellectual promise, "a perfect gentleman," as Jane Carlyle later thought approvingly.[3] This was a good recommendation for looking kindly on another member of the family fond of natural history: Henslow would have been just as inclined to be agreeable to Darwin as Darwin was to him. Erasmus's role as an intermediary was given material substance when he came to Cambridge late in 1828 to receive his medical degree and stayed for two weeks with Darwin in Christ's. Eager to introduce Darwin to some of the friends and places he had enjoyed as an undergraduate, he surely paid a call on Henslow with his younger brother in tow.

Nevertheless, Darwin did not attend Henslow's or any other professors' lectures during his first year at Cambridge. Although Fox regularly went to the botany course through 1828 and encouraged Darwin to do the same, Darwin did not pay his guinea for registration until the following year, after his cousin had left. His name appeared in Henslow's list for the courses held from 1829 to 1831 inclusive.[4] These botany lectures were the only formal instruction in natural science undertaken during his entire Cambridge career.

II

Henslow's background was tailor-made for an academic life. After a conventional upbringing in the English upper-middle classes, Henslow, the son of a solicitor and grandson of Sir John Henslow, surveyor and master of the royal dockyards at Chatham, showed such aptitude for natural history that he was allowed, as a schoolboy, to help Dr. Leach of the British Museum catalogue the national collection of crustaceans.[5] Moving on to Cambridge, he graduated from St. John's College in 1818 with a high place in the mathematical honours list. He then became a fellow at the same college, followed by ordination into the Church of England in 1824. During this period, he emerged as one of the few men in Cambridge seriously interested in natural history, notorious for the huge, untidy collection of specimens spilling out from his college rooms at St. John's.

After that came the professorships. Though Henslow did not deliberately court trouble over these appointments, it accompanied him without fail. Professors at that time were essentially superfluous figures, because all the teaching for examinations was carried out by college tutors and there was no official requirement for undergraduates to attend any of the professorial courses offered around the university; indeed, students usually avoided them unless they harboured an extracurricular interest in the topics taught or thought them useful for their honours exams. Much the same air of cosy inactivity embraced the occupants of the professorial chairs themselves: William Lax, an appropriately named professor of astronomy and geometry from 1795 to 1837, never, as far as is known, delivered a single lecture; and Francis Barnes, who held the Knightsbridge chair of moral philosophy from 1813 to 1838, was equally remiss. Even the most conscientious teachers, like Adam Sedgwick, the Woodwardian professor of geology, who mustered a regular audience of fifty, were required to give only four lectures a year. Sedgwick greatly exceeded the demands of Dr. Woodward's bequest by giving an annual course of thirty-six geological lectures from 1819 until 1871, when failing health finally compelled him to appoint a deputy.[6]

Professorships were not even permanent offices until the administrative crisis surrounding Henslow's first appointment to the mineralogy chair. Before then, positions were filled on an ad hoc basis by internal nominees who might—or might not—have an acquaintance with the subject. Genial, poetic Sedgwick had little practical grasp of his new field when first awarded Woodward's geological chair in 1818.[7] He learned as he taught. Henslow, on the other hand, knew a great deal about mineralogy and its interrelations with geology and chemistry after being taught by Sedgwick and the chemistry professor James Cumming and was keen, like his friend Sedgwick, to revive the prestige of a university teaching appointment.

Still, Edward Daniel Clarke's mineralogical chair had been a personal endowment, and there was general reluctance to go to the expense and inconvenience of establishing another professorship which might not attract paying customers. For more than six months, Henslow was kept on tenterhooks as senior members of the university vacillated about the chair's future existence, until at last a regulation was passed to permit an appointment. By then, however, the college masters were too agitated to think straight. They put up no less than three straw candidates to run against Henslow—who was already nominated and supported by Sedgwick and a coterie of other prominent reformers. After a bitter campaign, Henslow was ultimately elected on a technicality.

Neither he nor his friends prospered by the experience, for the affair continued to seethe through a university court case in 1823 and in fierce public letters from Sedgwick to Cambridge newspapers until further inflamed in 1825 by the death of Thomas Martyn, the elderly professor of botany. Rashly, Henslow again stepped forward, admitting as he did so that though "he knew very little about it, he probably knew as much of the subject as any other resident in Cambridge."[8] This time, the University Senate was quicker to avoid dispute and found to its relief that the botanical chair comprised two positions, one of which was independent of the university and financed by the crown; Henslow was appointed to this one (retaining his mineralogy chair for two more years), and the university position was allowed to lapse. Exhausted by it all, the heads of houses reluctantly agreed in 1827 to take independent legal advice about future procedure.

To the new professor's credit, he emerged as one of the most respected figures in his field: a zealous, socially concerned, hard-working Anglican don. In his hands, botany became a crusade for transforming the role of professors and a way of reinstating the neglected merits of a scientific training. Personally, too, the episode cemented his growing friendship with Sedgwick. Their mutual religious commitments, their faith in academic reform, and the underlying rapport of the English intelligentsia drew them together as closely as any overlapping professorial subjects did, and the pair became central figures in the small group of liberal Anglicans who steered university life for half a century—the "gentlemen of science" then emerging as leaders of the Broad Church movement, advocates for the Romantic poets and German philosophy, and mentors to the generation of thinkers who ultimately dominated Victorian culture, a generation including Tennyson, Thackeray, Fitzgerald, and Darwin, as well as important mathematical physicists like James Clerk Maxwell. Not least in Henslow and Sedgwick's joint undertakings was the foundation of the Cambridge Philosophical Society in 1819, brought into existence for promoting natural philosophy in the university and progressing to become the single most important influence in the training of most of Britain's future physicists.[9] Henslow took his religious duties equally seriously, both in college and in the parishes of later years.

Moreover, Henslow was a political animal as well, willing to bring all his energies to bear on redressing imbalances inside and outside the academic system, readily using influence to promote his own causes and prepared to stand by his principles. Originally a Tory, he changed sides with Palmerston in 1828, worked on the Whigs' behalf for general electoral reform, and somewhat naïvely tackled the problem of bribery for votes in an encounter with the Tory public that ended in the slogan "Henslow—Common Informer" being daubed on Corpus Christi College walls. On another occasion he tried to save two body-snatchers from being dismembered by a Cambridge mob. No one, he argued, however horrible, deserved to be kicked to death in the street. Darwin took a small role in these proceedings by running for help at Henslow's request to a nearby college.

To many students and university colleagues during the second quarter of the century he consequently represented the very type of an upright, scholarly man: an exemplar in his commitment to education; a successful pioneer in teaching the whole range of botanical sciences and revitalising the functions of the professoriate; and a contemporary, if local, hero for his staunch

Christian and liberalising political principles. "The striking feature in Professor Henslow," said his friend and brother-in-law Leonard Jenyns, "was that every advantage he possessed he gave to the public."

Darwin felt much the same. "He never took an ill-natured view of anyone's character," he wrote fondly in 1861, "though very far from blind to the foibles of others."

> It always struck me that his mind could not ever be touched by any paltry feeling of vanity, envy or jealousy. With all this equability of temper and remarkable benevolence there was no insipidity of character. A man must have been blind not to have perceived that beneath this placid exterior there was a vigorous and determined will. When principle came into play, no power on earth would have turned him an hair's breadth.[10]

Even so, Henslow did not envisage spending the whole of his life as a heroic bachelor don as the college rules stipulated, and soon after acquiring the mineralogy chair, he resigned his fellowship to marry Harriet Jenyns, the sister of his friend Leonard, bought a house in Cambridge, and became curate of Little St. Mary's, a high-ranking though low-paid university preferment for favoured sons. A few years later he transferred to a benefice in Berkshire (popularly supposed to be a reward for political services from Lord Brougham), but continued to live and teach in Cambridge. After that again, he took up a crown living in Hitcham, Suffolk, coming back to Cambridge for a few months each year for the Easter term's teaching commitments.

When Darwin first came into contact with him, Henslow was thus at the height of his university career, with the number of people attending his lectures running to sixty or seventy each session, his lists packed with the names of influential senior members of the university, including other professors such as William Whewell, Sedgwick, and George Peacock, and many of the tutors and recently qualified reverends and fellows of various colleges. For a time it was one of the most stimulating courses available, drawing, with Sedgwick's geology course, a wide and appreciative audience. Some men, notably Charles Cardale Babington (called "Beetles" Babington because of his enthusiasm for entomology), attended faithfully year after year. When he reappeared for a fourth time in 1831, Babington's persistence was acknowledged with a free course. At first Henslow's informal aide-de-camp, he soon became the professor's official assistant and then successor.[11]

As might be expected, Henslow held strongly revisionist views about the content of a botanical education. He delivered lectures daily through the spring (Easter) term and followed a cycle of his own devising that covered the theory of classification, "vegetable anatomy," and plant physiology, ranging from the function of sap to the processes of germination. He insisted on some basic knowledge of the chemical properties of plant tissues and, since the course additionally served the medical community, careful study of materia medica and other "useful" plants.

Like the Edinburgh comparative anatomists, he was also well read in contemporary continental science, paying great attention to the Swiss botanist Augustin de Candolle's attempt to apply Geoffroy's and Cuvier's principles to plant morphology and embryology. Candolle's *Théorie élémentaire de la botanique* (2d ed., 1819) and *Organographie* (1827) were recommended texts in his printed syllabus for 1828.[12] To judge from a wide-ranging review he wrote in 1833 on another authoritative work by Candolle on the same subjects, Henslow was capable of supplying Candolle's deficiencies and of giving his own interpretation of many preexisting puzzles about the ways in which plants worked.[13]

To these lecture topics he added brief discussions on hybrids, monstrosities, adaptations to different environments, and the various means of fertilisation. Traditional plant taxonomy did not delay him much. It was only necessary, he considered, insofar as it helped in understanding larger philosophical issues like geographical distribution or the physiology and morphology of plants. His was, in essence, a very active, vital botany based on appreciating plants as living organisms.[14]

Lectures were therefore supplemented with practical instruction in recognising and dissecting plants, an innovation in Cambridge circles, and with a number of field excursions, sometimes on foot or in stagecoaches, and on other occasions on a barge hired for the day to drift downriver to Ely, ending with a meal in an inn and hearty singing. "Most jovial we then were," related Darwin, always fond of the convivial side of natural history. More than just botany was learned on these trips. Henslow used to pause every now and then "and lecture on some plant or other object; and something he could tell us on every insect, shell, or fossil collected, for he had attended to every branch of natural history."[15]

The social high point of the course was an excursion in the late spring to Gamlingay heath, some twenty miles to the west of Cambridge, full of scented sweeps of lily-of-the-valley and animal rarities like the natterjack toad. For this, coaches were hired to transport the members of the botany class who did not ride, plus the several ladies—mostly wives and sisters— who also attended. Breakfast and dinner rooms were booked at country inns, and a band was hired to help the evening festivities along. According to the expenses listed in Henslow's papers, about sixteen or twenty people usually attended at a cost of twelve shillings each, to include gratuities to the ostler, page-boys, and band. These trips were begun in 1827 and continued without a break until 1852. They were a beacon in the memories of many botanical students, including Darwin.

A more sophisticated development was Henslow's introduction of intellectual soirées. His "Friday evenings" began in February 1828 and continued
during full term until 1837, attracting famous men and students alike. When
he eventually called a halt, obliged by the move to Hitcham Rectory to
change the habits of a decade, there was such a blank in the university's
scientific calendar that a formal structure sprang up to replace it: the Cambridge Ray Club was established, according to Babington, with the intention
of serving as a similar kind of discussion group.[16]

Henslow's soirées were informal affairs of no more than ten or fifteen
people eased by the homely surroundings of a family man and by Mrs.
Henslow serving tea, as was usual in the polite evening parties of early-
nineteenth-century England.[17] Sometimes curious natural history specimens
were displayed: Henslow possessed an eclectic array of skulls, arrow-heads,
exotic skins, wasps' nests, and rare fungi that periodically appeared on
the tables, and guests were encouraged to bring their own finds along if
sufficiently interesting. Other times there were visitors to fête or local politics
to debate. Serious talk about science was the norm, each guest mingling
and conversing freely, the professors happy to meet a few kindred spirits
among the general run of claret-swilling undergraduates, the favoured students eager to be given an opportunity, as Darwin later put it, of becoming
"slightly acquainted with several of the learned men of Cambridge—
which much quickened the little zeal which dinner parties & hunting
had not destroyed." Leonard Jenyns claimed Henslow's parties had an
"immense importance in diffusing taste for science, no less than for incit-
ing young men to intellectual pursuits." Moreover, said Miles Berkeley,
another botanical friend of Henslow's, they were "extremely agreeable and
interesting."[18]

Darwin got an invitation to attend these soirées through his cousin Fox,
although he did not go regularly until late in his university days, by which
time he was well acquainted with Henslow from lectures and excursions.

In fact, the last two terms at Cambridge—the ones after passing his degree
examination in January 1831—were the months he really came to know
Henslow closely. During those final weeks he took long walks with him and
joined the family dinner table, becoming such an obvious favourite that he
was called by some of the other dons "the man who walks with Henslow."
Henslow seems to have enjoyed his company as much as Darwin appreciated Henslow's. The two matured into close friends in the intimate fashion
special to a pupil and his teacher.

III

By then, Darwin was ready to seek out a mentor. All his early life had been spent in the accommodating shadow of some older, more knowledgeable figure, graduating from the all-encompassing spell of his father, by no means the ogre of post-Freudian considerations, to that of his brother Erasmus in the homemade chemistry lab and anatomical theatre, and thence to Robert Grant in Edinburgh and Fox at Christ's. Other older people hovered protectively in the background: jolly Mr. Owen of Woodhouse, Caroline and Susan Darwin, and his silent but understanding Uncle Jos. Each of these nurtured different aspects of his character and continued to do so, for Darwin was not a man who could ever stand completely alone. His early life was characterised by a constant need for this kind of quasi-parental support, and he often felt most comfortable in the company of older people who drew him out and encouraged him to shine. They, in return, may have warmed to his unstinting youthful appreciation. Darwin's greatest gift at this time was not so much the ability to understand nature's secrets, if he had it to any degree as an undergraduate, but a capacity to identify the people capable of giving and inspiring in him the loyal affection he desired. On such affections his ultimate success as a naturalist depended.

He soon became deeply attached to Henslow. The admiration was total, leading him from a dedicated attendance at successive botany courses, rivalled only by Babington in his persistence over the years, to a request for private tutorials in mathematics before his finals; and from a grateful acknowledgement of Henslow's attributes as a teacher to enthusiastic declarations to Fox that "he is quite the most perfect man I ever met with." He had never come across anyone he would so much like to emulate in later life. "The more I see of him the more I like him."

Crucial to the unprecedented intensity of this attachment was a passing occasion which illuminated all of Henslow's perceived qualities and brought out a stark contrast between him and Darwin's only other comparable scientific acquaintance, Robert Grant. The two men, Darwin decided, could hardly be more different. The incident, moreover, crystallised feelings which for the most part had run unacknowledged until then. It was a watershed in his emotional life generally unremarked by historians.

Henslow, like Grant, was fully aware of the advantages of using microscopes to investigate the cellular structure of organisms and was himself just as much inclined towards a functional interpretation of tissues as Grant, although he, unlike the Scotsman, believed in the ultimate authority of God's laws. For Henslow, it was perfectly possible to incorporate the radical-materialist "philosophical anatomy" of French anatomists into a conventional natural theological context.

He consequently required his students to pay attention to the minute anatomy of plants in botany lessons and to examine the sexual organs and process of fertilisation—only recently and partially disclosed by Giovanni Amici's and Robert Brown's researches—under a hand lens or microscope. It is more than likely that Henslow also told his students about the fierce debate initiated by Brown over the nature of the granular material visible in pollen grains in relation to reproduction and the definition of life.[19] Henslow's observations seemingly confirmed Adolphe Brongniart's assertion that some of this granular material was analogous to the spermatozoa in animals and carried the necessary information for inheritance. Brown strongly disagreed.

Functional investigations like these were bound to intrigue Darwin, particularly in the way they dovetailed with his previous interest in the reproduction of simple marine animals. He believed himself fairly adept in microscopical work; and his discoveries about the fertilisation of *Flustra* (itself very like a seaweed, although actually an animal) and the leech *Pontobdella* can only have encouraged him to think that plants offered some of the same novelties bearing on important questions about life and reproduction.

Certainly as soon as he possessed a microscope, through his friend Herbert's generosity, he turned to his former Edinburgh notebook in which the small successes from the Firth of Forth were recorded and began adding new observations on the pollen and cellular structure of geraniums and orchids—clearly working out on his own some of the points raised under Henslow's botanical instruction.[20] He may even have begun to ponder the discrepancy between Grant's assertion that plants and animals were joined by an intermediate group called zoophytes, identified by the release of motile "eggs" during sexual reproduction, and Henslow's conviction—firmly delivered in the opening lecture of successive botany courses—that the chemical properties of plants and animals showed how they were categorically separate beings.[21] Only one of them could be right. Which one, Darwin wondered.

And when Henslow set the class to observe plant fertilisation, Darwin diligently applied himself:

> Whilst examining some pollen-grains on a damp surface I saw the tubes exserted, and instantly rushed off to communicate my surprising discovery to him. Now I do not suppose any other Professor of Botany could have helped laughing at my coming in such a hurry to make such a communication. But he agreed how interesting the phenomenon was, and explained its meaning, but made me clearly understand how well it was known; so I left him not in the least mortified, but well pleased at having discovered for myself so remarkable a fact, but determined not to be in such a hurry again to communicate my discoveries.[22]

Inadvertently, he found himself in the middle of a replay of seeing *Flustra* larvae move across a watch-glass. This time, however, the outcome was completely reversed. There was no trace of the sudden professional jealousy that so shocked him when he rushed with similar excitement to Grant: no hint of the cold withdrawal indicating that a pupil's work was in reality owned by the teacher, no string of sarcastic remarks covering a beginner with confusion. Darwin never forgot the generosity Henslow showed at that moment, all the more vivid for his being saved from certain embarrassment. Henslow's benevolence was unbounded, he said later, a whole world apart from Grant's possessive appropriation of nature's curiosities. In circumstances almost exactly paralleling his former dance with discovery, Henslow protected where Grant attacked. "He had a remarkable power of making the young feel completely at ease with him. . . . Nothing could be more simple or cordial and unpretending than the encouragement he afforded. . . . however absurd a blunder one might make, he pointed out clearly and kindly that one left him in no way disheartened, but only determined to be more accurate next time. In short, no man could be better formed to win the entire confidence of the young, and to encourage them in their pursuits."[23]

Henslow was everything Darwin hoped a scientific mentor could be, the antithesis of the once-admired friend who provided an unwelcome introduction to the "jealousy of scientific men."

IV

Henslow's evening parties provided Darwin with plenty of other opportunities to discover more about the ethos of Cambridge men. The professors he met there and the way they talked and walked with him meant a good deal in personal terms and helped direct his aspirations towards the standards they publicly adopted for themselves. Henslow, he came to realise, was only one of several notable men reshaping the university.

In general, these academic reformers were members of St. John's and Trinity, the largest, richest colleges in Cambridge and the two least dominated by the aristocracy. "Johnians" active in Darwin's day included a number of influential figures, among them Henslow; John Haviland, professor of medicine between 1817 and 1851; and John Herschel, the mathematician and astronomer who although living elsewhere played a central role in developing a new curriculum for the university and in enhancing government cooperation with practising natural scientists and philosophers.

Trinity produced a more pugnacious field: George Pryme, the subversive classics scholar whose first action after graduation was to offer unofficial lectures in political economy and who triumphed in 1828 when the University Senate was forced to establish a chair for him in that subject; James Henry Monk, Regius Professor of Greek, who insisted classics should be made an honours examination subject in 1822; Adam Sedgwick, the first of the Cambridge men known as the "Northern Lights," a bluff Yorkshireman and liberal Anglican priest whose only preferment was the canonry at Norwich, and whose rapprochement between geology and religion helped create much of the early-nineteenth-century view of the natural world; William Clarke, professor of anatomy; Joseph Romilly, the university registrar, fond of smoking cigars and discussing politics "till one in the morning," young enough to be bewitched by Sedgwick's "fascinating Miss Clarke," to bet on the outcome of the chancellor's medals, and get "awfully pigeoned"; Richard Sheepshanks, George Peacock, and George Biddle Airy (the "professor of stars," in Romilly's admiring words), mathematicians and astronomers of great significance in British science in midcentury; Julius Hare and Connop Thirlwall, sprightly German scholars whom Leonard Jenyns once saw leaping over a ditch at the bottom of his garden; Thomas Spring Rice, a Trinity graduate of 1811, secretary of the treasury in Grey's Whig ministry and chancellor of the exchequer in Melbourne's; and William Whewell, the most brilliant of the "Northern Lights," at that time the professor of mineralogy in succession to Henslow and destined to be the central figure in the academic rerouting of nineteenth-century Cambridge.

The son of a master carpenter from Lancashire, Whewell was a large, physically powerful man, so burly he was once or twice mistaken for a prize-fighter, with a brusque, energetic manner to match. In politics, unlike the others, he was ostentatiously Tory, but this did not impede the thrust of his reforming zeal. Anecdotes abounded about his omnivorous interests, especially when marshalled into two enormous historical and philosophical works surveying the development of European science from antiquity to what he provocatively called the age of reform. His *History of the Inductive Sciences* (1837) was held in such high contemporary regard that he and it reached some kind of personal apogee in being acted out—and quickly identified—in a Christmas game of charades at Lord Northampton's house in 1838.[24] "Science was his forte and omniscience his foible," quipped Sydney Smith, accurately enough. Whewell never developed any narrow scholarly speciality, taking pains to remain as familiar with moral philosophy, German literature, international law, and "Niebuhrising" techniques of historical research as with natural science, astronomy, advanced mathematics from France, and the theory of the tides: an accumulation of interests that induced Peel to make him master of Trinity in 1841, whence he emerged as one of the natural leaders of the university community and supplied an opening for carrying through some of the more dramatic changes in the world of higher learning.

Over a twenty-year period, and in the company of Charles Babbage of "calculating engines" fame, and William Hopkins, the mathematical and physical geologist, both from Peterhouse, and James Hildyard of Christ's, Whewell and his friends briskly pushed Cambridge into the modern world.

Being allowed to associate with figures from this circle at Henslow's parties was uplifting as well as flattering to the serious side of Darwin's personality. "When only a few were present I have listened to the great men of the day conversing on all sorts of subjects, with the most varied and brilliant powers." Thinking of himself, he added, "This was no small advantage to some of the younger men as it stimulated their mental activity and ambition."[25] Philosophical luminaries like Whewell let him listen to their high-flown monologues as they walked back to their colleges from Henslow's house on Parker's Piece. "Next to Sir J. Mackintosh [a friend of Josiah Wedgwood's] he was the best converser on grave subjects to whom I ever listened." Whewell praised Henslow's version of botanical science, seeing at first hand the way he encouraged students in framing generalisations and drawing up new "laws" from observations. Botany like this, he emphasised in an important essay, was ideal for including in a liberal education.[26]

In similar vein, the talk at Henslow's parties encouraged Darwin to read John Herschel's book on the principles of natural science, *A Preliminary Discourse on the Study of Natural Philosophy,* first published in 1831 and naturally the subject of detailed discussion among Herschel's Cambridge colleagues, who, to a man, held strong views about the way science should be conducted. Darwin read it with "care and profound interest," learning to respect, as the author and his scientific friends did, the idea that nature was governed by laws—laws that were often difficult to discern or to capture in mathematical terms, but to understand which was the highest aim of natural philosophy. The orderly sequences of scientific thought set out by Herschel, the delicate interplay between observations and theory, and the successive mental steps—Herschel's process of "induction"—by which researchers sought to attain a single unifying explanation for the phenomena, one that they could regard as a fundamental "truth" of nature, manifested everything that was believed about the scientific process in the early nineteenth century; and although Whewell later came to provide a different model, altogether more idealistic and Germanic in style, which also enjoyed great fame during succeeding years, it was to Herschel's philosophy of science that most of the significant work of the period paid homage. Darwin thought the book was inspiring. "If you have not read Herschel in Lardners Cyclo—read it directly," he cried to Fox.

From them too, Darwin imbibed something of contemporary natural theology, a system of ideas with which he developed a close but ambivalent relationship. Originally devised by theologians of the late sixteenth century as a way of proving the existence of God through the apparent "design" evident in nature, this long-lasting argument was brought to a crescendo by William Paley in his works on moral philosophy (1785) and the natural world (1802). Paley believed that the world was so full of design there must be a designer in the same way as a watch found on a path indicated the existence of a watchmaker (rather than a negligent owner). All of the "perfect adaptations" or "contrivances" Paley saw in nature were correspondingly understood as features specially created by God to fit each and every being for its role in an overall plan; a plan, he went on to say, characterised by stability, by inbuilt hierarchies, and by orderly arrangements reflecting the social and moral structure of Britain.

Though not without its theological and political critics in Britain, this form of thinking rose dramatically in the Napoleonic era to become the dominant doctrine of those favouring social stability and maintenance of the political status quo: the ideology, in short, of the British governing classes, and of Cambridge dons in particular. Darwin found Paley's logic irresistible while revising for his examinations despite flirting with alternatives during his time at Edinburgh.

By 1830 or so, however, Cambridge men were increasingly inclined to criticise Paley for his emphasis on Jeremy Bentham's utilitarian principles, suggesting his books should be removed from the students' compulsory reading lists,[27] and a more sophisticated version of liberal Anglican natural theology was gradually brought into being. Science, claimed men like Herschel, Sedgwick, and Henslow, with its privileged access to the laws of nature, spoke to the rest of the world about God's ultimate truths. To study nature was to study the work of the Lord. There was therefore little conflict, they asserted, between natural philosophy, as it was then understood, and religious doctrine, if the latter was broadly interpreted; and it was perfectly possible for an ordained cleric of the Church of England—Whewell, say, or Sheepshanks, or Airy—to follow the most abstruse inquiries into the ways of the physical universe with a clear theological conscience. "No opinion can be heretical," declared Sedgwick to the Geological Society of London in 1831, "but that which is not true. . . . Conflicting falsehoods we can comprehend; but truths can never war against each other. I affirm, therefore, that we have nothing to fear from the results of our inquiries, provided they be followed in the laborious but secure road of honest induction. In this way we may rest assured that we shall never arrive at conclusions opposed to any truth, either physical or moral, from whatsoever source that truth may be derived."[28]

For Sedgwick, as for the others, there was no apparent disharmony between science and religion. Science, in a sense, *was* religion.

This famous—and famously slippery—British compromise enabled many early-nineteenth-century scholars to pursue their researches without eliminating either biblical or scientific authority. Moreover, in their confident eloquence, words like Sedgwick's gave a magnificence and purpose to science that resonated powerfully with youthful enthusiasms such as Darwin's. Unlike the sceptical philosophers he had encountered in Edinburgh, these men made the study of nature a divine quest: a romantic exploration of forces, powers, laws, and truths that appealed to him at the deepest imaginative level. Darwin did not go so far as Sedgwick or Henslow in correlating abstract laws or the apparent plan of nature directly with theology: in this, insofar as is known, he took a position similar to that of his father and grandfather Erasmus Darwin, thinking of the creator more as an external force who brought the world into existence and permitted it to run according to inbuilt natural laws. But, as he insisted right through to old age, he was strictly orthodox in his beliefs as an undergraduate and during the *Beagle* voyage, and was at that time entirely serious in intending to take Holy Orders. It came as "a sort of a shock," recorded his son George, "when during the *Beagle* voyage he first met someone who openly avowed disbelief in the flood."

In the Broad Church surroundings of liberal-traditional Cambridge, at a time when religious authorities stood on the cusp of moving from literalism to a metaphorical reading of the Bible, it was easy for Darwin to pour all his emotional yearnings and admiration for nature into this form of natural theology, one which encouraged the pursuit of knowledge without too many obligations to think about God or the original creation.

Naturally he experienced doubts about the depth of his personal faith. Darwin talked to John Maurice Herbert in 1829 about the vows required of a priest, worrying that he could not honestly say yes when asked by the ordaining bishop if he was, in the words of the service, "inwardly moved by the Holy Spirit."[29] He expressed similar doubts to Henslow, who told him in reply that he personally "should be grieved if a single word of the Thirty-nine Articles were altered." Darwin was probably consulting Henslow in the knowledge he would soon need to declare his own belief in the same articles before receiving his degree. But these self-examinations were unremarkable in a conscientious prospective clergyman—essential even. They did not signify incipient scepticism or some kind of alert probing into the inner recesses of Victorian belief. Darwin was impressed by the sincerity and the philosophical rigour that Cambridge professors brought to bear in understanding nature and wished to associate himself with them. The natural theology they promoted, for all the faults he subsequently saw in it, became the baseline from which the majority of his future researches emanated.

V

Contact with Henslow therefore brought Darwin into the world of intellectual Cambridge and exposed him to some of the deeper philosophical issues that were to preoccupy him for many decades. That Darwin was ready to be directed in such a way is evident from the admiration he displayed for Henslow. In lectures, at parties, during field trips, or on their private walks, nothing was too much to do for his mentor.

His admiration took on extreme proportions at times. One or two of the other students attending botany courses at some point or another remembered Darwin not just as the professor's favourite but also as someone teetering on the edge of exhibitionism. Only he, it was thought, would go to such inordinate lengths to locate and produce with triumph the full text of a Latin quotation that Henslow mentioned in class as "one of exquisite beauty." Henslow did not recall all the words, yet Darwin had got it traced before the next lecture, ready to read out loud and to reflect, pedantically, that "there were botanists before Linnaeus."

Darwin found it just as difficult to know when to stop during field excursions. "We had a very amusing expedition to Gamlingay heath in search of Natterjacks," wrote John Medows Rodwell. "Darwin was very successful in detecting the haunts of these pretty reptiles and catching them. He brought several to Prof. Henslow who said laughingly—Well Darwin, are you going to make a Natterjack pie?"[30]

Rodwell could not hide a satisfied smirk at another exaggerated display:

> In order to clear the ditches we were provided with several jumping poles with which we had to swing ourselves across. One object of our search was to find the Utricularia, a specimen of which caught his keen eye, and in order to secure he attempted to jump the ditch on the opposite side of which it grew. Not however having secured sufficient impetus for the leap, the pole stuck fast in the middle in a vertical position of course with Darwin at the top. Nothing daunted however he coolly slid down, secured the prize, and brought it, all mud besmirched as he was to the amused Professor.[31]

Rodwell also noted how Darwin was singled out as Henslow's assistant in class, helping the professor arrange specimens and getting the room ready for lectures. "It was obvious that Darwin was Henslow's favourite pupil and that he saw in him prognostications of future distinction and eminence as a naturalist. . . . Professor Henslow used to say 'What a fellow that Darwin is for asking questions!'"

This blatant favoritism was noticed by William Allport Leighton as well. He reported in jaundiced terms on the mutual admiration between professor and pupil. "Darwin hung upon the Professor's lips and words and no doubt he influenced him much as to his voyages and explorations in the *Beagle*. I remember that the Professor in the concluding remarks at the close of his course of lectures said he hoped his teaching had influenced many to perseverance—certainly he knew it had influenced *one*."[32] No one doubted that Henslow meant Darwin.

Nor did Beetles Babington take kindly to Darwin's helping Henslow arrange the lecture hall—a job he considered his own kingdom and his route to an eventual professorship. According to Babington, it was he, not Darwin, who "assisted Prof. Henslow in putting things in order before and after the lectures."[33] Neither man bothered to hide his dislike of the other: theirs was a long-standing difference originally rooted in mutual competition for water beetles, and matters came to a head when Darwin discovered that one particular natural history supplier—a Mr. Harbour—was giving Babington first choice of the insects coming in. Harbour was "a d—d rascal," Darwin exploded, and he vowed never to buy from the man again. Each wanting to have the pick of the beetles, the two treated each other warily ever afterwards. How Henslow coped with two possessive students rushing to set out the plants before class was left unrecorded.

It seems that the Darwin who inspired indulgent affection in some acquaintances was perfectly capable of generating ill feeling in others. His manner outside his favoured circle appears to have been aloof, snobbish in a certain withdrawn way, persistent, often liable to be misunderstood. Leighton saw how the Cambridge undergraduate resembled the inward-looking schoolboy he once knew: Darwin was "reserved & proud—but it was patent to all that his mental and intellectual powers were greatly developed and he seemed to be pondering in his mind some great results."

Henslow also noticed an air of supercilious disdain. It worried him sufficiently to warn Darwin.

> If I may say so, one of your foibles is to take offence at rudeness of manners & of any thing bordering upon ungentlemanlike behavior, & I have observed such conduct often wound your feelings far more deeply than you ought to allow it—I am no advocate for rudeness God forbid, & still less for any thing dishonorable, but we must make abundant allowances for mal-education, early contamination, & vulgar feelings, if we really intend to pass smoothly through life.

Darwin had failings like anyone else. Where he was best served by his friends was in the way they were prepared to see these as positive traits. Already, he was able to create a private ambience in which he felt safely protected from the outside world.

VI

For his own part, Henslow was amused by Darwin's attentions, seeing in his student's lavish enthusiasms an extension of his own passion for nature. Darwin at Cambridge was very like the man Henslow had been some ten or fifteen years before. He reminded Henslow of the days in 1814 when he spent his time rushing out from his own undergraduate rooms in St. John's in search of specimens: an uncomplicated period when the most pressing object in life was to collect and understand the myriad ways of natural beings.

Darwin mirrored the younger Henslow in other ways as well. He, like Henslow, intended reading for the church; and perhaps would follow Henslow's footsteps by joining the university teaching community in due course.

Most of all, Darwin yearned to travel. Late in his time at Cambridge he read Alexander von Humboldt's exciting account of his expedition with Aimé Bonpland through the Brazilian rain forest and beyond. Humboldt's *Personal Narrative* of this journey, made in 1799–1804, was immensely evocative, not merely in his fine descriptions of the jungle and the views from the Andes but also for the grand theories of nature he proposed, each one documented with cultural and historical cross-references and a full armory of measurements that inspired readers to ponder some of the most important philosophical, artistic, and scientific questions of the age. Together with John Herschel's work, this book influenced the young Darwin more than any other. The two authors stirred up in him a "burning zeal to add even the most humble contribution to the noble structure of natural science."

What is less generally known is that Henslow too longed to be an explorer. Reading François Levaillant's *Travels from the Cape of Good Hope into the Interior Parts of Africa* (1790) at the age of fourteen or fifteen, he had been swept away by the idea of following the Frenchman's track. He periodically indulged in tropical daydreams—daydreams that reflected his encroaching age and family commitments as much as any strictly scientific ambition. Levaillant's extraordinary journey through South Africa began after a shipwreck which left him with nothing but his gun, ten ducats, and the clothes he was wearing. It was the first work fully to bring the wonders of Africa to drab Europeans. "Long after he had given in to the wishes of his relations," wrote Jenyns about Henslow, "he still continued to think much upon the subject, read with the greatest interest many other African travels that were published from time to time, and the volumes procured to gratify this taste continued to occupy a place on the shelves of his library to the day of his death."[34]

The botanist's quiet demeanour masked a fiery heart, as Darwin and close friends recognised. It was here, in his longing to escape from Cambridge responsibilities, to revel in the heat, the difference, the freedom, that the underlying steel of Henslow's personality could be glimpsed. All other forms of temptation—academic jealousy, professional ambition, sins of the flesh and of the spirit—were resistible in their fashion. Quelling the travelling urge was the hardest thing he ever did.

How Henslow must have struggled when Darwin impulsively began to talk about getting up a natural history expedition to Tenerife, the largest of the Canary Islands and in Humboldt's words a scientific paradise: particularly when Darwin insisted on reading out what he called the most glorious passages from the book during botany field trips.[35]

Completely gripped by the idea of recreating Humboldt's experiences, Darwin spent his last months at Cambridge fantasising about his projected excursion. The trip was not envisaged as a formal natural history affair, since few scientific expeditions were anything other than informal at that time, apart from official projects arranged by the British Admiralty or other government departments. Darwin had rather more of a collecting holiday in mind, on which a few university friends would pay for a commercial passage and then explore the islands at their own cost for a month or two: a natural history equivalent of a tour through the fine arts and antiquities of continental Europe.

Such private forays were commonplace in his period, and many of the wilder areas of Europe as well as other parts of the world were habitually traversed in the eighteenth and early nineteenth centuries by groups of British naturalists sturdily combining their vacations with intellectual affairs. Even the furthest reaches of highland Britain were methodically combed, to the point that Beetles Babington was not unduly surprised one day in July 1832 when after struggling to the top of Mount Snowdon, the highest mountain in Wales, he found someone from his own Cambridge college already there collecting insects.[36]

Darwin hoped to go after graduation. He was sure his father would allow the additional expense, especially when Erasmus had spent a whole year drifting around Switzerland and Germany after finishing his London training, ostensibly furthering his medical education but actually considering the continental fashions and reading Goethe. Now back at The Mount, Erasmus had just announced his intention to live in Paris for the following winter. (He did not.) Darwin anticipated travelling in the same way his brother did before returning to Cambridge to study for Holy Orders.

"At present," he told Fox in April 1831, "I talk, think, & dream of a scheme I have almost hatched of going to the Canary Islands.—I have long had a wish of seeing Tropical scenery & vegetation: & according to Humboldt Teneriffe is a very pretty specimen."

Much the same song was sung to Caroline. "All the while I am writing now my head is running about the Tropics: in the morning I go and gaze at Palm trees in the hot-house and come home and read Humboldt: my enthusiasm is so great that I cannot hardly sit still on my chair. . . . I never will be easy till I see the peak of Teneriffe and the great Dragon tree; sandy, dazzling, plains, and gloomy silent forest are alternately uppermost in my mind.—I am working regularly at Spanish; Erasmus advised me decidedly to give up Italian."

"I have written myself into a Tropical glow," he sighed before concluding.

Several student friends were eager to join him. Henslow and Marmaduke Ramsay, a tutor at St. John's, fell under the same exotic magic. In truth, Ramsay was far more likely to go than Henslow, who had too many Cambridge and parish ties; yet both pupil and mentor solicitously nurtured the idea of exploring the wilds together. "I hope you continue to fan your Canary ardour," Darwin wrote to Henslow in July. "I read & reread Humboldt, do you do the same, & I am sure nothing will prevent us seeing the Great Dragon tree. . . . I am very anxious to hear how Mrs Henslow is.—I am afraid she will wish me at the bottom of the Bay of Biscay, for having been the first to think of the Canaries."[37]

Henslow's chance of going was, as they both conceded, "very remote." Another baby confirmed it. Passions ran high enough, though, to carry Darwin over his initial disappointment. He would go instead with Ramsay and two naturalist friends of Henslow's, William Kirby and Richard Dawes. His spirits were not more than temporarily dampened either by literally missing the boat: when he made inquiries about passenger ships in July he discovered they left for the Canaries exclusively in June. The scheme was not given up, however, merely postponed till the following year.

All through those last months at university, from April to July 1831, Darwin worked "like a tiger" to get to Tenerife, encouraged at every turn by a professor vicariously reliving his own dreams of freedom and exploration. Some of the basic requirements were bothersome: learning Spanish was "intensely stupid." It was far more atmospheric sitting at the foot of a palm tree in the university botanic garden dreaming of days to come or pressing his friends to listen to yet more extracts from the *Personal Narrative*.

"Many is the walk I had with him in the meadows between Cambridge & Grantchester, & many is the wretched animal that he unearthed from a rotten willow tree or some other obscure hiding place," remembered Frederick Watkins of Christ's. "I do not forget the long & very interesting conversations that we had about Brazilian scenery & tropical vegetation of all sorts. Nor do I forget the way and the vehemence with which he rubbed his chin when he got excited on such subjects & discoursed eloquently of lianas & orchids & other treasures of the almost impenetrable forest."[38]

In more realistic moments Darwin wondered why these loyal friends did not wish him already far away on his desert island.

VII

These halcyon days of scheming and dreaming were important for reintroducing Darwin to the study of geology. He could not hope to walk over the volcanic cones of the Canaries, said Henslow, without a proper knowledge of this most basic and majestic of sciences. Humboldt had written how he considered the Pico de Teide on Tenerife essential for understanding the origins of all volcanoes, likening it to other mountains whose names rang with images of the sublime: Cotopaxi, Etna, Vesuvius, Stromboli, and Chimborazo, then thought to be the highest mountain in the world. Humboldt's graphic account of climbing Chimborazo as far as he could go—the highest any European had then achieved—deeply impressed his readers. The island of Tenerife, he said, presented many crucial geological questions. Further than this, Humboldt asserted that the curious plant life, the blue haze of the evenings, the white pumice ash mimicking snow on the mountain top, all depended on the island's volcanic origin. Tenerife offered geologists a "vast field to inquiry."[39]

At first it was Henslow—a former professor of mineralogy, after all—who promised "to cram" Darwin in geology, and from Darwin's letters to Fox it does appear that Henslow taught Darwin how to use technical instruments like a clinometer and explained the trigonometry that lay behind calculations of the inclination of rock beds.

Some of the arid geological rules set out by Robert Jameson in Edinburgh probably sprang into life with this fresh new focus; and in a rush of enthusiasm, Darwin spent twenty-five shillings on a clinometer modified to Henslow's specifications in Cary's instrument shop—the same one in London where Herbert had purchased his Coddington microscope. "I put all the tables in my bedroom at every conceivable angle & direction," he boasted to Henslow from Shrewsbury. "I will venture to say I have measured them as accurately as any Geologist going could do."[40]

But it was Adam Sedgwick who really gave him a taste for geology and initiated him into the arcane rituals of practical fieldwork. Here again, Henslow stepped in to ask if Sedgwick would take Darwin with him for part of his customary field excursion in the summer vacation of 1831—at that point in Sedgwick's research entailing an expedition to north Wales. As a favour, Sedgwick agreed: no doubt he could make Darwin useful, and in any case it was only for a week or ten days; he always enjoyed company. Still, it was that trip in particular, thought Darwin later on, that "set me up wonderfully." Even the British penchant for understatement could not hide the marked impact that Sedgwick exerted on him.

Sedgwick was then in his prime as a geologist. A rugged, individualistic northerner, dedicated to the university's improvement and to the natural theological wonders of the world about him, he was altogether more prominent, more abrasive, more political, and more poetic than Henslow. An acquaintance of William Wordsworth, with whom he occasionally rambled through the Lake District, and one of the teachers of Alfred Tennyson during his time at Trinity College, Sedgwick brought to his studies many heightened features of Romanticism. Never so happy as when he was striding out across the hills with an agreeable companion, "pounding the porphyries," all the while theorising, talking, admiring nature's beauties, and declaiming on the meaning of the rocks, his geology was cast in the grandest of moulds. He aimed for the large view, the all-embracing hypothesis that would explain the earth's history, the scientific truths that would, he believed, reveal God's intention and allow mankind to come to know its maker. "I am thankful," he wrote in an autobiographical sketch composed in his eighties, "that I have spent so much of my life in direct communion with nature, which is the reflection of the power, wisdom, and goodness of God."[41]

The stones in his pockets, he was fond of protesting, kept him from soaring into heroics. Nonetheless, his most significant ability as a geologist lay in taking the imaginative leaps necessary to discern regional patterns in merely local details. This ability enabled him to determine some of the underlying structure of the Lake District, an area of immense geological complexity in Britain; and provided new ways to distinguish the slanting, secondary cleavage of rocks from the sedimentary layers in which they were originally laid down. Early in his career he also traced Old Red Sandstone in Scotland. Then—in the company of Roderick Impey Murchison, a recent friend and convert to geology from fox-hunting—he reassessed the older rocks of the Alps during a summer tour in 1829. Afterwards he began questioning the Wernerian, water-based geology publicised by Robert Jameson and adopted a predominantly igneous view of the origin of the oldest formations. "For a long while I was troubled with water on the brain," he admitted; "but light and heat have completely dissipated it."[42] In the same year, his position as a leading geologist was endorsed by his election— repeated again in 1830—as president of the Geological Society of London.

On the whole, Darwin's previous contact with him had been brief. It is doubtful, for instance, whether he attended any of Sedgwick's lectures, although one or two anecdotes subsequently told to Francis Darwin in the 1880s by university friends suggest some kind of formal connection. These accounts are probably based on a conflation of memories after a lapse of more than fifty years. There seems no reason to disagree with Darwin's statement: "I was so sickened with lectures at Edinburgh that I did not even attend Sedgwick's eloquent and interesting lectures. Had I done so I should probably have become a geologist earlier than I did."[43]

What is more likely is that Darwin learned from talking with Sedgwick at Henslow's Friday evenings, maybe calling on him at his rooms in Trinity, reading the books recommended on an informal basis by the two professors, discussing the lectures that other friends attended, and almost certainly joining Sedgwick's popular "equestrian" outings, most of which took place during April and which often included people not specifically taking the geology course. Sedgwick's lectures always finished before the end of March,[44] and it is known that Darwin became interested in the subject only in the spring of 1831: "In the spring Henslow persuaded me to think of Geology & introduced me to Sedgwick."[45]

This is not to deny the pleasure he derived from Sedgwick's teaching. James Heaviside of Sidney Sussex recalled how Darwin "ardently took up the subject." Though neither Heaviside nor any of his literary and artistic friends, who included Thackeray and profligate Henry Matthew, took any particular interest in geology, they could recognise gusto when they saw it. "I can remember," said Heaviside, "how genially he bore with the chaff of those, who like myself & Matthew knew nothing about the subject, as to Moses being a better authority on Mundane cosmogony than he is the Geologist."[46]

Rodwell also discussed Sedgwick's lectures with Darwin, who remarked to him: "It strikes *me* that all our knowledge about the structure of our Earth is very much like what an old hen would know of the hundred-acre field in a corner of which she is scratching." Again, Darwin exclaimed, "What a capital hand is Sedgwick for drawing large cheques upon the Bank of Time."[47]

Geological field days were bound to catch his attention. On these occasions Sedgwick conducted a group of "60 or 70 academic horsemen" through the countryside round Cambridge and lectured at prearranged intervals on the history of the earth. "These were grand days with us," Sedgwick reminisced. "We used to meet at Castle Hill or some commanding ground and after a short lecture on the geology as seen in the distance, mount our steeds. Many of the men were excellent riders, and go right across country to our next point perhaps St Ives or Ely . . . (there were one or two ugly tumbles in these excursions) . . . till the inner man wanted replenishing. They were merry dinners those."

The intention was not to flood the riders with detail but to tell a clear and logical story, moving steadily from present-day surroundings back into the distant past. "I cannot promise to teach you all geology," he used to say, "I can only fire your imaginations."[48]

Few occasions could have been more inviting to the hunting and shooting Darwin. A mixture of natural history, galloping about on horses, convivial company, and awe-inspiring thoughts about the world around him was exactly what he responded to the most. One or two of these geological outings would have been more than enough to encourage him to take up private study with all his customary enthusiasm.

Darwin's crucial moment of contact with Sedgwick, however, came with the end-of-term invitation generated by Henslow. Sedgwick was then dallying with the idea of collaborating with William Conybeare in expanding Conybeare's *Outlines of the Geology of England and Wales* (1822), and he and Murchison had arranged to study Wales together as a preliminary to that and other publications. In the event, their independent trips that summer ultimately led to their deciphering of the two great geological systems with which they became indelibly associated: soon christened the Silurian and Cambrian systems after the ancient British and Welsh tribes of the area, these formations became the respective life work of the pair and subsequently the focus of heated controversy and estrangement.[49] Irretrievably at odds over their individual intellectual property by 1836, Sedgwick and Murchison were never afterwards reconciled.

At the very least, Sedgwick hoped in north Wales to modify and fill in what he suspected were errors in the national geological map compiled by George Greenough in 1820. Though Greenough's work was acclaimed for the scope of the undertaking, which involved considerable cooperative effort among local specialists and initiating new techniques of colouring areas according to the diagnosis of the rock formations,[50] it was necessarily vague in some particulars. People out in the field were accumulating alterations and corrections even as the map was being compiled; and Sedgwick, as much as anyone, appreciated how far practical work had taken geology during the ten years it was available. Greenough himself was gathering material for a second edition, already asking Henslow for corrections for the chalk beds of East Anglia.[51] Though there is no record of Sedgwick's being similarly asked, it is likely that he was well aware of the map's limitations.

Sedgwick also looked to Wales as a place where the fossil record could be traced back to its uttermost limits. A major factor in that concern was the publication of the first volume of a geological work by Charles Lyell, a clever young barrister-turned-geologist in London, who argued that there had been no discernible sequence of progress in the fossil record or in the rocks themselves. Lyell proposed that James Hutton's system of uniformity should be applied rigorously throughout geology, asserting that previous geological processes acted with the same intensity as those in the present era and that the fossil record was but an incomplete chronicle of living worlds once containing representatives of all organic groups. Lyell hinted that life, just like the earth itself in his new scheme, had always existed in some form or another.[52]

Sedgwick, on the other hand, in concert with many other geologists and natural theologians who criticised Lyell's view, was convinced that the facts as he knew them revealed a series of self-contained stages through which the earth came to approach the present system of things: a sequence of now-extinct floras and faunas, each appropriate to the successive conditions of the earth, coming into existence, turn by turn, from the simplest, at the dawn of time, to the most complex, in the modern era. In the face of this evidence it seemed nonsensical for Lyell to assert that fish or mammals were alive at the time of the oldest known fossiliferous rock. Sedgwick took prolonged and detailed issue with these aspects of Lyell's thesis in his presidential address to the Geological Society delivered in February 1831. "If the principles I am combatting be true, the earth's surface ought to present an indefinite succession of similar phenomena. But as far as I have consulted the book of nature, I would . . . affirm that the earth's surface presents a definite succession of dissimilar phenomena." He concluded that "Mr Lyell has, unconsciously, been sometimes warped by his hypothesis." To find the earliest known fossiliferous rocks was to demonstrate, if he could, that life had some kind of simple, and created, beginnings.

VIII

The trip began for both of them at Shrewsbury, conveniently en route to the Welsh rocks. Sedgwick went to stay at The Mount for a few nights, and on 5 August 1831 they left together in his gig for Llangollen.

Sedgwick's visit to the family caused a definite stir: it was the first time that Darwin had brought an eminent person home for supper, and it lasted long enough for Dr. Darwin to come out with the diagnosis that Sedgwick was a confirmed hypochondriac. Susan, on the other hand, was bowled over. This gregarious bachelor don brought with him all the bustle and glamour of intellectual society, particularly attractive to Susan, who had little chance of meeting clever men.[53] Her manner must have been noticeable over the dinner table. Months later, her younger brother was still making high-spirited remarks about whether there was any announcement about a forth-coming Mrs. Sedgwick.

Privately, Darwin was hardly complacent either. He secretly practised his geology in the fields around home before Sedgwick got there, hoping to impress him before they took to the hills together, and was chastened to find it a great deal harder than he expected.[54] He bought a copy of Greenough's map in reduced format in a travelling case for his own use in the field.[55] And when Sedgwick arrived he tried to entertain him in an appropriately geological fashion by telling him of the gravel pits near Shrewsbury. But Darwin's story of the labourer who found a tropical shell in the gravel brought only a peal of laughter and the remark that this could not be true. If the shell was genuinely embedded there, said Sedgwick, it would overthrow everything that was known about the superficial deposits of the Midland counties. There was no evidence to suggest tropical species had lived on the site at the time the gravel was laid down. "It must have been thrown away by someone into the pit."

Recounting the story later, Darwin remembered being astonished that Sedgwick was not more delighted by his strange fact. "Nothing before had ever made me thoroughly realise, though I had read various scientific books, that science consists in grouping facts so that general laws or conclusions may be drawn from them." What Sedgwick went on to explain to him was that there must be a great deal of mutually supportive material for scientific theories of all denominations. Once such theories were established, it took more than an isolated shell to change them.

Darwin's consternation must have been obvious. Six months later, in a letter written when his son was sailing across the Atlantic on the *Beagle,* Dr. Darwin slyly reminded him with a smile that he doubted if there were any shells in the gravel pit that would interest him now.

And from the way Darwin continued to hold this salutory episode in mind, it evidently had a marked effect on his scientific practice. If nothing else, it warned him to hold his tongue: to keep his ideas quiet until sufficient evidence came in. During the expedition with Sedgwick he tried as hard as he could to do well, putting into practice the lesson so recently learned.

Sedgwick wanted to travel along the Vale of Clwyd, following the point of contact between the limestone cliffs and the underlying Old Red Sandstone that was shown on Greenough's map, up to Great Orme's Head on the north coast. Thereafter, he intended tracing the sandstone down to Bangor, perhaps taking a quick look at Anglesey on his way to confirm Henslow's survey of 1818, and maybe squeezing in a few days' entertainment in Dublin before returning to Cambridge in early September.

Darwin accompanied him for the first week or so of this itinerary, leaving Sedgwick somewhere around Capel Curig (near Bethesda) in order to trek, on his own, through the central massif of Wales to Barmouth, where Herbert and some other university friends were once again studying mathematics and enjoying themselves in the holidays.

In order to make him useful, Sedgwick taught Darwin as much and as wide a variety of topics as he could in the time available. On the way to St. Asaph, he showed him the caves of Cefn, where vertebrate fossils, including a rhinoceros tooth, had been found (Sedgwick unearthed one for himself from the floor of the cave) and explained the significance of the fossil corals seen in these particular limestone beds. He taught him how to recognise rock formations by the kind of vegetation and surface features they exhibited, gave him extensive practice in measuring the dip of the escarpment they were following, and demonstrated the way to mark up stratification and inclination on a map and how to make field drawings of sections. The trip ended with an individualised lecture on cleavage and stratification in the great slate quarry of Penrhyn.

As they walked and talked, Darwin learned a thing or two about Sedgwick as well. They started from their inn one morning, and had walked in silence for a mile or two when Sedgwick suddenly stopped. Darwin thought he had offended him in some way. But Sedgwick vowed that he would return, certain that "that damned scoundrel" (the waiter) had not passed on to the chambermaid the sixpence given to him for the purpose. Uncertainly, Darwin did his best to be reassuring: a volatile professor in the middle of nowhere was not an easy item to deal with. But he managed to persuade Sedgwick to give up the idea of returning, since there was "no reason for suspecting the waiter of perfidy." Scientific fieldwork plainly included more than just making measurements.[56]

All this practical advice was meant to make a geologist of Darwin, one suitable, as Sedgwick believed, to get the most out of an expedition to Tenerife; but it actually provided the initial expertise necessary to transform him into a powerful geological thinker during the *Beagle* voyage. "Tell Prof. Sedgwick," Darwin wrote to Henslow from Rio de Janeiro in May the following year, "he does not know how much I am indebted to him for the Welch expedition,—it has given me an interest in geology, which I would not give up for any consideration." More than a year after that he was still asking Henslow to "tell him I have never ceased being thankful for that short tour in Wales."[57]

Most of all, like the teacher he was, Sedgwick gave Darwin confidence. Coming into St. Asaph, he was puzzled by the absence of the usual clues relating to the presence of Old Red Sandstone: there was plenty of reddish soil, yet did this really indicate the rock beds he was after? He decided to send Darwin off on his own to make a short traverse in search of the Old Red that was shown on Greenough's map running along the southern edge of the escarpment. He would meet him at Colwyn, having travelled along the other edge of the limestone similarly searching.

Out on his own for the first time since leaving Shrewsbury, Darwin could not find any trace of the desired rock. He was more than a little anxious by the time he returned to Sedgwick, because it was easy to miss details in the field and hard to contradict an acknowledged authority like Greenough. He had scoured the countryside for elusive corroborative signs.

Yet Sedgwick was very pleased with him, congratulating him that evening in Colwyn and explaining how his researches would require the revision of a major portion of the national map. Sedgwick too had not seen "a particle" of Old Red. The band up to Orme's Head was "pure fiction," he told Murchison in September. To Darwin's delight, he further told him how the structure of the Vale of Clwyd could now be reinterpreted on the basis of their work not as the complex structure proposed by Greenough, but as a simple trough that had at some point been "stretched." Other material evidence such as the lack of limestone pebbles in the valley could now be put into proper perspective.

In truth, the work was not nearly as easy as either Sedgwick or Darwin liked to remember, because the baseline, as recorded by Sedgwick, was not readily defined: "It was a hard summer's work—I think I never got over so much geological ground in one year before."[58] Despite this, Darwin had been helpful and in retrospect trustworthy: few professors would have accepted a major negative claim like Darwin's without backtracking to check on the data. Rodwell, who later came to know Sedgwick well, recalled that "Sedgwick often spoke of him [Darwin] as then being a promising student of Geology."

This moment of personal success encouraged Darwin greatly: "it made me exceedingly proud." The experience turned his thoughts positively towards theoretical geology and showed him the way scientific propositions were created and revised.[59] He was pleased at having made a significant observation and intrigued by the almost magical metamorphosis of scientific theory his information had brought about: he saw Sedgwick, single-handedly and in the space of an evening's talk, reframe the geology of the Vale of Clwyd, saw the interplay between accredited theory, field data, and guesswork, and recognised that he could play a part in the process.

For him, the evening had long-lasting effects. His chagrin at Sedgwick's brusque response to the tropical shell in the gravel pit was transformed into a fleeting but thoroughly practical awareness of the philosophical structure of science. He went on his way to Barmouth with his wits sharpened and a good deal more intellectual purpose in his step than he had had rattling down the family drive six or seven days earlier.

Tenerife, however, was still uppermost in his thoughts. Back in the devoted company of Herbert at Barmouth, Darwin energetically discussed the number of days he could possibly wear a shirt without washing it.

THE CAMBRIDGE NETWORK

CRAMBLING over the rocks in Cwm Idwal, Darwin was untroubled by anxious thoughts about the future. His occupations for the next few years were pleasantly sorted out. He had come to an arrangement with his father that he would return to Cambridge in October to begin the specialised reading necessary for entering the church, an arrangement that seemed generally acceptable despite his occasional unfocussed religious scruples and the family tendency on the male side towards free thought. Back at university, he hoped to walk and talk again with Henslow and arrange the visit to the Canaries. After that he expected to settle down as a country parson like his cousin Fox or the entomological Leonard Jenyns, surrounded by books, animals, and children, perhaps acquiring a college living in due course.

Only Erasmus was sceptical. The whole idea was absurd, he kept saying, finding every conceivable opportunity to poke fun at his brother's naïve visions of parsonages and asking with heavy irony which theological tracts he recommended today. A D.B.—the university degree of Bachelor of Divinity—really stood for "dammed bitch," he jibed.

Beyond this, Darwin planned nothing except shooting and socialising during the long vacation and—if he could engineer it—some "lovering" with Fanny Owen when she reappeared from a visit to Exeter. October, though not unpromising, seemed a long way off. "At Capel Curig I left Sedgwick and went in a straight line by compass and map across the mountains to Barmouth, never following any track unless it coincided with my course. I thus came on some strange wild places and enjoyed much this manner of travelling. I visited Barmouth to see some Cambridge friends who were reading there, and thence returned to Shrewsbury and to Maer for shooting;

for at that time I should have thought myself mad to give up the first days of partridge-shooting for geology or any other science."[1]

Letters from Henslow were welcome events in the holidays, and on returning home on 29 August 1831 after two weeks of shooting with Uncle Jos at Maer, still full of the geological work with Sedgwick and longing to tease Susan ("anything in coat and trousers from eight years to eighty was fair game to Susan," he once unfairly said),[2] Darwin was pleased to find a note from Cambridge waiting for him. Among other things, he hoped for news about a Stilton cheese "fit for eating pretty soon."

But this letter was different. Written on 24 August, it was about a proposed "trip to Terra del Fuego & home by the East Indies." Henslow had been asked to recommend a suitable young man interested in science and natural history to accompany a surveying ship leaving England in the autumn, and he thought Darwin just the person they were looking for. The voyage, as Henslow understood it, was to last two years and, as he put it in his letter, "if you take plenty of Books with you, any thing you please may be done—You will have ample opportunities at command—In short I suppose there never was a finer chance for a man of zeal & spirit."[3]

The position was not strictly a professional one. Captain Robert FitzRoy, he said, "wants a man (I understand) more as a companion than a mere collector & would not take any one however good a Naturalist who was not recommended to him likewise as a *gentleman*." Henslow therefore approached Darwin

> not on the supposition of yr. being a finished Naturalist, but as amply qualified for collecting, observing, & noting any thing worthy to be noted in Natural History. . . . Don't put on any modest doubts or fears about your disqualifications for I assure you I think you are the very man they are in search of.[4]

The ship was due to leave four weeks later.

II

It did not take much for Darwin to realise that offers like this were most unusual. Henslow wanted him to go straight to London and consult his Cambridge colleague George Peacock—who was living in town during the long vacation and had reported the opportunity directly to Henslow from the Admiralty—about further particulars. There was a strong possibility that Captain FitzRoy might start making alternative arrangements.

Nor did it take much curiosity to wonder what kind of naval man could initiate such an invitation. Why did FitzRoy want to take a complete stranger around the world for two years—a gentleman companion, no less, not an experienced collector? None of the family could begin to venture a guess: not even Dr. Darwin, pessimistically shaking his head.

Robert FitzRoy, however, was acting entirely true to his personal type. He was an idiosyncratic, difficult young captain, only four years older than Darwin, who had already sailed in the *Beagle* once before. There were plenty of reasons for his wanting non-naval company.

FitzRoy had joined the navy as a boy soon after his mother's death and was educated at the Royal Naval College at Portsmouth.[5] Like Darwin, he carried the name of a famous family, in his case the aristocratic line of the Dukes of Grafton, originally stemming from the illegitimate children of Charles II and Barbara Villiers. The Graftons owned vast estates in England and Ireland and were prominent Tories and members of the royal court: the fourth duke, FitzRoy's uncle on his father's side, took part in the coronation procession of William IV staged in the summer of 1831, accompanying the king's regalia as hereditary position dictated. There was an equally influential uncle on the other side of the family in the shape of his mother's half-brother, the third Marquis of Londonderry, the heir to Lord Castlereagh (another uncle), who had killed himself in 1820 by slitting his throat after a long and increasingly troubled political career.

With relations like these it is not surprising that FitzRoy's promotions came relatively soon and smoothly. Graduating from the Portsmouth college with a gold medal, in 1819 he joined a peace-keeping force in the Mediterranean, and he was then posted to the South American fleet at Rio de Janeiro, which was protecting British interests in the area. Aristocratically at ease in high-ranking naval circles, he became a favoured aide of Admiral Otway, the head of the station. He was also one of the first technically competent lieutenants produced by the Admiralty—one with strong scientific interests and good mathematics. This distinguished him markedly from the individuals usually found making their way through the officer classes.[6]

But he was still lucky when a "death vacancy," as the navy called it, arose in 1828. In December of that year, Pringle Stokes, the captain of a small converted coaster named the *Beagle*, shot himself, driven to the edge by surveying duties in Tierra del Fuego. His crew were coming down with scurvy, the maps and charts were a labyrinth of errors leading them endlessly in circles, the storm-lashed coastline was too desolate to be endured any longer. "The soul of man dies in him," he wrote in the logbook, and put a pistol to his head.

When Captain King, the overall commander of the expedition, managed to get the *Beagle* and his own ship, the *Adventure,* back to port on the Argentine coast, Admiral Otway gave the *Beagle* to his protégé FitzRoy and sent the convoy off again to complete the southern survey.

"What think you of your old brother Bob being a captain of a Discovery ship," FitzRoy wrote in surprise to his sister in England; "not perhaps quite that but nearly so—for much of the coast is very little known.... We are ordered to collect everything—animals—insects—flowers—fish—anything and everything we can find, so you may suppose I shall have no leisure time to complain of.... Will it not be a most interesting employment?"[7]

Behind the bravado, he hated this particular pair of dead man's shoes. Nor did he complete the survey in any effective sense. Obsessive about detail, overanxious about justifying his early promotion, inexperienced as a captain and as a nautical surveyor, he had many things to worry about, including the crew's idea that the previous captain still sailed with them in the form of a ghost. Even the simple task of collecting "anything and everything" went dangerously awry, escalating into a misguided adventure that dominated his private life for the next five years and marked the beginning of a series of impossible situations dogging his career. FitzRoy, it turned out, had an aristocratic knack for creating his own disasters. He spent the closing days of his life mentally disturbed and ended them with a gory suicide, just like his uncle.

On this occasion, the newly commissioned captain had a small boat, essential for surveying the shallows, stolen by a group of Fuegians from a campsite on shore. Convinced it was being hidden locally, FitzRoy took several hostages in retaliation, all of whom escaped except for one girl and two men who seemed willing to remain on board. Giving up his boat as a lost cause, he conceived the grand plan of "collecting" the three Fuegians instead. He would take them back to England, educate them, and return them, at his own expense if necessary, with sufficient equipment to set up an Anglican mission station. He would bring civilisation to the uncivilised, as he thought, and help Tierra del Fuego step onto the nineteenth-century ladder of progress.

Never one to do things by halves, FitzRoy flung himself into this new project with autocratic naval enthusiasm. A fourth Fuegian aged about fourteen was purchased for a single mother-of-pearl button, prompting the sailors to call him Jemmy (James) Button, and FitzRoy began compiling a vocabulary of Fuegian words, the first ever attempted. As abruptly, he ordered the dead body of a man to be weighed and measured like a piece of meat for natural-historical purposes. A pickled human carcass already floated in a barrel in the *Adventure*'s hold, destined for the Royal College of Surgeons in London.

European cultural chauvinism of the most obvious kind ran underneath FitzRoy's elevated, if patronising, aims. Rendered plausible by the gloss of science and glamorised by the drama of travelling where few Admiralty ships had been before, his plan fitted into a long-standing pattern of importing human curiosities to display in Georgian and Victorian exhibition halls. It also interlocked with the missionary movements of the times, which represented in its most literal form the developing imperial ethos of the British nation. The human occupants of a country were thought to be perfectly legitimate objects for Englishmen to collect and study: just as legitimate as foreign stones and flowers.

FitzRoy's survey ship consequently returned to England with four Fuegians on board. Blind to all the difficulties that followed, the captain never once admitted that he might have made a mistake. One of the Fuegians died of smallpox. No one was interested in his mission project. New postings failed to materialise from the Admiralty. He had trouble locating a residential school suitable for his visitors. This catalogue of mishaps arose out of a fundamental misjudgement that FitzRoy naturally preferred to see as dedicated humanitarian activity.[8]

Yet he did have influential friends and relations. Just as he was settling the final details of an independent shipping contract in July to sail to Tierra del Fuego to fulfil his plans in the absence of any official interest, Francis Beaufort of the Hydrographer's Office—who took a professional interest in advancing FitzRoy's technical career—and his uncle, the Duke of Grafton, persuaded the Admiralty lords that the earlier survey should be completed. They made a good case for a second expedition, particularly in light of the lifting of trade restrictions between Britain and a newly independent confederation of Latin American states brought about by George Canning in 1824, and emphasised that the southern parts of Patagonia and Chile were potentially significant in commercial and naval terms. It was important too, as Canning, and then Palmerston, recognised, to forestall French and North American interests in the area. To chart these waters could easily become an exercise of the greatest economic and political importance.[9]

At very short notice, FitzRoy accordingly found himself captain of the Beagle for a second expedition. The three remaining Fuegians were hastily included when the duke's philanthropic friends proposed sponsoring the mission project; and it was arranged that a privately funded volunteer would travel on the ship to establish an Anglican outpost in South America with the returning Fuegians' help, under the Admiralty's general sanction.

This time, however, the expedition consisted of only one ship and FitzRoy was fully in charge. Eager as he was, he knew this would stretch him to the limit. He had seen what it was like in the far south, recognised the responsibilities and dangers, and was well aware of the Beagle's physical inadequacies— the compactness that made it so seaworthy also made for cramped internal quarters and restricted space in the hold.

Furthermore, he would be alone. Although thrown into close proximity with the ship's company, he would have no commanding officer to consult, no second captain to share the rigours of a long voyage, no one of his own social standing and intellectual persuasions to join in the tribulations and excitements of exploration. Captain Stokes, in whose cabin he was again sailing, had blown his brains out rather than continue under those conditions. FitzRoy, moreover, feared for his own sanity, believing himself very like his uncle Lord Castlereagh, who had teetered on the edge of madness for several weeks before cutting his throat. Overwork and stress drove his uncle to it, thought FitzRoy: he suspected he too might tumble into the same kind of extreme depression under the same kind of circumstances. He was afraid of being overwhelmed.

Early in August 1831, he took at least some of these worries to the person he knew best in the Hydrographer's Office, Francis Beaufort. Was there room on the *Beagle* for someone from the outside world who would share his scientific tastes and make good use of his time on a surveying expedition—a gentleman, of course, who could dine with him as an equal, share his expenses, and help maintain a semblance of normal life beyond the pressures of the South American survey?

With touching simplicity, he asked Beaufort to find him a friend.

III

A request like that, however, does not often end in an open invitation to a Cambridge arts graduate to go round the world. The convoluted chain from FitzRoy through to the letter rack in the hall of The Mount was the result of a complex social procedure, far more intricately laced than a mere happy chain of coincidences. There was no apparent reason why Darwin should be invited rather than his cousin Fox, or Henslow, or someone else entirely.

The invitation, in truth, was a dramatic manifestation of the Cambridge intellectual network in action. It was the network that caught the drift of FitzRoy's inquiries and transformed his suggestion into material reality, the network that sprang into action to find a suitable candidate. Darwin was not the first person to be approached, and FitzRoy later hesitated to accept him. Though always considering it "the greatest piece of good fortune" and completely justified in personal terms to say so, Darwin was singled out as the recipient of this largesse for distinctly different and socially observable reasons.

When Darwin first read Henslow's letter, the offer had already travelled a long way from its source, coming to him via George Peacock on the behalf of Francis Beaufort, the Hydrographer of the Admiralty. Peacock was a fellow of Trinity College, Cambridge, a respected tutor and lecturer in mathematics. A lifelong friend of Sedgwick's, a strong advocate for university reform, and devotedly Whig in his politics, he had a friendly relationship with Beaufort. He thought Beaufort was the only man in London capable of bringing the British navy's scientific attainments up to date.

In this he was quite right. Beaufort's offer to Darwin was an incidental result of far larger plans concerning the modernisation of the navy. It was Beaufort—friendly, careful, and ultimately extremely powerful, ceaselessly negotiating with the British treasury and a succession of foreign secretaries, always emphasising the need for new ships for civil purposes in conjunction with the money to make proper cartographic surveys—who forced senior members of the Admiralty out of their post-Napoleonic complacency and gave ships and their officers something useful to do. Though the Hydrographer's Office had been established in 1795 and its operations saw Britain safely through Trafalgar, it was in a dispirited and ineffective state when Beaufort took over early in 1829. Two years later he succeeded in separating it administratively from the rest of the Admiralty and was champing to start a major programme of improvement. He wanted his men fully trained in science and mathematics, familiar with theoretical issues like the earth's magnetism and movements of the tides, competent to make measurements for purposes broader than mere Admiralty concerns, and able to report with authority on the prospects of British trade and commercial developments in far-flung countries. Many of these ambitions were realised by mid-century: "No one thought of instituting a scientific adventure without applying to him," declared Captain Portlock in a public tribute after Beaufort's death.[10] More than anyone else he established the naval framework for the great age of Victorian colonial expansion.

Peacock empathised deeply with Beaufort's scientific and technical aspirations. He had known him since 1827, when, in the company of Cambridge notables like John Herschel and Charles Babbage, they formed the nucleus of an influential pressure group acting behind the scenes wherever relations between British science and government policy were involved. Their primary aim was to introduce what were perceived as much-needed reforms to the Royal Society of London, the premier society for science in Britain, and to establish stronger connections between the society and government departments.[11] Babbage's blistering attack in 1830, ostentatiously titled *Reflections on the Decline of Science in England,* focussed alarmingly on the lack of any coherent policy for British science; and John Herschel stepped forward as a nonaristocratic candidate for president of the society in opposition to the Duke of Sussex, younger brother of William IV. Although Herschel was not elected, his supporters, Babbage, Peacock, and Beaufort among them, felt something had been achieved: the election was hotly contested; the council listened to ideas for administrative reform; and the exclusive system of courtly scientific patronage was shaken. Peacock and Beaufort joined the society's council that year, initiating a modest degree of further improvement.

If not entirely successful, these underground machinations did produce one important consequence. A group of like-minded individuals materialised in an informal way that united academics from Cambridge University with London professionals. These included such men as Beaufort and reforming politicians favourably inclined towards science like Robert Peel, out of office since 1827 and once mooted as a possible president of the Royal, and Leonard Horner, the progressive M.P. and educationalist from Edinburgh, vice-president of the Geological Society in 1828, and founder and first warden of London University on its opening in the same year.

These were men espousing reform to a greater or lesser degree in science, education, and politics. They also held the power to get things done.[12] Cambridge dons like Peacock had confidence in Beaufort. Beaufort in turn depended on the collegiate scientific network to support his own project of transforming the hydrography department. Canny political exertion along these channels allowed him to plan a revitalised naval regime.

IV

The second *Beagle* expedition was to be Beaufort's biggest exercise so far. He lavished proprietorial care on it and paid minute attention to the programme laid out for the officers to undertake. The survey, he anticipated, would be a showpiece for the Hydrographer's Office. Nothing was too much trouble.

So when FitzRoy came to him with the idea of a scientific companion, he willingly supported the plan. He quickly informed Peacock about the likelihood of an opening on a surveying ship and asked him to find "a savant."[13]

At first, Peacock misunderstood the precise nature of what was being suggested, and his letter to Henslow spoke of a vacancy for an official naturalist. He must have written again soon afterwards with slightly different details which stressed FitzRoy's wish only for a scientifically inclined gentleman-companion.

Several of the students and younger fellows known to Peacock in Cambridge colleges met this requirement. He thought Leonard Jenyns might like to go. "What treasures he might bring home with him, as the ship would be placed at his disposal, whenever his inquiries made it necessary or desirable; in the absence of so accomplished a naturalist, is there any person whom you could strongly recommend: he must be such a person as would do credit to our recommendation. Do think on this subject: it would be a serious loss to the cause of natural science, if this fine opportunity was lost."[14]

Actually, Henslow—a mere thirty-five years old—thought briefly of taking up the offer himself. He was still secretly longing to accompany Darwin and Ramsay on their proposed trip to Tenerife. But "the expression on his wife's face," the new baby, and collegiate and parochial affairs persuaded him to pass it on to Jenyns, altogether freer from restrictions and well qualified for a general natural history undertaking.

Jenyns took a day to think it over before deciding he ought not to leave his parish at Bottisham so soon after being appointed. He did not "think it quite right to quit for a purpose of that kind, as on account of my judging that I was not exactly the right person, either in point of health or other qualifications."[15] Yet he was so near accepting that he packed up his clothes.[16] Jenyns always regretted his unimaginative decision and in future years found it difficult to listen to Darwin's stories about the voyage, even more so when fame as a scientific traveller and writer was heaped on him. The final ignominy came when Darwin later asked if Jenyns would describe the fish he had collected on the voyage, although Jenyns generously undertook the task. A few months earlier and he would have gone without a second thought. But in 1831, unaware of the magnitude of what he was about to give up, Jenyns bowed out gracefully. He and Henslow passed the invitation on to Darwin.[17]

V

Darwin did not take half as long as Jenyns to make up his mind. It was the most exciting thing that had ever happened to him. Incomparably better than a few months in Tenerife, this proposal was a dramatic opportunity to get out of Shropshire to do the things he yearned to do, to see the world and make something of himself. How could he refuse? "I immediately said I would go."[18]

Unfortunately, Dr. Darwin did not see it in quite the same light. Nearly despairing of his idle son's ever settling down to a career, anticipating all kinds of shipwreck, death, and disease as any parent would, he thought Darwin should refuse. Sailing ships were just like gaols, he said, repeating Samuel Johnson, with their brutal discipline, filthy conditions, and the additional disadvantage of being drowned. This advice was given in such a way it seemed best not to ignore it.

Next morning Darwin wrote glumly to Henslow:

Mr. Peacocks letter arrived on Saturday, & I received it late yesterday evening.—As far as my own mind is concerned, I should think, *certainly* most gladly have accepted the opportunity, which you so kindly have offered me.—But my Father, although he does not decidedly refuse me, gives such strong advice against going,—that I should not be comfortable, if I did not follow it.—My Fathers objections are these; the unfitting me to settle down as a clergyman,—my little habit of seafaring,—the *shortness of the time* & the chance of my not suiting Captain FitzRoy.—It certainly is a very serious objection, the very short time for all my preparations, as not only body but mind wants making up for such an undertaking.—But if it had not been for my Father, I would have taken all risks. . . . Even if I was to go, my Father disliking would take away all energy, & I should want a good stock of that.—Again I must thank you; it adds a little to the heavy, but pleasant load of gratitude which I owe to you.—[19]

He could not bear staying cooped up with the disappointment. That same morning he set off for Maer to drown his feelings out shooting with Uncle Jos.

VI

Before Darwin disappeared, however, his father found time for some serious thought. His fears for his son's safety in the age of tall ships were not exaggerated, and his doubts about the value of the exercise were probably justified in view of the wasted time at two universities. On the other hand, the invitation reflected the esteem that Cambridge professionals held for him, and he knew enough about the ways of the world to be sure that an offer like this would not be repeated. Darwin had showed unexpected docility in acknowledging the offer ought to be rejected. The doctor recognised that a real longing had been swallowed in deference to his own wishes.

The upshot of it was that he subtly, perhaps half unconsciously, provided an opportunity for the decision to be revoked. "If you can find any man of common sense who advises you to go," he said in exasperation, "I will give my consent." They both knew he meant Uncle Jos. A note to Josiah Wedgwood from the doctor confirmed it. "Charles will tell you of the offer he has had made to him of going for a voyage of discovery for 2 years.—I strongly object to it on various grounds, but I will not detail my reasons that he may have your unbiassed opinion on the subject, & if you think differently from me I shall wish him to follow your advice." Just as Darwin was leaving, the doctor scribbled on the bottom, more for his own benefit than for Wedgwood's: "Charles has quite given up the idea of the voyage."[20]

But in this new light and safely over at Maer, everything naturally took on a different appearance. The Wedgwoods expressed much more enthusiasm for the idea than Dr. Darwin, and the rest of the day was spent deep in discussion. Surprisingly, the strongest support came from bookish, stay-at-home Hensleigh, who "heartened him up" to the point that he afterwards called himself "a sort of godfather" to Darwin's exploits.[21] By early evening everyone was urging him to reopen the case with the doctor.

The first thing to be done, thought Uncle Jos, was for Darwin to list his father's objections. To this Wedgwood would add his "unbiassed opinion":

as invited. In the meantime, Darwin should write to apologise ("I am afraid I am going to make you again very uncomfortable"), assuring Dr. Darwin he was "not so bent on going, that I would for one *single moment* hesitate, if you thought, that after a short period, you should continue uncomfortable."

Darwin's list was short and evocative, the turns of phrase straight from his father's mouth the night before. It was on a separate piece of paper, ready to push over the table to his uncle. "I have given Uncle Jos, what I fervently trust is an accurate & full list of your objections, & he is kind enough to give his opinion on all.—The list & his answers will be enclosed."

(1) Disreputable to my character as a Clergyman hereafter
(2) A wild scheme
(3) That they must have offered to many others before me, the place of Naturalist
(4) And from its not being accepted there must be some serious objection to the vessel or expedition
(5) That I should never settle down to a steady life hereafter
(6) That my accommodations would be most uncomfortable
(7) That you should consider it as again changing my profession
(8) That it would be a useless undertaking[22]

Wedgwood treated each statement with proper consideration, although barely suppressing a smile at the curious discussion between father and son which had evidently taken place: where were the fears of death or the inevitable loneliness and separation from loved ones at home? Darwin only remembered the things that touched a nerve, his past idleness and future profession conspicuous among them. Nevertheless, these were the objections as given, and Wedgwood did his best to turn them to Darwin's advantage.

He certainly knew how to handle his brother-in-law. His letter appealed directly to Dr. Darwin's innate sense of order, to his rational, logical approach to the morass of everyday life. Others who knew him less well might have played on his fatherly feelings, on opportunities lost by the older generation that the next could relive or experience in their place, on being ungenerous or overcautious.

Wedgwood appreciated that Dr. Darwin was none of these. The best way to deal with him was also the way that came intuitively. He presented the case as would a man of business: one side of the balance sheet was in his hands, and he went through it seriatim, reckoning up the profits and losses. Like a ledger-clerk in the company offices, Wedgwood employed his reason without evident emotion.

My dear Doctor
  I feel the responsibility of your application to me on the offer that has been made to Charles as being weighty, but as you have desired Charles to consult me I cannot refuse to give the result of such consideration as I have

been able to give it. Charles has put down what he conceives to be your principal objections & I think the best course I can take will be to state what occurs to me upon each of them.

1—I should not think that it would be in any degree disreputable to his character as a clergyman. I should on the contrary think the offer honorable to him, and the pursuit of Natural History, though certainly not professional, is very suitable to a Clergyman.

2—I hardly know how to meet this objection, but he would have definite objects upon which to employ himself and might acquire and strengthen, habits of application, and I should think would be as likely to do so in any way in which he is likely to pass the next two years at home.

3. The notion did not occur to me in reading the letters & on reading them again with that object in my mind I see no ground for it.

4. I cannot conceive that the Admiralty would send out a bad vessel on such a service. As to objections to the expedition, they will differ in each mans case & nothing would, I think, be inferred in Charles's case if it were known that others had objected.

5—You are a much better judge of Charles's character than I can be. If, on comparing this mode of spending the next two years, with the way in which he will probably spend them if he does not accept this offer, you think him more likely to be rendered unsteady & unable to settle, it is undoubtedly a weighty objection—Is it not the case that sailors are prone to settle in domestic and quiet habits.

6—I can form no opinion on this further than that, if appointed by the Admiralty, he will have a claim to be as well accommodated as the vessel will allow.

7—If I saw Charles now absorbed in professional studies I should probably think it would not be advisable to interrupt them, but this is not, and I think will not be, the case with him. His present pursuit of knowledge is in the same track as he would have to follow in the expedition.

8—The undertaking would be useless as regards his profession, but looking upon him as a man of enlarged curiosity, it affords him such an opportunity of seeing men and things as happens to few.

You will bear in mind that I have had very little time for consideration & that you & Charles are the persons who must decide.[23]

Both letters went off early in the morning of 1 September, and the two men tried some shooting—the opening day of the partridge season was a convenient if uncertain distraction. It was not easy, though, mustering their customary ardour. "I shot one partridge on the 1st," Darwin later complained to a friend. "Devilish dear"—hardly worth the game licence.[24] Josiah Wedgwood's mind was also running on other things. At ten o'clock he bundled Darwin into his carriage determined to argue the point in person.

But there was no need, as they discovered after arriving at The Mount. Dr.

Darwin had changed his mind. More than that, he would give "all the assistance in my power."

"All things were settled," cried Darwin. Without examining his feelings any further, he sat down and wrote for the first time to Francis Beaufort to tell him that, contrary to his previous letters to Henslow and Peacock—and if the appointment was not by now already filled by another—he was "very happy to have the honor of accepting it."[25]

VII

From then on the family leaped into action. Events had moved fast since Henslow's letter was opened, and they did not slow down for another six weeks at least: the time from Peacock's first letter until Dr. Darwin's consent was only seven days; on 1 September 1831 Darwin accepted the offer; and by the 5th he was on his way to Cambridge to consult Henslow and thence up to London to meet Peacock, Beaufort, and in due course his new captain, Robert FitzRoy.

Henslow took his position as mentor seriously, arming Darwin with letters of introduction to various London naturalists who could recommend appropriate equipment and advise him about desirable specimens to collect. Beaufort filled in the gaps, both personally and indirectly, by sending him to the homes of retired naval officers like Sir John Richardson, an expert on the natural history of the Arctic, and to the head of the Royal Navy medical department in the hope of acquiring some "apparatus free of expense."[26] Darwin bustled and hustled through London, seeing the eminent men of metropolitan science, freely asking for and receiving information, choosing instruments and glassware, buying books and preserving papers, debating the merits of iron nets and oyster trawls, hastily learning elementary astronomy in the evenings as "it would astound a sailor if one did not know how to find Lat & Long.," and generally making himself known to others, fulfilling all Henslow's expectations that he was just the person the Admiralty had been looking for. "You can have no idea how busy I am all day long. . . . I am as happy as a king," he wrote to Cambridge.[27]

"For about the first time in my life I find London very pleasant," the family in Shrewsbury was told: "hurry, bustle & noise are all in unison with my feelings."

The sisters busied themselves with Darwin's urgent requests for clothes, including strong new shoes and shirts, the shirts to be marked DARWIN for the ship's laundry, and a proliferation of conflicting instructions on how to pack everything into as small a box as possible.

Dr. Darwin provided money. His offer of assistance was not an empty one; and although his daily account books for the period are lost, the cost of equipping his son ran to around £600, roughly comparable to two years at Cambridge University. The Admiralty, moreover, expected Darwin to pay for himself during the expedition, and the doctor was here agreeing not only to send him around the world for two years (it eventually stretched to five) but also to pay the bill. It was more expensive than keeping him on at Cambridge, he ruminated, but he might learn to manage his affairs with more prudence than he had showed so far. Darwin's "spend-penny" attitude had left debts of £200 at university, which Dr. Darwin disapprovingly paid off during the course of the summer; and right up to the end of November, Henslow was still juggling with Darwin's complicated directives about tutor's fees and furniture rentals. Several unpaid bills that the doctor did not know about were also waiting to be settled privately when he returned in October. Fanny Owen caught the general air of careless prodigality when she said Darwin's voyage was a pretty desperate way of avoiding paying his tailors.[28]

Dr. Darwin, inwardly resigned to the extravagant habits of his younger son, was not going to stint now that the decision was taken. He wanted him to be well equipped, safe, and adequately provided for. However, Darwin was also allowed to indulge his fondness for technical gadgets and given the money to buy one or two costly instruments, including a portable dissecting microscope as recommended by the botanist Robert Brown. He tried consoling his father by saying, "I should be deuced clever to spend more than my allowance whilst on board the *Beagle.*" The answer came back promptly. "But they all tell me you are very clever."[29]

Among the flurry of spending and ordering, Henslow's friend the ornithologist and bookseller William Yarrell was an oasis of pennypinching calm. He advised and supplied many travellers in his time and operated on the philosophy that you never need all the things you take, advice which Darwin found "quite invaluable." Yarrell took Darwin round the shops and bullied about prices. "Hang me if I give 60£ for pistols," exclaimed the budding naturalist under his care. Together they bought a case of pistols and an excellent rifle for only £50—"there is a saving," he told his father triumphantly, for FitzRoy's firearms were sure to cost £400 at least.[30] The point was not lost on Dr. Darwin, who sent Yarrell a brace of partridges from the Wedgwood estate in gratitude.

VIII

The only drain on these heady times was Darwin's forthcoming meeting with Captain FitzRoy. Each was openly apprehensive about the other.

While the Cambridge network was vibrating with messages about the *Beagle* opportunity, FitzRoy quite understandably had second thoughts about sharing his life with a stranger, however much a natural philosopher he might be, and asked someone else—it is not known who—to accompany him for at least part of the voyage. He may have invited Harry Chester, youngest son of Sir Robert Chester, who in 1831 was a clerk in the Privy Council Office, since a Mr. Chester was once mentioned to Darwin and FitzRoy did possess a friend by that name; but in the absence of any corroborative letters his identity remains uncertain.[31] It is equally possible that the "friend" was a useful fiction dreamed up by FitzRoy to provide an excuse—"the want of room"—in case Darwin turned out to be unacceptable.

The first that FitzRoy heard about his proposed companion was through Francis Beaufort, who painted a glowing picture in a letter on 1 September 1831 apparently written before receiving any news from Darwin himself. "I believe my friend Mr Peacock of Trin[y] College Camb has succeeded in getting a 'Savant' for you—a Mr Darwin grandson of the well known philosopher and poet—full of zeal and enterprize and having contemplated a voyage on his own account to S. America," Beaufort wrote cheerfully. "Let me know how you like the idea that I may go or recede in time."

The two naval men met soon afterwards to discuss this and other matters relating to the *Beagle*'s sailing, and Beaufort probably took the opportunity to stress the desirability of FitzRoy's taking a Cambridge-educated enthusiast rather than any high-society friend he might have approached in the interim. Though Beaufort did not at that stage know Darwin personally, the network already ensured that he came with appropriate recommendations. Moreover, Beaufort felt he had certain connections with the Darwins through his sister Frances, who had married Richard Lovell Edgeworth, an intimate friend of Darwin's grandfather Erasmus, and more directly through bringing his mother over from Ireland in 1803 to consult Dr. Darwin about a skin disease (porphyria ran in the Beaufort family). Apparently the doctor was more concerned about her general health than her skin, but either way she lived until the age of ninety-four with no further complications.[32] Beaufort could speak with some authority about the family's respectable place in scientific and county affairs.

Beaufort's private system of influence operated from the Cambridge end as well. Darwin's suitability formed the subject of a letter received by FitzRoy from his cousin Alexander Charles Wood, an undergraduate at Trinity College, Cambridge. Wood's tutor was the ubiquitous Peacock, and it was at his instigation that Wood—who barely knew Darwin—wrote to FitzRoy to recommend him. Wood did take the precaution, however, as a relative, to point out that Darwin was a Whig.[33]

Like any strong-minded individual, FitzRoy balked at all this pressure. He wrote back to his cousin Wood saying he believed the place was already filled. Up at Cambridge consulting Henslow, Darwin received Wood's news a few days later. Thunderstruck, he complained that although the letter to Wood was "*most* straightforward & *gentlemanlike,*" he could not, under the circumstances, contemplate sailing. For two hours or so, he gave up the scheme completely while Henslow rumbled resentfully that Peacock was "very wrong" in misrepresenting the situation. A "discouraging letter from my captain," Darwin informed Fox, was the cause.[34]

In this highly charged atmosphere, he set off for London to meet FitzRoy. Unexpectedly, he found him charming, even though the fraught situation with the friend was explained and the lack of room discussed in detail: FitzRoy was "open & kind . . . there is something most extremely attractive in his manners, & way of coming straight to the point. . . . I like his manner of proceeding."[35]

But there can be no doubt that FitzRoy did his best to put Darwin off, making him aware the trip was not a pleasure cruise. It was sure to be stormy, expensive, uncomfortable, and—to Darwin's real disappointment—perhaps not completely around the world, since FitzRoy intended completing his survey come what may and would cancel their scheduled visit to the South Sea Islands if more time was needed for working in Tierra del Fuego. He gave Darwin ample opportunity to stand down. It would be easy to leave the voyage at any major staging post.

Yet both young men must have made themselves as agreeable as possible, for during the course of the interview FitzRoy warmed to Darwin, shifting his ground to admit that if he could accept all these inconveniences he would be pleased to have him aboard as a guest. "Mr. Chester" evaporated. Only five minutes before Darwin came in, said FitzRoy, he had had a note to say his friend was "in office" and could not go. The lack of room was not such an impossible problem.

What bothered FitzRoy more, he confessed, was whether Darwin "would bear being told that I want the cabin to myself when I want to be alone,—if we treat each other this way, I hope we shall suit, if not probably we should wish each other at the Devil."[36]

Whatever Darwin made of these naval tactics, his doubts disappeared. He was impressed by FitzRoy's cultured authority and direct way of speaking. "You cannot imagine anything more pleasant, kind & open than Cap. FitzRoy's manners were to me," he told Henslow. "Gloria in excelsis" was the most moderate thing he could think of saying.[37]

The two dined together later that day, and the future looked much more rosy. Darwin's relief pitched him dramatically towards adulation. "I think he really wishes to have me," he told Henslow; "Cap. FitzRoy is every thing that is delightful, if I was to praise half so much as I feel inclined, you would say it was absurd, only once seeing him."[38]

For his part, the captain also eased up. His misgivings were forgotten, and the space—always a genuine handicap—was now considered well within the usual range of difficulties in shipboard life. Writing to Beaufort that evening, FitzRoy admitted that "I like what I see and hear of him, much, and I now request that you will apply for him to accompany me as a Naturalist. I can and will make him comfortable on board, more so perhaps than you or he would expect, and I will contrive to stow away his goods and chattels of all kinds and give him a place for a workshop."[39]

With this point established, Darwin at last felt free to cry, "Woe unto ye beetles of South America."

IX

And so it was fixed. He had passed through the strangest test of his abilities he ever experienced. It was exhausting in every conceivable way: "I have had a most tremendous hard week of it."[40]

The qualifications that brought him, instead of Jenyns or even Henslow, up to London were plainly somewhat different from those that swayed FitzRoy in his final decision. Darwin was chosen not because he was noticeably good at natural history, although this was a factor in ensuring he was put forward for the voyage by his Cambridge professor, nor because he was an aspiring "savant," well trained at university, but because he was an amiable young man of good social standing who looked as if he would be easy to live with. Whatever Peacock and Beaufort may have said or wished to believe about the *Beagle* voyage, FitzRoy's need was for a companion.[41] Darwin's acceptance of this invisible emphasis on his upbringing, education, and family background indicates that he was for at least some of the time the man FitzRoy thought he was: gregarious without being unpleasantly hearty, socially adept, with refined manners and country-based interests in riding and shooting, clever without being overbearing, enthusiastic about the prospect of a voyage and new sights to see, tactful about the need for privacy. There were elements too of ingratiation—of his ready deference to the captain's authority, a willingness to be servile.

Where FitzRoy had once wavered, he now opened up to Darwin with the unpredictable warmth that characterised all his personal relationships: "an ardent friend to all under his sway," stated his new companion, rather taken aback. Yes, he told Darwin, he had felt "a sudden horror of the chances of having somebody he should not like on board the vessel." His letter to Cambridge was intended "to throw cold water on the scheme."[42]

FitzRoy even revealed, only partly as a joke, that Darwin had also run a risk of rejection because of the shape of his nose. As a passionate believer in phrenology and its sister system of physiognomy, which concerned itself with analysing character as seen in the face, FitzRoy thought Darwin's broad placid features lacked inner resolution.

> He was an ardent disciple of Lavater, and was convinced that he could judge a man's character by the outline of his features; and he doubted whether anyone with my nose could possess sufficient energy and determination for the voyage. But I think he was afterwards well-satisfied that my nose had spoken falsely.[43]

With these small confessions and intimacies, the two tentatively started seeking a place in each other's world. FitzRoy began to feel some of his fears about the voyage receding: the idea of having Darwin on board was something he could start looking forward to. For Darwin—preoccupied with the realisation he was truly going to sail with the *Beagle,* that all the difficulties were overcome, his family expressing their love for him through the inadequate medium of shirts and banker's drafts, Henslow writing useful letters, and his quirky "beau ideal of a captain" asking him "to give me a trial"—the time passed in an excited blur.

"Every body seems ready to assist me," he gratefully observed.[44] Well aware of who was responsible for this remarkable turn in his fortunes, he could only say to FitzRoy: "I shall always recollect your kindness in helping me in every possible way to my end with the truest pleasure."[45]

TRAVELLER

Of the 57 months that the *Beagle* was at sea
42 were spent in the waters of South America.
Of these, 27 were spent on the east coast,
and 15 on the west.

MILES 3000

KILOMETRES 3000

Scale at Equator; scale increases with latitude

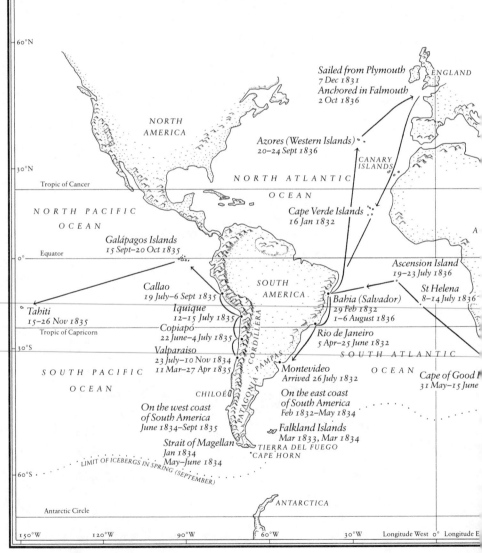

60°N

NORTH
AMERICA

Sailed from Plymouth
7 Dec 1831
Anchored in Falmouth
2 Oct 1836

ENGLAND

Azores (Western Islands)
20–24 Sept 1836

CANARY
ISLANDS

30°N

Tropic of Cancer

NORTH ATLANTIC

OCEAN

NORTH PACIFIC
OCEAN

Cape Verde Islands
16 Jan 1832

Galápagos Islands
15 Sept–20 Oct 1835

Equator 0°

Ascension Island
19–23 July 1836

SOUTH
AMERICA

St Helena
8–14 July 1836

Callao
19 July–6 Sept 1835

Bahia (Salvador)
29 Feb 1832
1–6 August 1836

Tahiti
15–26 Nov 1835

Iquique
12–15 July 1835

Tropic of Capricorn

Copiapó
22 June–4 July 1835

Rio de Janeiro
5 Apr–25 June 1832

30°S

Valparaiso
23 July–10 Nov 1834
11 Mar–27 Apr 1835

SOUTH ATLANTIC

SOUTH PACIFIC
OCEAN

Montevideo
Arrived 26 July 1832

OCEAN

Cape of Good F
31 May–15 June

CHILOÉ

On the east coast
of South America
Feb 1832–May 1834

On the west coast
of South America
June 1834–Sept 1835

Falkland Islands
Mar 1833, Mar 1834

Strait of Magellan
Jan 1834
May–June 1834

TIERRA DEL FUEGO
CAPE HORN

LIMIT OF ICEBERGS IN SPRING (SEPTEMBER)

60°S

ANTARCTICA

Antarctic Circle

150°W   120°W   90°W   60°W   30°W   Longitude West 0° Longitude E

THE
VOYAGE of the *BEAGLE*

December 1831–October 1836

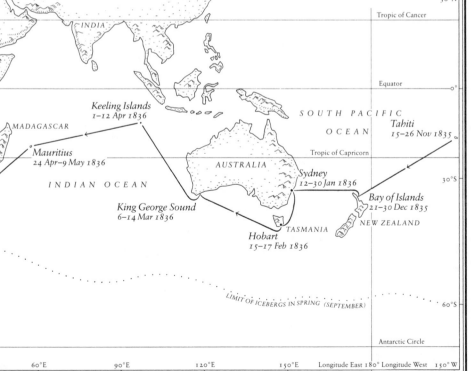

60°N

30°N

Tropic of Cancer

INDIA

Equator

0°

Keeling Islands
1–12 Apr 1836

SOUTH PACIFIC

Tahiti
15–26 Nov 1835

OCEAN

MADAGASCAR

Mauritius
24 Apr–9 May 1836

Tropic of Capricorn

AUSTRALIA

Sydney
12–30 Jan 1836

30°S

INDIAN OCEAN

Bay of Islands
21–30 Dec 1835

King George Sound
6–14 Mar 1836

NEW ZEALAND

TASMANIA

Hobart
15–17 Feb 1836

LIMIT OF ICEBERGS IN SPRING (SEPTEMBER)

60°S

Antarctic Circle

60°E   90°E   120°E   150°E   Longitude East 180° Longitude West   150°W

NEW HORIZONS

ARWIN'S first week at sea defied description. Seasickness struck hard and suddenly on entering the Bay of Biscay, a notorious trouble spot in European waters. "The misery is excessive," he whimpered when next well enough to pick up a pen. "It far exceeds what a person would suppose who had never been at sea more than a few days.—I found the only relief to be in a horizontal position."[1]

At first, he swung unhappily in his hammock while the officers began working on sea charts on the table beneath. When that became too much he lay on the table itself. Soon, however, FitzRoy settled him down on the sofa in his cabin and engaged him in idle chat: just the thing for "cheering the heart of a seasick man," thought Darwin gratefully. As the ship ploughed onwards, they discovered a mutual enthusiasm for Jane Austen (her novels are on everyone's table, said FitzRoy, assuming Darwin knew he meant solely people like the Londonderrys, the Jerseys, and the Graftons) and for tropical scenery. But these pleasant diversions did not help him forget his stomach. Nor was it much consolation to be told that this run across the bay was one of the three or four worst passages at sea that FitzRoy had ever experienced.[2] The captain wisely refrained from confessing that it was also the first time he had steered a ship out of the English Channel.

Swirling around with the seasickness in Darwin's head were shrieks from sailors being flogged. His father's words about ships and gaols could hardly have been more accurate. FitzRoy defensively explained he was not as much of a martinet as some captains he knew but flogging was a weapon he had no qualms about using to establish order right from the start.[3] Four sailors were beaten with the cat-o'-nine-tails: one for drunkenness (twenty-five lashes);

one for disobeying orders (thirty-four lashes); one for drunkenness and insolence (forty-four lashes); and one for neglect of duty (thirty-one lashes). Leg irons were clapped onto five more.

Darwin barely possessed the energy to know what he thought about this except that he had somehow stepped into an Old Testament version of hell: the screams mingled with his own nausea in a sickening whirlpool of revulsion. FitzRoy's punishments seemed too severe for the behaviour they punished, and his sympathies were torn between the captain, so kind where Darwin's own well-being was concerned, and the beaten men. Was this a taste of the years to come? "I often said before starting, that I had no doubt I should frequently repent of the whole undertaking; little did I think with what fervour I should do so.—I can scarcely conceive any more miserable state, than when such dark & gloomy thoughts are haunting the mind as have today pursued me."[4]

Such a brutal start to the voyage of a lifetime was almost unendurable. Indeed, the shock to Darwin's system was so obvious that FitzRoy fully expected him to leave at the first convenient landfall. "He was terribly sick until we passed Teneriffe, and I sometimes doubted his fortitude holding out against such a beginning of the campaign."[5]

II

Actually, there had been plenty of time for Darwin to mull over the potential disadvantages of the voyage before the ship set sail. After the first thrill of the invitation died down and the flurry of his preparations was completed, he found little else to do but wait—and worry. September's blur of activity and the high emotion of a succession of sentimental farewells faded into a dreary November and December spent kicking his heels at the royal dockyards in Plymouth while FitzRoy supervised endless alterations to the decks and internal quarters of the Beagle. When at last these were deemed sufficient by their fastidious captain, bad weather kept them harnessed to shore—not just one but three attempts to leave over as many weeks were aborted by winter storms blowing up the Western Approaches. When the Beagle eventually sailed on 27 December 1831, the excitement had completely disappeared and the occupants were, Darwin remarked, as phlegmatic as if setting out on a day's excursion to France. He felt a bit cheated. "I did expect to have felt some of the same heart-sinking sensations which I experienced when I first had the offer of the voyage," he grumbled.[6]

Those months at Devonport were among the worst in Darwin's life. He arrived in Plymouth late in October expecting to leave within a dozen days or so, adding an extra week to his time with Erasmus in London precisely to avoid spending too much time in harbour. "What a glorious day the 4th of November will be to me—My second life will then commence, and it shall be as a birthday for the rest of my life,"[7] he wrote ecstatically before boarding the coach.

But it was soon clear that refitting and loading would not be finished until well into November. He could not unpack or stow his goods because the cabin he was to share with others was still only half built, nor could he settle down to any other constructive activities. "My chief employment is to go on board the Beagle & try to look as much like a sailor as ever I can," he complained to Henslow on 15 November. "I have no evidence of having taken in man, woman or child."[8]

Despite the mutterings, there were several things to occupy him at first. He explored the *Beagle* as much as he was able, picking his way through the carpenters, sailmakers, and deliverymen trying to unload hogsheads of rum and flour. FitzRoy was already feeding the crew as if they were aboard: the monthly rations he served out ran to twenty-six pieces of beef and fifty-two of pork, a barrel of cocoa, and vast quantities of bread, peas, vinegar (an antiscorbutic), tea, soap, and sugar.[9]

The ship, Darwin discovered, was as tiny as FitzRoy had said, fully reflecting its humble origin as a coastal carrier, a mere ninety feet long with a capacity of roughly 242 tons. Three masts and a few small cannon had been grafted on some years before to turn it into what the navy called a ten-gun brig. But it looked more like a wreck than a vessel commissioned to go round the world. Tired of stooping wherever he went, and well aware that the wood was half rotten from the previous voyage, FitzRoy insisted that the upper deck be raised to give more headroom in the living quarters below and that the hold be reorganised to suit his own purposes. He also took the opportunity to turn the room where Pringle Stokes had shot himself into a storage area and created a new, smaller cabin for himself as captain. The gunroom, the poop cabin, the midshipmen's berths, and the men's mess were all refitted. Up on the deck, boxes and housings for the ship's scientific equipment sprouted wherever there was least interference from sea motion and natural magnetism: almost a guarantee that they would impede any other routine shipboard occupation. "Perhaps no vessel ever quitted her own country," recorded FitzRoy proudly, "with a better or more ample supply (in proportion to her probable necessities) of every kind of useful provision."[10]

Into the remaining space seventy-four people were expected to stow themselves. As well as the captain, his crew, and Darwin, there were two other supernumeraries—an instrument-maker and an artist, both in FitzRoy's private employment—plus a volunteer missionary and the three Fuegians due to be returned to their proper home. There was no room left for a padre even if FitzRoy had wished to relinquish his right to conduct Sunday services: under naval rules a captain was God anyway. There was not much room for

Darwin either. "The corner of the cabin, which is my private property, is most wofully small.—I have just room to turn round & that is all," he told Henslow. His height was a great inconvenience, agreed the officers. How many more cubic inches was he planning to cram in? asked First Lieutenant Wickham. Despite this, "our Cabins are fitted most luxuriously with nothing except Mahogany: in short every thing is going on as well as possible. I only wish they were a little faster."[11]

Darwin was to share the poop cabin with two of the survey officers, John Lort Stokes and Phillip Gidley King. Stokes had travelled on the first *Beagle* expedition as a midshipman and was now promoted to mate and assistant surveyor. His main responsibility was to look after and redraft the navigational charts which were the object of the voyage, and these were tightly packed in large lockers lining the poop cabin's wall. To one side were books: more than a hundred of them, Bibles, dictionaries, poetry, novels, and reference works, all privately owned by members of the ship's company and made available for lending to others.[12] The rest of the space was dominated by Stokes's huge but necessary chart table, over which Darwin and King nightly hung up their hammocks. Taller than the rest, Darwin removed one of the drawers on the wall every evening to make room for his feet. Stokes slept in a bunk bed tucked away under the stairs just outside the door.

This restricted space was subdivided with rigid naval formality. Even the allocation of the chairs and the places where the three men were to sit were established straight away, never to change for the whole duration of the voyage. Darwin, who was in no position to argue, fell in with the arrangements but was relieved to find Stokes an affable man with no wish to monopolise the table. Midshipman King, a boy sailor aged fourteen and the eldest son of Captain King of the previous expedition, afterwards stated that Darwin always sat on the right-hand side of the table, closest to his personal set of drawers, as Stokes, in his turn, occupied the place by the door with his naval papers close to hand.[13]

Beyond these short-lived preliminaries, there was nothing else for Darwin to do in Devonport except make himself agreeable. Never one to waste time or sentiment on his men, FitzRoy had thrown Darwin and Stokes together in the same lodgings in Clarence Baths. Within the week, Darwin therefore began helping Stokes with his surveying instruments, mostly by marking the time and taking observations on the dipping needle while Stokes calibrated the ship's chronometers for their initial readings before departure. Together they went to the gardens of the Plymouth Athenaeum, the local literary and philosophical society founded in 1812, to set up a small "astronomical house" which was the starting point for the chain of measurements the *Beagle* was to draw around the globe.

To his chagrin, Darwin found his Cambridge education a poor substitute for Stokes's practical expertise. "I want your advice de Mathematicis," he admitted to Henslow at that time. "After looking at my 11 books of Euclid, & first part of Algebra (including binomial theorem?) I may then begin Trigonometry after which I must begin Spherical? are there any important parts in the 2^d & 3^d parts of Woods Algebra.—It is almost a shame to ask you, but I should be much obliged if you would write to me pretty soon."[14]

It was a far cry from measuring the table top at Shrewsbury. "I suspect when I am struggling with a triangle I shall often wish myself in your room, & as for those wicked sulky surds, I do not know what I shall do without you to conjure them."[15]

Patiently, Stokes taught him how to use scientific equipment all over again, this time with enough accuracy to satisfy both the navy and FitzRoy himself. The captain—as the subsequent inventor of the FitzRoy barometer that came to dominate Victorian meteorological activities—was an exacting taskmaster where instruments were concerned. Slowly, Darwin improved enough to offer to take barometric readings for him, a job which he intermittently carried out throughout the voyage. He had to buy his own barometer, though. FitzRoy did not allow ordinary mortals to touch his instruments.

The days were punctuated by social engagements with the captain. Right from the start, FitzRoy included Darwin in his necessary round of the admirals, savants, and country gentry in Plymouth. He also asked him to dine once or twice in his own lodgings so that they could become better acquainted. Accustomed to talking and walking with the great men of Cambridge, Darwin felt at ease on these elevated occasions, possibly because FitzRoy treated him "like a child," promising to put him ashore whenever there was a storm.[16] This sense of ease obviously showed. The captain assured Francis Beaufort that "Darwin has not yet shown *one* trait which has made me feel other than glad when I reflect how much we shall be together."[17] Dining with the junior officers, on the other hand, was decidedly unpleasant. On the one evening that Darwin was invited, they tormented him with tall stories about crossing the line and the "williwaws" of Tierra del Fuego, pointedly making their conversation "rough & . . . oftentimes so full of slang & sea phrases that it is as unintelligible as Hebrew to me." He felt unwelcome and a complete outsider. To his eyes the professionals appeared frivolous and unhelpful, as crudely boisterous as the freshest of university freshmen: "very troublesome for me," he told Caroline.

But idleness and delay rubbed on everybody's nerves, especially the captain's. As time pressed on and little progress seemed to be made, FitzRoy's mood worsened until he could bear it no longer. He erupted on a boring afternoon in Plymouth after frittering away the day shopping with Darwin. Suddenly, Darwin came face to face with FitzRoy's mercurial temper—and with his candour in apologising afterwards.

> At Plymouth before we sailed, he was extremely angry with a dealer in crockery who refused to exchange some article purchased in his shop: the Captain asked the man the price of a very expensive set of china and said "I should have purchased this if you had not been so disobliging." As I knew that the cabin was amply stocked with crockery, I doubted whether he had any such intention; and I must have shown my doubts in my face, for I said not a word. After leaving the shop he looked at me, saying You do not believe what I have said, and I was forced to own that it was so. He was silent for a few minutes and then said You are right, and I acted wrongly in my anger at the blackguard.[18]

Other disagreements followed during the years of the voyage. At least two of them were just as memorable as the first, but none involved the same quality of petulance that so shocked the younger man standing in a china shop. Darwin saw in FitzRoy's outburst the workings of aristocratic privilege: the absolute power of the British ruling classes. He said nothing because FitzRoy so clearly held his immediate future in his hands.

Privately, he resolved to speak out if there was ever another similar occasion; and so he did, later in the voyage, upsetting the well-ordered stability of the ship's social relations until FitzRoy again delivered a magnificent apology. To the end of his life Darwin always remembered these bad-mannered incidents, the worst aspects of the captain's temper. There was another, darker side, he realised, to his "beau ideal" of a naval man.

III

Over and above desultory activities like these there was plenty of opportunity for anxious thoughts. Darwin worried about leaving home for so long and about his compatibility with his new companions. He missed the cosy ambience of Cambridge. His future began to look bleaker, lonelier, and more uncertain than he had expected. What would happen to everyone while he was away? What might happen to himself? Fears about his ability to carry out what was expected of him also ran riot—although in truth he overestimated the extent that either FitzRoy or Henslow anticipated striking new results in natural history. He wondered about Fanny Owen. Should he have said something positive about marriage?

Not surprisingly, his doubts and anxieties dissolved into a range of minor physical disabilities. The skin around his mouth exploded in a nervous rash; and he began experiencing what he believed were heart tremors, pains in his chest that he thought must be signs of some incipient disease. Torn by conflicting emotions, he was simultaneously convinced that he was too ill to go and that he could not let himself be thwarted now.

In later life, Darwin was capable of discussing these pre-voyage afflictions with some insight:

> These two months at Plymouth were the most miserable which I ever spent, though I exerted myself in various ways. I was out of spirits at the thought of leaving all my family and friends for so long a time, and the weather seemed to me inexpressibly gloomy. I was also troubled with palpitations and pain about the heart, and like many a young ignorant man, especially one with a smattering of medical knowledge, was convinced that I had heart-disease. I did not consult any doctor, as I fully expected to hear the verdict that I was not fit for the voyage, and I was resolved to go at all hazards.[19]

He did confide in friends like Fox and Whitley, far away in the Midlands and unlikely to veto his expedition. Yet the difficulties of maintaining a self-imposed silence closer to home made the illnesses—and the fears—seem much worse than they really were.

Left to his own devices in this way, in turn bored, nervous, irritable, and impatient, Darwin did what many people in his position have done. He opened a diary. With considerable lack of imagination, he wrote "Monday, October 24th. Arrived here in the evening after a pleasant drive from London."

He had never felt any urge to record his feelings before. For him, as for others, it took some kind of crisis in his personal life to propel him into action. Only a dramatic upheaval could convince him of the need to make a record of the times he was living through. Faced with a long voyage, fully aware that a new kind of shipboard adventure was starting, emotions at bursting point, painfully conscious that he was stepping out into an unknown world without his usual solicitous empire of family and friends, Darwin plainly believed the occasion should not pass unremarked.

But he felt awkward writing about himself. In the first few pages he stuck closely to charting the simple chronology of his daily occupations. As the days went by, however, he managed to overcome this self-consciousness and began using his diary for recounting events in longer, more contemplative detail. Thrown upon his own resources, no friends as yet among the junior officers, FitzRoy preoccupied with a multitude of necessary affairs, the personal doubts and dangers gathering momentum, his family far away, and the practical difficulties of a sea voyage becoming ever more apparent, Darwin found his journal a comfort. In its pages he recreated the friendly conversations he would have had with his sisters or Erasmus if they had been there to share the experience, describing his impatience and "panic on the old subject [of] want of room" and his awareness of being an uneducated "shore-going fellow" always in the way of the ropes and other paraphernalia on deck, and acknowledging that all his thoughts "are now centered in the future & it is with great difficulty that I can talk or think on any other subject."[20]

Naturally these views also found their way into letters, but Darwin was here developing the foundations of a personal style. Impressed with the magnitude of the recent changes in his life, he learned to observe and describe the people and places he saw in and around Devonport. He learned to think about his feelings and how to express them in a good-humoured, unpretentious way. He found he had an eye for an anecdote or amusing incident, often featuring himself as an ignorant "Landsman" or the butt of someone else's nautical joke. The task of writing entries became easier and easier, and by December, still tied to the port by bad weather and other delays, he was capable of expressing thoughts that would, even in October, have been difficult for him to catch in words. Gradually, over the months, he developed an ability to make his life and diary into a continuum so that the book and the keeping of it became an important aspect of the reality it chronicled. He began to create himself as the man who joined the *Beagle* expedition.

IV

All the various elements of his pre-sailing frustrations were brought to a head by a letter from Fanny Owen, closely followed by another when she heard that the *Beagle* was delayed in leaving. Full of gossip, as he had come to expect, her mind running on weddings and her sister Sarah's final walk to the "halter," she offered her fond farewells:

> Pray my dear Charles do write me one last adieu if you have a spare half hour before you sail—I should like very much to send you some account of us now & then during y^r absence if I knew where to direct to you? You cannot imagine how I have *missed* you already at the Forest, & how I do long to see you again—may every happiness & pleasure attend you dear Charles, and return to us as soon as *you can* I *selvishly* say!—I miss poor Sarah very much it seems like a dream I can hardly yet believe she is really gone! I have no news really to tell you. I wish I had. . . . what a steady *old sober body* you will find me when you return from your Savage Islands—Miss Fanny Sparling, is going to marry *Dry Corbett!!!* This is said every where as a positive fact. . . . If you have time write to me my dear Charles——how I do wish you had not this horrible *Beetle* taste you might have staid *"asy"* with us here I cannot bear to part with you for so long—[21]

She enclosed a "leetle purse" decorated with her own embroidery "in remembrance of the *Housemaid* of the *Black Forest.*"

Folded small and carefully put away with the others, this letter went with Darwin on the *Beagle*. How many times it was unfolded and read again in the next few months can only be imagined, but it is known for sure that Darwin's affections, deeply moved at the moment of departure, were always kept secret. Not from Fanny, who appeared to be relatively well informed about his feelings or capable of making a few shrewd guesses. She did her best to be reassuring. "You say what changes will happen before you come back—& you hope I shall not have quite forgotten you—I doubt not you will find me in *status quo* at the Forest only grown *old* & *sedate*—but wherever I may be whatever changes may have happen'd *none* there *will* ever be in my opinion of you—so do not my dear Charles talk of *forgetting*."[22] And not really from his sisters, who knew there was something significant in the Woodhouse air.

These inner feelings were primarily kept secret from his *Beagle* companions. FitzRoy was too recent an acquaintance to be told, and perhaps in Darwin's opinion not the best person to share sentimental thoughts with. There is nothing to suggest that Darwin ever revealed his romantic hopes and fears to FitzRoy or to the other naval officers at any stage of the voyage. Oddly enough, FitzRoy might have welcomed the opportunity. He too had an attachment. Mary Henrietta O'Brien was the daughter of an Irish country gentleman, formerly a major general in the army, whom FitzRoy met during the stressful months in London spent trying to find support for his Fuegian mission. Almost nothing else is known about her. Darwin, for one, had no idea that his captain was in love and that, even before the *Beagle* left Devonport, FitzRoy had resolved to ask her to marry him on his return. This he was to do, and less than two weeks after his ship finally docked in Plymouth on 4 October 1836, she would accept his proposal.[23] But the two travellers, as straitlaced and reserved as only English gentlemen can be, managed to circumnavigate the globe together without a single hint about the state of their hearts passing their lips.

Wistful recollections of what he was leaving behind began to eclipse all other sensations. The voyage was like going into exile, he told Fox.

Why I shall be an old man, by the time I return, far too old to look out for a little wife. What a number of changes will have happened; I suppose you will be married & have at least six small children.—I shall very much enjoy seeing you attempting to nurse all six at once,—& I shall sit by the fire & tell such wondrous tales, as no man will believe.—When I think of all that I am going to see & undergo, it really requires an effort of reasoning to persuade myself, that all is true,—that I shall see the same land, that

Captain Cook did. I almost doubt the truth of the old truism, that man may do, what man has done,—when I think that I, an unfortunate landsman, am going to undertake such a voyage.—[24]

"Oh Lord what a jolly place Cambridge is," he sighed to Whitley in the next post. "But it is all over, so there is no use thinking about it. But I cannot help it; I suppose jolly old Herbert and F Watkins are up there.—I swear I would go without my dinner to sit by & see you three eat one. As for old Herbert, I will beat him in telling lies when I come back, if I dont may all men cry eternal shame on my soul.—I wish you three men the quickest the largest & the best digestions of any men in the united kingdoms."[25]

V

When the *Beagle* at last left Britain, Darwin was already homesick, depressed, and ready to question the wisdom of his entire enterprise. FitzRoy's prediction that he might leave at the first port of call was well founded. Even Henslow's words of farewell rang hollowly in his ears. Inside the first volume of a smartly bound set of Humboldt's *Personal Narrative,* the professor had proudly written: "J. S. Henslow to his friend C. Darwin on his departure from England upon a voyage round the world. 21 Sept. 1831."[26]

As chance would have it, an odd combination of circumstances made it impossible for Darwin to jump ship. Furthermore, when an opportunity did eventually present itself, Darwin was feeling so much better, seduced by the warm, still nights of the tropics and his first sight of fish playing round the bows, that he refused to acknowledge that the thought of leaving might have earlier crossed his mind.

To begin with, the *Beagle* failed to stop at Madeira, a place normally used for taking on fresh food and also a centre of British society abroad, being much favoured by holiday-makers and invalids who needed to winter in warmer climates. Only three months further into the year, Darwin's cousin Charlotte Wedgwood and her husband, Charles Langton, were to combine a honeymoon tour in Europe with some valetudinarian weeks on Madeira. Had he left the ship in Funchal, Darwin could have filled his time usefully and enjoyably until their arrival. But the *Beagle* did not even get close to the island. Despite the Admiralty's instructions to anchor in the bay, FitzRoy felt there was such a heavy sea running it was not worth the extra effort. For his part, Darwin was "much too sick even to get up to see the distant outline."

They made instead for Tenerife, an alternative location for the chronometric measurements ordered by the Admiralty, and not much further off. It was here, if anywhere, that Darwin might give up and leave the voyage. The potent image of Humboldt's Tenerife that had inexorably drawn Henslow,

Ramsay, and Darwin together during the previous year at Cambridge in order to plan a natural history expedition would not be easy to resist; and it was Humboldt's words that had inspired Darwin's intense desire to travel, a wish so often expressed and so deeply felt at Cambridge that it became an integral part of his passion for nature. FitzRoy thought it highly likely that Darwin would not come back on board ship after tasting this naturalist's paradise.

But the *Beagle* did not call at Tenerife either. The consul in Santa Cruz was afraid of naval visitors bringing the seeds of cholera to this isolated community, and recent outbreaks in a number of crowded English cities convinced him of the need to impose strict quarantine regulations on incoming ships. FitzRoy was not prepared to wait in harbour for the statutory dozen days and gave the order to make due south for the Cape Verde Islands.

Bitterly disappointed by the turn of events, Darwin could only express the depth of his despair to his diary. "I must have another gaze at this long wished for object of my ambition.—Oh misery, misery . . . we have left perhaps one of the most interesting places in the world, just at the moment when we were near enough for every object to create, without satisfying, our utmost curiosity."[27]

Luckily, it was at this point that his seasickness began to ease. The relative calm of the subtropical ocean, the air "still & deliciously warm," the only sounds "the waves rippling on the stern & the sails idly flapping round the masts," and the sky "so clear & lofty," combined to help him get on his feet again. Leaving Tenerife without landing (a "real calamity" for him, noted FitzRoy in his logbook), was not as insupportable as it might have been: there was the prospect of fishing for scientific specimens as the ship glided gently towards equatorial waters, trawling for plankton and jellyfish with one of his interestingly complicated iron-and-gauze contraptions, unpacking his microscope and papers, time for reading, working, and admiring the fine moonlit nights.

"No one could withstand such delightful weather," he told his diary, and almost as if echoing a new compact with the sea, the pale grey morning mist lifted as the *Beagle* nosed its defiant way out of Santa Cruz harbour. Out on the deck taking a final, regretful look, Darwin acknowledged the grandeur of the view behind him and the prospect of other unseen lands to come, the sun tinting the snowy peak, "the scene most beautiful & varied." Such moments "can & do repay the tedious suffering of sickness."[28] Optimism flooded over him. He meant to stay with FitzRoy till the distant end.

Despite this spirited resolve, Darwin never managed to find his sea-legs. Just as FitzRoy feared, the ocean was a cruel enemy to him throughout the expedition and he always felt "wretchedly out of spirits & very sick" whenever the *Beagle* sailed. Some weeks were better than others, as might be expected, yet even on the last leg of the voyage, with only four months left to go before turning up the Channel again, Darwin was still complaining, "I positively suffer more from sea sickness, now, than three years ago."[29] The same thoughts were expressed more vehemently to Fox: "I hate every wave of the ocean," he protested, "with a fervour, which you who have only seen the green waters of the shore can never understand. I will take good care no one shall ever persuade me again to volunteer as Philosopher (my accustomed title) even to a line of Battle Ship."[30] Writing home to the calm, spacious comforts of Shrewsbury, he declared: "I loathe, I abhor the sea and all ships which sail on it. Not even the thrill of geology makes up for the misery and vexation of spirit that comes with sea-sickness."

This continued handicap was no secret on board the *Beagle*. Stokes remembered Darwin's discomfort vividly. "Perhaps no one can better testify to his early and most trying labours than myself. We worked together for several years at the same table in the poop cabin of the *Beagle* during her celebrated voyage, he with his microscope and myself at the charts. It was often a very lively end of the little craft, and distressingly so to my old friend, who suffered greatly from sea-sickness. After, perhaps, an hour's work he would say to me, 'Old fellow, I must take the horizontal for it,' that being the best relief position from ship motion; a stretch out on one side of the table for some time would enable him to resume his labours for a while, when he had again to lie down."[31]

Other shipmates like Alexander Burns Usborne, the master's assistant, agreed he was such a "dreadful sufferer" that the slightest reduction in the amount of sail would earn the watch-officer some heartfelt personal acknowledgement. Up to the end of the journey, FitzRoy was writing home that "Mr Darwin is a martyr to confinement and sea-sickness when under way."[32]

Nonetheless, Darwin's subsequent fame has tended to obscure the rather obvious point that during the voyage itself his stomach upsets were unimportant in the overall economy of the ship. To most of the officers on board, seasickness was unremarkable, a routine inconvenience that extra personnel like Darwin had to deal with each in his own way. Many experienced sailors had their uncomfortable times. It made no difference to them whether Darwin felt good or bad, whether he stayed or went: the *Beagle* would have continued on its course, as planned, even if its guest had left at the first or second port of call. FitzRoy would have been piqued by the failure of his careful arrangements, but he would have carried on regardless. The ship was an independent entity with a life and purpose of its own. Darwin's presence, and his sicknesses, were peripheral to the real functions of the voyage.

VI

The Admiralty's requirements were naturally paramount. No Royal Navy ship was ever sent out without an expressed purpose that had been checked, counter-checked, and approved by several government offices and, at the last hurdle, financed by the British treasury. The *Beagle* expedition, like all such voyages, was assigned many tasks to fulfil, and the ship's route was closely supervised by the Hydrographer's Office on behalf of the Admiralty lords. FitzRoy had to report back to London at regular intervals and to the major British outposts dotted around the globe, each time checking and revising his instructions as advised by superior officers. Seagoing captains had to work to a plan.

The Admiralty's primary aim lay in obtaining a geographical and hydrographic survey of Tierra del Fuego and the southern coasts of South America. Yet the ship's instructions included a great deal more than that, undoubtedly at Beaufort's insistence. The voyage was also the first full-scale attempt made by the British to plot the course of an entire circumnavigation by marine chronometers. The striking feature of this venture was that Beaufort was able to force it through reams of Admiralty red tape. At his insistence, FitzRoy's ship was equipped as a mobile base for scientific instruments which were going to be used in counterpoint with other measurements taken on land, in the observatories or other stations established by Britain in the southern hemisphere.

To that end the *Beagle* carried a set of clocks that ran on Greenwich Mean Time throughout the voyage, and officers recorded the time intervals between predetermined stations, back-checking with the sun, stars, and existing navigational charts. If all went well, FitzRoy would arrive back at Greenwich with a series of readings taken in sequence around the globe adding up to twenty-four hours exactly.

Few captains could have been more eager or better qualified than FitzRoy to throw themselves into this kind of instrument-based science. He was one of a very small number of naval officers to arrive at their position through the technological and mathematical training offered at the Royal Naval College rather than through patronage—although in the end FitzRoy relied on patronage just like the rest. Beaufort chose him with these qualifications in mind. The more accurate the timepieces, and the more of them there were in case of mechanical failure, the better the results; and FitzRoy's first action after being put in command was to insist on increasing their number. Whereas the Admiralty provided eleven chronometers of various kinds, convinced that this ought to be adequate for even the most scrupulous time-keeping, and at Beaufort's demand grudgingly borrowed a handful more from other government departments, FitzRoy considered it essential to supplement the official quota with another six, commissioned and paid for out of his own pocket. These were bedded in sawdust rather than hung on the Admiralty's gimbals, and then mounted in special housings as close to the centre of the ship as possible. Only FitzRoy and George Stebbing, the specialist travelling attendant from Plymouth, were allowed to touch them.

Twenty-two chronometers were surely enough, thought Beaufort in the privacy of the Hydrographer's Office, while applauding the thrust for accuracy lying behind FitzRoy's precautions.

In other areas, Beaufort could not afford to be so compliant about the captain's relish for the advancing technology of science. Lightning conductors and a large new galley-stove were improvements he was pleased to make. He also authorised the testing of an experimental device for measuring depths, and allowed the ship to stock supplies of meat preserved in tin cans. (The depth device proved more successful than the canned meat which exploded.) He asked FitzRoy to try out one of his own inventions as well—the Beaufort wind scale devised by him as a way of quantifying the force of winds at sea.[33] The *Beagle* was therefore the first ship to go out from Britain capable of specifying with mathematical exactitude the strength of gales it experienced. But Beaufort finally drew the line when FitzRoy wanted to replace the *Beagle*'s guns—good solid iron cannon, veterans of Trafalgar— with expensive brass ones that did not interfere with his fancy new compasses.

There was no stopping the captain's obsessions, however. Faced with Beaufort's refusal to comply with his request about the guns, FitzRoy provided two nine-pounders at his own expense, quietly bringing them on board and getting rid of some of the iron cannon when he was far away in Rio de Janeiro, out of reach of officialdom.

FitzRoy's initial duty was to take the *Beagle* across the Atlantic to Bahia (now Salvador) in Brazil to resolve a discrepancy between French and British measurements of the line of longitude. Then he was to survey the coastline from Buenos Aires to Port Desire and, after the southern winter, to explore as much of Tierra del Fuego as possible before running through to the west. While in Tierra del Fuego, he had permission to set up the Anglican mission that was the original incentive for the expedition. He hoped to land the three English-speaking Fuegians in the western arm of the Beagle Channel, where they had been picked up during the previous voyage, along with Richard Matthews, the volunteer missionary from London. The ship would return at intervals during the next few surveying seasons to monitor progress.

After that, he had to take chronometric measurements at various specified locations in the Pacific and Indian oceans. Accordingly, the *Beagle* was to make brief calls at Tahiti, New Zealand, Sydney, and Hobart in Tasmania, before sailing through the coral islets of the Indian Ocean, where Beaufort had a few knotty navigational problems of his own that he wanted investigated. Then they were to return via the Cape of Good Hope. The voyage should last two to three years, thought Admiralty officials, depending on the weather and the technical difficulty of the work. Beaufort, concerned about results, gave FitzRoy a free hand to extend or compress the survey as he saw fit—as long as he did not go too far over budget.

Far more significant in contemporary terms were the political implications of the voyage. Expeditions like this were invariably drawn up to fulfill complex administrative and national purposes in which geographical exploration and the rhetoric of discovery were only parts—albeit essential parts—of the developing infrastructure of empire. Cook's voyages of the 1770s, for example, though replete with scientific achievements, including the astronomical observation of the transit of Venus, were essentially aimed at claiming Australia for the crown. Joseph Banks's botanical activities during Cook's first voyage established the potential for British settlements—and a penal colony—in New South Wales; and subsequent expeditions to the area claimed other important lands for Britain, including New Zealand and as many of the Pacific islands as the race with France would allow. Captains Flinders, Parry, Beechey, and Ross similarly set out from Britain with colonial expansion as part of their remit.[34] The whole point of the British Admiralty's desire to chart southern Latin America was to enable informed decisions to be made on naval, military, and commercial operations along the unexplored coastline south of Buenos Aires and to enable Britain to establish strong footholds in these areas, so recently released from their commitment to trade only with Spain and Portugal. Were there gold or diamond deposits as there were in Brazil? They knew there was guano, the raw material of a vast fertiliser industry for early-nineteenth-century Britain, and important salt pans. By skilful manoeuvring the British foreign minister George Canning had managed until then to keep France out of much of South America; but he needed more definite commercial links to add weight to the British position in the European balance of power, as well as to protect an estimated £150 million of English money invested in speculative South American ventures.[35] His successor Viscount Palmerston deftly maintained the same policy. In his hands, Spain and Portugal were diverted from absolutism, and a federation of free South American states beckoned alluringly.

So it was no coincidence that the same coastline was surveyed by a French expedition under the command of Du Petit Thouars at exactly the time FitzRoy made his way through the area, and that French naturalists like Alcide d'Orbigny and Claude Gay were independently working in Patagonia and Chile collecting information and specimens for the Paris Muséum d'Histoire Naturelle. Another survey concentrating on the Río de la Plata under Lieutenant L. M. Barral was carried out in 1830–32. And the French were not alone. The United States was a powerful commercial threat to Britain after the lead taken by President Monroe in recognising the Argentine states' trading independence. The Russian naval explorer Otto von Kotzebue hovered in the Pacific Ocean. A German naturalist was unexpectedly discovered by Darwin working away in deepest Chile.

It was not unreasonable for Beaufort to send out additional British ships after the *Beagle* left. Captain Paget of H.M.S. *Samarang* took the same route around South America as the *Beagle,* unintentionally shadowing FitzRoy's footsteps through 1831–35, and Captain Beechey of H.M.S. *Sulphur* was commissioned to survey the west coast of Central and South America in 1835. More than 250 British merchant ships carried manufactured goods to the area during the same period.[36] The *Beagle*'s captain was inextricably engaged in the emergent business of colonisation.

FitzRoy was also responsible for his crew and for the protection of British nationals at the ports they called at. The *Beagle* was involved in several incidents, including military action in Montevideo and a major naval blockade off Buenos Aires. The Falkland Islands, ceded to Britain by Spain in 1771 and then annexed by Buenos Aires in 1820, were a necessary stopping place at which the flag literally had to be shown. A government fine was to be exacted from the queen of Tahiti. Local consuls and government officials had to be visited, messages passed on, the state of the dominions judged, and rival political leaders assessed. FitzRoy was obliged to think politics and negotiate his ship through government policy as well as fulfil the more practical investigations of the survey. His official Admiralty instructions, individually tailored for this particular surveying expedition, and including all such government requirements, were always to hand in the cabin and were regularly referred to and discussed by FitzRoy and his closest officers.

A naval ship was in another sense an emissary, a floating reservoir of British news and views, the bringer of letters and newspapers from home or from ports further down the coast, a vehicle for taking on temporary passengers or filling vacancies, a place for official parties and receptions, always alive to colonial society overseas. Many residents depended on the social and political vigour that ships brought with them; and other places, though perfectly self-contained, welcomed the excitement. Much of Rio de Janeiro's high society revolved around the British admirals and officers stationed there, as to a lesser degree did the life of expatriates in Valparaiso, Montevideo, and Bahia. This kind of overseas society was hardly provincial. Visiting captains were part of an extended network of government officials, retired gentlefolk, shipping agents, managers, and commercial entrepreneurs that included not only figures like Captain King, the previous commander of the

Beagle, now residing on his family estates in Bathurst, Australia, but no less than two great astronomers: John Herschel, who arrived in Cape Town in 1834 to make his southern observations, and Thomas Maclear, the British royal astronomer, who ran the observatory there. Small towns in Chile possessed their local gentry pursuing occupations appropriate to their standing, and larger cities like Buenos Aires, Valparaiso, and Montevideo sported libraries, museums, botanic gardens, theatres, and opera houses. The ship itself was an integral part of the colonial network. Darwin may have been alone in some literal manner, a solitary naturalist pursuing his individual researches, but he travelled along the strands of a well-organised web of empire where the commitments and interests of British society constantly met and accompanied him.

Responsibilities like these, moreover, came early in a naval officer's career. FitzRoy was twenty-six years old, Stokes was nineteen, John Clements Wickham, the first lieutenant, was the oldest officer on board at thirty-three. Darwin was twenty-two. It is worth emphasising that the voyage was undertaken by young men confident of their youthful ability to get things done. They had few doubts about their capacity to withstand all the privations of nineteenth-century sea travel. FitzRoy wanted desperately to succeed: to produce the best surveys, keep the best ship, complete the exercise more efficiently than required. Less ambitiously perhaps, Wickham and Stokes hoped to keep their place on the promotion ladder and eventually command their own ships on similar projects. Everyone on board had aims for the future. Darwin too, though seeing few such clear objectives at the start, regarded the voyage as a tremendous opportunity. Like the others, he intended to make the most of his time on board.

VII

The chance came sooner than he expected. After turning away from Tenerife, the *Beagle* made for the Atlantic island of St. Jago, one of the charred volcanic outcrops of the Cape Verde group, about 450 miles from the coast of Africa. For Darwin, this desolate location turned out to be one of the most important landings of the whole expedition. St. Jago was the first place he disembarked—the first foreign soil he stepped on as a natural history explorer— and the island carried a special light in his affections for that reason. More than this, it was the place where he began pulling together all his diverse early natural history experiences and took a deliberate step into the world of investigative science. It always glowed in his memory as the site of a philosophical and personal initiation.

While FitzRoy and the others busied themselves with chronometric and astronomical observations, Darwin spent the time in a tropical fervour.

From the first, he thrilled to the dramatic scenery, a striking combination of barren volcanic cones and lush, verdant valleys. St. Jago and its tiny neighbour Quail Island were the greenest of the islands, which were more usually streaked white by sand from the Sahara. He revelled in the sight of coconut palms and orange trees, wasted no time about buying a banana in the market ("maukish & sweet with little flavor"), and plunged into a valley beside the harbour of Porto Praya to recreate Humboldt's vibrant Canary Island experiences:

> Here I first saw the glory of tropical vegetation. Tamarinds, Bananas & Palms were flourishing at my feet.—I expected a good deal, for I had read Humboldt's descriptions & I was afraid of disappointments: how utterly vain such fear is, none can tell but those who have experienced what I to day have.—It is not only the gracefulness of their forms or the novel richness of their colours, it is the numberless & confusing associations that rush together on the mind, & produce the effect.—I returned to the shore, treading on Volcanic rocks, hearing the notes of unknown birds, & seeing new insects fluttering about still newer flowers.—It has been for me a glorious day, like giving to a blind man eyes.—he is overwhelmed with what he sees & cannot justly comprehend it.—Such are my feelings, & such may they remain.—[37]

Awash in new sensations, Darwin then turned to the natural history of the island with unconcealed delight. Barely knowing where to start, he collected everything he could find, especially the sea animals in the rock pools stretched along the foot of the coastal cliffs, each strange new form gathered with increasingly satisfied cries of delight. An octopus entranced him by blushing furiously as it scuttled for cover. Born and raised in the heart of the English countryside, Darwin had no idea that this animal changes colour; in fact, he thought he had discovered something new and eagerly returned the next day armed with coloured reference cards to test its ability. He managed to catch another one to take back in a box to his cabin in the *Beagle*. What else might octopuses do, he wondered; and, obligingly, it glowed in the dark. He crowed over his discoveries in a letter to Henslow and was embarrassed to be told how well known these attributes really were.

It was not long, either, before recollections of the heady pleasures of geological work with Sedgwick came rushing back, amplified this time by a great deal more background information gleaned from his systematic reading in the subject in Devonport and at sea. Free from the mental turbulence and ill health of the previous weeks, and longing to do something intellectually stimulating, Darwin was ready to bring everything he ever learned to bear on the physical structure of this obscure little landfall.

Within two days, Darwin believed he understood the geological history of the island, a major claim for an inexperienced amateur to make after such a brief examination of a new area and frivolous if it had not been for the restless ingenuity that he unleashed on this first independent geological problem. It could have been a rerun of his apparent octopus discovery. But Darwin fizzed with possible interpretations, bubbling with a multitude of ideas about what might have happened in the past, his mind "a perfect *hurricane* of delight & astonishment."

Looking at the most pronounced geological features of the land around him, he decided that a stream of molten lava had formerly flowed over the bed of the sea, baking shells and pieces of coral into a hard white rock. Since then the sea bottom must have been elevated by some subterranean force which brought the rocks up into the air, making an island whose cliffs were interlaced with a prominent white band. Irregularities in the band suggested successive volcanic activity and some partial subsidence. All this, he inferred, must have taken place quite recently in geological terms. The shells in the white rock were the same as those of live creatures on the beach below.[38]

What Darwin was proposing was an interpretation quite unlike those current among the majority of his more experienced contemporaries. Robert Jameson, his former teacher at Edinburgh University, believed most volcanic structures were extremely ancient—not unreasonable in view of the venerable mountains of Scotland—and would not have entertained the possibility that islands had changed their level in recent times by many feet. Sedgwick and Henslow, although not nearly so conservative in their geology as Jameson, were just as cautious about allowing the possibility that great changes had taken place in geological periods relatively close to the present day. None of them would have thought it likely, either, that land could rise up out of the sea so gently and regularly that bands of rock remained parallel with the horizon: the very nature of subterranean activity implied that uplift was usually accompanied by fractures and strong irregularities. A more feasible circumstance to explain the horizontal bedding of the cliffs at St. Jago was a gradual withdrawal of the waters—not an elevation of the land.

Darwin was evidently thinking big and thinking differently from those who had first taught him.[39] Out on his own at last, traversing ground no geologist had studied before, burning with the proprietorial sensations felt by all fieldworkers, well aware that this was "his" country, free to be understood and made his own, he was sure he was right. He was knowledgeable enough to realise that his views differed radically from the general run entertained by his teachers, but no matter. That was part of their charm.

Deeply stirred by the excitement of hard scientific thought, he succumbed to the full force of ambition. To chase a theory through the mind like this was marvellous: an intoxicating combination of effort, skill, caution, and bravery—

and in this case too, a healthy dose of ignorance which encouraged imaginative leaps in the geological dark—were called into play in turn, beguiling in
their sudden rushes and withdrawals, completely fulfilling at their moment
of coherence into a likely answer. He caught a glimpse of his own powers
and recognised a new kind of desire—the wish to make a contribution to the
world of philosophical natural history.

He remembered the moment till the day he died. Sitting on the beach on
nearby Quail Island, leaning against the rock face whose origins provided
such cerebral enjoyment, "ripe tamarinds & biscuit" for lunch, Darwin
decided to write about his findings.

"It then first dawned on me that I might perhaps write a book on the
geology of the various countries visited, and this made me thrill with delight.
That was a memorable hour to me, and how distinctly I can call to mind the
low cliff of lava beneath which I rested, with the sun glaring hot, a few
strange desert plants growing near, and with living corals in the tidal pools at
my feet."[40]

With these happy thoughts he took his first—and very determined—step
into the world of science, full of youth and *brio*.

VIII

It would be wrong, however, to suggest that Darwin came to his conclusions
unaided or that his future progress was always so briskly positive. The
theories of Charles Lyell, as put forward in his *Principles of Geology* (1830–33),
were crucial to Darwin's understanding of the structure of St. Jago and
central to all his other activities during the rest of the voyage. In one of the
most remarkable interchanges in the history of science, Lyell's book taught
Darwin how to think about nature.[41] Without Lyell there would have been no
Darwin: no intellectual journey, no voyage of the *Beagle* as commonly
understood. His influence—and his impact—on the young traveller can hardly
be overestimated.

Darwin had read only part of Lyell's *Principles* by the time he landed on
St. Jago, but he was already delighted with the grand theoretical schemes he
found there. FitzRoy had made a present to him of the first volume before
they left England, a gift reflecting FitzRoy's interest in the subject, and also
the fact that he had met Lyell some months earlier when the geologist asked
for several observations to be made in South America on his behalf. Teasingly,
FitzRoy gave Darwin another present at the same time in the shape of an
English grammar.[42] Like Stokes, he put little faith in a Cambridge education.
Inscribed in the front and dated 1831, the grammar went into the poop cabin
book locker along with Lyell.

Previous to this, Darwin probably heard of Lyell's views from Sedgwick during their excursion in Wales, particularly in relation to the fossil record. Sedgwick no doubt reiterated his scathing opinion of Lyell's palaeontology as delivered in his presidential address to the Geological Society that same year. More ambivalently, Henslow had also recommended that Darwin get a copy of the work before setting sail, but warned him "on no account to accept the views therein advocated."

What the two university professors disliked so much was Lyell's insistence that the earth's changes were not necessarily progressive in nature. Lyell's earth was forever on the move, but the movements, he emphasised, were not going anywhere, were not directed to any future point or coloured by their first beginnings. There was no obvious correlation between the Christian story of a beginning and an end and geological history: no correlation between the broadly directional account given in the Bible and the widely accepted geological theory of a gradually cooling earth progressively adapted for successive batches of living beings each more complex than the last and culminating in the creation of mankind. Everything, Lyell said bluntly, could be explained without this kind of theological underpinning. He thought large sections of the earth's crust were pushed up or depressed relative to sea level according to the pressure from internal molten rock, and that these changes by themselves accounted for all the different phenomena usually attributed to the gradual cooling of the earth's core. Elevation was part of a continuous fluctuation of the earth's surface and was always balanced at some place or another by reciprocal and compensatory subsidence. The system was not directed by any external force nor regulated from within. Instead, Lyell's earth was self-balancing and self-contained. In modern terms, it was "steady-state."

Further to this, Lyell declared that fossils were no sure guide to the course of earth history either. He claimed that the increasing perfection of flora and fauna usually discerned in the rocks was an illusion: a mere artefact brought about by a combination of wishful thinking and incomplete evidence. Complex animals and plants might have lived very early in geological history, he asserted, and have escaped our notice. The remains of fish or mammals might be discovered in deposits usually thought far too early for them. It was unwise, he went on to say, to base the whole of geology on the idea of a progressive advance, each improved creation coming after the next. Sooner or later the serpent of transmutation would rear its head and no one—least of all the geological natural theologians—would have the intellectual backing to stop it. Genuinely aghast at the thought of animal ancestry, Lyell saw the dangers lurking in directional geology and hoped his scheme of "non-progress" would help maintain an unbridgeable divide between mankind and beasts.[43]

This concept of a self-balancing, nonprogressive earth lay at the heart of Lyell's method, subsequently labelled "uniformitarianism" by William Whewell. Lyell explained how all geological agencies such as volcanic activity or the weathering effects of the sea, wind, or rain never change in intensity—that geological forces always act at the same rate, both nowadays and in the past. Nothing could happen faster or slower than today. No agents other than those seen today could have existed. Taken as strictly as Lyell intended, this view specifically excluded the idea that there might have been some intensely active epochs long ago when mountain ranges were built or continents rose up out of the sea. If the geological timescale was expanded to an enormous length, so long that it became unnecessary to think of the earth's having a beginning or an end, all these geological features could be explained as having happened gradually. Major geological events had certainly taken place, Lyell conceded, but only at the same rate as the forces acting today.

Still, Lyell's arguments were not nearly as new as he asserted. Many of the recommendations were commonplace in early-nineteenth-century science, and, apart from one or two naturalists immersed in continental theories like Jameson, the majority of British geologists—Sedgwick and Murchison among them—considered Lyell's advice on these matters superfluous.[44] Jameson himself thought it redundant. "Although Lyell is amusing," he wrote condescendingly, "it is not what geologists want."[45] Equally, Lyell's ideas about balance and uniformity were similarly unoriginal, since he propounded the doctrine put forward in 1795 by the Edinburgh philosopher James Hutton, elaborated afterwards in more readable form by John Playfair. Both Whewell and William Fitton took him to task for skating so lightly over the innovative work of his predecessors.

But Lyell turned history to his advantage by giving a long and cleverly argued account of the course of geological endeavour from antiquity to the nineteenth century in which everyone who held the same general idea as he did was praised and the rest dismissed as "unscientific" in blatantly one-sided style.[46] Like the Whig historians whom he admired greatly, he recreated the history of his subject from the position of the author, not just as one in which the past creaked painfully towards the present, but also as a story in which certain inviolate truths of nature and liberal principles of thought (as seen by Lyell) were progressively revealed to scholars through the ages. Lyell's "history" of geology was as prejudiced in his favour as it was comprehensive. In particular, he struck out at the vested interests of the clergy inside the universities; and even though he claimed to have "cut out all the bits that a bishop could object to," he went to great lengths to show that geology should be studied without the aid of the established church.

Without severing his ties to the British establishment, without relinquishing his faith in an original and active creator, and unwilling to jeopardise the traditional hierarchies of education and British intellectual life, he ridiculed contemporary attempts to keep biblical truths to the fore when considering the history of the earth. Whiggish and self-serving it certainly was; but his book also called for a reduction in overt natural theology in science. The pages rang with the firm conviction of a man who knew his mind and intended to convince others.

Young and susceptible, Darwin was tremendously impressed. Lyell's glittering prose style, his rich and varied knowledge, his succinct synopses of what was already known about the structure of the earth, his tart characterisation of current controversies and the salient points at issue, his inclination to discuss large issues and ask fundamental questions without risking the label of atheist or political radical, the clarity of his vision, his wit, and the well-integrated nature of the geological history that he evoked were avidly absorbed. Henslow and Sedgwick, though inspiring in their way, had never touched quite the same responsive chord. Loyal as he remained to these his first teachers, Darwin's heart opened out to a very different way of understanding things.

Moreover, when he came to make his first solo excursion into theoretical geology on St. Jago, he found that Lyell's system worked. It helped him analyse and draw appropriate conclusions, and showed him how to test his theories. The *Principles* dangled a key to comprehension. "I had brought with me the first volume of Lyell's *Principles of Geology,* which I studied attentively; and this book was of the highest service to me in many ways. . . . The science of geology is enormously indebted to Lyell—more so, as I believe, than to any other man who ever lived. . . . I am proud to remember that the first place, namely St Jago, in the Cape Verde Archipelago, which I geologised, convinced me of the infinite superiority of Lyell's views over those advocated in any other work known to me."[47] Lyell supplied him with the idea of the gradual elevation and subsidence of landmasses, movements that were taking place even in modern times. This was the anchor of all his forthcoming views.

Darwin went on to geologise through South America, on the Galápagos and Keeling islands, around Sydney, Hobart, and Cape Town, fully convinced of the value of Lyell's interpretation of earth history. He made sure he acquired the next two volumes of the *Principles* during the course of the voyage and worked eagerly to understand the world as if he were Lyell. "I have always thought that the great merit of the *Principles* was that it altered the whole tone of one's mind, and therefore that, when seeing a thing never seen by Lyell, one yet saw it partially through his eyes."[48] Admiration swiftly deepened into profound respect for the man who so stimulated and expanded his own mental boundaries.

Lyell acquired his first and, at that time, only scientific disciple.

IX

Darwin's pleasure in his interpretation of the St. Jago rocks and his joy in discovering an intellectual guide were obvious to FitzRoy. "A child with a new toy could not have been more delighted than he was with St. Jago," he wrote in amusement to Beaufort. "It was odd to hear him say, after we left Porto Praya, 'Well I am *glad* we are *quietly* at *sea* again, for I shall be able to arrange my collections and set to work more methodically.' "[49] Darwin himself burbled happily to his family.

> I do not believe, I have spent one half hour idly since leaving Teneriffe: St Jago has afforded me an exceedingly rich harvest in several branches of Nat: History. . . . Geologising in a Volcanic country is most delightful besides the interest attached to itself it leads you into most beautiful & retired spots.—Nobody but a person fond of Nat. history can imagine the pleasure of strolling under Cocoa nuts in a thicket of Bananas & Coffee plants, & an endless number of wild flowers.—And this Island that has given me so much instruction & delight, is reckoned the most uninteresting place, that we perhaps shall touch at during our voyage.

Nothing could have been more satisfying. He had seen his first palm tree and experienced something of the lushness of the tropics; had devised an explanation for the physical structure of his first landfall; had decided to write a book about this and the geology of other countries shortly to be visited; and was invigorated by the knowledge that many of the specimens waiting in jars and boxes on the *Beagle* were probably new to science or inadequately described in published sources. At last he was reaping the excitement anticipated so long ago in Shrewsbury. His journey had truly started.

LOSS AND NO LOSS

AILING over to Bahia from St. Jago, Darwin and FitzRoy eased into a steady routine which hardly varied through the ensuing years. Like a couple starting out in a marriage, they did their best to be agreeable; and like any newlyweds they quickly found relations were much smoother if they did not spend all their time together.

They ate breakfast together at eight, then each spent the daylight hours pursuing his own interests and obligations. It seemed odd to Darwin's lively imagination—still filled with the boyish adventure stories of his youth—that the captain spent long periods tied to his desk rather than striding around in full dress uniform giving orders like Nelson. By far the greatest proportion of FitzRoy's time was taken up with naval paperwork and administering shipboard justice. Sometimes he was not seen for the whole morning, in which case Lieutenant Wickham might tactfully ask Darwin "whether much hot coffee had been dished out today," meaning how was FitzRoy's temper. (Second Lieutenant Sulivan varied the question by innocently wondering how much sugar went in.) It was a brave junior who dared to interrupt while FitzRoy wrestled with accounts or fusty Admiralty regulations.

Yet the captain was also intensely proud of his men and of his ship, putting herculean effort into turning the *Beagle* into a showcase of neatness and efficiency on behalf of the hydrography department—always a poor relation in the warmongering hierarchies of naval service. He took every possible opportunity to display the crew's combined artistry when coming into port. "We came in first rate style alongside the Admiral's ship," wrote Darwin in breathless admiration after his first few months at sea, "& we, to their astonishment, took in every inch of canvass & then immediately set it again: a sounding ship doing such a perfect manoeuvre with such certainty & rapidity, is an event hitherto unknown in that class." Full of burgeoning naval pride, Darwin joined in the show, hanging on to a rope in each hand, putting another between his teeth, and letting go when Wickham shouted the order. Both he and FitzRoy positively glowed in the light of congratulatory words from the warship's commander.

Most of Darwin's scientific work was carried out in the poop cabin which comprised his living and sleeping quarters. There, on the giant table, he and Stokes would get on with their occupations, the one patiently marking up charts with the results of trigonometric observations and coastal excursions in the whaleboat, the other balancing preparations under his microscope, making drawings, drying and preserving specimens, attaching paper labels to each leg, bottle, or box, writing snatches of letters in between the chores of a natural history collector. "I find to my great surprise that a ship is singularly comfortable for all sorts of work.—Everything is so close at hand, & being cramped, makes one so methodical, that in the end I have been a gainer. . . . if it was not for sea-sickness the whole world would be sailors."[1]

Other time was spent on deck, examining the contents of his trawl, admiring the seagoing birds, puzzling about a snowstorm of butterflies or the red colour given to the sea by millions of minute organisms swirling in the current. Later in the voyage, Darwin also had fossil bones to clean and number, the making of barrels and wooden boxes to supervise, sometimes a fish to catch for supper with his special London hooks, and more often than not the jokes of the junior officers to contend with.

He was ridiculously easy prey for naval humour, as the crew found out on April Fool's Day when one of them called out, "Darwin, did you ever see a Grampus?" Rushing onto the upper deck in a transport of enthusiasm, he was greeted with an empty sea and a roar of laughter from the whole watch.

He was not alone in being the butt of these practical jokes, for even FitzRoy had to submit occasionally. The ceremony held as the ship crossed the equator was a traditional occasion for a crew to torment their captain, and Darwin, as FitzRoy's closest companion, was equally vulnerable. "Crossing the line" in the years after Trafalgar was a boisterous—often cruel—initiation into the "Kingdom of the Deep" in which ordinary jack-tars took any chance that presented itself to even the score with figures of authority. Far from being an empty, purely symbolic gesture, it was customary to push King Neptune's upper-class victims as far as they could go. Darwin and FitzRoy considered that they got off lightly with only a couple of buckets of water tipped over them. But Darwin could not avoid being shaved:

They then lathered my face & mouth with pitch and paint, & scraped some of it off with a piece of roughened iron hoop.—a signal being given I was tilted head over heels into the water, where two men received me & ducked me.—at last, glad enough, I escaped.... The whole ship was a shower bath: & water was flying about in every direction: of course not one person, even the Captain, got clear of being wet through.[2]

FitzRoy glumly recorded that it was one of those traditional amusements of which the omission might be regretted.

The two refined young gentlemen were united by the patrician feeling that they should unbend for these vulgar revels and comfortably in agreement that it was a thoroughly disagreeable practice. "What fools these sailors make of themselves," Darwin said. He was surprised to hear afterwards that he had been exempted from the worst excesses because of his "high standing on board as a friend and messmate of the captain."[3]

He usually took his midday meal with FitzRoy, following the ritual check of the chronometers which the captain supervised daily at noon. After this they would sit down to their papers: FitzRoy to the logbook and then to his personal journal and letters; and Darwin to the various daily details of his natural history work. These hours, though regulated by the changing of the watches, were their own, for neither had a place in the ordinary business of keeping ship. When engaged with others in an onshore surveying party, they took regular turns mounting the evening guard, and Darwin liked sitting up overnight on these dramatic occasions. But there was no such call on their time on the *Beagle* itself.

After Darwin's paperwork was finished he usually joined Wickham or Sulivan for some conversation as they continued with their evening duties. Like the rest, he soon started teasing Sulivan about his propensity to spout blank verse during the night-watch, and listened time and time again to Sulivan's story about the medal he had won for public speaking at school. On tropical evenings he would sit on a boom with Phillip Gidley King, charmed by "the delightful sensation of tropical airs, wafted out of the sails overhead."[4] Every now and then, he was invited into the gunroom to join these officers for a meal, providing them, him, and FitzRoy with some necessary variety. Before long his low opinion of the officers was completely reversed. There never was such a fine body of men, he boasted to the family: "I like the officers much more than I did at first,—especially Wickham & young King, & Stokes & indeed all of them."[5] And so the days went by. Sundays were slightly different in that FitzRoy conducted a long and suitably pious church service to which everyone on board was summoned.

Paperwork, however, was the most usual occupation. Taking the captain as his example, Darwin consciously strived to get into the habit of recording the day's events. As a naval officer was required and trained to do, FitzRoy rarely let an afternoon pass without completing his log and personal journal.

Darwin, too, composed a logbook, filling page after page of foolscap with geological observations compiled from his field notebooks while his memory was fresh.[6] He also opened a comparable log of zoological and botanical observations.[7] By default, the latter came to be almost exclusively concerned with zoology, since Darwin's botany was not up to anything more arduous than taking specimens and making notes on the overall appearance of the vegetation; however, this "zoological diary" was rich in remarks of a more general kind on the local habitat, plant cover, soil, and physical geography of the places visited, as well as the behaviour, colours, voice, preferred food, and other information about the animals he saw. As in FitzRoy's log, details were compiled as a record which could be used by someone else: they were the information naturalists might need to identify or explain Darwin's materials. The routine of this daily writing soon became second nature to him, so much so that while he was staying on shore or travelling overland on collecting excursions he usually attempted to "keep ship's hours," making a deliberate effort to write up his books as FitzRoy had shown him.

To these scientific papers, he added his diary and letters back home. The diary (Darwin called it his "journal," sometimes also his "logbook") was the more significant in serving as a repository of information that was copied out, often word for word, in long, descriptive letters to his sisters and friends. There was, however, a close interplay between the two, and Darwin saw little advantage in dividing scientific and personal doings between them. His journal became very like an extended epistle to his family, and he did, on several occasions, refer to it in letters as another, more authoritative source of his activities written for the family to read. Yet the letters were the only place he could talk of private family feelings. He and his sisters corresponded regularly through the five years of the voyage, exchanging gossip and affection freely. "You must excuse my queer letters," he apologised to them, and "recollect they are generally written in the evening after a long day's work. . . . I take more pains over my Log Book,—so that eventually you will have a good account of all the places I visit." Parts of the journal were sent back to Shrewsbury as supplements to the regular bulletins he gave in letters.[8] Caroline made sure every scrap was saved. Her unspoken fear was that each letter might be his last.

This plethora of written material was one of the unsung achievements of Darwin's activities on the *Beagle* voyage. In keeping such copious records, he learned to write easily about nature and about himself. Like FitzRoy, he taught himself to look closely at his surroundings, to make notes and measurements, and to run through a mental checklist of features that ought to be recorded, never relying entirely on memory and always writing reports soon after the event. Like FitzRoy, he became accustomed to thinking about himself as the central character of his text—the captain of his personal natural history travels, the man responsible for planning and executing collecting trips—and accustomed to explaining his course of action, even if it was only a half-hearted justification of money spent on some expedition into the interior. Although this was ordinary practice in naval affairs, it was for Darwin a basic lesson in arranging his thoughts clearly and an excellent preparation for composing logical scientific arguments that stood him in good stead for many years afterwards.

The daily discipline was severe, and again, he learned from FitzRoy to give it priority. He tagged and numbered specimens, made notes about their location and time of capture with other details where necessary, and prepared duplicate copies of his lists so that nothing would be irretrievably lost. Darwin had not done this as an amateur specimen-hunter in either Edinburgh or Cambridge, and was no doubt advised by Henslow and others on the wisdom of the practice. FitzRoy played an important if unacknowledged role in showing just how the undertaking could be carried out.

FitzRoy's evident approval and encouragement of Darwin's activities also generated an atmosphere in which the officers and crewmen felt it their duty—"captain's orders"—to help him at every opportunity. Darwin carried "a sort of halo of sanctity," wrote Stokes, created by dining at FitzRoy's table. He was the only person on board, for instance, who could address FitzRoy by his surname in the intimate manner of personal friends. He came from the cream of English intellectual society and unquestioningly took his place in its upper reaches.

These social niceties were not lost on any of the people concerned, for it was precisely that kind of distinction that enabled nineteenth-century relationships to run smoothly through the hierarchies on which they were based. On an English ship, where the social stratification was so much more pronounced, the overall success or failure in creating a unified, functioning body of men could very well depend on the minutiae of what people called each other or where they had gone to school. Because of this, it took a couple of months at sea before the junior officers felt they could stop calling Darwin "sir." The change was achieved only by inventing the nickname "Philos," standing for "Ship's philosopher," a label lightheartedly bestowed one day by FitzRoy. It was seized by his companions as one which would ease their interchanges with Darwin while still according him superior status.

Being the captain's friend meant everything.

II

The first row was not long in coming, however. Early in March, FitzRoy and Darwin argued fiercely, so fiercely Darwin thought he ought to return home. All the courtesy generated on board was temporarily flung to the winds in the most emotionally tempestuous moment of the voyage.

Landing at Bahia (Salvador) was the immediate cause. Stepping off the *Beagle* at its mooring in the harbour, Darwin was horrified to find himself in a full-fledged slave society. His hackles automatically rose. Portugal was still legally transporting Africans to Brazil, and no steps towards emancipation would be made until 1858. The scene was a "scandal to Christian nations," Darwin declared to Henslow.

Slavery inflamed all his most passionately held beliefs about human nature. It was the one social issue guaranteed to upset and annoy him throughout his long life. He had no problems with the idea of self-interested commercial expansion through plantation crops, for example, or the grinding poverty, factory children, and indentured servants to be found at home. Like the majority of people he knew, he bowed to the capitalist ethos of the British ruling classes without a qualm. But the actual state of slavery agitated powerfully humanitarian instincts in him. He could not think about it, let alone see it for himself, without boiling over in righteous anger.

Moreover, his Darwin-Wedgwood family background entitled and prepared him to express strong condemnation. Each of his grandfathers had taken a pronounced abolitionist stand in the 1780s and 1790s, as did his father, brother, and sisters in relation to the nineteenth-century emancipation movement, and he now felt similar crusading emotions coursing in his veins. In fact, the first Josiah Wedgwood and the first Erasmus Darwin were central figures in rousing public opinion in Britain during the crucial anti-slavery years at the end of the eighteenth century, along with family friends like Sir James Mackintosh and other influential Whig campaigners. Wedgwood's design, in blue-and-white china, of a Negro in chains below the famous phrase "Am I not a man and a brother?" (which he coined) affirmed all the outraged feelings of the era and was adopted by the Anti-Slavery Society soon after 1787. (It must also be said that the mass production of these cameos was an astute commercial move capitalising on the philanthropic feelings surging through upper- and middle-class Britain.)[9] The first Erasmus Darwin issued his own tirades in *The Botanic Garden,* in which he praised Wedgwood's effort to bring the potter's art into the service of "virtue":

> *The slave, in chains on supplicating knee,*
> *Spreads his wide arms, and lifts his eye to Thee;*

With hunger pale, with wounds and toil opress'd,
"Are we not brethren?" Sorrow chokes the rest.[10]

These stirring words and images were an integral part of Darwin's
upbringing. He was more than familiar with the history and achievements of
the anti-slavery campaign, and had met some of the main protagonists as a
boy at Uncle Jos's house. The milestones that marked the progress of
emancipation were to him family events, telescoped and romanticised in
Wedgwood and Darwin household legend to make it seem as if the poet and
the potter had forced abolition just the day before yesterday. It was in truth a
long-drawn-out process, still unfinished in Darwin's time, first introduced to
Parliament as a motion to inquire into the transport and sale of slaves as early
as 1788. Britain banned trading in its dominions only in 1807. The effects
were not seen until 1811, when Henry Brougham carried a bill that made
human cargo a capital offence.

Passing the laws did not resolve the problems either. Abolishing British
trade merely aggravated the traffic run by other nations, especially since
France, Spain, and Portugal delayed taking legal action for years. Nor did
abolition make life any easier for existing slaves in British dominions. By
1820 or so, it was plain to stalwarts of the anti-trading movement like
William Wilberforce that actual slave-holding should be abolished in British
territories overseas. Under his aegis, and whipped up by an avalanche of
printed material constituting Britain's first experience of mass public propaganda, the reforming zeal which began life as a minority principle among a
small band of liberals and evangelicals became a national, pervasive obsession that captured the imagination and energies of millions.[11] Britain's civilising
mission was in large part thereafter portrayed as a drive to purge the
"uncivilised" world of its pagan, slaving habits.

Darwin was travelling the world just when these mass philanthropic
movements climaxed in Britain. In 1828 the free people of colour in the
colonies were placed on a footing of legal equality with whites, a policy
mostly intended to benefit the indigenous blacks in South Africa. It was a
start, at least, for public speakers like Brougham, Buxton, and Mackintosh.
Agitation for full emancipation quickly followed: the "great deed of the
Emancipation of the Slaves," as Caroline Darwin cried. Even so, it was only
Earl Grey's ministry in the first reformed Parliament of 1832 that took the
question of full emancipation in hand. "All parties seem to agree that some
strong measure in favor of Emancipation of the Slaves will be carried this
session," Caroline told Darwin from Shrewsbury; "& I am sure that alone is
enough to make one value the present Ministers."[12] Hurrah for the honest
Whigs, exclaimed her brother on the *Beagle*.

So Darwin was not surprised to hear horrific stories about Brazilian slavery recounted by Captain Paget of H.M.S. *Samarang* when he came to dine with FitzRoy in Bahia harbour: facts so revolting, said Darwin, that if he had read them in England, he would have thought them made up for journalistic effect. "The extent to which the trade is carried on; the ferocity with which it is defended; the respectable (!) people who are concerned in it are far from being exaggerated at home," he confided to his diary.

> I have no doubt the actual state of by far the greater part of the slave population is far happier than one would be previously inclined to believe. Interest & any good feelings the proprietor may possess would tend to this.—But it is utterly false (as Cap Paget satisfactorily proved) that any, even the very best treated, do not wish to return to their countries.—"If I could but see my father & my two sisters once again, I should be happy. I can never forget them." Such was the expression of one of these people, who are ranked by the polished savages in England as hardly their brethren, even in Gods eyes.[13]

In his view, slaves were men and women with the same feelings as anyone. Personal experience told him so. His memories of kindly John Edmonstone in Edinburgh were at the front of his mind: the freed slave who took his master's name to Europe and taught Darwin how to stuff birds.

It was all the more shocking when he discovered that FitzRoy did not share his horror at Paget's stories. Although FitzRoy did not by any means endorse slavery, he saw nothing wrong with paternalism and its associated systems of tied and virtually unwaged labour. Brought up on a large landed estate with servants and family retainers, he was immersed in the patrician lifestyle of the Tory aristocracy, with its almost feudal relations between lord and peasant. It was hard for him, as it was for many wealthy Englishmen, to equate wage slavery with chattel slavery. The Grafton and Londonderry estate workers, in his opinion, were well looked after. In many respects they were like slaves: though ostensibly freemen, they were not entitled to vote in elections, for they did not own property; they occupied tied cottages; their livelihood came entirely from above. Household servants were exchanged between estates, children were born into service. What FitzRoy encountered in Brazil was to his mind not all that different. Complacently, he assumed slaves who were well looked after were happy slaves, better off than if living or dying in dirty poverty.

He therefore seemed unbearably myopic and self-satisfied in accepting the word of a great *estancia*-owner who said his slaves did not wish to be free. Calling them all before him, the owner had asked if they would rather be free. No, they answered.

Horrified, Darwin inquired of FitzRoy whether he thought that the answers of slaves in the presence of their master were worth anything. In response FitzRoy exploded, saying that as Darwin doubted his word, they could not live together any longer.[14] Storming out of the cabin, he vented the rest of his anger on Wickham.

Later that afternoon, his ears still burning, Wickham came by to ask if Darwin would like to eat in the mess-room in future. It was clear that Wickham thought the honeymoon was over. But Darwin was not going to back down: he was frightening in his absolute firmness. He was offended. He was accustomed to the great men of Cambridge and the people met at his uncle's house listening benignly to his comments and generously discovering something interesting in what he said. FitzRoy was not prepared to play these indulgent games. It came as a shock to Darwin to find his opinions easily tossed aside and his interventions construed as personal rudeness.

Yet FitzRoy's moods were volatile. A handsome apology arrived before nightfall with the request that Darwin "continue to live with him." By mutual agreement they avoided the subject of slavery ever afterwards.

That evening Darwin recorded the only harsh thoughts about the captain made during the entire voyage—and these strategically anonymous.

> From instances I have seen of people so blindly & obstinately prejudiced, who in other points I would credit, on this one I shall never again scruple utterly to disbelieve. As far as my testimony goes, every individual who has the glory of having exerted himself on the subject of slavery, may rely on it his labours are exerted against miseries perhaps even greater than he imagines.[15]

III

After leaving Bahia, the *Beagle* sailed gently up and down the Brazilian coast from March to July 1832 taking soundings and checking the accuracy of Admiralty charts for the area. Darwin was not needed during these strictly practical weeks, so as soon as the ship called at Rio de Janeiro he rented a cottage "in a beautiful village about 4 miles from this town" where he could collect specimens and, as he explained to Caroline, "escape cauking & painting & various other bedevilments which Wickham is planning." Though his relations with the captain were back on an even keel, the holiday might do both of them good, he thought. The *Beagle*'s artist, Augustus Earle, and Phillip Gidley King came on shore to keep him company. Fuegia Basket, the Fuegian woman travelling with the *Beagle,* stayed there too for a time.

The idyll had hardly started before fresh setbacks occurred. He learned that Fanny Owen was engaged to be married to someone else. A few weeks later, he discovered that the surgeon on the *Beagle* was offended by his scientific activities and was returning to England in high dudgeon. Shocked and puzzled by the unexpected turn of events, he was forced to reassess both his relationship with the distant world of Shropshire and his functions on board ship.

Letters had been accumulating at the British naval station in Rio de Janeiro since January, and when the *Beagle* arrived there in April, Darwin, like the others, fell on this first contact with home with eager anticipation. There were two long letters from his sisters, another from his cousin Charlotte Wedgwood, and a welcome note from Henslow relaying news about Cambridge friends and some breezy remarks about the poor showing of noblemen in the final examinations that year. Are you still a Whig? inquired Henslow. Erasmus had told him about Darwin's "beau ideal of a captain" whose Tory charm could easily convert a susceptible passenger; "I shan't change my principles myself," he stated, amused at the echo of his own political volte-face in younger days.[16] The Reform Bill and the prospect of a new government meant readjusting everyone's established values.

Caroline Darwin, reliable as always, wrote of her affection for Darwin and how much she missed him. Charlotte's letter was more of a revelation. Hidden in the account of her brother Hensleigh's wedding to Frances Mackintosh, she deftly inserted the information that she too was to be married: not to Erasmus, as the Darwin side of the family half hoped, but to an impoverished curate of two weeks' acquaintance. Her letter was filled with talk of livings and parsonages, weddings and honeymoons.

"England is gone mad with marrying, you will think," sympathised Darwin's younger sister Catherine. She took it upon herself to break the news about Fanny Owen's accepting a proposal only a few days after the *Beagle*'s departure: "in the course of a secret ride, Fanny meeting him at the Queen's Head."

Just as startling was the information that the new man in Fanny's life was Robert Biddulph, the dashing aristocrat who only the year before had assiduously courted her sister Sarah. Worse for his reputation was an earlier broken engagement to someone they all knew, Isabella Forrester of Willey Park in Shropshire. Catherine reported that Biddulph's "dissipated, gambling character" was apparently much reformed; and he intended standing for his father's safe parliamentary seat in Denbighshire as a liberal in favour of "gradual reforms in Church and State."[17] Mr. Owen, Darwin's convivial shooting companion of the autumn, had agreed to the match. Under the circumstances he could do little else, implied Catherine sourly. His strong-willed daughter presented him with a horse-riding *fait accompli*.

Catherine knew that no amount of jaunty description would neutralise the shock for her brother. She felt an injustice had been done. "You will find her a *motherly old married woman* when you come back. I hope it won't be a great grief to you, dearest Charley, though I am afraid you little thought how true your prophecy of 'marrying and giving in marriage' would prove. —You may be perfectly sure that Fanny will always continue as friendly and affectionate to you as ever, and as rejoiced to see you again, though I fear that will be but poor comfort to you, my dear Charles."[18]

As she expected, Darwin was stunned. Anguished thoughts of home, love, marriage, Fanny, Charlotte, and his three protective sisters whirled around that afternoon until he was exhausted by emotion. Then he wrote to Caroline, always his consolation in a storm.

> It is seldom that one individual has the power [of] giving to another such a sum of pleasure, as you this day have granted me.—I know not whether the conviction of being loved, be more delightful or the corresponding one of loving in return.—I ought for I have experienced them both in excess. —With yours I received a letter from Charlotte, talking of parsonages in pretty countries & other celestial views.—I cannot fail to admire such a short sailor-like "slicing" match.—The style seems prevalent, Fanny seems to have done the business in a ride.—Well it may be all very delightful to those concerned but as I like unmarried women better than those in the blessed state, I vote it a bore: by the fates, at this pace I have no chance for the parsonage.... it positively is an inconvenient fashion this marrying: Maer wont be half the place it was, & as for Woodhouse, if Fanny was not perhaps at this time Mrs Biddulp, I would say poor dear Fanny till I fell to sleep.—I feel much inclined to philosophize but I am at a loss what to think or say; whilst really melting with tenderness I cry my dearest Fanny why I demand, should I distinctly see the sunny flower garden at Maer; on the other hand, but I find my thoughts & feelings & sentences are in such a maze, that between crying & laughing I wish you all good night.—[19]

He was hurt and his heart was full.

Nevertheless, his heart was quick to recover. In one sense, of course, there was nothing to be done: Fanny was already married by the time he read the letter. In any event, he did not mourn too seriously or too long over lost love. After the first surprise wore off, he defiantly came to the conclusion that he and Fanny Owen had been unsuited to each other anyway. She enjoyed whirling her way through dances, weddings, trips to Bath and Harrogate, picnics, and fox-hunting in their seasons, always eager for the next excitement. Although Darwin liked many of the same kinds of activity, he would have found it impossible to keep up with such an existence as a married man. Fanny had also chosen an aristocrat to marry—"it is certainly what the world calls a very great match for her," ruminated Mr. Owen—and would live in a castle on the border of Wales. After his recent brush with FitzRoy, Darwin was feeling none too warmly towards aristocrats at that moment. Her winter seasons, spent in a grand house in Grosvenor Square, promised to be full of political entertaining, a future far more glamorous and society-based than the one Darwin wished for himself. In effect, whatever the tentative understanding may have been between them, it was irrevocably destroyed by the alarming promptness and implications of her choice. In the space of a few weeks apart, they had turned into different people.

Curiously, Fanny's father had much the same thought. In his unassuming way he had considered Darwin a prospective son-in-law, a man like himself content with slow-running country affairs; and he felt real regret that his daughter harboured quite different desires. An air of bemused solidarity with Darwin crept over him. He wrote to him as soon as he could expressing sympathy and reassuring him of his continuing affection.

By the time the letter arrived, Darwin's first romance was as much over for him as it was for Fanny.

IV

As if this news were not disturbing enough, there was more to come. During a short absence from Rio on a collecting excursion, Darwin became the centre of a disagreement between FitzRoy and the senior surgeon of the *Beagle,* Robert McCormick.

McCormick had until then scarcely featured in Darwin's day-to-day routine. As the ship's medical man, he was at Devonport during the boring months before departure, where the two first made acquaintance, and naturally enough travelled on board the *Beagle* across the Atlantic. Neither of the two men felt inclined to become friends in this period despite several interests in common, not least their medical background and fondness for natural history. Relations—though perfectly polite—were lukewarm at best.

"We jog on very amicably," reported Darwin. Privately he thought McCormick was "an ass." Only thirty-two years old, the surgeon already displayed the preoccupation with status, accommodations, and uniforms that later ruined his chances of promotion. "At present he is in great tribulation, whether his cabin shall be painted French Grey or a dead white—I hear little excepting this subject from him."[20]

Nor did Darwin see enough of him on the *Beagle* to make the resulting clash directly personal. Although they were different in almost every respect, with widely divergent intellectual views, social background, and private commitments, these incompatibilities were more or less ignored within the small confines of the ship and never led to quarrels between them. McCormick and Darwin geologised together on St. Jago, taking long walks into the interior and climbing the central mountains. These were pleasant enough excursions, said Darwin, and there is nothing to suggest that they were entered into unwillingly by either participant. McCormick, as much as Darwin, was pleased by the novelty of meeting with the fabled baobab (upside-down) tree on the outskirts of Porto Praya, a sight they had both regretted missing when the ship failed to call at Tenerife. Just as he had heard Humboldt describe doing, McCormick gamely climbed and carved his initials on St. Jago's ancient specimen, with the date; and in order to collect a flower for their individual herbarium sheets they both shot wildly at the only blossom until it fell to the ground.[21]

But Darwin found it hard to resist comparing his own bold new Lyellian approach with McCormick's conventional natural history techniques. Patronising self-satisfaction underpinned his casual dismissal at the end of a letter to Henslow: McCormick was "a philosopher of rather an antient date; at St Jago by his own account he made *general* remarks during the first fortnight & collected particular facts during the last."[22]

While this outwardly polite choreography was going on, McCormick began nurturing a grievance about the favours FitzRoy lavishly bestowed on Darwin. The problem as the surgeon saw it was simple: was it he or Darwin who was the *Beagle*'s naturalist? As McCormick saw it, custom decreed that he should be the expedition's natural historian, and to all intents and purposes he was right. By tradition, and usually also by inclination, the ship's doctor was the man most obviously concerned with natural history during a naval voyage. The *Beagle* survey was no exception. Darwin was not responsible for bringing together a natural history collection for the Crown, nor was Darwin appointed, or even called, the *Beagle*'s naturalist except in his own imagination and in a few informal letters from FitzRoy to Beaufort. In the absence of any specific instructions from the Admiralty, it ought to have been McCormick's official duty to fill that role.[23] One or two letters exchanged between FitzRoy, Darwin, and Beaufort before the *Beagle* sailed suggest the point was tacitly agreed among them: "the Surgeon's collection would be at the disposal of Government." This, thought Darwin, made it easier for him, as a paying guest, to retain possession and disposal of his own private collections. His appointment was "not a very regular affair," he admitted to Fox before sailing.

McCormick was therefore surprised, and then outraged, when Darwin started an extensive natural history collection on St. Jago under FitzRoy's benevolent eye. Subsequently, it was Darwin's nets and trawls hanging over the side of the ship, Darwin's microscope set up in the poop cabin, Darwin who sat at the captain's table discussing books in a friendly fashion in the evenings. McCormick's traditional natural history role was usurped by someone who seemed to him nothing more than a callow youth from Cambridge.

His dissatisfaction reached a climax with one of FitzRoy's characteristically imperious gestures. Much preferring Darwin's company to McCormick's,

FitzRoy ignored the surgeon and took only his dining companion with him when setting out on a mid-Atlantic adventure.

More for the thrill than anything else, the captain had decided to land a small party from the *Beagle* on St. Paul's Rocks, halfway between the Cape Verde Islands and the Brazilian coast. Uninhabited except for dense flocks of seafowl, and previously unvisited by any scientific recorder, they were an alluring target for a restless naval man and an eager friend. Drenched in their attempts to get ashore from the launch and exhilarated by the slippery, fragmented bareness of the rocks, Darwin and FitzRoy had a marvellous morning of it, whooping and killing birds with abandon. The boobies and noddies (species of gannet and tern) were so stupid, declared Darwin, that he could have killed any number of them. "Lend me your geological hammer?" asked one of the men. "No, no," replied Darwin, "you'll break the handle." But hardly had he said so when, overcome by the novelty of the scene, and the example of those around him, away went the hammer, with all the force of his own right arm.[24] Poking around under the untidy birds' nests, Darwin found that spiders were the only other living beings occupying the rocks. The isolation in natural history terms was almost absolute.

None of them paid any attention at all to the members of a second launch, which included McCormick. This second launch was waved away and told to circle about catching fish for dinner.

When, at Rio de Janeiro, the ship's carpenters then began making packing cases for Darwin's first consignment home, McCormick was deeply offended, to a point that would make reconciliation difficult. He was resentful that the voyage, which at first had seemed a perfect opportunity to fulfil his own ambitions, was instead a period "which I can only look back to with unavailing regret, as so much time, health, and energies utterly wasted."[25]

V

McCormick's irritation was completely centred on professional responsibilities, a situation that would not have occurred if Darwin's interests had lain in some other scientific field such as geomagnetism, stellar astronomy, or theories of the tides. The problem was entirely to do with competition for a niche in the problematic and disorganised realm of professional science then emerging in nineteenth-century Britain.

McCormick wanted more than anything to accompany "scientific voyages of discovery" and become famous as an exploring naturalist.[26] After training as a working pupil with the noted London surgeon Sir Astley Cooper, he partially fulfilled this ambition in 1827 by sailing as an assistant-surgeon with Edward Parry on the *Hecla* in search of the North Pole. He was not very easy to please, however. Three overseas commissions followed, but each time McCormick considered himself insufficiently appreciated and got himself invalided home, a naval euphemism for personal disagreements and dissatisfactions.

Taking leave from the navy on half-pay early in 1830, he then set out to enhance his scientific standing by attending the classes of Robert Jameson in Edinburgh, with whom Darwin had studied a few years earlier. McCormick was not intending to take a full medical degree, as Darwin had once planned, since Edinburgh lectures were available to anyone who paid for tickets and Admiralty men were encouraged to take official leave to attend; "Only Scotchmen have any chance with the head of our department," McCormick grudgingly acknowledged. As well as listening to Jameson's natural history lectures, he went to university courses on the practice of medicine and midwifery, with a little chemistry and botany thrown in, and extracurricular tuition in anatomy delivered by John Lizars. Back in London by May 1831, he seemed a good catch when Beaufort was casting around for suitably qualified men for the *Beagle*.

Jameson was pleased to hear of McCormick's appointment and, like McCormick, assumed he would be taking on all the usual natural history duties of a naval surgeon. He wrote to him in November 1831, just before the *Beagle* sailed, giving him clear instructions about the kind of information he should concentrate on. In lectures and field excursions in and around Edinburgh, Jameson always insisted on the need for careful observations. The advice to McCormick was no different. "The exploratory expedition will be a most delightful one," he said warmly, "& the more particularly to yourself from the numberless opportunities it will afford for the advancement of natural history. . . . Every dept. in all the Kingdoms of nature in the countries you are about to visit possess a high degree of interest more especially to the naturalist of Europe. Your collection therefore ought to be ample. . . . I shall take it kindly that you write me from time [to time] informing me of the progress of your voyage in which I feel particularly interested. I have heard from Naval Officers here that Capt. FitzRoy your Commander is a capital officer and excellent man & that you are most fortunate in being appointed to serve along with him."[27]

With its careful counsel and encouraging tone, this could have been a letter from Henslow to Darwin. Certainly, McCormick believed himself as appropriately educated and capable as Darwin. He had every intention of getting together a fine natural history collection. With visits to Jameson's natural history museum in Edinburgh, the Royal College of Surgeons, and the British Museum still uppermost in his mind, he meant to make his name by distributing the best and most valuable trophies among these three prominent institutions.

VI

The point about collections would hardly have been important had not specimens been such very marketable commodities. Under other circumstances, Darwin and McCormick could perhaps have reaped their individual harvests without professional conflict. But in the entrepreneurial world of early-nineteenth-century natural history, the possession of a substantial collection from faraway places, full of rarities and undescribed species, the enviable harvest of inland expeditions or of long periods dredging in foreign seas, frequently made the collector a scientific celebrity. Finds like these could easily generate fresh discoveries in anatomy and physiology, or lead to the identification of new species and genera; standard taxonomic schemes and catalogues might have to be revised; papers and scientific articles would be written. As often as not, new species ended up with a Latin or Greek name paying tribute to their collector. William Kirby expressed the secret hopes of hundreds of British naturalists with his aphorism that once named, an animal or plant becomes a possession forever. In this way Francis Masson's South African plants were the sensational high spot of the Royal Botanic Gardens at Kew after 1792. Hugh Cuming's magnificent shell collection pushed him into the scientific limelight in 1839.

If all else failed, the specimens possessed commercial value. Though neither McCormick nor Darwin intended exploiting their finds in this way, they were well aware that exotic material could be sold for handsome prices among the members of a wide-ranging network of independent dealers, natural history agents, shop-owners, and merchants who profited by the national passion for cabinets of curiosities and private collections. Darwin's useful London friend William Yarrell was one such respected natural history businessman; Cambridge's Mr. Harbour and the Pieman were two others, of a different but no less versatile sort.

Moreover, science was much more of a public spectacle than its later history would suggest, far removed from the institutionalised endeavour conjured up by modern practitioners, and natural history was one of the most widely appreciated aspects of this generalised interest in the external world. All kinds of collections became popular public displays in Britain during these years, scientific material falling indiscriminately into a miscellaneous spectrum of stage shows, art exhibitions, pageants, theatres, circuses, painted panoramic displays, fireworks, magic lanterns, freak shows, funfairs, and the crammed glass cases of civic museums. Many of these exhibitions were staged in London's Egyptian Hall, located on Piccadilly, or in cosmopolitan arenas like the pleasure grounds of Ranelagh and Vauxhall Gardens.[28] William Bullock's museum and Pidcock's menagerie at Exeter Change were only two out of hundreds of natural-history-based exhibits put on show in the capital in order to profit from scientific and public attention. Museum specimens such as Darwin and McCormick hoped to collect blended almost indistinguishably into this culture of open spectacle. Card-playing pigs and five-legged cows were merely the showman's tip of the iceberg; and icebergs themselves (wooden, to be sure) appeared in Vauxhall Gardens after Captain Ross's search for the Northwest Passage in 1829–30. John Gould, for example, the ornithologist who later identified Darwin's bird specimens, mounted a remarkable array of hummingbirds viewed by both royalty and crowds of enthusiastic commoners before it was transferred to the London zoological gardens as a permanent freelance exhibit: entry fees to the birds' kiosk enabled Gould to live relatively well in London and to finance his other collecting expeditions. The Regent's Park zoo was opened in 1828 similarly to capitalize on the public yearning for all kinds of displays, closely followed by the British Museum's admission of working people into its new building in Bloomsbury at sixpence a time. Intense public interest accompanied George Catlin's long-running show of anthropological paintings fronted by living native American Indians during the 1830s, and Andrew Smith's touring exhibition of stuffed animals which he had collected during years of government service in South Africa. Gould, Catlin, and Smith were as well known among the general British populace as in their own professional circles. Their collections helped them become self-financing and famous.

To this should be added the surge of interest in consumer goods which gripped the nation during the early years of the nineteenth century. Natural history, with its emphasis on the physical objects of nature, fitted the contemporary ethos as no other science could hope to do. Whether dealt with by experts or amateurs, the subject was almost entirely based on tangible things—on specimens of rocks and plants, on stuffed animals, drawers of minerals, serried ranks of butterflies and moths, jars of marine invertebrates, fern cases, aquariums, crates of bones—as completely as late Georgian and early Victorian homes were full of the new goods of the manufacturing era, or as the Crystal Palace later in the century displayed the combined products of the world's industries, the zenith of a cultural preoccupation with material possessions.[29] Where Disraeli spoke of the "shopocracy" over which he was meant to preside, naturalists of the period could well have made play with the idea of "thingery." To study nature was to collect physical parts of it; to appreciate and to understand the natural world was to see its various objects named and displayed.

A natural history collection consequently possessed intrinsic social value as well as solid financial worth. It was an article of scientific commerce which an astute collector could use for furthering his or her status in scientific society. Many travellers were recognised as "experts" upon their return—if not in lasting terms, at least in the eyes of their immediate contemporaries. In the early days of empire, a few years spent travelling in out-of-the-way places could easily provide sufficient material for a visiting European to write an account of the country or make notes on its flora and fauna, and eventually invite questions from individuals at home eager to know more. Countless expatriates and colonial officials otherwise lost to history became, for a short while, authorities on some point relating to the natural history of their area, or contributed information to the natural history journals proliferating in London and elsewhere. Many of Darwin's contemporaries and later correspondents belonged to this group of people at some time or another; Richard Thomas Lowe, for example, a former friend from Cambridge, lived on Madeira as a curate to English visitors in 1832 and soon became knowledgeable about Madeiran plants and animals. Similarly, to accompany a voyage of exploration meant a chance to become an authority on a particular group of organisms, as Robert Brown was on the plants of the southern hemisphere, or on a specific area, as Sir John Richardson was on the Arctic or Phillip Parker King on New South Wales. Both Darwin and McCormick consulted these and comparable specialists when making their preparations to embark.

Most important, specimens could be donated to prominent institutions. Some collections were private property, owned by the collector or his sponsor, and were theirs to do with as they wished. Other material was more usually the property of the Crown, almost invariably the Admiralty, which required objects to be placed with an official body, usually the British Museum or some other significant London institution. The East India Office ran its own museum in the city centre, as did lesser-known bodies like the London Missionary Society and the Royal United Services Institution in Whitehall. Ownership boundaries, however, were not always clearly defined, and individual collectors, Darwin included, could expect to benefit from the interlacing of private and public property in an eventual round of strategic donations.

Even before he sailed, Darwin made this clear to Henslow, who had hoped the *Beagle* material would end up in the museum—as yet tiny—he had established for the Cambridge Philosophical Society. Smoothly, Darwin disabused him. He had no intention of giving his material to a "country collection, let it be ever so good." He intended giving it to some public body, probably "the largest & most central collection."[30] Only there would his specimens receive the attention he believed they would deserve. What was the point of collecting if the objects, and the objects' collector, were not appreciated properly? He was risking his life to get them.

And when Beaufort subsequently proposed putting Darwin on the Admiralty's books for victuals, in essence providing a free passage, Darwin's immediate response was not gratitude but anxiety that he would forfeit absolute control over his cargo. He complained afterwards that "my only difficulty is about the disposal of my collection when I come back."

As Darwin, Beaufort, and Henslow acknowledged, the advantages offered by an intimate acquaintance with nature outside Europe, plus a practical monopoly on certain key topics supported by a large and potentially disposable collection of specimens, went a long way towards helping collectors join the community of British savants on their own terms.

In particular, in view of McCormick's case, a choice collection and a growing reputation as an expert helped outweigh some of the social disadvantages that many middle-class British naturalists experienced. British science was then governed by snobbery. It was thought vulgar to receive money for researches, and the handful of salaried personnel employed for natural history duties in museums or elsewhere were usually regarded as coming from lower social strata where one had to work for a living.[31] Only the upper echelons of "keepers" in the British Museum and senior figures at the Royal Institution or Royal College of Surgeons were exempted from such class-based categorisations, and this by virtue of receiving appropriately nonmanual (though nonuniversity) professorial status. Lest anyone inadvertently mistake Richard Owen, the curator of the Royal College of Surgeons collection, for a menial employee, he insisted on wearing his Hunterian professor's gown on all conceivable occasions. No portrait or photograph of Owen is without it.[32]

Even though this hierarchical scale of scientific practitioners was under attack from diverse quarters, both high and low, during the 1820s and early 1830s, Francis Beaufort still felt justified in remarking that lucre was not what philosophers set out to gain and, besides, science should not be a trade.[33] Darwin himself was a typical example of a rich young gentleman following his private enthusiasms as a self-financing guest of the government.

The prime exceptions to these social rules were the officer classes of the British army and navy. A naval surgeon from a middling kind of background with interests in natural history or a sea captain with astronomical or geophysical leanings could hope for preferential treatment from the Admiralty and for the respect of London's scientific gentlemen, often joining them as an acknowledged specialist. Edward Parry, John Ross, James Clark Ross, Robert Brown, John Richardson, and Edward Sabine had all done so. Five of these serving officers ultimately earned knighthoods for their dedication to national science and accounted for four fellowships and one presidency of the Royal Society between them.

No wonder then that Darwin's natural history activities were such a sore point with McCormick. Everything on board seemed to encourage Darwin's private collection rather than the surgeon's. Further than this, FitzRoy was making arrangements to ship Darwin's things home by the official routes available to the Admiralty, a considerable gift to Darwin, who had expected to pay all his own expenses. In McCormick's eyes, Darwin was receiving much more than he deserved—not only the benefits of the captain's blessing on board ship and free transport of cargo but even the right to retain ownership of these valuable commodities when they arrived in England. By making a bigger and better collection with the indulgent approval of the captain, Darwin was demolishing all McCormick's justified hopes for social, scientific, and professional advancement.

"Having found myself in a false position on board a small and very uncomfortable vessel," McCormick wrote in frustration, "and very much disappointed in my expectations of carrying out my natural history pursuits, every obstacle having been placed in the way of my getting on shore and making collections, I got permission from the admiral in command of the station here to be superseded and allowed a passage home on H.M.S. *Tyne*."[34] He stalked off to buy a parrot as a souvenir before leaving the *Beagle* full of rancour, only four months out of Plymouth.

"He is no loss," Darwin informed Caroline with a barely hidden sneer. "As for the Doctor," Henslow read, "he has gone back to England,—as he chose to make himself disagreeable to the Captain & to Wickham."[35]

McCormick could not even bring himself to record this brief encounter with Darwin in his autobiography.

NATURALIST ON
THE *BEAGLE*

ARWIN did not care. By then the lush tropical forest enveloped him, green and still. Only Milton and Humboldt, he thought, possessed words for what he was experiencing. A copy of *Paradise Lost* slipped easily into his pocket, ready for reading while resting on a convenient log. "Delight," he wrote in his journal, "is a weak term to express the feelings of a naturalist who for the first time has wandered by himself in a Brazilian forest.... such a day brings a deeper pleasure than he can ever hope to experience again." It was like stumbling across a scene from the *Arabian Nights*. "A most paradoxical mixture of noise and silence pervades the shady parts of the wood. The noise from the insects is so loud that it may be heard even in a vessel anchored several hundred yards from the shore; yet within the recesses of the forest a universal silence appears to reign." He was entering paradise with Milton as a guide.

Darwin had already tasted something of this pleasure at Bahia, where even the torrential afternoon rains beguiled him. "I can only add raptures to the former raptures.... each new valley is more beautiful than the last," he said weakly.

I believe from what I have seen Humboldts glorious descriptions are & ever will for ever be unparalleled: but even he with his dark blue skies & the rare union of poetry with science which he so strongly displays when writing on tropical scenery, with all this falls far short of the truth. The delight one experiences in such times bewilders the mind,—if the eye attempts to follow the flight of a gaudy butter-fly, it is arrested by some strange tree or fruit; if watching an insect one forgets it in the stranger flower it is crawling over,—if turning to admire the splendour of the scenery, the individual character of the foreground fixes the attention. The mind is a chaos of delight, out of which a world of future & more quiet pleasure will arise.—I am at present fit only to read Humboldt; he like another Sun illumines everything I behold.—[1]

Settling down in Rio de Janeiro in April 1832, he wanted nothing more than time to luxuriate in these sensations and hastily made arrangements with FitzRoy to stay on shore for ten to twelve weeks while the *Beagle* went about its duties. The cottage in Botofogo soon became the centre of a happy tropical existence—like a holiday from school, he said.

Living so close to Rio was exhilarating in itself, and the *Beagle*'s artist, Augustus Earle, was lively company. Earle had visited the city once before as a roving, penniless artist while making his way from Tristan da Cunha, New Zealand, and Calcutta to London, with interludes spent painting portraits of Australia's first colonial governors for money.[2] When first employed by FitzRoy, he was unsuccessfully promoting his paintings of Maoris, and was glad to go overseas again. Earle knew far more about Rio than was probably good for either of them or for teenaged Midshipman King. He showed Darwin and King the sights, each one more glamorously foreign to English eyes than the last, and propelled them through the crowded streets to find the best churches, the Catholic cathedral, the baroquely crumbling palaces, the grand hotels and theatres, and more and more breathtaking vistas. A constant procession of Negro slaves, interspersed with half-castes, priests in cone-shaped hats, and rich Latin ladies in their carriages pressed by on either side. Earle made an excellent guide, said Darwin as they dined in high spirits one evening at a *table d'hôte*. But few of his previous friends were still around. "Dead & gone" was the invariable answer: driven to drink by conducting business in such a hot climate, the doctor's son naïvely recorded.

Darwin visibly loosened up by the hour. Heat, colour, and exoticism mingled delightfully as far as he was concerned. Within a few days he arranged to join an eccentric Irishman named Patrick Lennon who was about to visit his coffee plantation a hundred miles away to the north. They would stay at *vendas* or *estancias* each night until the journey ended, making use of the simple system of hospitality that upcountry residents generously fostered. Despite this, getting a passport proved tricky, and Darwin came to regard all the city's officials with contempt. However, "the prospect of wild forests tenanted by beautiful birds, monkeys & sloths, and lakes by cavies & alligators, will make any naturalist lick the dust even from the foot of a Brazilian." In the end, they made a party of six or seven Europeans, all mounted on horseback, with a black boy as their guide. Earle stayed behind nursing a bout of rheumatism. Seldom did a more quixotic set of adventurers start out, sighed Darwin romantically.

The trip, like others which came after, was a revelation. It provided aesthetic experiences quite the equal of anything felt in Bahia or St. Jago. "Twiners entwining twiners—tresses like hair—beautiful lepidoptera—silence—hosannah," he noted as he rode along. Life and death never seemed more intense than now. The scene forcibly reminded him of an engraving of the Brazils which Henslow once showed him where infinite numbers of lianas and parasitic plants clambered over the living trees next to a riot of decaying, fallen trunks. Such sublimity unavoidably led to exalted thoughts. The vaulting canopy was like a cathedral for nature: "It is not possible," he wrote, "to give an adequate idea of the higher feelings of wonder, admiration and devotion which fill the mind. I well remember my conviction that there is more in man than the mere breath of his body."[3]

They passed through slave country. Darwin was still seething about the injustices recounted by Earle and the naval men he met in Rio and Bahia. In Botofogo, Earle came back one night telling him that the woman who lived opposite kept a thumbscrew to crush the fingers of her female slaves: he had seen the stump of a joint on a girl's hand. He learned how the *maticans* or slave-hunters were sent out to catch escaping labourers and treated their victims like animals when they were caught, slicing off the ears as proof of death, just as Darwin used to do with dead rats for his father. "The Brazilians, as far as I am able to judge, possess but a small share of those qualities which give dignity to mankind," he complained. "Being surrounded by slaves, they become habituated to the harsh tones of command & the sneer of reproach."[4] He was aghast at the barbarity of people he would otherwise have thought civilised gentlemen.

Listening to the travellers in his own party, he heard about runaway slaves managing to find illegal employment—a sure sign, he thought rebelliously, that Negroes would work for wages when free and a good antidote to the argument that they were constitutionally lazy. Not long after, the party passed under a precipice from which an old woman had once thrown herself rather than be recaptured. In ancient Rome, he reflected, this would have been called noble patriotism; here it was seen as "brutal obstinacy." Most appallingly, when they arrived at Mr. Lennon's plantation, his riding companion disintegrated into a raging tyrant. Darwin had at first thought him "above the common run of men." He was dismayed by the threats now streaming out: Lennon would take all the slave women and children from their menfolk and sell them at the market at Rio, including a much-loved mulatto child illegitimately fathered by the plantation agent. "Picture to yourself the chance, ever hanging over you, of your wife and your little children—those objects which nature urges even the slave to call his own—being torn from you and sold like beasts to the first bidder!"

The full horror of it struck him hardest on the way back to Rio. Crossing a ferry manned by a Negro, Darwin unthinkingly waved his arms in an effort to make him understand where he wanted to go. The man thought Darwin was going to hit him. "Instantly, with a frightened look and half-shut eyes, he dropped his hands. I shall never forget my feelings of surprise, disgust, and shame, at seeing a great powerful man afraid even to ward off a blow, directed, as he thought, at his face. This man had been trained to a degradation lower than the slavery of the most helpless animal."[5]

Thoughtfully, he returned to Botofogo to mull over man's inhumanity to man. He did not like being cast as a brutal slave-driver.

II

Natural history collecting seemed far less stressful. A tropical forest was a gold mine to a naturalist, he exclaimed, and the life was not a particularly hard one. "Got up at 4 oclock to go out hunting," he wrote on 4 June 1832:

> The person who keeps the hounds is a priest & dean—the pack only consists of five dogs, their names Trumpeta, Mimosa, Clariena, Dorena & Champaigna; the huntsman is a black man & performed the other offices of body servant & clerk.... At about seven we arrived at our hunting ground, & put up the horses at a small farm house situated in the middle of the woods.—The hunting consists in all the dogs being turned into the forest & each separately pursues its own game.—The hunters with guns station themselves in the places most likely for the animals, such as small deer & pachas (like guinea pigs) to pass by.—And in the intervals they shoot parrots & Toucans &c.—I soon found this very stupid & began to hunt my own peculiar game.[6]

With a score of profound bows, putting his hand to his heart for good measure and repeating *"Monte, monte obligado,"* Darwin proceeded home after a memorable day.

It was pleasant dabbling in brooks, turning over stones, or picking up shells on the beach, and the practical demands of dealing with the resulting material were absorbing. Walking or riding out into the countryside, catching and preserving animals, his geological hammer, shotgun, nets, and pistols much in evidence, busy with drying papers and chemicals at every conceivable moment, all gave him great satisfaction. He delighted in carrying out dissections and making the fiddly preparations required before items could be packed away, and proved himself adept in examining the details of living animals that usually disappeared in preserved specimens. The smaller the organism, the greater his appreciation of the complexities of life. He was always ready to tease out its mysteries under the travelling microscope bought in London with Robert Brown's advice.

This congenial mixture of hand, head, and heart led to some wonderful moments. Deep in the forest, he hunted for things under logs and stones, probing through the leaf litter for fat, pale worms and peering into the furled rainwater traps of bromeliads for small insects or spiders. "I am at present red-hot with Spiders, they are very interesting, & if I am not mistaken, I have already taken some new genera," he told Henslow excitedly.[7]

During the same expedition, a handful of beautifully coloured flatworms were revealed rippling under the decaying wood of a shady tree-lined spot. Darwin could hardly believe these were true planarians, since the great majority were usually aquatic. Careful work at his microscope and an exhaustive search through his reference books nevertheless persuaded him that these and another kind found at the seashore were entirely new to science. He fired off another missive to Cambridge. "Amongst the lower animals, nothing has so much interested me as finding 2 species of elegantly coloured true Planariae, inhabiting the dry forest! The false relation they bear to Snails is the most extraordinary thing of the kind I have ever seen.—In the same genus (or more truly family) some of the marine species possess an organization so marvellous,—that I can scarcely credit my eyesight."[8]

Far away in England, older, wiser, and closer to a university library, Henslow was not nearly so certain. It seemed much more likely to him that Darwin was mistaken. Were they slugs and the marine one perhaps a *Doris*? he replied. He told Darwin he would send, via Erasmus, a copy of Cuvier's *Anatomie des mollusques* which had all these species accurately described.[9]

Watching his box in Botofogo, Darwin stoutly persevered in his original opinion and continued searching for all kinds of flatworms whenever he could during the rest of the voyage. Of the fifteen species he succeeded in obtaining, twelve were genuinely terrestrial and one was the sole representative of a new genus.[10] These were among the first animals he studied in proper scientific detail when he arrived home, partly because he wished very much to continue his own researches into invertebrates and to bring the results before the zoological community as fast as he could, but also to prove to his dubious teacher that he had been right in his initial judgement. To think independently from Henslow after this carried with it a strong whiff of the defiant student.

None of this collecting work was carried out in an intellectual vacuum. He brought with him a selection of authoritative natural history books from the *Beagle's* shelves. These included an important new encyclopedia of the living world edited by the French naturalist Bory de Saint-Vincent and other French scholars, the *Dictionnaire classique d'histoire naturelle* (1822–31), which ran to seventeen volumes and was full of articles by different experts giving the most advanced views of the day on their subjects. Other volumes used by Darwin were Lamouroux's *Exposition* of sea anemones and polyps (1821) and Lamarck's *Histoire naturelle des animaux sans vertèbres* (1815–22), seven volumes on the identification, classification, and functions of molluscs and other invertebrates. If Darwin found his specimens or something comparable listed in the catalogues available to him, he usually made a dissection and provisional identification, acquiring in the process a fair idea of the scientific interest of each new set of organisms. Letters to Henslow filled any gaps; and Erasmus excelled in locating and sending the books his brother asked for. Darwin furthermore read as widely as he could among explorers' tales, struggling through Spanish texts where necessary, and again and again reading Humboldt until he knew the feelings expressed there as if they were his own. He was, in fact, no more divorced from mainline scientific ideas than he was from ordinary English society.

Tactile satisfactions, as well as the fun of believing himself right, were complemented by a growing sense of wonder. "Whilst seated on a tree, & eating my luncheon in the sublime solitude of the forest, the pleasure I experience is unspeakable," he told Catherine.[11] The flowers were "enough to make a florist go wild." Astonishing beauties were found everywhere, down to the smallest complexities of gnats and worms. Darwin was often intensely moved by the intricacies of nature in its many guises, impressed by the exuberant profligacy of it all. "I am quite tired having worked all day at the produce of my net," he told his diary on one occasion. "Many of these creatures so low in the scale of nature are most exquisite in their forms & rich colours.—It creates a feeling of wonder that so much beauty should be apparently created for such little purpose."[12]

His feelings of admiration were enhanced by an easy sympathy with living beings other than himself. During these few months in Rio de Janeiro, he allowed his inbuilt tendency towards anthropomorphism full rein. A turtle suddenly glimpsed wheeling through the glassy depths made him gasp with incredulity—and then laugh because "nothing certainly could be imagined worse for surprising an animal than a boat full of midshipmen." Flowers invited him to bury his head in their petals, guinea-pigs reproached him for finding them tasty. It was a shame to kill armadillos when they were "so quiet." Sometimes the rocks themselves were like people, hiding their secrets or teasing him with gnomic clues.

Thereafter, he gave human attributes to almost every species he met, including flatworms and beetles: a trait that blurred the dividing line between man and beast. He felt himself part of a single world united by the same kind of mental responses. Guinea-pigs and turtles were capable of feeling many of the same emotions as a naturalist, and he—as the naturalist—believed he could understand what they were thinking. More than this, he enjoyed characterising himself, the eccentric English traveller, as the main curiosity. The rat-traps and other contrivances in his pockets, he suggested, were assuredly a greater wonder to local people than anything their woods contained.

This deepening appreciation of the individuality of animals and plants was important too in making him aware of his own insignificant place in nature. The forest was "a temple filled with the varied productions of the God of Nature," of which mankind was but a single species. Admiration and humility combined, making him conscious that he—and the rest of the human race—was just a small part of a much larger interlocking system of life on earth.

III

Darwin left Rio de Janeiro full of regret and gratitude. But it was good to see FitzRoy and the *Beagle* men again and satisfying to sail out of the harbour with the cheers of the crews of the *Samarang* and *Warspite* ringing in their ears. Everyone on board appreciated that the real "wild work" of the survey was about to start. After a call at Montevideo and Buenos Aires, FitzRoy intended sailing down to Patagonia to chart the coastline as far as he could before restocking at Buenos Aires and then on to Tierra del Fuego when the southern summer arrived. "Every thing shows we are steering for barbarous regions," Darwin cried. "All the officers have stowed away their razors, & intend allowing their beards to grow in a truly patriarchal fashion."

His boyish wishes for some unremitting wildness were fulfilled sooner than expected. As they sailed into the harbour of Buenos Aires early in August, a guard ship fired at them—a blank shot as it turned out, but they did not know that. Darwin was convinced he heard the ball whistle through the rigging. Fulminating to Wickham about this insult to the British flag, FitzRoy carried on regardless: he had many faults, but cowardice was not one of them. But he was brought to a halt by a quarantine boat. As in their ineffectual call at Tenerife, they were prevented from going any further by the harbour authority's fear of cholera. So FitzRoy ostentatiously loaded up all the cannon on one side of his ship and turned back to hail the guard ship on his way out to sea. "If you dare fire a shot when we enter port again," he shouted, "we shall send our whole broadside into your rotten hulk."

Back at Montevideo by nightfall, FitzRoy complained so heatedly to the captain of the British warship stationed there that the other officer promised to take his frigate, H.M.S. *Druid,* up to Buenos Aires and demand an apology. "Oh I hope the guard-ship will fire a gun at the frigate," breathed Darwin along with the rest of the crew; "if she does, it will be her last day above water."[13]

Scarcely had the *Druid* disappeared up the River Plate on its mission of gunboat diplomacy when the chief of police from Montevideo begged FitzRoy, as the only English captain left in port, to help quell a sudden local rebellion. Negro soldiers were holding the central fort, which also contained the town arsenal. It looked as if they might run riot and attack the houses of local residents.

FitzRoy's blood was already up, and he rose magnificently to the occasion. He sent fifty well-armed sailors (almost the entire complement of active servicemen on the *Beagle*) marching through the town, followed by Darwin, who secretly longed to swish a cutlass or put a dagger between his teeth. But it was pretty tame, Darwin said afterwards: the mutineers capitulated easily and the *Beagle* men were left with little to do except cook beefsteaks in the courtyard. As soon as FitzRoy's neutrality was compromised, he sent the crew home. Darwin departed with a bad headache: "there certainly is a great deal of pleasure in the excitement of this sort of work—quite sufficient to explain the reckless gayety with which sailors undertake even the most hazardous attacks."[14] He was disappointed in not seeing any gunfire. Writing home to Beaufort about this incident, FitzRoy approved of Darwin's warlike behaviour. "Darwin is a regular trump. . . . He has a mixture of necessary qualities which makes him feel at home, and happy, and makes everyone his friend."[15]

Soon afterwards, they filled the *Beagle*'s hold with dry stores and got going for the expedition south. The pampas, Darwin discovered, meant long, dull days sailing along a line of sandy hillocks, without any break or change. Since he was not involved with the technical work in any way, he used the time to write and dissect, in between bouts of seasickness. When they arrived at Bahía Blanca, situated at 39°S, he was glad enough just to get off the ship even without the extra lure of fresh exploring.

Bahía Blanca was just about as far south as regular Spanish contacts then reached. The country was ostensibly run by Argentine authorities, and several great *estancia* owners ranched cattle there. But violent disputes over landownership and unofficial war with the native Indians made the place dangerous: the Indians tortured all their prisoners, said Darwin, and the Spaniards shot theirs. Nevertheless, there were small troops of soldiers patrolling the area under the overall command of Juan Manuel de Rosas, the Argentine general. Rosas's army of adventurers had been privately funded and trained by himself, a ruthless force entirely independent of the state; and Rosas himself was practically an independent ruler whose help was sought by rival political parties. His army was more or less commissioned to exterminate the Indians. "The soldiers pursue & sabre every man," Darwin said. Women were massacred in cold blood. "Everyone here is fully convinced that this is the justest war, because it is against barbarians. Who would believe in this age in a Christian, civilized country that such atrocities were committed?"[16]

Being English made no difference. Riding out with a party of sailors to visit the *comandante* in charge of the Bahía Blanca settlement, FitzRoy and Darwin aroused all kinds of military suspicion. An old major stopped them before they ever got to the *comandante,* alarmed by FitzRoy's courteously bland comment that the fine large bay would hold a whole fleet of battleships. Then the major took exception to Darwin's description of himself as *un naturalista,* an expression unheard of before. James Harris, the temporary pilot for the *Beagle,* who accompanied them, had explained this as "a man who knows everything." Further attempts to allay the soldiers' anxieties proved useless. They had to return to the *Beagle.*

During less frustrating trips into the plains, Darwin characterised himself as "a great wanderer," catching precisely the cheerful air accompanying all his overland excursions.[17] Galloping here and there, enjoying the rough outdoor life and examining the countryside with fresh, honest enthusiasm, was for him a great pleasure, not far removed from university vacations spent riding out to Woodhouse or Maer for the autumn shooting. Much of the natural history work he undertook in Argentina and elsewhere was conducted in this carefree fashion. Catching birds, avoiding South American "lions," shooting, riding, collecting, and looking forward to the thrill of "a few revolutions" tumbled together in an agreeable series of occupations that pleased his soul as well as furthering his understanding of the land itself. As he joked to Henslow before setting sail, he was only changing from hunting foxes in Shropshire to llamas in South America.

One animal in particular became associated in his mind with this breezy period and its youthful approach to nature. This was the South American rhea, more usually called an ostrich by the sailors, although the lack of taxonomic affinity with the real ostrich was well known. These ungainly, rather silly birds captured Darwin's imagination. They were shy, wary, and solitary, and easily confused by a group of men on horseback. Chasing them was irresistible. "When seen on the brow of a hill against the clear sky they form a fine spectacle. . . . if, after approaching close, you suddenly gallop in pursuit—it is beautiful to see them, as a sailor would express it, 'up with their helm' & make all sail, by expanding their wings right down the wind."[18]

Always alive to the peculiarities of animal behaviour and amused by the absurdities intrinsic to such large flightless birds, Darwin made particular efforts to establish the exact sequence of events relating to the ostriches' egg-laying and nesting habits. Riding around Bahía Blanca one day, he was puzzled to see individual eggs lying randomly on the sand when all the others were grouped, twenty or more, in proper nests. It was the result, he was told by the gauchos riding out with him, of several females coming together to fill a nest—just a shallow hollow in the sand—after which a single male would incubate and look after the young. If no cock bird could be found, the females seemed to lose heart, laid their individual eggs anywhere on the pampas, and abandoned them.

Darwin, brought up on traditional British ideas of marital life, and thinking perhaps of his own failed relations with Fanny Owen, anxiously pondered how the females could possibly balance the number of eggs and nests with available males: there seemed little chance of there being enough nests for all the prospective fathers. Attempting to work out these calculations statistically, he soon gave up in a rush of empathy for the paternal feelings of the male ostrich forever searching for a nest to look after. The scattered eggs, he recorded pensively, were called by the Spaniards *huachos:* orphans or foundlings.

Darwin's evident ability to ride, use guns, and enjoy himself is often forgotten in discussions of his years on the *Beagle.* Yet to those around him at the time, he liked nothing better than a ride across the pampas, learning to throw the *bolas* and smoke *cigarritos* with the gauchos, shooting and fishing not only for the purposes of his collection but also to provide food for himself and the *Beagle* crew. He had some good sporting in Patagonia, he told Caroline; "but in this line I never enjoyed anything so much as Ostrich hunting with the wild soldiers, who are more than half Indian. They catch them by throwing two balls which are attached to the ends of a thong so as to entangle their legs: it was a fine animated chace." Flinging the *bolas* round his head like the rest of them, Darwin succeeded in tripping up his horse. "The Gauchos roared with laughter; they cried they had seen every sort of animal caught, but had never before seen a man caught by himself."

Hunting and shooting came easily to him. Natural history collecting, after all, was not so very far removed from hunting: the two activities were different expressions of a single urge for possession and inspired in Darwin ardent responses that were familiar in some degree to every one of his colleagues on the *Beagle.* All the officers and most of the ordinary sailors knew how to hunt and shoot. Their lives—and their stomachs—depended on the accurate use of firearms; and no one saw any harm in combining the procuring of food or self-defense with capturing a few local souvenirs like puma skins or sharks' teeth. Darwin's occupations were remarkable only in that he did these things all the time. Many of the others would have liked to be rich enough and sufficiently friendly with the captain to spend their hours similarly.

His early prowess during the English partridge season therefore served

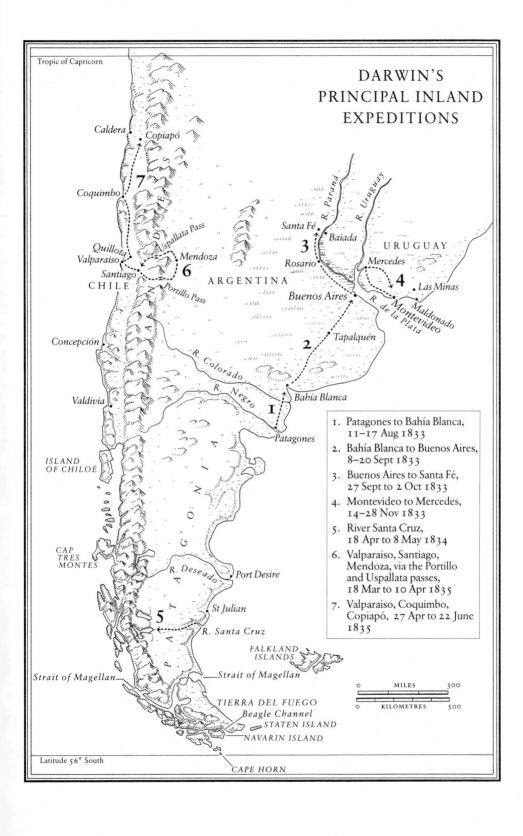

Tropic of Capricorn

DARWIN'S
PRINCIPAL INLAND
EXPEDITIONS

Caldera
Copiapó

Coquimbo

7

Quillota   Uspallata Pass
Valparaiso   Mendoza
Santiago   6
CHILE   Portillo Pass

Santa Fé
Baiada
URUGUAY
Rosario   Mercedes
3
4   Las Minas
ARGENTINA   Maldonado
Buenos Aires   Montevideo
Tapalquén   R. de la Plata

Concepción   R. Colorado

2

R. Negro
Valdivia   Bahía Blanca
1
Patagones

ISLAND
OF CHILOÉ

R. Paraná   R. Uruguay

A N D E S

CAP
TRES
MONTES

R. Deseado   Port Desire

5

St Julian
R. Santa Cruz

Strait of Magellan

FALKLAND
ISLANDS

Strait of Magellan

TIERRA DEL FUEGO
Beagle Channel
STATEN ISLAND
NAVARIN ISLAND

Latitude 56° South

CAPE HORN

P A T A G O N I A

1. Patagones to Bahía Blanca,
   11–17 Aug 1833
2. Bahía Blanca to Buenos Aires,
   8–20 Sept 1833
3. Buenos Aires to Santa Fé,
   27 Sept to 2 Oct 1833
4. Montevideo to Mercedes,
   14–28 Nov 1833
5. River Santa Cruz,
   18 Apr to 8 May 1834
6. Valparaiso, Santiago,
   Mendoza, via the Portillo
   and Uspallata passes,
   18 Mar to 10 Apr 1835
7. Valparaiso, Coquimbo,
   Copiapó, 27 Apr to 22 June
   1835

0   MILES   300
0   KILOMETRES   500

him well. During these first months in Argentina, Darwin became a valued member of the shooting parties sent out by FitzRoy to find something to eat, describing his culinary booty with pride in letters home. Fuller, Stokes, and Bynoe, the acknowledged marksmen of the crew, welcomed him on their expeditions to fell deer, cavia, and the nervous, excitable guanaco, which constituted the greater portion of their fresh meat during their time in the south.

> I am spending September in Patagonia, much in the same manner as I should in England, viz. in shooting; in this case however there is the extra satisfaction of knowing that one gives fresh provisions to the ships company. —Today I shot another deer & an Agouti or Cavy.—The latter weighs more than 20 pounds; & affords the very best meat I ever tasted.—Whilst shooting I walked several miles within the interior; the general features of the country remain the same, an undulating sandy plain covered with coarse herbage & which as it extends, gradually becomes more level. —The bottoms of some of the vallies are green with clover: it is by cautiously crawling so as to peep into these that the game is shot.—If a deer has not seen you stand upright, generally it is possessed with an insatiable curiosity to find out what you are; & to such an extent that I have fired several times without frightening it away.—[19]

To his shame as a sportsman, he shouted at one deer until it ran off.

This kind of useful participation in the *Beagle*'s kitchen economy continued on board ship with his fishing lines and trawl, although there was strong competition among the sailors to land bigger and better spoils. The captain's table was usually the first to benefit, and Darwin and FitzRoy dined on fresh tuna, turtle, shark, and barracuda (spelled "Barrow Cooter" in Darwin's diary) in turn. There was hardly any opportunity for salt beef and biscuit, he assured the womenfolk at home. More likely to appear on the menu were ostrich dumpling and armadillo. "The former would never be recognised as a bird but rather as beef,—the armadilloes when (unlike the Gauchos' fashion) cooked without their cases, taste & look like a duck.—Both of them are very good." He was ready to try almost anything, although some changes in diet were difficult to accommodate for any length of time—the gauchos ate far too much meat and not enough salt, he protested feebly.

This robust side to Darwin's character was an important feature of his day-to-day mode of living and undoubtedly facilitated his integration into the *Beagle*'s company. Uncomplicated enthusiasm for life and a vigorous disposition endeared him to the officers. "With my pistols in my belt & geological hammer in hand, shall I not look like a grand barbarian?" he asked them. FitzRoy too saw the strength of character. His messmate, he explained in a letter to his sister Frances Rice Trevor, was "a good pedestrian, as well as a good horseman; he is a sensible, shrewd, and sterling good fellow. While I am pottering about in the water, measuring depths and fixing positions, he wanders over the land—and frequently makes long excursions where I cannot go, because my duty is Hydro- not Geo-graphy."[20]

IV

Despite these gentle protestations, FitzRoy was with Darwin when the major natural history excitement of the first voyage south occurred. Sailing aimlessly round Bahía Blanca bay one day in September 1832, the two rounded a headland called Punta Alta and noticed some broken bones and shells embedded in the low-lying silty banks. Could they be fossils? asked FitzRoy.

Quickly pulling the launch over and scrabbling through the soil with bare hands, they found they had chanced on a natural mausoleum. There were many more bones further in, the fossilised remains of animals from long ago turned into stone by chemical percolation through the silt. Not surprisingly, Darwin could barely contain himself. Like any young naturalist of the period, he passionately hoped to find animal relics from an earlier age, the larger the better. Now, happily up to his elbows in earth, he anticipated that these would be sensational. All the way back to the ship and late into the night, tusks and thighbones as tall as a man danced about in his head, until even FitzRoy felt obliged to change the subject if they were to get through dinner in good order.

The next morning Darwin returned with axes and sailors from the *Beagle* to start chipping through the soft sedimentary deposits.

"I have been wonderfully lucky with fossil bones," he crowed on the sixth day. "Some of the animals must have been of great dimensions: I am almost sure that many of them are quite new; this is always pleasant, but with the antediluvian animals it is doubly so."[21]

Incomplete skeletons of three big animals were at last revealed, along with a number of miscellaneous smaller bones, mostly teeth, from local South American species, primarily armadillos and tree sloths, which he recognised more or less straight away. A mysterious "head of some large animal, imbedded in a soft rock" took a whole afternoon to dig out; but dig it out he would. "I did not get it on board till some hours after it was dark." All the effort of excavating and loading the great skull into the launch, the ropes and pulleys over the side of the ship, the colourful curses, were ignored in his moment of triumph. "Notwithstanding our smiles at the cargoes of apparent rubbish which he frequently brought on board," said FitzRoy, "he and his servant used their pick-axes in earnest, and brought away what have since proved to be the most interesting and valuable remains of extinct animals."[22] Wickham and several of the younger *Beagle* ratings were swept up by the melodrama of this chase for fossils, longing to join in whenever possible and eager to catch news of any possible cliff-hammering campaigns; and the rubble Darwin spread out on deck became a fertile source of amusement. Picking a path through the philosopher's stones—"dirt," he called it—was something Wickham always recalled with brusque affection when asked about Darwin's *Beagle* days.

Darwin thought the biggest jaw—the one that gave them such trouble—and the large bony plates found with it belonged to either a *Megalonyx* or a *Megatherium,* powerful animals the size of a small elephant, which Cuvier, and then William Clift of the Royal College of Surgeons in London, had described some twenty to thirty years earlier. He was not working entirely from memory here, although the extinct animals he once learned about in Jameson's Edinburgh museum were possibly useful points of reference.[23] More immediately, his copy of Bory de Saint Vincent's encyclopedia, the *Dictionnaire classique,* provided full descriptions of both these extinct species with pictures to help the identification.[24] Another smaller jawbone containing a tooth convinced him he had recovered the remains of a *Megatherium,* although he was mistaken in following the dictionary's opinion that this animal was covered with a carapace like an armadillo. When the experts in London subsequently set to work they decided the plates belonged to something else—itself a creature relatively new to science named *Hoplophorus,* like a giant armadillo or glyptodont.

It was impossible to doubt that these bony giants were extinct. The *Megatherium,* for example, had been the subject of an exhaustive study that convinced Cuvier in 1795 of the fact of extinction. No one on the *Beagle* would have suggested that the animals still roamed the Argentine plains.

Yet the overall nature of the other remains and the composition of the silty beds in which they were found created difficulties in understanding why and when they disappeared. The bones were mixed up with fossilised seashells that appeared to Darwin identical with shells of living creatures on the shores of South America. The conglomerate itself was of indeterminate age but probably quite new in geological terms. If the bones and shells were contemporary, it meant these enormous animals had been alive in the very recent geological past, so recent, he said, that the shells were still in existence: a point hard to accept, since the conditions of the country had seemingly not changed much. If not contemporary, how had the bones got into deposits of a subsequent era?

No answers emerged before the *Beagle* moved off to its next engagement in spite of the theories spilling out from captain, crew, and Darwin alike—enough to account for a whole museum of bones if necessary. The specimens needed to be packed and shipped to England for a proper analysis.

Please be careful with the numbers inked onto the pieces, Darwin implored Henslow. "*Many* points *entirely* depend on the numbers being carefully preserved."[25]

V

With the discovery of the fossils came a general assumption that Darwin was now the man most concerned with natural history on the voyage. From then on he was given all the practical advantages of an official naturalist to the expedition, with the added benefit of being entitled to keep possession of his material when the *Beagle* returned. He did not replace McCormick, nor in any strict sense could he, not possessing a commission in the navy; moreover, there were others on board equally willing to take on the surgeon's customary tasks in natural history. Nonetheless, it was Darwin who became the person most obviously authorised to form a collection, and the crew thereafter generally deferred to him.

Yet almost every officer on the ship had a liking for natural history and the outdoor life. The way that Darwin smoothly rose to the top of a body of amateur naturalists on board ship reflected nothing so much as his position in relation to FitzRoy. First Lieutenant Wickham was something of a botanist. Second Lieutenant Sulivan was a good geologist, of no mean ability to judge from his studies of the Falkland Islands, and he collected plants assiduously. Benjamin Bynoe, the assistant surgeon (promoted to acting surgeon after McCormick's departure), was another capable field naturalist and supervised the gathering of wild celery and cranberries in Tierra del Fuego in order to replenish the ship's supply of antiscorbutics. He went on to make botanical collections both on the *Beagle* voyage and elsewhere that displayed real interest and a knowledge of plants. Bynoe also collected geological specimens, as he had done on the previous expedition.[26] John Lort Stokes took pride in the skill with which he could stalk game, reflecting a boyhood spent in the countryside, and the twelve-year-old volunteer Charles Musters, on his first voyage, thought there was nothing better than splashing through the shallows around Botofogo Bay shooting snipe.

Even FitzRoy and lesser mortals like the two midshipman, Phillip Gidley King and Arthur Mellersh, made natural history collections. FitzRoy's steward, Harry Fuller, and Edward Hellyer, the ship's clerk, for example, collected birds. Hellyer drowned in the Falklands in March 1833 while attempting to retrieve an interesting specimen shot for his collection. FitzRoy's bird skins, given to the British Museum in 1836, were essential to Darwin after his return to England when he discovered that the Galápagos Islands possessed different species of mockingbirds and finches: Darwin had mostly ignored the precise geographic locale when gathering his own specimens.[27] FitzRoy gave the museum its only representative of the (now extinct) Falkland Islands fox, the *"loup-renard"* of Bougainville, and imported several native dogs from Tierra del Fuego and Patagonia, one of which was still alive in the zoological gardens in London in 1840.[28] He brought a tortoise home from the Galápagos as a pet, and the skin of a puma shot by Mr. Stewart; and he kept rare breeds of South American rabbits on board until they escaped by chewing through their boxes. While in New Zealand he purchased the jaws of an enormous shark killed by an English whaling crew just as it was about to crunch the men's launch, but what he did with them remains unknown.[29] And like Darwin, FitzRoy had a special interest in geology, reading several of the major texts in this field, including Lyell's *Principles*. FitzRoy collected lava on Ascension Island and fossil shells in Patagonia, again for the British Museum. This scientifically inclined captain made a useful collection of mineralogical specimens and thought carefully about the interpretation of the various landforms and other geological features seen on the voyage.

Despite their own inclination to accumulate private collections, these men made a habit of bringing back the most interesting objects for Darwin's opinion. They copied out charts or geological sketches for his use, sometimes also helping with his observations. Wickham and Sulivan were generous with their natural history information, which seems to have been mostly Darwin's for the taking—the only exceptions were Sulivan's plants, which he regarded as something special and dispatched periodically to his father and on to the London botanist John Lindley for identification. Their trained surveyor's eyes identified rock formations for Darwin's notes when the *Beagle* stood too far out to sea to make geological explorations, and their joint experience of working in the same area during the first *Beagle* survey kept him well primed about natural history sites to visit. Darwin also took any advice that Benjamin Bynoe cared to offer.

The ordinary sailors on board similarly gave Darwin the benefit of their experience, and several of the visiting pilots and harbour masters, no doubt impressed by his obvious status on board, provided help and information. Edward Lumb, an English merchant in Buenos Aires, for instance, gave Darwin living quarters in his house in 1833 (it was strange to see Mrs. Lumb making tea, Darwin reported, after months in the wild) and arranged for a cargo of fossil bones to be sent to England after his guest's departure. Lumb's friend Mr. Hughes, sailing from Buenos Aires to Liverpool, saw this consignment of specimens (or perhaps a second one) through English customs free of import duty: another considerable favour to Darwin. In Chiloé, a local surveyor named Charles Douglas collected beetles for him while acting as a pilot and interpreter to FitzRoy, and compiled records of local earthquakes at Darwin's request which were forwarded and used by him in later days.

Towards the end of the voyage in September 1835, Alexander Usborne, the master's assistant on the *Beagle,* made a complicated reconnaissance of the Peruvian coast to complete Darwin's study of the geology of South America at a time when the *Beagle* itself, with Darwin and FitzRoy aboard, was sailing onward to the Galápagos.[30]

As FitzRoy later pointed out, Sulivan, Bynoe, and the rest gave up any possible claims they had on the natural world to help Darwin perfect his personal collection. The official collection, assembled under FitzRoy's orders after McCormick's departure, was allowed to take second place to Darwin's numerous barrels and boxes. Darwin, FitzRoy rumbled darkly in post-*Beagle* days, should not forget the generosity extended to him by captain and crew alike. It seems only too evident, however, that he did.

VI

Darwin made full use of the freedom that underwrote these independent circumstances and after rejoining the ship for its departure from Bahía Blanca established a pattern of natural history work that he maintained throughout the rest of the voyage. His prime objective was to stay on land for as long as possible. Sometimes the ship's itinerary permitted only a few hours on shore. More often than not, he could make arrangements for riding expeditions of several days' duration or spend weeks working at his collections while staying in lodgings or as the guest of expatriate Englishmen.

One rather obvious point about this distribution of his time is that his journey on the *Beagle* was not so much a voyage at sea as a series of miscellaneous travels on land. Although he was away from home for five years, Darwin was at sea for a combined total of only eighteen months in all, with the longest single stretch aboard being forty-seven days. A more usual ocean run was between eight and eighteen days. FitzRoy and his crew undoubtedly spent much longer times on the ship than Darwin, who had a privileged position as FitzRoy's guest. It seems that the guest took advantage of this convenient situation: he was on land for a grand total of three years and one month. Some of these intervals extended to four months, as when Darwin travelled in the Río Negro area of Patagonia or made a major geological tour of the Andes, setting out from an old Shropshire friend's house in Valparaiso. On another occasion he spent three and a half months based at the same friend's home in Valparaiso. Most of his shore visits were longer than a fortnight, and only five out of a total of thirty-seven landings were less than a week in length. So the colourful picture of FitzRoy and Darwin cooped up in a small boat for weeks on end or of Darwin delving into his psyche alone on deck out in the middle of the ocean may indeed be true, but only in part. There comes the more mundane but inescapable conclusion that Darwin was on shore, exploring the countryside and going about his business, for roughly three-fifths of the expedition.

During these periods ashore he worked like a man possessed: most of his life was literally crammed into the days spent safely out of the reach of seasickness on firm land. In one respect the itinerary of the *Beagle* forced this intensive programme upon him. FitzRoy occasionally retraced his steps if the course of the survey required it or if bad weather delayed him, but such events were haphazard and not to be depended on. Darwin was obliged to complete his tasks before the *Beagle* left because there was no guarantee that the ship would ever return to the same area. It was imperative to work at full pitch.

Yet he also experienced the deepest pleasure imaginable in carrying out his self-imposed natural history tasks and wished for nothing more than the opportunity to work as hard as he could at the occupations he enjoyed most. It was satisfying to realise that these piecemeal diversions were his job for the next few years. "Naturalising is doing my duty," he happily told himself; "if I neglected that duty I should at the same time neglect what has for some years given me so much pleasure."[31] At the end of the voyage he was still writing to his sisters that "such pursuits are sources of the very highest pleasures I am capable of enjoying."

Before landing in any new area, Darwin laid out his plan of action carefully, taking advice from FitzRoy and other colleagues and the books available to him. The first requirement, however, was money.

He found it essential on arriving in a major port to go straight to the local bank or English agent to draw cash on his father's account through the international banking system. He kept Dr. Darwin informed about the *Beagle*'s schedule and from time to time supplicated him—with increasing energy as his scientific ambitions escalated—with pleas for money orders to be available at forthcoming ports for immediate encashment. Since the ship's route ranged across some of the most untouched regions of the globe, each visit to a bank became more and more important.

And inevitably, his outgoings were considerable. Darwin paid the captain £50 a year for his food and soon took on the additional cost of a servant, at first sharing one of FitzRoy's cabin staff—a young assistant to the bird-collecting steward, Harry Fuller—and then employing a member of the crew, Syms Covington, as his personal attendant at £60 a year. Seventeen years old, universally referred to as one of the ship's "boys" and, as Darwin put it, "fiddler and boy to the Poop cabin," Covington remained with Darwin as servant, secretary, and natural history assistant during the voyage and well beyond, only leaving his employment when Darwin married. Deaf in one ear, notwithstanding (or possibly because of) which he was a good shot, and possessed of a clear round handwriting, Covington became an essential adjunct to Darwin's scientific work—the unacknowledged shadow behind every triumph. "I do not very much like him; but he is, perhaps from his very oddity, very well adapted to all my purposes."[32] Covington's own diary of the *Beagle* voyage reveals a phlegmatic character and a tendency toward bemusement at the escapades of his buccaneering "Don Carlos."

Darwin also paid for his food and lodgings on shore. Over and above these anticipated expenses, there was still the financing of natural history expeditions to consider. He usually hired a local guide, horses, and baggage mules for as long as was necessary, and occasionally commissioned help with his actual collecting while staying for any length of time in a single place. "A few reales," he once wrote from Maldonado, "has enlisted all the boys in the town in my service; & few days pass, in which they do not bring me some curious creature."[33] Sometimes he gathered a large party of people around him for a long expedition. Sometimes he took just a single guide and Covington. But he always travelled with someone, for FitzRoy never allowed a member of the ship's company ashore on his own unless the *Beagle* was berthed in a large city where the men could more or less look after themselves. It was unsafe to travel alone, and Darwin was told to consider the hiring of companions an essential precaution.

The captain's orders did not prevent Darwin from feeling guilty every time he asked his father for money: five years spent touring the world as a gentleman-naturalist was bound to be expensive. The net total of the drafts he requested from Shrewsbury added up to a little under £1,200, a sum that should be judged against Covington's annual salary of £60 and Darwin's lavish pre-*Beagle* allowance of £100 a year and the £600 or so spent outfitting him for the voyage. Darwin was costing his father more than twice as much as if he had stayed in England, a point that did not pass unnoticed either in South America or in Shrewsbury. His letters home were always full of elaborate justifications for the latest bout of extravagance interlarded with high-flown and probably sincere promises to reimburse Dr. Darwin later. No wonder Darwin took such care of his specimens: they cost his father a fortune. In the most basic of ways they were the final products emerging from Dr. Darwin's investment.

But he knew his father would pay. The money turned into the kind of joke that was only possible in wealthy families: Darwin forever promising to control his expenditure and protesting he could hardly spend a thing when the *Beagle* was making one of its longer cruises; while at the same time Dr. Darwin solicitously arranged for his London bank to honour each and every dubious-looking South American call on his account. The family bankers, Robarts, Curtis & Co., of Lombard Street, were instructed to pay every bill without a query.

VII

Since Darwin was well situated, well financed, and well looked after by his family and *Beagle* friends, it is no surprise that his collecting successes on the *Beagle* voyage were many and various. Modelling his activities on the comprehensive intellectual range of Alexander von Humboldt, he eventually succeeded in mastering an equivalent breadth of scientific and personal concerns. He recorded everything he saw in the natural history line and much from other fields such as ethnology and political economy, and gathered a comprehensive series of specimens from most of the places visited. The material went to Henslow in Cambridge, who agreed to act as a kind of receiving officer. Henslow performed the necessary function of unpacking the cases on receipt to check the contents of bottles and boxes and to see that unwanted insects had not destroyed Darwin's prizes. Most things were arriving in pretty good order, he reassuringly wrote early in 1833 after receiving the first consignment. But what on earth was in packet 223? he asked doubtfully. "It looks like the remains of an electric explosion, a mere mass of soot—something very curious I dare say." Towards the end of the voyage, Henslow ran out of space and was obliged to rent an unused lecture room in the university to lay out the items adequately. There were eight consignments in all, plus one box of bones (or perhaps two) sent independently by Edward Lumb from Buenos Aires.

Advice given earlier by Henslow, Richardson, Brown, and the other naturalists Darwin had met in the British Museum or sought out in London and Plymouth was well heeded, for he collected carefully and with much thought. His longstanding interest in small and seemingly insignificant animals encouraged him to focus on these and other organisms that might normally be overlooked. He concentrated on insects, many of them minute, including moths and other night fliers rarely collected; and then by extension on small reptiles, fish, inconspicuous mammals like mice and shrews, and diminutive organisms such as spiders, corals, barnacles, molluscs, and soft-bodied invertebrates of all kinds. He fully indulged his boyhood passion for birds.

Little things became the key to his researches. He was blissfully content grubbing around under stones, turning over logs, peering behind bits of bark. "I *fancy,*" remarked FitzRoy about Darwin's first collection from Rio de Janeiro, "that, though of small things, it is numerous and valuable, and will convince the Cantabrigians that their envoy is no Idler."[34] All Darwin's previous enthusiasms manifested themselves in this scavenging for tiny animals.

Darwin also tried hard to gather plants for Henslow, hunting out bizarre fungi or cacti; and he methodically dried and pressed specimens of the flowering plants he encountered. Battling with a large palm leaf and a small piece of paper on which to attach it, he occasionally felt his botanical specimens were not sufficiently appreciated by their recipient, especially when he was subsequently told to fold them in quite a different way. But he continued. Even so, although Henslow was pleased with the plants that arrived for him, he never managed to find time to classify them properly, eventually passing bits and pieces on to his taxonomist friends and the remainder to Joseph Dalton Hooker at the Royal Botanic Gardens, Kew. Out in South America, Darwin had already forgotten how much Henslow's interests mostly lay in living organisms, not in these laboriously accumulated herbarium sheets.

Still, Darwin did not try to send live plants and animals back to England, compensating for the lack of technical sophistication in nineteenth-century travelling cases by packing mainly dried bulbs and seeds in boxes filled with sand. One such box containing wild potato tubers from the Chonos Archipelago stimulated Henslow and then Fox into suggesting they might serve as uninfected stock in the opening years of the Irish potato blight.[35] Actually Darwin would have dearly liked to bring some of his trophies home alive—a monkey at the very least—but it was almost impossible to dispatch or carry exotic species over the Atlantic without special precautions, and wild animals and plants usually died from the experience. Yet the combined attentions of all the *Beagle*'s naturalists managed to keep a Falkland fox alive for several months, as also some indigenous dogs from Tierra del Fuego, a few South American rabbits, and FitzRoy's tortoise. Many of the crew were used to dealing with pigs, goats, chickens, and turtles brought in at various stages for the cooking pot and probably enjoyed varying their duties by attending to curious new animals. But only the dogs, a fox skin, and an empty tortoise shell arrived in Plymouth.

Along with this, Darwin made extensive geological collections supplementing his researches in that field and providing the requisite information about deposits where fossils were found.

Throughout it all he showed no qualms about shooting birds and animals, energetically digging up rare plants by the roots, collecting armfuls of living corals and seashells, and dining off turtles, alpacas, and armadillos with all the gusto of an unconcerned sailor. Though Darwin ultimately came to hate killing animals, there was little evidence of this during the early years of the voyage itself; and even Darwin came to believe he gave up his shooting habits only as his "primeval instincts" slowly yielded to the acquired tastes of a civilized man.[36]

On the contrary, like any young Turk, he was capable of sweeping into a new area, taking everything he saw, and sweeping out again. Compassionate ideas about leaving nature as it was, or of giving a set of specimens to local institutions, such as they were, never entered his head. When visiting the Museo Público de Buenos Aires, the first natural history museum established in South America, he patronisingly recorded how bad it was compared to those at home, "although esteemed as second to none by the inhabitants."[37] The botanic garden in Rio hardly deserved the name. But he could see no reason to sacrifice his own hard-won collections for the sake of improving the state of South American science. After all, the Madrid Museum made no apologies for exhibiting a complete *Megatherium* skeleton fifty years before any Argentine establishment.[38] National and personal motives came first. And Darwin did not give away his specimens to interested South American acquaintances lightly. The only recorded instance came when he wrote to Henry Stephen Fox, the senior British diplomat in Rio de Janeiro, about the geology of the Andes. Darwin enclosed a few rock specimens, "of little value," he modestly feared, before launching into some complex questions about elevation he wanted answering.[39] It was obvious that Darwin gathered material entirely with himself and some nebulous vision of national pride in mind. He intended to make his collections as complete as possible, and he intended to take them back to England.

In this, Darwin was but a typical actor on the expanding geographical stage of early-nineteenth-century Europe, bringing to his work unthinking assumptions of superiority that encouraged him to believe the natural commodities of unexplored countries were his to claim by intellectual and cultural right. The distinction between collecting, hunting, and plundering was never very clear in the activities of any naturalist in this period. Darwin's overall ethos hardly differed from that of a commercial trader gathering his wares, or souvenir-collectors such as the junior officers on the *Beagle,* on the one hand, or of British officials sent out to reconnoitre the larger potential of foreign territories, like FitzRoy, on the other.[40] The declared scientific nature of the voyage and the argument that geographical exploration contributed to the general advancement of learning, however sincerely maintained, was only the outer varnish of a far deeper and more widely shared conviction that European countries—Britain in particular—were fully justified in exploring and exploiting the rest of the world. The absolute right to curiosity expressed their absolute control. The ultimate aim was always national expansion.

VIII

The *Beagle* made way for Buenos Aires in October 1832, sweeping along at night on a luminous sea. Darwin felt like a real mariner at last. "The vessel drove before her bows two billows of liquid phosphorus, & in her wake was a milky train.—As far as the eye reached, the crest of every wave was bright; & from the reflected light, the sky just above the horizon was not so utterly dark as the rest of the heavens.—It was impossible to behold this plain of matter, as it were melted & consuming by heat, without being reminded of Miltons description of Chaos & Anarchy."[41]

The guard ship at Buenos Aires treated them with more respect the second time around, and their business was completed quickly. Darwin went to the theatre ("I did not understand one word") and to the museum ("very poor"), and visited a local curiosity in Donna Clara, a former convict woman who had made good by marrying a man of property. At the same time he struck up a pleasant friendship with Robert Hamond, a young naval lieutenant from the *Druid* in Montevideo, who had come to join the *Beagle* for its next cruise south. The two of them had plenty of opportunity to parade the squares looking at Spanish ladies. After seeing these "angels gliding down the streets," Darwin realised English women could neither walk nor dress. "It would do the whole tribe of you a great deal of good to come to Buenos Ayres," he groaned to his sisters.

After a few more days getting stores in Montevideo, and a grand ball, they were off again, this time for Tierra del Fuego.

chapter

10

ALMOST ANOTHER
SPECIES OF MAN

O all intents and purposes, the three Fuegians travelling on board the *Beagle* were the expedition's prize specimens. Like some rare form of animal they had been collected by FitzRoy, transported to England, turned to goals quite beyond the horizons of Tierra del Fuego, and exhibited to the king and queen, and were in the process of being shipped back to their country of origin to fulfil the captain's visions of establishing Christianity in the far south. Just like any precious object destined for a botanic garden or museum case, they were carefully looked after all the while. Although FitzRoy would never have contemplated publicising the Fuegians as literal exhibits in a money-making London show or parading them at meetings of scientific societies, he did, when requested, display them privately during their time in England, so much so that the terminology of a natural history collection held real meaning for him: he did indeed consider the Fuegians as material to be assessed and discussed, trained and repatriated almost as a new and improved kind of domestic animal.

Because of this, the three were necessarily the subject of interested speculation in London. As they might have made a trip to the new zoological gardens in nearby Regent's Park, FitzRoy's aristocratic friends and relations came to look at the Fuegians working on their infant primers in the schoolmaster's house in Walthamstow. So did various members of the English missionary societies and a succession of philanthropic ladies who collected equipment for the projected mission station in Tierra del Fuego. The Fuegians furthermore bowed and curtsied to King William and Queen Adelaide just like the other human curios and circus turns that the royal couple loved to see in private performance.

Having been displayed, the Fuegians were also examined. FitzRoy at one stage took them to a phrenologist to have their heads read. His intention was to make sure that their characters and moral attributes were equal to the task he envisaged for them. All three, the phrenologist concluded, possessed several marked "animal" traits that would be difficult to eradicate, even through education. Their intellectual bumps—those associated with civilised mankind—were found to be small, whereas their "propensities"—the parts of the brain believed most characteristic of a barbarian—were large and full. At the same time, as if to emphasise a growing gulf between observer and observed—between collector and specimen, aristocrat and savage—the solitary pickled corpse brought home in a barrel from the first *Beagle* voyage was dissected at the Royal College of Surgeons.[1]

Even the names given to the three captives—Fuegia Basket, Jemmy Button, and York Minster—were nonhuman in their terms of reference. Baskets, buttons, and architectural features were more appropriate to dogs than people. Their real names, as recorded in FitzRoy's *Narrative* of the first *Beagle* voyage, were Yokcushlu (Fuegia), Orundellico (Jemmy), and El'leparu (York).

Through all this the Fuegians accepted FitzRoy's wishes with placid indifference. If they were regarded as biological specimens they did not appear to notice or care. But it was still a deeply exploitive moment in the relations between north and south. FitzRoy felt quite within his rights to take—and educate—people for religious purposes beyond their ken. He was sure he had acted reasonably, always believing the Fuegians accompanied him willingly and that this was justification enough for initiating his experiment.

In one sense, of course, this kind of experiment was not unusual. There had been any number of such exotics brought to Britain since Captain Cook co-opted the Tahitian Omai from the South Seas in 1775. After two years of socialising in London and having his portrait painted by William Parry, Omai returned home exhausted on Cook's last voyage. Several of these strange imports became celebrated in fashionable circles, although never as social equals. "Tono Maria," an Indian woman from Brazil with a wooden plug in her lower lip, was renowned in 1822 as the "Venus of South America," while in the same year 58,000 visitors paid to gaze upon a family of Laplanders accompanied by live reindeer in the Egyptian Hall. Twenty years later, a troop of "Ioways," complete with feathered headdresses, made a triumphant progress through society, culminating in breakfast with Disraeli.[2]

On a less public scale, individuals or small groups of people arriving from foreign missions for an English education were also common enough by the 1830s. The practice began on a large scale with Zachary Macaulay, who returned from Sierra Leone in 1799 with twenty-five Negro children to be taught by a schoolmaster in Clapham. The children went on to help the Church Missionary Society's work in Africa. In reverse, the missionary and translator Hannah Kilham acquired her first grasp of West African languages from two native sailors being educated by a mission in Tottenham.

Few of these visitors from abroad were volunteers. Yet like so many of their sponsors, or kidnappers, FitzRoy was animated by missionary zeal and a simplistic belief that his aboriginals were just as much free agents as Englishmen, perfectly capable of deciding whether they wished to sail to Plymouth or not. "They understand why they were taken, and look forward with pleasure to seeing our country, as well as returning to their own," he wrote.[3] It never crossed his mind that there had been no choice at all.

II

Everyone on board the *Beagle* was fascinated by the returning Fuegians.

The oldest of them was York Minster, who from the start seemed dangerously difficult to handle. "His disposition was reserved, taciturn, morose, and when excited violently passionate; his affections were very strong towards a few friends on board; his intellect good," reported Darwin.[4] York was about twenty-eight or thirty years old by the time the ship arrived back in Tierra del Fuego. Both Darwin and the captain felt uneasy in the presence of this sullen, muscular man, especially since it was obvious he understood a great deal more English than he cared to divulge. It was "singularly difficult" to extract information from him. At the schoolmaster's house he was hard to teach, disliked learning to read, and was reluctant to take a hand in the garden work believed necessary to train the Fuegians for mission life. FitzRoy anxiously referred Darwin to the phrenologist's opinion that York was "disposed to cunning and caution. . . . from possessing a strong self-will, he will be difficult to instruct, and will require a great deal of humouring and indulgence to lead him to do what is required."[5] The only time York showed any spark of interest in his new situation, the captain confessed, was when first travelling through London in a private carriage. He saw the stone lion in front of Northumberland House and "certainly thought [it] alive and walking there."

Jemmy Button was also passionate, but his was an altogether softer, weaker character. Simple-hearted, affectionate, fond of a good joke, short, fat, and vain, he was the ship's favourite. The expression on his face, claimed Darwin (unconsciously echoing the physiognomical theories that had once made FitzRoy doubtfully view the Darwinian nose), immediately revealed a "nice disposition."

He was merry and often laughed, and was remarkably sympathetic with anyone in pain: when the water was rough, I was often a little sea-sick, and he used to come to me and say in a plaintive voice, "Poor, poor fellow!" but the notion, after his aquatic life, of a man being sea-sick, was too ludicrous, and he was generally obliged to turn on one side to hide a smile or laugh, and then he would repeat his "Poor, poor fellow!" He was of a patriotic disposition; and he liked to praise his own tribe and country, in which he truly said there were "plenty of trees," and he abused all the other tribes: he stoutly declared that there was no Devil in his land.[6]

Jemmy took pride in his Anglicised appearance and after the first *Beagle* voyage rapidly graduated from the rough canvas outfit of sailors to smart London clothes. Now, like any ambitious city clerk of the period, he oiled his thick black hair and enjoyed fancy pattern-work on the braces for his trousers: "he used to wear gloves, his hair was neatly cut, and he was distressed if his well-polished shoes were dirtied." Darwin's characterisation edged towards music-hall stereotype. "He was fond of admiring himself in a looking-glass; and a merry-faced little Indian boy from the Rio Negro, whom we had for some months on board, soon perceived this, and used to mock him: Jemmy, who was always rather jealous of the attention paid to this little boy, did not at all like this, and used to say, with rather a contemptuous twist of his head, 'Too much skylark.' " The self-important servant, aggrieved at a joke against himself, was a stock character from stage and literature that all the Englishmen on board could recognise and lavish proprietorial affections on. Jemmy did not bruise British illusions in the way York Minster did.

Nevertheless, Darwin was fully alive to the differences between Europeans and those who merely mimicked their ways, even if it was a predominantly indulgent and paternalistic contrast that he drew. The Anglicised Fuegians possessed attributes that were quite distinct, he thought, from those of civilised mankind.

In particular, their mental world was a mystery. No amount of questioning by him revealed useful information about their religious beliefs, although it was evident that all three were, as he put it, "superstitious." They thought it very bad luck to kill a bird on the wing, for instance. Their talk of devils, however, was irredeemably mixed up with biblical teachings learned in Walthamstow. Darwin was also exasperated by the Fuegians' inability to comprehend any questions involving what an Englishman would consider a plain alternative. He regarded their lack of any distinction between yes and no, or black and white, as enigmatic in the extreme. His frequent use of the word "simple" in this context reflected the popular Western view that the aboriginal mind was generally undeveloped and unorganised, often childlike in its immediacy.

The most striking physical difference was that Jemmy and York had remarkably good eyesight, a point that interested Darwin personally as well as biologically, because he was accustomed to think of his own eyesight as exceptionally strong: those "telescopes you call eyes," Erasmus used to say. Only five or six of the crew could see as far or further than Darwin. But the male Fuegians' sight was much superior, a fact they turned to their advantage. "They were quite conscious of this power; and Jemmy, when he had any little quarrel with the officer on watch, would say, 'Me see ship, me no tell.' " Jemmy also surprised Darwin by protesting that the sour wild berries Bynoe was expecting them all to eat as preventives against scurvy were far too sweet. Much later on, Darwin came to believe these acutely developed senses were essential for preserving life under adverse conditions, and wrote in his *Descent of Man* of them as important features characterising primitive tribes and early human beings in the evolutionary hierarchy. For forty years he remembered how impressive Jemmy's and York's natural powers were compared to his own.

The third and last was Fuegia Basket, by then a young woman of twelve or thirteen. She was, in Darwin's words, "a nice, modest, reserved young girl, with a rather pleasing but sometimes sullen expression, and very quick in learning anything, especially languages. This she showed by picking up some Portuguese and Spanish, when left on shore for only a short time at Rio de Janeiro and Monte Video, and in her knowledge of English."[7] It would not be difficult, said FitzRoy, to make her a useful member of society: it had been Fuegia who softened the hearts of visitors to Walthamstow with her unassuming manners. The same social transparency stimulated Queen Adelaide to give her a bonnet and ring (appropriately plain) as souvenirs of her royal audience. Fuegia Basket wore them often.

Like the others, she was short in stature. One day, less circumspectly than usual, Darwin told his diary that Fuegia "daily increases in every direction except height." She nearly capsized the launch, an officer remarked, and had to be shifted from side to side like a bundle of dirty clothes every time the boat tacked.[8] Fuegia was said to be engaged to be married to York Minster. Conventional English assumptions must have coloured this interpretation of their wishes, since there is no evidence that a Christian ceremony was proposed or intended. However, York Minster was very possessive about Fuegia. "He had long shewn himself attached to her," said FitzRoy, "and had gradually become excessively jealous of her goodwill; if he was not sitting by her side, he grumbled sulkily; but if he was accidently separated, and obliged to go in a different boat, his behaviour became sullen and morose."[9]

Despite FitzRoy's efforts to like them all equally, he still preferred the fourth Fuegian, Boat Memory—the hostage named for the stolen whaleboat on the first voyage and the only one who died in England. He regretted Boat's death—by smallpox, in the face of all his elaborate medical precautions— and brooded over the probable future of the mission station without him. "This poor fellow was a very great favourite with all who knew him, as well as with myself. He had a good disposition, very good abilities, and though born a savage, had a pleasing, intelligent appearance. He was quite an exception to the general character of the Fuegians, having good features and a well-proportioned frame."[10] But this mournful talk was meaningless to Darwin, who knew only the three on board the *Beagle*.

III

By December 1832, the *Beagle* was ready to embark on its first working cruise in Tierra del Fuego. FitzRoy planned setting up his mission during this three-month tour of duty in some suitable location over at the western end of the Beagle Channel, where he formerly had taken York and Fuegia captive. It would be sweet work, he caught himself thinking, to establish the Anglican faith in the very waterway he had discovered during the first expedition and had named after his own ship. To that end, the subscriptions raised by members of the Church Missionary Society financed a young missionary, a catechist as yet unqualified called Richard Matthews, to take up residence in Tierra del Fuego. Well-meaning friends of FitzRoy's provided stores and equipment. The venture was in this sense an independent charitable enterprise, not directly sponsored by the society, whose official attentions were exclusively turned towards West Africa, the Antipodes, and the Far East. FitzRoy himself promised everything else needed in the way of labour and wood for the settlement.

Anglican missions were almost always run on practical lines, and FitzRoy was only one of many philanthropic aristocrats who sincerely believed Christianity was indistinguishable from civilisation. The inculcation of the one, he thought, would inevitably lead to the blessings of the other; cultivation of the land would lead to cultivation of the mind; clothes and rows of beans inexorably brought savages closer to Christ. "Religion is strictly and essentially a civilizing process," John Angell James said in a famous sermon in 1819, and "the Bible and the plough" was an expression so familiar in nineteenth-century overseas work that it could have served as the motto for any one of the numerous societies proliferating in London and the provinces. Matthews was to establish a core of Christianity by showing the native Fuegians how to farm the land and build wooden houses, giving the people clothes, promoting cleanliness, and, if all went well, teaching some basic English and the precepts of the established Anglican Church. The captain's three Fuegians would be there to help him. The overall hope as expressed in the letter Matthews carried with him from Dandeson Coates of the Church Missionary Society was "to attempt to teach them such useful arts as may be thought suited to their gradual civilization."[11] His efforts, in short, were aimed at leading aboriginal culture towards northern values.

Not surprisingly, Darwin did not fully recognise the crusading ardour burning in FitzRoy's heart until the *Beagle* arrived in Tierra del Fuego. Before then, with the comfortable liberalism of English Whigs, he found the polite manners and cheerful disposition of Jemmy Button and Fuegia Basket completely unremarkable. Even York Minster's behaviour was of a type familiar to English experience—Darwin had met enough coachmen and canal labourers to know that surliness was not confined to foreigners or savages. The three Fuegians appeared to him like solid country peasants, deferential and mostly easy to deal with. More than this, however, he was ready to believe them as intelligent as the next person, a point he made himself in remembering the interesting talks he once had with John Edmonstone, the Negro taxidermist in Edinburgh. "The American aborigines, Negroes and Europeans are as different from each other in mind as any three races that can be named; yet I was incessantly struck, whilst living with the Fuegians on board the *Beagle,* with the many little traits of character, shewing how similar their minds were to ours; and so it was with a full-blooded negro with whom I happened once to be intimate."[12]

The shock of seeing genuine wild men as the *Beagle* ran down the eastern tip of the continent never thereafter left him.

> I shall never forget how savage & wild one group was.—Four or five men suddenly appeared on a cliff near to us,—they were absolutely naked & with long streaming hair; springing from the ground & waving their arms around their heads, they sent forth most hideous yells. Their appearance was so strange, that it was scarcely like that of earthly inhabitants.[13]

From the very first sighting, Darwin was dazed; the absolute primitiveness sent him reeling. "They are as savage as the most curious person would desire," he announced to Fox in disbelief.[14]

As he grasped for metaphors, the only remotely appropriate pictures that came to mind were of animality and devildom: images entirely outside the human realm and indicative of his inability to adjust to what he was seeing. Smeared with red and white paint, hair lankily hanging, their only garment a dirty guanaco skin thrown over the shoulders, gesticulating wildly in the mist, the Fuegians made him think of the devils in *Der Freischutz:* "like the troubled spirits of another world," he declared to Henslow.

The simile was apt. The theme of Weber's melodramatic opera was a young wanderer in search of magic bullets to win a shooting contest and the love of his future bride. First performed in London in 1824, and seen by Darwin in Edinburgh in the same year, the high point was a scene in the "Wolf's Glen," where the magician's forge was sited. Staged with many novel lighting effects, including green and red smoke, and ghostly props that played to the British audience's fondness for spectacle, the Glen was a gothic, pre-Wagnerian set piece that had caught Darwin's vivid adolescent imagination.[15] The civilised world of Shrewsbury and country parsonages was indeed far behind him; in his mind, Milton, Humboldt, and Shakespeare were abandoned in favour of the sheer sensationalism of theatre. Weber, not *Paradise Lost,* provided the analogy for the supernatural other-world of his Fuegian experience.

Fires blazing on each and every headland as they passed—whether to attract the ship's attention or to spread the news of their arrival, Darwin could not guess—added to the otherworldly effect. Most of the men they could see were running: running so fast that their noses bled and their mouths frothed, which mingling with the red and white paint made them seem "like so many demoniacs who had been fighting." He was truly in Magellan's "land of fire," he told his diary. "The sight of a naked savage in his native land is an event which can never be forgotten."[16]

He thrilled to the barbaric glamour of it all, the "surrounding savage magnificence" of the country matching what he felt to be the raw brutishness of the inhabitants, feeling at last that he was on a real voyage of discovery, sailing to the uttermost ends of the earth. The very names of the bays and mountains paid tribute to the perilous travels of Captain Cook, Joseph Banks, and the explorers of old like Magellan, Anson, and Narbrough. Mountainsides dropped precipitously into the arms of the sea and giant glaciers broke directly on the water while naked men ran along the grey stone shoreline. A menacing air—not unwelcome to Darwin at this stage of the voyage—hung over them as the *Beagle* progressed. Wary tribesmen perched on a "wild peak overhanging the sea," while men on the hills inexplicably kept up a "loud sonorous shout." Taking his turn on the night-watch, Darwin revelled in desolate aboriginal nature.

> There is something very solemn in such scenes; the consciousness rushes on the mind in how remote a corner of the globe you are then in; all tends to this end, the quiet of the night is only interrupted by the heavy breathing of the men & the cry of the night birds,—the occasional distant bark of a dog reminds one that the Fuegians may be prowling, close to the tents, ready for a fatal rush.[17]

When the captain sent a party to communicate with the indigenous Fuegians gathered at the *Beagle*'s first anchorage in Good Success Bay,

Darwin found the experience "without exception the most curious & interesting spectacle I ever beheld."

These east-coast Fuegians had probably met Europeans before, because after some initial cautiousness they accepted presents of red cloth and entered into an exchange of greetings with alacrity, slapping Darwin and several of the sailors heartily on the chest and inviting them to return the compliment. Though FitzRoy felt too self-conscious to unbend in front of his crew, Darwin acted out these signs of friendship with enthusiasm. Since the whole experience was in his eyes theatre of the purest kind, he threw himself into his supporting role, an extrovert foil to the captain's haughty embarrassment. He and an old man walked along the shore "patting our breasts & making something like the same noise which people do when feeding chickens."

The Fuegians also knew what guns were, since nothing would tempt them to take one (unloaded for the occasion) into their hands. Two or three of the officers, Darwin slyly reported, were evidently "taken for Ladies" although sporting large naval beards. Their white skin was carefully examined by the Fuegians. "An arm being bared, they expressed the liveliest surprise & admiration."

The Fuegians' chief concern, however, was to obtain knives, and this they showed by acting as if they had meat in their mouths and pretending to cut instead of tear it.

Jemmy and York Minster provided another kind of puzzle.

Jemmy Button came in the boat with us; it was interesting to watch their conduct to him.—They immediately perceived the difference & held much conversation between themselves on the subject.—The old man then began a long harangue to Jemmy; who said it was inviting him to stay with them:— but the language is rather different & Jemmy could not talk to them. . . . They noticed York Minster (who accompanied us) in the same manner as Jemmy, & told him he ought to shave, & yet he has not 20 hairs on his face, whilst we all wear our untrimmed beards.—They examined the color of his skin; & having done so, they looked at ours. . . . Their whole conduct was such an odd mixture of astonishment & imitation, that nothing could have been more laughable & interesting.—The tallest man was pleased with being examined & compared with a tall sea-man, in doing this he tried his best to get on rather higher ground & to stand on tip-toes: he opened his mouth to show his teeth & turned his face en profil; for the rest of his days doubtless he will be the beau ideal of his tribe. . . . In the evening we parted very good friends; which I think was fortunate, for the dancing & "skylarking" had occasionally bordered on a trial of strength.[18]

It was difficult to work out who was more interested and surprised: Darwin, as a visitor from the other side of the globe, at first full of "grave astonishment" and then finding it all ludicrous; or the Fuegians, perplexed by the sight of white, hairy sailors singing and waltzing on the shore. That day he was acutely aware of himself as an object of curiosity, as much a natural history specimen as the other living beings on the beach, a phenomenon to be considered by these strangers with surprise, suspicion, and amusement. The whole situation was indeed laughable. But it was also humbling.

In bringing about this meeting, FitzRoy had no motives beyond establishing friendly relations before moving on to the survey work and mission station. Yet it had a deep effect on almost everyone concerned. The captain was disillusioned because the Anglicised Fuegians did not behave as he expected. York Minster snorted rudely at the other Fuegians, calling them monkeys, and Jemmy Button assured FitzRoy that these people were dirty, not at all like his own tribe. "Fuegia was shocked and ashamed," wrote FitzRoy in his journal; "she hid herself, and would not look at them a second time. It was interesting to observe the change which three years only had made in their ideas, and to notice how completely they had forgotten the appearance and habits of their former associates; for it turned out that Jemmy's own tribe was as inferior in every way as the worst of those whom he and York called 'monkeys—dirty—fools—not men.'"

It was also irritatingly evident to FitzRoy that York understood much more than he indicated. He was no help as a translator. "York betrayed this by bursting into an immoderate fit of laughter at something the oldest man told him, which he could not resist telling us, that the old man said he was dirty, and ought to pull out his beard."[19]

To Darwin, the episode was gripping in a different way. Naïvely, he recounted his surprise that Jemmy was almost another species of man compared with those who were his literal relatives. "I could not have believed how wide was the difference, between savage and civilised man. It is greater than between a wild and domesticated animal, in as much as in man there is a greater power of improvement."[20] Where was the noble savage of his grandfather's day or the unclothed Adam of the Bible? Expostulating to Caroline, he found it hard to acknowledge blood relationship with such wild people. "An untamed savage is I really think one of the most extraordinary spectacles in the world. . . . In the naked barbarian, with his body coated with paint, whose very gestures, whether they may be peacible or hostile are unintelligible, with difficulty we see a fellow creature."[21] Thinking over Jemmy's good qualities, he found it remarkable that he was a member of the same race, and once doubtless possessing the same character as the "miserable, degraded savages whom we first met here."

IV

Even so, Darwin did not slip into the contemporary solipsism of believing the aboriginal Fuegians really constituted another species separate from his own. He did not, beyond the purposes of metaphor, seriously consider them to be animals or devils. Unlike Louis Fraser, a naturalist on the Niger expedition a few years later, Darwin did not shoot down a native boy in mistake for a monkey. Possessing, as he did, substantial knowledge of contemporary comparative anatomy and the classificatory sciences, he was not lured into blurring the line between mankind and apes by postulating an intermediary but taxonomically separate group in which dark-skinned peoples were placed. Several prominent men of the previous generation had put forward such a scheme, including the English surgeon Charles White and Edward Long, a historian of Jamaica. In Germany, writers like Christoph Meiners and Georg Forster, the erudite son of Cook's second travelling naturalist, argued that Negroes were necessarily a distinct species, as had Julien Virey in France.[22] Up in Edinburgh, there were hints that Robert Knox, the anatomist implicated in the Burke and Hare scandal, was a firm believer in several different species of human beings, a theory on which he lectured and published during the 1840s. Authorities from former eras such as Lord Kames and even in a sense Linnaeus endorsed a similar polygenist view of human origins.[23]

Both Darwin and FitzRoy, on the contrary, were absolutely certain that all human beings came from the same stock—that there had been only one original species of mankind, however diverse human beings now appeared to be—and recoiled from the idea that primitive races were intrinsically different from civilised Europeans. Their certainty was at once humanitarian and biblical. Both of them at that time believed in the Mosaic account of creation, though FitzRoy more literally than Darwin, and both of them took an elevated paternalistic view about the ultimate interrelationships of mankind. Darwin's notions emerged out of his family's generally Unitarian and Whig attitude to human nature, where FitzRoy's were based on Tory landowning concerns and a pronounced commitment to philanthropy. But they met at the same place. Neither could give any credence to the idea that the differences between races—great as they appeared—were sufficient to suggest more than one family of humans.

Racial distinctions, Darwin also knew, fuelled many outspoken justifications for slavery. They gave Europeans, both formerly and in his own time, a quasi-scientific backing for exploitive trading practices and the brutal use of native races in the creation of plantation wealth. If "savages" were as innately different from Europeans as some people argued, there was every reason to deny them the capacity to benefit from European values and believe it impossible that they could ever become civilised. Indeed, the views on mankind which Darwin brought to bear on the Fuegians were intimately interlaced with his abhorrence of slave labour. Though the native Fuegians were not slaves, he saw them, and pondered their characteristics, with the same unflinching, egalitarian gaze. They too were just as much brothers under the skin.

Of course, Darwin had moral inconsistencies of his own about slavery that were just as glib as the ones FitzRoy let slip in Bahia, and in any case, few nineteenth-century figures escaped the quagmire of stolid British hypocrisy about slavery. Anti-slavery movements had become an irresistible form of cultural imperialism in the early years of the century, full of images of national superiority. Not only that, but the continued persistence of slavery in the United States, South America, Africa, and elsewhere provided the British with an undeniable sense of self-righteousness. Anti-slavery turned into a national talisman which distinguished the good (the British) from the bad (the rest).[24]

In the light of Darwin's real abhorrence of slavery, these cultural dissimulations have often been passed over without remark. Yet Darwin saw no incongruity in the wide-scale employment of servants, for example, and was as patronising as the next man about the lowly nature of the uneducated masses in Britain or the indigenous people he met in various parts of the globe. His father's fortune was built on the backs of entrepreneurial companies that exploited cheap labour—a family business sense which continued unabated in his own later endorsement of joint-stock railway companies. Both grandfathers also belittled the role of human labour in advancing British prosperity.[25] Though Wedgwood's employees were in principle free to come and go, they were in practice tied to his cottages, to his insurance societies, and to his wages. In truth, with more than fifteen thousand people living at the Etruria works at the time of Wedgwood's death in 1795, the site resembled nothing so much as a displaced plantation town with its big house and separate workers' quarters. And Darwin never questioned the legal ties binding FitzRoy's seamen—officers and boys as well as sailors—to naval service. The money-making classes of Britain perpetuated forms of human bondage which seemed to many critics merely a variant of slavery—the new system of slavery that Lord John Russell decried in 1840.[26]

However, everything of an ethical nature taught to Darwin at home was designed to inspire horror at the idea of buying and selling human beings as chattels. His father, his Wedgwood aunts and uncles, and particularly his sisters Caroline, Catherine, and Susan, who were active in charitable organisations throughout their lives, gave him a firm belief in the essential unity of mankind. He hated slavery with all the outraged zeal that a freeborn Englishman could muster. Like countless others, his commitment was buoyed up within a general cultural framework of British heroism and Christian ardour in confronting and suppressing this barbaric custom in hostile regions of the world.

V

Darwin had no foundation for believing that Negro slaves or native Fuegians were in some way closer to animals than he was. It was this rejection of separate origins that made the whole experience of Tierra del Fuego so painfully interesting to him. Aboriginal tribesmen were of the same clay as Europeans, as were the slaves in Brazil, and the barrier between a state of savagery and one of civilisation was remarkably small. Darwin had already come across several instances during his travels where the varnish of civilisation was stripped away by circumstance. By now he was only too ready to believe civilisation itself a tenuous phenomenon.

In the most immediate sense, he saw his *Beagle* friends, and himself, toughen up round the edges during their time in Tierra del Fuego. They wore thick, heavy clothes as protection from the climate. They quickly hardened to living on shore in impromptu tents made from the ship's sails and became capable of tracking, shooting, and gutting their own food for cooking on makeshift campfires. Oh for the luxury of a shingle beach, Darwin lamented to Caroline during one tour of duty: pebbles were much more yielding for a bed than cold flat earth. After twenty days in an open boat scudding through the shallows around the Beagle Channel, he felt like a bear in an overcoat, grizzled and rough. FitzRoy was once taken for a pirate (a laughable mistake, cried Darwin), and Darwin called himself in turn a chimneysweep or a grand "banditti." The big black beard, specially grown against the cold of Tierra del Fuego, was so long he could see the end of it when clasped in his fist.

These hardships were more frequent and more serious than the escapades Darwin enjoyed describing in letters. One night he was left stranded on shore with a handful of sailors when the sea was too rough for FitzRoy to send a launch to pick them up. "It was very cold, but by all huddling in a heap, we managed pretty well till the rain began, & then we were sufficiently miserable." The misery lasted for two days: "I never knew how painful cold could be. I was unable to sleep even for a minute from my body shivering so much." On another occasion, the whaleboat—their solitary link with the distant *Beagle*—was nearly smashed by waves from a calving glacier. Only a sixth sense brought on by fear of destitution made Darwin turn and rush to pull the boat further up the beach. Gratefully, FitzRoy recorded that this prompt action saved their lives; and, still thankful to be alive the following day, he named a large expanse of water Darwin Sound—"after my messmate who so willingly encountered the discomfort and risk of a long cruise in a small loaded boat."[27] FitzRoy was eccentric but thoughtful in his generosity; his course during this one surveying excursion can be traced 150 years later by the names given to the landmarks he passed: Stokes, Sulivan, Darwin, Wickham, Usborne, and Midshipman Stewart, as well as Admiral Otway, Queen Adelaide, Francis Beaufort, FitzRoy's sister Mrs. Rice Trevor, and his uncles Grafton and Londonderry, all received a geographical tribute, despite clear Admiralty instructions to the contrary; neither could FitzRoy resist creating a geological corner around Clarence Island with the names of Lyell, Buckland, Greenough, and Fitton. His whole naval enterprise, as well as the Admiralty's claims on the area, were manifested in the simple—or more correctly, the symbolic—act of naming. Darwin Sound and Mount Darwin stood silent testimony to his growing regard for his dining-companion.

Furthermore, the *Beagle* twice rescued stranded sailors. One pair were long-term fugitives living rough in Patagonia after deserting their ship. "I dare say they were worthless vagabonds," said Darwin, "but I never saw more miserable ones; they had for some days been living on Muscles &c, & berrys & had been exposed night & day to all the late constant rain & snow.—What will not man endure!"[28]

Another time, after anchoring in some remote cove, they thought they had stumbled across Robinson Crusoe himself when the *Beagle*'s lookout saw a man waving a shirt on shore. He belonged to a group of six American sailors who had run away from their ship fifteen months beforehand not knowing where they were. "Excepting by this chance they might have wandered till they had been old men," wrote Darwin soberly, "& probably would not have been picked up." They were in good condition, he added, from having some knives for hacking at seal meat. But he had never seen expressions so heartbreakingly anxious as theirs when trying to get into the boat: "before she landed they were nearly jumping into the water."[29] Death and the threat of death seemed more pressing in this part of the world. Just as the tropics showed life in all its vibrancy, the southern lands were frightening in their hostility, their atmosphere rank with decay.

Shipwrecks and garish tales of cannibalism abounded, all adding to Darwin's private feeling of coming closer to the edge of existence than before. He could not help but wonder how he might cope with similar exigencies. Could he live on berries?

The ephemeral nature of civilisation struck him most forcefully when he compared the three Anglicised Fuegians with members of their original tribes. These people had been transformed into virtual Europeans in less than four years. Jemmy Button polished his shoes and made jokes, Fuegia Basket wore jewellery and an English bonnet. Their language, faith, and aspirations had altered, as he believed, to reflect an English education, short and basic as it was; and they themselves seemed to feel markedly different from their former compatriots. FitzRoy had single-handedly done what thousands of years of living in Tierra del Fuego had conspicuously failed to do, literally recreating them in a new form. When Darwin likened that process to the difference between wild and domesticated animals he consequently employed far more than a simple farmyard metaphor: he saw what he thought was an authentic transformation of personality from aboriginal brutishness to the softer, tamer, more civilised nature of Western humanity, "domestic" in all its senses.

Reflections like these were underpinned by his strong commitment to the idea of progress—progress, the theme of the age.[30] In all areas of English life, a large proportion of people believed in a universal and inbuilt tendency towards improvement: improvement in manufacturing, in commercial life, in science and art, in technology, and in social relations. Even those individuals who brought the absence of progress to public notice—as in brutal working conditions, the exploitation of women and children, and the lack of general enfranchisement—were committed to the idea that improvement was possible; and philanthropic groups felt responsible for providing the means of improvement to groups that could not effect it for themselves. This could be seen most obviously in missionary work overseas, but also in the proliferation of all kinds of small charitable associations for the middling, artisan, and labouring classes ranging from Coal Clubs and Friendly Societies to Associations for the Relief of the Ruptured Poor. At the individual level, Smilesian self-help was just around the corner. Popular phrenology already showed people how the "education" of particular areas of their brains was one way to "better" themselves.[31]

For FitzRoy, and then for Darwin, such a concept of cultural progress became real during the Beagle voyage in the most dramatic fashion imaginable. Jemmy, York, and Fuegia were virtually English. "What a scale of improvement is comprehended between the faculties of a Fuegian savage & a Sir Isaac Newton," wrote Darwin in his diary in amazement.[32] "To those who have never seen man in his savage state," echoed FitzRoy, it was "one of the most painfully interesting sights to his civilised brother." A voyage such as the Beagle's which took them to remote countries inhabited by races scarcely known in Europe brought the notion of progress home with a vengeance.

The ability to change like this, to advance from a state of "savagery" to the world of English manners or, alternatively, to degenerate into a hardened

PATAGONIA

Skyring Water

FitzRoy
Channel

Otway
Water

Magellan

TIERRA
DEL FUEGO
DAWSON I.
Admiralty Sound

Barbara
Channel

Cockburn
Channel

MT. SARMIENTO

MT. DARWIN
Beagle
Channel
Murray Narrow

Desolation Bay
STEWART I.
Whaleboat Sound
LONDONDERRY I.
Darwin Sound
YORK MINSTER I.

HOSTE I.

Woollya
NAVARIN I.

Nassau
Bay

STATEN I.

FALSE CAPE HORN

WOLLASTON I.

Latitude 56° South

CAPE HORN

MILES   80
KILOMETRES   125

slave-master or berry-picking refugee, was to FitzRoy and Darwin, as to many others in pre-Victorian society, a natural feature of the human condition. Though a vast gulf lay between civilised and uncivilised races, it always remained a possibility that the gulf could be bridged. The possibility of change linked all mankind, according to circumstance, along the arc of culture.

Darwin's intense interest in the ability of human beings to change like this was fundamental to his later conversion to evolutionary theory. The attention he paid to the contrasts and to the similarities between civilized and uncivilized races of human beings during the voyage created an intellectual context in which ideas about a real evolutionary connection could take root and subsequently flourish. Without this experience in Tierra del Fuego—the experience of comparing Anglicised Fuegians with wild tribesmen and -women, of comparing native Fuegians with himself—he would never have had the breadth of vision to include mankind as an integral part of the natural world, or to have registered any form of continuity between the most urbane and cultivated Englishmen and savages: between FitzRoy and Jemmy's wild brother, between the Darwin sisters and naked Fuegian women. The opportunity to see primitive groups dramatised for him the animal nature of human beings. By seeing men and women under a great variety of circumstances, he managed to shed all illusions that there was any group of human beings on earth exempt from the most basic of impulses.[33]

And of all Darwin's varied experiences during the voyage, it was this recognition of the connections between humans around the world that moved him the most: more than the geology or zoology, more than the stars over the Andes, or even the lush abandonment of the tropics. He was forced to acknowledge that the gauzy film of culture was nothing but an outer garment for humanity, acquired or lost in response to the individual milieu, and he began to appreciate the ephemeral, manmade nature of civilisation. Not only was he glad to have been born an Englishman, he was also struck by the full extent of the ambition behind FitzRoy's intentions for founding a mission station, understanding now the powerful urges that drove him on in his project.

"It is an interest," he told Caroline, "which almost repays one for a cruize in these latitudes; & this I assure you is saying a good deal."

VI

FitzRoy's mission station was set up, not without preliminary difficulties, in January 1833. Before then, violently bad weather forced the captain to abandon his plan to settle Matthews further west, for the practical reason that he could not get the *Beagle* over there. It took the experience of sailing twenty-four days to travel twenty miles after they rounded Cape Horn, and a near-fatal wave (two hundred feet high, Darwin recorded in horror), before FitzRoy admitted defeat and ordered a return along Ponsonby Sound.

This was Jemmy Button's territory, at the heart of the Yaghans' region, more fertile and pastoral than the other mountainous areas. The site FitzRoy eventually chose was in Woollya Sound, a sheltered area dotted with islands, off the Beagle Channel, the same cove where Jemmy said he used to live. Although coming from a different tribe, York Minster and Fuegia Basket decided they would live here with Jemmy and Matthews.

After all the preparations, landing in Woollya was an anticlimax for everyone. The years in England had taken their toll on Jemmy.

> We were sorry to find that Jemmy had quite forgotten his language, that is as far as talking; he could however understand a little of what was said. It was pitiable, but laughable, to hear him talk to his brother in English & ask him in Spanish whether he understood it. I do not suppose, any person exists with such a small stock of language as poor Jemmy, his own language forgotten, & his English ornamented with a few Spanish words, almost unintelligible.[34]

There was not much sympathy for Jemmy's linguistic predicament. Cultural dissonance was similarly pronounced in the way that the much-travelled Fuegian was reunited with his family. Two horses in a field could not have been less interested in each other, Darwin noted with some asperity. Jemmy did not seem sad to hear of the death of his father—"me no help it," he flatly remarked. To Darwin, who spent sentimental nights dreaming of his friends and family, and of his future reception when he walked in the door at Shrewsbury, this was unaccountable. "The most curious part," he wrote, searching for some common point of empathy, "was the astonishing distance at which Jemmy recognised his brother's voice."[35]

Once Jemmy's relatives arrived from the other side of the bay, building work began in earnest. Three large wooden wigwams were constructed and two gardens dug and planted, the Fuegian men impassively sitting all day long watching their womenfolk—who had been co-opted as soon as they materialised out of the forest—and the sailors working. "They asked for everything they saw & stole what they could," grumbled Darwin. At first understandable, this habit rapidly grated on Darwin's nerves. Young and old, men and children, never stopped repeating the word "Yammerschooner," which meant, he said, "give me." "After pointing to almost every object, one after the other, even to the buttons on our coats, and saying their favourite word in as many intonations as possible, they would then use it in a neuter sense, and vacantly repeat 'yammerschooner.'"[36]

Determined to look on the bright side, FitzRoy consoled him with the thought that none of the *Beagle*'s sailors could have resisted the urge to beg or steal if similarly surrounded by valuable goods—by gold and diamonds rather than nails, he grandly proclaimed. The captain seemed generally inclined to regard the indigenous Fuegians—the raw material of his plan—with an indulgent smile. Ancient Britons, he wrote optimistically in his log, were covered with woad and animal skins when the Romans first arrived. Even so, he was reluctant to let the train of thought take him too far. On discovering that one of Jemmy's relatives was the doctor of the tribe, he was quick to dismiss him as "a pretended prophet . . . conjuring and pretending to cure illness." For FitzRoy, as for Darwin, the British way of medicine was unquestionably superior.

One or two English-style evenings were spent singing songs around the campfire, the Fuegians streaming with perspiration from the unaccustomed heat and making Darwin laugh in the way they were always a few bars behindhand in the chorus.

After three days of this, the atmosphere turned nasty. One old man mimed the unmistakable action of cutting up and skinning a human body, and the entire company—about 120 of them—retired overnight into the hills. Only FitzRoy's Fuegians remained, from whom no explanation was forthcoming.

The next morning the Fuegians returned and an appearance of quiet normality prevailed. Sufficiently relieved to let goodwill overcome caution, the captain thought it safe enough to leave Matthews for a trial run while he took the crew away to resume surveying work. If he had doubts, he did not care to show them, although at dinner Darwin gently expressed his own reservations: Matthews's energy seemed to Darwin inadequate for "so arduous an undertaking." Robert Hamond was more encouraging, telling the captain it was a pity fine fellows like the native Fuegians should be left in "such a barbarous state." These words, faithfully repeated in the ship's logbook, helped FitzRoy overcome the feeling that he might be the victim of "individual caprice or erroneous enthusiasm"; so much so that when the missionary's goods were unloaded and it became glaringly obvious that no serious thought had gone into furnishing the station, he still ploughed on with his decision to leave. London ladies had no idea of the kind of people or country they were dealing with, he muttered to Darwin. "The choice of articles showed the most culpable folly & negligence," his friend loyally agreed:

> Wine glasses, butter-bolts, tea-trays, soup turins, mahogany dressing case, fine white linen, beavor hats & an endless variety of similar things shows how little was thought about the country where they were going to. The means absolutely wasted on such things would have purchased an immense stock of really useful articles.[37]

Keeping their jokes about top hats and table napkins to themselves, the sailors moved Matthews's inappropriate stores into the central house, made sure he had an adequate supply of gunpowder and cloth for barter, checked that the fences were secure, the corn planted properly, and the fish drying, and left him to it.

With its sturdy wooden houses and vegetable patch, the mission station expressed all the moral virtues dear to FitzRoy's heart. Blind to everything except his own imagination, he happily pictured Matthews a few years hence surrounded by fields and hedges with a crowd of busy, decent Fuegians at his feet.

Unfortunately the South American project did not live up to these elevated ideals. Matthews was soon intimidated by the large numbers of Fuegians who flooded into his area, stealing mission property and making him fear for his life. The settlement, he emotionally told FitzRoy when the *Beagle* returned a few weeks later, ought to be abandoned before he was killed.

In fact, Matthews ran towards the captain's launch screaming with terror and refused to go ashore again. At the very moment the *Beagle* had appeared round the headland, the Fuegians had been forcibly plucking out the hairs of his beard one by one, using mussel shells as pincers.[38]

FitzRoy took Matthews on board. None of the English-speaking Fuegians wished to rejoin the ship. Reluctantly, he decided to leave them there in Woollya Sound, safe, as he supposed, with Jemmy's family and the few others who joined them. The station as such would have to be abandoned.

Slipping back about two weeks later, the ship's company was heartened to find the three still in some sort of English order. Jemmy had given clothes to his mother, and York was busy making a canoe. Perhaps some benefit, FitzRoy thought, however slight, might result from leaving them there, even though the grander plan had faded. Perhaps Matthews might have renewed courage for another try next year. Perhaps the first step towards civilisation had been made, he dejectedly speculated in his logbook. Turning the *Beagle* towards the Patagonian coast to take up the rest of his naval duties was the hardest thing he was ever obliged to do.

Darwin too found it melancholy leaving "our Fuegians." There was one solitary comfort, he wrote, and that was that they appeared to have no personal fears. He reflected sadly on the fact that the three were now in essence Europeans, not Fuegians.

> I am afraid whatever other ends their excursion to England produces, it will not be conducive to their happiness.—They have far too much sense not to see the vast superiority of civilized over uncivilized habits; & yet I am afraid to the latter they must return.[39]

Darwin's interest in mankind never waned from that point onwards. He was already caught in the profound mental and moral dilemma that was to plague not only him but all the later readers of his books describing the place of human beings in the natural world. On the one hand, the misery, squalor, and animality that he saw in the Fuegian people had such an impact he constantly declared how difficult it was to believe "that they are fellow creatures placed in the same world." The higher powers of the intellect never came into play, for "to knock a limpet from the rock does not even require cunning, that lowest power of the mind." How little must the mind of one of these beings resemble that of an educated man, he reflected further. The gap seemed unbreachable.

On the other hand, he knew in practical, emotional, and theoretical terms that these people were at root the same as he, "essentially the same creature."

"UN GRAND GALOPEADOR"

N the middle of 1833, when the *Beagle* was again surveying the eastern coast, Darwin started out on a long expedition across the pampas which he remembered as one of the high points of the voyage. He was exhilarated by the unconfined feeling of riding over boundless plains and sleeping out under the stars. Though the scenery was relatively uninteresting after the previous year's experiences in the Brazilian rain forest and in Tierra del Fuego, some of his most intense emotions were permanently stirred.

He intended following a line from the small settlement of Patagones, near the estuary of the Río Negro in Patagonia, to Bahía Blanca, where he would temporarily meet up with FitzRoy, and then on to Buenos Aires. The distance was about five hundred miles, all of it through Indian territory, and a dangerous choice in view of the continual violence between Spaniards and the indigenous Indians. The unsettled atmosphere was getting worse as arguments escalated between General Rosas and inflammable government factions. Nevertheless, Darwin reckoned that the chain of *postas* strung out across the country, each one manned by small troops of Rosas's soldiers, promised some basic security. These refuges would enable him to penetrate further inland than any European who had previously travelled in the area. "There is now a bloody war of extermination against the Indians," he told Caroline triumphantly afterwards. "So fine an opportunity for geology was not to be neglected, so that I determined to start at all hazards."[1]

His companions on the journey were an English trader called James Harris, who had served as an intermittent temporary pilot for the *Beagle* the year before and was then on his way to Buenos Aires, a peon or guide (in Darwin's employment), and five gauchos who were proceeding to General

Rosas on business. Covington did not travel with him on this occasion. The expedition took six weeks. "Every body seemed glad of companions in this desolate passage."

Striking out towards the Río Colorado, where General Rosas was stationed, the party set off in high spirits. In particular, the gauchos, with their colourful costume of ponchos and petticoats—impressively foreign to his provincial English eyes—and their fierce, independent existence, patently dazzled Darwin. He thought them the natural aristocrats of South America.

> They are generally tall and handsome, but with a proud and dissolute expression of countenance. They frequently wear their moustaches, and long black hair curling down their backs. With their brightly coloured garments, great spurs clanking about their heels, and knives stuck as daggers (and often so used) at their waists, they look a very different race of men from what might be expected from their name of Gauchos, or simple countrymen. Their politeness is excessive: they never drink their spirits without expecting you to taste it; but whilst making their exceedingly graceful bow, they seem quite as ready, if occasion offered, to cut your throat.[2]

The five formed by far the most picturesque group he had yet beheld.[3]

These men told Darwin a great deal about the country they were riding through, and he appreciated the fresh perspective gained on the manners and social mores of a people so very different from any other he had encountered. By then his Spanish was up to a level where he could understand and make himself understood: he had worked hard at it during the early part of the voyage and was, in his own estimation, pretty fluent. Still, some words were better left alone, he discovered, when an Indian they met on the road eyed him speculatively and asked the others was he a *gallego*—in the Indian's lingua franca, was he worth robbing? "Your entire safety in this country depends upon your companion," he thankfully wrote in his diary.

Through the gauchos Darwin briefly met General Rosas, learned much about his military activities, and heard the landowners' and government's complaints about marauding Indians. The situation seemed incredibly complex to him. He was initially predisposed towards the Indians, in the high philanthropic style of his anti-slavery sentiments, and thought the native *caciques* were so persecuted that it counterbalanced their butchery of the settlers. But he rapidly changed his mind after passing through the ruins of fine farming estates destroyed by Indians on the rampage. All his upper-class English feelings about the sanctity of property swept to the fore. Brutality had to be matched with brutality. "It is clear to me that Rosas ultimately must be absolute Dictator (they object to the term king) of this country."

Something of Rosas's growing importance was similarly conveyed by the

way Darwin's party was obliged to halt in the general's encampment by the
Río Colorado for several days. Sentries thoroughly checked their travelling
papers; and the oddity of having an Englishman pass through was sufficient
to merit an interview with the general himself. Harris filled Darwin up with
alarming anecdotes beforehand.

> General Rosas is a man of an extraordinary character; he has at present a
> most predominant influence in this country & probably may end by being
> its ruler. He is said to be owner of 74 square leagues of country & has
> about three hundred thousand cattle.—His Estancias are admirably man-
> aged & are far more productive of corn than any others in the country. He
> first gained his celebrity by his laws for his own Estancia & by disciplining
> several hundred workmen or Peons, so as to resist all the attacks of the
> Indians. He is moreover a perfect Gaucho:—his feats of horsemanship are
> very notorious; he will fall from a doorway upon an unbroken colt as it
> rushes out of the corral, & will defy the worst efforts of the animal. He
> wears the Gaucho dress & is said to have called upon Lord Ponsonby [the
> British minister in Buenos Aires] in it; saying at the same time he thought
> the costume of the country the proper & therefore most respectful
> dress.—By these means he has obtained an unbounded popularity in the
> Camp, and in consequence despotic powers.[4]

The meeting passed without a smile, but Darwin got what he wanted: "a
passport and order for the government post horses, & this he gave me in the
most obliging and ready manner. . . . I was altogether pleased with my interview with the terrible General. He is worth seeing, as being decidedly the
most prominent character in S. America."[5] In fact, in 1835, two years after
the *Beagle* left the area, Rosas succeeded in taking all public authority in
Argentina into his own hands and assumed the position of a popular saviour.
Thereafter he was an unambiguous dictator, and it is probable he would have
continued as such until his death if ambition had not led him into war with
his neighbours, a war ending up with his government being overthrown in
1852 and the defection of all his generals. After that crushing defeat, he took
refuge in England, where he lived on peacefully in Southampton.

Proceeding onwards from Rosas's camp, the travellers made for Bahía
Blanca at some speed. Each night they camped outdoors. The great gaucho
saddle, the *recado,* provided everything they needed. "There is high enjoyment in the independence of the Gaucho life—to be able at any moment to
pull up your horse, and say, 'Here we will pass the night.' The deathlike
stillness of the plain, the dogs keeping watch, the gipsy-group of Gauchos
making their beds round the fire, have left in my mind a strongly marked
picture of this first night, which will not soon be forgotten."[6]

Darwin drank his *maté* and smoked his cigar with the best of them;

and then he lay down to sleep "as comfortably with the Heavens for a Canopy as in a feather bed.—It is such a fine healthy life, on horse back all day, eating nothing but meat, & sleeping in a bracing air, one awakes as fresh as a lark."[7]

It was even more picaresque when four soldiers joined them as an escort between *postas*.

> At night, when they were sitting round the fire & playing at cards, I retired to view such a Salvator Rosa scene.—They were seated under a low cliff, so that I could look down upon them; around the party were lying dogs, arms, remnants of Deer & Ostriches, & their long spears were struck in the ground; further, in the dark background, were horses tied up, ready for any sudden danger.—If the stillness of the desolate plain was broken by one of the dogs barking, a soldier leaving the fire, would place his head close to the ground & thus slowly scan the horizon. Even if the noisy Teru-teru uttered its scream, there would be a pause in the conversation, & every head, for a moment, a little inclined.[8]

As a conscientious Englishman he was swept by embarrassment when the black soldier in command of the next *posta*—the most obliging man in the world, he said—would not sit down to eat with him and his travelling party.

Darwin's sense of danger was not exaggerated. A few days later he was truly terrified for the first time in his life. As they neared Bahía Blanca, his guide saw three people on horseback in the distance who "dont ride like Christians." The distant figures dismounted as soon as they were spotted—suspicious in itself, thought Darwin—and one slunk off behind a hill. The guide suspected they were Indians, possibly from the same gang that had recently killed two gauchos in the area:

> The Gaucho said, "We must now get on our horses, load your pistol" & he looked to his sword.—I asked are they Indians.—Quien sabe? (who knows?), if they are no more than three it does not signify.—It then struck me that the one man had gone over the hill to fetch the rest of his tribe; I suggested this; but all the answer I could extort was, Quien sabe?—His head & eye never for a minute ceased scanning slowly the whole horizon.—I thought his uncommon coolness rather too good a joke; & asked him why he did not return home. I was startled when he answered: "We *are* returning, only near to a swamp, into which we can gallop the horses as far as they can go & then trust to our own legs.—So that there is no danger."—I did not feel quite so confident of this & wanted to increase our pace.—He said, no, not until they do.—When any little inequality concealed us, we galloped, but when in sight, continued walking.—At last we reached a valley, & turning to the left galloped quickly to the foot of a hill, he gave me his horse to hold, made the dogs lie down, & crawled on his hands & knees to reconnoitre.

He remained in this position for some time. At last, he burst out laughing. "Women!" he exclaimed. The wife and sister-in-law of one of Rosas's majors were out searching for ostrich eggs.

Darwin's rush of relief came with a vengeance. Death had never seemed closer or more likely before. The whole episode cut so near to the bone that—unusually—he never managed to see the funny side of the story, even several days later when he recovered from the shock and described it with a wan smile in his diary. He could not steel himself to mention the incident in letters home to the family.

II

The weather made it difficult for a rendezvous with FitzRoy in Bahía Blanca bay, although Darwin caught sight of the ship, with its shape curiously altered by refraction, over the mudbanks. Impatiently, he set off for a few days' fossil-hunting in nearby Punta Alta, where he had found his monsters the year before. Soon, however, a launch came out to see if he was there, carrying Mr. Chaffers, the master, and a reassuring letter from FitzRoy.

My dear Philos
  Trusting that you are not entirely expended,—though half starved, —occasionally frozen, and at times half drowned—I wish you joy of your campaign with Gen Rosas—and I do assure you that whenever the ship pitches (which is *very* often as you *well* know) I am extremely vexed to think how much *sea practice* you are losing;—and how unhappy you must feel upon the firm ground.
  Your home (upon the waters) will remain at anchor near the Montem Megatherii until you return to assist in the parturition of a Megalonyx measuring seventy two feet from the end of his Snout to the tip of his tail—and an Ichthyosaurus somewhat larger than the Beagle.—Our wise ones say that you are not enough of an Archimedes to accomplish the removal of this latter animalcule.
  I have sent,—by Chaffers,—to the Commandant.—On *your* account, —and on behalf of *our* intestines,—which have a strange inclination to be interested by beef. If you have already departed for the Sierra Ventana— tanto mejor—I shall stay here,—at the old trade—"quarter-er-less four" . . .
  Send word when *you* want a boat—*we* shall send, *once* in *four* days. Take *your own time*—there is abundant occupation here for *all* the *Sounders*,—so we shall not growl at you when you return.
    Yours very truly Robt FitzRoy

PS 2^d (Irish fash) Have you yet heard from Henslow—or about your collections sent to England? P.S. I do not rejoice at your extraordinary and outrageous peregrinations because I am envious—jealous,—and extremely full of all uncharitableness. What will they think at home of "Master

Charles" "I do think he be gone mad"—Prithee be *careful*—while there's *care* there's no *fear*—says the saw.[9]

As FitzRoy anticipated, Darwin spent the next few days successfully searching. Some of his fossil finds that second summer were spectacular. He located more *Megatherium* bones, some of which composed nearly a complete skeleton, and marked them carefully for Covington and a sailor to dig out later. More of the puzzling armour turned up as well. Other fossils crumbled in his hands and practically broke his heart because they could not be excavated whole. "The bones were very large, I believe belonging to the Mastodon," he lamented. "They were so completely decayed & soft, that I was unable to extract even a small bone."

None of the new material was associated with marine shells: Darwin's first bones remained an anomaly he still had to explain.

As circumstances would have it, Darwin had by then received the second volume of Charles Lyell's *Principles of Geology*—the volume which spelled out Lyell's detailed account of the history of the fossil record and gave an explanation of issues like extinction. This volume, sent by Henslow, arrived at Montevideo in November 1832.[10] Walking over the same ground as before freshly armed with a persuasive battery of Lyellian interpretations, Darwin now had several definite ideas to explore as well as a better knowledge of the surrounding country. He decided his giant animals must have lived and become extinct during the previous geological epoch but one. The bones found while he was waiting for FitzRoy probably became fossils when the eastern seaboard slowly sank into the sea and were only exposed to view through a subsequent, equally gradual, elevation of the land. The other bones, the first ones, found in 1832 along with marine shells, were credited with a slightly different history in that he thought the animals must have been swept into the sea by rivers when the coastline of the pampas was further inland than today. Then, covered with estuarine sediments and the debris of marine shells, they were raised above the surface like the rest.

In this way, he argued in his notebook, land mammals could be found entombed with littoral molluscs. The disparity between animals and shells, the former becoming extinct while the latter evidently continued through to the present day, was explained by supposing, along with Lyell, that warm-blooded animals and marine invertebrates spent different lengths of time on earth. Lyell, much more than any other of his contemporaries, was convinced that there had been no large-scale mass extinctions of animals and plants in the past, and that species came to the end of their natural span by gradually diminishing in numbers until they petered out in twos and threes, leaving no descendants. Some species, by all sorts of combinations of circumstances, could exist longer than others, he thought. Cold-blooded animals in particular tended to exist in the fossil record for more extended periods than warm-blooded ones like mammals.[11] The turnover of shells was consequently slower than that of mammals, or, as Darwin put it, "the longevity of the species in the mammalia is upon the whole inferior to that of the testacea."[12]

Darwin followed Lyell in believing extinction was both gradual and individualised, not involving the destruction of any other associated forms of life. "With respect to the *death* of species of terrestrial Mammalia in the S. part of S. America," he explained, "I am strongly inclined to reject the idea of any sudden debacle."[13]

Yet what could these giants possibly have lived on? he wondered. Sitting up late with FitzRoy, the "whole day consumed in telling my traveller's tales," he endlessly discussed what the largest animals might have eaten, fascinated by their great size in relation to the sparse vegetation of the present era. The teeth he collected indicated that most of them were herbi-vores and insectivores—relatives of elephants, llamas, armadillos, and rodents. But the surrounding country was of a "very desert character." Lyell's gradual-ism and uniformitarianism required that there were no sudden alterations in the landscape, and Darwin could find no evidence that the countryside had once been heavily forested or had changed in any remarkable way: no indication that the animals died out from lack of food, for example. Perhaps there was some inbuilt aging device which meant a species ultimately came to the end of its natural life span: "as with the individual, so with the species, the hour of life has run its course, and is spent," he ruminated later. He could not decide.

But there was no doubting the delight he took in it all. "I wish any of you could enter into my feelings of excessive pleasure, which Geology gives, as soon as one *partly understands* the nature of a country," he rhapsodised to the family. "There is nothing like geology: the pleasure of the first days partridge shooting or first days hunting cannot be compared to finding a fine group of fossil bones, which tell their story of former times with almost a living tongue."[14] If he did not ask about his nephews and nieces, he said, it was only because he was too busy with his own children, Masters Megatherium and Mastodon.

III

After a week or so with FitzRoy at Bahía Blanca, he was off again, eager to complete his expedition. *Posta* by *posta,* the travelling party trekked across the pampas, making a detour for him to study the geology of the Sierra de la

Ventada, and to investigate a surprising Cambridgeshire fen in the middle of endless grassland. For geology like this, he told Fox cheerily, one required six-league boots. Wheeling vultures were a constant reminder of the underlying dangers: the birds were waiting, he said, for the Indians to murder a few more people. "Ah when the Indians come, we shall have a feast," he imagined them croaking.

FitzRoy enviously thought Darwin's life to be much more exciting than his own routine occupations. While his guest galloped, he measured his way up to Buenos Aires by inches. Moreover, the separation made it hard to keep in touch.

Two hours since, I received your epistle dated 26th, and most punctually and immediately am I about to answer your queries (mirabile!!) But firstly of the first—my good Philos why have you told me nothing of your hairbreadth scapes & moving accidents. How many times did you flee from the Indians? How many precipices did you fall over? How many bogs did you fall into? How often were you carried away by the floods? and how many times were you kilt?—that you were not kilt *dead* I have visible evidence in your handwriting. . . . Since the day of that note the Beagle has been two days at Maldonado—one day here [Montevideo] and about a week between this & Cape Corrientes.—Not having any Stone pounders on board—nor any qualified person (the *Mate* being absent)—I could not think of landing,—so *you* have yet a *chance*. . . . Still you get no answer— *"What is the Beagle going to do—will you tell me, or not?"*—Philos—be not irate—have patience and I will tell thee all. Tomorrow we shall sail for Maldonado—there we shall remain until the middle of this month;—thence we shall return to Monte Video—to remain quietly, *if possible,* until the end of the month.—I will try all I can to get away from the River Plate the first week in November but there is much to do—and I shall not be surprised if we are detained even until the middle of November.—However— weather is of such consequence, that every long day gained will tell heavily—and I hope & will try hard to be off *Early* in November—therefore do not delay your arrival *here* later than the *first few* days of November, at the farthest.[15]

The stirring pace of this kind of life clearly got into Darwin's blood, because when the group arrived at Buenos Aires in late September he continued travelling on to Santa Fé, another three hundred miles further inland. There was a river to the north, he explained sheepishly, the banks of which were reputed to be so thickly strewn with great fossil bones that the inhabitants built corrals with them. "My object in all this galloping, is to understand the geology of those beds which so remarkably abound with the bones of large & extinct quadrupeds."

This northern area was much more densely populated than his path from

Patagones and Bahía Blanca, and Darwin consequently travelled from house to house, rather than between military outposts, meeting upcountry settlers as he went. However, like any stout English squire, he could hardly believe how provincial these expatriate Spanish and Portuguese landowners were. The usual British correlations of landownership with wealth, furnishings, and style did not apply here, since the houses of local gentlemen were frequently "not so good as cowsheds"; and their manners, despite being hospitable and correct, were characterised by what Darwin bluntly considered ignorance. He entered these homes with more than a touch of amusement. "I possessed two or three things which created unbounded astonishment,—principally a small pocket compass."

> In *every* house I entered I was asked to show its powers, & by its aid told the direction of various places.—This excited the liveliest admiration, that I a perfect stranger should know the road . . . to places where I had never been.—At one house, a young woman who was ill sent to entreat me to come to her room & show her the compass. If their surprise was great, mine was much greater to find such ignorance; & this amongst people, who possess their thousands of cattle & *estancias* of great extent.[16]

English matches—"promethians" in the terminology of the time—were another glamorous accessory, especially when he shamelessly played to the gallery by igniting them between his teeth: "to see this the whole family was collected; and I was once offered a dollar for a single one." Slightly embarrassed, he asked Erasmus to send him out some more.

In one local household his host was a military captain of limited horizons, and Darwin unfairly made fun by pontificating about how the earth was round and that a hole, if deep enough, would open on the other side.

> The Captain at last said, he had one question to ask me, & he should be very much obliged if I would answer him with all truth.—I trembled to think how deeply scientific it would be,—"it was whether the ladies of Buenos Ayres were not the handsomest in the world." I replied, "Charmingly so."—He added, I have one other question—"do ladies in any other part of the world wear such large combs." I solemnly assured him they did not.—They were absolutely delighted.—The Captain exclaimed, "Look there, a man, who has seen half the world, says it is the case; we always thought so, but now we know it." My excellent judgement in beauty procured me a most hospitable reception; the Captain forced me to take his bed, & he would sleep on his Recado.[17]

Darwin's diary entries for this trip reveal how his views on women were equally entrenched. The Spanish ladies he met often behaved in ways he considered egregiously inappropriate. One elegant hostess expected him to take a morsel off her own proffered fork. Another time a gaucho woman accompanied him all day dressed and riding like a man. "Till dinner I did not guess she was otherwise." And he only guessed because she started to flirt with him—a "creature of a woman," he recorded in consternation. Darwin was condescending at best towards these local figures, sometimes cruel in the way he judged nonindigenous people by British social standards. Cultural as well as scientific chauvinism ran powerfully underneath his experiences.

By the time he rode into Santa Fé, he was unwell, from overexertion he thought, and extremely anxious not to miss FitzRoy's deadline at Buenos Aires. Though unable to collect his hoped-for corrals of bones, his baggage did include one of the most surprising specimens of the entire time he spent in South America: a fossil horse tooth. Horses were not native to South America. They had been imported with the conquistadores. Could they have once lived in the pampas, he wondered, and then become extinct? But there was no time to investigate further. Almost immediately he felt obliged to turn around, catching a passenger boat back down the Paraná River. He had not realised how far inland he had travelled. Even so, the journey downstream took a long time, far too long, in fact, requiring him to disembark and hastily ride the last twenty miles overland.

Entering Buenos Aires from a landward direction, intending to meet FitzRoy in the harbour, Darwin was surprised to find his way blocked by soldiers. A party of Rosas's men had cordoned off the city, preventing provisions going in, and intending ultimately to overturn the governor. Cross, anxious, and exhausted, Darwin was unable to think very fast. A few words in the *comandante*'s ear about his recent audience with the general would have to do. As he hoped, "magic could not have altered circumstances quicker than this conversation did." He was allowed into Buenos Aires, alone, without his passport or luggage. "I may thank kind providence I am here with an entire throat," he wrote miserably from his ransacked lodgings that night. Yet there was no FitzRoy, no *Beagle* at the quay. The ship was safely in Montevideo having avoided the blockade entirely. Unfortunately for him, he was trapped inside the city when he would far rather be out. "Here is a pretty series of misfortunes, & there are plenty of smaller ones to fill up the gaps.... I wish the confounded revolution gentlemen would, like Kilkenny cats, fight till nothing but the tails are left."[18] Worse, his servant Covington, who was staying on a nearby *estancia* finishing some collecting jobs for him, looked as if he might also be stranded. "I shall be obliged to send some small vessel or boat to smuggle him off the coast," Darwin told Caroline in exasperation. Covington was in fact cut off for several days before Darwin managed to bribe a man to smuggle him through the blockade. At last the two of them boarded a packet ship making for Montevideo, glad enough to escape from "so miserable a town."

Astonishingly, FitzRoy was not even ready to move the *Beagle*. He planned to stay in Montevideo for another month. After a few days fidgetting around and feeling his great escape was insufficiently appreciated, Darwin impatiently set off to complete his geological investigations, this time making for Mercedes in Uruguay. "I have really now been struggling for a whole week," he explained helplessly to Caroline,

> but there is a very interesting geological formation on the coast of the Uruguay, & every day I hear of more facts respecting it.—When I think I never shall be in this country again, I cannot bear to miss seeing one of the most curious pieces of Geology. . . . I have drawn a bill for 50£.—I well know, that considering my outfit I have spent this year far more than I ought to do. . . . The sort of interest I take in this voyage, is so different a feeling to any thing I ever knew before, that, as in this present instance I have made arrangements for starting, all the time knowing I have no business to do it.[19]

Short as it was, the trip was well worth his while, because he began to understand the structure of the whole stretch of country from Santa Fé through to Montevideo. Moreover, real excitement came when he stayed overnight at an *estancia* where there was half a skull of a *Megatherium,* "very perfect," already excavated and cleaned, resting on the ground. Two shillings and it was his. The landowner apparently knew the whereabouts of more skulls further inland, so Darwin paid him for a second head and the cost of sending them both downriver. His friend the English agent Edward Lumb, who lived in Buenos Aires, could easily be persuaded, he thought, to forward them to England when they arrived. Darwin appreciated the scientific value of items like these and had no scruples about buying bones if necessary, even from sites he had not seen. Acquisition, in such cases, was the overriding aim.

IV

These last four months were deeply satisfying to him on all counts. "Since my last letter to you (middle of July, when I sent off some specimens)," he told Henslow, "I have been, as they say here, un grand galopeador." He went on to list his achievements. Good manners nonetheless came to the fore when dealing with Cambridge professors. "I am very anxious to hear from you. . . . I want much to hear about your family—L. Jenyns, your lectures, excursions, & parties &c.—respecting all of which I have so very many pleasant recollections, that I cannot bear to know nothing."[20]

Now, FitzRoy was making preparations for another season's surveying in Tierra del Fuego, to be followed by sailing over to the Falklands, and then back to the coast of Patagonia somewhere round Port Desire. They set off in

December 1833 with twelve months' provisions loaded into the *Beagle*, meaning to run through the Strait of Magellan when their work was completed. FitzRoy had purchased a schooner to accompany them, which would make the surveying process quicker and better, and this scudded along behind. He named it the *Adventure,* after the other ship on the first *Beagle* voyage, and put Wickham in charge as the captain. Rashly, he had paid for it out of his own funds, hoping to be reimbursed later by the Admiralty.

Another change on board affected Darwin more directly. Augustus Earle was too ill to carry on as ship's artist, and a replacement was fortuitously located in Montevideo. Conrad Martens was a "stone pounding artist—who exclaims in his sleep 'think of me standing upon a pinnacle of the Andes—or sketching a Fuegian glacier!!!' " said FitzRoy. "By my faith in bumpology," he told Darwin, "I am sure you will like him." Darwin did: like all birds of that class, he wrote home, Martens was full to the brim with enthusiasm. Yet Darwin's mind was mostly focussed on what lay ahead. Address your next letters to Valparaiso, he informed his sisters. "We shall for the future be much amongst volcanic rocks."

First, however, came the survey work and a chance to revisit Woollya Cove and see how Jemmy and the other Fuegians were getting on. The whole crew felt keenly interested in their prospects.

During this cruise, both Darwin and FitzRoy paid much more attention to the comparative anthropology of Patagonia and Tierra del Fuego than before, and in truth they had more time to do so. FitzRoy took the *Beagle* methodically up and down the coast from Port Desire (Deseado) to the Strait of Magellan several times, carefully charting the estuaries and inlets, allowing landing parties on shore for several days at different places, and coming to a rest at Port St. Julian (a few miles north of Santa Cruz) for two weeks in January. The Patagonian Indians—the fabled giants of early travellers' tales—were most impressive, the travellers thought. They resembled the few friendly Indians who joined General Rosas's troops, Darwin said, although more painted and much wilder in general appearance. "They are all clothed in large mantles of the Guanaco, & their long hair streams about their faces. . . . One man was ringed & dotted with white like a Fuegian."

These men were what the captain and philosopher later characterised as Horse-Indians or Horse-Patagonians, contrasting them with the tribes further south who primarily went on foot. They were also semi-civilised, familiar with Westerners from the sealing and whaling boats calling in. FitzRoy took three on board the *Beagle*. "At tea they behaved quite like gentlemen, used a knife & fork & helped themselves with a spoon.—Nothing was so much relished as sugar." Like Darwin they felt uncomfortable with the sea-motion and soon wanted to be landed. Neither these Patagonians,

FitzRoy and Darwin simultaneously noted, nor the foot Patagonians used canoes, although in several other features they seemed very like the Fuegians. The two Englishmen wondered how the tribes were historically related.

Before then the ship's company celebrated Christmas at Port Desire. FitzRoy put the whole crew ashore, erected a makeshift tent, and distributed prizes to "the best runners, leapers, wrestlers." These Olympic games, reported Darwin, were very amusing; it was ridiculous to see the schoolboy eagerness with which the burly, full-bearded sailors competed. There was one game he had never encountered before, a naval version of "tag," or "it," crudely called "slinging the monkey," in which a midshipman was suspended upside-down on a makeshift frame and vigorously swung around as the men tried to hit him. Anyone struck by the monkey in return had to take his place. The scene was sketched by romantic Conrad Martens, losing much of its fierceness in the process.

A few days later, Darwin walked with some of the officers to investigate an Indian grave on top of a hill. They found an immense pile of stones but no bones underneath. Other piles of stones round about suggested the area was an ancient burial ground. "It is said that where an Indian dies he is buried; but that subsequently his bones are taken up & carried to such situations." But as in his inquiries into Fuegian religious beliefs, Darwin had very little information to go on. Sheer guesses took over. However, these and the other geological walks he took proved very interesting. He became fascinated by the empty wastelands. "There is not a tree, and, excepting the Guanaco, who stands on some hill top a watchful sentinel over his herd, scarcely an animal or bird. All is stillness & desolation. One reflects how many centuries it has thus been & how many more it will thus remain.—Yet in this scene without one bright object, there is a high pleasure, which I can neither explain or comprehend."[21]

At Port St. Julian, Darwin found the remains of another large fossil mammal, later named *Macrauchenia patachonica,* about the size of a camel with many of the features of a llama. Darwin believed he was digging up a mastodon: the bones of one hind leg, he told Henslow, were very perfect and solid. The location was very far south for mastodons, he went on, and a good distance from the *Megatherium* country around Bahía Blanca, but he was sure this animal and *Megatherium* were "fellow brethren in the ancient plains." It was not until some time after his return that he found out he was wrong and had to revise what he thought about these animals.

He also proved physically stalwart, surprising even FitzRoy in his powers of endurance, brought to a head in an incident when only he could push on to collect water for an inland exploring party. Ambitious as always, FitzRoy had overestimated his own ability to carry scientific instruments into the desert, insisting on bringing with him heavy meteorological gauges as well as a double-barrelled shotgun. "A glass of water would have made me quite fresh," explained FitzRoy impatiently afterwards, "but it was not to be had." He was obliged to stop where he was while Darwin went ahead for water. Yet the lake they saw in the distance was not water. It was a "field solid of snow-white salt." Returning to the tired men with the bad news, Darwin found the captain still too exhausted to go back or forward. So a group of them proceeded to walk back to the *Beagle* for help. "After some hours two of my boat's crew returned with water, and we were very soon revived. Towards morning we all got on board, and no one suffered afterwards from the over-fatigue, except Mr Darwin, who had had no rest during the whole of that thirsty day—now a matter of amusement, but at the time a very serious affair."[22]

Darwin had walked twenty miles further than FitzRoy. He spent the next two days feverish in his hammock.

His shooting skills were much in evidence too. He shot the ship's Christmas lunch: a fine large guanaco of 170 pounds which fed the whole contingent well. Two or three days afterwards, Martens made his own contribution of an ostrich.

Long beforehand, Darwin had been told about a possible second type of ostrich, smaller and more distinctively marked than the ones common around Bahía Blanca and Maldonado, one that was confined to the southern regions of Patagonia beyond the Río Negro. It was called the "Avestruz Petise," he noted in his zoological diary, apparently misunderstanding the Spanish, because although *avestruz* means "rhea," the word *petiso* was used merely as a diminutive.[23]

Darwin badly wanted to collect a specimen, a yearning intensified by his seeing what the gauchos assured him were the abandoned eggs of one on the plains further north. It was rare, its reality was disputed, and much more than that, the French naturalist Alcide d'Orbigny, who preceded Darwin in exploring Patagonia for natural history purposes from 1826 to 1833, had failed to find one, though he "made great exertions to procure this bird." The *Beagle* party heard much of Orbigny's work from James Harris when they first arrived at the Río Negro, and Darwin, though always publicly generous towards him, worried for fear Orbigny would pre-empt a great deal of what he wanted to do in the natural history line. "By ill luck the French government has sent one of its Collectors to the Rio Negro,—where he has been working for the last six month, & is now gone round the Horn.—So that I am very selfishly afraid he will get the cream of all the good things before me," he growled to Henslow.[24] Nothing could have been more attractive than combining a difficult collecting exploit with the relish of scoring a national and personal first. But he had not caught a glimpse of one yet.

"When at Port Desire, in Patagonia (lat. 48°)," he wrote, "Mr Martens shot an ostrich."

> I looked at it, forgetting at the moment, in the most unaccountable manner, the whole subject of the Petises, and thought it was a two-third grown one of the common sort. The bird was cooked and eaten before my memory returned. Fortunately the head, neck, legs, wings, many of the larger feathers, and a large part of the skin, had been preserved. From these a very nearly perfect specimen has been put together, and is now exhibited in the museum of the Zoological Society.[25]

Only the inedible pieces cast aside from the cooking pot were left for Darwin's packing case. Still, he made the best of a lost opportunity and, on his return to England, was gratified when the taxonomist John Gould named the new species after its eater. The *Rhea darwinii* that nearly got away became one of Darwin's best-loved anecdotes from the expedition.

V

They were too busy going backwards and forwards along the coast to sail to Tierra del Fuego until February, and then they needed to survey Wollaston Island at the eastern tail of the continent first. There, everyone was shocked to see how primitive the southernmost Fuegians were. "I can scarcely imagine that there is any spectacle more interesting & worthy of reflection than one of these unbroken savages," wrote Darwin humbly in his diary. What pleasure in life could these naked people enjoy? "They cannot know the feeling of having a home—& still less that of domestic affection." And where had they come from? "What could have tempted a tribe of men leaving the fine regions of the North to travel down the Cordilleras, the backbone of America, to invent & build canoes, & then to enter upon one of the most inhospitable countries in the world.—Such & many other reflections must occupy the mind of every one who views one of these poor savages."[26] He was most pitifully struck by seeing a woman nursing her baby, both of them naked in the rain.

When they at last arrived in Woollya Cove in March 1834, three canoes came out to meet the captain's launch. The occupants were unrecognisable. Only "a sudden movement of his hand to his head (as a sailor touches his hat)," said FitzRoy, "told me it was indeed Jemmy Button." How altered he was, he exclaimed. "I could almost have cried."[27]

Darwin was equally dismayed.

> It was quite painful to behold him; thin, pale, & without a remnant of clothes, excepting a bit of blanket round his waist: his hair, hanging over

his shoulders; & so ashamed of himself, he turned his back to the ship as the canoe approached. When he left us he was very fat, & so particular about his clothes, that he was always afraid of even dirtying his shoes; scarcely ever without gloves & his hair neatly cut.—I never saw so complete & grievous a change.[27]

Jemmy was hurried below decks to get some clothes; and in half an hour, said the captain, he was "sitting with me at dinner in my cabin, using his knife and fork properly, and in every way behaving as correctly as if he had never left us." But FitzRoy and Darwin were sad to hear he had not the least wish to return to England, although the offer was repeatedly made. To their eyes there was nothing left to hold him in Tierra del Fuego: the settlement had disappeared and he was once again living in a state of nature; unwillingly, they saw him as a "naked, thin, squalid savage" again. Furthermore, although Matthews had come back with them for a second try at a settlement, there was no more likelihood of its succeeding than on the first attempt. York Minster had robbed Jemmy of all his stores and absconded with Fuegia.

Still, Jemmy had a wife, to whom he had taught some English. She would not visit the *Beagle* and sat waiting miserably in the canoe until he reappeared from the captain's cabin. Jemmy's brother, "Tommy Button," who accompanied her, constantly called out, at her request, for Jemmy to come up from below.

It was obvious to them all that there was no point in pursuing the mission project any further. The whole scheme was no doubt begun on too small a scale, reflected FitzRoy, and he had done as much as any one individual could be expected to do. A final exchange of gifts—clothes for Jemmy, otter skins for FitzRoy and some other remembered friends, and two spear heads "made by himself for Mr Darwin"—and FitzRoy brought his Fuegian undertaking to a close. "Perhaps a shipwrecked seaman may hereafter receive help and kind treatment from Jemmy Button's children; prompted as they can hardly fail to be, by the traditions they will have heard of men of other lands; and by an idea, however faint, of their duty to God as well as their neighbour."[27]

Every soul, echoed Darwin, was as sorry to shake hands with Jemmy for the last time as they were glad to see him. "I hope & have little doubt he will be as happy as if he had never left his country; which is much more than I formerly thought."

VI

After this, FitzRoy and Darwin found the Falklands depressing, more so when they went ashore together with the other officers in an exploring party and stayed with an enterprising sealer overnight. Robert Hamond told how the group quickly decided to return to their hammocks the following day. "I spread my bag on the table, Bynoe on chairs, the captain on an old sofa and Darwin on the floor, of which he soon bitterly repented, for we had no sooner got asleep than out came the rats, not one or two, but I think 50, for in my life I never heard such a noise or squeaking, and by one consent we set up a prodigious roar of laughter, which for the time put the rats to flight; but it was no laughing matter for poor Darwin, he lay on the floor at their mercy for he dare not show his nose out of his bag, for they were running all over him sniffing and smelling about; he never lay on the floor again."[28]

Left to his own form of natural history, Darwin made two or three rainwashed sorties across the islands. Picking him up again after a few weeks, FitzRoy then made for the Patagonian coast to pull the *Beagle* ashore for repairs. It seemed to him that the ship's keel had been wrong since they grazed a rock in Port Desire. He chose the estuary of the Río Santa Cruz, a few degrees north of the Strait of Magellan, in the empty Patagonian desert. They could camp there undisturbed for as many weeks as needed. And indeed, when they beached the *Beagle* he found several feet knocked off its keel. Martens, blithely immune to these kinds of naval problems, transformed the leaning belly of the ship into his finest picture of the voyage.

FitzRoy was altogether less enthusiastic. He was itching to do something else beyond looking at charts and was bored with the idea of supervising weeks of routine repairs. He longed for excitements comparable to Darwin's treks with the gauchos. Restlessly, he decided to go exploring. He would take a party of men right into the heart of the country along the course of the river: no one else had negotiated this except for his predecessor Pringle Stokes of the earlier *Beagle* survey, who managed only some thirty miles before turning back; and FitzRoy thought the river's source might well be in the foothills of the Andes, so far to the west they were not even dimly perceptible across the desert. The notion of treading where no other naval officer had gone before was very tempting—FitzRoy was always vulnerable to the glamour of geographical discovery—and easily excusable on a surveying voyage. The ship's carpenters did not need him to deal with the *Beagle*'s peeling copper bottom, he told himself. Wickham could look after it.

FitzRoy promptly collected a willing group of sailors and officers, including Darwin, Bynoe, Martens, and Stokes, and loaded up three of the whaleboats with provisions. The party was united by the impractical but passionate wish to touch the Andes from the other side: an entirely "glorious scheme," said Darwin.

The expedition turned out to be unexpectedly gruelling. The men were forced to abandon their oars and sails on the second day, when the river's fierce downstream currents opposed every action. From then on they pulled their boats by ropes, yoked together in teams with collars like tow horses, but

(1) Is reputable to my character as a Clergyman hereafter

(2) A wild scheme

(3) That they must have offered to many others before me, the place of Naturalist

(4) And from its not being accepted there must be some serious objection to the vessel or expedition

(5) That I should never settle down to a steady life hereafter

(6) That my accomodations would be. Most uncomfortable

(7) That you should consider it as again changing my profession

(8) That it would be a useless undertaking

Darwin's list of his father's objections to the voyage.

Maer Hall in Staffordshire, the Wedgwood family home, where Uncle Jos persuaded Darwin to accept the *Beagle* offer. This sketch is by Charlotte Wedgwood.

Robert FitzRoy, temperamental captain
of the *Beagle*.

Living on board ship was like being
in gaol, said Samuel Johnson, with
the added disadvantage of being
drowned.

The traditional ceremony of crossing the line, drawn by Augustus
Earle, the *Beagle*'s artist.

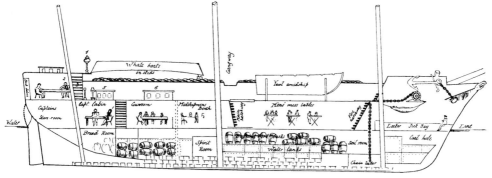

H.M.S. Beagle 1832

1 Mr Darwin's seat in Capt. cabin
2   "   "   " Poop
3   "   "   drawers   "   "
4 Azimuth Compass
5 Captain's skylight
6 Gunroom

A drawing of H.M.S. *Beagle* made by Phillip Gidley King, showing
the poop cabin he shared with Darwin (top left).

(Darwin Museum, Downe)

The richness of the tropical forest mesmerised Darwin.

(J. B. von Spix and C. von Martius, *Atlas zur Reise Brasilien* 1823–31,
courtesy of the Syndics of Cambridge University Library)

His first encounter with slavery was horrifying.

Both of Darwin's grandfathers were prominent in the anti-slavery movement. It was Josiah Wedgwood who coined the phrase "Am I not a man and a brother?"

Facing page: "English women can neither walk nor dress," he told his sisters.

Darwin lived in a cottage beside Botofogo Bay for two months, working and collecting.

Alcide d'Orbigny was a rival collector. "He will get the cream of all the good things before me," Darwin feared.

(A. d'Orbigny, *Voyage pittoresque* 1837. Wellcome Institute Library, London)

Darwin's fossil finds were spectacular, including parts of a *Megatherium*. Such finds eventually led him to question the fixity of species.

(W. Buckland, *Geology and Mineralogy* 1836. Wellcome Institute Library, London)

Most of this rare southern rhea was cooked and eaten before Darwin realised it was a species he wanted to collect.

(*Zoology of the Beagle* 1838–42)

Take a view, my dear Sir, through these glasses, and you will see that the whole face of nature is as blue as indigo. —

The . Theory .

A contemporary caricature of Charles Lyell offering coloured spectacles to a sceptical fellow geologist. Darwin had no such doubts about Lyell's ideas.

(By permission of the Director, British Geological Survey)

A copy of Lyell's *Principles of Geology* went round the world on the *Beagle*. Inside the front cover Darwin wrote, "Given me by Capt. F.R."

(Darwin collection, courtesy of the Syndics of Cambridge University Library)

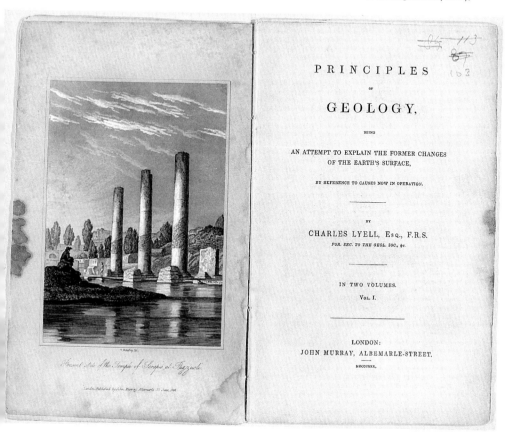

PRINCIPLES

OF

GEOLOGY,

BEING

AN ATTEMPT TO EXPLAIN THE FORMER CHANGES
OF THE EARTH'S SURFACE,

BY REFERENCE TO CAUSES NOW IN OPERATION.

BY

CHARLES LYELL, Esq., F.R.S.

FOR. SEC. TO THE GEOL. SOC., &c.

IN TWO VOLUMES.

VOL. I.

LONDON:

JOHN MURRAY, ALBEMARLE-STREET.

MDCCCXXX.

Present State of the Temple of Serapis at Puzzuoli.

T. Bradley Sc.

London Published by John Murray, Albemarle St. June 1830.

FUEGIA BASKET. 1833. JEMMY'S WIFE 1834.

JEMMY IN 1834. JEMMY BUTTON IN 1833.

YORK MINSTER IN 1832. YORK IN 1833.

FUEGIANS.

T.Landseer sc.

The three Fuegians who were resettled in an Anglican mission. FitzRoy's sketch shows Fuegia Basket (top), Jemmy Button (middle), and York Minster (bottom).

(R. FitzRoy, *Narrative* 1839. Wellcome Institute Library, London)

The *Beagle* (background) and its temporary schooner the *Adventure* working in the Strait of Magellan.

(R. FitzRoy, *Narrative* 1839. Wellcome Institute Library, London)

Woollya Cove in the
Beagle Channel,
where the mission
was set up.

(R. FitzRoy, *Narrative*
1839. Wellcome Insti-
tute Library, London)

Christmas Day in Patagonia.

(R. FitzRoy, *Narrative* 1839.
Wellcome Institute Library, London)

Repairing the *Beagle*. A drawing by
Conrad Martens, the replacement artist.

(R. FitzRoy, *Narrative* 1839.
Wellcome Institute Library, London)

(*top*) FitzRoy and Darwin discussed geology as they
explored the inland course of the River Santa Cruz.

(R. FitzRoy, *Narrative* 1839.
Wellcome Institute Library, London)

(*bottom*) Lieut. Wickham's sketch of the ruins at
Concepción after the earthquake.

(R. FitzRoy, *Narrative* 1839.
Wellcome Institute Library, London)

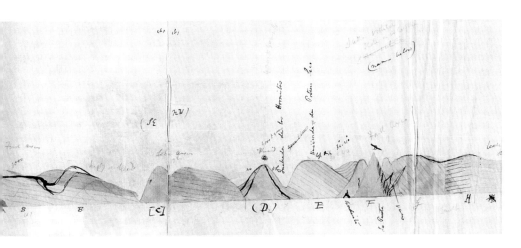

(*top*) Darwin studied volcanoes, but not as closely
as Claude Gay, another geologist working in Chile
at the same time.

(C. Gay, *Historia fisica y politica de Chile. Atlas* 1854.
Wellcome Institute Library, London)

(*bottom*) Part of Darwin's geological diagram
of the Andes.

(Darwin collection, courtesy of the Syndics
of Cambridge University Library)

The guanaco was a continual source of fresh meat.

(A. d'Orbigny, *Voyage pittoresque* 1837. Wellcome Institute Library, London)

Charles Island, in the Galápagos. The impact of visiting these islands lasted a lifetime.

(R. FitzRoy, *Narrative* 1839. Wellcome Institute Library, London)

Trekking across the Andes was one of the most
exciting experiences of the voyage.

(A. Caldcleugh, *Travels in South America* 1825)

A contemporary engraving of the Galápagos
tortoise by R. Harlan, who gave it the name
Testudo elephantopus.

(*Journal of the Academy of Natural
Sciences of Philadelphia* 1826.
Wellcome Institute Library, London)

The land iguanas were "ugly animals, of a
yellowish orange beneath and a brownish
red colour above."

(*Zoology of the Beagle* 1838–42)

Birds Pl. 39

The Galápagos finches did not catch Darwin's attention until he returned home. Although this pair came from James Island, he did not bother to label them as such.

(*Zoology of the Beagle* 1838–42)

Erasmus Darwin, who introduced his brother to London intellectuals after the voyage. By George Richmond, 1841.

(Darwin Museum, Downe)

Darwin's sketch of how he imagined coral reefs forming as the ground sank gently beneath the sea.

(Darwin collection, courtesy of the Syndics of Cambridge University Library)

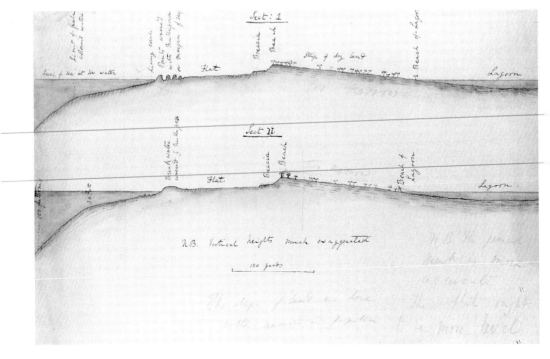

working against a much stronger body of water than the smooth canals of industrial Britain. For eleven days they toiled on, taking turns at the ropes, all the time crossing a series of featureless steppes that reached out in front and behind them as far as they could see.

Hunger soon joined tiredness. "The curse of sterility is on the land," wrote Darwin. "The very waters, running over the bed of pebbles, are stocked with no fish: hence there are no water-fowl, with the exception of some few geese and ducks." Shooting for game was foiled by the ever-present vultures picking the carcasses clean before the men could retrieve them; and the current pulled their nets away empty. Letting themselves get careless on a crucial hunting expedition, Darwin and Stokes only managed to stampede the herd of guanaco they were stalking. "I shall always remember," Stokes wrote later, "the emphatic manner he made use of [his favourite curses] in trying in vain to stop a herd of Guanacos rushing down a pass in the lava cliffs on the St. Cruz River in Patagonia, he with his geological hammer & myself with a gun and very nearly were we both run over."[29] After this, FitzRoy put them all onto half-allowances of ship's biscuit. "This same half allowance, although really sufficient, was very unpleasant after our hard work," complained Darwin; "& those who have not tried it will alone exclaim about the comfort of a light stomach & an easy digestion." Further on they began getting cold: the nights were frosty. And their temporary camps were stealthily reconnoitred by Indians while they slept. One hundred and forty miles inland the captain halted because of lack of provisions.

When they stopped, the Andes seemed tantalisingly close. FitzRoy reckoned they were within twenty miles of the foothills and was sorely disappointed that although the summits could be seen white above the cloud he could not safely take his men any further. There was not enough food for any more days going forward when they had to provide for the return as well. "We were obliged to imagine their nature and grandeur," said Darwin sorrowfully, "instead of standing as we had hoped, on one of their pinnacles & looking down on the plains below."

Unconcerned about himself, FitzRoy plunged on, accompanied by Stokes and Darwin, for another mile or two to gaze wistfully into the distance. "At last then the Andes were in sight!" he wrote in his journal. They were the first Europeans, he later discovered, to penetrate the country so far to the west. FitzRoy subsequently made the expedition the subject of a scientific paper contributed to the Royal Geographical Society when he got home, and it played a significant role in the society's award of the "Royal Premium" to him in 1837 for his geographical achievements.[30]

Almost everyone was discontented with this adventure. It took only three days to return downstream, making all the hard work pulling at the boats seem pointless. They were hungry and Darwin's boots were ruined. In addition, the inland geology scarcely varied from that of the coast: the stepped plains appeared to be made up from a series of incalculably thick deposits of smooth round porphyry pebbles embedded in grit, gravel, and mud; "terribly uninteresting." Further inland these beds were capped by a thick, level field of lava which fell into rugged cliffs and ridges where the river cut through it. It was just the scenery for wildmen and lions, thought Martens, who went on to embellish the view with a huge—and imaginary—puma ready to pounce. In some places, mostly near the coast, there were occasional pockets of crushed and mangled seashells.

Geologically speaking, however, the tour was helpful to Darwin in "affording so excellent a section of the great modern formation of Patagonia," almost like walking through a cut-away diagram of the different layers. Darwin interpreted the rock formations much as Lyell would have done: as having been laid down on the seafloor and then elevated gradually above the water. The great flat lava beds also indicated a slow and steady origin, seeping out from surface vents, perhaps themselves underwater.

More surprisingly, in view of his later intensely biblical beliefs, FitzRoy agreed. At this time FitzRoy was just as taken with Lyell and his geological theories as Darwin. He discussed the nature of the eastern deposits at some length with Darwin, and the history of the fossil mammals, undoubtedly also reading the next installments of Lyell's book when they arrived at Montevideo in 1832 and the Falklands in 1834.[31] Such amiable concurrence does not fit readily with the usual tale of conflict between Darwin and FitzRoy, particularly in relation to their religious beliefs. The real relationship was altogether more striking.

While he was captain of the *Beagle,* FitzRoy was apparently much inclined to believe Lyell's revisionist anticlerical arguments. According to a memoir on geology written by him in 1838, FitzRoy then possessed a "disposition to doubt, if not disbelieve, the inspired History written by Moses" and thought that many biblical events were based in myth or were probably fabulous.[32] Much of this "unease," as he later characterised it, was attributed to his reading works written by "men of Voltaire's school" who contradicted—by implication, if not in plain terms—a literal understanding of the scriptures.

In particular, FitzRoy doubted the existence of a Noachian flood—the traditional stumbling-block for Protestants since the seventeenth century.[33] Few British naturalists of FitzRoy's time were, in truth, believers in a literal biblical deluge. Even the Reverend J. S. Henslow's beliefs were stretched on the point, as shown by a paper he wrote in 1823 proposing extravagantly arcane physical phenomena to make possible a sudden increase in rainwater.[34] Most practising naturalists and geologists favoured a compromise between

Genesis and geology as worked out by a succession of eminent natural theologians, in which it was accepted that the biblical account of a forty-day flood of global extent was not literally accurate, and that geological deposits indicating an unmistakable watery past were relics of a "diluvial" period, pushed back in time to a point predating the appearance of mankind, and longer and more localised than the words of Genesis dictated.[35] Adam Sedgwick's presidential address to the Geological Society in 1831 made this position clear. The Book of Genesis was allowed to become something of a metaphor for creation and more liberally interpreted by broad churchmen and relatively lax sectors of the public alike.

But FitzRoy, always his own man and uncomfortable with any form of tactful compromise, preferred to confront the issue anew, boldly grappling with fundamental theological questions on his own terms. He could not believe that the extensive gravel and clay deposits of Patagonia, hundreds of feet thick and apparently originating in relatively calm water, had been laid down in forty days. Lyell's secular proposals seemed altogether more probable.

He said as much to Darwin while they tramped the coastal plains puzzling over the sequence of deposition. To understand these deposits was important in relation to the fossil mammals and FitzRoy was as keen to unravel the conundrum as Darwin.

> While led away by sceptical ideas, and knowing extremely little of the Bible, one of my remarks to a friend, on crossing vast plains composed of rolled stones bedded in diluvial detritus some hundred feet in depth, was "this could never have been effected by a forty days' flood,"—an expression plainly indicative of the turn of mind, and ignorance of Scripture. I was quite willing to disbelieve what I thought to be the Mosaic account, upon the evidence of a hasty glance, though knowing next to nothing of the record I doubted: and I mention this particularly, because I have conversed with persons fond of geology, yet knowing no more of the Bible than I knew at that time.[36]

He suggested to Darwin that the "barren shingly plains" over which they endlessly walked on their upriver expedition had been gradually deposited underwater: "how vast, and of what immense *duration,* must have been the action of those waters which smoothed the shingle-stones now buried in the deserts of Patagonia!"[37] He reflected on the crushed shells, collecting samples and working out the mathematics of the depth and weight of water needed to contort them, putting his knowledge of William Whewell's new theory of the tides to good use. He used his sophisticated barometric measurements to demonstrate the remarkably level surface of the steppes.

Darwin must have been pleased to have such a geologically inclined captain. He too thought the entire eastern plain had been slowly and

relatively recently elevated, probably in conjunction with igneous movements underneath the Andes. "The geology of this district abounds with
interest," he wrote to Catherine; "the recent elevation of this whole side of
S. America can be most clearly proved."[38] Rather more ambitiously, he told
Henslow how glad he was to make such an extensive inland survey:

> I conjecture (an accurate examination of fossils may possibly determine the
> point) that the main bed is somewhere about the Miocene period (using
> Mr Lyell's expression), I judge from what I have seen of the present shells
> of Patagonia.—This bed contains an *enormous* field of Lava.—This is of
> some interest, as being a rude approximation to the age of the Volcanic
> part of the great range of the Andes.—Long before this it existed as a Slate
> & Porphyritic line of hills.—I have collected tolerable quantity of informa-
> tion respecting the period, (even numbers) & forms of elevations of these
> plains. I think these will be interesting to Mr Lyell.—I had deferred reading
> his third volume till my return, you may guess how much pleasure it gave
> me; some of his wood-cuts came so exactly into play, that I have only to
> refer to them, instead of redrawing similar ones. I had my Barometer with
> me; I only wish I had used it more in these plains.[39]

VII

In June the *Beagle* went through the Strait of Magellan, past the great snowy
Mount Sarmiento. Icebergs and glaciers abounded, and the mountains rose
so steeply out of the water there was hardly anywhere to anchor. Such
"enormous, still, & hence sublime masses" almost defied description.

> The dark ragged clouds were rapidly driven over the mountains, nearly to
> their base; the glimpses which we had caught through the dusky mass were
> highly interesting; jagged points, cones of snow, blue glaciers, strong
> outlines marked on a lurid sky, were seen at different distances & heights.—
> In the midst of such scenery, we anchored at C. Turn, close to Mount
> Sarmiento, which was then hidden in the clouds. At the base of the lofty &
> almost perpendicular sides of our little cove there was one deserted
> wigwam, and it alone reminded us that man sometimes wandered amongst
> these desolate regions; imagination could scarcely paint a scene where he
> seemed to have less claims or less authority; the inanimate works of nature
> here alone reign with overpowering force.[40]

Darwin saw a whale rising before they passed out between the East and
West Furies into the Pacific.

A NEW MISTRESS

ROM the Pacific Ocean the Andes looked much less forbidding, reflecting Darwin's pleasure in the forthcoming change of scene. A better climate made a great deal of difference, he thought. "How opposite are the sensations when viewing black mountains half enveloped in clouds, & seeing another range through the light blue haze of a fine day: the one for a time may be very sublime, the other is all gayety & happy life."

They made first for the island of Chiloé and then for Valparaiso. "After Chiloe and T. del Fuego we felt the climate quite delicious; the sky so clear & blue, the air so dry & the sun so bright, that all nature seemed sparkling with life." In Valparaiso harbour there were fine views of the mountains and of the volcano Aconcagua, and the town was picturesquely composed of groups of whitewashed houses with tile roofs. "Very pretty" said Darwin.

The travellers were delighted by the cosmopolitan civility of the residents as well. After only a few days, Darwin had met several English people who were interested in the same subjects as himself, "no way connected with bales of goods & pounds shillings & pence." It was as surprising as it was pleasant, he said, to be asked what he thought of Lyell's geology.[1]

The town was altogether the nicest they had visited since Rio de Janeiro: a "sort of London or Paris, to any place we have been to." Admittedly a few disadvantages accompanied their reentry into human society: "it is most disagreeable to be obliged to shave & dress decently," they complained. Despite this, Darwin looked forward to breathing clear, dry air, and eating some hearty meals. Rocks and mountains were not half so attractive at that moment as good roast beef, he told Henslow. He was glad to hear that FitzRoy planned to stay there at least two months to repair the *Beagle* again and to complete some of his own dealings in relation to the survey. Darwin wanted to write and read letters, open his boxes from Shrewsbury, look at presents from the family, and go travelling. "The little political books are very popular on board," he thanked Catherine. "Everything came right in the box; the shoes are invaluable, tell Erasmus he is a very good old gentleman for doing all my commissions, but he would be still better if he would write once again.—Four letters are too much, it will frighten him, so I will change my demand into two, & they may be as short as he likes, so that they really come from him." He sent a message to his father, important as always: "I have drawn a bill of eighty pounds."

Darwin took up residence on shore in the house of an acquaintance from Shropshire, a slightly older schoolfriend called Richard Corfield who was a shipping agent and independent merchant in Valparaiso. Inevitably, his father's name was on Dr. Darwin's list of financial patients back home. Corfield was a pleasant, undemanding man, the same age as Erasmus and with many of the same urbane interests, full of useful information about the area and eager to provide introductions should Darwin need them. His life was interestingly luxurious, based on sharing the expenses of a spacious colonial house with another gentleman. A similar establishment in England would have cost twice as much to keep up, remarked Darwin. Corfield displayed few regrets over leaving Shropshire. "He is as hospitable & kind in deeds as a Spaniard is in professions,—than which I can say no more. It is most pleasant to meet with such a straitforward thorough Englishman, as Corfield is, in these vile countries.—He has made his house so pleasant to me, that I have done less during the last fortnight, than in any time since leaving England."[2] Several Chileno señoritas, he joked to Catherine, were very obligingly anxious to become the señoras of this house.

Through Corfield, Darwin met Robert Edward Alison, another English merchant, who later helped him with his researches; and further Englishmen discovered on Corfield's ubiquitous social round flattered him with their readiness to discuss scientific books or give their opinion on European politics. The last English newspapers the *Beagle* men had read were full of Lord Grey's resignation—"& we cannot guess who will succeed him."

After a while, however, Darwin's thoughts inevitably turned to the mountains. He could not have given up such a chance to indulge all his strongest inclinations. "I find in geology a never failing interest," he told his old Cambridge friend Whitley. "It creates the same grand ideas respecting this world, which Astronomy does for the universe."[3] He wished his cousin Fox would become a "smatterer" in the science—"she will soon be the favourite mistress & one easy to be wooed."

Setting out with Covington from Corfield's house in August 1834, Darwin made his first expedition through the central valley of Chile to the capital, Santiago. On his way he climbed and camped out for two days on the Bell of Quillota, standing at a height of 6,200 feet, on the very edge of the Andes. Up on top, the sunset was glorious, he wrote. The whole undulating country and the ocean were laid out as if on a map, with the two great ranges of the Andes behind him, more like a wall than a chain of separate peaks and valleys. "Who can avoid admiring the wonderful force which has upheaved these mountains, & even more so the countless ages which it must have required to have broken through, removed & levelled whole masses of them?"

By then he was well prepared to come to some general conclusions about the geology of the Andes. In fact, his ideas went far beyond his practical knowledge, "& most gloriously ridiculous ones they are. I sometimes fancy I shall persuade myself there are no such things as mountains, which would be a very original discovery to make." Mainly he thought the underground upward thrusts which once created the Andes simultaneously lifted up the eastern plains. The whole continent, he mused, was affected by elevationary forces, which pushed it up out of the sea in stages. He could almost see the peaks emerging out of the water. When the thick low fog rolled in over the valleys around Valparaiso it beautifully represented a former ocean washing up against the mountainsides, "the white vapour curling into all the ravines," filling up the little coves and bays. "Here & there a solitary hillock peeping up through the mist showed that it formerly had stood as an islet."[4] Afterwards, in imagination, he always saw the ocean lapping at the summits of the Andes, shaping and scouring the mountains, excavating valleys, leaving mementoes of its presence in the form of shingle, seashells, and the beaches cast up high and dry on the hillsides.

Pushing on through the Quillota pass to Santiago, where he intended meeting Alexander Caldcleugh, another friend of Corfield's who had formerly helped Captain King with the geology of Juan Fernández, Darwin stopped for several days to inquire about the "rage for mining" that pocked the surface wherever he went. Near the summit of the Bell of Quillota he had found a pit where someone had once searched unsuccessfully for gold. Scarcely a spot elsewhere escaped the hunt for valuable minerals. One copper mine that Darwin visited was superintended by an émigré Cornish miner—"shrewed but ignorant." This man explained the local method of mineral extraction. Listening carefully, Darwin found his account entirely archaic, a combination of a few small European improvements in machinery indiscriminately mixed with labour practices out of the distant past. He was astonished to hear that in some mines water was removed by men carrying it up the shafts in skins on their backs. To such a son of the Industrial

Revolution, these methods were inconceivably primitive, neatly exacerbated by the ignorance of the Cornishman himself. Now that George Rex was dead, the miner asked Darwin, how many of the family of Rexes were yet alive? "This Rex certainly is a relation of Finis who wrote all the books," Darwin added drily.

Further inland, a gold mine run by an American was more than 450 feet deep. The labourers here carried the ore up to the surface on ladders. Each man, Darwin was told, conveyed on his back a Chilean measure of stones equivalent to 104 pounds, a figure that Darwin later revised to around 200 pounds. They were naked "excepting drawers," pale, poor, and miserable: shocking in their grinding servitude.

Agricultural workers, he discovered, fared even worse. "Poverty is very common with all the labouring classes," he exploded. "This must be chiefly owing to the miserable feudal-like system by which the land is tilled." He did not hesitate to assume that Britain arranged its affairs better, conveniently forgetting how his grandfather Wedgwood streamlined the pottery factories by turning men into machines. Darwin thought only of the cottages and ostensible interest in welfare expressed by the Etruria estate management. Exploitation was much more horrifying when it was encountered abroad.

His tour ended in a hotel in Santiago:

My dear FitzRoy,

I arrived at this gay city late last night, and am now most comfortably established at an English hotel. My little circuit by Quellota and Aconcagua was exceedingly pleasant. The difficulty in ascending the Campagna is most absurdly exaggerated. We rode up 5/6ths of the height to a spring called the Aqua del Guanaco & there bivouacked for two nights in a beautiful little arbor of bamboos. I spent one whole day on the very summit, the view is not so picturesque as interesting from giving so excellent a plan of the whole country from the Andes to the sea—I do not think I ever more enjoyed a days rambling. From Quellota I went to see some Copper mines beyond Aconcagua situated in a ravine in the Cordilleras. The major domo is a good simple hearted Cornish Miner—It would do Sulivan good to hear his constant exclamation "As for London—what is London? they can do anything in my country." I enjoyed climbing about in the mountains to my hearts content, the snow however at present quite prevents my reaching any elevation. . . .

My ride has enabled me to understand a little of the Geology—there is nothing of particular interest—all the rocks have been frizzled melted and bedevilled in every possible fashion. But here also the "confounded Frenchmen" have been at work. A M. Gay has given me today a copy of a paper with some interesting details about the Geology of this province published by himself in the Annales des Sciences—I have been very busy all day, and have seen a host of people. I called on Col. Walpole, but he was in bed—or said so. Corfield took me to dine with a Mr Kennedy, who talks much about the Adventure & Beagle; he says he saw you at Chiloe—I have seen a strange genius a Major Sutcliffe. He tells me as soon as he heard there were two English surveying vessels at Valparaiso, he sent a book of old voyages in the Straits of Magellan to Mr Caldcleugh to be forwarded to the Commanding Officer as they might prove of service. . . . He is full of marvellous stories; and to the surprise of everyone every now & then some of them are proved to be true.—

My head is full of schemes; I shall not remain long here, although from the little I have yet seen I feel much inclined to like it. How very striking & beautiful the situation of the city is—I sat for an hour gazing all round me from the little hill of St Lucia. I wish you could come here to readmire the glorious prospect—I can by no means procure any sort of Map,—you would most exceedingly oblige me if you would get King to trace from Miers a little piece of the country from Valparaiso to a degree south of R. Rapel—without any mountains. I do not think it will be more than 1/2 an hours work—I have some intention of returning to Valparaiso by the Rapel.—If you would send this *soon* and half a dozen lines, mentioning if you should know anything about the Samerangs movements, it would assist me in my schemes very much—

Adios, dear FitzRoy, yr faithful Philos., C.D.[5]

II

Two weeks later Darwin was ill, too ill to write either letters or diary. He blamed some sour wine which struck his stomach violently on the return journey from Santiago to Valparaiso: "this half-poisoned me." He just managed to get back to Corfield's house before collapsing. Once there, Benjamin Bynoe, the *Beagle*'s surgeon, came in to dose him with calomel (mercurous chloride) to purge the fever. Anxiously, FitzRoy took over Darwin's arrangements to send a consignment of specimens to England on board H.M.S. *Samarang* and plied him with books and good advice. Equally important, as Darwin's recuperation dragged on over the weeks, FitzRoy delayed sailing until he was perfectly well again. Only a few months previously the captain had pensively read the burial service over the purser's body out at sea, a man warmly respected by them all. He had no wish to perform the same ceremony for his scientific companion. Two others from the *Beagle* had died of fever earlier in the voyage.

Darwin's sickness, and his subsequent descent into debilitating exhaustion and loss of appetite, lasted for six weeks: an intensely difficult time. The first major illness in his life, it came as a shock to him, particularly after so many months spent reaping the benefits of a strong constitution. As the first significant episode in a lifetime subsequently tied to ill health, it may also have played a part in the ailments he came to suffer long after the conclusion of the *Beagle* expedition.

Possibly Darwin was somehow infected by a benchuca bug during his expedition to Santiago, a notorious carrier (in its faeces) of South American sleeping sickness, later identified as Chagas' disease. But he only recorded being bitten by benchucas some months after this illness, over towards Mendoza, and that incident was not followed by any of the fever typical of sleeping sickness infections.[6] The illness in Corfield's house was the only major bout of ill health he experienced during the voyage.

Moreover, Darwin afterwards had plenty of opportunity to ask his London doctors about such an overseas infection and to consider the possibility for himself. Malaria and other periodic fevers, for example, were well known, if difficult to prevent or alleviate, and even without a named diagnosis Dr. Darwin and the family could have accommodated the information that he returned with an intermittently incapacitating foreign disease. Chagas' disease was endemic in Chile, and the characteristic symptoms of infection— the red swellings and goitres—would not have gone unremarked by Corfield or his Valparaiso friends. Yet there was no serious suggestion that a South American disease could be to blame, although once or twice in extreme old age Darwin attributed his breakdown in health to this Valparaiso attack.[7]

Darwin's post-*Beagle* illness (or, more likely, combination of illnesses) was seemingly rooted in other, less obvious causes. Sour new-made wine seems as good a reason as any for his disorders in Chile, and his story of pushing onwards towards Corfield for eight days easily accounts for his feverish prostration. Acute food poisoning followed by overexertion and then Bynoe's doses of toxic emetics would have incapacitated the hardiest.

Recuperating took a lot more out of him than he expected. Laid up in bed from 26 September to the end of October, Darwin thought seriously about going back to England, making a detour en route to investigate the Andes, to be sure, but still planning to move on faster than FitzRoy apparently intended. Suddenly the voyage seemed interminable, the prospect of the boat and the oceans unbearable. "I find being sick at stomach inclines one also to be home-sick," he moaned unhappily to Caroline. "I suspect we shall pay T. del Fuego another visit; but of this good Lord deliver us: it is kept very secret, lest the men should desert; every one so hates the confounded country. Our voyage sounded much more delightful in the instructions, than it really is."[8]

And even though FitzRoy was delaying sailing on his account, he found it difficult to return to the *Beagle* from Corfield's comfortable English oasis; all the harder when he heard from Wickham how depressed and difficult FitzRoy had been in the interval. Mostly the trouble was of the captain's own devising, but that did not make it any easier for his companions to bear. FitzRoy genuinely thought he was going mad.

In truth, all of FitzRoy's deepest fears about coping with the demands of the voyage materialised at this time. Exhausted after his lengthy tour in the storm-lashed south and upset by the purser's death, FitzRoy arrived in Valparaiso only to meet a crisis in his financial affairs and shabby treatment from the Admiralty. Neither Beaufort nor any of the lords of the Admiralty supported his ad hoc purchase of the *Adventure,* the schooner which had accompanied the *Beagle* since leaving Maldonado in July 1833. He was told to sell it and decommission the men. Moreover, he was criticised for spending such a long time surveying the east coast and Tierra del Fuego. The money would not be reimbursed.

Instead of exploding with righteous anger, FitzRoy crumpled. He was not so rich that he could afford to waste as much of the family inheritance as he had, nor had he really expected his judgement of his own naval needs to be questioned in this way. He withdrew into his cabin. A few days later he asked for medical advice from Bynoe, telling him he thought he was becoming deranged. His uncle Lord Castlereagh's ceaseless official duties and eventual suicide evidently preyed on his mind, along with Pringle Stokes's pistol, and the Admiralty's lack of support—all the "blue devils" he worried about from the start.

Days later he emerged, gaunt and depressed, to resign. He did not feel able to continue as captain under such a burden of mistrust from the authorities, and appointed Wickham as his replacement. He had no wish left to carry on with the survey.

To his credit, Wickham talked FitzRoy out of this extravagantly pointless action, intuitively finding the words for both soothing the captain's pride and appealing to his extreme punctiliousness. At just the right moment, Wickham refused to take over.

"We have had some strange proceedings on board the Beagle, but which have ended most capitally for all hands," wrote Darwin afterwards.

Capt FitzRoy has for the last two months, been working *extremely* hard & at same time constantly annoyed by interruptions from officers of other ships; the selling the Schooner & its consequencs were very vexatious: the cold manner the Admiralty (solely I believe because he is a Tory) have treated him, & a thousand other &c &c has made him very thin & unwell. This was accompanied by a morbid depression of spirits, & a loss of all decision & resolution. The Captain was afraid that his mind was becoming deranged (being aware of his heredetary predisposition). All that Bynoe could say, that it was merely the effect of bodily health & exhaustion after such application, would not do; he invalided, & Wickham was appointed to the command. By the instructions Wickham could only finish the survey of the Southern part & would then have been obliged to return direct to England.—The grief on board the Beagle about the Captains decision was universal & deeply felt.—One great source of his annoyment was the feeling it impossible to fulfil the whole instructions; from his state of mind, it never occurred to him, that the very instructions order him to do as much of West coast, as *he has time* for & then proceed across the Pacific. Wickham (very disinterestedly, giving up his own promotion) urged this most strongly, stating that when he took the command, nothing should induce him to go to T. del Fuego again; & then asked the Captain what would be gained by his resignation: Why not do the most useful part & return as commanded by the Pacific. The Captain, at last, to every ones joy consented & the resignation was withdrawn.[9]

FitzRoy's letter to Beaufort had not got as far as the next ship out of Valparaiso.

III

While this shipboard drama was going on, Darwin made his own lightning plans. As soon as he heard of FitzRoy's resignation, he decided to leave the *Beagle* for good. He would examine the Andes properly and return to England from Buenos Aires. His recent bout of homesickness made the settled calm of The Mount seem very attractive: "would this not have been a fine excursion & in 16 months I should have been with you all." The lure of being on his way home far outweighed any regret at FitzRoy's misfortune—a thought in itself surprising and rather shaming, brought about by prolonged ill health and a wish for Shropshire, he hoped a few days later, instead of ingratitude.

As it was, Darwin felt relieved when the captain took back his customary position, more so when Wickham persuaded FitzRoy to abandon any intentions to return to Tierra del Fuego. A far more manageable plan was devised incorporating the welcome idea of surveying the coast of Chile as quickly as possible and turning into the broad Pacific Ocean as soon as they could. For the first time, there seemed to be a real prospect of returning to England in the not so distant future. This news, relayed to Darwin still in bed at Corfield's house, "has done me more good than a pint of Medicin."

There was little enough good humour to share around. FitzRoy's spirits were still so low after his illness that it was hard for Darwin—himself tired and depressed—to remain equable in the face of the captain's moods. Only a few days after Darwin returned to the ship from Corfield's house the two of them argued. FitzRoy complained bitterly about feeling obliged to give a party on board ship to thank all the local residents who had helped him in recent months. Darwin saw no need under the circumstances.

He then burst out into a fury, declaring that I was the sort of man who would receive any favours and make no return. I got up and left the cabin without saying a word, and returned to Conception [actually Valparaiso] where I was then lodging. After a few days I came back to the ship and was received by the Captain as cordially as ever, for the storm had by that time quite blown over. The first Lieutenant, however, said to me: "Confound you, philosopher, I wish you would not quarrel with the skipper; the day you left the ship I was dead-tired (the ship was refitting) and he kept me walking the deck till midnight abusing you all the time."[10]

As FitzRoy apologetically said to Beaufort, "Mr Darwin has been ill, as well as myself, though from a different cause."[11]

After these tired and emotional outbursts, it was really only the dramatic impact of experiencing volcanoes and earthquakes in action that set FitzRoy and Darwin back on their mental feet again. When the *Beagle,* with both of them aboard, sailed along the coast towards Chiloé, they saw two volcanoes erupt and soon afterwards experienced a major earthquake. All Darwin's thoughts about returning home evaporated and he hastily gathered up the remnants of his most ardent geological desires. Witnessing such powerful forces at work was galvanising. He wanted desperately to work out the causes of these, nature's most "terrible effects."

The main volcanic eruption took place in southern Chile at the beginning of 1835 while the *Beagle* men were surveying the large offshore island of Chiloé. For ten weeks the crew had admired the scenic effects of the mountains as seen from the island, finding the interplay of clouds and colours far more rewarding than their rain-sodden work at the instruments. It was peculiar, noted Darwin, that from their vantage point the range appeared semicircular because of visual distortion. The most prominent peak they could see was Mount Osorno, standing out in dark relief against the night sky some seven thousand feet high, its perfect, snow-covered cone inspiring FitzRoy to commission an appropriately sublime drawing from Martens: almost his last commission from FitzRoy before he left the *Beagle* to travel and then to settle in Australia in 1835. This "most beautiful mountain" delighted them all at Christmas time by "spouting out volumes of smoke."

Then in January, Osorno and its nearest companions in the range began giving signs of preparing to do more than merely smoke. Far away, still safely surveying on Chiloé, the men of the *Beagle* watched.

The eruption when it came lit up the water with a long bright shadow. "It was a very magnificent sight," Darwin gloated. Borrowing FitzRoy's telescope, he could see huge lumps of stone in the middle of the "great red glare of light," giant dark objects ejected and falling down. Most of the ship's audience stayed on deck until three o'clock that night watching the earth at its most awe-inspiring. Towards morning the volcano "seemed to have regained its composure."[12]

Seeing a full volcanic eruption was astonishing to Darwin, bringing home to him the vulnerability of the ship and its passengers. The earth never appeared less benign; and Darwin abruptly came to appreciate the underlying ferocity of nature and the way in which the world was merely a temporary refuge for mankind. Intensely powerful geological forces like these created fear and respect. Nature, he recognised, was not just a pleasant afternoon in Valparaiso or Cambridge. It was breathtakingly all-powerful. He could hardly bear to think he might miss something still more spectacular after they had left the area, and he gave elaborate instructions to Charles Douglas, a kindly English surveyor living on Chiloé, for recording further eruptions.[13]

Douglas's information was preempted by the earthquake that followed a few weeks after.

By then the *Beagle* had moved on to the small town of Valdivia on the Chilean coast, where everyone, Darwin included, welcomed the congenial social whirl that the local intendant provided for them. Darwin filled the time with shopping and short excursions into the surrounding hills. He also attended the intendant's ball, where he noticed the ladies' ability to blush when they flirted—a modesty which the pretty girls on Chiloé, he cynically commented, had not yet acquired.

Walking in the forest around Valdivia a day or two after this ball, Darwin was forced to confront the question of how far he truly believed in Lyell's moving crust of the earth. Up until then he rarely thought of these movements as something potentially real. Blithely, and perhaps understandably in view of his origins in the solid British shires, he assumed the earth was firm under his feet. But all his residual assumptions about the earth's stability dissolved in an instant:

This day has been most remarkable in the annals of Valdivia for the most severe earthquake which the oldest inhabitants can remember.—Some who were at Valparaiso during the dreadful one of 1822, say this was as powerful.—I can hardly credit this, & must think that in earthquakes as in gales of wind, the last is always the worst. I was on shore & lying down in the wood to rest myself. It came on suddenly & lasted two minutes (but appeared much longer). The rocking was most sensible; the undulation appeared both to me & my servant to travel from due East. There was no difficulty in standing upright; but the motion made me giddy.—I can compare it to skating on very thin ice or to the motion of a ship in a little cross ripple. An earthquake like this at once destroys the oldest associations; the world, the very emblem of all that is solid, moves beneath our feet like a crust over a fluid; one second of time conveys to the mind a strange idea of insecurity, which hours of reflection would never create. In the forest, a breeze moved the trees, I felt the earth tremble, but saw no consequence from it.—At the town where nearly all the officers were, the scene was more awful; all the houses being built of wood, none actually fell & but few were injured.[14]

Covington thought the sensation was something like a ship "in a gentle seaway." The trees waved to and fro, and the water "came up of a sudden."[15]

The other officers and residents exchanged excited reports during the rest of the day, and towards nightfall Darwin and FitzRoy compiled a fairly complete picture of what had happened, confirming the direction of the shock waves and establishing the accuracy of statements about unusual tidal movements. Some weaker follow-on shocks which occurred later in the evening felt disturbingly as though the *Beagle* were touching bottom.

Much more havoc was apparent when they called at Concepción, further up the coast. The town was razed: "nothing more than piles & lines of bricks, tiles & timbers—it is absolutely true there is not one house left habitable." A tidal wave had strewn timber, furniture, and other wreckage over the ruins. "Besides chairs, tables, bookshelves &c &c in great numbers, there were several roofs of cottages almost entire, store houses had been burst open, & in all parts great bags of cotton, Yerba, & other valuable merchandise were scattered about."[16] One small islet in the harbour showed the physical effects almost as clearly. The ground was riven by cracks nearly a yard wide, and where the earth was soft, large masses had fallen in. Harder rocks were shattered into small fragments. "I believe this earthquake has done more in degrading or lessening the size of the island, than 100 years of ordinary wear & tear," Darwin recorded.

Surveying the desolated township and shattered rocks, Darwin braced himself to work out the pattern of geological forces responsible for the destruction. He found it the "most awful yet interesting spectacle" he had ever beheld.

Over the days afterwards he pieced together an account that suggested the earthquake had reverberated across four hundred miles of countryside with Concepción more or less at the centre. Shock waves came roughly from the east, leaving cracks running in a north-to-south direction where, as Darwin supposed, the tops of the undulations had been. Reports filtered in that the volcano of Antuco, a little to the north of Concepción, had also been very active and that there had been more than one tidal wave, possibly even three, the last of which drowned cattle grazing at the head of the bay. Actually, as FitzRoy afterwards recorded in the *Beagle*'s logbook, all the volcanoes in the area, from Antuco to Osorno, were active to some degree immediately after the earthquake.[17]

The remains of the Catholic cathedral were to Darwin the most morbidly interesting sight of all. The magnificent frontage which had originally faced northeast was now "the grandest pile of ruins I ever saw." The side walls were left standing, for the shock waves were apparently so specific in direction that only the front collapsed, sheared off from the others "as if done by a chisel." There must have been some secondary twisting, noted Darwin, since the square ornaments on the coping were turned sideways.

> I have not attempted to give any detailed description of the appearance of Concepcion, for I feel it is quite impossible to convey the mingled feelings with which one beholds this spectacle.—Several of the officers visited it before me; but their strongest language failed to communicate a just idea of the desolation.—It is a bitter & humiliating thing to see works which have cost men so much time & labour overthrown in one minute; yet compassion for the inhabitants is almost instantly forgotten by the interest excited in finding that state of things produced at a moment of time which one is accustomed to attribute to a succession of ages.—To my mind since leaving England we have scarcely beheld any one other sight so deeply interesting. The Earthquake & Volcano are parts of one of the greatest phenomena to which this world is subject.[18]

One other phenomenon was very noticeable to Darwin and FitzRoy. The main beach in Concepción harbour and the islets of Santa María and Quiriquina seemed to have been elevated above the previous high-water mark—or the sea had receded. Here was an opportunity for FitzRoy to use his instrumental skills to good effect, and he spent several days making finely calibrated measurements of the heights of various levels and landmarks. His observations, along with the "visible evidence of dead shell-fish, water-marks, and soundings, and . . . the verbal testimony of the inhabitants," led him to state that the land was raised nearly eight feet above its previous level.

Two months later, when a curious visitor to the *Beagle* questioned his results, FitzRoy made an impromptu return for more measurements and concluded that the effect was permanent.

Believing he was right on both counts, FitzRoy settled down to prepare a comprehensive report on the earthquake, gathering together the different bulletins sent in to the British consul at Concepción and collecting his own information from ship captains and responsible government officials in the area. Since British scientists yearned for authoritative first-hand documents like these, authenticated by a reliable Englishman on the scene, FitzRoy lost no time in sending a report to Francis Beaufort with the wish that it should be passed on to Lyell to see "if it would be useful to the Geological Society," and part of his report was read to the Geological Society some six months later on 18 November 1835.[19] He also sent an eight-page memorandum detailing his evidence for elevation and its probable cause in localised volcanic activity—just the thing to please Lyell and a reflection once again of the interest FitzRoy took in understanding geology in an essentially Lyellian fashion. Not surprisingly, Lyell, who was the president of the Geological Society that year, was gratified to receive the papers: he was pleased that a naval captain was reading and acting on his work at such a distance as well as taking the trouble to substantiate one of his most crucial theoretical points; and he wrote soon afterwards to Beaufort asking him to get the next passing Admiralty man to etch marks in the rocks at Concepción so that a measure of future movement might be made. FitzRoy's heights were an invaluable starting point. And though the sheets of information arrived too late to be read as an official communication at one of the Geological Society's winter meetings, Lyell went on to praise FitzRoy's efforts in his presidential address delivered in February 1836.[20] He was keen to advertise what seemed to be such a conclusive proof of recent land elevations. FitzRoy's memorandum was then sent by Lyell to the *Nautical Magazine* for publication in March 1836.[21]

IV

Quite content to let FitzRoy concentrate on this public documentation of the earthquake's effects, Darwin allowed himself to speculate wildly about the different phenomena he was directly experiencing. It seemed as if Lyell's scheme, already familiar to him in book form, was being acted out in front of his eyes. Abstract theory suddenly materialised into a striking geological performance, complete with sound effects and movement..

Indeed, Lyell's *Principles* laid out the framework. Set in motion by the movements of rock melted by the earth's internal heat, elevation, earthquakes, and volcanic activity represented a chain of events stretching through geological time and over a large geographical area. If eruption was suppressed, argued Lyell, liquid rock under the crust would be forced against the roof of its reservoir, raising and shaking the land overhead. When the melted matter cooled and solidified—as all igneous material eventually did—the land surface would remain permanently elevated until the next bout of underground activity. Lyell's proposals therefore accounted for the fact that volcanoes and mountain chains were often associated with evidence of raised landscapes and why such regions were typically fractured by earthquakes. He also explained the presence of granite at the core of existing mountains as a natural result of consolidation after elevation.

Darwin's achievement was to provide the first detailed information supporting and extending these essentially theoretical assumptions, supplementing Lyellian dynamics with his own case histories drawn from the southern hemisphere. Darwin came to believe that if the volcanoes of a mountain range were in some way connected deep below the surface they would tend to erupt together or in sequence. Pressure not relieved by eruption might be dissipated through the fracturing and shifting of strata, causing earthquakes. At a less intense level of activity, molten rock would be constantly injected into the basal zones of mountains, thereby lifting the ground level "slowly and by little starts." Though the power of the geological forces was very great and the overall effects mighty, he felt sure that the process was as piecemeal as Lyell spelled out, each renewed bout of activity causing only a small increment in height, for the most part a change in level as small as the few feet indicated by the island of Santa María in Concepción harbour. Century after century, epoch after epoch, these increments slowly accumulated, the whole interrelated system effecting a gradual shift in the level of one of Lyell's crustal blocks.

Darwin first pulled these thoughts together in his diary. Mount Osorno, the earthquake at Valdivia and Concepción, and the small but certain proof of elevation in Concepción harbour were, he mused, different parts of the same underground phenomenon.

> Many geological reasons have been advanced for supposing that the earth is a mere crust over a fluid melted mass of rock & that Volcanoes are merely apertures through this crust. When a Volcano has been closed for some time, the increased force (whatever its nature may be) which burst open the orifice might well cause an undulation in the fluid mass beneath the earth; at each successive ejection of Lava a similar vibration would be felt over the surrounding country; these are known gradually to become less & less frequent, & with them probably the earthquakes, till at last the expansive force is counterbalanced by the pressure in the funnel of the Volcano.—Where Earthquakes take place without any volcanic action, we may either imagine that melted rock is injected in the inferior strata, or that an abortive attempt at an eruption has taken place beneath the Volcano.—[22]

Each individual effect could be linked in a single explanatory scheme based on the uplift of a vast segment of the earth's crust.

V

The mightiness of such geological forces naturally remained fresh in Darwin's mind throughout the rest of his time in Chile. "I wish some of the Geologists who think the Earthquakes of these times are trifling could see the way the solid rock is shivered," he cried to Henslow.[23] Total devastation was no laughing matter: "the earthquake & volcano are parts of one of the greatest phenomena to which this world is subject." A hundred people died in Concepción, he recorded, the remainder saved only by their ingrained habit of rushing outside at the first underground tremble. "If beneath England a volcanic focus should reassume its power, how completely the whole country would be altered. What would become of the lofty houses, thickly packed cities, the great manufactories, the beautiful private and public buildings? If such a volcanic focus should announce its presence by a great earthquake, what a horrible destruction there would be of human life,—England would become bankrupt; all papers, accounts, records, as here would be lost: & Government could not collect the taxes."[24] Full of Lyellian images of the cyclical return of all geological conditions, he ended the reverie gloomily. "Who can say how soon such will happen."

After this, Darwin always felt as if he had looked into the earth's history and glimpsed the internal workings of nature. Everything he subsequently saw in South America was turned to the purpose of providing evidence for this all-absorbing theory of elevation. He searched for inland beds of shells or beach debris wherever he went, finding a striking series of shell deposits south of Valparaiso at heights of 60 to 230 feet above the sea, and another similar site further north near Copiapó. He was easily able to explain the origins of these beds in the light of Lyell's ideas; so easily, he started wondering why no one else saw it as clearly as he did. The local inhabitants, for instance, believed the shells could not be seashells because of their mountain location. Country folk in Chile were just like the philosophers of old in their mistaken doctrines, he concluded, and rather like some of the non-Lyellian thinkers he expected to find at home. "It is amusing to find the same subject discussed here as formerly amongst the learned of Europe concerning the origin of these shells, whether they were really shells or were thus born by Nature." The easiest answer to give, he discovered, was to say God put them there—an explanation less and less likely to his mind but convenient under the circumstances.

By far the most important series of observations in this line were made in March and April 1835, only ten days or so after the earthquake, during Darwin's second and longest expedition across the Andes. The tour itself was the most significant piece of geological work he undertook on the voyage, and the scenery was the most breathtaking. That he should also discern natural phenomena neatly fitting into his developing schemes reveals just how sophisticated his science had by then become. More than at any other time in South America, Darwin almost willed the geological evidence he most needed into existence. His educated eye chose, and then transformed, selected parts of nature into relevant information.[25]

For this expedition he left the *Beagle* surveyors continuing their work along the coast and set off into the mountains, travelling from Corfield's house in Valparaiso to Mendoza and back again by a different route, taking in both the Portillo and Uspallata passes. He hoped to find evidence of uplift or other consequences of the large-scale interrelated forces he thought were at work in the recent period. But the expedition was also an adventure matching the thrill of riding out with the gauchos. The threat of snowstorms was imminent and altitude sickness very likely; there were precipices and clusters of wooden crosses marking graves; frozen mules beside the track and stories of men dying of *punado,* or altitude sickness. Darwin's bravado was high. "From what I have seen I believe the real danger is nothing, & the apparent very little." *Puna* was cast aside with derision. The only sensation he claimed to feel at the highest points was a slight tightness in the head and chest that reminded him, more than anything, of running back to school on a frosty day after leaving The Mount. "There was a good deal of fancy even in this," he joked in his diary; "for upon finding fossil shells on the highest ridge, in my delight I entirely forgot the puna."

The scenery made up for any temporary inconveniences. He was romantically stirred by the sight of a mule train making its way down the steep mountainside towards the coast, and hearing the wild cries of the muleteers—so diminutive with nothing but a backdrop of peaks to compare them with. "When we reached the crest & looked backwards, a glorious view was presented. The atmosphere so resplendently clear, the sky an intense blue, the profound valleys, the wild broken forms, the heaps of ruins piled up during the lapse of ages, the bright coloured rocks, contrasted with the quiet mountains of snow, together produced a scene I never could have imagined. Neither plant nor bird, excepting a few condors wheeling around the higher pinnacles, distracted the attention from the inanimate mass.—I felt glad I was by myself, it was like watching a thunderstorm, or hearing in the full orchestra a chorus of the Messiah. This one view stands distinct in my memory from all others."[26]

As he told Henslow, "it is worth coming from England once to feel such intense delight." There was a transparency in the air and a stillness that gave him the sensation of being in another world.

The illusion continued as his travelling party climbed up over the passes through the perpetual snow. Intense colour was the most unexpected thing, said Darwin. On each side stood bold conical hills of red granite, intersected by the deep blue of a glacier—not thought to occur in these mountains. Vast piles of purple detritus spilled into the valleys making their own mountains thousands of feet high. The moon and stars were magical, the clouds silver, the rising sun a giant orange disc divided by a distant horizon as level as the ocean; and the profundity of the sky was everything Humboldt had ever described. As the party sat round the evening campfire, Darwin's flannel waistcoat added to the fantastical effect by crackling with static electricity in the dark. Even the baggage mules left coloured footsteps behind them: not blood as Darwin first thought, nor dust from the red porphyritic rocks, but from the countless airborne spores of a lichen crushed underfoot. On their return across the Uspallata pass, there were "white, red, purple & green sedimentary rocks & black lavas . . . broken up by hills of porphyry of every shade of brown & bright lilacs. All together they were the first mountains which I had seen which literally resembled a coloured geological section."

Descending into the plains on the other side was an inevitable anticlimax. Ever since FitzRoy abandoned their exploration of the Santa Cruz River, Darwin had half hoped to find some marked change in the countryside close to the foothills on the Andes' eastern flanks. But the trip to Mendoza only confirmed that the plains there were just like the rest of Patagonia except "up an ascent." The animals were the same species that he knew from before, the same ostriches and armadillos, animals typical of the flatlands and not seen on the western seaboard. This made him think that the mountains acted as a dividing line between two different kinds of fauna: a literal wall rather than the metaphorical wall he had envisaged some months earlier; a wall over which he had just laboriously climbed, and therefore he could testify to its imposing substantiality. But even this interesting thought did not alleviate the familiar sterile dreariness remembered from Patagonia. Darwin's rides from town to town were "devoid of all interest." An attack of benchuca bugs was equally dispiriting, the great black bugs of the pampas that wriggled in the crevices of cheap and dirty houses. "It is most disgusting to feel soft wingless insects, about an inch long, crawling over ones body; before sucking they are quite thin, but afterwards round & bloated with blood, & in this state they are easily squashed." His heart, he was afraid, was in the mountains.

Coming back over the Uspallata pass was easily more enjoyable, not least for the evidence of former Inca habitations high up in places that were now absolutely barren. Although giant animals like his Patagonian fossils might be presumed to live out their lives feeding on scrub, he was reluctant to believe mankind could have once existed in these mountain wastes without any trace of water. At first he imagined the ruins were hide-outs for Indians when the conquistadores came. Then he wondered if they were even older and if it was possible that there had been a change in climate. The cause of any such change, he began to think, might be the gradual elevation of the mountains: look how long Druidical remains persist in the wet climate of England, he wrote; how much longer would ancient mud walls last in the dry cold air of alpine Chile. He suspected the thought was nearly absurd. The slopes could hardly have risen thousands of feet during the reign of mankind.

Most remarkable, however, the geology of the easternmost range seemed to him to be composed of the same relatively recent deposits as in Patagonia and parts of the west coast, although baked harder, stretched, fractured, and distorted by being pushed up into the shape of mountains. As he recorded in his diary and in letters to Henslow, this conclusion became impossible to ignore after two days spent geologising in the Uspallata pass. Right at the summit of the mountains the strata were tossed about like the crust of a broken pie. But they were composed of the same basic elements as the flat deposits on either side.

Moreover, even as he was arriving at this radical theoretical position, he happened to find a small "forest" of silicified trees still standing upright. To Darwin, these represented larger memorials of the thin layers of silicified wood characteristic of the west coast deposits, especially around Concepción and on the island of Chiloé, places he knew he had studied thoroughly. To his surprise the silicified wood also mirrored a similar vestigial layer in Patagonia.

> During two days of careful examination I said to myself at least 50 times, how exactly like, only rather harder, these beds are to those of the upper Tertiary strata of Patagonia, Chiloe, Concepcion, without the possible identity *ever* having occurred to me.—At last there was no resisting the conclusion.—I could not expect shells for they never occur in this formation; but Lignite or Carbonaceous shale ought to be found.... How do you think I succeeded? In an escarpment of compact greenish Sandstone I found a small wood of petrified trees in a vertical position, or rather the strata were inclined about 20–30 to one point & the trees 70° to the opposite one.—That is they were before the tilt truly vertical.... 11 are perfectly silicified, & resemble the dicotyledonous wood which I have found at Chiloe and Concepcion: the others 30–40 I only know to be trees from the analogy of form & position; they consist of snow white columns like Lots wife of coarsely crystall. Carb. of Lime. The longest shaft is 7 feet. They are all close together within 100 yd. & about same level; no where else could I find any.... I hardly expect you to believe me, when it is a consequence of this view that granite which forms peaks of a height probably of 14,000 feet has been fluid in the Tertiary period.... If when you see my specimens, sections & account, you should think that there is pretty strong presumptive evidence of the above facts: it appears very important: for the structure, & size of this chain will bear comparison with any in the world. And that all this should have been produced in so very recent a period is indeed wonderful. In my own mind I am quite convinced of the reality of this.[27]

In effect, he was proposing that this eastern range of the Andes had been made during a recent geological epoch at a time broadly contemporaneous with the formation of the upper strata of the west coast and plains of South America. The silicified trees were roughly the same age (actually a little younger) as his fossil mammals from the east. When the trees were alive they grew on relatively flat land at a low level, land much the same as the underlying beds of Chile and the great Patagonian formations; since then the surface had sunk beneath the waves and various thick sedimentary deposits were laid down; these strata were then pushed up six or seven thousand feet into the form of mountains. Subsequent weathering and dendation eroded away all but a few scattered traces of the sedimentary rocks and exposed the well-preserved fossil trees to view. The upthrust, he thought, probably took place in conjunction with the elevation of the plains of Patagonia. If one was to include the evidence of human habitations, as he now believed he might, the process of elevation was apparently continuing through to the present day.

These suggestions were more Lyellian than even Lyell would have dared to make. Nevertheless, Darwin's evidence was good and apparently supported his audacious conclusions. "Since leaving England I have never made so successful a journey. . . . I cannot express the delight, which I felt at such a famous winding up of all my geology in S. America," he reported to Susan. "I literally could hardly sleep at nights for thinking over my days work. —The scenery was so new & so majestic: every thing at an elevation of 12000 ft. bears so different an aspect, from that in a lower country. . . . This last trip has added half a mule's load [of specimens]; for without plenty of proof I do not expect a word of what I have above written to be believed."[28]

VI

Darwin knew he was putting forward an extremely bold interpretation, proposing huge structural changes in recent as well as more remote geological epochs. Yet he was also sure he was right, certain that the igneous rock at the core of the eastern range had been injected into the nucleus of the mountains, elevating them bit by bit during the Tertiary Period. The whole process must have consisted of innumerable repetitions of small-scale elevations like those he saw in the bay at Concepción. Enormous peaks emerged, he told his sisters, foot by foot after the Patagonian monsters became extinct.

Nothing after this could amaze him; no hypothesis was too improbable for his fertile imagination. For the rest of the time he spent in Chile he abandoned himself to a heady extravaganza of untrammelled speculation, theory cascading after theory. Imaginary mountains rose thousands of feet out of the water only to sink and rise again, eruptions and earthquakes rent the crust, molten lava poured out over pebble beds, precious metals crystallised into secret veins deep in the bowels of the Andes, and seawater relentlessly edged further and further over the surface.

If parts of the range were as new as he thought they were, almost anything could have happened in the past. Geology was a kind of gambling, he cried to his cousin Fox, with all of its marvellous excitements. "I often mentally cry out 3 to one Tertiary against primitive."[29] It required the same outlandish hunches and a penchant for backing an unlikely outsider. He danced from hypothesis to hypothesis and thoroughly enjoyed himself.

He was convinced that the majestic story of nature could be explained by the accumulation of little things. Though clear enough to him through Lyell's writings, this notion was given physical reality by Darwin's geological researches in Chile and became the hub of all his later biological thinking.

VII

He arrived back at Valparaiso in high good humour towards the middle of April 1835. This time he made a special effort to be careful with FitzRoy's feelings, and when the *Beagle* called in on its way to Coquimbo he went on board specially to tell the captain some good news from home. FitzRoy's temporary posting in the rank of naval captain was official: he now became a full captain in rank and income as well as title.

For his part, FitzRoy could gladly report that his survey of the south coast was finished. They were soon to be off in a northerly direction, first to Coquimbo, Iquique, and Lima, and then out into the Pacific. "He is fully determined nothing shall induce him to delay the voyage a month," Darwin told his sister Susan cheerfully. "Our voyage now will solely consist in carrying a chain of longitudes between important positions." To Henslow he said he felt as if he had been let out of school early and was planning a ten-week holiday. He arranged to travel up the coast by land, meeting FitzRoy at Copiapó (just north of Coquimbo): another journey of around four hundred miles during which he wanted to examine "all that preeminently curious country abounding with mines."[30]

He cashed a banker's draft for £100, asking Susan to remind his father how necessary it was to have the money in hand in case of accidents: "horses stolen—I robbed—peon sick, a pretty state I should be 400 or 500 miles from where I could command money."

My father will believe that I *will* not draw money in crossing the Pacific, because I *can* not.—I verily believe I could spend money in the very moon.—My travelling expences are nothing; but when I reach a point as Coquimbo, whilst my horses are resting, I hear of something very wonderful 100 miles off, a muleteer offers to take me for so many dollars, & I cannot or rather never have resisted the temptation.[31]

He also wanted to go to Coquimbo to see the famous steps or shelves in the mountainsides, described by the traveller Basil Hall in 1824, and tentatively identified as raised beaches by Lyell in the *Principles*. When he got there, Darwin quickly established Lyell's point and brought home evidence of marine shells, oysters, and half-fossilised sharks' teeth from one of the terraces, at an altitude of 250 feet.

Otherwise he soon got bored with the Chilean deserts. "Excluding the interest arising from geology such travelling would be downright martyrdom. . . . I shall be very glad when once again settled on board the Beagle.—I am tired of this eternal rambling, without any rest." He himself noticed the attractions of an outdoor life wearing off. It was impossible to sleep in local houses, he complained, because of the fleas. "Before I was fully aware of this, I have risen in the morning with my whole shirt punctured with little spots of blood, the skin of my body is quite freckled with their bites. I never formerly had any idea what a torment in these hot, dry climates, these ravenous little wretches could be.—But gracias a dios one month more & farewell for ever to Chile; in two months more farewell South America."

chapter

13

ISLANDS

HE *Beagle* finally left South America in September 1835: "We shall go round the world like a Flying Dutchman, & without doubt if this was the third instead of the fifth year the cruise would be delightful," Darwin told Susan. "I am quite impatient to get into a glowing hot climate." The prospect made him "twice as fat & happy" as he had been for some months before.

With thoughts like these running through his head, it was good to contemplate the immediate outlook. The first port of call was the Galápagos Islands, a small cluster of fifteen or so islets straddling the equator some six hundred miles off the coast of tropical Ecuador. No one who went there, Darwin later said, could ever forget them; nor did he. The archipelago was remarkable, a "little world within itself." There, he respectfully acknowledged, "we seem to be brought somewhat near to that great fact—that mystery of mysteries—the first appearance of new beings on this earth."

Darwin himself was only too ready to pay tribute to the strangeness of the islands and the role they played in formulating his evolutionary theories. They famously became "his" islands, their name inextricably tied to Darwin's throughout his life and beyond.

Yet even Darwin found it difficult to disentangle his subsequent views from his actual experiences on the Galápagos: from what he thought about the animal life around him at the time; and what he at first hoped to see there. In this regard, it is often forgotten just how intently he looked forward to investigating the geology of the island. Much of his anticipation was admittedly the effect of having left South America for good. He was longing for a change in scenery and different activities to occupy his time.

But his scientific interest was fully engaged as well because the islands promised a new kind of geological situation. First of all, they were islands, not continental landmasses. The group was of volcanic origin and, he thought, geologically recent. Mountainous and studded with craters, the landscape was said to be composed entirely of volcanic rocks in various stages of decomposition, and at least two of the larger islands were covered with sheets of naked lava, signifying continuing geological activity. Only a few years previously the English naval captain George Byron (uncle of the poet) reported seeing a volcano that "burns day and night" and lava pouring onto the bubbling sea. A well-thumbed copy of Byron's account of his voyage round the world told the *Beagle* men that the archipelago presented as wild and desolate a scene as imagination could picture: the place was like a new creation.[1] "I look forward with joy & interest to this," gloated Darwin happily to Henslow, "both as being somewhat nearer to England, & for the sake of having a good look at an active Volcano.—Although we have seen Lava in abundance, I have never yet beheld the Crater."[2]

For Darwin, phenomena such as these suggested one thing only: new land was being brought into existence. The geological forces he envisaged raising the South American continent and fuelling the processes of mountain building were, he thought, manifested here as a series of volcanic eruptions. At first hidden on the seafloor, these lava flows must have accumulated steadily around each vent, eventually emerging above the surface of the water as steeply inclined volcanic cones. Perhaps the process was accelerated by a general elevation of the seabed, thought Darwin, since elevation often accompanied eruption. Where there had once been "unbroken ocean" there was now a constellation of new islands exposed to whatever the sea and sky brought along. In the Galápagos, Darwin could examine the origins of new land and judge the path of its subsequent history; he could study the effects of denudation and weathering and assess the rate at which base rock disintegrated into soil; he could witness the transformation of the earth's raw materials into a fully diversified topography. This was the very stuff of Lyellian geology. "I look forward to the Galapagos with more interest than any other part of the voyage," he wrote to Fox. "They abound with Volcanoes & I should hope contain Tertiary strata."[3]

Of course, he also welcomed the chance to investigate the animal and plant life of the archipelago. Island populations were fascinating things at any time, and the Galápagos were known to possess a rich variety of species that lived nowhere else on the globe. It might be possible to see how animals and plants colonised new lands, how bare rock was clothed and peopled with living organisms. Lyell had written at length on the problem of accounting for the origins of island species in the second volume of his *Principles*. Was it by immigration from other nearby areas? Or did new land have new species?

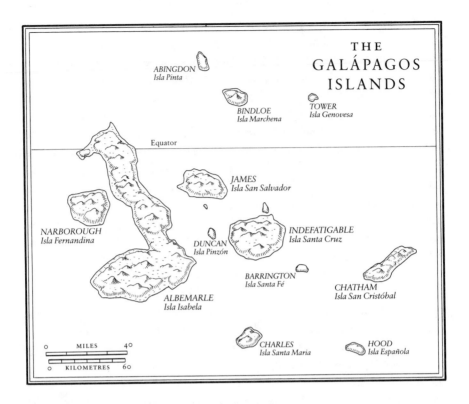

THE
GALÁPAGOS
ISLANDS

ABINGDON
Isla Pinta

BINDLOE
Isla Marchena

TOWER
Isla Genovesa

Equator

JAMES
Isla San Salvador

NARBOROUGH
Isla Fernandina

DUNCAN
Isla Pinzón

INDEFATIGABLE
Isla Santa Cruz

BARRINGTON
Isla Santa Fé

CHATHAM
Isla San Cristóbal

ALBEMARLE
Isla Isabela

MILES   40

KILOMETRES   60

CHARLES
Isla Santa Maria

HOOD
Isla Española

Certainly, Lyell said, quoting from James Cowles Prichard's *Physical History of Mankind,* there were no large animals on isolated oceanic islands like the Galápagos, because it was too far for them to be washed by currents or for their transport on natural rafts. There was little evidence to suggest to Lyell that such remote islands were once connected to the mainland, although that did seem part of the answer for islands closer to continental landmasses. Salt water, Lyell went on to say, often presented an insuperable barrier to terrestrial species, especially mammals, with the exception of flying animals like birds and bats.[4]

Most emphatically of all, Lyell roundly condemned the notion that transmutation could account for the connections and differences between various animals and plants distributed over the globe on islands and continents. The whole thrust of his careful assessment of geographical distribution patterns was to contradict the idea of transmutation, which he considered impossible in practical terms as well as theologically subversive. Two kinds of elephants in different countries, two or three species of monkey scattered over the Indian islands, were, to him, the natural result of organisms being created ideally suited to their situations. To allow any kind of self-generated change, he argued, undermined the orderly hierarchy of nature and cut away any special religious meaning from the separate status of mankind. A given species had a real existence in nature, he insisted, and although frequently varying within itself, it never transformed itself into anything that could be called a new species.

There could be no doubt about Lyell's target. His severest attacks were reserved for the transmutationary scheme proposed by Lamarck some twenty years earlier. Point by point, he worked his way through Lamarck's scheme, arguing that it was false on every level. He paused only to criticise English geologists foolish enough to assume anything like a progressive sequence of organisms in the fossil record. The onslaught ended with a withering remark—an effective Lyellian tactic much used elsewhere—aimed at reducing Lamarck and his theory to terminal oblivion. The French naturalist, he cried in astonishment, would have people believe that a small gelatinous body was capable of being transformed into an oak or an ape; and that the orang-utan could slowly "attain the attributes and dignity of man."[5] For one who believed in the divine creation of human beings, the thought of an orang under his skin was inconceivable. Nevertheless, and unfortunately for the future of his argument, Lyell in conducting it set out a detailed summary of all the problems in classification, distribution, anatomy, and philosophy that other theories of evolution—Darwin's included—eventually attempted to resolve.

Everything Darwin had seen up till then went to confirm in his own mind Lyell's point that most animals and plants spread only as far as geographical barriers allowed them to. But he already knew that Lyell (or rather Prichard) was wrong about there not being large land animals on the Galápagos. The islands were notable for the "ugliest living creatures" Captain Byron ever saw, the big lizards or iguanas special to that location. Moreover, there were the giant tortoises from which the islands took their name.

Darwin's interpretation of the geology of this region therefore raised fundamental biological questions even before he landed, the answers to which would, he thought, reinforce his overall theory of land movements. Added to this, he was agog to see the monstrous animals chronicled by earlier travellers—the land and sea dragons of a former age.

II

In 1835 the Galápagos Islands belonged to the new state of Ecuador, which had annexed them three years before. Their past history, however, linked them closely with Spanish and English adventurers, and they were more generally called the Islas Encantadas on old sea charts—enchanted in the sense of being bewitched, as sailing ships had difficulty making headway from island to island because of powerful currents in the straits. Separated by these deep and narrow sea channels, the islands were mostly in sight of one another. The climate was noticeably moderate, thanks to the blend of ocean water from the warm west and cold south, and the animals and plants presented a curious amalgam of arctic and tropical forms.[6] Darwin noted with astonishment how penguins, fur seals, and sea lions lived side by side with tropical birds, flying fish, cacti, and flamingoes. As far as he knew there had never been any aboriginal human population.

By then, too, the islands' natural advantages were widely appreciated. Pacific voyagers and pirates since William Dampier's buccaneering day had depended on them for fresh food and water, and particularly for the tortoises, which would stay alive and fat in a ship's hold for months on end. Sealing and whaling fleets visited regularly to stock up with these ready-packed provisions, sixty to seventy vessels a year, recorded Darwin, sufficient to justify small settlements on one or two of the islands. A British official had lived for five years on Charles Island in lieu of an Ecuadorian governor; pigs and goats were for sale; letters could be sent. Every passing captain called in at Post Office Bay on Charles Island, where a box was set up on the beach, from which he took any letters he thought he might be able to forward. One whaler coming through not long after the *Beagle*'s visit had Herman Melville on board, and his impressions of the "Encantadas" are part of the saga of the great white whale. "Little but reptile life is here found," wrote Melville. "The chief sound of life is a hiss."

The *Beagle* came up to Chatham Island first. Everything was black, Darwin noticed in surprise. The beach was black lava, buckled and rippled like an ocean of stony waves, giving way to a low horizon of black cones: "what we might imagine the cultivated parts of the Infernal regions to be." It was a shore "fit for Pandemonium," in the captain's opinion. The two agreed it reminded them of the smoky industrialised Midlands, "the Iron furnaces of Wolverhampton." Dismal heaps of broken lava, piles of cinders, large circular pits, fumaroles, stacks, and chimneys made it a port of call suitable for Vulcan.

Yet they had a remarkably good time after anchoring in the bay. Fish, sharks, and turtles swarmed around the ship, "popping up their heads in all parts." Fishing made everyone very merry, wrote Darwin: there was loud laughter and the heavy flapping of fish on every side. After a hearty dinner, they all went on shore to catch tortoises, broadly joking in the launch about who was likely to lift up and carry the biggest.

Darwin saw no tortoises of any size, small or large, that day as he walked for several miles along the coast, collecting as he went. The birds intrigued him, especially the red-footed booby, which perched in the trees on inappropriately webbed feet. Blue-footed boobies swooped and dived, catching fish from heights of eighty feet or more, and tiny yellow warblers filled the bushes a few yards away from the seashore. These birds were so unaccustomed to human beings that they hopped up to within three or four feet of Darwin and his companion, undeterred by pebbles gently lobbed at them. Darwin pushed a large hawk off the end of a branch with his gun, and Phillip Gidley King caught a dove in his hat. They must have thought he was a *galápago,* Darwin told King, hiding a smile behind his beard.

Oddest of all were the seagoing iguanas. They swarmed over the rocks by the edge of the sea like so many rats, although much larger. Unlike any other lizard known to Darwin, they went into the sea to feed.

> These islands appear paradises for the whole family of Reptiles. Besides three kinds of Turtles, the Tortoise is so abundant that a single ship's company here caught from 500–800 in a short time.—The black Lava rocks on the beach are frequented by large (2–3 ft) most disgusting, clumsy Lizards. They are as black as the porous rocks over which they crawl & seek their prey from the sea.—Somebody calls them "imps of darkness." —They assuredly well become the land they inhabit.[7]

The iguanas' feeding habits fascinated Darwin throughout the visit. He threw one into the water time after time until he was convinced—along with King and Covington, dubiously watching in the background—that they did not like being in the sea any longer than necessary. In all essentials they were land animals merely taking their meals in the ocean. Darwin then proceeded to dissect several specimens to identify the stomach contents, a smelly job that quickly obliged him to shift the operation from Stokes's chart table to the rocks ashore. He was interested, he defensively told his diary, to discover that the iguanas were vegetarians and ate only seaweed.

With Covington in tow, Darwin spent two more days exploring the geology of the northern part of Chatham Island. He was disappointed that the volcanic craters were entirely inert, seemingly burnt out centuries ago and now little more than rings of ashes. The thin, weedy vegetation was disappointing too, mostly leafless shrubs and a handful of flowers so ugly and insignificant, he complained, that they would better become the Arctic Circle than an equatorial island. Still, some unusual species of cacti grew further inland. In between the cinders and the cacti lay the tortoises' ponderous paths, something like goat tracks, wrote Darwin, if they were not so strongly suggestive of a main road tamped down by the regular passage of weighty feet.

Turning up one of these inviting paths, he at last met tortoises face to face.

One was preoccupied in eating a cactus, and he took the opportunity to measure its circumference at seven feet; the other did not care for his and Covington's attempts to gauge its weight by heaving at its shell and gave them a "deep & loud hiss" before staggering off. It was an entirely Cyclopean scene, Darwin fantasised. "Surrounded by the black lava, the leafless shrubs & large cacti, they appeared most old-fashioned antediluvian animals; or rather inhabitants of some other planet." Unlike most tortoises, they did not withdraw into their shell. Like the birds, they showed little fear of human beings.

FitzRoy soon moved the *Beagle* to Charles Island, where there was a small Ecuadorian penal colony under the eye of Nicholas Lawson, the official British resident. Darwin only managed to ascend the central mountain in the four days that FitzRoy stayed there. Yet he found evidence confirming that the lava forming this island originally erupted under water, although so long ago that it presented a much smoother surface than on the other islets, and had weathered into soil supporting a more copious plant life. Not since Brazil, he remarked, had he seen such tropical vegetation. But there were notable differences in the way the trees were draped with long wispy lichens instead of lianas and an odd lack of insects.

The sensation of isolation up on the mountain was overwhelming. "The inhabitants here live a sort of Robinson Crusoe life," he remarked; "the houses are very simple, built of poles & thatched with grass,—part of their time is employed in hunting the wild pigs & goats with which the woods abound; from the climate, agriculture requires but a small portion."[8] It was interesting to hear that this island once had had a Robinson Crusoe of its own, one Patrick Watkins from Ireland, a refugee from civilisation who had arrived early in the nineteenth century before any of the Ecuadorian settlers. Watkins built a crude hut and managed to grow crops of potatoes and other vegetables, which he exchanged for rum with passing ships, mainly whalers. His appearance was wretched, reported Captain Porter of the United States Navy in 1815: his red hair and beard were matted, his skin burnt, and he was so wild and savage he filled everyone with horror. He once abducted a Negro sailor from an American ship to serve as a Man Friday, although the sailor got the better of him and escaped.[9]

Darwin was alert to the evocative imagery such a tale of privation and isolation could convey. The account of Crusoe's shipwreck and his meagre existence had struck many chords as the *Beagle* passed through the harshest regions of South America. During the first voyage of the *Beagle,* FitzRoy had even briefly been to Juan Fernández, the Pacific island where Alexander Selkirk, the original castaway on whom Defoe based his book, had lived alone for five years. The power of the story underpinned much of Darwin's imaginative involvement with his own *Beagle* voyage. Islands and castaways coloured the final, seagoing period of his journey as dramatically as geological elevation dominated the land-based, continental part.[10]

Crusoe's self-contained world had been built up with material saved from his shipwreck. Already sensitive to the problems of geographical distribution presented by the species he was seeing on the Galápagos, Darwin began to wonder if the animals and plants might be in turn a sort of living flotsam from South America, surviving as castaways. Perhaps every species on the islands was its own kind of Robinson Crusoe, making do with what it found? He industriously collected all the organisms he could and pondered how they had got there. "It will be very interesting," he told himself, "to find from future comparison to what district or 'centre of creation' the organized beings of this archipelago must be attached."[11] Darwin's souvenir from the Galápagos reflected the same tenor of opportunism. He acquired a fearsome-looking pipe made out of the legbone of an albatross. Unused, like most souvenirs, this accompanied him back to England.[12]

Moving on to Albemarle Island, the *Beagle* men found it distinctive for possessing a second, completely land-based iguana—another hideous animal, explained Darwin in his notebooks, coloured orange, red, and yellow, with spines along the back, and a facial expression that resulted in a "singularly stupid appearance." Like the sea lizards, it was vegetarian. It was not uncommon, though at first startling, to see two or three of them some way up a tree browsing on leaves, their tails dangling.

These lizards were just as tame—or phlegmatic—as the other iguanas, and the temptation to tease them was irresistible. Darwin waited till one was half buried in a burrow before pulling its tail. "At this it was greatly astonished, and soon shuffled up to see what was the matter; and then stared me in the face, as much to say, What made you pull my tail?"

James Island was the last. FitzRoy left Darwin on shore with Benjamin Bynoe and three other men while he went off to survey the northernmost islands. From the 8th to the 17th of October, Darwin crisscrossed the island, searching out many of the specimens that later posed the evolutionary puzzle—and then supplied its key. Even without this, the interior had hardly been explored before. The fauna and flora of the wet central uplands of all the islands, for instance, were virtually unknown in European scientific circles. Darwin and Bynoe's trip up into the mountains consequently resulted in two uniquely valuable plant collections. They also found many tropical ferns and epiphytes dripping with condensed vapour from the clouds hanging over the peak. Among them flew mockingbirds, doves, and a number of finches.

Darwin had already collected some of the Galápagos birds from a pond

on Charles Island, but there were many more to be taken on James, particularly of the smaller kinds now known as Darwin's finches. These smaller
birds were very diverse in their habits. Some lived exclusively on plant seeds
or cactuses, and mostly stayed on the ground, whereas others occupied the
trees and ate either insects or leaves. All of them possessed beaks appropriate
to their diet, long and pointed or compact and heavy. Darwin divided them
into separate subfamilies on the basis of these beaks, as most field naturalists
would have done, calling some "Grosbeaks," others "Fringilla" (true finches),
and putting the cactus-eaters into the category "Icterus," a separate family
including orioles and blackbirds. Just how far he was misled by their confusing characteristics is illustrated by his misclassification of the warbler-like
bird resident on the islands as a "wren."[13] He did not have any reason to
think that some varieties might live only on particular islands, or that their
idiosyncratic beaks might suggest some sort of evolutionary differentiation.

In fact, Darwin later stated that the possibility of the different islands'
possessing separate species was only drawn to his attention by Nicholas
Lawson. Lawson informed him that "the tortoises differed from the different
islands, and that he could with certainty tell from which island any one was
brought"—their shells were characteristically flanged or flared according to
their home location. The evidence for this percipience, as FitzRoy noted,
was scattered around Lawson's garden in the shape of flower pots. "I did not
for some time pay sufficient attention to this statement," said Darwin; "and I
had already partially mingled together the collections from two of the
islands." Even when taking a ride on a tortoise lumbering up the hill to water,
he failed to notice anything distinctive about its shell. All he discovered was
the creature's extreme slowness—about four miles a day, he calculated. "I
never dreamed that islands, about fifty or sixty miles apart, and most of them
in sight of each other, formed of precisely the same rocks, placed under a
quite similar climate, rising to a nearly equal height, would have been
differently tenanted."[14] Oddly enough, the differences between the islands
seemed to be an obsession with Lawson. When the French naval captain
Abel Dupetit-Thouars called at the Galápagos a few years later, in 1838, he
too was told all about "les différentes productions de cette île" by the governor.[15]

Darwin did, however, notice that the mockingbirds he collected from
Charles and Chatham islands were different from each other, which made
him pay particular attention to the ones he saw on James, finding these
different yet again. They were all apparently related to another species he had
seen in several places in South America. In his field notes he commented:
"This bird which is so closely allied to the Thenca of Chili (Callandra of B.
Ayres) is singular from existing as varieties or distinct species in the different
Isds.—I have four specimens from as many Isds.—There will be found to be

2 or 3 varieties.—Each variety is constant in its own Island.—This is a parallel fact to the one mentioned about the Tortoises."[16]

Neither this point nor Lawson's information about the tortoises' shells stopped him in his tracks. Darwin found it interesting but not problematic, and saw no reason at the time to collect or make notes about island variants, even when he had the opportunity to study them closely. Though well aware of transmutationary schemes, both through Lyell's writings and further back in time through his acquaintance with Robert Grant of Edinburgh and his own grandfather's expansive theories, he felt no sudden need to think about the possibility of evolution. He experienced no legendary moment of revelation.

Other more pressing thoughts occupied his mind. Pushing his way through the wet leaves of James Island, he discovered the bleached skull of a ship's captain, killed by his mutinous crew.

Everything spoke to him of isolation. He was wrapped in a cluster of ideas involving private worlds, aboriginal nature, and hardships overcome. He was Robinson Crusoe, wandering through lands uninhabited by human beings, sleeping rough on bare volcanic rocks. The scarcity of fresh water, the skull, the mad Irish hermit: all these contributed to a powerfully evocative vision of primitive nature. Giant tortoises and outlandish lizards gave it an antediluvian air: the land that time forgot. Relations between humans and the rest of nature were also different here, for the animals were not afraid, treating him as one of themselves. It is no exaggeration to suggest he found on the Galápagos his own Garden of Eden, in the same way that the *Beagle* was his ark.

The irony was that he did not come to understand the meaning of what he saw until long after the ship sailed away from the archipelago.

III

A few more days surveying and the *Beagle* turned towards Tahiti: a "most charming spot," Darwin told Henslow. He felt little inclination to ruminate about the Galápagos Islands. The prospect of the South Sea Islands was far more exciting. For the one and only time on the voyage, he was moved in anticipation to quote Homer. "A new Cytheraea has risen from the ocean," he said in a letter home. Only Tahiti was beautiful enough to resemble the island where Aphrodite was born in the foam. His fine sentiment was only slightly spoiled by coming secondhand from the French navigator Bougainville, via Admiral Kotzebue, not from his own ill-remembered schooldays. Still, he had been looking forward to this part of the voyage for years.

It was a long passage to Tahiti, the longest of the expedition so far, which gave Darwin and FitzRoy an opportunity to read all the books on the South Seas that had been sitting unopened on the captain's shelves since leaving

Plymouth. A break in routine like this was wholly welcome, an indulgent pleasure for the two independently driven companions. Out on the deck in the sunshine, most of the usual formalities about dress and manners relaxing in the heat, the sails creaking, fresh pork and turtle soup for supper, they discussed the islanders they were soon to meet and the differing reports given by previous travellers. Like Darwin, FitzRoy had never been this far into the Pacific. He was absorbed by the idea that Polynesians might be the "eastern ancestors" that Chilean Indians worshipped, and was greatly interested by the prospect of seeing what various missionary activities had made of the moral—or what was more often considered the immoral—situation on the Society Islands generally. He relished the chance of following so completely the tracks of Captain Cook. Darwin, after contemplating the prospect of a "boundless ocean for five & twenty entire days" (why did they call it the "Pacific" ocean? he grumbled), settled down to dream of wild and beautiful scenery. He wished to make up his own mind about the Tahitians' "moral state." Such a judgement, he wrote with some self-awareness, would depend mostly on what he had previously heard.

Both men were interested by the account of Tahiti given by the Russian explorer Otto von Kotzebue, who had last visited the island in 1824, eleven years before the arrival of the *Beagle*. They were also reading Captain Beechey's *Narrative of a Voyage to the Pacific* (1832) and classic texts like William Ellis's important but idealised *Polynesian Researches* (1829), against which Kotzebue was partly reacting. In his book *A New Voyage Round the World* (1830), Kotzebue came down heavily against the English missionaries stationed in Tahiti and criticised the general course of Anglican proselytising in the South Seas. He accused the missionaries of a stultifyingly narrow outlook, of having killed the innocent gaiety of the islanders, of an unscrupulous thirst for power, and of causing strife in the internal affairs of the islands.[17] Furthermore, he attacked the London Missionary Society for letting what he called uneducated sailors manage church affairs in the islands, a direct hit at the policy of deploying "mechanic" missionaries without divine orders or a university education.[18] Most of the South Sea Islands' projects were run by this London Missionary Society, as Kotzebue knew. He was a respected naval explorer, observer, and scientific writer, and his criticisms were not to be taken lightly.

Despite a personal predilection for the rival, strictly establishment Church Missionary Society (the London Missionary Society was too low-church for the captain's traditional tastes), FitzRoy wanted to see what English philanthropy had achieved in the light of Kotzebue's views, especially since his own failed project in Tierra del Fuego still smarted painfully. Darwin was also concerned by the Russian's claims, although predisposed to take a much more liberal view of the missionaries after reading Ellis's favourable account and by the memory of his grandfather's uninhibited writings about the Tahitians' sex life. All of the first Erasmus Darwin's fervent beliefs in the naturalness of sexuality had come to a crescendo in his *Loves of the Plants* (1789), in which he introduced a Tahitian marriage ceremony to explain the reproductive processes of the Linnaean class Polyandria and brought the poem to a thundering close. Having learned some of his childhood botany from these verses, the younger Darwin could barely look at a tropical plant without seeing in his imagination undulating Tahitian maidens. His grand-father based his imagery firmly on Cook's encounter with South Sea Island life.[19] How far, Darwin wondered, had things changed since Cook and Banks arrived to observe the transit of the planet Venus?

Sailing up to Tahiti, FitzRoy and Darwin found little evidence for Kotzebue's dire claims that the islanders had become a gloomy race living in fear of the English. Instead, they disembarked into the middle of what they called a happy, merry throng.

Darwin was charmed:

> In nothing have I been so much pleased as with the inhabitants.—There is a mildness in the expression of their faces, which at once banishes the idea of a savage,—& an intelligence which shows they are advancing in civilization.—No doubt their dress is incongruous, as yet no settled costume having taken the place of the ancient one.—But even in its present state it is far from being so ridiculous as described by travellers of a few years standing. . . . The common people when working, have the whole of the upper part of their bodies uncovered; & it is then that a Tahitian is seen to advantage.—In my opinion, they are the finest men I have ever beheld;—very tall, broad-shouldered, athletic, with their limbs well proportioned. It has been remarked that but little habit makes a darker tint of the skin more pleasing & natural to the eye of a European than his own colour.—To see a white man bathing along side a Tahitian, was like comparing a plant bleached by the gardeners art, to the same growing in the open fields.—Most of the men are tattooed, the ornaments so grace-fully follow the curvature of the body that they really have a very elegant & pleasing effect. . . . The simile is a fanciful one, but I thought the body of a man was thus ornamented like the trunk of a noble tree by a delicate creeper.[20]

Tahitian women, he went on to say, were some way "inferior to the men": they were in great need of a "becoming costume," though the habit of wearing a flower in the hair was pretty, he conceded. Strait-laced in words at least, Darwin must have been the only man ashore, apart from an equally strait-laced FitzRoy, who objected to this flower-decked nudity. Perhaps he would have written more if his diary had not been intended for reading aloud by his sisters, cousins, and father. It seems likely that most of what he really thought was easier to express when describing the men.

Darwin also saw no incongruity in repeating a turn of phrase he had previously used for describing the inhabitants of Tierra del Fuego. This time, however, he put it in reverse. Where he characterised the Fuegians' primitiveness as unbearably wild, too savage to contemplate, he thought the Tahitians' unsophisticated state made them natural gentlemen, the "finest men I ever beheld." He found no problem in thinking of one group of natural human beings as savages and of another as noble. In the first case, he saw himself as inexpressibly superior, the educated product of a long process of civilization; in the latter, as he artlessly said, he felt like an overdomesticated, etiolated greenhouse plant. No matter which way he approached it his English ideology was always in the right. Like those of countless other travellers in similar situations, his metaphors invariably supported his prejudices.

The hospitality extended to the *Beagle* visitors on Tahiti was universal. Darwin entered several of the houses, and afterwards he and FitzRoy joined a "very pretty scene" on the beach, where circles of women and children around a fire were singing songs related to the ship's arrival: "one little girl sang a line which the rest took up in parts, forming a very pretty chorus, —the air was singular & their voices melodious." It made him unequivocally aware that he was, at last, seated on the palm-fringed shores of an island in the South Seas.

As soon as FitzRoy began his measurements on Point Venus, the same promontory where Cook and Banks had worked, Darwin made a two-day trip into the interior. Even in the Andes, he had never had such a vertiginous experience, edging along narrow paths in the wake of his guides, hanging on to the hillside, climbing up precipitous cliffs, and at one point moving from one level to another up a tree trunk notched and leaned against the mountain wall as a makeshift ladder. Waterfalls cascaded around him.

> Suspended, as it were, on the side of the mountain, there were glimpses into the depth of the neighbouring valleys; & the highest pinnacles of the central mountains towering up within sixty degrees of the Zenith, hid half the evening sky. Thus seated it was a sublime spectacle to watch the shades of night gradually obscuring the highest points. . . . The Tahitians with their naked tattooed bodies, their heads ornamented with flowers, & seen in the dark shade of the woods, would have formed a fine picture of Man inhabiting some primeval forest.[21]

As for the missionaries' influence, Darwin noticed approvingly that his guides said a prayer before retiring to sleep, not just for his benefit, he hoped; and they showed every sign of guilt when he unintentionally forced them to break their temperance vows by accepting a tot of rum when it was offered.

Tahitian moral resolve was stiffer when Darwin wanted to try the hallucinogenic *ava* plant, notorious in earlier days for enlivening tribal ceremonies. Darwin chewed it alone ("acrid & unpleasant"), since his companions had long ago given it up at the missionaries' request.

Over the days, FitzRoy and Darwin developed a much more generous opinion of the Tahitian missionaries than Kotzebue had. Charles Wilson, a relatively uneducated "mechanic" missionary, had been running the station at Matavai with the help of George Pritchard and Henry Nott, the Bible translator, since 1801. The London Missionary Society, which had been involved with the Society Islands since the days of its foundation in 1795, took considerable pride in the way these and previous missionaries overcame a succession of difficulties, drink and *ava* among them.[22]

All three missionaries seemed "sensible agreeable gentlemen," and the two visitors were soon united in their outrage at Kotzebue's apparently groundless attacks. Wilson's quiet exterior hid "a great deal of most unpretending excellent merit."[23] There was no reason to believe the islanders were afraid of any of them or disciplined too harshly. In particular, FitzRoy, who had been commissioned to exact payment of a fine from the new queen of the Society Islands, Pomare II, felt that she and her chiefs were politely at ease with Mr. Wilson, perfectly willing to pay her dues to the British government. The captain was sufficiently impressed by Queen Pomare's regal demeanour to invite her to a formal dinner on board the *Beagle;* and he and Darwin independently recorded their impression that her behaviour, and that of her party, was "extremely correct: their habits and manners perfectly inoffensive." The group had absorbed evangelical preachings so completely, said Darwin wryly, that they disapproved of the "merry comic songs" sung for them by the sailors. Surely one very noisy one could not be "Hymeni," remarked the queen. Some hastily devised "grave performances" were greeted with more approbation.[24]

FitzRoy plainly believed that a mission education provided the queen and her elders with European manners suited to their high social standing. Ordinary Tahitians, on the other hand, were perceived as cheerful, unruly children. He described—with exasperated amusement—how difficult it was making his chronometric measurements while crowds of interested spectators jostled to look inside the instrument tent.

Full of notions of noble savages and the stable, hierarchical, pastoral England he thought he remembered, Darwin too was greatly pleased by what he saw. The missionaries, he fancied, had succeeded in turning the settlement of Matavai into something like a country village in Shropshire. The hymn or "hymeni" singing was "decidedly pretty," the Sunday church services "filled to excess by tidy clean people of all ages & sexes." FitzRoy was also overcome enough to compare two chiefs of inferior rank with respectable English farmers. "A more orderly, quiet inoffensive community I have not seen in any other part of the world," he wrote.[25] English moral values and an approximation of English social structure were what both of them expected mission work to achieve. Tahiti was a success story. It reinforced FitzRoy's belief he had been right to try to set a similar enterprise in motion in Tierra del Fuego; and Darwin's diary echoed the same unthinking assumption that civilisation meant an idealised form of British hierarchical behaviour. Perhaps Kotzebue's attack, Darwin pointedly remarked, originated in disappointment that the celebrated licentiousness of Tahitian women was no longer evident. It was useless to argue against such men, since "they expect the Missionaries to effect what the very Apostles failed to do."[26]

IV

Everyone left with regret. "The kind simple manners of the half civilized natives," Darwin wrote to Caroline, "are in harmony with the wild & beautiful scenery. . . . In every respect we were delighted with Tahiti, & add ourselves as one more to the list of the admirers of the Queen of the Islands."[27]

Three long weeks of misery followed, crossing the sea to New Zealand. There was no more geology, but plenty of seasickness. Homesickness too: "hitherto the pleasures & pains have balanced each other; of the latter there is yet an abundance, but the pleasures have all moved forwards & have reached Shrewsbury some eight months before I shall." Think how amiable he was towards FitzRoy and the others, he grumbled to Caroline, when the ship was pitching against a heavy sea. Resignedly, he supposed it was necessary to sail over the great ocean in order to understand its immensity.

And when they got to New Zealand, he was too weary to let the lush green landscape, the curious natural history, and the exotic inhabitants ignite his imagination. The country was renowned for its bloodthirsty Maori warriors (though the term "Maori" was not then in use) and for fierce tribal antagonisms. It was also relatively unknown to the West in natural history terms. Yet he barely raised sufficient interest to hope to catch a kiwi, the mysterious flightless bird that came out at night to eat insects, tentatively identified from a feathered Maori cape by the French naval commander Jules Dumont d'Urville.

New Zealand was the religious preserve, so to speak, of the Church Missionary Society, the society which had helped FitzRoy with his Fuegian project. Whereas the London Missionary Society, the senior association in Britain, and the Wesleyan Missionary Society dominated activity in the South Pacific from Tahiti westward to Fiji, the Church of England, and the Church Missionary Society, was confined to a single diocese—the diocese of

Australia, embracing the rudimentary British colonies of New South Wales and New Zealand.[28] The *Beagle* arrived several years before George Augustus Selwyn was sent out to become the first bishop of New Zealand. At that time, there were only three or four mission stations in the North Island, located around the Bay of Islands, dating from Christmas Day 1814, when the Reverend Samuel Marsden preached the first sermon that a tattooed Maori assembly had ever heard.[29]

Kotzebue's anathemas had not been extended to these missions in the Bay of Islands, but were superseded in any case in Darwin's and FitzRoy's eyes by what Augustus Earle, the *Beagle*'s former artist, had written and told them before he left the ship because of illness in 1832. The same rebellious cynicism which led Earle to reject most conventional values and travel the globe in search of an idealised primitive society drove him to lambaste the New Zealand missionaries' behaviour towards the local inhabitants. Earle knew what he was talking about: he had lived as a native with a Maori woman for nine months in 1827. His highly sensationalist *Narrative* relating his adventures was published in England in 1832, just before he returned to London from Montevideo, becoming a *cause célèbre* in its day, although Earle did not live long enough to benefit much from its financial success.[30] The *Beagle* carried a copy of this outspoken *Narrative* on board, as well as one or two of the disapproving English literary reviews, the *Quarterly* in particular being mentioned by Darwin. The men's recollection of Earle's wayward personality easily filled in the unvoiced gaps.

Earle, like Kotzebue, had nothing good to say about churchmen or colonisation, about English prudery and social snobbery overseas, and said it forcefully. Moreover, he possessed considerable knowledge of Maori customs, speaking with feeling of their fine physical appearance, friendliness, and artistic gifts without minimising the turbulence of pre-colonial society and its cruelty. His particular complaint was humiliating rudeness from the missionaries Henry and William Williams, rudeness both to himself and to the tribesmen they were meant to be converting. The whole ethos of the Church Missionary Society, in short, was brutally attacked.

The subject was still very much alive when the *Beagle* arrived, not least because Earle's book was sent to the Williams brothers a few weeks after publication, causing them to defend themselves vigorously in a barrage of letters to church superiors.

So when FitzRoy discovered he had few official responsibilities to carry out except for seeing to the chronometers, he and Darwin decided to observe the work of the missions for themselves. FitzRoy also intended leaving the *Beagle*'s own missionary, Richard Matthews, at one of the stations in the Bay of Islands, where a brother lived. After the Fuegian debacle, Matthews wanted to fulfil his calling in a family atmosphere. He was finding it increasingly difficult even to say good morning to the captain without feeling guilty.

Walking over to Paihai, the largest mission station in the country and one accompanied by quite a big settlement of Europeans, FitzRoy and Darwin met Henry Williams. He gave them a kind welcome. The settlement was a pleasing reminder of home, with English garden flowers climbing over the whitewashed verandas and all the Maori huts hidden away on the outskirts of town.[31] The situation was not nearly as bad as Earle had led them to expect, especially after Williams told them his side of the contentious story. "I should think in no part of the world a more war-like race of inhabitants could be found than the New Zealanders," Darwin stated. He thought the missionaries had done a great deal in improving the Maoris' moral character "and still more in teaching them the arts of civilization."

> We are quite indignant with Earle's book, besides an extreme injustice it shows ingratitude.—Those very missionaries, who are accused of coldness, I know without doubt that they always treated him with far more civility, than his open licentiousness could have given reason to expect.[32]

They went next to Kororarika, the largest settlement. There they were shocked to find English people living in squalor as profound as that of Maoris. A great number of these poor white émigrés were the very refuse of society, complained Darwin: drunkards, addicted to all kinds of vice. Proper laws, he said, were quite unknown. Furthermore, by introducing the local inhabitants to drink, money, and what FitzRoy called "the most abandoned, profligate habits," this unruly element in the settlers' community (escaped convicts for the most part, they thought, or whalers) had wiped out many of the missionary successes among the Maori. Every resident was as vicious and degraded as the next, they dourly reported.

This was also their first chance really to look at the indigenous inhabitants. Inevitably, they drew comparisons with the Tahitians—unfavourable for the most part. A single glance at the respective facial expressions, said Darwin, convinced him that "one is a savage, the other a civilized man." The tattoos made it worse, he acknowledged. Even so, there was a look in the New Zealanders' eyes which suggested nothing to him but "cunning & ferocity." The Maoris, as Darwin and FitzRoy saw them, were "filthily dirty & offensive: the idea of washing either their persons or their clothes never seems to have entered their heads." Their lives operated on a simple, if brutal, system of revenge. "If the state in which the Fuegians live should be fixed on as zero in the scale of governments, I am afraid the New Zealand would rank but a few degrees higher, while Tahiti, even as when first discovered, would occupy a respectable position."[33] Altogether, Darwin concluded, the village of Kororarika was a disgusting scene.

Their depression was lifted by an expedition to Waimate, where the missionaries William Williams and Richard Davies lived in an English-style farming community. Here FitzRoy finally said goodbye to Matthews, whose brother had been in Waimate for some years. The men stationed in this mission, again a Church Missionary Society project, were politely interested to hear of FitzRoy's work among the Fuegians and insisted that instead of courting failure he had shown remarkable enterprise.[34] FitzRoy was deeply touched and was from then on a close and admiring friend of the New Zealand missions, a relationship which was relatively unimportant during the *Beagle* years but put him in an awkward position when he later returned as governor and was faced with the land crisis set into motion by the treaty of Waitangi. FitzRoy's wish to satisfy all the parties concerned led him to bankrupt the country, with two bloody massacres along the way. The dirty settlement of Kororarika was one to suffer.[35]

According to FitzRoy's account of this visit, Williams and the other professionals freely acknowledged that the missionary system in New Zealand needed to be different from procedures already established in Tahiti, Sierra Leone, and South Africa. The Maoris were hard to handle and accustomed to a fierce native government. Progress was slow and uncertain. Despite this, FitzRoy was impressed to find English tea (the explorers' cliché) served in the midst of men who had once eaten human flesh.[36] Darwin discovered his own cliché in a game of cricket played out in front of the farmhouse.[37] Around the mission were stables, a threshing barn with its winnowing machine, a blacksmith's forge, and on the ground ploughshares and other tools; in the middle was "that happy mixture of pigs & poultry which may be seen so comfortably lying together in every English farmyard."

> When I looked at this whole scene I thought it admirable.—It was not that England was vividly brought before my mind; yet as the evening drew to a close, the domestic sounds, the fields of corn, the distant country with its trees now appearing like pasture land, all might well be mistaken for such.—Nor was it the triumphant feeling at seeing what Englishmen could effect; but a thing of far more consequence;—the object for which this labour had been bestowed,—the moral effect on the native inhabitant of New Zealand.[38]

The two took their leave of these workers in the field full of admiration for their courage and humility. Teacups, verandas, and cricket bats had blazed a way into primitive society. Nonetheless, "I believe we were all glad to leave New Zealand; it is not a pleasant place."

V

Australia, by contrast, was the epitome of civilisation. Sydney harbour in January 1836 presented every appearance of a great capital city: windmills, warehouses, forts, big stone houses, a botanic garden, a civic museum, carriages in the streets with uniformed servants behind, and "superb villas." Even the prices of articles in the shops were "villainously dear." Large towns were the same the world over, said Darwin dismissively, as he made arrangements to gallop off into the hinterland. But he thought it was a wonderful colony. Writing to Susan, he had nothing but praise. "Ancient Rome, in her imperial grandeur, would not have been ashamed of such an offspring. . . . Can a better proof of the extraordinary prosperity of this country be conceived than the fact that 7/8th of an acre of land in the town sold by auction for 12,000£ sterling? There are now men living, who came out as convicts (& one of whom has since been flogged at the Cart's tail round the town) who are said to possess without doubt an income from 12 to 15,000 pounds per annum."[39]

He repeated this impressive information to Henslow, to Fox, and again in his diary: the country was a "very paradise to the worshippers of Mammon." Moreover, he thought the scene on the medallion made by the first Josiah Wedgwood out of clay brought from New South Wales, and the verses written by Erasmus Darwin on "Hope's visit to Sydney cove," in which he prophesied a bright future for the new colony, had all come true. He dallied with the idea of living there himself. "It is an admirable country to grow rich in; turn sheep herd & I believe with common care, you must grow wealthy." On the whole, though, he did not wish to settle in a place where every other man was sure to be "somewhere between a petty rogue & bloodthirsty villain."

Leaving FitzRoy shopping in Sydney, and after paying a call on Conrad Martens, who had settled there in 1835,[40] Darwin rode out to Bathurst, in the Blue Mountains, for the geology. He noticed nothing remarkable in the one hundred miles he travelled over, not even a kangaroo, he muttered, although he did kill and skin a platypus for his collection. The most interesting thing was meeting a party of Aborigines who showed him how they threw spears so accurately that they could pierce his hat fixed more than thirty yards away. These men appeared far from the degraded beings they were usually thought to be, Darwin noted. For a few coins he bought two boomerangs, one for himself, one for Henslow. He also visited Govett's Leap, on Martens's recommendation, to admire the stupendous view from the cliffs.

All the wild animals of this part of New South Wales had seemingly been exterminated by imported dogs: the emu had been banished to another region and the kangaroo was scarce. The woods, too, were remarkably uniform—hill after hill of the monotonous, never-failing eucalyptus. Yet lying on a sunny bank before riding into Bathurst, Darwin reflected on the strange character of Australian species compared to those of the rest of the world. Everything here was very different. "Surely two distinct creators must have been at work," he mused idly; if he let his reason rather than his religious belief dictate the terms, he would readily assent to that view. Still, he was startled to see in the sand in front of him the conical pit of a "Lion-Ant," just like the ones he knew from home. Watching the insect catch ants and flies in its trap, he was convinced it belonged to the same genus as the European one. "Now what would the disbeliever say to this? Would any two workmen ever hit on so beautiful, so simple & yet so artificial a contrivance? It cannot be thought so.—The same hand has surely worked throughout the universe."[41] Was it one hand at work, uniting the living kingdoms, however disparate they looked? Or did each country, so to speak, generate its own particular creatures? Without knowing it at the time, Darwin was edging towards the kind of questions which ultimately led him to evolution. Australia was a puzzle that occupied his thoughts more and more in the years to come.

On his way back to Sydney, Darwin stayed a night at Dunheved, the estate of Captain King, the captain of the first *Beagle* survey.[42] King was graciously anxious to help and entertain him, and the two spent an afternoon walking about the farm and discussing the natural history of Tierra del Fuego. Phillip Gidley King, the captain's son and Darwin's cabin mate since leaving Plymouth, was also present, released from his midshipman's service on the *Beagle*. King the father was grateful to Darwin for being his son's friend. Here it was just like being back in English high society: possibly grander. King took Darwin off to a neighbouring estate for lunch. "When we called I suppose there were twenty people sitting down to luncheon. There was such a bevy of pretty ladylike Australian girls, & so deliciously English-like the whole party looked, that one might have fancied oneself actually in England." But unlike Thomas Henry Huxley, visiting Sydney eleven years later on a comparable natural history expedition, Darwin did not come home with a female heart in his collection.

More in character, he splashed out on buying two watercolours from Martens, one of the Santa Cruz River and another of the *Beagle* in Tierra del Fuego, at three guineas each. He would not have bought them, he apologised to his father, if he had known how expensive the trip to Bathurst would be.

Moving on to Hobart, he liked Tasmania much better than Australia: there was altogether less likelihood of meeting convicts driving in their carriages, "revelling in wealth." The *Beagle* stayed for only ten or eleven days early in February, but everything to him seemed engaging. "You would be astonished to know what pleasant society there is here. I dined yesterday at the Attorneys General, where amongst a small party of his most intimate friends he got up an excellent concert of first rate Italian music. The house large, beautifully furnished, dinner most elegant with *respectable!* (although of course all convicts) servants.—A short time before they gave a fancy ball at which 113 people were present.—At another very pleasant house where I dined, they told me, at their last dancing party, 96 was the number.—Is this not astonishing in so remote a part of the world?"[43] If he was obliged to emigrate, he wrote in his diary, he would certainly prefer this place to New South Wales: the climate and aspect of the country almost alone would determine it. Most important, the island community was well governed.

It was curious, he reflected, how travelling and seeing the British colonies made him appreciate what "wonderful people the English are."

VI

FitzRoy's next task was to head round the Great Australian Bight (King George's Sound) into the Indian Ocean, making for the Keeling or Cocos Islands, where the surveyors were to take more chronometrical observations and to investigate, if they had time, the coral reefs which surrounded the islets. The captain was as homesick as Darwin and vowed to make this part of the voyage as short as possible.

There was in fact only one more thing Darwin really wanted to do in the natural history line, something he had hoped to study from the very start and had thought about intermittently since the ship surveyed the western American coast. It had become a much more tantalizing issue on Tahiti. There Darwin glimpsed—and did not have the time or a boat available to sail out to see more closely—his first coral reef: a reef encircling the green spires of Eimeo (Moorea) with a line of brilliant white surf where the waves "encountered the wall of coral." Inside the surf was a glassy lagoon out of which the mountains rose abruptly. The effect was very pleasing, he said, just like a framed engraving.

The pictorial image conveyed everything he wanted to find out about coral islands. He was puzzled by the conjunction of battering waves, quiet lagoons, and palm-clad mountains out in the middle of the ocean. Underneath it all, he knew, lay innumerable, minute coral polyps, incessantly building up their stony frameworks. Were the islands a monument or tombstone? he wondered. How could the polyps raise up such a structure, and why usually in a circle? The result was one of great natural beauty. Nowhere else on the voyage could he hope to examine living corals, their colourful reefs, and associated islands: nowhere else could he so indulge scientific and aesthetic appreciation simultaneously.

Darwin had encountered several theories attempting to explain the way coral reefs were built up from the ocean floor, and had taken trouble throughout the voyage to collect and understand the life cycle of marine polyps of all shapes and sizes. "I have lately determined to work chiefly amongst the Zoophites or Coralls," he remarked to Catherine on his way to Valparaiso. "It is an enormous branch of the organized world; very little known or arranged & abounding with most curious, yet simple, forms of structures."[44]

That these small gelatinous animals also constructed large submarine edifices was nothing less than marvellous. Lyell discussed the point in his *Principles,* suggesting that since the polyps could live only in the top few fathoms of water, where there was light and warmth, they must build their calcareous frameworks on the rim and bowl of submerged volcanic craters. Captain Beechey addressed the same question in his book of travels, as did Jean-René Quoy and Paul Gaimard in their authoritive account of the zoology of Freycinet's voyage. Since no sailor liked to leave reefs or submerged craters uncharted, FitzRoy was asked by Francis Beaufort to investigate Lyell's suggestion if possible. This looked as if it would be one of the most interesting parts of the circumnavigation, reported the *Athenaeum* before the *Beagle*'s departure, particularly in the way it afforded "useful inquiries" of a scientific nature.[45] Lyell himself was interested in the outcome, writing to Beaufort late in 1835 with a message for Beechey to collect specimens of the living polyps and any submarine volcanic rocks.

Somewhat surprisingly, Darwin had already considered Lyell's theory of volcanic underpinnings, rejected it, and devised his own Lyellian alternative to account for the origin of these and other reef-based islands.

About six months beforehand, long before he even saw a reef, and while still wandering through the Andes, he dreamed up a scheme that integrated coral reefs into a larger theory of the earth as a whole. What Darwin had in mind was that the elevation of land in South America was bound to be balanced by comparable subsidence elsewhere, the geological ups and downs together constituting one of Lyell's self-regulating oscillatory movements of the earth's crust. Common sense suggested that the place to find subsidence was in the sea, and he turned to consider the Pacific and Indian ocean basins, quickly deciding these vast expanses of water must conceal a subsiding seafloor. If lowering of the ocean floor was matched by coral polyps building their reefs up to the surface, there was no need to suppose a substrate of volcanic ridges and craters to account for the surface shapes. Instead, a volcanic island with a fringing reef attached to its shore might gently subside while the coral polyps kept on building up towards the surface. The result would be reefs dead at the bottom and alive at the top, the whole construction apparently separated from the subsiding central island: in effect, a ring around the island such as he saw at Eimeo. If subsidence continued to the point where the island disappeared below the waves, only the coral circle would be left to show where it once existed—with some drifting sand dunes and a few scattered palm trees, this constituted the curving horseshoe of an atoll.

Reefs ought to range, he proposed airily, from simple fringing and "barrier" constructions built up around the edge of an island to the complex lagoons and crescents composing atolls. Such a series of coral formations—fringing, barrier, and atoll—spread out over a great sweep of the ocean would indicate a large, generalised area of subsidence matching, size for size, the elevation of its nearest continental neighbour. He felt no need to invoke Lyell's unseen volcanic craters: coral polyps, subsidence, and time could do it all. "The subject of coral formation has for the last half year, been a point of particular interest to me," he told Caroline at the end of April. "I hope to be able to put some of the facts in a more simple & connected point of view, than that in which they have hitherto been considered. The idea of a lagoon island, 30 miles in diameter being based on a submarine crater of equal dimensions, has always appeared to me a monstrous hypothesis."[46]

Darwin was the first to recognise that his theory emerged out of an analogy drawn with the geological processes he had witnessed in the Andes.[47] Indeed, he recalled the moment with unashamed pleasure: it was the first time he worked in such a predictive fashion and went to confirm, in his own mind at least, the superiority of the geological views he developed under Lyell's bookish guidance.

> No other work of mine was begun in so deductive a spirit as this; for the whole theory was thought out on the west coast of S. America before I had seen a true coral reef. I had therefore only to verify and extend my views by a careful examination of living reefs. But it should be observed that I had during the two previous years been incessantly attending to the effects on the shores of S. America of the intermittent elevation of the land, together with the denudation and the deposition of sediment. This necessarily led me to reflect much on the effects of subsidence, and it was easy to replace in imagination the continued deposition of sediment by the upward growth of coral. To do this was to form my theory of the formation of barrier-reefs and atolls.[48]

His ideas about elevation and subsidence, sedimentary deposition and erosion, intermeshed effectively with the concept of small changes having large effects. This ever-moving, "little-by-little" approach was translated into a vision of reefs slowly building up to the surface, inch by coralline inch, accumulating the necessary height as the land unceasingly subsided below it, the coral formation mimicking the deposition of a geological stratum under water. Biological and geological forces acted in concert to bring about what he called one of the most remarkable alterations in the natural world.

Of course, Darwin would not have been nearly so cheerful if his ideas had, in practice, turned out to be wrong. Much of his delighted self-congratulation lay in realising that reefs, once seen and analysed, fitted his theory perfectly. Keeling Island was a chain of low coral reefs in the form of a circle on which sand had accumulated and formed strips of dry land barely two or three hundred yards wide. One could wade from island to island when the tide was low, reported Darwin, except for crossing the entrance to the basin or lagoon; and the lagoon itself was so shallow there was barely enough depth for the *Beagle* to anchor. The brilliancy of the colours made it all very attractive, he enthused. "As in the sky here & there a white cloud affords a pleasing contrast, so in the lagoon dark bands of living coral are seen through the emerald green water. Looking at any one & especially a smaller islet, it is impossible not to admire the great elegant manner in which the young & full grown Cocoa-nut trees, without destroying each others symmetry, mingle together into one wood: the beach of glittering white calcareous sand, forms the border to these fairy spots."

Waist-high in the warm central waters with Covington by his side, or bouncing about on the choppy waves outside attempting to drop a plumbline, Darwin obtained most of the evidence he needed for geological purposes and had a good time besides. One day the sea was smooth enough for him to wade over the flat surface as far as the breakers. "In some of the gullies & hollows, there were beautiful green & other coloured fishes, & the forms & tints of many of the Zoophites were admirable. It is excusable to grow enthusiastic over the infinite numbers of organic beings with which the sea of the tropics, so prodigal of life, teems." Covington waxed lyrical in his diary as well. "The water always being clear the beautiful branches of coral can be seen from the ship's side; the fish constantly passing & repassing amongst the coral, has a most beautiful effect."

A couple of days afterwards, FitzRoy took them in the *Beagle*'s launch to measure the reef's windward side. The waves there were far more dangerous and considerably grander to Darwin's mind, so dangerous that FitzRoy eventually called off the deep sea sounding because of the difficulties of negotiating between the winds and the surf. But the *Beagle*'s surveyors did discover there was a sharp drop on the seaward edge, suggesting that the reef rose up almost straight from the ocean floor; and the bits of coral scraped off far below with the ship's sounding leads were as dead as Darwin hoped. The rest of his investigations revealed delicate fanlike species in the protected lagoons. They would not be there at all, he reasoned, if the floor had once been a volcanic crater exposed to the abrasive force of the surf.

Confidence, gratitude, and admiration at nature's marvels combined in an epiphany for the voyage:

> I am glad we have visited these Islands; such formations surely rank high amongst the wonderful objects of this world. It is not a wonder which at first strikes the body, but rather after reflection, the eye of reason. We feel surprised when travellers relate accounts of the vast piles & extent of some ancient ruins; but how insignificant are the greatest of them, when compared to the matter here accumulated by various small animals. Throughout the whole group of islands, every single atom, even from the most minute particle to large fragments of rocks, bear the stamp of once having been subjected to the power of organic arrangement.[49]

Trying hard to be modest, he thought his answer considerably better than Lyell's.

HOMEWARD BOUND

Y the time the *Beagle* sailed away from the Keeling Islands, Darwin's self-perception and his wishes for the future were very different from those that had run through his mind on leaving England. The allure of a scientific life had taken hold. He wanted to become a proper geologist and naturalist: not just a travelling collector of specimens but an expert who could analyse the hidden depths of the earth and talk with men like Lyell as an equal. His work on the structure of coral reefs had confirmed it.

Simultaneously, the idea of becoming a clergyman was dissolving. Darwin's religious faith apparently stayed pretty much as before, waning in intensity perhaps yet still sufficiently concrete to give spiritual meaning to the natural wonders he saw; and his belief in the value of missionary activities within the Anglican Church was unshaken by the fiasco in Tierra del Fuego. But he had come to think he could make a contribution to the world of philosophical thought without also being a parson.

In later life, Darwin was the first to see the paradoxical side of this situation and remarked how ludicrous it was that he had once planned to take Holy Orders.

Yet despite these myth-making words of old age, and the wish expressed by numerous contemporaries and social commentators to find a lifelong secularism in his endeavours—to juxtapose his science and religion as irreconcilable opposites—Darwin's rejection of the church as a career during his *Beagle* days was not a rejection of God, at least not at first.

The situation was considerably more complex than that. Darwin was then, and always remained, sensitive to the ultimate aims and beliefs of certain broad-church clergymen, especially Henslow's and to some extent

Sedgwick's, and to the devotions of his wife and family, without feeling any need later on to subscribe to the same views himself. One of his best friends in middle age was the clergyman John Brodie Innes; and he made concerted efforts to interest Charles Kingsley and Baden Powell, among other noted clerics of the day, in his evolutionary writings—in these two cases with great success. Nor were any of his arguments with FitzRoy over religious or doctrinal issues: these came later. His natural history investigations were then and for several years afterwards rooted in the same natural theological traditions that he and other Victorians eventually overturned.[1] And in the social sense as well, Darwin retained many of the outward concerns of the clergyman he might have become without actually being one, eventually taking up some of the unspoken duties of a village squire and country parson when he went to live at Down.[2] He avoided any internal scourging of feeling, any moment of catharsis. The process of abandoning a church career that took place during the *Beagle*'s travels round the world was gradual, gentle, and silent; it was barely chronicled in his diary and letters. His intention to be a clergyman and his father's wish were never formally given up. They died "a natural death," he said afterwards.

II

All through South America, in fact, Darwin had written freely to his sisters and friends like Fox about parsonages and his expected life among the green fields of a country living: familiar images that cheered him up when home-sick. "Although I like this knocking about," he wrote to Shrewsbury from Brazil, "I find I steadily have a distant prospect of a very quiet parsonage, & I can see it even through a grove of Palms."

Susan wrote back encouragingly. "I am very much pleased to find the quiet parsonage has still such charms in your eyes, it is so delightful to look forward & fancy you settled there."

Only Erasmus was horrified, seeing much more clearly than his brother that it was the external trappings drawing him towards the life of a vicar. "I am sorry to see in your last letter," he roused himself sufficiently to write, "that you still look forward to the horrid little parsonage in the desert. I was beginning to hope I should have set you up in London in lodgings some-where near the British Museum or some other learned place. My only chance is the Established Church being abolished."[3] Erasmus recognised that clergydom attracted Darwin because of its security: the security of a house and home, the prospect of an unassuming, diligent wife, time for his hobbies, and a useful, relatively undemanding niche in social affairs.

Perhaps Darwin came to see something of this himself as the voyage progressed. Certainly his remarks about a clerical future dwindled into a coded expression representing all the other feelings of homesickness and longings for female company that mingled with his growing desire to be in the English countryside again. Sometimes he felt normal life was passing him by: the life he would have had like that of his cousin Fox, with its courting, marrying, and the surprising news of babies (though Fox, Caroline reported, suffered greatly when his first child was stillborn). The hypothetical parsonage became a personal myth, reassuring to himself and his sisters. It promised that an ordinary, non-travelling existence would at some point become a reality.

Caroline was quick to see the hidden messages in Darwin's hopelessly idealised talk of fields and firesides.

> I can conceive no thing more extraordinary and interesting than to be quietly living in a Brazilian cottage,—but do not let the cottage put the parsonage out of your head, a far better thing, and which we were rejoiced to hear continued to be a vista to your prospects. I hope you will in all probability find Fanny Wedgwood [their cousin] *disengaged* and sobered into an excellent Clergyman's Wife by the time you return, a nice little invaluable wife she would be.[4]

His sisters went on to write regularly to him about the Shropshire girls they hoped would still be single when Darwin returned, always evaluating them, as he tended to do himself, according to their suitability for a parsonage. None of them forgot Fanny Owen ("I cannot say Mrs Biddulph," objected Darwin), and her arrivals and departures and the birth of a daughter were chronicled for his information. She was, however, very much "an old married woman." Charlotte Wedgwood was changed, not much for the better, the Darwin sisters complained. So they shifted their matchmaking attention to the two youngest Wedgwood girls, Fanny and Emma, known as the "Dovelies," with a hopeful passing glance at the younger Owens, one of whom they thought had turned into a regular beauty. Their list of eligibles was reduced when Fanny Wedgwood died of cholera in 1832.

The spiritual emptiness of the imagery was also easy to see in Darwin's letters to Fox. Tell me how you contrive to live on such a stationary, slow-sailing craft as a Parsonage, Darwin teased him from Rio de Janeiro. Six months later, he was not so sure. There was the prospect of children romping beside Fox's vicarage chair and petticoats rustling.

> Poor dear old England. I hope my wanderings will not unfit me for a quiet life, & that in some future day, I may be fortunate enough to be qualified to become, like you a country Clergyman. And then we will work together at Nat. History, & I will tell such prodigious stories, as no Baron Munchausen ever did before.—But the Captain says if I indulge in such visions, as green

fields & nice little wives &c &c, I shall certainly make a bolt.—So I must remain contented with sandy plains & great Megatheriums.

In the end he stopped referring even to parsonages, although fields and nice little wives still haunted his imagination. To give his life to science, not the church, was now his private ideal.

There was, to be sure, no pressing reason for the two vocations to be mutually exclusive. He could have done both if he had persevered with his father's wishes. His Cambridge professors, for instance, provided a sterling example of men who combined natural philosophy and religious commitment, to their evident enjoyment and prestige.

But there was another, far more powerful image of the future to conjure with during Darwin's personal as well as literal voyage, one much more appealing in its youthful dedication to the realm of ideas and spiced with an attractive dash of rebellion. He was very taken with the thought of becoming someone like Lyell, a gentleman-expert who wrote about nature without bowing to anyone, least of all to the proprietors of contemporary theology. On the contrary, Lyell constantly and often amusingly pointed out how he interpreted natural phenomena without such aid while still maintaining a clearly expressed faith in the Creator. How far Lyell really dissented from the traditional consensus or was purely self-serving in his literary effects is hard to say: possibly only Darwin, reading and rereading between the lines of the *Principles,* saw him in this attractive light. In practice, Lyell offered a halfway house to thinkers like Darwin who could not find the courage or see any need to abandon everything in a single swoop.

Lyell, as Darwin understood him, was not tied to a university college fellowship and could speak his mind. He was not tied to a vicarage or to the church patronage system. He was free to marry. He was free to think. It was important also that although Lyell was much the same age as Henslow, he presented a much sharper, livelier view of science, history, and nature, and addressed some of the grandest themes science invoked. To a young man revelling in the world of reason and working independently, this stimulating author appeared the very essence of intellectual autonomy.

The impact of Lyell, indeed, can hardly be overestimated in assessing the state of Darwin's mind on religious matters. To follow Lyell as slavishly as he did in geological affairs was to become deeply impressed with the kind of secularised science offered by the *Principles;* and to adopt Lyell's wide-ranging philosophical programme was to free his mind to deal with personal beliefs in new ways. These beliefs were already loosening their hold on him, although they were far from being discarded. The man who spoke to Darwin through the pages of his book became a model for what he might glimpse in the future. As the parsonage among the palms crumbled, there was the figure of Lyell beckoning behind it.[5]

Hesitantly, Darwin tested the family waters from time to time, explaining to his father that the interest he took in the natural history of the voyage was "so different a feeling to any thing I ever knew before." He was working very hard at science, he emphasised, "at least for me"; and he thought it would be a pity after going so far, "not to go on & do all in my power in this my favourite pursuit."

> And it appears to me, the doing what *little* one can to encrease the general stock of knowledge is as respectable an object of life, as one can in any likelihood pursue.[6]

Although Dr. Darwin and the sisters did not particularly want to acknowledge it, a conversion was taking place. Darwin was coming to make the most important transition in his emotional journey. Without it, none of the other steps he took during the passage home would have been possible.

Drifting away from the church as a career, however, did not necessarily call into question Darwin's faith in an original Creator. Darwin always insisted that he believed in some form of God throughout the *Beagle* voyage and for a period beyond. In his *Autobiography* he says that he was in the end very unwilling to give up the last shreds of "my belief" and that this act took place some years after his return. But it is also clear that his kind of belief, though orthodox, was a very loose, English-style orthodoxy in which it was far less trouble to believe than it was to disbelieve. Accepting the basic story of Christianity was much easier than grappling with doubt. For Darwin, as for countless others, belonging to the Church of England was as much a statement of social position and attitude as it was a profession of any particular doctrine—particularly so for the liberal, gentrified section of society to which Darwin belonged. He used to say he had been so orthodox on the voyage that he was laughed at by some of the officers for quoting the Bible as an unanswerable authority on a point of morality: "I suppose it was the novelty of the argument that amused them."[7]

He did admit that the religious sentiment was never strongly developed in him. During his travels, he recalled, he came gradually to discredit the Old Testament as a literal source: he now saw it as a text no more to be trusted as an authoritative record of real events than the sacred books of the Hindu or "the beliefs of any barbarian." It was correspondingly difficult to believe in divine revelation. Like other men and women of the period, but especially in his case because of his developing analytic and scientific attitude toward natural phenomena, he wanted proof before he would believe—proof that the Bible was true. He remembered inventing absurd scenarios in which ancient manuscripts were discovered in Pompeii that confirmed "in the most striking manner" all that was written in the Testaments. But he knew he was not serious. His study of the religious customs of wild tribes like the Fuegians or the Patagonian Indians—and his experience travelling from country to country generally—played a much larger part in generating a feeling of theological relativity. Such a position was reinforced by his meetings with Spanish families during his American expeditions. Darwin was haughtily disparaging about the credulity expressed by Catholics all over South America and wickedly indulged in a form of religious role reversal by playing up to their shocked suspicions that Protestants were devils or worse. On some occasions, he knew he appeared to them as much an outlandish heathen as a "Musselman."

The New Testament too, "beautiful as is the morality," could not be taken wholly literally. It seemed to him to depend in part on the interpretation put on metaphors and allegories. Doubts rose in his mind about the practice of referring inexplicable facts to higher authority. Miracles, for example, bothered him, as they notoriously did many people throughout the nineteenth century.[8] No sane man could believe in miracles, he decided—"the more we know of the fixed laws of nature the more incredible do miracles become."

Yet he went to church regularly throughout the voyage, attending the shipboard ceremonies conducted by FitzRoy and services on shore whenever possible. He and Hamond spent some hours in Buenos Aires waiting to hear if they could receive communion from the English chaplain stationed there before going to Tierra del Fuego. As Hamond said, "we were both then young and looked on that ordinance as many young did, and do, as I suppose they do now, as a sort of vow to lead a better life. Our request met with so cold a response and the necessity put on us of engaging others to come with us, that our purpose was not carried out, but it shewed a disposition of mind I was glad to dwell on. Of course this was too delicate a passage in life to mention in public."[9] There seems no reason to assume Darwin's wish for communion was purely for show. It more accurately reflected the various contrasting sides to his faith—at once determined by social position and expectations, an unquestioned duty to behave in what he thought was the correct way, but also including a belief in higher authority and elements of private dissent. The *Beagle* Darwin, though occasionally doubtful, was by no means a thorn in the side of the church.

Neatly crystallising these issues was Augustus Earle's last and greatest picture. Its title is *Divine Service as It Is Usually Performed on Board a British Frigate at Sea* (1837), and it probably portrays the *Beagle* company, for it is a subtle panorama of the wide range of theological opinion that could be embraced by just such a set of travellers. The captain is seated in a flag-draped chair below decks intent on the Bible before him. Except for his grey sailor's queue, he looks like FitzRoy. A woman close by, otherwise unusual on a ship, is probably Fuegia Basket in her royal bonnet. Another figure, who must be Darwin, sits to one side hardly looking at his book although following the words for all that, and the junior officers, the young midshipmen, and sailors show varying degrees of intentness. To the right someone slumps in civilian clothes, half asleep, his top hat tossed on the floor. Earle was not one to bow to conventions like these.

III

As the ship made for Mauritius (Ile de France) in May 1836, the wildest and most exotic parts of the voyage were over. The point became evident when the *Beagle* docked at Port Louis, a thriving harbour surrounded by cultivated fields, sugar-cane plantations, bookshops, opera houses, and tarred roads, all very French even though the island had been taken over by the British some twenty-five years before. "Music & reading bespeak our approach to the old world of civilization," said Darwin in anticipation. He and FitzRoy read their copies of Bernardin de Saint-Pierre before arriving: both his natural history book about the island, which was in the *Beagle* collection, and his pastoral romance *Paul et Virginie,* set in the glades of Mauritius. "It will clearly be necessary to procure a small stock of sentiment on the occasion," wrote Darwin to Fox. "Imagine what a fine opportunity for writing love letters.—oh that I had a sweet Virginia to send an inspired epistle to.—A person not in love will have no right to wander amongst the glowing bewitching scenes."[10]

All these finer emotions signified something of Darwin's imperceptible shift into being a different kind of man—a man deliberately leaving behind the rough naval life as he gradually neared his home country, deliberately prepared to allow his more sensitive feelings to take over. He had already virtually given up shooting, viewing his former exploits as the activities of a barbarian, or at least of an uncouth, unthinking oaf let loose overseas. As his life of the mind expanded and took over, perhaps this was inevitable. Nevertheless, he decided that killing animals for pleasure was wrong. His hunting-shooting days were behind him. The future would be devoted to altogether more civilised, thoughtful, and intellectual preoccupations.

On Mauritius, Stokes and Darwin were invited to stay for a couple of days at the house of John Lloyd, the surveyor-general, a clever man who had formerly surveyed the Isthmus of Panama for imperial purposes. Lloyd owned an elephant, the only one on the island, and Darwin was entranced by his offer of taking it out for a ride in search of inland coral rocks. "The circumstance which surprised me most was the perfectly noiseless step: the whole ride on so wonderful an animal was extremely interesting." The rest of his visit, though not matching an elephant for novelty, was similarly "idle & dissipated."

After Mauritius, South Africa came next, the last major port before they turned into the Atlantic and made for home. FitzRoy brought the *Beagle* into Simonstown harbour, about twenty miles from Cape Town, in May 1836. He intended to stay for a month to take his chronometrical readings at the British observatory and confer with the English astronomers John Herschel and Thomas Maclear, who were then living at the observatory making their southern observations. Darwin thought there was no point remaining on the *Beagle* for such a long time: he had had enough of hammocks for the time being. As soon as he decently could he hired a gig and set off to look at Cape Town.

He particularly wanted to see the game animals of the African savannahs, the lions, gazelles, and rhinoceroses he had read about in travellers' tales. Lloyd's elephant had revived his curiosity about his own fossilised giants from the pampas. How could such beasts live successfully in the bare South African plains? "Having seen so much of that sort of country in Patagonia, Chili, & Peru, I feel myself to a certain degree a connoiseur in a desert, & am very anxious to see these."

When he viewed the sun-bleached earth on the edge of the Karroo, with hardly a tree breaking the horizon, he acknowledged that an animal's size cannot bear too much relation to the amount of fodder it needed. A meagre diet was evidently sufficient for rhinoceroses and for his fossils too. Other factors must have caused *Megatherium,* and all his other extinct specimens, to die out.

He had never seen such an uninteresting country, he said afterwards, unfairly extrapolating from his short excursion. He returned to Cape Town rather dispirited. But he met "several very pleasant people" during his last few days there, including Andrew Smith, the English army naturalist, who had just returned from an expedition into the interior with a new species of rhinoceros. Smith took Darwin on a couple of short geological rambles to show him the most important sites, and told him a great many things about the wildlife he had missed.

He also dined out several times with Maclear, with Lady Caroline Bell, and once with Herschel: this last, he said, was the most memorable event which, for a long period, he had the good fortune to enjoy.[11] "I felt a high reverence for Sir J. Herschel, and was delighted to dine with him at his charming house at the Cape of Good Hope. . . . He never talked much, but every word which he uttered was worth listening to. He was very shy and he often had a distressed expression. Lady Caroline Bell, at whose house I dined at the C. of Good Hope, admired Herschel much, but said that he always came into a room as if he knew that his hands were dirty, and that his wife knew that they were dirty."[12] (Herschel's passion for gardening may have been as much responsible as his notorious shyness.)

They saw each other a few times subsequently in Herschel's Dutch farmhouse outside Cape Town, and Herschel showed Darwin a "pretty garden" full of Cape bulbs of his own collecting. Growing bulbs and proselytising for public education filled the days of this gauche and brilliant scientist, and astronomy the nights. During his residence at the Cape—a privately funded expedition lasting from 1834 to 1838—Herschel made the most significant observations of his life's work, concentrating on star clusters, nebulae, and binary stars, but also mapping sunspots and watching the return of Halley's comet in 1835.[13] Darwin was secretly delighted that such a famous man, a man whose philosophical writings he fervently admired, was so awkward, so ordinary, in the flesh.

In his diary Herschel mentioned meeting Darwin at a dinner party which included FitzRoy and several others, although going into few details. According to Herschel, the conversation mostly concerned itself with Andrew Smith's recall to Simonstown on medical duties.[14] Herschel and Darwin probably talked about Lyell, however, whom Herschel knew personally, and perhaps a little about Darwin's geological theories as well. Herschel was a capable physical geologist, well qualified to discuss rival ideas of the earth's internal heat, the patterns of former climates, and the causes of elevation and subsidence. Possibly the two ranged more widely into the relations between science and religion. Herschel had recently finished reading a copy of the fourth edition of the *Principles,* sent to him by Lyell, and wrote to him in London about the way he dealt with the origin of species. He thought Lyell was on the verge of attributing even the origin of species to natural causes. Though Herschel did not want to believe in anything other than a miraculous origin for living beings, the force of analogy almost required Lyell to say what his theory demanded. In his reply (which arrived after Darwin's departure), Lyell explained that he had not wanted to appear too heterodox: "I should have raised a host of prejudices against me." Like his friend Whewell, Lyell tried to get the best of both worlds by thinking of the miraculous origin of life as something that was itself under God's natural law. This interesting letter, and Lyell's reply, soon became semi-public information in the small world of geological London, and completely public property in 1837 when Babbage published parts of them in his *Ninth Bridgewater Treatise.* But neither Lyell nor Herschel really wished to expose himself in this way to the hazards of scientific truths conflicting with theological certainties.[15]

Either way, Darwin's underlying religious views were different from Herschel's. Politely, he kept them quiet. The great man was too great, too hospitable, to engage him in controversial after-dinner arguments. Metaphysi-cal brawling was not a feature of Darwin's developing scientific personality. He went on his way grateful and flattered at having met one of the most eminent English scientists of the day.

The Cape Colony did, however, set him thinking about missionaries again. Missionaries at the Cape, with John Philips, the political activist, at their head, seemed to be attacked from every quarter. They were charged with exacerbating hostile racial conflicts between Dutch and British settlers and the Bantu tribesmen; criticised for their lack of control over supposed converts; and accused of lining their own pockets by taking advantage of a close relationship with aborigines to buy land at cheap prices and then selling it on at a profit to Europeans. Much of the blame for the turmoil of the 1830s—the economic hardship following on from slave emancipation in 1833, the sixth Frontier war of 1834, the Great Trek of 1835, the English legislation detailing the civil rights of the indigenous peoples—was uncere-moniously laid at the doors of the African mission houses.[16]

Fresh from their South Pacific and South American experiences, FitzRoy and Darwin felt these criticisms were unfounded. Talking over their activities at the end of the month in the captain's cabin, they were reminded of the adversities suffered by mission men in New Zealand and the injustice done to those stationed on Tahiti by Kotzebue. So when they sailed away from Cape Town at the close of June 1836, they spent the first few days jointly composing a brief notice for a South African evangelical newspaper describ-ing the favourable impressions they had received of mission activity in New Zealand and Tahiti. This notice was only a few pages long and entitled "A letter, containing remarks on the moral state of Tahiti, New Zealand, &c."[17] Chiefly composed by FitzRoy and made up from extracts from their respec-tive diaries, it was sent to the *South African Christian Recorder* and pub-lished in September, a few weeks after they left the colony.

This letter was notable for being the first conscious effort that either of them made to put something into print: a forgotten contribution to the mission controversy, forgotten by Darwin in later life when cataloguing milestones in his development as a thinker, and often forgotten by historians. Doubtless it was embarrassing for Darwin to recall that his first published work was on the mission question, or difficult linking himself again with FitzRoy after their paths diverged. Doubtless the paper was a passing whim of the captain's. But the physical evidence of their joint publication remains.

In the notice the two told how they had seen missionaries working hard under difficult conditions with never a thought for self-advancement. Charles Wilson of Tahiti, they reported, had the "sincere and naturally impressive manner of a kind-hearted honest man earnestly performing his duties." The

Williams family in Waimate had "superior characters" with an "air of honesty and that outward tranquillity which is the result of a clear conscience and inward peace." Credit should be given, they thought, for what had been achieved against almost insuperable odds. Moreover, added Darwin darkly, repeating a thought that FitzRoy had expressed earlier in relation to Tierra del Fuego and one not far removed from their own nautical circumstances, some shipwrecked sailor would be thankful for even the slightest moral improvement in races renowned for murderous behaviour. Who could deny dutiful servants of God and the promoters of English moral values the opportunity of buying a smallholding for the maintenance of their families? There is land enough for everyone, they declaimed; must a missionary seek out only the worst?

Even though this joint outpouring was only a letter to a small colonial newspaper, itself established only the year before and directed exclusively to the evangelical community, and consisting merely of a series of quotations from their diaries, it reveals what a remarkable accord had built up between the two men during the course of the voyage. Apart from its intent to defend the Anglican missionaries, the paper also represents the culmination of a set of discussions, experiences, disappointments, excitements, and developing opinions shared by Darwin and FitzRoy. Their interest in mission activity, to be sure, was only one aspect of a long and basically friendly association on board the *Beagle*. Yet the interest was hardly irrelevant to more central matters. It brought to a focus important issues concerning human origins, questions about the relationship of mankind with the natural environment, and moral themes of progress and improvement. By wishing to give credit to missionaries for taking the first and hardest steps in spreading European values throughout the world, they were openly subscribing to a particular view of human nature, a view based on the concepts of racial unity and a capacity for progress through education and the alleviation of external circumstances. Darwin's opinions—which reflect the emancipationist, liberal views of his father and grandfather before him—were endorsed for rather different reasons by FitzRoy. FitzRoy—like his father and grandfather before him—believed in the high-Tory, Christian ethic in which paternalism provided the motive for supplying direct aid to primitive societies. United by their mutual concern for these aboriginal groups and steeped in the same kind of European cultural chauvinism, they met on the common ground of British philanthropy at a time when optimism and high-minded ideals were vital outer garments for what were already becoming the exploitations of the imperial era.

IV

Once the *Beagle* left South Africa, it became harder and harder for all on board to submit to their usual routines. The thought of arriving home in three months or so made it impossible to concentrate.

Darwin was intensely homesick. "For the last year, I have been wishing to return & have uttered my wishes in no gentle murmurs; but now I feel inclined to keep up one steady deep growl from morning to night.—I count & recount every stage in the journey homewards & an hour lost is reckoned of more consequence than a week formerly." He had done everything he had wanted to do and more besides. Now, like the others, he was ready to return. Understandably, he started saying he was not the travelling kind: that his time on the *Beagle* was harder than that of a convict sentenced to seven years' transportation. From the ship his thoughts moved inexorably to its captain. FitzRoy's unusual and "noble character" was sadly flawed with "strong peculiarities of temper," he complained to Caroline. He often wondered what FitzRoy's future held. "Under many circumstances I am sure, it would be a brilliant one, under others I fear a very unhappy one."[18]

All his enjoyment in the constant change of scene had gone. "I confess I never see a merchant vessel start for England, without a most dangerous inclination to bolt.—It is a most true & grievous fact, that the last four months appear to me as long as the two previous years, at which rate I have yet to remain out four years longer.—There never was a ship so full of homesick heroes, as the *Beagle.*—We ought all to be ashamed of ourselves."[19]

With this came other anxieties about what Shrewsbury would be like when he arrived home. "How changed every body & every thing will be by the time I return," he groaned to Fox. "You a married clergyman, ave maria, how strange it sounds to my ears. I wonder when I shall see you. . . . Five years is a sadly too long period to leave one's friends & relations; all common ideas must be lost & one returns a stranger, where one least expects or wishes to be so.—I hope at least it will not happen with you & me."[20] How strange it will be, he wrote pensively to his sisters, seeing his friends as married men with families.

He told the womenfolk at home that they would not recognise the ancient, brown-coloured gentleman coming through the door. The thought was unconsciously echoed by Susan, who, after reading the last instalment of his journal, could hardly fancy Darwin was her brother "going through such hazardous enterprises." All three women, perhaps Dr. Darwin too, were poignantly conscious of the way Darwin's life had moved on while they were left at home. Many an hour was spent now, said Caroline, wondering if our little spot of a house and garden was too confined—"it will be as if you were awakened from a dream when you find everything & everybody just as you left them except all 6 of us being pretty considerably aged—Pincher & Nina inclusive." However, even if it was only for his own peace of mind, he issued early instructions to them about sending his heavy overcoat and leggings in a suitcase to wait for him at Plymouth. Sulivan provided a temporary address. In the meantime, he sorrowfully remarked, he was going to bed to dream of England.

For all his fears, Darwin was actually remarkably well informed about what was happening at home. His sisters had promised to take turns in writing letters every month until he returned, a promise they faithfully kept and to which Darwin always bore grateful testimony. Their long "gossipaceous" letters gave him a strong sense of what was going on—not only in political terms, when the Reform Bill and Emancipation were making their way through Parliament, but also in relation to the ups and downs of local existence, the incidental Shropshire news that would have been impossible to recapture several years later. There were anecdotes about Shrewsbury scandals, tight-lipped references to the black sheep Sir Francis Sacheveral Darwin, who spent his grand tour in Europe "disfiguring & mutilating all the statues he came across," the latest information about marriages and broken engagements, the books the family were reading, and Dr. Darwin's new hothouse. There was affectionate abuse of Erasmus, too lazy to write, hypercritical of his cousins' new husbands and wives, alternately immersed in the cultural life of the capital and plagued by the duties of dinner parties. "You really must not blame me if Eras does not write to you for I regularly send him a dun in every postscript," exclaimed Susan. "He is now quite buried alive in a little Lab he has set up in his lodgings which makes him quite forget times & seasons.—If he comes down at Easter I will stand over him & torment his heart out about writing to you."

Month by month Darwin heard of Marianne's babies (always boys, the sisters grumbled), one of whom was named Charles in his honour, and of Dr. Darwin's chesty cough which turned into gout, the mushrooms that gave them all stomach-ache, Susan's riding tour in Wales, the banana tree bought for the hothouse and called the Don Carlos tree, the plan to take a house in London for the season, and Erasmus's fatal attraction for his cousin Hensleigh's wife—"she is quite as much married to him as to Hensleigh, and Papa continually prophecies a fine paragraph in the Paper about them."

Darwin was astonished at the number of events which took place: "I assure you no half famished wretch ever swallowed food more eagerly." He came to depend on their regular instalments. The girls were the "very best of sisters."

Still, the *Beagle*'s long haul across the Pacific and Indian oceans had created a large gap in everybody's mail: there were no letters waiting for the ship at Sydney, nothing at Mauritius. And at Cape Town, instead of the mountain of post they all hoped to see, they received only the letters that were meant to be there. None of the missing letters had caught up. "Nine months' letters are wandering over the wide ocean," Darwin cried melo-dramatically, "which we shall not receive till some time after reaching England." His disappointment was aggravated by the annoying suspicion that a letter from Erasmus was among them.

Moreover, the nearer Darwin got to England the more uncertain he felt about his future. "I do so earnestly desire to return, yet I dare hardly look forward to the future for I do not know what will become of me," he confessed to Fox. "Your situation is above envy; I do not venture even to frame such happy visions.—To a person fit to take the office, the life of a clergyman is a type of all that is respectable & happy; & if he is a naturalist & has the 'Diamond beetle,' ave maria, I do not know what to say."[21]

He tried to explain these feelings to Caroline from Mauritius. If he was going to make best use of his *Beagle* investigations he would need some time either in London or Cambridge to work at writing. "I am in high spirits about my geology,—& even aspire to the hope that my observations will be considered of some utility by real geologists. I see very clearly it will be necessary to live in London for a year, by which time with hard work, the greater part, I trust, of my materials will be exhausted. Will you ask Erasmus to put down my name to the Whyndam or any other club; if, afterwards, it should be advisable not to enter it, there is no harm done. The captain has a cousin in the Whyndam, whom he thinks will be able to get me in.—Tell Erasmus to turn in his mind for some lodgings with good big rooms in some vulgar part of London."[22] Though he was coming back, he did not necessar-ily want to stay in Shrewsbury.

At last a hint from Susan showed that Dr. Darwin recognised his dilemma. Erasmus had bought a house in London. In her mind Susan linked the two philosophical brothers together, just as much as the doctor probably did.

Poor Eras' troubles about housekeeping are quite pathetic, first of all he was excessively puzzled how to get an old woman into his house without furniture, or furniture into his house without an old woman; & then after he had accomplished that difficulty he had to carry 13 cab loads of glass bottles &c from his Lab.—Still each letter is full of the *"eternal botherations"* as he calls them & now we are busy breaking in a horse to send up to London for him; as his beautiful grey horse is dead who I suppose lived & died since your days. Papa & we often cogitate over the fire what you will do when you return, as I fear there are but small hopes of your still going into the church:—I think you must turn professor at Cambridge & marry a Miss Jenner if there is one to be had.[23]

Dr. Darwin, she implied, had no objection to his becoming an independent scholar, like Erasmus; although perhaps without the same amount of fuss.

Darwin jumped on this information with relief. Apart from anything else he could easily imagine himself living close to his brother. "I am quite delighted at hearing Erasmus is turned house holder," he wrote from Cape Town; "I hope I shall be able to get lodgings at no great distance, & then London will be a very pleasant place." Possibly Cambridge might be better, since "I can not make myself cockney enough to give up thoughts of a quiet walk on an autumnal morning in the real country."[24] Quickly, he wrote another letter to Erasmus, a long and heavy one about himself, he said afterwards, from St. Helena, in which these and other problems were probably discussed. (The letter has not been found.) In the meantime he asked Henslow if Sedgwick would propose him as a member of the Geological Society of London: "I am very anxious to belong."

The future seemed to him altogether more positive than it had for some months previously, especially when the letters from Shrewsbury at last caught up with the *Beagle* in July 1836 on Ascension Island in the Atlantic. Their news could hardly have been more welcome or timely.

It happened that Henslow was so pleased and interested in Darwin's information from South America that he had concocted out of the letters sent to him a small scientific paper on natural history, running to some thirty-one pages.[25] These extracts from Darwin's letters were read out loud by Henslow at one of the meetings of the Cambridge Philosophical Society on 16 November 1835, nearly seven months before Darwin heard about it. Darwin's name was thus brought before some of the most notable natural scientists of the day—the Cambridge dons and fellows he used to know and would come to know—serving to generate interest in his endeavours and a general buzz of anticipation about his impending return. Sedgwick, Whewell, Peacock, William Hallowes Miller (the new professor of mineralogy after Whewell), Jenyns, and the rest were present. Henslow then got the paper printed by Cambridge University Press as a pamphlet and sent it round to his friends. Dr. Darwin, said Caroline, proudly distributed other copies to Darwin's school and university contemporaries.

Henslow had done more than this. The pamphlet spurred him on to reactivate the Cambridge network that once had sent Darwin overseas to take full advantage of what their envoy was now achieving, asking his friend Edward Newman, editor of the *Entomological Magazine,* to print the entomological parts of Darwin's paper in his journal, which he did in April 1836, and then persuading Sedgwick to read a shortened selection from the same extracts of letters at a meeting of the Geological Society on 18 November

1835. Despite getting Darwin's name wrong in the printed proceedings (F. Darwin), and in the index (T. Darwin), and crediting him with being a graduate of St. John's rather than Christ's College, Cambridge, the paper went down very well with the members. Charles Lyell was in the presidential chair.[26] Hearing about Darwin's work on elevation and subsidence was music to his ears that evening. "How I long for the return of Darwin!" Lyell cried to Sedgwick afterwards. "I hope you do not plan to monopolise him at Cambridge."[27] He was particularly eager for more details on the geology of South America from this young man who seemed to know the *Principles of Geology* as well as the author did. Writing to Francis Beaufort at the Admiralty, Lyell asked him to communicate with Mr. Darwin: he particularly wanted to know "all the latest intelligence of the geology of Patagonia and Chile."[28]

Sedgwick too was pleased to hear of Darwin's geological investigations: they sounded very promising. Privately, he told Samuel Butler (Darwin's former headmaster and an old college friend of Sedgwick's) that the young traveller was doing "admirable work in South America and has already sent home a collection above all price." There had been some risk, Sedgwick knowingly added, that he would turn out an idle man. But if God spared his life "he will have a great name among the Naturalists of Europe."[29] The Darwin sisters breathlessly repeated the last sentiments word for word straight from Butler to their brother.

Another surprise, warmly retold in these letters by each sister in turn, was that Henslow had sent Darwin's *Megatherium* head to William Clift at the Royal College of Surgeons, where it caused much palaeontological excitement by supplying information about a part of the jaw missing on both the London and Paris specimens. William Buckland, professor of geology at Oxford, dean of Westminster, and the leading bone man of the day, had come to see the fossils and took some with him to display at the Cambridge meeting of the British Association for the Advancement of Science in 1833. Buckland and Clift, reported his sisters, were very eager for more.

V

To cap it all, FitzRoy looked over Darwin's shoulder one day and suggested his diary might be published as a description of the natural history of the voyage. FitzRoy was committed to publishing his own narrative drawn from the ship's logbook, and to editing an accompanying volume based on Captain King's account of the first *Beagle* survey. Darwin's journal would make a third to complete the set. "Of course I have said I am perfectly willing," he told Caroline proudly; "he has read over the part I have on board & likes it. I shall be anxious to hear your opinions, for it is a most dangerous task, in these days, to publish accounts of parts of the world, which have so frequently been visited. It is a rare piece of good fortune for me, that of the many errant (in ships) naturalists, there have been few or rather no geologists. I shall enter the field unopposed." Yet Caroline might think he overstepped the mark. "I assure you I look forward with no little anxiety to the time when Henslow, putting on a grave face, shall decide on the merits of my notes. If he shakes his head in a disapproving manner I shall then know that I had better at once give up science, for science will have given me up.—For I have worked with every grain of energy I possess."[30] There was also the proposed geological text still at the back of Darwin's mind since the day on St. Jago: "here was a second book in prospect!"

He seemed, as his letters began to attest, to be becoming the very man he wanted to be, even before the *Beagle* journey ended. Some of his fossils were already in the right hands, his views were politely advertised in the right circles, his contact with Lyell was already assured: Henslow had done far more to give him professional status than he could ever have hoped to do himself, and much more quickly. The social and intellectual network which had chosen him for one set of reasons was apparently busy finding a place for him—for different reasons—to fill as an equal. Sedgwick, Lyell, Henslow, Buckland, and even FitzRoy all had vested interests in Darwin as a future colleague: they wanted the information only he could give them about his natural history travels; and they were not averse to playing cards in the game of scientific politics to secure him for their own position on the intellectual spectrum, be it Cambridge versus London, or natural theology against secular geology. Through the judicious placing of choice specimens and some careful editorial work, his friend and former professor had constructed a public figure who now only had to return—not always a certainty in the age of tall ships—to take his place in scientific society. In this sense, Henslow acted almost as an agent or business manager for Darwin, and completed his self-appointed task with skill. Never forgetting this assistance, Darwin believed that Henslow had made him what he was. For many grateful years afterwards Henslow was always his "Chief Lord of the Admiralty."

Confidence, independence, and a growing sense of vocation manifestly converged to set these last months of Darwin's voyage apart from the years before. Doubts about his own ability, of course, crossed his mind regularly, and he was not so cocksure that he failed to imagine what it would be like if his notes turned out to be worthless. Apprehension and self-deprecation had their moments just as much as ambition and scientific vigour.

Nevertheless, all his hopeful thoughts of doing something useful in science, of making an opening for himself in intellectual life, of having theories to explain, that had gradually worked their way into his life during the voyage now intermeshed in a satisfying way with a deepening sense of having found his vocation: a vocation glowing with youthful idealism and ambition, stripped of any lingering wish to enter the church or of fantasies of parsonages, fired by what he imagined Lyell was like as a man, and gratifyingly confirmed, at least in the more private regions of his mind, by the messages that came late, though not too late, over the ocean from home.

"Towards the close of our voyage," he wrote in his *Autobiography,* "I received a letter whilst at Ascension, in which my sisters told me that Sedgwick had called on my father and said that I should take a place among the leading scientific men."

> I could not at the time understand how he could have learnt anything of my proceedings, but I heard (I believe afterwards) that Henslow had read some of the letters which I wrote to him before the Philosophical Soc. of Cambridge and had printed them for private distribution. My collection of fossil bones, which had been sent to Henslow, also excited considerable attention amongst palaeontologists. After reading this letter I clambered over the mountains of Ascension with a bounding step and made the volcanic rocks resound under my geological hammer![31]

"All this shows how ambitious I was," he concluded defiantly.

VI

What Darwin did not recognise until considerably later was how far he was also capable of drawing free from his acknowledged sources. He had diverged from Henslow long ago over the nature of terrestrial flatworms in Brazil and was looking forward to confirming his own point of view. He diverged from Kotzebue and Earle after witnessing mission projects in action, and experienced a sea change of opinion about the nature of primitive mankind, finding close links between savage and civilised races which other authorities at home publicly rejected. He found the courage to disagree with the captain over slavery. He believed he had a fresh new understanding of the reproduction of corals and other marine invertebrates. He gradually dissociated himself from his father's plan that he should become a clergyman. He even diverged from Lyell in certain areas. He could improve on Lyell's theory of subterranean movements. He could demonstrate the steplike elevation of the Patagonian plains, the recent origins of part of the Andes, the volcanic nature of the Galápagos Islands, and the formation of coral reefs. He could supplement much of what Lyell had to say about the geographical distribution of animals and plants and had some interesting theories about the extinction of fossil mammals to put before a scientific audience. Lyell, he thought, overestimated the way organisms were beautifully adapted to their surroundings.

The scale of these problems and the verve with which he handled them were still vivid when Darwin settled down to writing and rearranging his notes as the ship ploughed across the Atlantic. Covington settled down at the table beside him to help sort the papers: the field notebooks, the numbered catalogues of specimens, his large zoological and geological logbooks, and the last remaining pages of his diary. Carefully, Covington rewrote many of Darwin's lists in his clear clerk's handwriting. Darwin concentrated on drafting other notes and short essays preliminary to distributing his specimens among the experts he hoped to consult. He did the bird list himself.

This time around, the birds of the Galápagos archipelago puzzled him much more than before. They did not seem to fit any of the conceptual schemes he used for other animals or birds: their status as species or varieties was very perplexing. Needing to write about them as one or the other in his ornithological notes, Darwin felt obliged to come to some kind of decision. But now, nearly six months later, the words he used, the tone of voice, the willingness to push harder than he pushed before, took him beyond his usual boundaries.

In these obscure private papers full of esoteric cataloguing details, Darwin made his first, extremely ambiguous statement about the possibility of evolution.

> When I recollect, the fact that from the form of the body, shape of scales & general size, the Spaniards can at once pronounce, from which Island any tortoise may have been brought, When I see these islands in sight of each other, & possessed of but a scanty stock of animals, tenanted by these birds, but slightly differing in structure & filling the same place in Nature, I must suspect they are only varieties. The only fact of a similar kind of which I am aware, is the constant asserted difference—between the wolf-like Fox of East and West Falkland Islds.—If there is the slightest foundation for these remarks the zoology of Archipelagoes—will be well worth examining; for such facts would undermine the stability of Species.[32]

As he said many years later to Otto Zacharias, the German entomologist who appears to have been the only man who thought to ask Darwin directly when he first thought of evolution, "vague doubts" about the permanence of species flickered across his mind.[33]

Confidence and knowledge had come far enough to open the door to doubt.

VII

The *Beagle* arrived in Falmouth on 2 October 1836, and Darwin left it as soon as the gangplank was down. A final storm in the Bay of Biscay had set the seal on his sailing life. "The stupid people on the coach did not seem to think the fields one bit greener than usual," he told FitzRoy in great good humour afterwards, "but I am sure we should have thoroughly agreed that the wide world does not contain so happy a prospect as the rich cultivated land of England."

He walked into The Mount just before breakfast on Wednesday, 5 October, five years and three days after leaving home. "Why," said his father, "the shape of his head is quite altered."

part three

NATURALIST

PARADISE LOST

IVE years was a very long time. When Darwin had time to look, he noticed how much England had changed. Railways were snaking across the land where stagecoaches had once gone, towns crept relentlessly outwards, shops, chapels, factories, and churches sprouted everywhere. Eighteen-year-old Queen Victoria was just about to ascend the throne, Lord Melbourne's Whig-dominated Parliament was dissolved, and the unveiling of an enormous Doric arch heralded the opening of London's Euston Station. "Let us now hope," declared Lord John Russell, "that we are going to have a female reign illustrious in its deeds of peace."

But the first issue of *Oliver Twist* revealed the miserable reality of life in Britain. Dickensian noise, discontent, agitation, and fervour spewed out under Russell's genteel, progressive optimism. Zealous Evangelicals and Benthamites pushed forwards with wide-ranging civil reforms at the same time as religious dissenters criticised establishment values and working men made their opinions vociferously known. Newspapers of all political hues, popular journals, Bible tracts, incendiary protest sheets, and educational volumes cascaded from the new steam presses. "This is the age of subdivision of labour," remarked the editor of the *Athenaeum:* "four men make a pin and two men describe it in a book for the working classes." England was the workshop of the world, claimed Disraeli: two nations, he went on to say, the rich and the poor. A huge colonial empire, as Darwin already recognised, glimmered on the horizon.

The Darwin family had changed as well. Caroline was already a matronly spinster at thirty-six, and Susan and Catherine, aged thirty-three and twenty-six respectively, were tending that way. The doctor, who had been in poor health for some years, was enormously fat, gouty, and short of breath. He had almost stopped his medical practice now, apart from treating long-standing friends and relations: Marianne's husband, Henry Parker, took over most of his patients and was physician to the Shropshire Infirmary. Erasmus owned a house in London and lived his own life.

Darwin too was different from before. Indeed, they all found it awkward to start with. Caroline half expected the same eager young undergraduate to reappear and only slowly came to terms with seeing a full-grown man in his place. He was awfully thin, she found herself saying stupidly, in lieu of all the other emotions. The other sisters openly hoped he would stay at home with them as a country gentleman, making their life much more sociable and agreeable: The Mount was terribly dull without any brothers around. Darwin, on the other hand, felt more like Father Noah emerging from the Ark with his animal family, a bemused survivor from the ancient world. Seeing Hensleigh Wedgwood walking up the street with a bandbox in one hand and a child in the other brought the gap home with a vengeance. His journey's end was puzzlingly strange to negotiate.

At first, however, Darwin naturally found little time or inclination for any kind of serious thought: everything was tumbling and shouting for attention. Immediately after landing, he rushed from place to place trying to satisfy his overwhelming need to see the people he knew best. He stayed at Shrewsbury for only ten days before running to Erasmus in London. Then it was off to Cambridge for Henslow, two weeks in London in order to meet Charles Lyell and be elected as a fellow of the Geological Society, four days with Uncle Jos and the Wedgwoods, another two weeks at The Mount, with a couple of days seeing Marianne on the way, and then two more weeks in London. "The busiest time of the whole voyage has been tranquillity itself to this last month," he gasped early in December. "I have talked and laughed enough for years instead of weeks, so my memory is quite confounded with the noise."[1]

Partly the problem was indecision about where to live and what to do next. He thought Shrewsbury was too remote for the exciting scientific activities he had in mind, yet Cambridge and London each possessed disadvantages of their own. He had to decide soon because two cases of specimens were due to be off-loaded at Woolwich despite the fact he did not know where to send them.

But he also displayed all the symptoms of intense overexcitement, almost manic in its fevered activity. He felt a strong urge to avoid at least some of the personal intimacies generated by his return. Family reunions were difficult enough in his imagination. Would his father start talking about the church again? Did his sisters really expect him to be unchanged? He was baffled by explaining events which happened to him three or four years before, totally unable to recapture the words and feelings of the expansive letters he wrote at the time. The same barriers were evident over at the Wedgwoods'. "He was shy," said Elizabeth Wedgwood to Hensleigh after Darwin's flying visit to Maer Hall. "We could not get on." Retreating safely into his new scientific persona, Darwin lectured the assembled cousins on Lyellian geology instead of supplying the cheerful exaggerations about man-eating lions they expected. Only Harry valiantly asked "whether we are going up or going down" before Uncle Jos stepped in with soothing agricultural chat about worms. It was so much easier dealing with dogs, thought Darwin reproachfully. When he walked into the yard on his first day home the old mongrel trotted up at his whistle as if he had never been away.

Darwin found the thought of visiting his university friends similarly daunting and avoided them for the time being. He wriggled out of going to see his cousin Fox on the Isle of Wight, with a wife and baby daughter to admire, and avoided a trip to Durham to congratulate Whitley on his recent marriage. He was far too busy, he wrote politely. Herbert's hearty invitations to meet him in London remained unfulfilled. "Faith I think I see & hear you now, on my having tried you with 'God save the King' or 'Cherry Ripe,' " reminisced Herbert affectionately. "By G— old fellow, I don't know, but isn't it the Hallelujah I heard in King's last Sunday? . . . We must have a meeting of the [Glutton] Club to welcome you on your return, when you must bring up your reports of Transatlantic cookery."[2]

There was too much to talk about, too much exposure. Such close attention made Darwin feel desperately self-conscious. It was impossible to spend the rest of his life, as it then seemed, telling people what he did during the voyage and how much he had missed them. More to the point, he resented the trivial demands of his long-awaited return, especially the obligation of paying calls on "stupid people . . . they neither cared for me, nor I for them."

As soon as he could, he bolted. He made for Cambridge, deliberately putting himself far away from the Midlands circle of friends and relatives, and almost as far away again from Erasmus and his new contacts in scientific London. He needed to work, he insisted: to have time on his own to sort out his *Beagle* material and think of the months ahead. Scooping up Syms Covington as a manservant and natural history assistant after the *Beagle* was paid off, he rented a small house in Fitzwilliam Street from 16 December 1836. Without fully realising it, he hoped to recapture the steady existence developed on board ship. He knew already he was happiest when left alone with his work.

Work, in fact, became Darwin's chief excuse for avoiding unsettling emotional exposure—a way of sidestepping the possibility of Dr. Darwin's veiled inquiries, of evading his sisters' wish to have him at home, and a useful ploy for missing dull Shrewsbury parties. It was also useful for avoiding his new scientific contemporaries before he was ready to see them and perhaps making a fool of himself. He discovered it was much easier to emphasise the pressure of his scholarly business: so much easier he soon believed it himself. His time was grievously destroyed by visits, he grumbled to a bewildered Fox from Cambridge. Instead of seeing his old friends, Darwin said, his weeks were going to be dedicated to hard scientific work: "I hope to extract a good many solid hours out of each day." Even interesting surprises like FitzRoy's sudden engagement drew only a work-related groan. Darwin flatly refused to satisfy Caroline's curiosity about the details, which included an intriguing rumour of an unnamed child and FitzRoy's withdrawing its promised inheritance. "It is a most inconvenient time to marry," Darwin impatiently snorted.

In actuality, there was plenty of work to do. The small house in Cambridge became Darwin's temporary centre for a storm of industry. He fired off letters to specialists in London, sent specimens to and fro, spread his papers out in careful piles over the floor, and frequently went out to see Henslow, or Sedgwick, or any one of his university acquaintances who might be able to help him. "Caroline rather puzzled me," wrote his elderly Aunt Sarah in a letter to him in December, "by saying that you have taken a lecture room at Cambridge, but I suppose you mean to employ it not exactly in its own line."[3]

Some of these negotiations were unexpectedly complex. Distributing his specimens was much harder than Darwin anticipated and naturally took precedence over anything else. Sitting at his desk in Cambridge, with Covington deftly copying manuscripts at his side, Darwin often wondered whom to approach next, which expert with enough time and knowledge would do proper justice to his collections. In letter after letter he tactfully probed the contemporary natural history scene, attempting to ascertain the names of the people best suited to his purposes. "I find, as you told me," he complained to Henslow, "that they are all overwhelmed with their own business." He began to think he would have to do the identifications himself. In between, he worked hard on a short geological paper to read before a scientific audience at the Geological Society of London on 4 January 1837, giving "Proofs of recent elevation on the coast of Chili." During this first appearance as a Lyellian thinker, his new friend Lyell looked on approvingly from the presidential chair.

Just as important as the specimens in the long run was the effort Darwin put into writing up his *Beagle* diary for FitzRoy—his proposed volume of natural history remarks which was going to accompany the captain's official narrative of the *Beagle*'s two voyages. FitzRoy had already begun writing his part, not letting marriage or a honeymoon interfere with his schedule, and Darwin started worrying that his own slowness might delay the publication—unnecessarily, as it turned out, since FitzRoy's early start quickly tailed off and Darwin's portion went to the printers long before the captain reached an end. In Cambridge, however, Darwin nervously waited for comments on his diary from relatives and began soliciting information about his specimens to add to the text. He intended rewriting everything from his *Beagle* diary in a better literary style, compressing some parts and expanding others, turning his day-by-day account of the voyage into a consecutive story interlaced with such scientific details as he could glean before publication. Not surprisingly, Darwin's intellectual horizons were governed by this work for the next nine months or more. It created the frame into which all his other thoughts and problems had to be slotted.

Writing such a book, moreover, was vital for his own peace of mind. Looking back over the voyage as an author gave him a wonderful chance to make sense of what he had seen, of finding unifying themes and achievements in the plethora of diverse and scattered observations. Darwin badly needed to decide what he had done with his life for those five years. The voyage had showed him more things than he had ever contemplated at Cambridge, and in ways impossible to conceive beforehand. He knew now that the external world was not the soft green object familiar to English eyes. Strong light and dramatic scenery told an altogether harsher tale, and internal pictures of volcanoes, earthquakes, and human beings dancing on the edge of savagery were unforgettable reminders that the earth generally eschewed gentleness. He had learned how to think and be independent. He knew about hardship, about empire, about cultural diversity and unity, about scientific persistence: a breadth of experience few contemporaries of the same age could match. He had already done more than many men achieved in a lifespan. But he felt a tension there too, tension between feeling like a stranger in Britain, like a mismatched newcomer whose recent life was full of adventures no one else could share, and his desire to be an acknowledged insider. He wanted to leap into everything opening up before him, to become a scientific star. The imaginative structure was in position. Yet it was going to take everything he could muster to put his notes and theories into some kind of order.

Without an overview he might lose sight of himself. Without an account of his journey that explained it to himself there was no prospective expert to speak of. Darwin needed to write himself out of being a mere collector and traveller—the rat-catcher of his father's gloomy predictions. His book about his travels was the construction of his future.

And he composed it in a white heat of enthusiasm from January to September 1837, sending the text soon afterwards to FitzRoy's printers. After more than a year's delay (to let FitzRoy catch up) it was published in the middle of 1839 as the third volume of FitzRoy's *Narrative* of the expedition under the title *Journal and Remarks, 1832–1836.* A few months later, Darwin's volume was reissued separately by the publishers with a different title, one which it carried for the rest of Darwin's life: *Journal of Researches into the Geology and Natural History of the Various Countries Visited by H.M.S. Beagle.*[4] This retrospective recreation of the voyage gave Darwin the larger view essential for making new kinds of sense out of his journey.

II

The first scientific topic Darwin grappled with in Cambridge was the one generating most interest among London naturalists: what would the experts make of his fossil bones? Unpacking the final consignment in Henslow's storeroom, he felt renewed paternal pride in his South American giants. They were even more exciting in England than when he and Covington had dug them out of the mud. Ever since his earliest finds had been announced by William Buckland at a meeting of the British Association in 1833, his entrance into the scientific community had been carried along on their bony surprises.

Darwin met Richard Owen, the man who would describe the fossils, at the end of October 1836 at an "early tea party" hosted by Charles and Mary Lyell. Lyell, who had met Darwin himself only a day or two beforehand, wanted to make a close friend out of him straight away, welcoming the idea of him as a colleague in geological arms. Even though Lyell's *Principles of Geology* was selling steadily and Lyell was working on a fifth edition as well as thinking of preparing a shortened version for publication in 1838, some of his ideas about uniformitarianism were taking a battering. Being president of the Geological Society of London for the year was no guarantee of immunity. Darwin was the first naturalist to use Lyell's "principles" effectively: his first, and in many ways his only fully committed, disciple. "The idea of the Pampas going up at the rate of an inch in a century, while the Western coast and Andes rise many feet and unequally, has long been a dream of mine," Lyell excitedly scrawled to him in October. "What a field you have to write on! If you cannot get here for dinner, you must if possible join the evening party."[5]

Lyell, said Darwin gratefully, "entered in the *most* good natured manner, and almost without being asked, into all my plans." Through him, he met all Lyell's favoured scientific friends, including William Lonsdale, the secretary of the Geological Society, and Leonard Horner, the Edinburgh politician who was Lyell's father-in-law and by then a well-known educational reformer and man of science in London. Darwin liked renewing his acquaintance with Horner on a relatively equal footing. It was even more enjoyable to be escorted around town by a prominent geological writer and president of a national society. Shall we dine at my club? asked Lyell. He was ready to discharge high-powered scientific gossip and flattering advice in the same breath. Darwin thought that if he was not already so much more inclined towards geology than the other branches of natural history, "I am sure Mr Lyell's and Lonsdale's kindness ought to fix me." No one else seemed nearly so friendly or so interested in his work. "You cannot conceive anything more thoroughly goodnatured."[6]

Owen, younger than Lyell and only five years older than Darwin, was one of the rising stars of British zoology, with ambitions and talents to match. He was at that time an assistant and son-in-law to William Clift at the anatomical museum of the Royal College of Surgeons in London, and was just starting to enjoy his new status as the college's recently appointed Hunterian professor. Tasting this kind of scientific success early in life, he was quick to catch at opportunities for more. Owen ultimately became England's greatest anatomist—the country's answer to Cuvier, trumpeted the scientific journals of the day—and the first director of the Natural History Museum, opened in South Kensington in 1882. He was very keen to examine any unusual fossils and smaller anatomical preparations in spirits that Darwin might like to pass on. Clift, he confided that evening, was unable to recognise any of the bones unpacked so far. When Darwin then heard from him how moribund the natural history departments of the British Museum were, and how Owen would smooth matters with gifts of casts and models, he gladly deposited them with this promising new acquaintance instead. Despite bitter differences later on, each was willing to capitalise on the other's burgeoning professional career. At the same time, and probably with Owen's advice, Darwin decided to give his mammal and bird collections to the Zoological Society of London. It was just as well, he thought with relief, that he had the right to dispose of his material as he wished. Otherwise, Owen warned him, it might well languish unused in the British Museum for years. Darwin had not spent five years away from home just to see his collections disappear into the Bloomsbury cellars.

By mid-December, Owen arrived at several significant conclusions. The *Megatherium* bones provided useful information previously unavailable because of the lack of specimens in Europe: Darwin's trophies added greatly to what was already known from Woodbine Parish's work, published in 1832.[7] The other bones belonged to animals more or less unknown to science.

Owen quickly discarded Darwin's opinion that the bony plates were part of a *Megatherium*'s armour and reattributed them to a new beast he named *Scelidotherium*—a large extinct armadillo. He pieced together fragments of another animal he called *Toxodon*.

When Owen received the second shipment from the *Beagle,* he was able to increase the list with a large extinct guanaco (*Macrauchenia*) and a big sloth (*Glyptodon*). More bones from the *Toxodon* turned up in the bottom of the crate, helping him identify that species as an enormous version of a South American capybara. He also set to rest Darwin's doubts about the horse tooth. Since horses were not native to South America, Darwin had hesitated to think they could be found fossilised in the same area. But they were, said Owen: "a most curious fact."

Thus clothed in proper Latin names, the size and variety of his animals impressed Darwin all over again. After seeing Owen in London at the end of the year, he told Caroline: "One animal, of which I have nearly all the bones is very closely allied to the Ant Eaters, but of the extraordinary size of a small horse. There is another head, as large as a Rhinoceros which as far as they can guess, must have been a gnawing animal. Conceive of a Rat or Hare of such a size—What famous Cats they ought to have had in those days!"[8]

Owen's identifications endorsed the idea of an affinity between the extinct species and their modern counterparts: something both Owen and Darwin described as a "law of nature" in which the fossil remains matched the animal groups currently living in the same area. Where there were live armadillos, there were likely to be fossil ones as well. This was not always the case, as excavations in Britain and France showed and as Darwin's fossil horse indicated. A spectacular cache of extinct rhinoceroses, elephants, and sabre-toothed tigers unearthed by workmen laying out Trafalgar Square just before Victoria came to the throne suggested a very different prehistory for the Thames basin; and jokes about the London "pea-soupers" killing off these animals made the point effectively. In South America, however, there appeared to be what Owen called a "persistence of type": an interesting consistency between past and present begging to be explained. For identifying this correlation and eventually describing Darwin's fossils in full, Owen received the Wollaston Medal of the Geological Society in 1838, the premier award of the society.[9] His first foray into fossil mammals proved entirely successful.

Although Owen changed his mind about one of Darwin's specimens in the space of a couple of months and told Darwin that the extinct guanaco was actually much more like a camel than a llama, the information did not interfere with Darwin's sudden interest in the fossils' relationship to modern species. Symmetry between old and new was already important to him, a reflection of Lyell's insistence on continuity over long periods of time. Such a chronological link nevertheless intensified some of the problems he faced with Lyell's interpretation of the fossil record. The point weaved through the chapters he was writing for his *Journal.* In private, he wondered why the giants were replaced by new animals built upon the same general plan.

Owen was not involved with this side of Darwin's researches, but he did touch on the larger problems of interpretation in letters describing the fossils, and early in January, Darwin came to London to get his advice at first hand—he wanted advice about the difficult *Macrauchenia,* for instance, previously a guanaco, then a camel, which now seemed to Owen intermediate between living tapirs and llamas, obliging him to rethink his understanding of pachyderms in general.[10] Drawn together by the bones, the two men became friends, and Darwin travelled to London from Cambridge several times more to sit with Owen in the evenings. The anatomist had many other similarly intriguing problems to talk about emerging from the anatomical lectures he gave at the College of Surgeons or from the rare animals he dissected for the Zoological Society's edification.[11] Sometimes their discussions took place standing over a carcass, since Owen's lodgings were above the College of Surgeons and were also his laboratory: the room at the end of the passage was often occupied by a half-flayed rhinoceros or dead orangutan formerly at the zoo. Otherwise, said Mrs. Owen patiently, when Darwin came to call it was "tea, muscular fibre and microscope in the drawing room."[12]

Lyell was just as keen to hear Owen's conclusions about the bones and mentioned them in his outgoing presidential address at the Geological Society in February 1837. He believed continuities like these between the ancient and modern world were useful grist to his uniformitarian mill. Gleefully, he invited Darwin up to town to hear him speak about "you & your new Llama, Armadillos, gigantic rodents, & other glorious additions to the Menagerie of that new continent."[13] Lyell also intended seizing the chance of stressing the significance of Darwin's January paper on elevation— another uniformitarian significance not lost on any of his audience. Darwin's work, Lyell announced, confirmed his own opinion that land levels could be greatly altered in modern periods.

Of course, Darwin came to London. Though elected a fellow only in the previous November, he had already agreed to join the council of the Geological Society, at Lyell's insistence, and this was the day of the annual election, followed by the president's speech. What was more, Darwin brought guests. With Erasmus and Hensleigh on either side, he was hopelessly impressed by Lyell's address. There was little enough about his *Beagle* work, he reported to Caroline, but he forwarded the printed text anyway. He felt honoured, in a naïvely youthful way, to be associated with Lyell and to have become part of this prestigious company of scientists. Lyell's theme of geological continuity was deeply attractive to him, intimately tied up as it was with an acknowledgement of the value of his own work. Afterwards, he wondered if his fossils showed some kind of real ancestry. "Tempted to believe," he wrote in a pocket notebook, "animals created for a definite time—not extinguished by change of circumstances."[14] Pages of close analysis in his longer manuscript followed.[15]

Stuck at home in Shrewsbury, the Darwin sisters shared in his triumph by post. They were beginning to realise that their brother aimed at becoming a gentleman-naturalist working on a par with university professors and famous experts. The idea was quietly pleasing. With nothing much else to do, they started reading up appropriate textbooks. "Can you (if a few words will do) tell me on what points it is that Lyell fully agrees with your views," asked Caroline indulgently. She knew biblical chronology was discarded by most geologists or that they "thought we did not understand rightly." These loyal Shrewsbury women were subsequently delighted to find an account of Darwin's zoological collections in the *Morning Herald* with the information that a new species of cat was named after him: *Felis darwinii*. Dr. Darwin thought this acknowledgement only right and proper. "Papa wants to know what gratitude the Zoological have shewn you: they ought at least to make you an honorary member."[16]

They liked to hear about Cambridge too. Darwin was not nearly as isolated as he had at first intended; he went out several times to colleges to dine with the fellows, and to Henslow's house on many occasions. At George Peacock's table he met "a dozen young lordlings" who were not half as bad as he expected. Sedgwick persuaded him to speak at a meeting of the university's Philosophical Society. Herbert came to celebrate New Year's Eve with him at St. John's. A prodigious snowball fight occurred. He lost a bet (a bottle of claret) by wrongly guessing the height of the senior common room ceiling in Christ's. And he amused Romilly with his talk of rationalising resources in Tierra del Fuego. "I met Mr Darwin," Romilly said; "he declares that in 'terra del fuego' whenever a scarcity occurs (which is every 5 or 6 years) they kill the old women as the *most useless* living creatures: in consequence when a famine begins the old women run away into the woods and many of them perish miserably there."[17] But Darwin felt melancholy walking through the courts of his old college—it was not half so merry a place as before, he told Fox.

His work, however, went well—a wonderful, tumbling rush of ideas fighting for expression. His book by now was revealing a single theme: the power of continuity as an explanation for diversity. Geology, as he and Lyell understood it, showed continuity. The story of the Fuegians metamorphosing into Europeans and back again showed it. The geographical distribution of the animals and plants encountered as he travelled westwards and southwards across the globe seemed to show it. The fossils showed it. So too did his preliminary paper on coral reefs sketched out in Cambridge at that time and discussed in detail during another helpful visit to Lyell. The past and present appeared to him to be welded together just as much as the living parts at the top of a reef were connected to their dead relatives at the bottom. Everything had roots that attached it to the past. Everything was connected, gradual.

Lyell caught more than a glimpse of Darwin's excited tumult. No other geologist of his acquaintance was so readily fertile in ideas, so keen to use the same wide-ranging theories as himself. "I could think of nothing for days after your lesson on coral reefs," he wrote enthusiastically after talking to Darwin in February. "It is all true, but do not flatter yourself that you will be believed, till you are growing bald, like me, with hard work & vexation at the incredulity of the world. . . . Your lines of elevation & subsidence will deservedly get you as great a name as De Beaumont's parallel elevations, & yours are true, which is more than can be said of his."[18] Lyell wrote more soberly to John Herschel expressing a genuine pang at being obliged to give up his own theory of reefs perching on the rim of submerged volcanic craters.[19] Darwin's theory was better, altogether more elegant and inspiring. In Darwin, he joyfully recognised, he encountered an equal.

Lyell's zest was infectious. By March 1837, Darwin's need for privacy had evaporated, and he moved to London, taking rented rooms in a house in Great Marlborough Street just down the road from Erasmus and large enough to hold Covington and the remaining boxes of *Beagle* specimens. There he was within walking distance of all the scientific institutions that interested him, including Lyell's house in Bloomsbury. This time he was ready to participate: ready to take an active role in Geological Society meetings and on the council; wining and dining with Lyell; collecting information about his collections; going out with Erasmus; and writing scientific papers about his *Beagle* researches whenever appropriate. Lyell welcomed his company willingly. "It is rare, even in one's own pursuits to meet with congenial souls," he said warmly, "& Darwin is a glorious addition to my society of geologists & is working hard & making way both in his book & in our discussions." He was a man after Lyell's iconoclastic heart. "I really never saw that bore Dr Mitchell so successfully silenced or such a bucket of cold water so dexterously poured down his back as when Darwin answered some impertinent & irrelevant questions about S. America."[20]

III

Such persistent and friendly approaches were irresistible. Already well advanced in his admiration for Lyell, Darwin threw himself into a closer friendship with happy abandon. "I saw more of Lyell than of any other man both before and after my marriage. . . . His mind was characterised, as it appeared to me, by clearness, caution, sound judgement and a good deal of originality."

> His delight in science was ardent, and he felt the keenest interest in the future progress of mankind. He was very kind-hearted, and thoroughly liberal in his religious beliefs or rather disbeliefs; but he was a strong theist. His candour was highly remarkable.[21]

He had a strong sense of humour too and often told amusing anecdotes. Sometimes he amused Darwin without knowing it: carried away by a train of thought, he would lay his head on the seat of a chair while still standing up, all the time descanting on coral reefs or volcanoes.

Lyell's only foible, Darwin ruefully recognised, was his fondness for high society, especially for eminent men, even better if they were titled. He used to discuss with his wife as a most serious question whether or not they should accept some particular invitation, and their own London parties were notable for bringing together many of the people who shone in early Victorian affairs. Darwin was not averse to this opportunity for social climbing. Through Lyell he met many men of the day: Roderick Murchison, the geological "king of Siluria," who got him to answer questions about Shropshire rocks the next time he went home; Robert Brown, the famous botanist, who encouraged him to call every Sunday morning; the astronomer John Herschel (for a second time) when he returned from the Cape of Good Hope in 1838; Herbert Spencer, whom Darwin found pompous though gifted; and Lord Stanhope, the historian, and his eccentric father, who said to him, "Why don't you give up your fiddle-faddle of geology and zoology, and turn to the occult sciences?" Lyell insisted Darwin should join the Athenaeum, the exclusive London club providing private dining rooms, a library, snuff, and select conversation in the heart of the West End, and Darwin was elected a year later, in 1838, along with Charles Dickens and a number of other "distinguished men" under a special ruling adding forty new members in a block.[22] Soon, an open invitation to attend Charles Babbage's glittering soirées dropped on his doorstep: there, he told Caroline, he would meet the best in the way of literary people "and a good mixture of pretty women."[23]

Moving to London made all the difference. Darwin's social life blossomed as he became known as one of the bright young men on the scientific circuit, a traveller returned. He easily reestablished his previous relationships with people like William Yarrell, the bookseller-cum-zoologist, and Francis Beaufort of the Admiralty, and generated new friendships inside the Zoological Society and Geological Society. He became special friends with the two talented museum taxonomists Owen and George Robert Waterhouse.

Living in London brought him closer to Erasmus as well. Erasmus took charge of his free hours and introduced him to his clever acquaintances, including Harriet Martineau, then at the height of her fame as a political author. Erasmus also knew Fanny Kemble, the actress (Mrs. Butler), and Thomas and Jane Carlyle, intellectual lions all: "*he* writes all the articles on German literature in the Foreign Quarterly and *she* is a little woman with a profusion of hair, one of Erasmus' married loves." In particular, Darwin found his cousin Hensleigh Wedgwood and his wife, Fanny, very agreeable company. Like Erasmus, he joined their extended family circle with pleasure, relishing the comforts of a cousinly intimacy and the couple's wide-ranging, highly cultured activities. Hensleigh was one of the serious-minded Wedgwoods, with a retiring nature, a powerful mind, and steadfast moral values: an intellectual version of his father, who was at the same time Darwin's Uncle Jos. His wife, Fanny, just as alert, channelled her abilities into literary society, gathering a devoted group of authors and reviewers, including Sydney Smith, Elizabeth Gaskell, Harriet Martineau, the Erskines, and Mrs. Reid, founder of Bedford Ladies College, around her. After he had known Fanny for a couple of months, Darwin's London circle expanded sufficiently for him to call on the lady novelist Anne Marsh, a distant relative on the Wedgwood side, and make firmer acquaintance with Dr. Henry Holland, a second cousin and close friend of the Hensleighs, a regular traveller and writer for the *Edinburgh Review*. Holland was a fashionable physician, one of several appointed to watch over Queen Victoria. Holland's pompous words of advice about Darwin's writing style in his *Beagle* diary were probably well meant. With the advantage of a closer look at the literary doctor, Darwin chose to ignore them.

Erasmus himself, that "dear good old brother," lived a life of fussy tranquility in Great Marlborough Street. "Going to Shrewsbury he considers a dreadful journey only to be undertaken once a year and, as far as anything further, as altogether impossible." He was idle, said Carlyle with his customary bluntness. Still, Carlyle thought he had something "original and sarcastically ingenious in him, one of the sincerest, naturally truest, and most modest of men." Erasmus's intellect was better than his brother Charles's, he also said. Jane Carlyle liked him from the start, and his terse, sardonic utterances were a great amusement to her. They appreciated each other's eccentricities. "Take me to Oxygen Street," she demanded, and without hesitation he drove her in his horse and cab to Oxenden Street.[24]

Yet Erasmus looked as if he might almost be thinking of getting married, or, as the family half-heartedly joked, Harriet Martineau was thinking of marrying him. She was a formidable prospect, with her ear-trumpet and strong opinions. "Our only protection from so admirable a sister-in-law," Darwin cackled unsympathetically, "is in her working him too hard. He begins to perceive, (to use his own expression) he shall not be much better than her 'nigger.' Imagine poor Erasmus a nigger to so philosophical & energetic a lady.—How pale & woe begone he will look.—She already takes him to task about his idleness."[25]

Actually Darwin quite liked Harriet Martineau, considering her agreeably interesting when he visited. She "managed to talk on a most wonderful number of subjects, considering the limited time. I was astonished to find how little ugly she is, but as it appears to me, she is overwhelmed with her own projects, her own thoughts and own abilities." She did not, in other words, fit into his idea of a winsome bride. But he enjoyed her company at Erasmus's dinner parties and found it relatively painless when she visited his lodgings to "look at me as author in my den"; she was not a complete Amazonian, he discovered, and she certainly recognised the same feeling of exhaustion that he had himself after thinking too much. Erasmus maintained, not altogether jocularly, that one ought not to look at her as a woman.[26]

Dr. Darwin of Shrewsbury, however, was irritated beyond measure at the thought of his oldest son's bringing this intellectual and politically utilitarian woman into the family. Rustling his copies of the *Westminster Review* crossly, he could barely be persuaded that the articles he objected to were usually by another author. Moreover, he got it into his head that Charles was an alternative candidate if Erasmus's courage failed. Boldly, the women at The Mount and Maer Hall teased him about his obvious prejudices.

But in Erasmus's eyes, marriage was essentially an enterprise for other people. Possibly he feared disappointment. Perhaps he was too lazy to be a husband. Nothing ever came of his relationship with Harriet Martineau, although they remained close friends for the rest of their lives. Erasmus arranged a private subscription to provide her with an income when she became ill and went to recuperate in Tynemouth and then the Lake District, and sent oysters and books from London whenever he could. He was the only one who dared confront her about her belief in mesmerism, and was always her "dear friend."[27] Their letters were later mutually destroyed.

And Darwin's attentions were already directed elsewhere. Leonard Horner had five unmarried daughters on his hands and was most conscientious in his invitations. Charles Lyell had married Mary Horner, the eldest daughter, in the summer of 1832. They usually spent their holidays travelling on the continent, making good use of Mary's linguistic skills and wide circle of German and Swiss acquaintances dating from the time the Horner family had lived in Bonn. What could be more appropriate, Horner hinted, than Lyell's newest and most promising geological friend choosing another one of his eligible girls?

Mrs. Horner made no secret of it. Her daughters were an exceptionally well educated, clear-headed brood, all of whom legitimately expected to marry members of the intelligentsia as Mary had. Frances's botanical knowledge was good enough to induce Robert Brown to accompany her on botanising expeditions over the Rottenberg Mountains, and she had an immense collection of specimens. Susan was an accomplished water-colourist and linguist. Katherine collected ferns and shells. The two youngest were avid conchologists. Individually, they brought a vigorous intellect to bear on cultural issues, manifested a decade or two later by a flurry of literary translations. In 1854, Susan published an anonymous memoir of Lajos Kossuth, the Hungarian president ousted from power a few years before and at that time living in heroic exile in England; afterwards she took on Colletta's *History of the Kingdom of Naples* (1858) and *Guiseppe Giusti and His Times* (1864), and she produced her own accounts of tours in Naples, Sicily, and Florence and a study of Greek vases. Frances translated Cesare Balbo's life of Dante in 1852 and went on to arrange the life and letters of her eventual husband, Charles James Fox Bunbury, while Katherine did the same for her brother-in-law Charles Lyell. Joanna and Leonora (only fifteen and sixteen when Darwin first met them) translated Oersted's *Soul in Nature* for publication in 1852 and Lepsius's *Letters from Egypt and Ethiopia* in 1853. Charles Koch's journal of a tour in the Crimea followed in 1855.

No wonder Horner wrote to tell his daughter Mary Lyell that the family had seen Darwin in London several times during the summer of 1837, but "not so often as we could have wished." Horner was "much pleased with him," Mary read: "I have not seen anyone for a long time with a greater store of accurate knowledge."[28] Pretty soon Erasmus started calling Mrs. Horner "Mother-in-law" when he talked to Charles, a sardonic twisting of Lyell's existing relationship with her into a potential one for his brother.

Frances, Susan, and Katherine—the three oldest—courted Darwin as well as they could. Science and natural history was an obvious way in. On one occasion Darwin sent them a botany book. *"The Botanists,"* they hopefully chorused in return, "present their best thanks to Mr Darwin for his kindness in advancing them in their pursuit by sending them a book with such interesting plates and which they intend to study with great attention. *The learned Linguists* feel also grateful for Mr Darwin's generous assistance—Ki te kahore hoki he mahi."

Having hardly expected to be addressed in Maori even by such an erudite group of Englishwomen, Darwin was intrigued. Once translated ("if you have nothing else to do"), the invitation to call more often was readily apparent. Call he did—all through 1837 he assiduously visited the Horners' house in Bedford Place. He was made so welcome that he could choose the time himself. "Allow me to say Monday," he asked Mrs. Horner. "If I do not hear to the contrary I will do myself the pleasure of coming that day.—You do not know how many solemn vows you make me break, by offering such pleasant temptations. But after Monday I verily vow, work I will, morning and evening."[29]

His assiduity was noticed by more than Mrs. Horner. Leonard Horner, whom Darwin met regularly at the Geological Society, was an eager marriage broker; and Charles and Mary Lyell pushed forward one or another of the sisters at their parties. Katherine seemed to be the favourite. Fanny Wedgwood similarly thought something was in the air, relaying gossip home to the womenfolk at Maer and Shrewsbury, along with a word or two about the state of Erasmus's heart. "I shall be very curious," replied Emma Wedgwood, "to know whether Susan and Catherine [Darwin] really like Miss Martineau." They seem to take very kindly, she said, to the idea of "their other sister." Which one of the Horner girls Emma referred to was left unsaid. It was clear that the Darwin-Wedgwood clan thought at least one engagement was brewing.

Never one to beat about the bush, Aunt Sarah Wedgwood sent Darwin a sum of money as an early wedding gift.[30]

IV

Even so, Darwin's *Beagle* specimens and his book were the main objects of his attention. Living in London, he hoped to find out how his bird and mammal collections fared. These he gave to the Zoological Society in January, although not before complaining about the lack of interest showed by individual zoologists. "I find the geologists all willing to render all assistance & exceedingly kind,—but the Zoologists seem to think a number of undescribed creatures rather a nuisance."[31] Worse, the fellows of the Zoological Society demonstrated a "mean quarelsome spirit," snarling at each other in meetings "quite unlike gentlemen." Should the society devote itself to running the zoological gardens in Regent's Park and breeding useful domestic animals, as traditionalist members insisted, or push to the forefront of scientific zoology?[32]

Nevertheless, giving the specimens away was better than classifying them himself, and Darwin soon appreciated that zoological fights created a stimulating atmosphere. After making his donation and attending a few meetings in the society's rooms in Bruton Street (he had been elected a corresponding member just before the *Beagle* left Britain in 1831, and would become a full fellow in 1839), he was able to co-opt the best of the zoological professionals. John Gould agreed to examine his birds. Darwin also asked Thomas Bell to identify the reptiles and George Waterhouse the insects and some of the mammals. William Martin, the superintendent of the Zoological Society's museum in Leicester Square, agreed to do the rest.

Darwin's contact with Gould was especially important. He was another rising museum expert like Owen: talented and becoming widely respected, actively making his name by classifying for the empire, yet not too grand to grasp the chance of identifying possible rarities. He was one of the few paid taxonomists in the country, working far harder and quicker than any comparable authority based in the British Museum.

Gould classified and exhibited the majority of Darwin's birds at Zoological Society meetings during January and February 1837, so Darwin did not have much of an opportunity to speak to him about them until after he moved to London early in March. He was already perplexed by Gould's announcement that the Galápagos finches constituted an entirely new group strictly confined to the Galápagos Islands.[33] Each bird represented a different species. All were unknown to zoological science.

When they met in March, Gould reiterated this opinion and told him how the various species also seemed mutually exclusive of each other from island to island. Gould could not be sure, because the finch specimens were inadequately labelled. The three species of mocking thrush certainly lived on separate islands.

Surprised, Darwin mulled this information over. If each island had its own birds, as Gould suggested, and the archipelago as a whole had its own roster of genera, his shipboard speculations about the instability of species were more accurate than he had thought. He originally thought they were varieties, but Gould now said they were not. Perhaps they could be either, depending on how he looked at it. Perhaps the birds had diversified into a range of forms through geographical isolation, each on a separate islet. Perhaps there was no logical difference between geographical variants and species. Was this suggestive of varieties turning themselves into species, or "non-creation," as he clumsily called it?

Either way, Darwin's evidence was uncertain. Because of his own carelessness about labels, one of the most interesting problems of the voyage was left hanging in midair. Darwin could not retrace his steps literally—the journey was an unrepeatable journey of a lifetime. Nor could Gould help any further on the anatomical side.

The only way forward was for Darwin to ask FitzRoy, and then, increasingly desperately, to approach Fuller, FitzRoy's shipboard servant, to give Gould access to their independent bird collections deposited in the British Museum.

But Darwin had barely seen FitzRoy during the months after disembarking except for taking tea one day to meet Mrs. FitzRoy. Neither of them really regretted it. Their connection was loosening fast: there was little in common now apart from a shared remembrance of the voyage and the future manuscript. And Darwin saw FitzRoy's faults much more clearly when he was not living with him. "The Captain is going on very well,—that is for a man, who has the most consummate skill in looking at everything & every body in a perverted manner." Lyell heard the same story. "I never cease wondering at his character, so full of good & generous traits but spoiled by such an unlucky temper.—Some part of his brain wants mending: nothing else will account for his manner of viewing things."[34]

FitzRoy nevertheless made the two sets of bird skins available to his old shipmate. First Gould, and then Darwin, pored over the captain's labels vainly trying to relate them to their own haphazard materials.[35]

Syms Covington also possessed four birds from the Galápagos, and these too were brought in to reconstruct the island localities. It was difficult work, nonetheless, dogged by errors, never completely certain. Darwin examined his master catalogue time and time again, and lists of names circulated from Gould to FitzRoy and back again to Darwin covered in question-marks. In the end, only two species of finches remained without any locality whatsoever: but the localities did not necessarily refer to his own specimens. The claims in Darwin's book manuscript represented a triumph of optimism over reliable information.

Quickly, the finches joined the fossils as extraordinary and intriguingly complex problems he yearned to solve. The more he puzzled, the more tortuous they became. Nor were the finches the end of it. A week later, on 14 March 1837, Darwin went to hear Gould talk at the Zoological Society about his South American "ostriches." The "Avestruz Petise," he learned, was not simply a geographical variety of the ordinary rhea as he thought. Gould found sufficient differences to consider it a separate species. The taxonomist called it *Rhea darwinii,* cheerfully disregarding the name given by Alcide d'Orbigny, who also searched for it in Patagonia— Gould's blatant nationalism always favouring the first Englishman to find something. Afterwards, the blushing discoverer stood up to read some notes about the rheas' eggs. The distribution of the two species, he said, showed that the *Petise* took the place of the common rhea in southern Patagonia.[36]

This moment more than any other in Darwin's life deserves to be called a turning point. Poised to insert the relevant information into his *Journal,* Darwin was tantalized by the week's results. Why should two closely similar rheas agree to split the country between them? Why should different finches inhabit identical islets? The Galápagos iguanas, he was further told by Thomas Bell, similarly divided themselves among the islands, and the heavily built tortoises with their individualised shells again came to mind. In a Lyellian world where living beings were tied to the geological conditions, or in a Paleyian world where animals and plants were perfectly adapted to their surroundings, things like this did not happen.

Suddenly, he caught at a parallel between what the rheas and finches expressed about the modern world and what his fossils were telling him. Where the birds were linked by being spread over a cluster of neighbouring islands, the extinct South American mammals seemed to be connected to modern species in a chronological sense. The geographical relationships mirrored other relationships through time. "The same kind of relation that common ostrich bears to Petisse," he wrote in a small private notebook, "extinct guanaco to recent: in former case position, in latter time." Lyell's general principles linking past with present could be applied to the biological world as much as to the geological.

Moreover, the physical resemblances between the animals made it hard to ignore the possibility of common ancestry. Everything he had laboured over during the weeks in Cambridge, the puzzles of the last few metropolitan days, all the effort to create some kind of shape out of his experiences, the confidence Lyell created in him, and the intellectually swashbuckling years on the *Beagle* itself, came together in the daring concept of transmutation. He abandoned himself to the idea of the jungle. Everything, mankind included, was part of one ancestral chain.

V

But Darwin had little to show for it at first. His earliest evolutionary thoughts were diffuse, undisciplined, rampant; and they primarily circled around the problem of how transmutation might actually work. Since the idea first sprang to mind as a solution to very specific natural history problems, he did not sweep off straight away into metaphysical questions about mankind and religion. These came soon enough. Right from the start he felt strangely comfortable with the thought of being an animal—the *Beagle* years had shown him, as nothing else could have done, how close to animality he really was. Instead, where other men pledged themselves to the idea of transmutation because of their philosophical commitment to progress in cultural spheres, Darwin mostly arrived at it through the organisms themselves. His intense curiosity about the manner in which things functioned—mechanical gadgets as much as living animals and plants—dominated. Did transmutation happen by jumps, one species suddenly changing into another? Or did a species split into two when geology and geography created unaccustomed barriers in the middle of a region? In the most literal of ways, Darwin wanted to know how the process might operate. How did an ape change into a man or two ostriches diverge from each other into separate species? If, after all, transmutation did not look likely at that mechanical level, he knew a thousand grander reasons for rejecting the entire notion.

Not much got written down. Nothing was said to friends. The atheistic tilt of even practical inquiries of this kind was perfectly obvious, as obvious to Darwin as it was to others. Moreover, he was not sure he was right, or on the correct track even if he was right. The last thing he wanted at that delicate professional moment was to be a laughing-stock or vilified for dangerous opinions. He knew it was not particularly unusual to think evolution could have occurred—contemporaries like Robert Grant and his own grandfather Erasmus Darwin had plainly thought the same way, as did several respected French anatomists; and there were plenty of phrenological, progressivist radicals shouting for self-generated political and social change in the human realm, urging transformations in the natural world as support for their views. Yet most of the men of his own professional standing who might have considered evolution invariably dismissed it. He had reason to believe Richard Owen had gone into the arguments as thoroughly as anyone, and then rejected the idea.[37] Even Lyell, who believed in natural causes for natural events, and half-hinted in the *Principles* that new species might still be appearing in the modern era, criticised any kind of transformist ideas, saying the facts of nature made it an impossible doctrine. For Lyell, as for others, God always stood rampant between man and apes.

Darwin's special achievement lay most of all in holding on in the face of this general consensus. He was not scared off by the lack of evidence or the frightening philosophical issues involved. His independence of mind was clearly crucial here: courage and an air of defiance too. Still, he could see the rocks ahead. He scribbled only a few scattered remarks suggestive of the way his thoughts were running in a small red notebook half-filled with old *Beagle* notes. A strong sense of appropriate behaviour, as much as insight, dictated caution.[38]

When Darwin had filled this red notebook towards the end of June he bought some more and reorganised himself. By then he was more assertive about transmutation, ready to start some serious speculating. One book was labelled "A" for miscellaneous geology, another (resuscitated from Edinburgh days) called "Zoology." The next was "B," exclusively given over to notes on the transmutation of species. Each one was the same size as his *Beagle* notebooks, just right for slipping into a pocket for making notes in the field; and each one was labelled and categorised to make sure nothing was lost that might one day be valuable.[39]

In the "B" notebook Darwin wrote his first halting words about evolution—or transformism, as he tended to call it. During a week's holiday in Shrewsbury at the end of June, and with the family copy of his grandfather's *Zoonomia* close to hand, he felt sure sexual reproduction held the key to the way animals and plants change their form.[40] If all organisms merely replicated their kind by vegetative budding or splitting, he wrote, history would show a succession of identical individuals holding no potential for alterations of any kind. Sexual reproduction, by contrast, generated change. Alive with thoughts like these, Darwin felt closer than ever before to his grandfather's liberally progressive views. There were, he proposed, "two kinds of generation . . . the coeval kind [where] all individuals absolutely similar; for instance fruit trees, probably polypi, gemmiparous propagation, bisection of Planariae &c. &c. The ordinary kind which is a longer process, the new individual passing through several stages (typical or shortened repetition of what the original molecule has done?). . . . therefore generation [is] to adapt & alter the race to *changing* world."[41]

Unlike his grandfather, however, Darwin added geology to sex. The Galápagos problem convinced him islands were directly involved in the process of change. If volcanic islands appeared fresh out of the waves and were colonised by animals and plants which then diversified, each on their own island, he had an answer, he thought, for the Galápagos: a thought which sent him scuttling to Henslow to prod him into identifying the plant specimens. Since the birds were unreliable evidence, his plants might prove more helpful. "Will you just look over the list of questions, & try to answer me some of them," Darwin pleaded. He could not stop himself running to Lyell either. "Has your late work at shells startled you about the existence of species?" he inquired in July; "the passages of forms do appear frightful—everything is arbitrary." As far as the Galápagos birds were concerned, "no two naturalists agree on any fundamental idea that I can see."[42] In this way, geography and geology became an integral part of his ideas of transmutation. "Animals differ in different countries in exact proportion to the time they have been separated," he recorded in his notebook. "Countries longest separated, greatest differences."[43]

He backed up the words with a scratchy diagram: a tree of life, ancestors at the bottom, modern species at the top. "Heaven knows whether this agrees with Nature—*Cuidado.*"[44]

VI

From then on, transmutation became the central, undisclosed hub of Darwin's life. By the time he was finished, eight years further down the evolutionary road, he had filled five notebooks up to the letter "E," or possibly "F," since some pages still in existence appear to come from a volume subsequently torn apart and left coverless, each one crammed with schemes and data, plus two labelled "M" and "N" for what he called "Metaphysics on morals & speculations on expression," and additional books and papers with names like "Old & useless." He devoted a separate exercise book to listing "Questions & Experiments." The sequence constituted his private, pocket-sized filing system: a record of secret mental endeavour on the heroic scale. Wherever Darwin went, one of these books went too, ready for catching elusive thoughts, for making notes in libraries, or recording useful conversations after a good evening's talk. He surreptitiously worked on them during boring scientific meetings. Out they came in the carriage going home.

They were his life; and the whole of his life flooded into the imaginative worlds he successively created in them. Everything he ever thought about the voyage was reassessed, everything he learned and was learning about nature found its place, everything to do with his personal hopes and fears also: he began thinking about the opposition he would face, the arguments he would use, the tight corners he would find himself in; he plunged into metaphysical questions more or less ignored by him previously, and immersed himself in a new range of literature that seemed relevant in the light of his developing views. He was shocked and delighted by his own audacity, buoyed up by the immensity of what he was proposing. Lamarck, Plato, Hume, and God jostled for attention. "Man from monkeys?" he asked himself. Yes, of course, and men make angels.

Right from the beginning, Darwin's idea of evolution was strikingly personalised. Though it was not the same theory that he would eventually put into print later in the century, and was not much like the theories he developed over the space of the next few years, he possessed the pivotal idea of change in living beings—and of real ancestral links between animals and mankind. He pulled together a wealth of information, he overflowed with hypotheses, and he was fairly confident he was right. There was no need yet in his mind for an extra key—the key of natural selection—to lock it all together. What he had at the moment was gripping enough. All his personal ambitions, social background, and code of behaviour, and a wealth of half-hidden dislikes, desires, and shortcomings, coloured the rush of thought as much as any scientific reasoning. The scope of his intellectual experience was obvious, and the notebooks crackled with an astonishing variety of ideas and information, little of which would have occurred to the Cambridge undergraduate six or seven years before. The *Beagle* expedition naturally was the baseline for all his speculations. His recent London activities and work on his *Journal of Researches* were just as readily incorporated.

Darwin lost no time, however, in coming to grips with other kinds of information available in London and the country. Friends and relatives helped his inquiries into species transmutation much more than they usually realised, and he rarely discarded an opportunity to question people while going about his daily routine. Evolution as such was never mentioned. Darwin kept that side of his researches carefully veiled. Yet it was easy enough to ask any passing individual about animals or plants—topics that most servants, country gentlemen, and London residents knew something about, if only by hearsay. He asked Mark, Dr. Darwin's coachman, for his opinion on dogs, and Thomas Eyton for his views on owls and pigs. He made Fox struggle with a deluge of farmyard questions of all shapes and sizes. He struck up a correspondence with his Uncle Jos about Staffordshire worms. When Darwin then discovered that his London hairdresser was interested in pedigree hounds, Mr. Willis of Great Marlborough Street appeared, just like the others, in his notebooks as a source of information about dog breeding, no doubt also recording the cycle of Darwin's haircuts. Standing at a city shop counter, or waiting for a horse to be harnessed, he routinely engaged apparently inconsequential figures in detailed discussions about natural history, an eccentric and sociable habit continuing without fail till the end of his days.

It was more than a habit—Darwin elaborated this way of proceeding into one of the most distinctive aspects of his life's work. When seeking information on any new topic, he learned to go straight to the breeders and gardeners, the zookeepers, Highland ghillies, and pigeon fanciers of Victorian Britain, who possessed great practical expertise and, as Darwin fondly imagined, hardly any interest in pursuing larger theoretical explanations. Through them he thought he could get closer to the real facts of nature. He did not want their explanatory notions, and if any were offered they were ruthlessly discarded. Being a gentleman—being able to use his social position to draw out material from people rarely considered scientific authorities in their own right—was important. His notebooks began bulging with details methodically appropriated from a world of expertise normally kept separate from high science.

Furthermore, Darwin relentlessly exploited the huge surge in publishing activity during the period. He made full use of the wide range of topographical and colonial literature issued by government departments and entrepreneurial publishers alike. Most of these texts related official accounts of land and sea surveys similar to the *Beagle* voyage—French, English, German, Russian, and American expeditions with nationalistic and broadly scientific purpose. Others described voyages and residencies in the Middle East, Australia, or India. Darwin's theory ultimately rested on the prolific literature of the British empire as much as it did on his inward soul-searching. There were scores of new journals for him to read, stretching from the publications of the Royal Geographical Society to the papers of the Bath and West of England Agricultural Society and the Asiatic Society. There was the boom in high-brow literary quarterlies and fortnightlies to embrace, a whole spectrum of periodicals concerned with farming, gardening, colonial statistics, naval observations and reminiscences, and popular natural history, as well as weekly reviews like the *Athenaeum,* newspapers, and an ever-growing specialist literature in geology, zoology, and botany. Darwin rode the crest of a wave of early-nineteenth-century printed papers, and his species notebooks took much of their irrepressible momentum from the eager anticipation with which he strode towards the weekly offerings piled high on the Athenaeum Club's tables.

Something of Darwin's mettle also showed through in the way he set off on a lifetime's programme of reading in areas formerly holding only faint attractions. He tackled David Hume, Adam Smith, and John Locke in turn; Herbert Mayo's *Philosophy of Living* (1837), Sir Thomas Browne's *Religio Medici,* and John Abercrombie's *Inquiries Concerning the Intellectual Powers and the Investigation of Truth* (1838) came between Gibbon and Sir Walter Scott; and he reread significant works like Herschel's *Introduction to Natural Philosophy.* Erasmus lent Darwin other books and was always ready to discuss their knotty philosophical problems with him.

Darwin's London friends came equally into their own. With all the seriousness of early Victorian thinkers, they earnestly sought out the moral meanings in contemporary writings. Many of the men's conversation was transcendently interesting, Darwin said, though more like a series of definitions than talk. Lyell often debated politics and education with him, criticising the injustices of American slavery or the vagaries of the church in Britain, and expatiated on the endlessly fascinating subject of geology. Lyell was not a man to write hysterically about a creator, either, and Darwin eagerly assessed his private notions against what Lyell said about transmutation. Methodically, Darwin settled down to read the fifth edition of Lyell's *Principles* (published in the summer of 1837) very carefully indeed. He was sorry to find his friend repeating the adage that variation in species only goes so far before it stops. Varieties, declared Lyell, can change a great deal but never deviate far enough to be called separate species. "If this were true, adios theory," Darwin wrote in the margin of his copy.[45] Nevertheless, he welcomed Lyell's attack on Lamarck and on transmutation in general as by far the most philosophical critique he had come across. He knew he would have to answer every point before he could categorically believe in the truth of his theory.

Meetings with Harriet Martineau at Erasmus's house and at the Wedgwoods' probably encouraged him to look at her stories, perhaps the ones on political and economic themes that first brought her into the public eye. These fictionalised *Illustrations of Political Economy* were so popular that Martineau republished them in book form under the title *Miscellanies* in several editions from 1832. Erasmus had sent some of them out to him on the *Beagle*. At other times he relaxed over *Childe Harold, Manfred,* and *The Giaour,* and dipped into George Crabbe. He felt obliged to read Carlyle's writings, since Erasmus had become quite a crony of his and was always talking about him. Thomas Carlyle, Erasmus said disrespectfully, was very much like any other Scotchman "except that he wore a green hat the size of a small umbrella." His wife was a "divine little woman." So Darwin tried *The French Revolution* and *Sartor Resartus,* neither of which he really enjoyed. "About this time I took much delight in Wordsworth's and Coleridge's poetry," he recollected, "and I can boast that I read the *Excursion* twice through."[46]

VII

Launching into this intensive study bearing on transmutation would have been enough for most men. The work Darwin covered in just a few months after March 1837, the scope of his inquiries, the struggle between caution and excitement, between faith and incredulity—all these were impressive and exhausting. Writing a volume for FitzRoy was similarly demanding.

But Darwin also itched to get on with the rest of his *Beagle* projects, particularly the geology book he dreamed of on the island of St. Jago. Time for polishing his theory of coral reefs needed to be squeezed in, and time for describing the pampas fossils, each of which he spoke about in short papers delivered at meetings of the Geological Society in May 1837. He worked on a completely new—though not unrelated—paper on earthworms at the same time, giving him another chance to dwell on the power of little things to produce great effects. Soon, he hardly knew where to stop. "I cannot bear to leave my work even for half a day," he confessed to Henslow while refusing yet another invitation. "Good Lord deliver us of our friends," Susan read. "If I do not work hard for the next two or three years, I never shall have done."

Truly he could not stop. Already he was too far into the compulsively driven life of an intellectual to retreat, hooked on the excitement that came with grasping for and achieving the answer, the incisive power. Living in London, identifying his *Beagle* specimens, and working on transmutation were a heady mix. Boldly, he set into motion an additional, extensive publishing project that gobbled up his few remaining hours.

Darwin's idea was to produce a series of books giving all his zoological and geological results in sequence.

He had been mulling this suggestion over since early in 1837, when

William MacLeay, one of the leading fellows of the Zoological Society, pointed out the advantages of bringing together the *Beagle's* zoological results in a single large volume. It would be a shame, said MacLeay, to let his descriptions slip piecemeal into the scientific domain, especially in such an expansionist age when the Admiralty and Hydrographer's Office put so much effort into grandiose exploring voyages. To publish a big book or several big books dedicated to the achievements of an expedition like Darwin and FitzRoy's was a sure sign of British authority on the global scale, and, as both MacLeay and Darwin knew, many professional men petitioned the army or navy for this purpose, often obtaining government grants for illustrated publications. Most of the seminal nineteenth-century texts in British natural history were produced in this manner, ranging from Tuckey's *Narrative of an Expedition to Explore the River Zaire* (1818) to John Richardson's *Fauna Boreali-Americana* (1829–37), and Captain Beechey's *Zoology* of 1839.[47]

It would be very pleasant, Darwin thought, to see "the gleanings of my hands, after having passed through the brains of abler naturalists collected together in one work." He could act as general editor to a small team of specialist naturalists and perhaps write a contribution himself. Like John Richardson's *Fauna Boreali-Americana,* the work could have coloured illustrations and be issued in parts over a number of years. Like Richardson again, Darwin hoped to get financial aid from the Admiralty—at least enough to cover the cost of producing plates. "The whole scheme is at present merely floating in the air," he told Leonard Jenyns before asking if he would take on the fish. "I daresay the egg from the want of a little government hatching will be addled."[48]

But the Cambridge network—efficiently expanded by his own thriving contacts in London's scientific circles—ensured his success. Darwin swept off to the Royal Hospital at Haslar to get Richardson's advice in person and solicited references from the presidents of the three most relevant learned societies in London: MacLeay helped him get Lord Derby's zoological approval; William Whewell, the incoming president of the Geological Society, made no difficulties for his former Cambridge acquaintance; over at the Linnean, the Duke of Somerset was agreeable. By June, Darwin had three influential signatures at the bottom of a glowing testimonial.

He sent his testimonial with a covering letter to Beaufort of the Admiralty. Taking no chances, Darwin simultaneously asked Henslow if either he or Peacock would have a word with the chancellor of the exchequer—their old political friend Thomas Spring Rice, the member of Parliament for Cambridge University. As always, Henslow did his best. His letter to Spring Rice showed how far he was prepared to back Darwin for public funding. And

Darwin's letter to Beaufort was interesting too in revealing just how far he had come to think of himself as an experienced naturalist—the official naturalist—on the *Beagle*. The whole expense of making collections "creditable to the country," he emphasised, "even to the purchase of materials for the preservation of the specimens, together with a salary for an assistant, has been willingly defrayed by myself."[49] Dramatically, he cast off the image of himself as FitzRoy's gentleman companion and reappeared in the new skin of a thoroughgoing specialist, richly deserving government favour for his efforts.

Darwin got his answer late in August, only a bit delayed by the hubbub of the general election after Victoria's accession. One thousand pounds was allocated out of public funds to cover his proposed text and illustrations. Spring Rice (reinstated as chancellor) told the treasury that Darwin's book would be of great advantage to the science of natural history—just as Henslow had told him. His political secretary repeated these encouraging words in the official notification.

Flushed with success at this good news, Darwin bounced much further than either MacLeay or Spring Rice envisaged. As soon as he heard of the award he resolved on making the money stretch to cover a geology book as well. Within a few days he signed a contract to that effect with Smith & Elder, specialists in large illustrated works and government publications. The negotiations were simple enough. He promised to supply the text and lithographed illustrations for a zoological book within two years, agreeing to finance it with pre-paid subscriptions and a cover price of £9, the cost of the plates coming from the treasury grant. He would then supply a volume of geological results to soak up the balance afterwards.

The problem lay more in fulfilling the agreement. In the space of six months, and without really thinking about it, Darwin had signed contracts to write two books and edit one large volume. He had no idea how he was going to fulfil these obligations as quickly as he had promised. With no publisher's advance and no future royalties in any of the agreements, there was scant financial recompense on the horizon. Moreover, he now realised he had been equally foolish in signing away his *Journal of Researches* on very poor terms to FitzRoy's publishers, Henry Colburn of Marlborough Street. Darwin found out about Victorian publishing the hard way. These early years became tied to what he angrily saw as profitless drudgery.

"I cannot leave London," he sighed to friends and relations. "I shall be hard at work as any galley slave during the next five weeks."

Not surprisingly, his production chain took much longer than five weeks. Darwin worked furiously through the rest of 1837, and for the next three years or more, editing *The Zoology of the Voyage of H.M.S. Beagle*, as it came to be called. The five years after that were dedicated to completing his geology. He superintended the *Zoology*'s text, wrote introductions for the different parts, and added notes from his various *Beagle* records about animal behaviour and habitats wherever appropriate, while also supervising the printers, proofreading the sheets, arranging artists for the plates, chivying the experts, and keeping them all moving forward within a tight self-imposed budget. At first he optimistically hoped to include his *Beagle* plants and insects. But he had to cut the project short long before that point. His friend Jenyns took on the fish, Owen the fossil mammals, Waterhouse the living mammals, Gould the birds, and Thomas Bell the reptiles. Darwin intended doing the marine invertebrates himself.

At the same time, the proof sheets of his *Journal* came rolling in. Overwhelmed, Darwin relinquished his intention to write up his marine invertebrates, realised that Henslow was unlikely to do anything with the plants, and sent the insects to friends, who published their conclusions elsewhere in specialist entomological journals.

VIII

Perhaps it was this unrelenting exertion that led Darwin to a sharp, decisive argument with FitzRoy in November. Perhaps an air of overweening certainty seeped in, or maybe something of his newly flattering idea of himself as an experienced naturalist to the voyage. Perhaps he was tired. Either way, overworked and harassed, Darwin unthinkingly dashed off a preface to his *Journal of Researches* and sent it to FitzRoy for his approval. The reply sent him reeling.

The captain made it plain that he was ready to break off all relations. The preface, he thought, displayed little acknowledgement of FitzRoy's role in taking Darwin round the world. Darwin's inflated talk of being "the naturalist" and having paid for his own collecting activities grated on FitzRoy's nerves. More than this, he was offended. Where were the names of the other people who had helped Darwin? All FitzRoy's pent-up resentments poured out in a tight-lipped exchange. "Captain FitzRoy will only venture to remark that there were obliging—disinterested—and kind-hearted officers on board the *Beagle*." Most people, he added in a second blast posted the following day, were aware that Darwin only went in the *Beagle* at FitzRoy's suggestion and depended on his giving up a part of his accommodation to a "scientific gentleman." Most people, he observed sternly, knew how much the other officers furthered Darwin's activities by giving him the preference on all occasions, especially Sulivan, Usborne, Bynoe, and Stokes. These men held the ladder, FitzRoy said, by which Darwin mounted to a position where his "industry—enterprise—and talent could be thoroughly demonstrated—and become useful to our countrymen—and—I may truly say—to the world."[50]

Most of all, he was hurt by the unfavourable comparison Darwin inadvertently drew between Captain FitzRoy's "wish" and Captain Beaufort's "kindness." Such a meagre acknowledgement of FitzRoy's remarkable generosity over five years was humiliating. The final straw came when Lyell told him that Darwin's volume was being published with FitzRoy's only for reasons of expediency. "He does not seem to consider," cried the tormented captain, "that the connection of your volume with mine—and mine with Captain King's—is one of feeling and fidelity."

Deflated, Darwin could only apologise. He resolutely soothed FitzRoy's ruffled feathers and added a much more grateful sentence or two to his preface, which he tactfully repeated in the preface to his *Zoology*. The affair was soon over. But Darwin did not like admitting he was wrong. He found it much easier to think of FitzRoy as irritable and touchy. He never mentioned the argument again except in his autobiography, and there only to emphasise FitzRoy's uncertain temper. The truth was he drove the pair of them "almost beyond mutual reconciliation."

In more ways than one, Darwin's voyage was well and truly over.

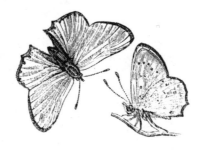

"A THEORY BY WHICH
TO WORK"

HEN the New Year of 1838 came around, Darwin was very hard at work and complaining much more about it. For one thing, Smith & Elder advertised the first part of his geology book and Darwin hastily thought he had better start writing it. For another, he needed to get an issue of the *Zoology* ready for publication every alternate month from February onwards. Yet his contributors were suddenly finding other things to do: John Gould was off collecting his own specimens in Australia instead of describing Darwin's birds; Richard Owen, after a brisk start, took the whole year to produce his second number on the fossil mammals; Thomas Bell seemed to have forgotten all about describing the reptiles.

Darwin was just as hard pressed in other areas too. In February, Whewell persuaded him to become secretary of the Geological Society, which entailed considerable administrative work and a regular appearance at the season's scientific meetings. Fully aware of the workload, Darwin had at first refused when Whewell asked him in 1837.[1] Now, however, he reluctantly agreed. And in March he completed a long analysis of the interconnections between volcanic activity and elevation in South America for reading in front of the same society.[2] Altogether the attractions of a fast intellectual life were beginning to pall. After hurtling along on the excitement of returning to England and joining the scientific community, he found the constant productive grind not nearly so much fun.

Darwin was frequently out of temper. The weather ate into his nerves, and he hated London's "abominable murky atmosphere." With his schedule, even walking with Henslow or Fox in the countryside appeared impossible dreams. There was no chance of getting to Shrewsbury for a holiday till the summer, he told Caroline. Dejectedly, he took up riding for the fresh air and relaxation. But he was determined to find fault with this as well. Although he was astonished to find "much pretty country" within three miles of London, and generally liked the exercise, his longing to get out of town ran deeper than anything a few rides in the park could alleviate. Spring and summer seemed about to pass him by.

Darwin was also ill. The stress of overwork was becoming more obvious, compounded by the complex, surging emotions arising out of his transmutation work—the secret notes, his shocked recognition of the full impact of what he was proposing. He was apprehensive of being misunderstood. "The noddle & the stomach are antagonist powers," he wrote plaintively to Caroline again. "What thought has to do with digesting roast beef—I cannot say, but they are brother faculties." He started experiencing palpitations of the heart. Doctors, he said, meaning Henry Holland and James Clark, *"strongly"* urged him to "knock off all work" and go and live in the country. "I believe I must do this . . . for I feel I must have a little rest, else I shall break down."[3]

Nevertheless he stayed in London and carried on—his ill health paradoxically acting as a spur to his imagination rather than a deterrent. The pace of his notebook entries increased dramatically through 1838. He finished "B" in March that year; filled "C" by June, completed "D" and "M" in October. Behind them all ran troubled musings on life, death, and religion. Man's place in nature, he repeated over and over, was not nearly as elevated as usually thought. "It is absurd to talk of one animal being higher than another. . . . People often talk of the wonderful event of intellectual Man appearing—the appearance of insects with other senses is more wonderful. . . . Who with the face of the earth covered with the most beautiful savannahs & forests dare to say that intellectuality is only aim in this world."[4] Insects were as marvellous in their way as men and women. Even human beings, he declared boldly, resulted from the unrolling of completely natural laws. "How far grander than idea from cramped imagination that God created . . . the Rhinoceros of Java & Sumatra; that since the time of Silurian, he has made a long succession of vile molluscous animals.—How beneath the dignity of him who is supposed to have said let there be light & there was light." But this was bad taste, he interjected.

Darwin's transmutation theories shifted just as powerfully into higher gear. In his "C" notebook, which he started in March 1838, he dwelled exhaustively on heredity, quickly pulling together a theory for the origin of inherited changes based on sexual reproduction and the "age" or "permanence" of bloodlines. The older the "line," he thought, the more likely the characteristics were to be passed on. Long isolation on an island, for example, or long-continued pure breeding in the farmyard would provide sufficient internal stability for that to happen. Mixed breeding between old and new races, or anything that unsettled the reproductive constancy of the line, like geological alterations, would introduce novelties and change. He pondered unceasingly on nature's fecundity, about the purpose of sex and sexuality.

A strong interest in women also crept into his notebooks. Ostensibly debating reproduction in corals and cuttlefish and the mating urge in dogs, Darwin unwittingly chronicled his own ambivalent desires. Women were much more of a reality—a possibility—for him after his return from the *Beagle*. Everyone he knew seemed to be married or getting married. To be sure, FitzRoy had jumped into matrimony with a rapidity born of naval desperation. Yet Bartholomew Sulivan found an admiral's daughter in January 1837. Caroline married her cousin Josiah Wedgwood (the oldest son of Uncle Jos) a little later in the year. Fox and Whitley had taken their chance when it came. John Cameron's wife, exclaimed Herbert, converted him into "the best of country parsons!"

Of Darwin's other friends, only Erasmus was in no rush to commit himself. And Erasmus had confused himself completely by falling in love with Hensleigh's wife, Fanny. Older than both Erasmus and Hensleigh by three or four years, Fanny Wedgwood was the daughter of Sir James Mackintosh and a cousin to the Wedgwoods on their mother's (Allen) side. Before marrying Hensleigh she had acted as Mackintosh's hostess in London while her parents' marriage quietly broke down, a great ally of her older (widowed) half-sister, Mary Rich. An extended family ménage was nothing new to her, nor was the concept of a difficult husband like Hensleigh any kind of surprise.[5] Erasmus, the rest of the family noticed apprehensively, was so constantly in the Wedgwoods' company that he practically lived with them.

Actually, Erasmus's sexual identity was mysterious, almost hermaphroditic. Too idle to go courting, he liked his womenfolk already trained up into wives, as it were. All through a long life he addressed Fanny Wedgwood as "Missus" or "Wifey," playing the attentive spouse in counterpoint to her real husband. It was Erasmus, not Hensleigh, who took Fanny out driving in his carriage, executed her errands, wrote notes about the tea parties he pretended to hate, exchanged caustic gossip about their mutual friends, expected sympathy for his bad chest, and nagged about her absence from the capital on family holidays. "If it were not for Letts' diary I should think it a century since you went," he complained. "If the present beautiful weather continues I shall be compelled to go and be happy in the country but at present I prefer being miserable in London. . . . Pray send me any comms. you want executing, as I have plenty of time, and am not really so dead as you always affect to consider me."[6] Erasmus was moreover devoted to Fanny's children, especially to Julia (nicknamed Snow). From the very strong affection he displayed for her, Snow might well have been Erasmus's child, although nothing confirms the suggestion.

To Darwin's mind, bursting with activity just down the road in Great Marlborough Street, Erasmus lived like a neuter bee, neither one thing nor the other: an old woman, his sisters said, too lethargic at thirty-four to take on anything requiring as much effort as a wife and family. He may, as their words half imply, have been a latent homosexual, a point supported by the apparent readiness with which Hensleigh Wedgwood and Thomas Carlyle allowed their wives to be escorted around town. Erasmus never married, growing older and fussier and iller. He was content with what he called his misanthropy from Marlborough Street.

Either way, Charles became his alter-ego: the one who thought constantly about sexual reproduction as the driving force of nature and smothered his feelings with work. Perhaps the basic animal form was female, he speculated in his notebooks, since offspring usually resembled their mother at birth and only later took on the distinguishing characteristics of breed and gender. Maleness might be added on afterwards. Or were the earliest animals and plants hermaphroditic, and did every species carry evidence of having lost one or the other set of sexual organs in the process of separating into two sexes? Nipples bothered him—why did males have them? Why should castrated cockerels take on female characteristics and old women take on male? Some kind of aboriginal hermaphroditism might explain these and the other cases he avidly hunted out from scientific and anthropological literature. Erasmus provided a shadowy backdrop to his musings.

Darwin had daydreams and anxieties too which seeped into his notebooks—anxieties about sexual attractiveness, female desire, begetting children, and the inheritance of bloodlines in human families. His own lack of any physical life was preying on his mind. All he did was write. "As for a wife, that most interesting specimen in the whole series of vertebrate animals," he told Whitley sadly, "providence only knows whether I shall ever capture one or be able to feed her if caught. All such considerations are hidden far in futurity, but at the end of a distant view, I sometimes see a cottage & some white object like a petticoat, which always drives granite & trap out of my head in the most unphilosophical manner."[7]

At last, on the back of a note from Leonard Horner written in April 1838, Darwin listed the advantages and disadvantages of getting married. Mrs. Horner's attentions had brought him to some kind of gentle boil. Not many advantages came immediately to his mind: work and money were far more pressing problems. "If I were moderately rich, I would live in London, with

[a] pretty big house," he grumbled, "but could I act thus with children &
poor?"[8] With a wife to support he would need a salaried position, perhaps a
professorship at Cambridge, where his private projects would have to take
second place. He could not bear to contemplate "hybernating in the country"
if he quit London's scientific circles. "My destiny will be Camb. Prof. or poor
man [in] outskirts of London, some small Square &c., and work as well as I
can." That way his work could still come first. He could not go on as Lyell
did, he added, merely correcting and expanding an old train of thought and
sacrificing all future natural history excursions. Not with his transmutation
notebooks crying so persistently for his attention. The prospect of this kind
of marriage looked so unappetising to him it was hardly worth pursuing any
further.

II

Far better, Darwin thought, to make the most of his active natural history life.
About then he decided to visit the Scottish Highlands in the summer for the
scenery and a chance to investigate the so-called parallel roads of Glen Roy.
This famous conundrum of British geology was discussed by Lyell in the
fifth edition of the *Principles*, which Darwin had just read.[9] All along the
sides of the glen and occasionally in other interlinked valleys in the mountains around Fort William and the Caledonian Canal, there were shelves as
wide as roads, or more mundanely, at least as well marked as sheep-tracks.
Their origins already interested several geologists, notably the Highland
experts John MacCulloch and Thomas Dick Lauder. These two men
independently considered the roads to be terraces formed when a hypothetical freshwater lake filled the valley. Lyell, on the other hand, thought they
might be relics of marine beaches, now elevated well above sea level, and
said as much in the *Principles*.

The thought of sea beaches appealed enormously to Darwin. He, after all,
had spent much of his time in Chile seeking examples of just such a
combination of circumstances, riding out to the "steps" of Coquimbo and
interpreting them as successive marine beaches.[10] Everything he had learned
on the *Beagle* suggested that Glen Roy's roads could be explained in the
same way. Furthermore, the trip might remedy some of his ignorance about
British geology. He did not know much about his own native rocks, he
realised, and as secretary of the Geological Society this ignorance was
regularly exposed to the sharpest cut and thrust of any London scientific
institution. He could easily include a visit to the volcanic sites around
Edinburgh in his itinerary. A few hills and clean air would do him a power of
good, he anticipated.

Before then, he amused himself by going to the zoo.

Two days since, when it was very warm, I rode to the Zoological Society, & by the greatest piece of good fortune it was the first time this year, that the Rhinoceros was turned out.—Such a sight has seldom been seen, as to behold the rhinoceros kicking & rearing, (though neither end reached any great height) out of joy.—it galloped up & down its court surprisingly quickly, like a huge cow, & it was marvellous how suddenly it could stop & turn around at the end of each gallop.—The elephant was in the adjoining yard & was greatly amazed at seeing the rhinoceros so frisky; He came close to the palings & after looking very intently, set off trotting himself, with his tail sticking out at one end & his trunk at the other, —squeeling & braying like half a dozen broken trumpets.—I saw also the Ourang-outang in great perfection: the keeper showed her an apple, but would not give it her, whereupon she threw herself on her back, kicked & cried, precisely like a naughty child.—She then looked very sulky & after two or three fits of pashion, the keeper said, "Jenny if you will stop bawling & be a good girl, I will give you the apple.—" She certainly understood every word of this, &, though like a child, she had great work to stop whining, she at last succeeded, & then got the apple, with which she jumped into an arm chair & began eating it, with the most contented countenance imaginable.[11]

Harriet Martineau was frisking round Erasmus just like the rhinoceros, he told Susan. She was outrageous. "Lyell called there the other day & there was a beautiful rose on the table, & she coolly showed it to him & said 'Erasmus Darwin' gave me that.—How fortunate it is, she is so very plain; otherwise I should be frightened."[12]

Late in June, Darwin consequently abandoned London for Scotland. He thoroughly enjoyed revisiting Edinburgh, tramping over Salisbury Crags again, laughing at the recollection of Jameson's field lecture of long ago.[13] The parallel roads too were just the kind of geological puzzle he loved best, where apparently mysterious phenomena could be explained with a single imaginative leap. After a few days of climbing through the area, he was sure his guess was right. He could find no evidence of any inland barriers formerly damming the River Roy, and not much reason to believe the shelves were the remains of a freshwater lake. He thought it was far more likely that the whole region had gradually risen up out of the sea. Glen Roy, he surmised, was an older and more symmetrical version of the elevated coast-lines he had seen in Chile.

Even so, however hard he looked he could not find any marine debris or fossilised shells on the shelves. Rather than give up his conclusions, Darwin adroitly turned this failure to his advantage. Since fossils were unlikely to be preserved, he told himself, their absence was far more likely than their presence. No shells did not necessarily prove him wrong: no shells, he argued, just meant he needed to use other, more positive evidence to support his theory. Even the most striking "negative" evidence could, with creative rethinking, be made to support his own contentions. Indeed, he was so accustomed to devising and "proving" similarly esoteric theories in South America—of looking at nature with a powerful battery of ready-made explanations in mind—that he did not allow anything as inconvenient as a few missing shells to spoil them.

In actuality, Darwin's confidence in his marine interpretation for Glen Roy was misplaced. His Lyellian eyes did not register the river outflows and other anomalies that soon stimulated a very different and generally more acceptable explanation based on freshwater lakes again. All the persistence and dogged determination that had generated such spectacular results in *Beagle* days blinkered him in Glen Roy. His idea of marine beaches was "a great blunder"—his greatest blunder, he crossly confessed afterwards.[14] The mistake came back to plague him little more than four years later.

Still, he was very much pleased with his work at the time. He was equally happy visiting Shrewsbury for a week or two on the way back to London, his affections pleasantly stirred by the idea of being at home. This time around, father and son talked to each other more freely than ever before, and Darwin consulted the doctor on a wide range of topics relating to human medicine and psychology, of direct concern to his species theories, pumping him for interesting stories about branches of the family virtually unknown to him. The flow of useful information came gushing out so freely that he opened two new notebooks to accommodate it, one coincidentally reaching the letter "D" for Darwin in his sequence, the other labelled "M" for "Metaphysical Enquiries." Afterwards the talk turned to religious belief and their shared lack of any strong feeling in that direction. Dr. Darwin advised his son never to let any future wife know the full extent of his disbelief: "conceal carefully" your doubts, he told him, they would only cause heartache. "Things went on pretty well until the wife or husband became out of health, and then some women suffered miserably by doubting about the salvation of their husbands, thus making them likewise to suffer."[15]

The expansive mood continued with frank discussions about money. Darwin redirected his anxious questions about marriage to his father—should he opt for married life and poverty in London ("like a prisoner") or married life and poverty in Cambridge ("like a fish out of water")? The doctor explained how it need not be either. His inheritance would ensure that Darwin would always be comfortably provided for.

Relieved and grateful, marriage suddenly seemed to Darwin more a question of freedom than poverty. He started to look at the issue differently. "Marry" or "Not Marry"? he asked himself as he divided a page of paper into a balance sheet: "this is the question."[16] Like the compulsive insect collector who still lurked under the skin, he settled down to add up the advantages and disadvantages of taking a wife. With no real candidate in mind, he inspected the idea for a second time as dispassionately as if he had a beetle before him. If he stayed unmarried, he wrote firmly, he would be free to do what he liked, free to choose his own company and listen to the "conversation of clever men in clubs." He could go into society or avoid it as he wished. He would have time to work. Being rich and single like Erasmus seemed a very attractive possibility.

Yet a wife offered the soothing charms of music and "female chit-chat," a constant companion for his old age, someone "who will feel interested in one" and take care of the house: solid Victorian virtues that Darwin expected any bride of his to possess. Such a wife was "better than a dog anyhow."

He found it much easier to list the disadvantages. Out they spilled, an extraordinary jumble of worries, delusions, prejudices, and preconceptions accumulated over the months through watching his friends, sisters, and cousins tread the same path. He would have to make conversation with women: no more peaceful reading in the evenings, he groaned. "Fatness & idleness—anxiety & responsibility—less money for books &c. If many children forced to gain one's bread." He would have to visit relatives and bend in every trifle. "Eheu!! I should never know French,—or see the continent—or go to America, or go up in a Balloon, or take solitary trip in Wales—poor slave—you will be worse than a Negro." Always there was the threat of a "terrible loss of time."

Ever practical, Dr. Darwin told him to get on with it, the sooner the better as far as having children was concerned. The cosy parsonage of Darwin's earlier days noiselessly emerged from beneath the surface. "Only picture to yourself a nice soft wife on a sofa with good fire, & books & music perhaps—Compare this vision with the dingy reality of Grt. Marlbro' St."

One cannot live this solitary life, with groggy old age, friendless & cold, & childless staring one in one's face, already beginning to wrinkle.—Never mind, trust to chance—keep a sharp look out—There is many a happy slave—

He had convinced himself. His sheet ended with mathematical certainty. "Marry—Marry—Marry. Q.E.D."

III

Yet whom to choose? If nothing else, Darwin was brutally honest about what he wanted. Romantic love was not necessary. No feminine names eased persuasively into his deliberations. Nor did he consider the possibility of a wife who might help his scientific activities or otherwise participate in his life of the mind. He had no need for an intellectual hostess like Mary Lyell or Mrs. Henslow. Erasmus filled that role to perfection, giving dinner parties in Darwin's honour and introducing him to interesting people without also demanding his opinion on clothes or hairstyles. He had no wish for a learned companion to translate German and Italian books in the evenings or re-arrange his shell collection as the Horner girls might do. The thought of being married to a bluestocking like Katherine Horner or Harriet Martineau suddenly appalled him. On the contrary, he wanted someone who would disturb him as little as possible. Clever women made him uneasy.

He looked instead to the solid, unflappable Wedgwoods. He had eight cousins on that side of the family, running from Elizabeth, the eldest, born in 1793 with a slight spinal deformity, to Emma, the youngest, born in 1808, the year before Darwin. Emma, so to speak, was the only one available. "Dear merry little Emma," an aunt once said indulgently, notably misreading her placid disposition. Her greatest asset was an exceedingly good nature, reflected another aunt. With her long brown hair looped around her face and gold spectacles perched on her nose, she reminded Darwin of his own sisters in their younger days or a plainer version of Charlotte.

Darwin may even have taken a conscious decision to aim for Emma in preference to one of the Horners before setting out from Shrewsbury to visit Maer late in July. Certainly it was during that visit, he later told Lyell, that he decided to try his chances. But as Emma explained afterwards, he did not make it at all obvious. Darwin stayed for only three days. He had barely seen her since his return from the voyage and was awkward and reserved in her company.

Emma knew her own mind rather better. Her interest in Darwin was awakened in May that year when she and a collection of relatives including Catherine Darwin stayed near Erasmus's house on the way to Paris, and again in Hensleigh's house on their return. "Charles used to come from next door, so we were a very pleasant, merry party," she told her Aunt Jessie. Artlessly she wondered on what principle men chose their wives. "He is so affectionate, and so fond of Maer and all of us and demonstrative in his manners, that I did not think it meant anything and the week I spent in London on my return from Paris, I felt sure he did not care about me, only that he was very unwell at the time."[17]

Darwin's July visit was equally mysterious. He helped Emma and Eliza-beth prepare for a charity bazaar, brazenly refusing to buy any of the ugly things they collected except when the honour of the Darwin family required it. Still, he managed to have a talk alone with her in the library one evening—a "goose" in the slang of the day, meaning an intimate chat—and wrote a self-conscious letter afterwards saying how much he looked forward to another. As for Emma, she had the feeling that if he saw more of her, "he would really like me."

There Darwin left it. He was oddly nervous of going any further.

Returning to London on 1 August, Darwin deliberately threw himself into relentless activity—a sure way of avoiding any awkward personal issues that agitated his mind. Principally he worked hard on writing up his results from Glen Roy, pausing only to consult Lyell in long geological letters and then in person as soon as Lyell returned from his summer holiday in Scotland. This essay was "one of the most difficult & instructive tasks I was ever employed on."[18] But he also continued drafting chapters for the geological book promised to Smith & Elder—chapters on volcanic craters and coral reefs, both requiring "much reading." He fretted about forthcoming numbers of the *Zoology,* finding crusty old George Robert Gray a poor ornithological substitute now that Gould had gone away. He wrote a long appendix for the *Journal of Researches,* which was still sitting on his desk waiting to be published, and irritated by FitzRoy's slowness, he turned it into a veiled reproof about how long ago the main part of his text had been ready for action. He let the delay rankle more and more, although he circumspectly dissuaded Whewell and Lyell from making his complaints public: as last year's argument about the preface had shown, FitzRoy's temper was easily ignited. Darwin took little consolation from hearing that Lyell's father had liked the proof sheets carried up to Scotland, and that Sulivan and Horner had enjoyed reading them too. He grumpily told Lyell that "my first born child" seemed "long since dead, buried & forgotten."

At the same time he devoured Lyell's new book on geology, the *Elements of Geology.* "I have read it through every word," said Darwin, overflowing with enthusiasm: "it must do good." Perhaps Lyell need not have pointed out the delay over Darwin's forthcoming *Journal.*[19] Darwin had a devil of a job pacifying FitzRoy, he reported, when the two met soon afterwards. Simultaneously, he compulsively started a diary recording his progress with work and the days lost to it by ill health, going right back to childhood as well as systematically laying out the itinerary of the *Beagle* journey and the London years so far.[20] He began listing the books he wanted to read and marking them off methodically when he had done so.[21]

The rest of Darwin's private life was crammed with furious work on transmutation. Two years of close investigation into species—their geographical distribution, their breeding, their adaptations and physical affinities—were coming to a pitch at precisely the same moment as his feelings oscillated wildly about marriage. Often now he sensed he was nearing a conclusion in his theoretical work. Yet it was as wayward and elusive as the idea of matrimony. In truth, all these frantic activities were a sign of mounting internal pressure to come to a decision about Emma. As he well knew, however, even if he made his decision about marriage, or recognised how far he had already moved towards it, he would still have to act—a discomforting thought that gnawed away at his nerves. "One *could* do it," he noted, "but other motives prevent the action."[22] It was easier to make himself far too busy to think about it: far too busy to write letters or pay another visit to Staffordshire. Courting would have to wait. But still he brooded about her, about species and sexuality, about women and faith. At the very least she would have to know about his speculations. More concretely, he worried that she might not have him. As he told his children much later on, he thought he was too ugly.

He read "a good deal on all subjects," as he truly said about these months back in London, and "thought much on religion."

IV

Darwin made light of his preoccupations to Lyell. "I have lately been sadly tempted to be idle," he wrote to him in September, "that is as far as pure geology is concerned, by the delightful number of new views, which have been coming in, thickly & steadily, on the classification & affinities & instincts of animals—bearing on the question of species—note book after note book has been filled with facts which begin to group themselves *clearly* under sub-laws."[23]

In particular, and without mentioning it to Lyell, he felt much more inclined than formerly to speculate on human origins. His theories necessarily included human beings, right from the day he first saw the inhabitants of Tierra del Fuego.[24] What did the power of "mind" really amount to? he now wondered. His memories of Jemmy Button, Fuegia Basket, and York Minster came back to haunt him, and he looked as closely at himself as he ever did in his life. Introspection seemed natural under the circumstances, and Darwin compiled a record of his earliest memories, calling it "Life—written 1838."[25] Through this he hoped to study the workings of his own mind—which he did with more honesty than he mustered for love. Nothing he could see fully separated human consciousness from that of animals. There was a chain of links between himself, Jemmy Button, and animals if he could only substantiate it. "Your arguments are good," he told himself, "but look at the immense differences between man [and animals]—forget the use of language & judge only by what you see. Compare the Fuegian & Ourang outang & dare to say difference so great."[26]

Facial expressions, he decided, showed some of these links across the animal-human divide. Each and every turn of the human head, he daringly proposed, revealed some sign of animal ancestry. A human smile found its roots in an animal's snarl, an expression of surprise from once cocking the ears. He even incorporated moral or mental attributes like blushing into the scheme, although he recognised these were not nearly so easy to explain. Blushing—and shame generally—was almost always understood as a specifically human quality, bestowed by the creator, and Darwin was forced to admit that animals did not blush in the same sense as humans did. Nevertheless he persevered, furtively documenting the blushes of his friends and relations, and promising himself time for searching through physiological texts for an appropriately animallike mechanism.[27] He watched Fanny and Hensleigh's babies as closely as Jenny, the orang-utan at the zoo. And once he went with Erasmus to shake hands with the monkeys at the Exeter Exchange: as thoroughgoing gentlemen as Mr. Lamarck would expect, said Erasmus. Not far below lay the helpless anthropomorphism of a country gentleman: "I cannot help thinking horses admire a wide prospect."

Even human thoughts, Darwin provocatively wrote in his notebook, were little more than secretions from the brain, no more wonderful than inert matter being subject to gravitation. "Oh you materialist!" he spluttered gleefully in conclusion.[28]

Changes in behaviour now seemed to him a very likely explanation for "fixing" advantageous alterations in an organism's physical structure. "Habits give structure . . . habitual instincts precede structure," he wrote in notebook "D." But in adopting that idea he knew he was treading on dangerously Lamarckian ground. He did not want to be ridiculed for proposing that animals and plants deliberately "willed" themselves into a new shape as Lamarck was popularly supposed to have done. He needed to emphasise unconscious, habitual behaviour. His own habits were as helpful in this respect as those of any other living being. "I kept my tea in right hand side" of a tea-caddy, he observed, "for some months & then when that was finished kept it in left, but I always for a week took off cover of right side, though my hand would sometimes vibrate. Seeing no tea brought back memory."[29]

Pursuing the same investigative threads, he tried recording a few of his dreams, hoping to discover something about the unconscious workings of the mind. One night he dreamed he ordered Covington to pack up and make for Shrewsbury—"very clear & pretty vivid & perfectly characterized dream, in continuation of waking thought." In another, he read an entire French book with total understanding. The dream was so vivid he was disappointed to wake up, he ruefully recorded.

On 21 September, he had another.

Was witty in a dream in a confused manner. Thought that a person was
hung & came to life, & then made many jokes about not having run away
&c., having faced death like a hero, & then I had some confused idea of
showing scar behind (instead of in front, having changed hanging into his
head cut off) as kind of wit, showing he had honourable wounds.—all this
was a kind of wit.—I changed I believe from hanging to head cut
off... because the whole train of Dr Monro experiment about hanging
came before me showing impossibility of person recovering from hanging
on account of blood.[30]

Unimaginatively, Darwin failed to analyse this gallows humour as far as he
might have done. But it did not take much to recognise that he was becoming deeply anxious about where his transmutation researches were taking
him. Fears in the night came to worry him. Insanity, he wrote in his "M"
notebook, must be very like a dream. Dr. Holland, whom he consulted on
the question, tended to agree with him. More than ever, Darwin felt his
heretical thoughts needed to be kept buried in the privacy of his notebooks.
No one could be told the full extent of the story—not even Lyell or Erasmus.

And what of his own awareness of being human? Could he honestly say
he believed in having a soul? Erasmus reminded him of Plato's belief that
"necessary ideas" arise from the pre-existence of the soul. Instead Darwin
opted to "read monkeys for preexistence."

V

All through August and September, Darwin ploughed through a wide range
of philosophical and metaphysical texts, following up references, checking
review journals, finding out what the best European minds had made of
some of the questions he was attempting to answer. His pocket notebooks
proved too small for exploring all the thoughts he wanted to record; and he
started composing longer and longer essays on the writing paper supplied
free in the Athenaeum Club's library. Day after day, he wrote out comprehensive notes on Mayo's *Philosophy of Living,* Staunton's *Embassy to China,*
Alison's essays on taste, Dugald Stewart on the sublime, Abercrombie's
Inquiries Concerning the Intellectual Powers and the Investigation of Truth,
his cousin Hensleigh's book on chance and free will, and Soame Jenyns's
Inquiry into the Origin of Evil. Every time a book was finished, he marked it
off on his list. Idle Erasmus interpreted this bookish, club-based schedule as
one agreeably like his own. "Charles is become quite an altered character,"
he told Fanny Wedgwood: "he lounges about most of the day, and can
hardly live out of the Athenaeum of which he is never tired of singing the
praises."[31]

If ever an individual was primed to make the most of another man's views at that time it was Darwin. One book invariably led to another as he searched for the next piece of his puzzle. David Brewster's review of Comte's *Cours de Philosophie Positive,* for instance, which Darwin read in the *Edinburgh Review* in September 1838, inspired him to hunt for papers by the Belgian statistician Adolphe Quetelet, whom Brewster mentioned in passing. Quetelet was famous for codifying the idea of an "average" man in 1835 and interesting to Darwin for "facts there mentioned about proportion of sexes at birth & causes." Luckily for Darwin's French, he found a long account of this work in the *Athenaeum* magazine. Before then he quizzed Babbage—who knew Quetelet well, and spoke French—about Quetelet's conclusions.[32] Similarly, Darwin's contact with Richard Owen led him towards a close and fruitful study of John Hunter's lectures as edited and published by Owen in 1837, particularly the volume containing Hunter's observations on animal physiology. Owen had added lengthy footnotes to Hunter's text explaining difficult biological points, which he was pleased to discuss further with Darwin in person. Darwin took the same range of problems to his zoological friends William Yarrell and William MacLeay. "Is there any law of variation—as Hunter supposes with monsters?" he asked them.[33]

So it is not too surprising that on 28 September 1838, Darwin began reading Thomas Robert Malthus's *Essay on the Principle of Population*—for amusement, he claimed, but clearly following up lines of inquiry relating to individual variation, averages, and chance, as well as seeking information on human population statistics.

Other reasons for reading Malthus were not far behind. A good case can be made for at least some of his initial interest lying in the fact that Malthus dealt with the question of the "fruitfulness of marriages," an issue running high in his notebooks. Practical statements relating to human fecundity were just the kind of details he sought at that moment. Underneath bubbled Dr. Darwin's warning that he should marry soon if he wanted healthy children.

Also, Erasmus's friend Harriet Martineau had built her literary fame on Malthus's back, to the point of being derided by the *Quarterly Review* as a "female Malthusian—an unmarried woman who declaims against marriage." Where Malthus wrote bleakly about an inexorable increase in population, at first in rebuttal to the utopian stance of William Godwin and Condorcet, and then expanding his argument in ever-bigger editions up to his death in 1834, Martineau presented a much more optimistic account of human nature amid the workings of capitalism, amalgamating Bentham's greatest-happiness principle, Adam Smith's laissez-faire doctrine, Malthus's population laws, and Riccardo's attack on the Corn Laws. Malthus, she complacently remarked, considered her one of the few people who properly understood his doctrine. Harriet Martineau had in fact nurtured a soft spot for Malthus since they first met. Despite her deafness and his speech impediment (originating in a defect in his palate), they discovered they could carry on a conversation with perfect ease.[34] Darwin no doubt heard a great deal about him when visiting the literary lioness "in her den."

Fanny Wedgwood had furthermore known Malthus well. Her father, Sir James Mackintosh, was professor of law at Haileybury when Malthus held the first professorship of political economy there. The families were also linked through Fanny's mother: Malthus liked Kitty Mackintosh's circle of Geneva friends and relations, which included her sister Jessie Sismondi, Mrs. Jane Marcet, and Pierre Prevost, who translated his writings into French. Malthus's daughter was a bridesmaid at Fanny's wedding to Hensleigh.[35]

Nor were Malthus's doctrines entirely unknown to Darwin personally. They were as pervasive in biology as they were in general nineteenth-century culture, intimately related to continuing debates within natural theology and social reform in the wider political sphere. Darwin came across them in the books by Paley which were a fixed part of the Cambridge degree course; and William Whewell discussed them in a paper delivered in 1829 at the Cambridge Philosophical Society. Lyell frequently described the Malthusian struggle to survive in his *Principles,* citing Augustin de Candolle's writings on the subject, as well as giving his own stirring descriptions of human endeavour and colonial warfare where the best fighter always won. More generally still, long reviews of Malthus's works, or of newly issued anti-Malthusian works, constantly appeared in the literary journals Darwin was methodically reading.[36] It would have been hard for him to avoid hearing about the principle of population while controversy raged over the new Poor Laws and when food riots, inflammatory addresses, and unprecedented economic depression flared in distant parts of the country. Every publication in the land discussed the Chartist question during that summer and autumn: every member of the "exasperated populace" knew his or her distress was aggravated by large numbers of people to feed and the high price of corn.

Malthus's argument was starkly simple. The natural tendency of mankind, he said in 1798, was to reproduce at such a rate that unless it was slowed down by some means the number of human beings inevitably outstripped the amount of food available to feed them.[37] He expressed this through juxtaposing the two presumed rates of increase: humans were capable of doubling their number over an approximate twenty-five-year period, he calculated, whereas agricultural production "could not possibly be made to increase faster than in an arithmetical ratio." There was an ineluctable disproportion between the geometric rate (1, 2, 4, 8, 16, etc.) and the arithmetic (1, 2, 3, 4, 5, etc.).

The number of individuals existing at any one time, however, seemed to him broadly balanced with the means of subsistence. He proposed that there must be strong and constantly operating "checks" on the increase of population: both "positive" checks, including early death, disease, famine, epidemics, and war; and "preventative" checks, including late marriage, "unnatural practices" like abortion and infanticide, and, in the most complete version of his scheme, sexual abstinence and moral restraint. Contraception for Malthus was not a possibility—like the solid country parson he was, he envisaged marriage as a commitment to unlimited procreation and as many children as God decreed. Boswell's contraceptive "armour" did not become part of political economy until much further into the nineteenth century. "All these checks," wrote Malthus decisively, "may fairly be resolved into misery and vice."

These abstract logical relationships became concrete in Malthus's discussion of social amelioration. If a man was given five shillings, Malthus claimed, instead of the eighteen pence he usually earned, the extra amount would not increase the quantity of meat or bread available for purchase, and competition between people with cash in their pockets would rapidly inflate food prices in the market. Hence William Pitt's proposal to increase the poor rate would merely increase population without increasing the means for its support. It would create more poor people than the country could provide for; or to be precise, more than the tax-paying middle classes were prepared to support through the usual channels of parish charity. Harassed by a Malthusian-inspired parliamentary outcry, Pitt withdrew his proposal in 1800. And in 1834 the passing of the Poor Law Amendment bill introduced what was to become the Victorian answer to this social and economic issue in the shape of the workhouse.[38]

Preoccupied with his own problems, Darwin never recorded what he might have thought about Malthusianism as it applied to human society except for a few passing words about "vice" being a word to describe innate passions now deemed "unnecessary" by civilised society.[39]

But he famously found that Malthus's inexorable numbers resolved his evolutionary questions. Overwhelmed by the instant recognition that comes to a prepared mind, Darwin saw that what Malthus said about checks to fecundity in the human world rang emphatically true for animals and plants also. Actually, Malthus discussed animals and plants in some detail: there was a vast overproduction of individual offspring in nature, he claimed in his Essay on Population and elsewhere.[40] Yet until Darwin read Malthus he never seriously questioned how the number of organisms living at any one time stabilised or held themselves roughly in proportion. Putting it as bluntly as Malthus did, why was the world not overrun with insects or frogs, given the number of eggs produced by each and every female? "I do not doubt," wrote Darwin wonderingly in his "D" notebook, "every one till he thinks deeply has assumed that increase of animals exactly proportional to the number that can live."

Malthus further explained how this apparent balance emerged out of death—out of what Darwin, extrapolating from both Lyell and the botanist Augustin de Candolle, called the "warring" of species. "Take Europe on an average, every species must have same number killed, year after year, by hawks, by cold &c.—even one species of hawk decreasing in number must affect instantaneously all the rest."[41]

The "war" acted as a chiselling, moulding force, destroying some individuals in order to maintain others in a delicately poised dynamic balance. Anything could tip the struggle one way or another; anything could create a "gap" in nature. That much Malthus made clear. Darwin's moment of insight came when he caught at the idea that the ones who died would be the weakest and the ones who lived the strongest—or best adapted.[42] Death, so to speak, could be a creative entity. It could preserve useful adaptations in some animals and plants while weeding out the remainder. Over a long period of time, favourable variations could become "fixed" in a population and a whole species might adapt to its current situation. If the situation changed—as he knew it almost always did—individuals might be driven along in a new direction by the same agency. Transferring Malthus's system of checks and balances from the human to the natural world provided a way of explaining how species must either change or die. Struggle both produced and explained adaptations. Differential death and survival maintained them in the population.

Without giving it a name, Darwin had hit upon the concept of natural selection. The words in his notebook practically leap from the page:

> One may say there is a force like a hundred thousand wedges trying [to] force every kind of adapted structure into the gaps in the oeconomy of nature, or rather forming gaps by thrusting out weaker ones. The final cause of all this wedgings [sic], must be to sort out proper structure & adapt it to change.[43]

At last, he said, here was a theory by which to work.

VI

The full impact of Malthus's *Essay on Population* became plain after Darwin finished reading it on 3 October. Excitedly, he set about rethinking his transmutation work.

First and foremost, he recognised that differential death rates gave him a mechanism for explaining the preservation of adaptations, until then a mysterious unknown quantity. Every individual death, bit by bit, contributed to a larger piecemeal shift in animal or plant form, with the result that each species became better adapted to external conditions. In this gratifying way, Darwin's longstanding belief in gradualism came back at him from the direction of Malthus. Whether it was sufficient on its own to account for all the phenomena recorded in his notebooks was something he would have to explore; and his confidence soared in anticipation. Here, perhaps, he had got what he was looking for.

Moreover, he saw a reassuring analogy between natural processes and what farmers and horticulturists did. Animal and plant breeders normally picked out the best variations in form, size, or colour in a wide sweep of offspring appearing over a number of generations, and used these individuals as the foundation stock for improved domesticated lines. This much Darwin had known for a long time, frequently considering breeders' activities as a key to how species might be made in the wild.[44] He had always thought it important to locate a symmetry between the normal world and animals and plants under domestication; and he usually evaluated the theories spelled out in his notebooks according to how well they explained information gathered from both the farming community and conventional natural history. He wanted to understand dogs and cabbages as much as finches and fossil bones, and he wanted an answer that served for all of them equally. Could it lie in Malthus?

In another sense, Darwin's whole enterprise emerged out of his countrified background. He felt most comfortable with ideas emanating from the practical rural base familiar to the English landed gentry, and his theories in turn were already closely intertwined with early-nineteenth-century agricultural and horticultural advances. His notebooks took much of their special tenor from the generalised explosion of interest in animal and plant breeding in Britain during the period, an interest that married commercial acumen with radical improvements and diversification through a wide range of livestock, fruit, and vegetables, in addition to garden flowers and domestic pets.[45] One of the essential footings of Darwin's work was data taken from the developers of new strains of pears and potatoes, of pigs and dahlias.

He therefore found it relatively easy to envisage an almost human force doing the same thing in nature—an "invisible hand" selecting the favourable or most advantageous variations in a wild population and letting the unwanted forms die. Suppose six puppies were born, he mused soon after reading Malthus, and it so chanced that some had slightly longer legs.[46] In the Malthusian rush for life, perhaps only two of these would live to breed. If some circumstance determined that long-legged dogs survived rather more frequently than any other, then in ten thousand years the long-legged race

would get the upper hand. "It is a beautiful part of my theory that domesticated races of organisms are made by precisely the same means as species—
but latter far more perfectly & infinitely slower."[47] For the rest of his working
life, Darwin put this parallel at the heart of his theory.

Further to this, Darwin's general understanding of the world around him
was of a kind that made Malthus's words, and the views on species that he
drew out of them, appear in the most vividly relevant light. The idea of
struggling to survive was ingrained in Darwin's personal outlook. He knew
all about hardship from his *Beagle* years. He knew about death, about human
wars of extermination, about famine, slavery, and disease. He had seen
native animals and plants, and native human beings, overrun by imported
tribes, his own tribe of Europeans victorious among them. He recognised
that nature was hard, that death was inevitable. He knew about his own
determination to overcome the rigours of exploration and about his growing
battle with ill health. To someone, moreover, so intimately familiar with
the ideology of an expanding national power, selection by death or survival
seemed an accurate description of what went on. Direct experience of
imperial expansion encouraged him to see struggle, war, and extinction as
inescapable truths of nature.

At another level, too, Darwin's new theory patently dovetailed with the
ethos of industrialised England—the commercial, entrepreneurial spirit of
unfettered competition that helped his grandfather Wedgwood and his finance-
minded father into making the most of their business opportunities. Darwin
saw competition abounding in the manufacturing society around him. It was
the adaptable entrepreneur who survived, the one who diversified or specialised
according to circumstance. The new Victorian public was already finding its
heroes among the engineers, the inventors, and the enterprisers: Charles
Babbage with his calculating machine, Louis Daguerre and Henry Fox Talbot
with their patented photographic process, John Joseph Parker with his improved
fountain pens, John Walker with his friction matches; and the men of steam
and machinery like Stevenson, Brunel, and Nasmyth.[48] For Darwin, the
balance of nature resembled an account book recording the financial affairs
of an entrepreneurial company, with adaptations acting like circulating capital,
representing past achievements and the wherewithal for future ventures. In
the unknown interlocking movements of the human mind, Darwin's social
and commercial contexts appear to have both generated and validated his
scientific ideas. Natural selection intuitively seemed the right answer to a
man thoroughly immersed in the productive, competitive world of early-
Victorian England.

VII

By the first week of November, Darwin was nevertheless at the end of his mental tether, overstretched by his startling visions, unwell, agitated, and tired. He needed a wife, he lamented, failing to recognise his headaches as a sign of anxiety about taking precisely that step. Finally, he decided to try his chances with Emma. Buying a ticket to Staffordshire made him feel sicker than ever.

Still, on Friday, 9 November, he started out for Maer Hall with Hensleigh and Fanny Wedgwood for company. Saturday was not an easy day at all, and on Sunday he spoke about marriage to Emma. Not unexpectedly, the event deflated both of them—Darwin was exhausted by the nervous strain, with a bad headache, and Emma was "too much bewildered" to feel any overwhelming sense of happiness. To Darwin's astonishment, she accepted him. Even so, the proposal caught her so unprepared that she went straight off to teach in the Maer Sunday school as usual. Darwin's exclamation in his diary that this was "The day of days!" was wildly misleading in its retrospective intensity.

The low-key atmosphere continued. Only Uncle Jos wept the traditional tears of joy when his nephew went formally to ask permission. No one else heard anything about it until evening, and then the news was broken in the privacy of Hensleigh and Fanny's bedroom. "I believe," said Emma afterwards, "we both looked very dismal." An elderly Wedgwood aunt thought something quite the reverse had happened: that Darwin had asked but received a rejection.[49]

Emma was equally unprepared to hear that so many of her female relatives had been hoping for this marriage. Her elder sister Elizabeth rejoiced "most sweetly," although it meant losing the only youthful company she had. Fanny Wedgwood and Caroline Darwin (herself married to the younger Josiah Wedgwood) were delighted, although Caroline had not thought the event so near. Aunt Sarah obligingly confided that she had "quite given it up in despair." Emma's favourite Aunt Jessie, over in Geneva, was as pleased as if she were going to be married again to Sismondi. Jessie was grateful Emma had chosen appropriately: "I knew you would be a Mrs Darwin from your hands; and seeing Charles did not come on, which Fan and I used to speculate on and expect in every letter from Maer, I began to fear it was Erasmus. . . . Everything I have ever heard of C. Darwin I have particularly liked, and have long wished for what has now taken place, that he would woo and win you." Blithely unaware of the unloverlike circumstances, she rattled on about how there was "no greater happiness this side of heaven than you are at this moment enjoying." Even Emma's invalid mother, who muddled up the two brothers' inclinations and expressed a momentary regret that Darwin had not captured Harriet Martineau as she had anticipated, amused herself with houses and wedding cakes. It was a match, Emma remarked tartly, "that every soul has been making for us, so we could not have helped it if we had not liked it ourselves."

It was a match Dr. Darwin liked too. The day after speaking to Emma and Uncle Jos, Darwin rode off to Shrewsbury to ask his father's permission. He hardly expected to be refused, nor was he. "Emma having accepted Charles," Dr. Darwin wrote thankfully to Josiah Wedgwood, "gives me as great happiness as Jos having married Caroline, and I cannot say more. On that marriage Bessy [Emma's mother] said she should not have had more pleasure if it had been Victoria, and you may assure her I feel as grateful to her for Emma, as if it had been Martineau herself that Charles had obtained."[50] For three or four days, the doctor echoed and reechoed Uncle Jos's astonished words, "You have drawn a prize!"

It was a match, moreover, of great convenience for everyone concerned. Despite Emma's friend Georgina Tollet's romantically trilling, "It is very like a marriage of Miss Austen's," neither of the protagonists seemed to feel much in love at that moment. The two had no obstacles to overcome, no delicate flirtations at picnics or dances, no misunderstandings wrenching the heartstrings. Darwin had barely seen her all year, and although, as he later told her, he had wanted to propose during his visit in August, he had been afraid to do so. His contact with her had been limited to three days in August and a few social calls in London in the spring, during which it was impossible to gauge his intentions. The "transparent" manner Emma later praised in him was not as transparent as all that. No wonder she was surprised.

Being cousins evidently made all the difference—he had known her all his life, so to speak, and felt no need to investigate further. The same surely applied to Emma. Intermarriages between the families were commonplace: the younger Josiah Wedgwood (Uncle Jos's son) married Caroline Darwin, Hensleigh married his cousin Fanny Mackintosh, and Harry took his cousin Jessie Wedgwood. There was a time when Hensleigh, Harry, and Frank had an eye for Susan Darwin, and Erasmus teetered between Charlotte, Emma, and Fanny—the Wedgwood daughter who died as a young woman. Henry Holland, another cousin, was once touted as an alternative for Charlotte. The same pattern ran through the previous generation, in which two Allen sisters married two Wedgwood brothers at the same time as a third Allen girl married Sir James Mackintosh and Robert Waring Darwin proposed to Susanna Wedgwood. In such a tight-knit and prolific clan, intermarriage was difficult to avoid.

Money made up an important part of the equation as well, although not quite so obviously. Much of the pleasure expressed by the two fathers was an inward sigh of relief that family fortunes would remain in the family. Like any recently wealthy line, both the Darwins and the Wedgwoods consolidated their financial interests by sensible marriages as much as by any other means and were apprehensive about fortune-hunters. Josiah Wedgwood was deeply in debt to Robert Waring Darwin, and their accounts were inextricably interlocked through mutual family trusts offset by company loans and private pensions for Wedgwood's two unmarried sisters and his brother John, the unsuccessful one of the family. Neither father wished to see his hard-earned portfolio frittered away by an unthinking daughter or son-in-law. Marrying inside, rather than outside, was an ideal way of avoiding these dangers; and they could afford to be correspondingly lavish in their arrangements. Josiah Wedgwood made over the sum of £5,000 to Emma, plus personal spending money of £400 a year while he lived, with the intention that the capital should go eventually to Emma's children. Since married women were unable to hold investments in their own name, Wedgwood did what he had done before for Charlotte and arranged a trust fund for Emma, nominating Erasmus and Caroline's husband Jos as her trustees. Dr. Darwin came up with stock to the value of £10,000 invested in canals, land, and railways, which would provide an income of roughly £600 a year.[51] This was enough—just enough, thought Darwin—to allow them to live as independent gentlefolk in London.

The couple's courting, curiously enough, came afterwards. Only when Darwin was fully into the swing of getting engaged, with his sisters and his father emphasising how lucky he was, did he feel safe enough to start saying something of what he thought. He had landed a wife without any real effort. "I have thought how little I expressed how much I owe to you," he wrote guiltily to Emma a day or two later; "and as often as I think this, I vow to try to make myself good enough somewhat to deserve you. . . . My own dear Emma, I kiss the hands with all humbleness and gratitude, which have so filled up for me the cup of happiness—it is my most earnest wish I may make myself worthy of you."[52]

Emma also needed time to adjust to her new circumstances. Once Darwin was gone, she found the idea of marriage to him much easier to contemplate. Her aspirations were amply fulfilled, she wrote to Aunt Jessie.

I must now tell you what I think of him. . . . He is the most open, transparent man I ever saw, and every word expresses his real thoughts. He is particularly affectionate and very nice to his father and sisters, and perfectly sweet tempered, and possesses some minor qualities that add particularly to one's happiness, such as not being fastidious, and being humane to animals. We shall live in London, where he is fully occupied with being Secretary to the Geological Society and conducting a publication upon the animals of Australia. I am so glad he is a busy man. . . . The real crook in my lot I have withheld from you, but I must own it to you sooner or later. It is that he has a great dislike to going to the play, so that I am afraid we shall have some domestic dissentions on that head unless I can get Martineau to take me sometimes. On the other hand he stands concerts very well. He told me he should have spoken to me in August but was afraid, and I was pleased to find that he was not very sure of his answer this time. It was certainly a very unnecessary fear.[53]

VIII

Back in London by 20 November, Darwin spent the following week writing letters and paying calls—all to explain his new situation. From the standpoint of work, the time was "wasted entirely," he recorded waspishly in his diary.

Lyell took the news with more enthusiasm than Darwin had expected. Darwin had wanted Lyell to hear it first from him, both because he was by now an intimate friend and because of Lyell's family ties with the Horners. The Horners, Darwin unwillingly recognised, might well feel slighted by his engagement, since neither Lyell, his wife Mary, nor any of the Horner women possessed any inkling of his having another prospective candidate for marriage in mind. In their eyes, and perhaps in the eyes of society in general, Darwin had failed to play entirely straight with them. Uneasily, he relayed the gist of his country visit to Lyell as soon as he could. Lyell's answer, which came back by return of post, was pleasing, "almost as affectionate as if from a relation." But Mary Lyell could not resist a word or two of reproach. "Your letter caused us some *surprise,*" she added in the postscript.[54] Embarrassed, Darwin knew precisely what she meant.

More embarrassments about the Horners arose a day or two afterwards. Mrs. Horner accosted Erasmus at an evening party, saying, "Oh, this is the reason he would not come near us of late." She looked like "an ill-used woman," Erasmus gaily told his brother. No doubt that was why Darwin avoided the party.

However, Darwin went to call, as he was honour-bound to do—an experience that made him uncomfortable, although he laughed about it later with Emma. "Mother-in-law" exacted a polite revenge for her miscalculation. Leonard Horner found the situation difficult as well and briefly wondered whether he ought to stop speaking to Darwin. Instead, he contented himself with a distant civility reeking of well-bred disappointment. Emma said it would be an added insult if she and Darwin moved into the house Erasmus found for them in Bedford Square just opposite the injured "Horneritas."

Yet Lyell's enthusiasm was real. He grew "quite audacious at the thought of having a married geological companion" and proposed that he and Darwin should leave their wives at home and talk geology every night over dinner at the Athenaeum. "Poor man, he would as soon eat his head as do such an action," went Darwin's reassuring message to Maer, "whilst I feel as yet bold as a lion." Emma, Darwin found, could give as good as she got. She was not going to read Lyell's book now, she retorted, especially as she began to think "he has such a bad heart." Mollification came with hearing how Lyell lectured Darwin on the importance of choosing their London visiting circle very carefully. Otherwise their evenings would be filled with paying calls on "every disagreeable or commonplace acquaintance" rather than going to the theatre.

Over the next few weeks, Darwin and Emma tried to say in letters the important things they had both left unsaid during their brief meetings. Darwin worried that he was selfish and unsociable, "a solitary brute," he warned her, and that she would find life with him dull in contrast to the large and friendly household at Maer. He would do his best, he promised, but the pointless social round of fashionable salons repelled him. He only enjoyed scientific society—meeting other men to talk about stones. The thought of evenings with Lyell at the Athenaeum was actually very attractive, though he joked nonchalantly about it. Most of all, he wanted to be left alone to get on with his work, a desire that automatically excluded Emma. Unconsciously making the best of a potentially disruptive situation, he clothed his confession to her in persuasively heroic images.

> How I do hope you may be as happy as I know I shall be: but it frightens me, as often as I think of what a family you have been one of.—I was thinking this morning how on earth it came, that I, who am fond of talking & am scarcely ever out of spirits, should so entirely rest my notions of happiness on quietness & a good deal of solitude; but I believe the explanation is very simple, & I mention it because it will give you hopes that I shall gradually grow less of a *brute*, —it is that during the five years of my voyage (& indeed I may add these two last) which from the active manner in which they have been passed, may be said to be the commencement of my real life, the whole of my pleasure was derived from what passed in my mind, whilst admiring views by myself, travelling across the wild deserts or glorious forests, or pacing the deck of the poor little Beagle at night.—Excuse this much egotism.—I give it you, because I think you will humanize me, & soon teach me there is greater happiness than building theories & accumulating facts in silence & solitude. My own dearest Emma, I earnestly pray you may never regret the great, & I will add very good, deed you are to perform on the Tuesday: my own dear future wife, God bless you.[55]

Intuitively, Emma recognised his apprehension about sacrificing time to the duties of marriage. She was good at making soothing noises. "I am sure it must be very disagreeable & painful to you to feel so often cut off from the power of doing your work & I want you to cast out of your mind all anxiety about me on that point. . . . You must not think that I expect a holiday husband to be always making himself agreeable to me."

But there were other issues she did want to talk about. She was anxious—melancholy, she said—that they differed over religion, "the most important subject." Darwin had obviously failed to follow his father's advice about carefully concealing any religious doubts he might hold. On the contrary, he must have mentioned at least some of his current tendency towards disbelief. He may even have explained how he was deliberately going against Dr. Darwin's advice—a good way to make an unpleasant admission more attractive to a lover. Emma was suitably grateful. "I thank you from my heart for your openness with me," she wrote at the end of November. "My reason tells me that honest & conscientious doubts cannot be a sin, but I feel it would be a painful void between us." She did not want Darwin to conceal his opinions merely from the fear of giving her distress.

Emma was devout in a quiet, steadfast way. She had been brought up as a traditional Anglican with few of the Unitarian leanings of her Wedgwood grandparents. Her father, like his brothers and countless other sons of the dissenting manufacturing elite, willingly embraced the conventional outlook of the Church of England as he turned himself into one of the landed gentry: "too Tory for these Radical times," Emma perceptively said in 1832 after his election as Whig M.P. for Stoke-on-Trent.[56] Josiah Wedgwood may also have gone some way along the road to scepticism. In a letter to Hensleigh in 1837, Emma wondered if their father was losing his faith: "I have felt so helpless & powerless to do anything but pray—hoping & hoping it is not possible God should finally leave a soul so full of all virtues."[57] Nevertheless, she and her older sisters carried out the various duties of an establishment family. They ran a Church of England Sunday school for local children, distributed food and basic medicines to villagers, and made useful items for charity bazaars.

She had a special request of Darwin. "It is perhaps foolish of me to say this much but my own dear Charlie we now do belong to each other & I cannot help being open with you. Will you do me a favour? yes I am sure you will, it is to read our Saviours farewell discourse to his disciples which begins at the end of the 13th chap of St John. It is so full of love to them & devotion & every beautiful feeling. It is the part of the New Testament I love best."

Unerringly, she chose a central text of Christian doctrine: the moment before the crucifixion when Jesus speaks of his love for his disciples, even for Judas, who betrayed him, and gives them the commandment to love one another as he loves them. Although the disciples doubted the likelihood of his resurrection, there was a place for them in his father's house. He would show them the way to everlasting life—to salvation.

Emma surely saw Darwin as one of the doubters who could, if they only stopped questioning, find themselves able to believe. She held firmly to a literal view of resurrection and salvation. This had crystallised most obviously at the time of her sister Fanny's death, just after Charlotte got married and Darwin sailed on the *Beagle*. Down at the far end of the family, thirteen years younger than her remaining sister, Elizabeth, Emma was desolated without Fanny. She and Fanny had done everything together, never apart for more than a week or two: united in disliking their London boarding school, united in learning the piano, in teaching Sunday school, and in paying lengthy visits to their vivacious Allen aunts.

Her death came as such a blow that Emma, then aged twenty-four, grasped at the idea of a future life with frightening intensity. The loss created a blank, she said afterwards, that stayed forever empty. "Oh Lord help me to become more like her and grant that I may join her with Thee never to part again," she noted at the time.[58] More than anything, she needed to believe that there was a heaven, and that, if she was good and kind, she would go there. Rejoining her sister after death became a primary personal motive for holiness. To imagine her future husband rejecting the prospect of salvation was harrowing: in the most basic of ways she recoiled from the thought that his doubts might brand him as one of the unsaved. She might not meet him in heaven. Eternal damnation was for her an unmentionable terror.

Unerringly, she also recognised something of the dichotomy characterising Darwin's mental life. His sense of duty to his fellows, his innate conservatism, his inbuilt appreciation of the values of gentlemanly society and unthinking acceptance of the advantages of Britain's hierarchies of power, lay uneasily together with the radical thrust of his philosophical views. He had yet to find a way to keep his life and work running smoothly together. Mostly, the problem was a consequence of the structure of English society—religion was as much a question of class and behaviour as doctrine, and a formal subscription to Church of England principles went hand in hand with his own position in society. For Darwin, as for Emma, it implied certain duties to perform. Though there was plenty of room among their circle of friends for private doubts about the finer points of theological dogma, and opportunities for some to step aside from the established church as had Dr. Darwin and Erasmus, few completely abandoned the conventions of normal Anglican-based life.

Darwin was still struggling to come to terms with this dichotomy when he proposed to Emma. No one knew better than he how far his changing views about species were leading him along the path of disbelief. No one knew better than he how far he was wedded to an entirely natural origin of man. Every time he opened one of his notebooks he felt the seductive call of a godless universe. Even his dreams warned him about wandering too far off the straight and narrow. Yet he also felt himself an integral part of the upper echelons of British society; and he was fully accepted as such by his scientific colleagues. For the moment, he could call on some residual belief in an external deity. But he still felt it was important to tell Emma his generalised uncertainty about a range of church axioms: how he rejected the Bible's status as an infallible text in relation to the history of the earth; and that he was no longer sure about miracles and revelation.

To a large degree, Emma accepted these confessions calmly. She was not so strait-laced that she could not admit a preference for avoiding one of "Allen's temperance sermons." She was not shocked by Lyell's tearing apart Genesis and geology. She contemplated Erasmus's scepticism with the same kind of indulgent resignation that all his actions inspired among the family: almost as if atheism were another of his eccentric foibles. She allowed herself a small joke at Darwin's scientific expense when she accused him of considering her merely as a specimen of "I dont know what, simia I believe." And she was amused by Fanny Wedgwood's penchant for charismatic preachers like Edward Irving of the Holy Catholic Apostolic Church, or Thomas Chalmers, and thought that Hensleigh's rigid insistence on not taking unnecessary oaths was an unfortunate setback to his professional advancement. Like her father, she was wary of religious enthusiasm, hoping that "the good sense of the Maerites" would keep such a disease at bay.

However, she was much more religious than Darwin and genuinely believed in the Anglican faith she was brought up in. She was relieved when Darwin complied with her request to read parts of the Bible and told her he felt "earnest on the subject." Luckily, he reassured her, "there were no doubts as to how one ought to act."

He was far more acerbic with himself in his notebooks. The only doubts he allowed during those weeks at the end of 1838 were whether his arguments for transmutation were fully effective. A hard edge suddenly flashed: an incisiveness about the full scope of a naturalistic view of the world which cut through the thicket of compromise and self-illusion he had carefully built up over the years. Fresh from thinking about Emma's religious beliefs, he confronted the raw bones of his theory. Did he really mean to threaten the status of the human mind and mankind's hopes for a moral meaning to life outside of life itself? Was the whole system of morality to go? The answer, he bravely concluded, was yes. Religious belief was merely a natural property of humanity. "Belief allied to instinct," he wrote on a slip of paper. Even better, he daringly ventured, the "love of the deity" was a mere "effect of organization." Emotions of terror and sublimity inevitably prompted a feeling that there was some external cause, one that primitive mankind could not help personifying and turning into a deity. "How completely men must have personified the deity."

Malthus had given him a fierce and destructive sword:

> When two races of men meet they act precisely like two species of animals,—they fight, eat each other, bring diseases to each other &c., but then comes the more deadly struggle, namely which have the best fitted organizations, or instincts (ie intellect in man) to gain the day.... Man acts on & is acted on by the organic and inorganic agents of this earth like every other animal.[59]

There was little space left for divinity or moral redemption in this bleak view of life.

MACAW COTTAGE

HE wedding took place on 29 January 1839 in the small church at Maer, two weeks before Darwin's thirtieth birthday. Emma was already thirty years old. It was a quiet occasion, attended by only a handful of relatives: so quiet, it probably seemed a little flat to the main participants. Darwin suffered his inevitable headache, and Emma got through the ceremony "stout-heartedly." The congregation was just as subdued. Elizabeth was glum at the thought of losing her sister's company, Mrs. Wedgwood was at home ill, and Caroline's baby was so seriously unwell that she could barely tear herself away. Erasmus stayed in London, "greatly comforted" by the news he would not be wanted. John Allen Wedgwood, the couple's cousin in common, who was the incumbent vicar of Maer, took them through the service promptly, and afterwards they all walked back to the house to say goodbye. There was hardly time for Emma to change her clothes and sit for a moment or two with her sisters before leaving for London.

Neither of them, it turned out, had "the steam up" for a honeymoon tour, although Darwin remained undecided right until the last moment. He had thought of visiting Warwick Castle. But Emma's matter-of-fact disposition and Darwin's inclination to start proper married life as soon as possible encouraged them to make straight for their new home. They ate sandwiches on the way and drank a bottle of water, as unceremonious a start, thought Emma, as ever could be wished.[1]

The same prosaic tone coloured their newly-wed existence. The house they had eventually decided to rent was in Upper Gower Street, close to the Bloomsbury area of London, and next to the buildings of University College. Considering what they were used to in the country, number 12 was very small, wedged into the middle of two facing rows of uniformly terraced houses developed by the Bedford Estate in 1789. However, the house was arranged on four floors with a long thin garden behind and room enough for a cook and servants at top and bottom. This area of London was very acceptable to them, neither too refined nor too plebeian, and strictly residential; the Bedford Estate allowed no shops, no public houses, and no mews for carriage horses. Gower Street itself was full of unostentatious professional people, predominantly minor solicitors, barristers, and clerks, along with one or two surgeons, a musician, and Thomas Jackson, a professor at the nearby college.[2] The remaining properties were rented by independent gentlemen like Darwin. Leonard Horner once lived there, and a few months later, in April 1839, Hensleigh Wedgwood took a house further down the street for a while. Coincidentally, Horner had rented the very same house that the Darwins moved into. Digging through his memory, Darwin at last remembered visiting him there a couple of years beforehand. Leonora and Joanna Horner longed to take another look inside, he told Emma.

"Macaw Cottage" they christened it after seeing the yellow curtains and gaudy blue walls topped off with red plush furniture. Emma doubted whether she could live with this startling colour scheme, and decided she would at least dye the curtains when she came up to town. Darwin wisely agreed. "The day of some signal reform must come, otherwise our taste of harmonious colours will assuredly be spoilt for the rest of our lives." But they lived with the colours for quite some time, as people do. Their household budget, although rapidly expanding to include all kinds of extra equipment and furniture, did not include unnecessary work on walls and curtains owned by a landlord.

Darwin moved in alone before the wedding. He paid the advance rent on 29 December and took up residence two days later, impatiently borrowing a pair of sheets from Erasmus and getting "the old lady here" to cook him impromptu bacon and eggs. "I was astounded," he wrote to Emma, "& so was Erasmus at the bulk of my luggage & the Porters were even more so at the weight of those containing my geological specimens.—The dining room, hall, & my own room are crammed & piled with goods."[3] Two or three days later he had tidied everything up to his satisfaction. He ordered coal, took receipt of the housemaid Mary, interviewed and appointed a butler (who stole the knives and was soon replaced by Joseph Parslow, who stayed with the Darwins until their old age), and went out for a celebratory geological supper with Lyell. These masculine dinners would not last much longer, they told each other conspiratorily. The following weekend, the Lyells called on him in his solitary splendour—although Lyell, Darwin remarked, was so full of geology rather than social chit-chat that he was obliged to disgorge. "We talked for half an hour unsophisticated geology, with poor Mrs Lyell sitting by a monument of patience.—I want *practice* in ill treating the female sex—I did not observe Lyell had any compunction: I hope to harden my conscience in time: few husbands seem to find it difficult to effect this."[4]

Actually, Darwin's initiation into absent-minded intellectualism had already begun. During the same Sunday visit, Mary Lyell asked him why he had forgotten an invitation to dine with the Horners a day or two previously. The whole party, she said, had sat waiting round the table at Bedford Square. Sheepishly, Darwin realised he had been happily eating his meal and reading the newspapers at his club. He seemed dogged by embarrassing *faux pas* with this well-meaning and likable family.

Still, he was as proud a householder as ever could be: "I declare I am just like a great overgrown child with a new toy," he informed Emma. Nothing could stop him enjoying the sensation to the full, not even Emma's pointed remarks about his waiting till she got there before rushing off to buy "lamps, all sorts of nice pots, pans, urns &c. &c." The elongated garden, he burbled, was ideal for half an hour's walk; the drawing room not so bad as they first thought. Emma's disappointment at being left out did not register. "I was surprized indeed," she eventually wrote in exasperation from Maer, "to find how soon you had moved into your new house & I dont wonder you feel triumphant. . . . I can fancy how proud you are in your big house, ordering breakfast in the front drawing room, dinner in the dining room, tea in the back drawing room & luncheon in the study, & occasionally looking through your window on your estate & plantations."[5]

Chastened, Darwin wrote back stressing that it was of course "*our* house": was not everything in it, he pleaded, "from me, the geologist, to the black sparrows in the garden . . . your own property." Yet the egotistical joy swirled onwards, right down to unrolling a London map and measuring with the compasses he usually dedicated to geological work exactly how far the house was from a public park. There was only a hundred yards difference between the house in Gower Street and another property they had looked at in Chester Square.

Emma was only slightly appeased: "I hope you will manage to finish Glen Roy now & get shut of it," she replied tartly. The household linen was on its way by canal.

With the wedding there also came wedding gifts. Harriet Martineau sent some of her own books for their embryo library: Emma said she supposed she would try to read them. Henslow came up with a silver candlestick and some good advice about marriage. William Whewell, president of the Geological Society to Darwin's secretary, gave them a copy of *Herman and*

Dorothea, one of Goethe's poems which he had translated into English and published privately early in 1839. If you can accommodate yourself to the canter of the verses, he wrote to Darwin, you will find in it a very pretty love story. And Darwin's old friend Herbert astonished them both with a "massive silver weapon which he called a Forficula (the Latin for earwig) & which I thought was to catch hold of soles & flounders, but Erasmus tells me is for Asparagus—so that two dishes are settled for our first dinner—namely soup & Asparagus."[6]

Soon after their arrival in London, Emma received a Broadwood grand piano, a present from Josiah Wedgwood. They met the van as they walked up Gower Street and Darwin shouted at the driver to find out whether he was going to number 12. "Besides its own merits," Emma expanded contentedly to Elizabeth, "it makes the room look so much more comfortable, and we expect Hensleigh and Fanny to be struck dumb today at our beautiful appearance. I have given Charles a large dose of music every evening, but he still seems to find an overture of Rossini's a very refreshing interlude."[7]

After this fatherly acknowledgement of her new status, Josiah Wedgwood asked if Emma would sit for a portrait when she was able. Elizabeth, who relayed the message, suggested she try George Richmond, the society artist who specialised in attractive portrait drawings. Richmond had already drawn Charlotte and Fanny (Mackintosh) Wedgwood. Undecided, Elizabeth thought James Holmes might be a better artist, though he was known to the family as a fool in other respects. "I will go and get it done when you have settled who is best," Emma agreed. But she did not get round to it until the following year, by which time Darwin had sat to Richmond for a pencil portrait of his own, paid for in December 1839. The couple ended up with two Richmond portraits apiece: Emma painted in water-colours in March 1840, as was Darwin, and then Emma again in a pencil sketch to match Darwin's in 1842.[8] No doubt a pair of pictures went off to both Maer and Shrewsbury. While Elizabeth was on the subject of pictures, however, Emma felt no compunction about asking for something in return. She said the blue walls in the drawing room looked much better with one of Charlotte's Welsh water-colours hung up. "If Charlotte should have any curiosity to know the size of Barmouth it is 13 inches by 8½. Ahem!"

The novelty of being young marrieds continued. They held their first dinner party, essentially for the practice, with the Hensleigh Wedgwoods and Erasmus invited. "Erasmus tells us it was a base imitation of the Marlborough Street dinners, and certainly the likeness was very striking. But when the plum pudding appeared he knocked under and confessed himself conquered very humbly. And then Edward [the new butler] is such a perfect Adantless in his best livery that he is quite a sight. Fanny and Hensleigh slept here, and Hensleigh went the next morning to the office."[9] Hensleigh had a job, after nearly a year of self-imposed seclusion. But the Wedgwoods brought bad news with them that evening. Caroline and Jos's baby had died just a few days after Emma's wedding at Maer.

There were formal social calls to pay too, and the pair trudged off in the February snow to see the Lyells. They in turn stayed in one afternoon to receive visitors. Only two callers came—a great relief to both Darwins. Such visits were pointless, they mutually thought, unless there was some personal significance or usefulness in the connection. Nevertheless, their high moral tone was only relative. They eagerly accepted an invitation to a soirée at Henry Holland's mansion early in February, representing Emma's first appearance in the world of society as a married woman. Parties at Babbage's house and that of Sir Robert Inglis (the Tory M.P.) followed.

Unusually for Darwin, spending money did not seem to bother him too much either during these first months of setting up house. His days were filled with shopping and paying small bills, all of which he carefully recorded in a pocket account book begun on 11 February. He intended keeping his household affairs as straight as any of his *Beagle* catalogues or species notebooks, especially now that his income depended on a regular return on capital investments and needed to cover Emma's expenses just as much as his own.

"Started with money in bank" of £573, he wrote in this account book, plus cash in hand of £36. The first week was a bit of a strain, with wages to pay, a constant procession of hackney coaches, medicine (at 4/6d), the anniversary dinner at the Geological Society (18/6d), a tip of £1 for Covington, and £7 advanced to Emma. But Darwin quickly got into the swing of it. Item by item, his list of small expenditures mounted up. Glasses, crockery, a coffee-pot, a table for the pantry, pestle and mortar ("For Edward"), beer and biscuits, shaving soap, tickets for the opera, bills from the picture framer, coal, Edward's board and wages, a toothbrush, hair oil and medicine, a present to the servants at the Zoological Society, a pickle pot, new stationery with "12 Upper Gower Street" printed on it, insurance, an umbrella, slippers, a china candlestick, "present to Covington on leaving me," haircut and soap, chimneysweep, books ("paid by Lyell"), the city's paving rate, Perryman pens, water rate, poor rate, turnpike fees: on and on went the entries, reflecting the multifarious expenses of setting up and maintaining a gentleman's London home.

Annoyingly, despite all Darwin's precautions, two shillings remained unaccounted for at the end of his first week. It happened again in April, when his sums were out by nine shillings, although this time to his credit. "Something wrong," he wrote in irritation. Eventually he got the system going efficiently, so much so that he never thereafter lost more than a few pence in his regular September totalling up. Alive to every penny spent, Darwin recorded each and every financial transaction that took place, however small, for the rest of his life. Obsessively detailed, cautious, and meticulous, these account books reveal more of his character than even his eventual autobiography. At the end of 1839, he reminded himself in relation to Christmas tips for the future, "give the tradesmen no more than 1/- apiece."[10]

Starting out together like this gave them some moments of high amusement. When the couple walked past the Athenaeum Club a day or two after moving to Gower Street, they saw Leonard Horner trying hard to avoid them. Darwin hailed him, only to hear Horner protest feebly that he thought they were incognito: "Charles said his face, trying to pretend not to see us, was the most comical thing he ever saw." A note came that evening from Horner describing the sensation this news created among his ladies—"Charles supposes the Horneritas made a great chatter." Soon afterwards the eldest girls went off travelling with their father on his Factory Commission investigations.

They did their best to please each other too. Darwin obligingly went to the theatre and professed to enjoy shopping and listening to Emma playing on the piano. One of his first gifts to Emma as her husband was a collection of sheet music for her evening performances on the Broadwood. Affectionately, he declared himself her "Nigger"—her slave. It seems clear that he shyly showed her the notes he had made on marriage the year before—his sheet of paper headed "This is the question" and ending with the remark "there is many a happy slave." Yet Emma soon learned to recognise the failings running underneath his general desire to please. "My Charles has been very unwell since Sunday," she told her sister Charlotte in March. "We went to church at King's College and found the church not warmed, and not more than half-a-dozen people in it, and he was so very cold that I believe it was that which has made him so unwell. We had Ellen Tollet to dine with us yesterday and go to the play, and I think it has cured Charles: at least he is much better today, and he was very much interested and clapped and applauded with all his heart. . . . I expect Charles to get quite fond of the theatre, but as to dinners and parties he gets worse I think. . . . Next week we dine at Dulwich and go to Blagrove's concert, which I am afraid will be a great deal too deep for Charles."[11] Darwin's illnesses were already something of an inconvenience in the way they came and went according to his social schedule; and he could not be relied on to share or even enjoy Emma's cultural interests, broad-based as they were. A few weeks of marriage had opened her eyes to the realisation that he mostly wanted a dull, quiet life.

Darwin, too, was forced to make adjustments, most obviously in suppressing his compulsion over neatness. Emma's personality was warmly untidy, to the point where she felt obliged to reassure her aunts and sisters that her wardrobe as a married woman would not embarrass the family pride. She saw no real reason to make the maids wear lace caps and was bluntly down-to-earth about London fashions. Darwin ended up keeping his study scrupulously tidy as some consolation, as he saw it, for the over-relaxed ambience of the rest of the house.

They were united, nonetheless, in one traditional newly married moment. Picking up a letter from the table, Darwin could not imagine who Mrs. C. Darwin was.

II

They quickly settled into a routine. Content as he was, Darwin had no intention of sacrificing his work to an unlimited period of genteel sociability.

He had promised Emma he would finish his lengthy paper on the geology of Glen Roy before getting married, which he did. It ran to nearly ninety pages of handwritten text, all carefully copied out by Covington before he left Darwin's employment at the end of December 1838. This, Darwin decided, was worth submitting to the Royal Society of London for possible publication, an indication of the high value he set on his interpretation of the parallel "roads" and how hard he laboured over it. It would also be his first attempt to move beyond the confines of the Geological Society towards wider scientific recognition. So in January 1839 he sent the completed manuscript to Lyell, who, as a fellow of the Royal, could forward it with a covering letter to one of the official secretaries. "I devoutly trust they will not ask me to shorten it," Darwin worried, "for long as it is, I believe there is scarcely a sentence that I have not considered whether I could strike it out without injuring the general argument."[12]

As he said, it was the argument more than anything that held the paper together. The shelves stayed the same no matter how they were understood. His point was to reinterpret—to revisualise—what was there. It was an instructive exercise, he said, and one which he thought he accomplished successfully. Indeed, he wondered why more people were not astonished at these strange formations. "I saw nothing in my peregrinations to the Antipodes nearly so curious in physical geography," he told Whitley. "I do not doubt they are old sea-beaches: & many most curious inferences may be, I believe, deduced from the fact."[13]

Darwin wrote to his beetling acquaintance from Cambridge, Albert Way, about the roads as well, hoping Way might be able to supply him with a drawing of the valley taken during one of his Highland tours. Way replied promptly. "In fact I have a sketch of Glen Roy which I took with some pains—& which I believe is tolerably exact, though not *so* exact or *so* artist-like as your purpose deserves. If it could be of use to you it is at your service. It is a long sketch quite enough for a quarto plate—with a good deal of detail but none of what the Art call Effect—that is, no heavy showers passing over the middle plane of the landscape, no powerful results of light & shadow, but such as it is, if it can help you I should be very glad."[14] Way duly turned up in Gower Street with the drawing, which Darwin gratefully included in his paper.

Darwin's rewards for his hard work came sooner than he had hoped. On 24 January 1839 he was elected a fellow of the Royal Society. Joining this elite body of men made him one of only eight hundred notable scientific figures worldwide. On 7 February the secretary (Samuel Hunter Christie) read part of his Glen Roy paper at a meeting in Burlington House, unfortunately mumbling and mutilating it as usual, the fellows complained.[15] On 14 February he paid his membership admission fee of £70. The rest of his paper was delivered by Christie at meetings held on 21 and 28 February.[16]

The full-length version was then sent on to a scientific referee for reporting on its suitability for publication, in this instance to Adam Sedgwick, who gave it a benignly favourable reading. There was no pretence of making an anonymous judgement here. Sedgwick knew the author was Darwin as much as Darwin knew Sedgwick was his referee, for anonymity was not an essential or regular part of the Royal Society's assessment procedure at that time and both sets of papers were appropriately signed. On the contrary, Victorian scientific convention usually required that the results of original research should carry the authority of a recognisable name.

But, as Darwin had feared, the length proved too much for Sedgwick, although he thought "it contains much original research, much ingenious speculation, and some new and very important conclusions." The text needed drastic shortening. "The discussions of the phenomena are good but require condensation, and they are too much scattered."[17] Sedgwick supplied a four-page report detailing the cuts he felt were necessary, probably also discussing them with Darwin when paying a social call at Gower Street on 29 March, two days after submitting his assessment to the society. He paused to take tea with the two of them, making himself pleasant to Emma, who remarked approvingly how "fresh and odd" he was. Either way, Darwin carried on regardless. All these polite scientific quadrilles seemed only natural to him now, an unremarkable part of the elevated world he had immersed himself in for several years. He ignored Sedgwick's recommendations almost completely and went ahead unedited and unshortened, each element of his argument safely preserved, right down to a long explanation of a "theory of expansion" which Sedgwick said was "unnecessary." Darwin felt sufficiently established by now to dismiss advice from older savants, however much he admired them personally. The paper went forward as he had written it. Then, after parting with so much money in one swoop to join the Royal Society, he eagerly bought a copy of the library catalogue for ten shillings. He avidly set upon it with his pencil, busily marking the books he wanted to borrow for his species theory.

Darwin similarly managed to complete two more numbers of the *Zoology* before getting married: one on mammals, written by George Waterhouse, and another on birds, written by George Robert Gray.

Symbolically, however, there was a kind of break. Soon after his marriage the tenor of his scientific work became more routine, more contentedly pedestrian, in many ways like a job with set hours. He was full of good intentions. On 5 February he began learning German, and on the 7th he turned again to his study of coral reefs. He conscientiously revised his earthquake paper for publication at the end of February in the Geological Society's printed *Transactions*. More on corals came after. "As you say you want to know all about us," he wrote apologetically to Caroline, "I will give you a specimen."

> Get up punctually at seven leaving Emma dreadful sleepy & comfortable, set to work after the first torpid feeling is over, and write about Coral formations till ten; go up stairs & find that Emma has been down stairs about half an hour, eat our breakfast, sit in our arm-chairs—and I watch the clock as the hand travels sadly too fast to half past eleven—Then to my study & work till 2 o'clock luncheon time: Emma generally comes & does a little work [needlework] in my room & sits as quiet as a mouse.—After Luncheon I generally have some job in some part of the town & Emma walks with me part of the way—dinner at six—& very good dinners we have—sit in an apoplectic state, with slight snatches of reading till half past seven—tea, lesson of German, occasionally a little music & a little reading & then bedtime makes a charming close to the day.[18]

Graciously he conceded that "Emma must find her life rather monotonous." Some of the urgency seeped out of his species work as well. He continued making notes in the two notebooks still in hand, "E" and "N," and wrote out copious disquisitions on mental and moral philosophy as before. But he spent fewer evenings furiously scribbling in the Athenaeum's library. His geological writings were quite enough to fill the working day; and he was frank in finding that tiring. In order to be thoroughly digested, his ideas about natural and artificial selection needed rather more time and attention than he could at that moment actually manage.

The species work therefore rematerialised in calmer undertakings. There were trips to the zoo with Emma on fine spring days, where Darwin studied monkeys or talked to the keepers while she waited patiently to one side, and snuff-filled conferences with Hensleigh and Erasmus, where she sat equally patiently waiting for them to finish. Thrown into the tightly-knit Wedgwood family with greater intimacy than before, Darwin also found more fuel for his evolutionary work in this context than he expected: Hensleigh had strong ideas about the development and history of language, for instance, and the doctrine of free will, on both of which topics he published well-thought-out studies; Fanny and her coterie of intelligent women friends had opinions on everything and anyone; and Darwin took advantage of ready access to the varied agricultural knowledge of his Wedgwood uncles. He observed Fanny's children, making observations on their development and behaviour. He asked Emma's sister Elizabeth about her failing eyesight, and approached their mutual maiden aunts for gardening lore. Nearly everyone in the family circle, he discovered, had something to say about animals and plants as experienced in their homes and gardens.

In particular, he initiated a wide-ranging programme of inquiry into the breeding and crossing of domestic animals and plants considered in a Malthusian light. This again was something all his relatives could understand and to some degree participate in. Though the overall thrust of his inquiries was secret, Darwin was perfectly open about his interest in variation and inheritance; and his family and friends began treating these enthusiasms with sympathetic indulgence. Darwin's science, Emma implied, was a personal foible, one of the things she found lovable about him. She was amused at his persistence about cucumbers at Maer or his intentness in ascertaining if the yew trees by the boathouse ever had any male flowers. When he managed to persuade old Abberley at The Mount to plant up special rows of beans to see how they sported, she knew his passion ran too deep to divert. Tolerantly, she found some curiosities of her own for him to put in his book about Fanny's baby's "nods and winks."

By now Darwin wanted much more detailed information on hybrid and cross-bred offspring. He pondered the problem of inheritance from many different angles, wondered if experimental crossing would ever prove the truth of his selection theory, and opened a new notebook of "Questions and Experiments," each page carefully arranged under subject headings.

This shifting intellectual focus encouraged him to strike up a correspondence with agricultural and horticultural experts of the day. William Herbert, vicar of Spofforth in Yorkshire (later dean of Manchester) and a leading authority on the breeding of ornamental lilies and plant hybrids generally, was an old friend of Henslow's. Darwin asked eagerly for an introduction to him after reading Herbert's big book on Amaryllidaceae in March. The introduction came as he knew it would, and towards the middle of April,

Herbert was awash with pages of esoteric botanical questions—all fit points to be investigated, he courteously agreed, but requiring more experience than the course of one man's life could provide. However, he obligingly tried to answer in a long reply sent to Henslow. When Henslow visited Gower Street for two or three days, bringing Herbert's letter with him, Darwin was so gratified, and found the information so stimulating, he fired off another batch of questions in June, carefully keeping a copy for himself to collate with the anticipated answers. The points raised about plant hybrids by the three of them in turn—Darwin, William Herbert, and Henslow—set out the parameters of what ended up as one of the longest and most demanding investigations into inheritance that Darwin would ultimately dedicate his experimental life to.[19]

Making the most of his contacts, Darwin then inveigled Henslow into approaching Lord Fitzwilliam on his estate near Cambridge, about the possibility of hybrid crosses between ferns: Fitzwilliam was renowned for his choice fern collection. Darwin thought ferns were basically asexual organisms and therefore unlikely to cross-fertilise each other. Henslow reported back that hybrids did not exist. Nor did Darwin take the Reverend William Herbert's replies as the last word on cross-breeding. He wrote out a set of parallel questions about animals and had it printed up as a questionnaire for distribution among his farming acquaintance. "If the cross offspring of any two races of birds or animals be interbred," he asked in this printed questionnaire, just as he asked Herbert in relation to plants, "will the progeny keep as constant as that of any established breed; or will it tend to return in appearance to either parent?" He wanted data, not theories of inheritance. He instructed the printers to leave a wide margin down one side for people to insert their handwritten answers.[20]

Only two people replied: Richard Sutton Ford, a Darwin family acquaintance living in Swynnerton, near Shrewsbury, and George Tollet, the father of Emma's friends Ellen and Georgina. Still, the questionnaire as a means of inquiry suited him well—a useful way of gathering information from the men (and sometimes women) scattered through Britain or across the expanding overseas colonial network. Pleased with his modest success, Darwin felt predisposed to use the same method of gathering information again—and again if necessary.

III

Intimacy with Emma brought its occasional problems. Early in their marriage, Darwin felt obliged to explain once more his lack of any serious religious feeling, and Emma began to realise the extent of the gap between them. She brooded anxiously for a while before writing her husband a long, generously tender letter. "The state of mind that I wish to preserve with respect to you, is to feel that while you are acting conscientiously & sincerely wishing & trying to learn the truth, you cannot be wrong."

But, she said sadly, "there are some reasons that force themselves upon me & prevent my being always able to give myself this comfort." She worried about his becoming an atheist.

> Your mind & time are full of the most interesting subjects & thoughts of the most absorbing kind, viz. following up yr own discoveries—but which make it very difficult for you to avoid casting out as interruptions other sorts of thoughts which have no relation to what you are pursuing or to be able to give your whole attention to both sides of the question. There is another reason which would have a great effect on a woman, but I don't know· whether it wd so much on a man—I mean E. [Erasmus] whose· understanding you have such a very high opinion of & whom you have so much affection for, having gone before you—is it not likely to have made it easier to you & to have taken off some of that dread & fear which the feeling of doubting first gives & which I do not think an unreasonable or superstitious feeling.
>
> It seems to me also that the line of your pursuits may have led you to view chiefly the difficulties on one side, & that you have not had time to consider & study the chain of difficulties on the other, but I believe you do not consider your opinions as formed. May not the habit in scientific pursuits of believing nothing till it is proved, influence your mind too much in other things which cannot be proved in the same way, & which if true are likely to be above our comprehension.[21]

She went on to say that she thought there was great danger in "giving up revelation." Casting off God's gifts, or not taking enough care to examine the case fully, might have terrible consequences on the Day of Judgement. "Don't think that it is not my affair & that it does not much signify to me. Every thing that concerns you concerns me & I should be most unhappy if I thought we did not belong to each other forever." She could not bear the thought that God might punish him for his doubts. He might not be saved.

Her letter put Darwin in an impossible situation, tearing him between two cherished commitments. Despite his pragmatic approach to marriage, he had come to love Emma dearly, more in those first months perhaps than at any other time in their married life. He had tried to be as honest with her as he dared. Yet he saw he would never be able to reveal everything, that she would always hope his faith was alive. It would crush her if he said what he really thought. He folded the letter up—her "beautiful letter"—and put it away dejectedly. "When I am dead," he wrote on the outside, "know that many times, I have kissed & cryed over this."[22]

IV

The rest of the year carried on in an up-and-down fashion. Sometimes they were social, mingling with interesting literary and intellectual figures, sometimes sedately dull at home. Early in April they held their first "learned party" for Henslow and his wife, who came to stay in Upper Gower Street for a few days. The whole occasion alarmed Darwin much more than Emma. On the Monday, Emma calmly recounted, the Lyells and Fittons came to dine with them at Gower Street; on Wednesday the Henslows went to the Lyells; on Thursday the Darwins and Henslows went to the Fittons. Tuesday was left free in case there was a wish to go to any "public amusement."

Emma's evening went off rather well, she thought. The rest of the company consisted of Leonora Horner (the youngest of the Horner girls), the geologist Dr. Fitton and his wife, and Henslow's old friend the botanist Robert Brown.[23] Emma hired an extra man to wait at table for the evening and listened resignedly to Darwin's agonising. "There never were easier guests," she said firmly, suppressing her own doubts about scientific gallantry. "We had some time to wait before dinner for Dr Fitton, which is always awful and, in my opinion, Mr Lyell is enough to flatten a party, as he never speaks above his breath, so that everybody keeps lowering their tone to his. Mr Brown, who Humboldt calls 'the glory of Great Britain,' looks so shy, as if he longed to shrink into himself and disappear entirely; however, notwithstanding these two dead weights, viz. the greatest botanist and the greatest geologist in Europe, we did very well and had no pauses. Mrs Henslow has a good, loud, sharp voice which was a great comfort, and Mrs Lyell has a very constant supply of talk. Mr H. was very glad to meet Mr Brown, as the two great botanists had a great deal to say to each other."

But "Charles was dreadfully exhausted when it was over, and is only as well as can be expected today. . . . He is rather ashamed of himself for finding his dear friends such a burden."[24]

Sometimes they were in London, sometimes not. After this dinner party they left London to go to Maer for two weeks and then on to Shrewsbury. Emma was pregnant and wanted to see her parents and Elizabeth, in addition to consulting Dr. Darwin as a prospective patient rather than a daughter-in-law. Planned as a treat, the trip was now something of a necessity, for she was very uncomfortable with morning-sickness. Matching her symptoms day for day, Darwin was equally unwell. He was exhausted and needed sympathy. Like many prospective fathers, he required full-time attention from his wife just when she felt most unable to give it.

They went for a second visit to Maer in August, moving on to Shrewsbury for more "doctoring" in September. Back in London for the autumn season, they decided to give up all parties: Emma got too tired. Darwin made no bones about liking the sudden peace: "we see nothing, do nothing & hear nothing, & this to my mind is the perfection of life.—I find I cannot stand going out in the evening."[25]

The most important event of Darwin's summer, however, was the publication of his *Journal* in June or July. "If I live till I am eighty years old I shall not cease to marvel at finding myself an author: in the summer, before I started, if anyone had told me I should have been an angel by this time, I should have thought it an equal improbability."[26] The set comprised four thickish volumes bound in dull blue-grey publisher's cloth bearing the general title *Narrative of the surveying voyages of HMS* Adventure *and* Beagle *Between the Years 1826 and 1836*: one volume of Captain King's writings about the first *Beagle* survey, edited by FitzRoy; one volume of FitzRoy's narrative about the second survey and the circumnavigation, with an accompanying volume of nautical addenda; and one volume of Darwin's natural history material, entitled *Journal and Remarks, 1832–1836*.

As authors, FitzRoy and Darwin naturally got their individual copies first, and Darwin presented one to Elizabeth Wedgwood while he was at Maer, although Elizabeth did not find time immediately to read it. Darwin gave another to Erasmus, self-consciously signing it "From the author."[27]

Yet his general response to the joint publication was afterwards uncharacteristically muted. The immediate history of writing the book had given him too much aggravation for its publication to be an unclouded pleasure now. Curiously, FitzRoy seems to have felt the same way. He was too busy, he said, to do anything more than glance at Darwin's volume. Mrs. FitzRoy was taking "various glimpses," and he went on to hint that his own attempts to dip in here and there revealed nothing "referring to me personally" that he objected to: "at any events neither I nor my wife have yet lighted upon anything that induces me to doubt in the smallest degree that I shall not be thoroughly at ease in that respect."[28] Darwin's gaffe was not forgotten. A month later, FitzRoy managed some more heartfelt congratulations.

Darwin was not surprised. FitzRoy's mercurial temper, he recognised, hid the beginnings of mental instability. The *Beagle* voyage and the captain's marriage had taken their toll on FitzRoy in different ways, making him overanxious about his naval prospects and touchy with colleagues generally. Scientific recognition did not come as quickly or as readily to him as it did to Darwin. Though FitzRoy was awarded the Royal Geographical Society's prize in 1837, and he published several well-received scientific and nautical papers, he evidently started feeling at least some of his own achievements sinking under the weight of Darwin's progress. It proved impossible for him to keep pace with Darwin's exhausting production rate for their *Beagle* manuscript, for instance. He was ill and fractious, not an auspicious climate for gracious interaction. And under the influence of his wife ("so very beautiful & religious a lady," muttered Darwin), FitzRoy plunged into religious enthusiasm. In particular, he reconsidered his views about geology. Living in London after the voyage ended, attending scientific meetings at the Geological Society and Geographical Society, listening intently to the debates over the history of the earth, and probably becoming much more aware of the full implications of Lyell's greatly expanded time scale for the world, the captain decided contemporary geological theories were not for him. They contradicted the literal word of God and ran counter to everything he and his wife believed about the Bible.

When he read Darwin's proof sheets as they became available, he was horrified at the way geological gradualism could turn the earth's history into an entirely secular story. He had harboured a viper in his bosom, he cried vehemently.

Passionately, and without Darwin's knowledge, FitzRoy dashed off a geological counterblast to neutralise what he considered the dangerously anti-biblical opinions about to be published under his general editorship. This was attached to his volume of the *Narrative* and published as Chapter 28 under the title "A Very Few Remarks with Reference to the Deluge."[29] How much his wife was involved in suggesting this course remains unknown, but the essay's tone, and the way FitzRoy directly aimed it at young sailors, point to the well-meaning educational commitments of Mary FitzRoy's philanthropising circle. Either way, FitzRoy lambasted the geological ideas put forward in Darwin's *Journal*. The Patagonian plains, the captain now asserted, showed no evidence of gradually rising out of the sea. The phenomenon could be just as well explained by the biblical flood.

Darwin barely knew whether to laugh or be offended. FitzRoy's chapter was outrageous, he told Lyell after reading the published volume in June. Lyell thought so too when he saw it in October: "it beats all the other nonsense I ever read on the subject," he spluttered. Shaking his head over the captain's vagaries among his friends, Darwin easily managed to dissociate himself from this kind of geological ranting. Very few geologists of the age would go so far as FitzRoy had in trying to squeeze the earth's history into six days of creation. "Although I owe very much to FitzRoy," Darwin said cautiously at this juncture, "I for many reasons, am anxious to avoid seeing much of him."

Floods apart, Darwin would have welcomed some financial benefit on sales of the set. But no money appeared. Even when his own volume sold out and was promptly reprinted by Colburn in August, the contract remained annoyingly unremunerative. To his chagrin, Darwin was eventually required to reimburse the publisher the sum of £21: a comfortable arrangement, was it not, he asked Susan wryly.

All Darwin had from the transaction was a handful of free copies to send around as presentation gifts, plus a number purchased for the same purpose. Still, this was the first time he was in any kind of a position to make himself welcome among the scholarly community by giving away copies of a book he had authored. For the first time he was able to participate in the central feature of Victorian intellectual life which drew authors together in a tightly integrated group. The copies Darwin sent out were not review copies distributed in hopes of a favourable article in one of the literary journals: that function was undertaken by his publisher, Henry Colburn, a man notorious in literary London for his constant, clever use of puffery. They were instead personal gifts, an acknowledgement of his friendship, gratefulness, or admiration. His presentations singled out the men and women he felt most obliged to and wished most to impress: Henslow, Lyell, Hensleigh Wedgwood, his brother Erasmus, Elizabeth Wedgwood and her father, Josiah. Others were tactical gifts to people he hoped to sweeten for some reason or another. Altogether, they were a demonstrable sign of his joining the community of authors as an equal.

One presentation copy went to William Buckland, professor of geology and the new president of the Geological Society after Whewell: a buffoon whom Darwin did not much like but met on a regular basis on the society's council. One went to Richard Owen, a close friend by now, from whom he was constantly learning fruitful points about comparative anatomy and the fossil record. Next on his list, the geologists William Fitton and William Lonsdale said their copies were a "most acceptable present." William Yarrell obligingly returned Darwin's compliment with a copy of the first volume of his own *History of British Birds*. Darwin "took the liberty" of sending his *Journal* to the Reverend William Herbert along with another barrage of botanical questions.

Others went overseas to Elie de Beaumont, the great French geologist, whose theories, despite their cataclysmic nature, were much respected in Britain and studied in depth by Darwin and Lyell; and to Carl Friedrich Hartmann, Lyell's friend and the erstwhile German translator of Lyell's *Elements of Geology*. After reading Hartmann's fractured letter of acknowledgement, Darwin silently gave up all hope of approaching him to make a translation of the *Journal*. Benjamin Silliman of Yale received a copy, probably on Lyell's advice, since Darwin did not know him personally. And late in the year a copy apparently went off to Admiral Krusenstern, the Russian navigator who had circumnavigated the globe in 1803.[30]

Most nerve-racking of all, Darwin sent one to Alexander von Humboldt. Humboldt was at that time living and working in Potsdam on his all-embracing philosophical interpretation of nature, the *Kosmos,* and had taken on almost mythic proportions in Darwin's mind. Everything Darwin drew out of the *Beagle* voyage was coloured with wildly adulatory thoughts about the man: about the scope of his heroic travels, his prose style in the *Personal Narrative,* his diverse scientific and artistic attainments, and the recollection of his power to fire the imagination of a Cambridge undergraduate. Darwin's *Journal,* such as it was, caught up and crystallised Humboldt's long-term effect on him.

Darwin awkwardly tried to convey something of this in his covering letter, expressing the hope that Humboldt might be coming to the British Association meeting in Birmingham in September so that he might meet him there. All his recent achievements and bravado deserted him; and he was suddenly shy, desperately wanting Humboldt to like his book for its own sake. He worried about looking foolish, especially since he did not know him except through his writings. And he was obliged to write in English, another embarrassment, despite his German lessons. Apart from everything else, there was symbolic *frisson* in the gift, a moment of historical aptness where one traveller paid tribute to another. He sent off his parcel to Prussia in trepidation.

Humboldt's highly laudatory reply consequently electrified him. The grand old man behaved just as grand old men were expected to behave, and warm congratulations poured from his pen like honey, praising Darwin's "excellent and admirable book."[31] Even allowing for continental forms of flattery, he was noticeably impressed, and he asked all kinds of detailed questions. But of course the flattery was the most welcome thing. "You told me in your kind letter that, when you were young, the manner in which I studied and depicted nature in the torrid zones contributed towards exciting in you the ardour and desire to travel in distant lands. Considering the importance of your work, Sir, this may be the greatest success that my humble work could bring. Works are of value only if they give rise to better ones. . . . You have an excellent future ahead of you." Humboldt went on to call Darwin's descriptive passages "happily inspired": Darwin was an "eloquent interpreter" of nature's facts. More than this, Humboldt claimed to judge impartially, valuing strength of intellect, solid and wide knowledge, and a felicitous literary disposition. "On all these counts, Sir, you rank high in my estimation." In Darwin, he recognised a major talent at work. Almost as an afterthought he asked Darwin to pass on his appreciation to Captain FitzRoy for these "fruits of his noble and courageous expedition."[32]

Darwin's spirits soared. Reading and rereading the letter soothed away many of his hidden doubts, not so much about his scientific results, although it was good to have Humboldt's detailed remarks and suggestions, nor really in relation to his writing style or the general approach to nature, which he could hardly change now. He understood the European tendency to exaggerate: "Few things in my life have gratified me more than hearing of his approbation, although I should have swallowed the dose quite as readily if it had been a little less strong: even a young author cannot gorge such a mouthful of flattery." It was more to do with feeling that he was passing a milestone—a sensation of having joined the inner circle of science, his views respected if not always accepted, his work valued as a contribution to the larger sphere he already moved in. He felt appreciated, and it was deeply pleasing.

And a healthy degree of self-interest was never too far behind. Darwin wrote an emollient reply telling Humboldt how he was "a mere amateur naturalist" when he left England and attempting his own flourish of compliments at the end. He was not averse to using Humboldt's remarks to chase Henslow about the Galápagos plants either. The main fault of the *Journal,* according to Humboldt, was the absence of any detailed botanical descriptions. "Do think once again of making one paper on the Flora of these islands," Darwin asked Henslow. "I do not think there will often occur opportunities of drawing up a monograph of more interest.—If your descriptions are frittered in different journals, the general character of the Flora will never be known, & foreigners, at least, will not be able to refer to this & that journal for the different species."[33] Henslow's descriptions of a single genus of cactus (*Opuntia*) and a few Keeling Island plants, an overall total of thirteen pages in two popular natural history magazines, were not good enough for a man who corresponded with Humboldt.[34]

V

Darwin's *Journal* in fact made him famous. The reviews were in the main extremely favourable, the romance of the *Beagle*'s travels in the far south and the Fuegian project capturing Victorian imaginations far and wide. William Henry Smyth, an explorer in his own right, complimented Darwin on his "fund of entertaining instruction" in the *United Service Journal*. Captain Basil Hall spoke enthusiastically of the book in the *Edinburgh Review,* quoting some of Darwin's geological results approvingly. William Broderip went further in the *Quarterly:* Darwin was a "first-rate landscape-painter with a pen," whose science provided "ample materials for deep thinking" and whose vivid descriptions "fill the mind's eye with brighter pictures than a painter can present." The *Journal,* Broderip suggested generously, was evidently written by "a strong intellectual man and an acute and deep observer."[35]

None of these reviewers was quite as keen on FitzRoy's contribution. Hall passed over the captain's volumes rapidly in order to praise Darwin's; and his throwaway line suggesting that FitzRoy's chronometric results could only be approximations was perhaps designed to cut to the quick. He pointedly ignored FitzRoy's deluge chapter in favour of a long extract from Darwin's account of the geological origins of the Patagonian plains.[36] Broderip took a different tack, and sarcastically congratulated FitzRoy for taking Darwin along with him. The captain, he wrote, ought to stick to his naval duties and not go into geology. "On this subject the gallant captain has got quite beyond his depth—but we content ourselves with this protest, and a strong advice to read Sir John Herschel's *Discourse on the Study of Natural Philosophy* before he ventures again in the same direction." And Smyth (politely refusing to name FitzRoy in person) devoted a substantial portion of his review to criticising literal views of biblical history.[37] It must have been galling for FitzRoy to find himself overlooked and undermined in this fashion. He had no wish to become known merely as the person who took Darwin round the world—a fate which seemed even then almost inevitable.

Henry Colburn did his best for both of them in the *New Monthly Chronicle,* a magazine conveniently owned and edited by him. Publisher's hyperbole came naturally to him. FitzRoy's *Narrative* was "beyond any question, the most valuable nautical and scientific work that has been given to the public for years." There was something for everybody: "to the scientific geographer and practical seaman, its value is measureless; to the geologist it suggests new theories, while strengthening the old; to the physiologists it affords the most ample details of imperfectly-known districts and unfamiliar objects; to the statist, a real body of facts hitherto unrecorded; and to the philosopher, a full account (amongst others) of tribes whose very stature and dimensions have been, until now, matter of dispute among travellers, and of a whole people purely aboriginal, and still intact in their native barbarity."

Only one review hit a sour note. An anonymous article in the *Athenaeum* took issue with Darwin's geological speculations. The reviewer was probably Samuel Pickworth Woodward, a geologist at the British Museum. He thought Darwin was too speculative, displaying "a spirit of bold generalization, of which the world, not without justice, is exceedingly mistrustful." Many of Darwin's theories were based on inadequate facts, he said. There seemed no reason, for example, for Woodward to accept Darwin's assertion that the dust in the air on St. Jago came from Africa; nor any reason to think his interpretation of the Andes' geological structure was anything more than an "exceeding bold speculation." If Darwin's suggestion was correct, the reviewer went on, at least a million years must have elapsed since ocean waves washed the feet of the Cordillera. The impossibility of this was obvious, he heavily implied.[38]

Undaunted, Darwin remained quietly pleased with himself. "The success of this my first literary child always tickles my vanity more than that of any of my other books," he wrote at the end of his life.[39] Moreover he was amused to see other authors capitalising on this perceived market with a flood of personal journals and "incidents of travel." At last, Erasmus conceded, he would have to stop saying that Darwin had never properly been abroad.

Other, subtler acknowledgements drifted into Darwin's professional life. People started asking his advice about natural history collections: how to collect and pack materials, what to look for, and what the London museums might be most interested in. Darwin advised Sir Thomas Livingstone Mitchell on the most desirable geological features to look out for when exploring the Blue Mountains in Australia during 1839 and identified rock samples for him on one of Mitchell's visits to England.[40] Before long, he was invited to help the Royal Society committee which was drawing up recommendations for research projects during Sir James Clark Ross's naval expedition, the first and greatest scientific survey of the Antarctic ice pack, that left Britain in 1839 and returned in 1843. The Royal Society's panel of experts compiled lists of requirements covering all scientific fields, and these were eventually published in pamphlet form. Darwin's *Journal* appeared in the list of recommended texts (the expedition's scientists were to give it their "attentive perusal"), and his and Lyell's personal influence was seen in the request for observations on elevated land, uplifted terraces, and erratic blocks. Specific instructions from Darwin included the need to check the white band of rock on the island of St. Jago and to compare the structure of St. Paul's Rocks with "Mr Darwin's account." Darwin also advised zoologists on board to collect floating marine mollusca and cephalopods by using dragnets, and at all times to dissect the living organisms.[41] One young medical man due to sail with Ross was Joseph Dalton Hooker, the son of William Hooker, the director of Kew Gardens. Hooker met Darwin in the street by accident (they were stiffly introduced by Robert McCormick, the *Beagle*'s former surgeon, who was recommissioned onto the Ross expedition or "palmed off on Ross," as Hooker put it) and was thrilled to be able to say how much he had benefitted from Darwin's *Journal*. Lyell's father had lent him the proof sheets in Scotland: Hooker slept with them under his pillow so that he would not lose any time in getting at them again in the morning. He hoped to be like Darwin, he ambitiously told his father.[42]

Scientific articles began arriving for Darwin to referee for publication in the same way as Sedgwick had reported on Darwin's study of Glen Roy earlier in the year. In part Darwin moved into this mutual circuit of reviewing and being reviewed because of his position as secretary of the Geological Society. But even when he retired from that position in February 1841 he was still a figure to reckon with, decidedly brisker than Sedgwick when given the opportunity to comment on other men's work. He displayed few of Sedgwick's professorial meanderings. One geological manuscript sent to him for assessment by William Shoberl, the senior publishing assistant to Henry Colburn, received a very curt analysis. The book, said Darwin, will never be highly esteemed by "*really* scientific men.... In order that a work of this nature should become of *authority* the author's name should be known as having worked in the department of science treated of, which is not the case in this instance."[43]

He similarly found it easier to ask for scientific favours. In geological terms, he was glad to be introduced to John Malcolmson, for example, a garrulous Scottish doctor on leave from the Madras Medical Establishment. Darwin asked Malcolmson many questions about Indian coral reefs, the elevation of coastlines in that region, the identity of the plants on the sand dunes of Coromandel, and fossil shells, and gathered from him the names of other people playing significant roles in the intellectual life of colonial India. Actually, Malcolmson proved too talkative once he got going. He was useful, though, in relation to Glen Roy, declaring himself a convert to Darwin's point of view and describing some other terraces around Strath Peffer spa.

Darwin wrote to William Henry Smyth, his reviewer in the *United Service Journal,* for a description of an otherwise unreported coral atoll. He got his answer. In November he tried exerting a little patronage of his own by asking William Hallowes Miller at Cambridge whether he would publish some of Bartholomew Sulivan's meteorological observations taken after the *Beagle* voyage had ended. Stealthily he prompted Miller with the information that Humboldt thought any fresh observations in the same parallel of latitude would be of great scientific interest.

And he made a special effort to go to the September meeting of the British Association for the Advancement of Science in Birmingham. This was an annual week-long event for the nation's "savants" which moved each year from city to city promulgating an attractive mix of reports on recent research, news of technological innovations, visits to places of interest, and plenty of opportunity for local worthies to mix with the best of British science and their wives and daughters.[44] All Darwin's scientific friends were there, most of them in some position of importance or another: Lyell, Horner, and Henry de la Beche were vice-presidents of the geological section, and Buckland was president; Whewell was the president of mathematics and physical science; Owen was the president of zoology and botany. Darwin himself was one of the three secretaries of the geological section. Peacock, Babbage, Herschel, and Murchison appeared on the high table in their role as founders and advocates for the Association. William Darwin Fox and Mrs. Fox were among the audience (more than fourteen hundred tickets were sold). But Humboldt was absent.

During this meeting, Darwin put himself forward for one of the British Association's committees on a subject not usually associated with him so early in his scientific career. Under the aegis of the two most prominent ethnologists of the age, James Cowles Prichard and Thomas Hodgkin, who both delivered impassioned speeches on aborigines at the meeting, this committee proposed the preparation of a standardised set of questions for travellers to answer about the primitive races they might encounter. Mankind, they proposed, could be viewed through these means as "an object of natural history."[45] Although Prichard and Hodgkin had their own philosophical and practical axes to grind, notably a crusade to protect the indigenous inhabitants of British colonies following on from the foundation of the Aborigines Protection Society in 1837 by Hodgkin,[46] Darwin's warm identification with the Fuegians encountered on the *Beagle,* his abhorrence of slavery, and his underlying admiration for the missionaries he met, as well as his public persona as a world traveller, easily persuaded him to join this committee. His naval experience was a help; his interest in circulating printed questions was already established.

The committee was awarded £5 for its labours and asked to present its questionnaire at the next meeting in 1840, which it did. Darwin's role in the process was no doubt small, but it was recognisable: several of the questions running through his species notebooks reemerged virtually unchanged on the printed forms. Which parental characteristics predominate in the offspring of mixed marriages? he asked. Is the mixed form permanent or does it revert? What is the proportion of the sexes at birth and among adults? Do primitive races keep any domestic animals, and "whence do they appear to have been derived?" Are the natives friendly? he continued. Do they practice infanticide? Are they polytheists?

These questions were printed and circulated during 1840, and reprinted in the British Association's reports for 1840 and 1841. Hodgkin masterminded its distribution overseas, using the facilities of the Colonial Office, the British Museum, the Royal Geographical Society, and other scientific bodies both foreign and local. Over the next five years he regularly reported the information that had been received.[47] Because none of these questionnaires appear in the Darwin archive, Darwin's early role in anthropological affairs has mostly gone unrecognised.

VI

Visiting Shrewsbury briefly after the British Association meeting, Darwin immediately searched out Prichard's *Researches into the Physical History of Man* and read as much as he could of the third edition (1837). He was impressed by Prichard's argument that human aborigines had mostly been exterminated by other races who had invaded their territory. This view was "profound," he said, important in relation to domestic breeds of animals, as well as reflecting what he remembered vividly from his experiences with General Rosas and the Araucanian Indians.[48] Prichard's writings suggested many other intriguing avenues to explore, each carefully noted by Darwin at the end of the volume. For a long time now he had wondered if human races might have diverged from a common ancestor because of some kind of differential resistance to disease and internal parasites. He hoped his new connection with an anthropological questionnaire would bring him his answers.

The year, he thought, had been very good for enjoying the sensation of achievement. He had a house, a wife, and a child on the way. He had a book and a rising position in scientific society. The overall vision of himself that he attempted to pull out of the *Beagle* experience was emerging satisfyingly complete. With the *Journal*'s publication he had become an established figure in English science.

MAN OF PROPERTY

HE baby was born in December 1839, a boy they decided to call William Erasmus in honour of a succession of ancestral William Darwins from Lincolnshire, and Darwin's brother. Emma's mother guessed quite wrong when she said he was bound to be named Robert. In the event, Darwin had spent several idle days during visits to Shrewsbury rooting through his father's collection of old family papers and afterwards wrote to Fox and to his sister Susan for further information about "our most ancient family." He wanted to have a seal made out of the family crest (three cockle shells) with the correct motto underneath, neither of which he could quite call to mind. Dr. Darwin was touched by his interest, which he secretly shared, and took the opportunity to give Darwin an old ivory box belonging to William Darwin of Cleatham, who died in 1682. "The pedigrees want filling up terribly; so ancient a family ought not to be neglected," Darwin told Fox, sure of a sympathetic ear. "Hensleigh Wedgwood made a curious discovery regarding our august family, which I must tell you, that a W. Darwin, my great grandfather, is described in the Phil. Transacts for 1719, as a person of curiosity, who discovered the remains of a giant, evidently an Icthyosaurus,—so that *we* have a right of hereditary descent to be naturalists & especially geologists."[1]

Darwin's pleasure in genealogy was more than a passing fad, although like many devotees he was really only interested in his direct family background. He liked excavating the Darwin line (hardly bothering with his maternal Wedgwood side) and expressed a wish to visit the old estates when he could. Something of his species work eased into these genealogical concerns as well, the two topics reflecting an interest in origins and lineages that was as readily applied to family history as it was to animals and plants. On the threshold of becoming a father himself, Darwin indulged in the commonplace activity of wondering whom the baby would be like and contemplating the chain of birth and death linking the family to history and the future.

Three or four days before Emma gave birth, he became ill with bad headaches and unspecified stomach problems. The coming baby was at least partly to blame: he found childbirth "a horrid affair at best." Emma's sister, who came up to London to help, had more on her hands than she had bargained for. "What an awful affair a confinement is," he moaned helplessly: "it knocked me up almost as much as it did Emma herself."[2] With no form of anaesthesia other than alcohol or morphine available for Emma's labour pains, the process was, no matter how routine or uncomplicated the delivery, bound to upset Darwin. His imagination made the occasion far worse than Emma herself considered it. Six babies further on, Darwin seized on the chance to use chloroform, administring it himself to Emma, and keeping her completely insensible, as he said, during the entire delivery, though he thought he was only relieving the pains.[3] It was a help to other people as well. "I was perfectly convinced that the chloroform was very composing to oneself as well as to the patient."[4]

But he was delighted and more full of wonder about their ensuing child than he had ever anticipated: the baby was a little prince, he crowed to Thomas Eyton in Shrewsbury, a great departure from the days when he told Fox that babies were "crying little wretches." Quickly abandoning the pompous label of William, they nicknamed him "Hoddy-Doddy" or "Doddy."

Darwin threw himself into his new situation wholeheartedly, surprising the rest of the family with his powerful fatherly affections and demonstrative behaviour. He was lavishly fond of his "little animalcule of a son," not afraid to hold him in his arms, kiss, or bathe him, quite unlike the usual idea of withdrawn or mysteriously absent Victorian fathers. Actually, the rush of sentiment he felt for William caught him unawares. Like many Englishmen he mostly showed emotion only when dealing with animals. "It is a great advantage to have the power of expressing affection," said Emma gratefully; "and I am sure he will make his children very fond of him."[5]

Darwin was well prepared to make the most of changed circumstances and started observing William's daily progress from the combined perspective of father and scientist. By now he could hardly experience anything in life without turning it to his own account, jotting it down for future analysis in the light of evolutionary theory. Perhaps his feelings did not seem properly real until he recorded them; or perhaps he could express his strongest passions only with written words rather than spoken ones. Certainly, very little passed through his mind without being captured by pen and ink. His mental life had become a collection of papers crammed into the drawers of his desk; his idea of living was already metamorphosing into the solitary act of writing it down.

A first baby was an obvious candidate for devoted attention, and William fascinated him on all counts. Inevitably, Darwin opened another notebook, this time an elegant vellum-covered pocketbook owned by Albert Way and probably left behind after his call at Gower Street about the Glen Roy drawing. "During first week," Darwin wrote proudly, William "yawned, streatched himself just like old person—chiefly upper extremities—hiccupped—sneezes, sucked, surface of warm hand placed to face seemed immediately to give wish of sucking, either instinctive or associated knowledge of warm smooth surface of bosom.—Cried & squalled, but no tears."[6]

On the eighth day William frowned; on the ninth he appeared to follow a candle with his eyes. Darwin closely watched the way he cried until he began to think that "squalling" was quite different from weeping tears. Tears, he tentatively suggested in his notebook, were secondary. The characteristic feature of real crying was a squarish, wide-open mouth associated with great heaves of the chest. Holding William up high in his arms to get a good look before passing him over to Emma, Darwin tried to catch the pattern of outraged wrinkles around his eyes.

Thereafter the boundaries between doting parent and ostensibly impartial observer crashed to the ground. Every sign of William's progress pleased Darwin in both the personal and scientific sense. The magic of human development captivated him as easily as any other eager father. "He is a prodigy of beauty & intellect. . . . I defy anybody to flatter us on our baby—for I defy anyone to say anything in its praise of which we are not fully conscious."[7] Writing to Fox to congratulate him on the birth of his first son, he said to give the boy a kiss—"that is if you are as fond of kissing babies as I am. Some fathers are more cleanly in their tastes."

Nevertheless, Darwin's purpose in making such attentive observations was undeniably utilitarian. He wanted William to reveal how human expressions and behaviour—and humans themselves—originated in animal ancestors. What was instinctive, he asked himself, and what was learned? William could have been a puppy or an infant monkey for all that Darwin distinguished between them: he was fascinated precisely because he could see how all three were similar in many respects. So he felt no compunction about making use of his family as scientific resources, of turning the children into facts. Ingeniously, he discovered a part of Victorian daily life to investigate that other scientists ignored. The natural history of babies, he decided, was essential to his proposals about evolution.

II

Not long afterwards, Darwin sank into a form of chronic ill health, feeling nauseated most of the time and suffering recurrent headaches; these were interspersed with bouts of actual vomiting and periods of unaccustomed debility. His symptoms were more intense and prolonged than those of the illnesses of the previous year. After six or eight weeks, he cried in despair, he thought they would go on forever.

Again, the baby was a part of it. Darwin worried tremendously about the responsibilities of being a father and husband—suddenly enmeshed in the predictable web of changing priorities, agitated about the money needed to support a family and what he ought to do about the future. He was furthermore beset with anxieties about keeping up with his publication schedules and the magnitude of the other tasks he set himself. There seemed little time for anything except work, and the more he tried to do, the less he managed. "Is it not mortifying, it is now nine weeks since I have done a whole day's work, & not more than four half days." A breakdown in his health seemed imminent. He was tired and depressed. "What detestable cold weather it has been of late," he complained to Jenyns. "It has been killing me by inches."

In February and March 1840, Darwin sought Henry Holland's medical opinion, recording the fee for three separate consultations in his account book. Holland identified Darwin's stomach as the direct enemy but told him the root of his troubles lay elsewhere. "His stomach rejects food continually," Maria Edgworth reported to her half-sister after a visit to London at this time, "and the least agitation or excitation brings on the sickness directly so that he must be kept as quiet as it is possible and cannot see any body."[8]

Holland probably diagnosed Darwin as a dyspeptic patient, a term of specialised usage in nineteenth-century medicine some distance away from its original meaning of upset stomach. For Holland and other early-Victorian doctors, the category of dyspepsia included marked physical weakness, loss of appetite, and most particularly a depression of spirits: what was generally called "nervous indigestion." Holland believed dyspepsia was aggravated by the patient's paying too much attention to his or her stomach (a "constant and earnest direction of the mind to the digestive organs"), and recommended various kinds of mental distraction: a tour on the Continent perhaps, or a new hobby or diversion.[9] If that proved ineffective, he dosed people with mercurous oxide—in the form of either calomel or the ubiquitous "blue pill" of British medicine boxes, an opium-based mixture which had a stimulating and usually purgative effect on the intestines and liver. Rattling his blue pills gloomily after his consultation, Darwin cautiously said, "Dr Holland thinks he has found out what is the matter with me, & now hopes he shall be able to set me going again."

Dispirited, he tried to resign from the post of secretary of the Geological Society on the grounds of ill health, only to find that the council was prepared to bend all the rules to keep him. He could come to meetings whenever he could manage, they told him: an unwelcome compromise for Darwin that meant he might legitimately miss the majority of society functions but would still have to work at official correspondence from his study at home. Much as he enjoyed being a public figure of sorts, these professional ambitions were already showing signs of being satisfied. He was coming to view this and the other positions he subsequently held as a duty rather than an opportunity to mould contemporary opinion or to participate in the inner politics of science. He was starting to appreciate the benefits of letting others carry out the necessary social functions of a scientist for him.

Early in April he gave up completely and travelled to Shrewsbury for his father's advice. He went on his own. Straight away he started to feel better, at least well enough to joke with Emma about his travelling companions in the train. They included an elegant female, "who pulled out of her pocket a religious tract in a black cover, & a very thick pencil—she then took off her gloves & commenced reading with great earnestness & marking the best passages with the aforesaid thick lead-pencil.—Her next neighbour was an old gentleman with a portentously purple nose, who was studying a number of the Christian Herald, & his next neighbour was the primmest she-Quaker I have often seen.—Was I not in good company? I never opened my mouth & therefore enjoyed my journey."[10] He was less successful in his travelling companions in the stagecoach from Birmingham to Shrewsbury. Rashly, Darwin pretended not to recognise Mr. Hunt, whom he and Emma knew as "an indomitable proser." The appearance of Mrs. Hunt put paid to that. "I shook hands with vast surprise & interest, & opened my eyes with astonishment at Mr. Hunt, as if he had dropped from the skies."

Dr. Darwin had discouragingly little to say about Darwin's illness except that he could take as much calomel as he wanted and should keep "absolutely quiet." Under his care, the vomiting stopped. Since Dr. Darwin was not the kind of man to exaggerate every stomach complaint into a major threat, his son was reassured that he would certainly "get quite well." Even Darwin was not melodramatic enough to think that he was dying.

Indeed, Dr. Darwin did not seem at all perturbed, although he found Darwin's condition as difficult to diagnose as Holland had. He may have wondered a little about typhoid fever—calomel was a favoured treatment for the internal problems which usually followed this disease, itself very difficult for doctors to recognise in its late stages and variable in its course.

Typhoid (enteric or gastric fever), as Victorian doctors knew, was typified by an insidious fever of uncertain duration, after which ulcerated patches appeared in the small intestine; subsequently patients were liable to relapse or experienced long-continued trouble with their stomach and bowels. These symptoms were recognisably different from typhus (gaol fever), with which typhoid was nevertheless often confused. In most cases the course of typhoid was marked by headaches and lassitude, sometimes a weak pulse, vomiting, and heart problems. Fatigue could bring the symptoms on again in susceptible persons. Perhaps Darwin experienced an attenuated form of the initial fever in London and then was prone to relapses, not a "carrier" in modern terms (someone who remains healthy), but never quite fully recovered.

Knowing his son rather better than the rest, Dr. Darwin at least recognised the stress he was undergoing and the self-absorbed manner in which it was expressed. "I was very well yesterday & today am looking so well," Darwin confessed, "that my father owned, he should not have known if I had been a new face, there was anything the matter with me." However, the doctor's diplomatic turn of phrase was replaced later on with brisker words. "I told him of my dreadful numbness in my finger ends, & all the sympathy I could get, was 'yes yes exactly—tut-tut, neuralgic, exactly yes yes'—nor will he sympathise about money, 'stuff & nonsense' is all he says to my fears of ruin & extravagance."[11]

The doctor did, however, weigh Darwin, something he always did when any of the family were at home, turning it into a diagnostic aid on which he placed great reliance: he possessed a sophisticated weighing machine that normally served his medical practice, and also a "weighing book" for all the patients measured since he first came to Shrewsbury. Darwin weighed in at ten stone eight pounds (148 pounds). He had lost a lot over the previous year, nearly ten pounds since 1839, and some eighteen pounds since his return from the voyage. He was thinner than Erasmus, he told Emma in surprise. Susan—still unmarried and acting as Dr. Darwin's housekeeper—consequently bustled around providing recipes for substantial puddings for him to take back to London. She promised to fill any jars Emma wanted to send with good strong country jam.

Darwin returned to London after his week of fresh air and family attention feeling considerably better: so much better that he accepted an offer to join the council of the Royal Geographical Society. Within the week, putting aside their usual excuse of indisposition, he took Emma to one of Babbage's evening parties. Soon afterwards they saw the Lyells and the Horners: by then all the Horners, except perhaps unmarried Katherine, had completely forgiven him; and Leonard Horner was a good friend for many years afterwards. The activities continued with a visit in May from Emma's Aunt Jessie and her husband, Sismondi, arriving from Geneva. The Darwins held a scientific dinner party for them in Upper Gower Street which included Alphonse de Candolle, also from Geneva, the son of Augustin de Candolle and a good botanist, and the Henslows.[12]

But the excitement, if it can be called that, was too much, and in June Darwin's sickness returned. He nearly despaired, thinking he would have to pass his whole life as a "miserable useless valetudinarian." This time Emma acted decisively and took the whole family to Maer, while her aunt and uncle stayed on in the house in Gower Street. Emma had not been feeling too well herself and suspected she was pregnant again: the unmistakable signs of morning sickness had begun as soon as William was weaned. Each member of the family needed looking after, she thought. Her sister Elizabeth was the one to do it.

Darwin's illness kept them at Maer for the whole summer and on through the autumn into November 1840. Emma anxiously recorded his symptoms in her diary: "C. trembling, cold fit, sick several times, faintness, numbness & shaking." Other times he was "languid." Without doubt she was concerned. There was nothing, she thought ruefully, that "marries one so completely as sickness."[13] During this illness she began to map out the emotional morass that was to become Darwin's continued ill health. Her natural inclination to look after the ones she loved escalated quickly towards taking on the role of his nurse and protector; and she was kind-hearted and probably overindulgent, since several members of the family said how much they liked being nursed by her.

With Darwin and Emma, however, the ill health became inextricably tangled up with the other emotions they came to feel for each other. Darwin needed her tender attentions most obviously when he was unwell, hardly at all when he felt spry enough to go to his clubs and societies, and she evidently found it easiest showing her feelings through sympathetic activity around the sickbed. Neither of them was particularly demonstrative, and there were few other fully acceptable routes to express affection available to them in the period. Illness bound them together as little else could do—Emma could not, and did not wish to, participate in Darwin's scientific or public work any more than Darwin wanted her to; their cultural interests divided them as much as they united; and neither displayed any passion for political or philanthropic causes. Both of them were used to curbing the outward expression of strong emotion. A kind of professional bad health therefore served as a ready avenue for them to say the things they needed to hear. In Darwin and Emma's case, the roles were cast from the start. One was a perpetual patient, the other a devoted nurse. "It is a great happiness to me when Charles is most unwell that he continues just as sociable as ever, and is

not like the rest of the Darwins who will not say how they really are," Emma
wrote to her Aunt Jessie; "but he always tells me just how he feels and never
wants to be alone, but continues just as warmly affectionate as ever, so that I
feel I am a comfort to him."[14] These feelings were reciprocated by Darwin.
"My own dear wife, I cannot possibly say how beyond all value your
sympathy & affection is to me.—I often fear I must weary you with my
unwellness & complaints." Piteously, he signed himself "Your poor old
husband."[15]

At Maer, Darwin used his time on the sofa effectively, reading his way
through the Wedgwoods' family library and arguing about mental philosophy with Hensleigh. When he felt sufficiently well, he walked around the
vegetable gardens and plantations, eager to follow up his inquiries into
cultivated plants and animals. Nicest of all, he discovered bees. Lying in the
banks of wild thyme out on Maer heath, he watched wild bees moving from
flower to flower. He knew they were collecting nectar to make into honey—
many of Uncle Jos's neighbours kept hives for that very purpose. But they
were also carrying pollen on their legs and fur, the unwitting emissaries in
the process of cross-fertilisation that Darwin believed essential for evolution:
industriously transporting the grains of change, he benignly thought.

His theories of plant reproduction, he soon realised during these summer
investigations, were far too simplistic. Even the most ordinary garden plants
presented intricate mutual adaptations between insects and flowers. The
wild thyme, for instance, when he examined it closely, revealed structural
adaptations in its sexual filaments which suggested it was sometimes
hermaphroditic and sometimes female, depending on the season. The male
parts, Darwin noticed, spontaneously shrivelled up and died at the point of
changeover: was this possible? he wrote to Henslow. If it was, he had
stumbled on a fascinating aspect of the sexual life of plants. He put down
question after question in his notebook for further investigation.

He passed other pleasant interludes watching William, whose rapidly
developing abilities enchanted him. Into the baby book went details of
William's first smile, his vaccination against smallpox, his curiosity in seeing
himself in a mirror, and, in triumph, his first word: "poor."

Unable to resist the temptation, Darwin also carried out experiments on
him in relation to his theories. He sneezed unexpectedly close to the baby
and made him cry. For an hour afterwards every noise made William flinch.
"I think he certainly has an undefined instinctive fear," Darwin recorded
complacently. Another day, Darwin issued a loud snoring noise which also
made William cry. "This is curious considering the wondrous number of
strange noises, & stranger grimaces I have made at him & which he has
always taken as a good joke. I repeated the experiment."

A drawing of the Geological Society in session. Darwin joined the Society as soon as he got back, and became its secretary in 1838.

(Geological Society of London)

The museum at the Royal College of Surgeons, where Richard Owen worked. This scene shows skeletons of the Mylodon (left) and Glyptodon (right), two species of extinct South American animals that Darwin collected.

(Illustrated London News)

The Athenaeum Club, where Darwin read the newspapers and worked in the library on evolution.

(Illustrated London News)

Charles Lyell, Darwin's lifelong
scientific friend.

(Wellcome Institute Library, London)

Richard Owen discussed all
kinds of natural history topics
with Darwin and identified the
Beagle fossils.

(Wellcome Institute Library, London)

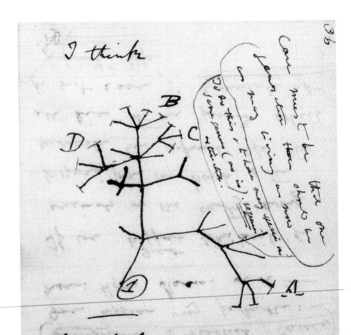

A page from Darwin's notebooks
showing his first ideas about evolution.

(Darwin collection, courtesy of the Syndics
of Cambridge University Library)

(*top*) Observations at London Zoo helped connect human and animal behaviour.

(T. H. Shepherd, *World's Metropolis* 1857. Wellcome Institute Library, London)

(*bottom*) The parallel roads of Glen Roy, in Scotland, were a geological puzzle Darwin tried to solve. The drawing is by his friend Albert Way.

(*Philosophical Transactions* 1839, courtesy of the Syndics of Cambridge University Library)

(*top*) "Marry [or] Not Marry. This is the Question."

(*left*) Emma Wedgwood. Darwin only plucked up courage to propose several months after deciding to get married. By George Richmond.

(*above*) Maer Church, where Darwin and Emma were married in January 1839. A watercolour by Emma's younger sister Frances.

Darwin and his eldest child, William. From a daguerreotype dated August 1842.

(Darwin collection, courtesy of the Syndics of Cambridge University Library)

In 1842 the family moved to Down House in Kent, "very solid throughout, though oldish and ugly."

(Darwin collection, courtesy of the Syndics of Cambridge University Library)

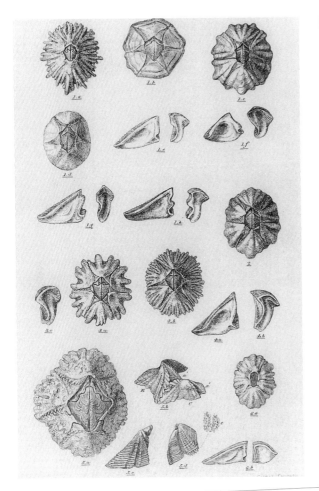

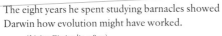

The eight years he spent studying barnacles showed
Darwin how evolution might have worked.
(*Living Cirripedia*, 1851)

(*top right*) Joseph Dalton Hooker became Darwin's
close friend after returning from the Antarctic
exploring voyage captained by James Clark Ross.
(Wellcome Institute Library, London)

Thomas Henry Huxley in 1857.
(L. Huxley, *Life and Letters
of T. H. Huxley* 1900)

(*top right*) Darwin's therapy involved vigorous treatments like this wet-sheet rubbing.

(*above*) Malvern, where Darwin went to try the water cure in 1849.

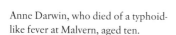

Anne Darwin, who died of a typhoid-like fever at Malvern, aged ten.

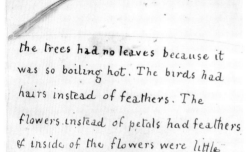

Page 3

A ray of the sun came to the moon & they jumped on the ray & away they slithered up to the sun, when they got to the sun

the trees had no leaves because it was so boiling hot. The birds had hairs instead of feathers. The flowers instead of petals had feathers & inside of the flowers were little grinning faces grinning at you.

Darwin gave his old notes to the children to use as drawing paper. This fairy tale has species notes on its back.

(Darwin collection, courtesy of the Syndics of Cambridge University Library)

Emma Darwin with Leonard in 1854.

(H. Litchfield, *Emma Darwin* 1904)

Darwin joined a pigeon-fanciers' club and went to meetings to learn about selective breeding. Portrayed is the annual show of the Philo-Peristeron Club in 1853.

(*Illustrated London News*)

And when Darwin picked him up from his bath he screamed violently: no doubt the unaccustomed situation, said the offended father, passing him back to the nursemaid. Later in the month Darwin wondered, "How can he find bo-peep amusing?"

The difference between instinctive and learned behaviour became very real as he watched his son grow.

III

When they came back to London in November fortified by their country visit, Darwin felt well enough to defend his geological work from the greatest challenge it had yet received. Ostensibly he only wrote a paper on erratic boulders, the large rocks found in places far from their original source. Yet Darwin's understanding of these rocks hinged on his idea of vast tracts of land once being covered by the sea, as in his South American geology. Louis Agassiz's explanation of erratic boulders was based on a rival theory of glaciers and giant ice sheets, which threatened to sweep aside every one of Darwin's oceans and elevations.

Like Lyell and some other contemporary geologists, Darwin had often wondered how erratic boulders had arrived where they were found. Darwin thought Lyell's suggestion that they were transported long ago as debris on free-floating icebergs was an attractive solution, a solution which had the great advantage of familiarity. Ever since Darwin was a boy in Shrewsbury he had been aware of the large rock, the "bell stone," incongruously situated in the middle of the town; and he remembered being told by an old man that the world would come to an end before anyone explained how it got there. "This produced a deep impression on me and I meditated over this wonderful stone. So that I felt the keenest delight when I first read of the action of icebergs in transporting boulders and I gloried in the progress of geology."[16] Darwin investigated Lyell's suggestion more thoroughly in his *Journal of Researches,* using it to explain the origins of the erratic blocks he saw in the Andes, the Falklands, and elsewhere.

He was stung into thinking about them again by the high excitement stirred up by Agassiz at the Geological Society in November 1840. Then still living and working in his native Switzerland, Agassiz visited Britain that year to study fossil fish in the Scottish Sandstones and to further his new views on glaciers. Taking the early work on ice movements by Charpentier and others as his baseline, Agassiz proposed that glaciers once extended much further than they do today. They were the primary agents in gouging out the huge U-shaped valleys in Switzerland, he asserted, scratching the rocks as they passed, and transporting and depositing stones as they moved inexorably onwards. When they melted they left behind banks of gravel and "till"

—moraines, in the technical vocabulary of geologists. To this, Agassiz added the idea that the Swiss Alps were formerly covered with an enormous ice sheet or *nappe,* which had retreated when the mountains were heaved up into their present form by a cataclysmic elevation. Erratic boulders, he claimed, were carried along on a sea of ice until at last they slipped down the slopes as the mountains rose.

These bold theories galvanised the geological community as never before. Agassiz's notions ran counter to everything British geologists thought about the recent past. British geologists had no need for an ice age when they already possessed adequate explanations based on water; nor did they need a cataclysmic upheaval of the Alps when they already believed these mountains had been in existence many eons before.[17] Lyell, Murchison, Buckland—everyone was involved. Everyone had an opinion.

For himself, Darwin found it hard to envisage glaciers as geological agents in the sense that Agassiz intended, and impossible to conceive of an enormous ice sheet, instead of ocean, formerly stretching out over Europe. Partly he recoiled from allowing a major event like this to feature in recent geological history: everything he valued in science persuaded him that nature worked gradually and in pretty much the same way throughout. Partly he was too far entrenched in his own version of geological history to see any merit in alternatives. His recent work on coral reefs, his *Journal,* his miscellaneous studies published by the Geological Society, and his proposed book were heavily committed to the watery, Lyellian scheme of things. So was his reputation. As he wrote to Lyell around this time, the sea was a much simpler hypothesis. "Floating ice seems to me to account for every thing as well as, and some things better than, the solid glaciers."

Yet Agassiz's enthusiasm for glaciers was readily absorbed by William Buckland. Buckland's "frost-bite," as Murchison called it, took him to Scotland in the autumn of 1840 to see if the drift deposits could be explained by glacier action. Agassiz went with him and showed him how they could. Everywhere they looked they saw Scottish counterparts to the ice-worn rocks and glacier debris of Switzerland. Up in Scotland on his annual holiday, Lyell too was won over to some degree, admitting that the silts and gravel beds near his father's house in Kinnordy were neatly explained by supposing they were glacial moraines. Both Buckland and Lyell announced their new views at a society meeting on 14 November, a meeting that Darwin came back from Maer specially in time to attend.[18] To Darwin's surprise, and then mortification, Buckland went on to say that Glen Roy was not a former arm of the sea, as Darwin had proposed in 1839, and the shelves were not marine beaches. The shelves were instead the remains of an inland lake dammed by a glacier. Darwin's geological life was called into question. The seeds were sown for a strongly worded answer.

Opportunely for Darwin, most of the members of the Geological Society were reassuringly sceptical of the more grandiose elements of Agassiz's theme: Greenough, De la Beche, Whewell, Sedgwick, Hopkins, and Murchison each in his way dissented from the glacier theory; and soon Lyell all but renounced it and returned to the fold. Buckland's eccentricities, on the other hand, made him easy to ignore: one geologist took advantage of the moment to circulate satirical verses about the society's president chatting to a helpful glacial boulder. When Murchison became president in his turn in 1841 he vigorously opposed the ice theory from the top. He had already used some of Darwin's Glen Roy work to supplement his interpretation of the ancient rock formations of Wales in his *Silurian System*.[19] It was a brave or iconoclastic geologist who persisted in going all the way with Agassiz, over the next few years at least.

Darwin decided to attack by reexamining erratic boulders. He had seen many of these rocks in South America and believed they were best explained as having been transported by icebergs floating in a cold and extensive sea: the same sea that he believed once spread over the pampas and Patagonia, and out of which the land emerged in gradual steps. Among a wide range of arguments and observations that he marshalled for his paper, he stressed the simple geographical fact that the rocks' distribution over the Argentine plains coincided with this former waterline. Privately, he tried to dissuade Lyell from flirting with the glacial theory, teasing him about how he, Darwin, was the only one left capable of "out-Lyelling Lyell." The links with his Glen Roy work were clear enough. To Darwin, erratic boulders meant icebergs, icebergs meant seawater, and seawater meant elevated beaches. He emphatically rejected an ice dam in Glen Roy. "I think," he told Lyell sententiously, "I have thought over whole case without prejudice & remain firmly convinced they are marine beaches."[20] He closed his ears when Buckland praised ice dams in his valedictory presidential address in February 1841.

Under it all he was shaken. "My marine theory for these roads," he told Fox, "was for a time knocked on the head by Agassiz's ice-work."[21] How far were his other theories likely to be undercut by things he had not thought of?

IV

The Darwins' next child was born in March 1841, this one a girl they called Anne Elizabeth. Once again Darwin was a "poor weak wretch," and once again they set out for Maer in the early summer. Once again he felt driven to resign from his position as secretary to the Geological Society, more successfully on this occasion; and he simultaneously stood down from the council of the Royal Geographical Society after only a year in the post.

As soon as he was safe at Maer, Darwin slipped back into the cosy routines of invalidism with some relief.

This time William was old enough to go with his nursemaid to Shrewsbury for a visit to Dr. Darwin and his aunts Susan and Catherine. Darwin followed a few days afterwards with his manservant Parslow. He wanted medical advice for himself and for William, who had a nasty cough and, it transpired, was being fed half a cup of cream every morning in London. "I will give you [a] categorical account," Darwin wrote to Emma when he arrived, knowing she would want to hear all the details. "First for my old beggarly self":

> I was pretty brisk at first, but about four became bad & shivery—wh ended in sharp headache & disordered stomach (but was not sick) & was very uncomfortable in bed till ten.—I was very very desolate & folorn without my own dear Titty's sympathy & missed you cruelly.—But today I am pretty brisk & enjoy myself. I think my Father looking rather altered & aged, though he & the two old chicks appear very well, & charmingly affectionate to me. Doddy's reception of me was quite affecting—He sat on my knee for nearly quarter of an hour, gave me some sweet kisses, & sniggered & looked at my face & pointing told everyone I was pappa. Everybody seems to like him—they say he is so meek & good.—When I had had him for about five minutes I asked him, where was Mama, & he repeated your name twice in so low & plaintive a tone, I declare it almost made me burst out crying.—He is full of admiration at this new house & is friends with everyone & sits on grandpapa's knees. . . . Dear old Doddy, one could write for ever about him.

Later in the visit William threw Darwin's walking-stick over the edge of the garden into the river and "cried Ta ta with the greatest sang-froid & walked away."

As always, the doctor's prescriptions were to the point: William's "motions are far from right," and he thought Darwin would not become strong again for several years. Darwin told Lyell that "It has been a bitter mortification for me to digest the conclusion that 'the race is for the strong'—and that I shall probably do little more, but must be content to admire the strides others make in science. So it must be, but I shall just crawl on with my S. American work & be as easy as I can," words that sadly echoed his species theory.[22] There was more. Dr. Darwin said the maids ought to wear decent mobcaps and Parslow should get his hair cut.

Seizing the family moment, Darwin asked his father about buying a house. "Macaw Cottage" was becoming a tight squeeze with two infants, a night nursery, a day nursery, assorted helpers, and Brodie, the children's nurse, to accommodate, and the adults were beginning to find London noisy and dirty. Darwin had insufficient capital in his own right to buy the kind of country house he desired. Delicately, he approached Dr. Darwin to see if he could borrow the necessary sum from him. Just like the other Shropshire gentlemen who raised cash from the doctor's private account books, he hoped for a useful financial outcome along with the medicine.

Dr. Darwin was doubtful but soon persuaded. He promised to advance Darwin £3,000 against his future inheritance and would charge him 4 percent interest for the privilege. But he was less authoritative, less certain, in his old age and could not believe Darwin would really buy a house without living in a new area for a few years first. It had taken him five or six years, he reminisced, to make up his mind about Shrewsbury when he came there in 1786.

Impetuously Darwin wrote to Fox telling him they were going to move straight away, a sentiment echoed by Emma in letters to her aunts and sisters. And as soon as they returned to London, rather earlier in the year than usual, they began investigating properties outside London near Windsor and Chobham. "I long to be settled in pure air, out of all the dirt, noise, vice & misery of this great Wen, as old Cobbett called it," Darwin told Fox in September 1841. "I am going to Westcroft (the name of one place) on Friday with a valuer & then mean to make an offer."[23]

He relayed the same news to Lyell, who was on the point of leaving England for a year's tour in North America. Not surprisingly, his friend was dumbfounded. Steeped in metropolitan society life, Lyell thought moving to the country was like going into exile: his own ancestral home was miles from anywhere in Scotland, and he made a point of visiting it only for a few weeks during the summer when nothing was afoot in London. He would miss Darwin hugely. Even though they had never put their bachelor threat about dinners into practice, they did spend many contented hours together at scientific meetings, enjoying the mutual pleasure of seeing things much the same way, gossiping about colleagues, and striking thoughts off each other's glinting intellect. Ordinary social engagements were similarly enlivened by the close feeling between them. "I cannot tell you," wrote Lyell sadly, "how often since your long illness I have missed the friendly intercourse which we had so frequently before & on which I built more than ever after your marriage.—It will not happen easily that twice in one's life even in the large world of London a congenial soul so occupied with precisely the same pursuits & with an independence enabling him to pursue them will fall so nearly in my way, & to have had it snatched from me with the prospect of your residence somewhere far off, is a privation I feel as a very great one—I hope you will not like Herschel get far off from a railway."[24]

Darwin sympathised. But as Lyell said, with a railway close to hand and Erasmus keeping a bedroom free for him in Great Marlborough Street, he anticipated few problems about getting into and out of London. He would do anything rather than stay on in the city.

Feeling decidedly better after his summer away, and with the thought of a move to the country to keep him occupied, Darwin resumed work in the autumn of 1841 on the manuscript of his geology book for Smith & Elder. This time he was determined to crack it. The project had expanded so much since he first proposed it that he had decided some time ago that he could only get through if the book was split into three. The first part, on coral reefs, was almost ready. Drawing up the maps had been the worst job, he thought; maps, and the extraordinary number of sources he consulted to find out the shapes of reefs occurring in different places over the globe. It proved much harder than he had expected to show that reefs genuinely appeared in clusters indicating areas of oceanic subsidence. "This book, though a small one, cost me twenty months of hard work, as I had to read every work on the islands of the Pacific and to consult many charts."[25] No human being would ever read it, he told Emma mournfully. On the contrary, she countered briskly, there was such a rage for geology she hoped for much better things.

At last it was done, and he sent the manuscript to Smith & Elder, his patient publishers, on 3 January 1842, four years after signing the contract. Proofs came and went by May. In his diary he counted up what the manuscript had cost him—and this was still only the first third of his projected geological study. "I commenced this work 3 years & 7 months ago. Out of this period about 20 (besides work during Beagle voyage) has been spent on it & besides it I have only completed the Bird part of Zoology, Appendix to Journal, paper on boulders & corrected paper on Glen Roy & earthquakes, reading on species & rest lost by illness."[26]

The news from Smith & Elder that his government grant was not going to be enough to cover the cost of publishing *Coral Reefs* as well as the rest of his *Zoology* was almost the last straw.

V

But he felt relieved at having finished something. Besides, he was still feeling quite healthy: healthy enough to go to Maer with Emma and the children in 1842 as they usually did in the summer for a month's holiday. If Darwin ever felt energetic during these wearying writing years, he felt it then in the summer of 1842. He had space to breathe and think before the obligations of proceeding with the next section of his geological book, or coming to grips again with the *Zoology*'s unending birds, fish, and reptiles.

Accordingly, while he was at Maer in May 1842, he gave himself the time to write out a brief sketch of his species theory. It had necessarily taken second place while his other tasks pressed into the foreground but never really left his mind; it was the mental landscape in which all his zoological and geological studies were ultimately situated. This time, however, his notebooks had been left at home. His sheaves of annotated papers lay undisturbed in Gower Street. All he had was the precious gift of two or three weeks of uninterrupted quiet.

He made the most of it. Darwin's species sketch poured out of him, page after page of scribbled pencil sentences, arrows and insertions everywhere, each section piling on to the last in a sequence he had been holding in his head for months, ready for the moment of delivery. Always the anxious outsider during Emma's childbirths, this was his own release and triumph.[27]

The resulting text was decidedly garbled, thirty-five folio pages of crabbed, elliptical scrawl. Darwin never considered it anything more than a first chance of setting out his theory as he currently saw it, an opportunity to arrange his thoughts unrestricted by the factual examples methodically collected and stacked far away in London. It was never meant to be read by others, never intended, at the time of writing, as something to use to convince friends or deter enemies.

His plan of attack was, however, clear. He went to considerable trouble to divide the various elements of his argument into a series of steps ascending towards the proposal that species were mutable. In this he believed he was following the rules laid out by Herschel and Whewell in their respective accounts of the correct way to do science: first giving the established facts about nature, followed by an analogy or extrapolation into theory, and then ending with the reasons why he thought his view was correct, or at least a worthwhile hypothesis.[28] So he began by listing the kinds of variation and selection occurring under domestication. Then, in the second section, he described variation in nature, admitting that it was less pronounced than any of the individual cases encountered in farmyards or gardens, but still an acknowledged feature of the natural world. Here he alluded to his own conviction that variations were mostly produced when the reproductive systems of animals and plants were in some way "unsettled" by changing environmental conditions or by different mixtures of species coming together for one reason or another. This, he recognised, was one of his major problems—failing to explain how variations actually occurred. It remained an important gap in his theory, never fully resolved.

By this time Darwin had come to use the expression "natural selection." Imagine a force in nature, he said, analogous to the hand of man in breeding domestic animals. This would be what he called a natural means of selection. "Who, seeing how plants vary in a garden [and] what blind foolish man has done in a few years, will deny [what] an all-seeing being in thousands of years could effect . . . either by his own direct foresight or by intermediate means?"[29]

Malthus's doctrine provided the mechanism for this natural selection. The most vigorous, skilful, or industrious individuals whose instincts are best developed, Darwin wrote, will rear more young, probably young which similarly possess useful qualities, and a greater number of these will survive. Gradually, and assisted by geographical isolation, individuals possessing the most successful adaptations would come to outnumber the rest. After a while they would be so different that they could be called a new species.

Embryology provided a kind of documentation of this ancestral diversification, he thought. As an embryo develops it passes through the approximate line of its life history: first appearing like a fish with gills, then like a reptile with branchiae, and on to a generalised mammalian form. Darwin's information was hazy on this point and his sketch no better. He spent many years afterwards working over this subject to his great advantage. Structural affinities like wings, flippers, and arms, and the existence of rudimentary or abortive organs like nipples in men, looked to him as if they might too confirm some of his views.

Darwin then proceeded to list the major difficulties in accepting these ideas and what he imagined would constitute the chief material contradicting his proposals. His choice was interesting, provocative, and at some point no doubt simultaneously useful and self-serving. The inability of species to cross-breed was one: if hares and rabbits were originally the same animal, how had they become mutually sterile? The origin of a complicated structure like the eye was another. Was animal behaviour inherited? There were no transitional forms in the geological record. There was no evidence of intermediate forms living in the present day. The intricate social structure of ants and bees seemed impossible on an evolutionary scheme. Darwin was apparently as good at spotting difficulties in species as he was on the subject of marriage.

In dealing with all of these questions, he depended heavily on the technique he had developed on the *Beagle* and in the years immediately afterwards. He stood each problem on its head until it was not so much of a problem at all: sterility was not nearly so universal or complete as people supposed, and was merely a by-product of other changes; fossils were so infrequently preserved that of course there would be gaps in the record; every intermediate stage had some other purpose that we can only guess at today; animal habits could be inherited and acted on by natural selection. This emphasis on negative argument was characteristic of all his work. But it was a dangerous game to play, as he later discovered.

Even so, Darwin did not anywhere acknowledge the most obvious and startling objection of all. He never mentioned God, nor mankind's special religious position. His wife's primary objection to his theories—and the objection that he knew would be paramount for close friends like Lyell, Fox, and Henslow—was resoundingly absent. This was surely deliberate, given his extensive philosophising about human beings in his notebooks and the way he built up evolutionary theory from his experiences of primitive races round the world; surely deliberate given his close attention to metaphysical questions and the nature of the human mind. Methodically, Darwin drained his sketch of any real confrontation with such emotive and difficult issues. His talks with Emma had warned him how delicately they needed to be handled.

More pragmatically, he may well have felt unable to provide an adequate answer to Emma's (and perhaps his own) religious difficulties, since he too still believed in some residual divine authority, albeit a God who did not act directly in nature. His easy glide from discussing the soulless forces of natural selection ("wedges") to an anthropomorphised selecting agent comparable to the Creator ("a being infinitely more sagacious than man, not an omniscient creator") suggested deep ambiguities lurking beneath the surface.[30] What Darwin had to say about mankind in his notebooks was almost too blunt, too shocking, for himself, let alone Emma. He had no end of theories about humanity occupying his brain: theories about the origin of language, about morality, religion, and race. But some of these were already overshadowed by confusing information gleaned from books and talks with men like his cousin Hensleigh. Certainly he felt his most workable hypothesis for racial divergence, which depended on differential resistance to disease, was beginning to look untenable, especially since the anthropological questionnaire sent out by Hodgkin a year or two before was not drawing in enough information to make his case. He was not sure what he was going to say about man yet. Taking the safest route out, he did not say anything: his natural caution, insufficient information, unwillingness to hurt his wife and friends, and procrastination reinforced each other effectively. Mankind was left for another time. Perhaps he knew already he would not take it up again unless absolutely forced by circumstances.

VI

With his sketch completed early in June 1842, all the bustle and rush of the last three years receded. In a way, Darwin's tide had symbolically turned. He felt as well as he ever did, his coral work was out of the way, and he had unburdened himself—allowed himself the "satisfaction," he said—of writing out a first draft of his species theory. The future looked busy but not impossible. There was another baby on the way and a country house to view when they returned to London. His botanical work at Maer was producing interesting material.

A sense of release swept in. He felt energetic enough to spend ten days exploring the wilds of Wales in June, leaving Emma and the children comfortably ensconced with Elizabeth at Maer. He went on his own, setting out from Shrewsbury in a gig as on the day he and Sedgwick took to the hills of Clwyd: the first time he had made any kind of geological field trip since tramping through Glen Roy as an unmarried man in 1838, and a diverting return to the scene of his student endeavours. He smiled ruefully at the difference a few years made. The last time he had gone to Capel Curig he had been twenty-one: before the *Beagle,* before Emma, before the transmutation of species. He had a lot to think about while relishing his long-lost activity in the blustery mountain air.

Still, he intended this to be more than an occasion for sentimental reminiscences. He wanted to consider for himself the evidence of former ice action that Buckland insisted was there in Wales for anyone with eyes to see. The glacial debate still raged in London, and Buckland's short essays of 1840 and 1841 had just appeared in the *Proceedings of the Geological Society.* By now Darwin was extremely anxious about the status of his explanation of Glen Roy. Did he depend too much on negative arguments—that the lack of any marine material on the shelves did not upset the hypothesis that they were sea beaches? All through his Glen Roy work—and, as he hazily began to realise, all through his species sketch as well—he asserted that absences cannot falsify. The absence of seashells did not necessarily mean the shelves were freshwater formations, any more than the absence of transitional forms in the fossil record implied that transmutation did not take place. Almost without thinking, Darwin tended to phrase his most original and important arguments in this counter-intuitive style. Agassiz said glaciers had blocked the river in Glen Roy and created a vast freshwater lake which, as it subsided, etched out and left the shelves; and Buckland agreed.[31] Erratic boulders strewn around, piles of gravel, the polished and heavily scratched rock faces: all these apparently supported the claim. Darwin therefore planned to retrace Buckland's route over Snowdonia to Caernarvon and Bangor looking for erratic rocks and glacial remains as he went, still determined to hang on to his marine theory.

In the course of this trip, almost repeating Lyell's experience of the year before, he was converted. But letters to America took too long, nor did Darwin really know where Lyell was, and he wanted to exhale some of his astonished feelings. Excitedly he wrote instead to William Fitton, safely fastened down in Bloomsbury. A volcano could hardly have left more obvious marks, he cried. "Pray if you have any communication with Dr Buckland, give him my warmest thanks for having guided me, through the published abstract of his memoir, to scenes, and made me understand them, which have given me more delight than I almost ever remember to have experienced, since I first saw an extinct crater.—The valley about here, and the Inn at which I am now writing, must once have been covered by at least 800 or 1000 ft in thickness of solid ice! Eleven years ago, I spent a whole day in the valley, where yesterday everything but the ice of the glacier was palpably clear to me, and then I saw nothing but plain water and bare rock."[32]

Nonetheless, Darwin's conversion only went so far. Paradoxically, he thought glacier action could be used to support his theory of icebergs distributing erratic boulders. Instead of seeing glaciers as an all-embracing alternative which required a fundamental reappraisal and possibly the rejection of his life's work—precisely what Agassiz proposed—Darwin acknowledged the glacial phenomena he saw around him by integrating them into his existing interpretation. He did what he customarily did when working on species. Rather than abandon a well-articulated framework, he preferred to rethink and then subsume any anomalous evidence.

In this case, Darwin's tactic also neutralised some of the power of Agassiz's alternative. Darwin considered erratic boulders, Glen Roy, and the species sketch as his intellectual property, so to speak, and he was not going to relinquish them readily. "I am the more pleased with what I have seen in N. Wales," he emphasised to Fitton, "as it convinces me that my views of the distribution of the boulders on the S. American plains having been effected by floating ice are correct. I am also more convinced that the valleys of Glen Roy & the neighbouring parts of Scotland have been occupied by arms of the sea, & very likely (for on that point I cannot of course doubt Agassiz & Buckland) by glaciers also." Confidently, he decided to write another paper when he got home on the effects produced by the ancient glaciers of Carnaervonshire, and on Welsh boulders transported by floating ice.

VII

Towards the end of July 1842, the Darwins' house problem became much more acute. They found London overwhelmingly dirty, crowded, and at times violent. Dickensian London was not a fiction. Of course, the Darwins' worries were distinctly upper-class. There was nowhere suitable for the children to play except for the nearby gardens of Gordon Square, for which they rented a key. Coal dust made the washing black. Horse dung in the streets dirtied their shoes. And Darwin's and Emma's health always seemed better in the country. They wanted grounds and trees of their own, a disease-free cow for the children's milk, and to live in less proximity to the servants. There was more traffic than they had expected in Gower Street.

Soon Darwin took Emma on an overnight trip to see a house situated in Down village in Kent (now Downe), about fifteen or sixteen miles from the centre of London.[33] This more or less met all Darwin's requirements, although it was too far away from a railway station to his liking and was "oldish & ugly." But he was prepared to compromise. The house was a former vicarage of sorts: large, countrified, with fields, rural walks, and fine trees around it. It had plenty of bedrooms and was in relatively good repair. To its great advantage it also came cheap: Darwin estimated the asking price at about £2,200, and told Susan and his father he thought he would be able to rent for a year to begin with.

Yet Emma was unimpressed. She did not like the bare chalky fields up on top of the Downs—the area looked desolate, she said. The views from the principal downstairs rooms were disappointing compared to the scenery of Staffordshire. The day was gloomy and cold, with a northeast wind. She had a toothache and pretty soon a headache too. It was hard to get excited over the field which Darwin repeatedly told her was "a noted piece of Hay-land," worth £2 an acre as a cash crop with no fertiliser put on it in the interval.

However, sitting in the carriage on the way back to London she came round to thinking the country had its charms. She agreed with Darwin that they should try to rent it. She wanted to move before the next baby was born. Otherwise she could foresee having to wait in Gower Street until the following summer.

But she was not particularly bothered when difficulties came up in the negotiations. She preferred the house in Surrey, and, from something her daughter Henrietta said in later life, she may have hoped Dr. Darwin would be more forthcoming with his money now that a purchase was looming. If Darwin had known the true size of his inheritance, Henrietta said, they would have enlarged their choice considerably.[34]

Renting turned out to be impossible, since the vendor's financial embarrassments dictated an outright sale. Darwin therefore rushed the transaction through, becoming friendly with Edward Cresy, the local surveyor and architect who acted on his behalf. By the end of August he owned a substantial property called Down House, and eighteen acres of land. He was about to turn into a Kentish hog, he crowed happily to anyone who would listen.

Emma moved on 14 September, and Darwin went a few days later. She liked the place a good deal better once she was there, he wrote to Catherine Darwin, and "Doddy was in ectsies for two whole days." As for himself, the dominant feeling was one of unmitigated relief. "I feel sure I shall become deeply attached to Down, with a few improvements—it will be very difficult not to be very extravagant there."

Erasmus, who hated the country, declared they ought to call the place "Down-in-the-Mouth."

Unfortunately, the move did not lighten Emma's troubles. Her third child was born on 23 September and lived for only three weeks. She was sadder than she outwardly admitted, confessing quietly to Fanny Wedgwood that she fancied the baby girl had looked like her mother, Bessy Wedgwood, and she hoped might have possessed the same pleasant personality as well. "It will be long indeed," she said, "before we either of us forget that poor little face." They named her Mary Eleanor and buried her in Down churchyard.

At the same time, Emma's father seemed as if he was going to die from a stroke. Hensleigh Wedgwood wrote from Maer to warn them. All the family rallied round, and even Dr. Darwin struggled out in his phaeton to minister to him. The doctor was himself almost an invalid, too frail to cope with seeing his oldest and dearest friend struck down. He broke into tears, Elizabeth told Emma: no one could have been kinder. Soon the physician from the Stoke infirmary politely took over. For a week or two Emma expected to hear of her father's death in every post.

But Josiah Wedgwood hung on for another year, bedridden like his elderly wife, his mental and physical powers virtually gone. Poor Elizabeth, said Emma, was left nursing the two of them, the only role left for a middle-aged spinster daughter. The strain was too much for Hensleigh, juggling his relatives and his own filial feelings. When the emergency was over and he was back in his own house in London, he too collapsed into a long nervous illness.

Hospitably, Emma took his and Fanny Wedgwood's oldest children to stay with her at Down for a month or two, so that Fanny could nurse Hensleigh without interruptions. Her first November in the country therefore filled up with children much bigger and more adventurous than William and Anne. They managed to get lost in the "big woods" nearby, requiring Darwin and Parslow to go hunting for them one evening. They hacked at the chalk outcrops, making their own quarry, and forcing Emma to write to Fanny for some different clothes that "won't mind being whitened all over." And when Ernest, aged five, the youngest Wedgwood there, refused to wear a hand-me-down coat of his brother's, Emma resorted to bribing him with a shilling: a useful trick she kept in reserve for her own offspring when it became necessary. The constant activity helped her get over the baby's death and her father's illness quicker than she had thought possible.

Darwin reacted to these melancholy affairs in the way that was becoming second nature to him: he started working, obliterating grief and his anxieties by throwing himself into his science. Two days before Mary Eleanor died he picked up his geological notes again, intending to bury himself in the second part of his book—or books—for Smith & Elder. The subject was volcanic islands. He had hardly looked at the papers since Covington had copied them out so long ago from his *Beagle* manuscript.

He similarly threw himself into being a country squire. First, he planted flowers, trying to make the place look more like Maer for Emma's sake. He felt happier about this unaccustomed aesthetic move when Erasmus came down from London to discuss the lack of views and performed wonders with artistically arranged sticks for a tree planting plan. Erasmus thoroughly enjoyed telling them about the horrors of his trek out from the metropolis ("Nature abhors a journey of 16 miles almost as much as vacuum"), matched only by the horrors of his expanding tea-party circuit in Bloomsbury. "I console myself for two mortal hours in the garden with a select little seraglio eating oranges and drinking tea. . . . there is no lack of desolate females in the world—I have got Mrs M. [Harriet Martineau's mother] on my hands to take back to Liverpool."[35] Erasmus also brought Darwin the news of Katherine Horner's forthcoming marriage—"which more particularly eases his conscience." In the end she had met and fallen in love with Charles Lyell's brother Henry, a happy solution for all. Undeterred, Darwin resolutely put milk cows into the field and a horse and cart in the stable yard.

Then he started building, extending the drawing room and Emma's bedroom above it as soon as he could in 1843, and afterwards adding a kitchen wing with better accommodation for the servants and a flight of back stairs. He set out the beginnings of a small orchard, soliciting advice from Fox about pear trees and the dangers of apple scab. A kitchen garden was next. He got Isaac Laslett, the useful jack-of-all-trades from the village, to dig him a cesspit behind the cow yard for liquid manure: "I hope to try one cask this spring," he informed his father brightly.

Soon he found the lane running outside the front of the house unpleasantly close; and he arbitrarily decided to move the track further away and have it lowered, a job involving the removal of two feet of earth over a distance of 170 yards. Darwin had the debris made into a bank between the house and road, on top of which he put a wall. "The publicity of the place is at present intolerable," he complained to Susan.

After this, he joined the parish council (the vestry), with a general interest in maintaining the genteel air of rurality which pervaded the village and its surroundings.[36] Unhesitatingly, he got involved in local politics. In particular, he seethed in patrician fashion about "Old Price," who was plotting some "atrocious doings with the village pool," doings which were made worse by the general suspicion that the same Price had secretly moved a fence at night so that his boundary took in part of another man's field. This fence helped Darwin become acquainted with neighbouring gentry, especially Sir John William Lubbock, who lived in the next village on a large estate called High Elms. Lubbock was a noted mathematician and astronomer, a fellow of the Royal Society, as well as the proprietor and working partner of a big banking concern in the City of London. With many mutual interests in European science and the world of high finance, the two relaxed in each other's company by conferring about buckets and the depth of their garden wells.

Indoors, Darwin arranged his study to his liking, with special wooden shelves in an alcove by the fire serving as an impromptu filing cabinet for all his different notes. He hung up pictures of Lyell, his father, and the two grandfathers, put all his books together according to their subject, and installed a mirror beside the window discreetly angled so that he could see who was coming up the drive. The room was his inner sanctum—a gentleman's retreat if ever there was, with dark walls and an enclosed atmosphere making it just the place for retiring to for hours, a smaller version of his rooms in Christ's College, Cambridge, or of the book-clad library in the Athenaeum. One curtained corner hid a lavatory enclosure where he could retch in private.

His habits became more squirelike and predictable too. Grandly, he invited Richard Owen to come and stay for a weekend with his wife and child, whom "our nurses could dress &c. &c." He asked Hugh Falconer, on leave from the East India Company's botanic garden at Saharanpur, to come by the same train. Sympathetically, he arranged for a prepaid fly to wait at Sydenham station for Edward Forbes, who was too poor and too proud to accept any obvious help over transport.

And he kept his snuff jar outside his study in the hall. By now he was severely addicted, and it was but a feeble attempt to reduce his intake: he carried a silver snuffbox in his pocket, for instance, and could usually think of a good reason to walk out into the hall if the box was empty. Sometimes when he was in the drawing room it would occur to him that the study fire must be burning low. The clink of the lid, said Emma, always gave him away.

VIII

Throughout 1843, Darwin worked hard on his volcanic islands and on his house.

In the winter, however, he turned again to his species sketch. He wanted to do it justice, to give the theory the treatment it deserved by incorporating the full range of his researches and spelling out his themes and arguments as persuasively as he could. Like the house, the sketch was his: his idea, his years of thought, his conscientious effort, his to do with as he wished. So far he had kept it secret from everyone except his closest friends and relatives. Even they did not know the full extent of his views or the careful edifice of support he hoped to put together eventually.

So as soon as his volcanic islands book seemed to be nearing a conclusion,

Darwin started enlarging and improving his earlier pencil sketch of 1842. He wrote clearly this time, methodically and comprehensively, covering nearly 230 pages over a period of five or six months.[37] Deliberately, he adopted the manner of a man who knew his words would be read. He tried to convince. He tried to persuade. He marshalled his evidence as effectively as he could. As he wrote, he sensed an audience, imaginary for the most part, but one that he addressed directly. Perhaps he was writing for Lyell or for Erasmus: the two men who he knew would not be unduly shocked at the way his thoughts were going. He may even have been writing for his father, inviting him to look at his son now: to look at what the *Beagle* voyage did for him, for his powers of reasoning and application. Once again he avoided dealing with any of Emma's concerns beyond adding a peroration glorifying the grandeur of an evolutionary view of life. On the contrary, his tone of voice was reassuring, conciliatory: the knowledgeable, persuasive manner of one respectable gentleman scientist persuading another in the smoking room of their London club.

When he finished early in July 1844 he sent the manuscript off to be copied out neatly. But he had no idea what to do with it now: it still seemed too heterodox to publish, still inadequately supported by the evidence he had spent so long collecting, still unfinished in his perfectionist eyes. Seeing it written out like this almost frightened him. He wanted to publish and he did not want to publish. How could he seriously put it before the public and his friends?

Turning to his papers, he wrote Emma the strangest letter of his life.

My dear Emma,
    I have just finished my sketch of my species theory. If, as I believe that my theory is true & if it be accepted even by one competent judge, it will be a considerable step in science.
    I therefore write this, in case of my sudden death, as my most solemn & last request, which I am sure you will consider the same as if legally entered in my will, that you will devote £400 to its publication & further will yourself, or through Hensleigh, take trouble in promoting it.—I wish that my sketch be given to some competent person with this sum to induce him to take trouble in its improvement, & enlargement.—I give to him all my books on Natural History, which are either scored or have references at end to the pages, begging him carefully to look over & consider such passages, as actually bearing or by possibility bearing on this subject.—I wish you to make a list of all such books, as some temptation to an Editor. I also request that you hand over [to] him all those scraps roughly divided in eight or ten brown paper portfolios: the scraps with copied quotations from various works are those which may aid my Editor.—I also request that you (or some amanuensis) will aid in deciphering any of the scraps

which the Editor may think possibly of use.—I leave to the Editor's judgment whether to interpolate these facts in the text, or as notes, or under appendices. . . .

With respect to Editors, Mr Lyell would be the best if he would undertake it: I believe he wd find the work pleasant & he wd learn some facts new to him. As the Editor must be a geologist, as well as naturalist, the next best Editor would be Professor Forbes of London or Mr Lonsdale (if his health wd permit). The next best (& quite best in many respects) would be Professor Henslow. Dr Hooker would perhaps correct the Botanical part—possibly he would do as Editor. The next, Mr Strickland.—Professor Owen wd be very good, but I presume he wd not undertake such a work. If none of these would undertake it, I would request you to consult with Mr Lyell, or some other capable man, for some Editor, a geologist & naturalist.[38]

Should one other hundred pounds make the difference of procuring a good Editor I request earnestly that you will raise £500. . . .

If there shd be any difficulty in getting an editor who would go thoroughly into the subject & think of the bearing of the passages marked in the books & copied out on scraps of paper, then let my sketch be published as it is, stating that it was done several years ago & from memory, without consulting any works & with no intention of publication in its present form.[39]

Reading between the lines was not hard. He would prefer to be dead rather than suffer the controversy which he knew would break over his head. He would prefer to be dead rather than deliberately hurt Emma's feelings, or, even worse, be the cause of her social ostracism. He would prefer someone else to put it before the public: someone else who could carry the argument by force of personality. He recognised that the weightiness of his proposals needed much more documentation than he provided, and he quailed at the labour involved. And though he clearly wrote the essay with publication in mind, he retreated at the last moment into the anodyne words of a posthumous publication, telling Emma what to put in her foreword if the worst came to the worst.

He had got himself over the hurdle of writing about transmutation. Now there loomed the far larger hurdle of publication.

FORESTALLED BUT FOREWARNED

HEORETICALLY, Darwin could have chosen anyone he wanted from the Victorian scientific community to edit his essay on species. His letter to Emma was only wishful thinking, after all, and he could have stipulated Prince Albert or Cuvier if he really thought either would be appropriate. He wrote with an opportunity to pinpoint the men in Britain—perhaps Europe and America as a whole—who were most likely to look favourably on transmutation and do justice to a radical new theory of nature that undermined everything usually believed about the human race. His list, it might be thought, would give the names of other secret evolutionists like himself or men already willing to risk a public advocacy of transformism.

But the men he chose were very different. Darwin's plan was not so much to find people predisposed to agree with him as it was to locate editors he could trust. This clearly included an idea of social respectability, even conventionality. His social topography did not, in this sense, represent a consensus of views on transmutation. Instead it was based on his estimation of people's competence. Darwin had several very good reasons for listing the names that he did. Editors for his essay, he believed, needed to be capable naturalists or geologists who would promote and further his views, not mere propagandists who might end up as a liability in themselves.

For this reason he ignored his former acquaintance Robert Grant, by then a well-known professor of comparative anatomy at University College in London, who could easily have put Darwin's transmutationary essay forward. Grant, he knew, was preaching organic change to his students. If nothing else, Erasmus, as a member of the governing council of University College, could keep him informed about Grant's latest activities. "I think Charles' old friend Prof Grant must have the hair growing the wrong way," Erasmus complained on one occasion. "He said the council couldn't appoint him professor as he was professor already, but in spite of that he will lecture, and what the offence is I dont know, but it looks like a bad beginning."[1] Grant's zoological lectures made the point about evolution devastatingly clear.[2] Yet his association with flamboyant medical reformers like Thomas Wakley and Darwin's recollection of his own early clash with him over scientific property stopped Darwin from even briefly contemplating the idea. The relationship had been dead for too many years to permit reviving it for such a purpose. Similarly, he never thought of including the names of any of the radical French anatomists whose broadly transformist writings were familiar to him. For a stolidly respectable Englishman it was unthinkable to go to France for this kind of assistance or to impose such a task without a previous personal introduction.

Nor did Darwin list any of the eminent scientific figures he did know, because he feared they would find his proposals distasteful. Sedgwick was getting more theological in his late middle age, insisting that a sense of personal responsibility was basic to human nature and would be wiped out by a general acceptance of utilitarian or materialistic doctrines: the contemplation of nature, he stipulated, ought to lead human minds towards God. Whewell was an equally devout Anglican don, the professor of moral philosophy at Cambridge since 1838, writing powerfully against transmutation in his *Philosophy of the Inductive Sciences* (1840) and giving his own version of natural theology in his Bridgewater treatise on astronomy. Herschel was almost too famous to ask. Even if Darwin had the courage, Herschel was renowned for calling the creation of species the "mystery of mysteries." Such acts of God, the astronomer stressed, were unfathomable to science.

Only Henslow among this group of older statesmen seemed to Darwin a possible editor, and that by virtue of their long-standing, deeply affectionate relationship rather than from any hope Darwin may have held that Henslow would actually approve of his arguments. Henslow was still exceptionally responsive to new ideas, his mind teeming with plans for reforming elementary botany teaching, building local museums, providing an education for working men, creating local insurance societies, and drawing up parish rules for land allotments, one for every villager.[3] Yet even Henslow was a doubtful candidate. Darwin felt it would be asking too much of their friendship to put this worthy parish priest on what he suspected might be a spiritual rack. Henslow never knew that Darwin put his name down for this potential torment.

He went instead for younger men, men more or less his own age who he knew were sceptical or prone to take a detached view of the interrelations between science and religion. Reluctantly, he recognised that Erasmus was far too lazy to get the essay published and not nearly enough of a naturalist to wade through the notes he wanted an editor to examine. Hensleigh would make an efficient executor, but he also lacked sufficient natural history knowledge for the work. Dr. Holland was too medical, too busy.

Lyell, naturally, was first: Darwin's ideal friend and confidant, whose wide-ranging mind already probed far into these kinds of problems, although he always at heart remained a firm believer in the existence of God. Lyell still stood resolutely behind his anti-evolutionary diatribe in the *Principles of Geology*. But Darwin admired his acuity and liberality in scientific affairs. The ties of friendship, and what Darwin considered Lyell's real ability to look behind the surface for nature's grandest organising concepts, convinced him that Lyell was everything he needed: "the best, if he would undertake it."

The other men listed by Darwin possessed qualities individually attractive to him. William Lonsdale was probably the most knowledgeable invertebrate palaeontologist of the era, friendly with Darwin through sitting on the council and various committees of the Geological Society, and more recently helpful in identifying Darwin's shells and fossil corals from the *Beagle* voyage. Lonsdale had spent fifteen years cataloguing the Geological Society's collection of specimens, generating the expertise which was crucial for resolving the great geological dilemma of the Devonian system which entangled Sedgwick, Murchison, Agassiz, and others in turn through the late 1830s and was partly continuing as Darwin wrote.[4] By identifying the intermediate character of fossil corals in the English southwest, Lonsdale showed how two apparently different rock formations, one in Devon, the other in Scotland, could be laid down at the same time: that they belonged to the same geological era. In Darwin's opinion, Lonsdale was interestingly open-minded about a progressivist view of the fossil record and capable of imaginative leaps in understanding the wider implications of geology. If anyone was going to be able to find appropriately detailed evidence for ancestral continuity over time, it was he.

Richard Owen was, of course, unmatched in comparative anatomy, his skills ranging from fossil mammals, as Darwin knew very well, to the internal organs of the pearly nautilus or the complex reproductive systems of Australian marsupials and egg-laying monotremes. Independent and unwilling to brook any rivals, Owen was not afraid to modify established classification schemes and create whole new orders wherever necessary. From 1839 he also showed marked interest in continuities, progress, and intermediate fossil forms, first puzzling over the anomalous position of Darwin's *Toxodon,* then confirming the identity of the very first known mammalian fossil (the Stonesfield mammal, a kind of marsupial shrew) in rocks formerly thought far too early for any such family.[5] Dinosaurs came next—an idea that Owen virtually invented when confronted with reconstructing large lizard-like bones.[6] Primates and anthropoid apes followed hard behind. Though not in any way a professed evolutionist, Owen certainly discussed the ways that the fossil record might—or might not—support transmutationary views in his important *Reports on Fossil Reptiles* (1839 and 1841) and dabbled privately in his own arcane theories of embryological change.[7] By 1844, Darwin knew Owen had no objection to the idea that the Creator may have worked through secondary causes, and he read Owen's publications on philosophical comparative anatomy, embryology, and classification with profound respect.

Hugh Strickland was more of a shot in the dark, since he was a very recent acquaintance. He was noted by Darwin's contemporaries for his promising ability as a rising young geologist and zoologist, full of reforming zeal about species names, active in forcing the Zoological Society to take account of avant-garde classification schemes, and youthfully aware of the potential of integrating the geological record with modern organisms. Darwin was impressed by him when asked in 1842 to join Strickland's committee for drawing up rules for scientific nomenclature under the auspices of the British Association for the Advancement of Science. His potential was never fully realised; he was run over by a train in 1853 while searching a railway cutting for fossils.[8]

Edward Forbes was even more talented, one of the most gifted men of the British natural history world, in turn a marine zoologist, a botanist, and, since early in 1844, employed by the newly established Geological Survey of Great Britain as a paleontologist.[9] He also lectured as professor of botany at King's College, London, and took over Lonsdale's cataloguing job at the Geological Society when he retired. By 1844, Forbes had published important papers on the geographical distribution of marine molluscs, explaining what these patterns might have to say about the differential preservation of fossil shells. He pretty much followed Lyell in adopting a gradualist universe and put forward an account of the way Britain's animals and plants arrived in waves from the continent during the previous and current geological epochs. Darwin had independently thought of much the same explanation.[10] Temporarily annoyed at being forestalled by Forbes, Darwin soon realised that he was a man mostly after his own mind. Clever, poetic, and the founder of a singing and dining club which greatly enlivened British Association meetings, although in Darwin's opinion far too caught up with transcendental ideas of the unity of type, Forbes possessed just the kind of informed, agile mind that Darwin appreciated. Ten years later he moved, with great acclaim, to take over Robert Jameson's natural history chair at Edinburgh University.

And last was Joseph Dalton Hooker, who had just returned from the

Antarctic expedition captained by James Clark Ross and had struck up a correspondence with Darwin in the closing months of 1843. Hooker was a dedicated botanist who used his medical qualifications as a lever to get appointed as an assistant naval surgeon to the Ross expedition, on which he hoped to collect plants and study the different vegetation of the globe. After four years of voyaging round the world, he proposed working at Kew, where his father was director of the gardens.[11] At that point, Henslow thought Hooker might like to have Darwin's *Beagle* plants, which were still lying unstudied in a room at Cambridge. The two travelling men quickly warmed to one another; and Darwin joyfully sensed that here was another scientific friend he could love as much as Lyell. Behind his dry botanical exterior and pebble spectacles, Hooker nurtured a good sense of humour and a powerful mind. He never balked at leaping over the highest metaphysical barriers.

Darwin admired Hooker's intellect so much that he soon broached the subject of transmutation with him. In January 1844 he cautiously described some of his views in a letter, wondering uneasily how Hooker would respond. Carefully, he phrased his remarks as a confession, as the unwilling confession of a guilty man, retrospectively restructuring what had happened to him in the most scientifically acceptable way that he could: for even though Hooker was eight years younger and presented no kind of professional threat, he ought to be treated seriously. "Besides a general interest about the Southern lands," Darwin wrote, tentatively trying out the feel of the words, "I have been now ever since my return engaged in a very presumptuous work & which I know no one individual who wd not say a very foolish one."

> I was so struck with distribution of Galapagos organisms &c &c, & with the character of the American fossil mammifers &c &c, that I determined to collect blindly every sort of fact which cd bear any way on what are species.—I have read heaps of agricultural & horticultural books, & have never ceased collecting facts—At last gleams of light have come, & I am almost convinced (quite contrary to opinion I started with) that species are not (it is like confessing a murder) immutable. Heaven forfend me from Lamarck nonsense of a "tendency to progression," "adaptations from the slow willing of animals" &c,—but the conclusions I am led to are not widely different from his—though the means of change are wholly so—I think I have found out (here's presumption) the simple way by which species become exquisitely adapted to various ends.[12]

"You will now groan," he added contritely, "& think to yourself on what a man have I been wasting my time in writing to. I shd, five years ago, have thought so."

But Hooker took it all in his stride. There may well be a gradual change in species, he replied unemotionally: "I shall be delighted to hear how you think this change may have taken place, as no presently conceived opinions satisfy me on the subject." Choice snippets of information about his plant collections followed.

Somewhat taken aback, Darwin was pleased at this matter-of-fact response and then overwhelmingly grateful. He felt sure Hooker would be one of the best and most erudite of sounding-boards for his theories, a botanical expert to rank beside Owen and Lyell in their own fields, and one moreover who was more forthcoming and thoughtful than Henslow, and with wider interests than William Herbert: a man who he judged could become the "first authority on that grand subject, that almost key-stone to the laws of creation, geographical distribution." After such an auspicious start, Hooker quickly became Darwin's intimate friend. "I can hardly tell you," Darwin gushed in relief, "how much all your facts & opinions interest me."

All these potential editors were situated at the liberal end of the Victorian social and intellectual spectrum, and Darwin believed they would treat him and his ideas fairly. Even so he did not tell any of them about the role they played in his plans. It is not clear whether Emma knew about the letter and its convoluted instructions—at least at the time Darwin wrote it. Nor did he risk letting them all into the secret of transmutation. That, he must have thought, would come of its own accord when he was dead.

He was not at all sure if this handful of respectable scientific contemporaries would be able to accommodate the view that mankind was the product of an ape.

II

With his letter written, and the essay neatly copied out by Mr. Fletcher in a nearby village, Darwin turned willingly to other duties. He felt no rush to publish. His theory, he believed, was still incomplete, needing much more time and effort than he was able to provide. Writing it out was enough for the moment. Like anyone who ever composed a list of things to do and then felt satisfied at the order temporarily imposed on chaos, he put it in a large brown portfolio and left it for another day on a shelf by his chair.

Besides, he was still tremendously busy. The last part of his geological book was calling stridently. Smith & Elder had published the *Volcanic Islands* volume in March 1844, which was the second part of his *Beagle* geology. Few geologists had talked to him about it, however, except for Leonard Horner, who wrote a long letter criticising his account of the origin of craters. Darwin's mistake, said Horner, lay in adopting a compromise position between Lyell and the continental geologists Elie de Beaumont and Christian Leopold von Buch. Where Lyell believed the shape of a volcanic cone originated in the successive build-up of layers of molten rock on the outside, the others argued that pressure from below pushed the rock into a cone until the centre collapsed and a vent was formed. Observations made on extinct volcanic craters were inconclusive either way. Still, Darwin thought he could resolve the discrepancy by proposing that some upthrust took place around the external rim and that layers of lava contributed to the rest. There was no collapse in the centre.

This abstruse debate had fuelled controversy about volcanoes for several decades, and Darwin's contribution, though sincerely meant and carefully worked out as always, hardly dented the surface. Horner did not think much of it. Nor did Darwin after reading Horner's letter. "I had no sooner printed off the few pages on that subject, than I wished the whole erased," he explained hastily. "I wish I had left it all out; I trust that there is in other parts of the volume more facts & less theory."[13] Nevertheless he complained to Lyell that the book "cost me 18 *months!!!* work & I have heard of very few who has read it."[14] He began to think geologists never read books—they only wrote them to show that they were serious.

The next volume was the final one in his trilogy and dealt with the general geology of South America. In it he hoped to describe in full the geological dynamics—the literal ups and downs—of the continent. He had struggled for years to publish his own interpretations of this area before Alcide d'Orbigny, his only rival in South American natural history. Yet d'Orbigny worked faster and more efficiently, because his geology was published in 1842, along with a large scientific study of the region. Some of Darwin's competitive urgency seeped away when he read the volume: he saw how d'Orbigny favoured catastrophes and watery debacles and recognised, with a sense of relief, that this approach would find only limited approval in Britain. His own Lyellian viewpoint, in which the pampas and Patagonian plains were thought to be the result of gradual elevation from the seabed, would be far more acceptable to the geological Englishmen he had come to know so well.

But he wanted to get it out. So after his essay was finished, he spent a few diverting weeks working on two short papers for natural history magazines, one on the dust which falls on ships far out to sea, another on the terrestrial flatworms he had discovered long ago in the Brazilian undergrowth. Then he took up his geological pen again in July 1844. In September he started priming Lyell. "I am astounded," he wrote, "and grieved over D'Orbigny's nonsense of sudden elevations. . . . What a pity these Frenchmen do not catch hold of a comet, & return to the good old geological drama of Burnet and Whiston. I shall keep out of controversy, & just give my own facts. It is enough to disgust one with geology,—though I have been much pleased with the frank, decided, though courteous manner, with which D'Orbigny disputes my conclusions, given unfortunately without facts & sometimes rashly in my Journal."[15]

Furthermore, Darwin had undertaken to supervise a German translation of his *Journal of Researches*. This German translation was relatively uncomplicated, because, as was usual for the times, the translator was expected to take on all the contractual obligations and expenses. Yet something of Darwin's growing prominence as a scientific writer emerges from his negotiations. Ernst Dieffenbach had written to Darwin early in 1843 asking if he could translate the *Journal*. He was a younger man, a physician and naturalist struggling to find some kind of congenial employment while in political exile. He hoped that translating a well-received scientific book like the *Journal* would help his future prospects. And not long afterwards he began using Darwin's name to bolster his wavering career: he persuaded Darwin to mention him to Lord Derby, the president of the Zoological Society, who often employed agents to collect specimens for his menagerie at Knowsley Hall; and he extracted a general promise of further references after briefly meeting Darwin in 1845. The relationship between author and translator, Darwin discovered, always demanded some kind of quid pro quo. Privately, Darwin called him the little devil-bach.

Yet Darwin conscientiously revised his text to include new details about his collections and provided several pages of corrections and alterations, which Dieffenbach incorporated, making the German version the first revised edition of his *Journal* since its release in 1839. Darwin was gratified to hear of its publication in 1844 and saw his own copy arrive at Down in April 1845. "I consider your having made my work known in Germany," he wrote graciously, "a full & ample recompense to such exertions as I made during our voyage."[16]

He was right to be grateful. This was the first and almost the only translation into any foreign language of any of his books until 1860, when a small selection from the *Journal* was published in French and the *Origin of Species* came out in German. Most of Darwin's early reputation in Germany was built on Dieffenbach's efforts—a reputation that gave Darwin the beginnings of an international stature and contributed markedly to the generally favourable response later given to his views by German naturalists. He could not have done this himself. As it was, Darwin depended on Emma to decipher Dieffenbach's introduction and one or two other passages.

Ungenerously, Darwin felt little inclination to offer the same service to other foreign nationals. When Adolf von Morlot wrote from Bern that same summer asking if Darwin would help him get an article on glaciers published, he met with a polite refusal. Darwin told him he could not provide introductions. Morlot pressed his case, eliciting a stronger refusal: no editor of respectable English scientific journals, Darwin emphasized, would publish his letters in their present form. "I know I shall appear to you unjust & unkind, & I am sorry for it."[17] Persistent, if not thoroughly thick-skinned, Morlot wrote once more in November, asking if he could publish extracts from Darwin's geological letters to him. The answer, again, was no.

Darwin's life, in fact, was becoming much more rigidly divided between public and private, with his intimate inner circle always taking precedence over the hopes or fears of other members of the scientific community personally unknown to him.[18] His move to Down was no doubt a feature in this withdrawal. Darwin liked his "complete rurality" and resented interruptions. Conducting his scientific life through letters suited his habits very well—he could keep people at arm's length, encouraging or dropping contacts as he wished, carefully choosing whom he wanted to interact with. He could pursue his researches just as readily with someone like Hooker on the receiving end of a letter as he could with a book in hand, probably more efficiently than by taking the train up to London and sitting in the British Library or the Geological Society. Nor did he have to depend solely on the people he already knew for this sort of private information. His *Journal* and other writings made him sufficiently well known that he felt justified in hunting out useful correspondents. He expected people to try to do as he asked. If not, he learned to move on fast when nothing came of it. Writing letters freed him from many of the usual encumbrances of scientific society: the interminable council meetings, the parties, the small talk over coffee and tea. Letters were safely impersonal. More than this, they were useful. They became his primary means of interaction with the outside world.

They were also the best way to sound out his friends on the issue of transmutation. As he did with Hooker, and had done with Lyell much earlier on, Darwin could choose when and how to reveal his thoughts and the words to use. Since neither Lyell nor Hooker abandoned him after hearing at least some of his subversive opinions, he cautiously tried similar words on someone else. Sitting in his Cambridge parsonage, Leonard Jenyns heard as much as Hooker did, and in the same convoluted confessional style:

I have continued steadily reading & collecting facts on variation of domestic animals & plants & on the question of what are species; I have a grand body of facts & think I can draw some sound conclusions. The general conclusion at which I have slowly been driven from a directly opposite conviction is that species are mutable & that allied species are co-descendents of common stocks. I know how much I open myself to reproach for such a conclusion, but I have at least honestly & deliberately come to it. I shall not publish on this subject for several years—at present I am on the geology of S. America. I hope to pick up from your book some facts on slight variations in structure or instincts in animals of your acquaintance.[19]

Jenyns, a vicar, appeared no more outwardly shocked than the others. Fortified, Darwin asked in another letter if he would like at some point to read his essay on the subject. Later in the year, he also wondered if Hooker would like to read it.

But in true Darwinian style his invitations were so hedged around with hesitations that both of his friends would have done well to identify an offer in there at all. Unsurprisingly, his essay stayed in its envelope on the study shelf at Down.

III

Having kept his secret for so long, divulging it only to these carefully selected friends, Darwin naturally felt he was the only man in Britain who possessed a fully worked out theory of transmutation.

That same autumn he was proved wrong—devastatingly wrong. Unknown to Darwin, an anonymous author was putting the finishing touches to a comprehensive work on the evolution of living things. This was published late in October 1844 under the title *Vestiges of the Natural History of Creation,* a thoroughgoing transmutationist tract which described not only the progress of the animal world from specks of living matter to men and women, but also the development of the astronomical universe and the mental life of mankind. The book swept the country as soon as it was issued, shocking and exciting a whole body of astonished readers. *Vestiges* became a *cause célèbre,* and "Mr. Vestiges" or the "Vestigarian" pilloried as an unidentifiable "practical Atheist." How could the mysterious author have reached broadly the same conclusions as Darwin?

The author was Robert Chambers, a folklorist, journalist, and publisher from Edinburgh, one of the most interesting thinkers of the early Victorian period. In his autobiography, he called himself an "essayist to the middle-classes," an aphorism accurately reflecting his wide-ranging activities and preferred milieu. Born into relatively modest circumstances in the Scottish borders, he and his brother William had worked hard establishing themselves as jobbing printers and booksellers in Edinburgh, and then they had set up in business together in 1832 as joint editors and publishers of *Chambers's Edinburgh Journal.* Their journal was an astute project in all senses. Capitalising on the surge in cheap publishing that accompanied the introduction of the steam press in the 1830s, and serving a market that desired wholesome and instructive reading at an economical price, the brothers issued it as a weekly magazine containing numerous short articles on literature, science, industry, and occasionally manners and morals, interspersed with stories and poems. It was exactly what a large proportion of the middling population, English as well as Scottish, had been waiting for, one of several similar mass publishing enterprises catching the earnest, self-educational tenor of the age.[20] *Chambers's Journal* was a complete commercial success, and the company went on to publish other worthy items, including Chambers's *Cyclopaedia of English Literature* towards the end of the century. More to the point, its success signalled an explosion of interest in popular science and gave a central role to capable journalists like Robert Chambers in moulding the widest possible sector of public opinion. Nonspecialist, self-educated, respectable people composed his essential audience.[21]

At first the brothers wrote all the material for their *Journal* themselves. Robert Chambers already had a reputation as the author of antiquarian and literary pieces of a Scottish nature: among many others, he wrote books on Edinburgh folk traditions, popular rhymes, Scottish songs, and a life of Sir Walter Scott, with whom he briefly worked as a clerk. He also broadly knew his way around science, expressing a particular enthusiasm for geology which emerged in a study of the ancient sea beaches of Scotland, published in 1843 in the *Edinburgh New Philosophical Journal,* and developed into a passion for charting glacial phenomena in the Lowlands from 1848 onwards. But his lively, eclectic interests took him further than this. Chambers read Lyell, talked with Sir Charles Bell about the nervous system, became friends with Dr. Neil Arnott, a London physician, Alexander Ireland, a Manchester journalist, and John Pringle Nichol, the populariser and radical astronomical thinker. In particular, he immersed himself in the science of phrenology, coming to know its leading proponent George Combe and his Edinburgh circle intimately, though he gently criticised Combe for not making enough concessions to religious feeling. Many of these interests fed directly into his articles for *Chambers's Journal:* an alert reader would have been familiar with a good part of the progressivist, all-inclusive self-help substance of *Vestiges* before it appeared.

Initially, or at least publicly, Chambers was against transmutation, finding Lyell's denouncement of Lamarck "so satisfactory as to require us to say nothing in addition." Yet his continuing relish for phrenology and Nichol's developmental history of the solar system—whereby the planets progressively condensed out of rotating gaseous nebulae—stimulated a ferment of novel ideas, making him change his tune. Phrenology spoke to him of the progress of the mind: a developmental process in which humanity could advance towards self-knowledge and a better state of things. Nichol's nebular hypothesis served as a secular account of the beginning of the cosmos and as a metaphor for similar progress in and on the earth.[22] Chambers decided to connect them by postulating a "law of development" that worked throughout nature, the universe, and society. He would describe all aspects of the known world from the formation of planets to the origin of mankind and the evolution of civilisation. Deliberately, and in attractively energetic language, he set out to say the things avoided by more conventional establishment scientists.

In 1841, Chambers moved north with his wife and family to St. Andrews: the Edinburgh business was not so demanding that he could not devote his time to study. There he worked on his book well away from the public eye, pulling together material from roughly the same sort of sources as Darwin, along with other evidence Darwin was not inclined to use. Much of his information came from review articles, journals, and secondary literature like encyclopaedias, reflecting his own commitment to educational printed matter that could be understood by any novice. He was just such a novice in many practical areas to start with, particularly in physiology, embryology, classification, and anatomy: most of his knowledge of these subjects came at second hand from books like William Carpenter's *Principles of General and Comparative Anatomy*.

In St. Andrews he also worked hard on creating the elaborate smoke screen that stood between him and his readers: a vital anonymity he never relinquished in his lifetime. While Mrs. Chambers copied the manuscript to disguise his handwriting, he approached a faraway London publishing firm for a contract, and his friend Ireland acted as an intermediary for all the negotiations. Later on, after the book's unexpected success, Ireland passed the profits through his own bank account before sending them on to Chambers. Rumours as to the author's identity of course abounded. But even on his deathbed, when asked if he was Mr. Vestiges, Chambers was reputed to have replied enigmatically, "So they say."[23]

Living behind the veil like this, Chambers felt free to spell out his evolutionary system in startling detail. His God was one who barely appeared in nature except as the ultimate architect: the provider of a plan for nature, the giver of a single "law" that drove it. He started with a description of an entirely secular origin of the planetary system, and then proceeded to explain the origin of life by similarly secular spontaneous generation.[24] In this he was greatly impressed by experiments conducted by a man called Andrew Crosse, who seemingly generated cheese mites by electricity. Not entirely gullible, Chambers was excited by the chamaeleon-like powers of electrical forces that scientists were then revealing. Nor was the spontaneous-generation controversy completely resolved. But he also wanted to believe. He wanted to believe living beings emerged out of the abyss of primitive time solely under the influence of physical agencies.

Thus emerging, Chambers's organisms developed into all the species known to man. The process was still continuing, he claimed. Information about how it happened, however, was very sketchy, mostly depending on the author's constantly reiterating the idea of an inbuilt tendency for development, but also introducing the concept of recapitulation and embryological divergence. Chambers's reading among French and German authorities led him to assert that an organism would customarily pass through most of its evolutionary history during embryological development. To this he added a twist, suggesting that if the process was stopped in the middle, or prolonged further, new kinds of species would appear. Moreover, he included the important qualifications worked out by Karl von Baer that embryos do not pass through stages resembling the adult forms of simpler organisms. Instead, the resemblance was to embryonic fish or reptiles at certain moments in their "foetal progress." Romping away with these ideas, he boldly proposed that a fish could give birth to a reptile, and a goose to a rat. The production of new species, he wrote, "has never been anything more than a new stage in the process of gestation, an event as simply natural, and as attended as little by any circumstances of a wonderful or startling kind, as the silent advance of an ordinary mother from one week to another of her pregnancy."

Chambers included in his book the classification scheme proposed by Darwin's Zoological Society friend William MacLeay, and taken up in greater detail by William Swainson. Known as the "quinarian" system, this scheme grouped organisms in fives and arranged them in a circle, not in a linear or branching series. Each circle of five by definition incorporated one "typical" species and one "aberrant" species, and there were many different kinds of analogies that could be drawn out between circles. For all its difficulties, the quinarian system goaded a great many naturalists, including Darwin, into asking precisely what the words "typical" and "aberrant" might mean in classification, and why naturalists usually thought in linear terms.[25] Chambers showed his partiality for aberrant forms by suggesting it was these that mostly gave birth to new lines of development. Monsters and abnormalities genuinely fascinated him, and he tried hard to integrate what he knew about their origins into his general embryological schemes. In this he was probably encouraged by his own physical abnormality: both Robert Chambers and his brother William had six fingers and toes on every limb. Early in life these extra digits were surgically removed, leaving Robert with a pronounced limp.

Chambers closed his volume with chapters describing the moral advancement of mankind, doing his best to allay fears that such a naturally operating universe undermined the notion of free will and of an organising God. Underneath lay an implicit, almost counter-cultural call. He turned his back on university learning, conservative politics, and the authority of organised

Anglican religion to speak for the ordinary men and women of Britain. He advocated the new Victorian values of hard work, progress, and gradual, mainly middle-class reform, in which the sciences played an integral part.

He was all set to cause a storm.

IV

Darwin was stunned. Reading *Vestiges* in November 1844 was a traumatic shock from which he only partially recovered. Hunched over a copy in the British Museum Library, with the three other books he had ordered left disregarded by his side, he hardly believed his eyes. The general thesis was exactly the same as his: that, as Darwin dispiritedly put it, "species are shown to be not immutable." The anonymous author marshalled many of the same lines of evidence that he had just painstakingly put together in his own essay, integrating geology, the fossil record, embryology, classification, comparative anatomy, and behaviour into a single scheme. In fact, he went further than Darwin by including mankind and the origin of life. What really hurt was that he also grasped the importance of Lyell's work in describing the geological past solely in terms of present-day forces and saw, as Darwin did, the symmetry of applying this view directly to the living world. Where Lyell had warned his readers about the religious and metaphysical dangers of doing this, and had constructed his elaborately circular account of the fossil record to circumvent any transmutationary interpretations, Mr. Vestiges went right ahead and did it. Darwin saw he was not the only man to think along these lines. He really did not want the company.

Yet these very similarities created a book quite unlike his own. *Vestiges* was journalistic, lively, all-encompassing. More than that, it addressed all the questions about man's relations with animals and God which naturally emerged from a transmutationist argument, all the moral questions Darwin carefully avoided in his own essay. Thankfully Darwin saw that *Vestiges'* treatment of these urgent themes, and its author's eagerness to accept the most astonishing stories as genuine, were the book's undoing in the eyes of high science.

Still, he considered the text very closely. It was the closest to a rival he had ever met. He was forced to acknowledge its existence, its impact, and show where he differed. Combined with the shock and resentment, this task seemed irritatingly tiresome.

"After the 'Vestiges of Nat. Hist. Creation,'" he impatiently wrote in a note to himself, "I see it will be necessary to advert to Quinary system, because he brings it in to show that Lamarck's willing (& consequently my selection) must be erroneous—I had better rest my defence on few English, *sound* anatomical naturalists assenting & hardly any foreign.—Advert to this subject after chapter on classification, & then show, from our ignorance of comparative value of groups, source of error."[26] Frantically he began thinking of ways to reveal *Vestiges'* reliance on doubtful theories. A few elitist punches would go a long way here, he thought ungallantly.

He was upset to hear how much Hooker enjoyed the read. "I have been delighted with *Vestiges,* from the multiplicity of facts he brings together," Hooker chattered in a letter late in December; "though I do [not] agree with his conclusions at all. He must be a funny fellow: somehow the book looks more like a 9 days wonder than a lasting work: it certainly is 'filling at the price,'—I mean the price its reading costs, for it is dear enough otherwise. He has lots of errors."[27]

Hooker went on to dissect some of these errors, adding with a smile that he could think of several popular fallacies unaccountably omitted. But he ruefully confessed his willingness to believe in some of them himself. "In one place he implies that species are made by the *will of the mother,* under which I wonder he does not quote a subject I have lately been struck with, & that is the real or apparent effect that a mental emotion of the mother might have on her unborn offspring.—I thought till lately that all these nursery stories were laid upon the shelf. All Sealers have told me that the young, taken out of the clubbed mother, bear similar club marks on their heads, & this they swear to. If you care to hear any thing on the subject I will go on at some future time. Do not think I am arguing this for the developement of species!"

After all, Hooker concluded, what was the difference between *Vestiges* and Lamarck, whom the anonymous author laughed at?

Darwin was stung. "I have, also, read the Vestiges, but have been somewhat less amused at it, than you appear to have been," he said stiffly. "The writing & arrangement are certainly admirable, but his geology strikes me as bad, & his zoology far worse."[28]

V

Worse was to come. *Vestiges* swept into British life as few scientific books have ever done. The first edition sold out so rapidly that three reprints were called for during the next twelve months. Some twenty other editions followed; it was published in America in 1845 and translated into German in 1851. The ordinary reading public fell on it, obtaining copies from railway bookstalls, sales booths, and circulating libraries and from a whole series of small, entrepreneurial printers and booksellers in county towns all over the nation. Many of these people saw *Vestiges* as a natural history sequel to George Combe's best-selling *Constitution of Man* (1828), and by 1860, around 24,000 copies had been sold.[29] Since it was also one of the first nonspecialist books about man's place in nature, it appealed particularly to Combe's artisan and middle-class readers. Evidently written by a self-made, solidly middle-class citizen, the book subscribed to the same forward-looking, progressive ethic as the majority of its readers. "One can scarce travel by railway or in a steamboat, or encounter a group of intelligent mechanics, without finding traces of its ravages," noticed Hugh Miller, who eventually wrote a refutation of *Vestiges* for the same audience poignantly called *Footprints of the Creator.*

Copies circulated just as widely elsewhere. Mary Somerville and Henry Crabb Robinson read it. Benjamin Jowett, Herbert Spencer, and Froude read it. The poets Tennyson, Fitzgerald, and Emerson were deeply impressed, each in his own way, Tennyson mournfully concluding that "nature is one with rapine," unconcerned about preserving either individuals or "the type." Samuel Smiles, Baden Powell, F. D. Maurice, the phrenological Combes, Benjamin Disraeli, and Abraham Lincoln—all these read it too. Frances Power Cobbe pinned her reformist faith to it at the age of eighteen. Leigh Hunt commended it in private. Erasmus Darwin's friend Fanny Kemble stated that "its conclusions are utterly revolting to me—nevertheless they may be true." And Florence Nightingale, discussing it with Lord and Lady Ashburton, "got up so high into *Vestiges* that I could not get down again, and was obliged to go off as an angel."[30] Until the moment when Darwin published the *Origin of Species,* Mr. Vestiges held his audience enthralled.

In fact, he held his audience so well he can rightly be credited with pushing evolutionary ideas into the foreground of British life. His themes became a fashionable talking point, deftly caricatured by Disraeli. One young lady in *Tancred* (1847) urged the hero to read *"Revelations."* "You know, all is development. The principle is perpetually going on. First, there was nothing, then there was something; then, I forget the next, I think there were shells, then fishes; then we came, let me see, did we come next? Never mind that; we came at last. And the next change there will be something very superior to us, something with wings. Ah! that's it; we were fishes, and I believe we shall be crows."

The reviews in current journals were also electrifying. The book was "a breath of fresh air to the workman in a crowded factory," shouted the reformist *Lancet.* "The doctrines advanced are not so new as the author seems to fancy, but they are none the worse for being thrown open to the general reader, instead of being, as hitherto, confined to the timid coteries of the so-called scientific world."[31] The *Examiner* went further. In this "small and unpretending volume," the reviewer said eagerly, "we have found so many great results of knowledge and reflection that we cannot too earnestly recommend it to the attention of thoughtful men." He agreed with everything *Vestiges* proposed, making sure *Examiner* readers knew exactly what he was talking about by reprinting long slabs of transmutationary text describing the early history of mankind and the mental constitution of animals.[32] The *Spectator* thought it was "a rather remarkable work" put together with more coherence than Lamarck had managed and "consequently possessing more plausibility."[33]

Antagonistic reviews fanned the flames further. The *Athenaeum* boasted the first strongly critical riposte, but others soon flooded out in serious literary magazines. Francis Bowen devoted fifty or so pages of the *North American Review* to a refutation of *Vestiges,* emphasising its atheistic tendencies; David Brewster in the *North British Review* followed the same line in stronger form, writing of it as "poisoning the fountains of science and sapping the foundations of religion." Charles Kingsley reviewed it negatively in the *Westminster and Foreign Quarterly.* How could *Vestiges* propose that mankind was the offspring of "a higher kind of monkey"? the *Athenaeum* shuddered.

Then came the pamphlets. First off the press in February 1845 was William Whewell with his *Indications of the Creator.* Reluctant to go into battle publicly, Whewell avoided reviewing *Vestiges* in any learned journals and refused to mention it by name in his *Indications.* Nevertheless, he pulled together extracts from his earlier writings directly countering transmutation and changes in animal morphology in order to demonstrate that science does not—cannot—concern itself with these kinds of final causes. "The mystery of creation," he said, "is not within the range of her legitimate teritory; she says nothing but points upwards."[34] Another pamphleteer was Samuel Bosanquet, whose small tract conveyed the sentiment that *Vestiges* possessed "all the graces of the accomplished harlot." Afterwards a Liverpool vicar, Abraham Hume, gathered responses to the book from famous men. "Brown shewed me a funny thing," laughed Hooker to Darwin when he heard of this. "Some Liverpool parson, after reading *Vestiges,* has written to all geologists for proofs on the contrary, & rather coolly printed all the answers. Every one, but De la Beche, referred said parson to their own works! I could not get the thing. I suppose you have read Bosanquet's answer, it is not half so *nice* as *Vestiges.*"[35]

John Herschel summed up the general contemptuous response from established scientists in his presidential address to the British Association for the Advancement of Science at Cambridge in June 1845. He made no bones about whom he was referring to: the recent author who invoked a "law of development" from crystals to living globules, and thence through polyps, fish, and reptiles, "up to man (nay for aught we know even to the angel)." The idea of a developmental law, he thundered to the assembled dignitaries, could never substitute for an explanation. "Take these amazing facts of geology which way we will, we must resort elsewhere than to a mere speculative law of development for their explanation."[36]

The storm swept up Darwin in its wake whether he liked it or not. "Have you read that strange unphilosophical, but capitally written book, the Vestiges?" he asked Fox in April 1845. "It has made more talk than any work of late, & has been by some attributed to me—at which I ought to be much flattered and unflattered."[37] Only his family could have made such a connection, Erasmus perhaps, or Erasmus and Hensleigh Wedgwood together, ganging up to tease Darwin about where he would find himself if he continued on his current path. Other names of possible authors were already flying around scientific London. Could it be Lyell or Owen? Owen himself thought it was Sir Richard Vyvyan, the Oxford-educated Tory baronet, once an M.P. and now a patrician geologist with learned and faintly obscure interests in psychology and electricity. Rumours abounded. The *Athenaeum* acidly suggested he must be a Scotchman, a wide reader but not much of an original observer: an outsider "who has mixed little with the men of science of his day." It did not take too long before Chambers's name was similarly paraded. Edward Forbes said as much to Darwin towards the end of 1845, noticing a repetition of a particular error in something Chambers wrote that also appeared in *Vestiges*. Later, both Hooker and Darwin saw a phrase or two from *Vestiges* repeated in *Chambers's Edinburgh Journal* in relation to the origin of a strangely anomalous cabbage on Kerguelen Land. Always, however, it was denied. Chambers found secrecy intoxicating as well as expedient.

There was not much Darwin could do except brood on the message so bleakly learned. He was forestalled: forestalled by a book which would injure his own arguments unless he divorced himself completely from *Vestiges*' style of popular progressive science. Morosely he decided never to fall into the same grandiose trap.

VI

Once again Darwin retreated into his study, more dispirited than he cared to admit. At least he could submerge himself in his private geological contro-versy with d'Orbigny safe in the belief that he was, on that point, absolutely right. Annoyed by *Vestiges,* he waspishly let off steam by criticising d'Orbigny's floods and Patagonian geology much more than the Frenchman deserved.

However, and in addition, he initiated another demanding project which probably owed some of its initial impetus to the rush of conflicting feelings sweeping in after he read *Vestiges* late in 1844. In February 1845, or perhaps a little earlier, he asked Lyell what he thought about putting out a second edition of his *Journal of Researches*. A new edition, Darwin suggested, could be expanded to include longer accounts of the Fuegians and take advantage of the revisions he had already drawn up for the German translation. As well as this, he would like to change publishers, and negotiate a contract which provided an income. "I should hope for a considerable sale," he said shrewdly to Lyell. All the reviews, and many private comments made to him over the years, led him to think the popularity of his volume propped up the sales of FitzRoy's set; and Henry Colburn had reissued his volume as a singleton to capitalise on this interest. He no longer needed the security of marriage to FitzRoy. "Many people to this day," he defensively asserted, "believe that my work is united to Captain King's and FitzRoy's."[38] Privately, he wanted to stand alone and be acknowledged again as a capable naturalist, an expert of quite a different character from Mr. Vestiges'. Piqued by *Vestiges'* runaway success, he allowed himself the satisfaction of thinking about a new and profitable book of his own.

Darwin asked Lyell to approach John Murray, the proprietor of the well-known London publishing house founded a generation before, and the man who published all of Lyell's books. Murray's firm specialised in general scientific literature as well as being one of the largest and most commercially sensitive popularisers of inexpensive literature for the reading public.[39] Books of travels, biographies, correspondence and memoirs, new editions of the classics, poems, Christmas books, and respectable novels streamed from its offices in central London. It was remarkably successful in establishing the new venture of issuing books in uniform series like the Colonial and Home Library, each item emblazoned on the front "Cheap literature for all classes." John Murray himself actively promoted science by retaining a succession of scientists on his list and publishing the annual *Report* of the British Association. He also published Samuel Smiles, Lord Stanhope, and Henry Sumner Maine, as well as the *Quarterly Review*. He was an erudite man, educated at Edinburgh University, with a strong interest in natural science. He liked to tell how he was one of the audience summoned by Murchison and Buckland to re-create, with an unwilling tortoise and some over-sticky dough, the circumstances under which an extinct reptile could have left footprints behind as a fossilised relic of its existence.

Lyell did as he was asked, and by the middle of March, Darwin had struck up an amicable business relationship with Murray based on mutual appreciation of each other's commercial sense.[40] This relationship lasted, to both men's evident satisfaction, through eleven titles and more than 150 different editions, to the end of Darwin's publishing life—beyond the grave if Murray's volumes of Darwin's correspondence and biographies are included.

Revising his *Journal* was more interesting than Darwin had expected. As always he went into it thoroughly, looking over his original notes and finding that many of his descriptions needed considerable overhauling. Hooker and Lyell read the old version through, with their pencils at the ready, and Emma did the same at home, correcting Darwin's prose with a liberality that made him a little anxious.

Furthermore, Darwin's species views stealthily crept into this revised English version.[41] He compared the indigenous Fuegians with animals, asking once again what pleasure in life these and some other peoples could possibly enjoy. Their human skills did not improve with experience: again something he compared to the fixed instinctive patterns of animal behaviour. Those Fuegians who examined the sailors' white arms were baldly likened to the orang-utan looking at visitors at the London zoo. One other sentence showed how far he had also turned into an English husband and father since the voyage. He had already described in the first edition his horror at seeing the Fuegians, these "most abject and miserable creatures," going unclothed in the rain. Now he recoiled at the thought of a woman nursing her baby "whilst the sleet fell and thawed on her naked bosom and on the skin of her naked baby!"[42]

More boldly, he mused on the isolation of the Galápagos Islands and the adaptations the animals and birds displayed. The publication of *Vestiges* did not completely break his confidence in his own evolutionary theory. But it plainly cramped his style. He was cautious about laying himself open to the kind of heated responses *Vestiges* generated and in which he partly joined himself; and he made his words sufficiently ambiguous to be read one way or the other. The archipelago was a "little world within itself," he said in the new edition.

> Considering the small size of the islands, we feel the more astonished at the number of their aboriginal beings, and at their confined range. Seeing every height crowned with its crater, and the boundaries of most of the lava-streams still distinct, we are led to believe that within a period, geologically recent, the unbroken ocean was here spread out. Hence, both in space and time, we seem to be brought somewhat near to that great fact—that mystery of mysteries—the first appearance of new beings on this earth.[43]

As for the finches, he presented the information that was mostly lacking before. "Seeing this gradation and diversity of structure in one small, intimately related group of birds, one might really fancy that from an original paucity of birds in this archipelago, one species had been taken and modified for different ends. In a like manner it might be fancied that a bird originally a buzzard, had been induced here to undertake the office of the carrion-feeding Polybori of the American continent."[44]

Already he was mapping out his ground. He was not going to be damned like Mr. Vestiges for being a "dabbler in science," or for taking up subjects "where their prudent cultivators have left them." But his remarks were left hanging as uncomfortably between the two worlds as he found himself. He dedicated the book to Lyell and sent it off with relief to the printers.

VII

Soon afterwards, Sedgwick burst out against *Vestiges* with more venom than he had ever showed in his life. Writing in the *Edinburgh Review* for July 1845, read by Darwin towards the end of September, Sedgwick denounced *Vestiges* in the most violent, peremptory manner imaginable, firing off an astonishing variety of personal, philosophical, and factual broadsides with the intention of utterly demolishing both this text and any general arguments for transmutation. It was a remarkably popular book, he conceded. But everything in it was shallow: it showed "the glitter of gold-leaf without the solidity of the precious metal." He saw no sign of any scientific expertise, no close study at the cutting edge of original research. Getting into his stride, he declared it was so bad it could almost have been written by a woman. But not even a woman could stoop so low as to put all the phenomena of the universe together as "the progression and development of a rank, unbending and degrading materialism."[45]

Above all, Sedgwick stormed, *Vestiges* rejected the word of God and the author "thinks he can make man and woman far better by the help of a baboon." The idea filled Sedgwick with inexpressible disgust. Such gross credulity and rank infidelity, he told Lyell in a private letter, could only breed deformed intellectual progeny. "If the book be true, the labours of sober induction are in vain; religion is a lie; human law a mass of folly and a base injustice; morality is moonshine; our labours for the black people of Africa were works of madmen; and men and women are only better beasts!"[46]

This was the way towards atheism and the collapse of Victorian society, he raged on in the *Edinburgh*. Who but an author whose mind had been warped by the "fetters of rank materialism" would dare to write such irreverent nonsense? Woe to the world, he concluded in his best fire-and-brimstone manner, if our knowledge was to be made up of idle speculations like these.

Although Sedgwick's review was published anonymously, as was the custom of the time, everyone in his circle knew he was the author. He emerged as the unofficial representative of a central group of university gentleman-philosophers and natural scientists anxious to demolish *Vestiges'* dangerous doctrines. Yet even Owen and Whewell, who stepped aside for Sedgwick to tackle the review, were shocked by his "threshing humour."[47]

Darwin was almost as appalled by Sedgwick's review as he was by *Vestiges*. He had never seen such fury unleashed before. All his private fears about being whipped by critics became frighteningly real. It was not possible to continue closing his eyes to the vehement opposition that was virtually certain to greet his own theories. Though Sedgwick's diatribe, as he complained to Lyell, smacked more of the pulpit than of a professorial chair, the Cambridge don had produced a devastatingly effective argument against the mutability of species. "I read it with fear & trembling," Darwin said woefully.[48]

Sedgwick, Darwin recognised in horror, was not only fervently against transmutation but also prepared to marshal every conceivable counter-argument from the most powerful authorities of the day. He spoke for the audience Darwin wanted to convince, using the words that the very same audience supplied. And the evidence Sedgwick brought in to demolish *Vestiges* was the same evidence that these men, as a group, were most likely to bring up as decisive facts against any theory of transmutation: a well-established consensus about the meaning of embryology, classification, anatomy, and palaeontology; the moral question of the origin of mankind and of religion too. These were the points Darwin would have to counter if he wanted to persuade. "I was well pleased to find that I had not overlooked any of the arguments," he told Lyell unhappily, "though I had put them to myself as feebly as milk & water."

He was shocked, moreover, by the ugly passion Sedgwick displayed. No gentleman of science should brawl in public like that, he thought. The author's wish to remain unknown did not give Sedgwick the right to blast him out of the sky like a pigeon. For these reasons Darwin was pleasantly surprised when Mr. Vestiges attempted to answer the grossest of Sedgwick's accusations in a book (again anonymous) called *Explanations: A Sequel to the "Vestiges of the Natural History of Creation,"* published at the end of 1845. The gentlemanly spirit of this answer, though not the facts, said Darwin, ought to shame Sedgwick.[49]

Nonetheless, the explosion from Cambridge almost annihilated him. Sedgwick summarised the opposition Darwin faced if he brought a theory of transmutation before the scientific public—opposition far more vehement than he had supposed existed from his few tentative confessions to friends. Formerly he had learned what transmutation was about from Lyell's impassioned demolition of Lamarck. Sedgwick's assault on *Vestiges* similarly revealed to him the ferocity of anti-evolutionary opinion in his circle. How could he proceed to publish after reading that transmutation was vile, full of "inner deformity and foulness"?

VIII

After this, Darwin recoiled into anxious self-examination and personal doubt. Despite all his careful work and reputation as a good naturalist, he felt exposed to some of Sedgwick's harshest accusations. What did he really know of comparative anatomy except that which he got from books and talks with experts? His knowledge of embryology, he guiltily thought, was as slight as that of *Vestiges*. His physiology was nonexistent. The technical world of plant anatomy, as Hooker unintentionally disclosed in every letter, was equally unknown territory. And classification was something he usually persuaded other people to do for him. Where was the fine-grained expertise in living animals and plants that Sedgwick demanded of acceptable theorists?

Perhaps Darwin would have ignored this part of Sedgwick's thunder if only Hooker had not come out with strong words along the same lines. The two men were corresponding about the vagaries of hasty French philosophers. Frédéric Gérard, whose pamphlet on species Hooker forwarded to Darwin, was the immediate culprit. Gérard had no idea, volleyed Hooker, how much labour was required to establish or destroy a "good" species: how much skill and judgement went into grouping individuals into useful categories. Nature was a muddle, Hooker went on, and species, though they certainly seemed to exist, were not easily defined on morphological grounds. Facetiously, he said he was glad Gérard's glib transmutation interested Darwin. "I am not inclined to take much for granted from any one who treats the subject in his way & who does not know what it is to be a specific naturalist."[50] All the pent-up furies of a taxonomist battling with thousands of herbarium sheets burst out: people who knew their material properly did not make outrageous claims like Gérard's.

Darwin took Hooker's words as a criticism of his own position. "How painfully (to me) true is your remark that no one has hardly a right to examine the question of species who has not minutely examined many."

> My only comfort is, (as I mean to attempt the subject) that I have dabbled in several branches of Nat. hist. & seen good specific men work out my species & know something of geology; (an indispensible union) & though I shall get more kicks than half-pennies, I will, life serving, attempt my work.—Lamarck is the only exception, that I can think of, of an accurate describer of species at least in the invertebrate kingdom, who has disbelieved in permanent species, but he in his absurd though clever work has done the subject harm, as has Mr Vestiges, and as (some future loose naturalist attempting the same speculations will perhaps say) has Mr D.[51]

Distressed, Hooker wrote back quickly to apologise. Nevertheless, continued Darwin in another letter, all that Hooker kindly said about his species work "does not alter one iota my long self-acknowledged presumption in accumulating facts & speculating on the subject of variation, without having worked out my due share of species." For the first time he doubted his ability to do the thing properly.

So on 1 October 1846, when Darwin posted his last geological proof back to the printers from Down, he went to retrieve his last remaining bottle of specimens from the *Beagle* voyage. The moment was ripe for some close analysis of a real animal—an opportunity to study classificatory theories by describing and cataloguing unknown species and to earn his taxonomic spurs the hard way, as Hooker seemed to imply. Out of the top came an unusual barnacle collected in the Chonos Archipelago, a small crustacean animal that lived embedded inside the shell of a mollusc found on the beach. Dusting off his zoological notes for the period, Darwin read how, in 1835, he thought it burrowed its way into the larger host when it was young. The larval form was almost unrecognisable as a barnacle. "Who would recognise a young Balanus in this illformed little monster. . . . It is manifest this curious little animal forms new genus," he had written.[52] More curious than this, he could hardly see the adult male. It lived unnoticed and much reduced in size inside the carapace of the female. Their respective growth and their sexual relations looked likely to be another one of his explorations into the reproductive unknown.

Hooker, long since forgiven for his taxonomic gaffe, was one of those useful friends who could turn their hand to anything, and during a weekend visit to Down to meet Bartholomew Sulivan in October 1846, in the occasional breathing spaces left between Sulivan's extended naval tales, he helped Darwin set up his microscope and make some preliminary studies of the anatomy of the unnamed barnacle. "Are you a good hand at inventing names?" Darwin asked him. "I have a new & curious genus of Barnacle which I want to name, & how to invent a name completely puzzles me." Together they decided to call it Arthrobalanus—"Mr Arthrobalanus" in subsequent letters, cheerily acknowledging its chief anomalous feature of possessing two penises and playing on the otherwise enfeebled, diminutive state of the male compared to the female.

Happily off on another hobby horse, Darwin planned to write a short paper identifying and describing his find, sending Hooker home with a few specimens to dissect at his leisure. Less than a week afterwards he wanted Hooker to answer more questions by post and to provide drawings. "The more I read," Darwin wrote to him, "the more singular does our little fellow appear." The number and position of the legs on the larvae, he realised, were crucial in identifying its nearest relations. Every day he tried harder to see things and got better at it; every day he found himself ranging through his varied natural history knowledge more and more widely to explain some of Arthrobalanus's anomalies. "I see you have not put in any trace of the oblique articulation between the head & sternum," he wrote to Hooker anxiously on 26 October. "Do you deliberately give it up? I certainly *thought* that there was one." A few days later he shouted with delight: "I believe Arthobalanus has no ovisac at all! & that the appearance of one is entirely owing to the splitting & tucking up of the posterior penis, of the inner membrane of sack."

He fished other barnacles out of the bottle for comparison. As you say, he murmured contentedly to Hooker, "there is an extraordinary pleasure in pure observation; not but what I suspect the pleasure in this case is rather derived from comparisons forming in ones mind with allied structures. After having been so many years employed in writing my old geological observations it is delightful to use one's eyes & fingers again."[53] Before long, he had finished his paper and sent it on its way to Richard Owen for his comments.

He was gripped. Just before Christmas he decided to make a full study of the entire order of barnacles.

DYING BY INCHES

ARWIN'S "beloved barnacles" lasted for eight more years, much longer than he anticipated, and eventually making him wonder whether the work was worth so much time. Edward Bulwer-Lytton was perfectly justified, he acknowledged ruefully, in caricaturing him as the absurdly preoccupied Professor Long in his novel of 1858, *What Will He Do with It?* His own family took it in their stride. "Where," said one of Darwin's small boys to another child when out visiting, "does your father do his barnacles?" Defensively, Darwin relished the air of eccentricity his investigations created. He was very fortunate, he joked to Emma, to have "an employment which I, at least, do not consider mere amusement."

And like a barnacle himself he settled down into middle age. Surrounded by the security of his house, his wife, the growing children, and his servants, he pushed the outside world away. Darwin discovered he preferred peace to anything else. He wanted to disengage himself from the tiresome bustle of normal adult life and went to enormous lengths to ensure that his days at Down were unruffled, building up a protective shell both physically, in his "great earthworks" and construction projects around the house and grounds, and psychologically, in developing a daily routine that required many quiet hours alone in his study. When he needed his friends, they were invited to stay. When he needed information, he wrote letters. Occasionally, he would emerge for a trip to London—he would go to Erasmus's house for the night, read a few books in scientific libraries, perhaps visit Owen or Lyell for a chat after breakfast, and collect his parcels from the Athenaeum Club. All of this he hugely enjoyed, and although he insisted on calling the visits a chore, they were not nearly so bad once he got going. He usually went alone. By now

Emma had learned to make her own arrangements for London shopping and trips to the theatre, and she invariably set off independently for the Hensleigh Wedgwoods' house in Cumberland Terrace. She hated Darwin's early starts, sometimes as early as five o'clock for a day in town, and his anxiety about getting to the station at least half an hour before the train was due to leave: all the fuss made the day more trouble than it was worth, she thought. Darwin welcomed the jab of intellectual stimulation he got from a trip to London. Afterwards he would retire again gratefully to the "absolute rurality" of Down.

This keen appreciation of solitude was understandable now that the household at Down was getting larger and noisier. Darwin and Emma had four children in 1846. By the end of 1850 there were three more, making a family running from William, the eldest at eleven years old, through the two girls Anne and Henrietta, to George (age five), Elizabeth (age three), Francis (age two), and the baby Leonard, born in January 1850. Nursemaids, housemaids, ponies, dogs, gardeners, stablehands, and governesses increased to match. Even Parslow the butler asked for help: on some occasions there could be "twenty pairs of little shoes to clean," he complained.[1]

Aunt Sarah Wedgwood came to live in the same village for the family company, and Emma's unmarried sister Elizabeth was often at Down House for weeks at a time. Charlotte (Wedgwood) Langton and Caroline (Darwin) Wedgwood lived close enough for regular visits; Fanny (Mackintosh) Wedgwood and her children were frequent guests, along with Emma's other assorted nephews and nieces; and Erasmus often came to stay despite his usual protestations of hating the country. "I have been extremely rural all this week," he complained to Fanny during one trip, "and have made several efforts to draw a donkey, but hitherto without much success." Alternatively, when Fanny was at Down, Erasmus wrote from London full of backhanded commiserations. "How is your cold? and is the house very cold? and do Emily Taylor's notes follow you to Down because if they don't your visit will be so pleasant you'll never come back and I shall have to fill her office."

Emma's diaries, in fact, were crammed with notes recording the comings and goings of a constant stream of relatives, sufficient to strike terror into the heart of even the most sociable of men. Without the formal, well-defined escape route supplied by his work, Darwin might have got sucked into a variety of time-consuming social occupations and parental outings. Although he generally liked company as much as Emma did, and enjoyed playing with his children, he nevertheless began arranging his days so that these kinds of intimate contact came only when he wanted them. The family was something to engage in when he had nothing else to do. By sitting in his study "doing" his barnacles, Darwin could be alone, getting on with his inner life, avoiding what he considered unnecessary demands on his time and attention.

More than anything, however, his preoccupation with barnacles was an indirect way of avoiding the full force of the religious and metaphysical implications of his ideas. Looking through a microscope provided the certainty of doing something useful without constantly coming up against difficult moral questions which he was at a loss to resolve. Looking at objects again made him realise how exhausted he was by the previous years of intellectual effort, too drained to marshal any sort of counter-blast to *Vestiges* or to Sedgwick's diatribes. He did not have much of an answer to his potential critics—nothing except personal conviction. In particular, he shrank from publishing his evolutionary essay, not so much from fear or irresolution, although these no doubt played their part in the fervid Vestigarian atmosphere, as from a much stronger sense of scientific caution. His theory was insufficiently documented, he thought in despair; not yet ready. Warily, he wanted to leave nothing to chance. If he encountered problems in seeing how transmutation might have taken place, how much greater and more potent would be the problems other people discovered in his work. For the moment he had had enough. He was too tired to think straight, astonished at where he had ended up. In ten years he had written four books, edited nineteen numbers of the *Zoology,* revised his *Journal of Researches* for a second edition, published twenty-five scientific papers and notes, filled six or eight notebooks on the most taxing philosophical issues of the age, read an extraordinary number of books, and composed an essay on transmutation running to 230 manuscript pages. There was nothing left in him to say. Throwing himself into a thoroughgoing practical occupation was a trusted remedy: Darwin did not have to confront God, or apes, or Emma, if he was busy with dissecting needles—at least not directly.

He relaxed for nearly the first time since disembarking from the *Beagle.*

II

Still, the extent of the barnacle project crept up unsuspected. Darwin only intended "to get out a little zoology & hurrah for my species-work."

He would perhaps have finished at the beginning of 1847 if Owen had not recommended his making a comparison between Arthrobalanus and a much wider range of species. Owen carefully explained his views on the existence of an abstract plan or "archetype" in living beings which allowed naturalists to see structural and functional relationships between organisms. Animal parts were basically the same throughout creation, he stressed, but individually modified for their particular function in different species: Surely barnacles mirrored an "archetypal" crustacean in some way or another? The species Arthrobalanus was exceedingly aberrant, was it not? Darwin should consider how far it was related to other, more conventionally arranged barnacles and to a typical crustacean: these were the kind of points thoughtful naturalists would expect to have answered if he intended publishing.

And of course Owen was right. Although Darwin already knew about Owen's archetypes and was well versed in similar views emanating from continental naturalists, he was suddenly nervous. When he arrived at Owen's house before breakfast on 7 January 1847 they talked it over exhaustively. Mrs. Owen patiently stood by. "He and R. had a long discussion on the subject of R.'s views on osteology and the archetype. After breakfast R. brought out his 'Broadsheet of Osteology' [synonyms of bones, showing the basic unity of form between them]. Mr Darwin quite saw the force of that."[2]

Owen's precise definitions enabled Darwin to disclose many more links between his specimens than he had expected. "I work out mouths and cirri carefully, muscular structure & tunics of the sack, & some of the structure of the viscera," he told Owen anxiously a few days later. "Whether this is worth doing I am not sure." It took hours to understand the complicated grooves and sutures in the shells, he complained more confidently in February; "I hope to heaven I am right in spending so much time over one object." This detailed anatomical work, however, was precisely what Darwin's contemporaries praised most in his resulting monographs. He was very thorough indeed.[3]

Darwin would also perhaps have finished a few months further along, in the summer of 1847, if he had not heard Louis Agassiz give a speech at the British Association meeting in Southampton declaring that a full study of barnacles (Cirripedia) was a "great desideratum." Coming from Agassiz, one of the finest naturalists of the age, a man on his way to take America by storm as the first professor of natural history in the country, the message hit Darwin forcefully. Though Darwin only met him briefly at the meeting, he always remembered the impact of Agassiz's words. Pragmatically, he ignored their diverging geological opinions. Ice ages and Glen Roy could wait until he had got what he needed about barnacles from this talented scholar.

He would no doubt have reached a conclusion the following winter after studying a good proportion of the pedunculate (stalked) barnacles if John Edward Gray from the British Museum had not steered him towards publishing an even wider survey. Gray helped Darwin pull off an extraordinary scientific coup in persuading the British Museum to lend him its entire Cirripedia collection. Moreover, Gray gave up his own half-finished researches so that Darwin could work on the group. There was a distinct air of favours being returned in these gentlemanly negotiations, since Darwin had previously supplied a handsome testimonial for Gray during his struggle to become the Keeper of Zoology in 1840: negotiations that Darwin was happy to ease along thanks to his appreciation of Gray's skill as a naturalist and the fact that he was the older brother of George Gray, Darwin's bird man for the *Zoology* book. Gray, moreover, anticipated administrative battles in the future, especially with Antonio Panizzi, the powerful librarian of the museum, who desperately wanted to co-opt Gray's natural history display space for books.[4] Darwin, Gray correctly believed, was a useful name to pull out when he needed it. Equally, Gray envisaged little time for cataloguing barnacles when a series of huge boxes started arriving in his department from John Rae's Arctic explorations.

Yet there was no reason for Darwin to assume that either Gray or the trustees would let uncatalogued material go outside. Darwin wanted much more than grudging access to the specimens. He wanted to have them at home in Kent. He wanted to dissect them, perhaps rendering them useless for further investigations. He wanted them all. In short, he hoped for exclusive command of the museum's unique national collection. That he managed to achieve this, with Gray's help, was a measure of how influential he had become in English intellectual circles.

But even a full survey of the museum's specimens would have lasted only for another year, maybe two. Darwin made arrangements to publish a volume describing his results with exactly that sort of time frame in mind, agreeing to send his material to the Ray Society, a small, privately run publishing association, for publication around 1850.

What really prevented Darwin from finishing was his discovery of the barnacles' sex life early in 1848. Their arcane sexual relations gripped him; he was puzzled, then intrigued. Examining the genera *Ibla* and *Scalpellum* in April and May that year, he was astonished to find that several of the species were not hermaphroditic—as was usual in barnacles—but possessed two separate sexes, male and female. The males were minute, rudimentary organisms, living virtually as parasites inside the carapace of the females. The male, he informed Henslow excitedly, was microscopically minute, even smaller than Mr. Arthrobalanus. "But here comes the odd fact, the male, or sometimes two males, at the instant they cease being locomotive larvae become parasitic in the sack of the female, & thus fixed & half embedded in the flesh of their wives they pass their whole lives & can never move again."[5]

He could afford a more knowing masculine smile to Lyell. The female "had two little pockets, in *each* of which she kept a little husband. I do not know of any other case where a female invariably has two husbands. . . . Truly the schemes & wonders of nature are illimitable."[6]

Through the rest of the spring and summer, Darwin looked carefully at the remaining hermaphrodite species in the same groups. His next discovery was even stranger. Some of these hermaphrodites possessed tiny "extra" males that seemed to complement the ordinary reproductive process, a kind of triple sexual arrangement, two parts male to one part female. Darwin's incredulity knew no bounds. "I have been getting on well with my beloved cirripedia," he cried to Hooker, far away in India.

> I have lately got a bisexual [two-sexed] cirripede, the male being micro-scopically small & parasite within the sack of the female. I tell you this to boast of my species theory, for the nearest & closely allied genus to it is, as usual, hermaphrodite, but I had observed some minute parasites adhering to it, & these parasites, I now can show, are supplemental males, the male organs in the hermaphrodite being unusually small, though perfect & containing zoosperms: so we have almost a polygamous animal, simple females alone being wanting.[7]

The astonishment came because he believed he had found a series of forms illustrating the gradual emergence of separate sexes from an unknown hermaphrodite ancestor. By putting all the living species together he could imagine what had probably happened during the course of their evolution: he could recreate their family tree, jumping from branch to branch in a flurry of delighted anticipation, dipping into the past as if it were in some sense a real entity before him, finding links and connections between his metaphori-cal twigs and leaves where other naturalists saw only the blanks of an unbreachable void. Through the sheer power of imagination he saw how species could be joined together by descent—a story of development linking geological antiquity with the present day. Some barnacles were ordinary hermaphrodites, as it were, possessing the usual male and female equipment, side by side, in each and every individual; others represented a stage of semi-hermaphroditism in which the male organs were still present next to the female ones but were reinforced by the tiny free-living extra or "comple-mental" males as Darwin called them. Further along the scale, a number of species had two sexes, the males similarly tiny and living attached to the female as "mere bags of spermatozoa." The process was one in which a hermaphroditic animal evolved into a hermaphrodite with an extra male, which in turn evolved into a two-sexed species comprising a female and a parasitic male.

Darwin was completely staggered, unprepared for any such contribution to his views. Nevertheless the find was another example of the way he sometimes almost willed appropriate evidence out of apparently intractable material: in one way or another he made it happen. Down among his barnacles he felt he was seeing evolution in action. This idea of an aboriginal hermaphrodite stood at the heart of his theories. Long before reading Malthus or constructing the idea of natural selection, Darwin thought there must have been some kind of divergence of the sexes from an ancestral hermaphrodite—an idea he worked out in the pages of his notebooks and subsequently pursued by examining the structure of aberrant flowers, particularly those with abortive stamens or pistils. Now the barnacles confirmed it. Their sexual relations seemed to him to mirror the probable emergence of single-sexed flowers out of plants with both male and female organs. Such a symmetry thoroughly pleased him. He would not—could not—have understood these relations without looking at his specimens with the evolution of sex in mind. As he went on to protest cheerfully to Hooker and Henslow, he thought the extra males were parasites at first, even throwing some of them out of his bottles as inconvenient distractions.

On another level, too, the new information explained one of his greatest difficulties in understanding transmutation—one of the many practical problems that plagued him for years before he felt ready to publish. He had often wondered about the origin of vestigial or rudimentary organs, cases in which some features of one sex appear in a rudimentary or nonfunctional state in the other. The wild thyme plants he collected from Maer Heath with their withered stamens featured among several similar cases described in his notebooks. Nipples bothered him. But at last Darwin saw an answer to why he—a man—should have nipples. On the principle of perfect adaptation, this curious feature of his own anatomy was entirely redundant. Child after child feeding at Emma's breast made that point ridiculously clear. With a start, Darwin realised that he carried on his chest the evidence of an ancestral divergence of the sexes. He was not just a "bag of spermatozoa" as he occasionally feared, like the diminutive males under his microscope, superfluous to the human domestic economy except for providing money and a means for procreation. Even the procreation, he sometimes thought plaintively, was restricted to the few intervals when Emma was not pregnant or nursing: only three months during the last eighteen. Women of Emma's background conventionally saw these maternal events as a signal to retire to their own bedrooms rather than taking advantage of their contraceptive properties.

Long ago, Darwin realised, he was once hermaphroditic. He carried both male and female within him. Everything alive was once hermaphroditic. Added to this, there was an evolutionary tendency for the sexes to diverge and specialise. The whole of nature was adapted to encourage sexual relations. Through his barnacles and the constant procession of babies at Down, Darwin thus stumbled onto one of his greatest insights, one that ran through his work for the rest of his days: nature abhors the idea of self-fertilisation.

"I never shd have made this out, had not my species theory convinced me that an hermaphrodite species must pass into a bisexual species by insensibly small stages," he crowed to Hooker jubilantly; "& here we have it, for the male organs in the hermaphrodite are beginning to fail, & independent males already formed. But I can hardly explain what I mean, & you will perhaps wish my barnacles & species theory al Diabolo together. But I dont care what you say, my species theory is all gospel."[8] Henslow heard the same shout of triumph. "I am in a very cock-a-hoop state about my anatomy of the Cirripedia & think I have made out some very curious points. My book will be published in two years by the Ray Soc., & will I trust do no discredit (see how vain I am!) to your old pupil & most attached friend."[9]

III

Flushed with his unexpected achievement, Darwin therefore reacted badly when John Edward Gray reentered the scene waving a couple of short papers about barnacles of his own. He thought Gray had given up his intention to publish work on this group and was disconcerted, to say the least. Worse than that, the species Gray described were dangerously similar to Darwin's interesting "polygamous" forms: what if Gray saw the same things from a nonevolutionary angle and spoiled his treasure trove?

Darwin simmered for a while and then exploded politely in the post. Gray's two papers trespassed on his own territory. Some of his friends, he said darkly, had warned him that Gray "intended to anticipate my work."

> I had resolved not to mention to you these communications (the first of which I received some months since) but now when coming to the determination of the species, I felt anxious to know what you intended doing, and I think you will admit that it was natural that I should wish that what little of novelty there yet remained in the subject, should be the reward of my work, which I assure you has been to my utmost every day.—I certainly should not have dreamed of undergoing the labour of making out all the close species if I had supposed that the most striking & therefore most interesting & easy forms were to be described before me; and this I hope you will consider a sufficient apology for my having spoken to you on this subject.[10]

Stiffly, Gray replied that he was only trying to be helpful. But he renounced all further activity in that field. He needed Darwin on his side. Panizzi was getting more troublesome about museum space by the day.

In October 1848, Darwin felt safe enough to repeat his news cautiously to Agassiz over at Harvard, a far stronger invertebrate anatomist than the museum-bound Gray or any of Darwin's indulgent scientific friends. By then he knew he was on to something quite remarkable. If he was wrong, Agassiz would soon tell him. If he was right, Agassiz would be impressed, would see him as a creditable anatomist. Yet the spectre of Gray still loomed. "I shd be glad if you would not mention my present results," he hesitantly asked, "partly because I shd like to have the satisfaction of publishing myself what few new points I have found out, & partly because one is more free to alter ones own views when they are confined to one's own breast."

Agassiz *was* impressed. Though he utterly rejected concepts of progressive development, sharing Sedgwick's horrified view of *Vestiges* and all it implied for the sanctity of a creator, and ultimately rejecting Darwin's theories of evolution as vehemently as any preacher, he was acutely aware of the value of comparative work among the lower invertebrates and respected Darwin's close attention to embryological phenomena. Like the majority of expert naturalists he honoured those men most who devoted themselves to original researches: Darwin's "works on the coral reefs, on the cirripeds, and his narrative of the voyage of the Beagle, show him to be a skillful and well prepared naturalist," he was to concede generously in later years.[11] He was perfectly willing to help Darwin with barnacles. In response he sent Darwin several North American species (some from Massachusetts, others from Charleston) and then a copy of his book on the natural history of Lake Superior when it was published in 1850. Deeply flattered, Darwin continued the correspondence as best as he could. He too recorded in later life that "when we met many years ago I felt for you the warmest admiration."

From then on Darwin committed himself to making a complete scientific survey of the group. He was convinced his barnacles would provide many of the facts he still wanted for evolutionary theory. Through them he might see how far his ideas could go, not only in relation to the origin of sex and the necessity for cross-fertilisation but also as they might explain structural resemblances, adaptations, and changes in the functions of organs, all the difficult anatomical questions raised in his evolutionary essay that were languishing partly unanswered. Darwin's concern to collect such "facts" was not a delaying tactic any more, if indeed it ever had been, but a vital part of his continuing scientific work. He glimpsed the possibility of proving his point—maybe not absolute proof, because this was always to elude him, but at least the most convincing demonstration of the effectiveness of his proposals he had yet come across. Barnacles might show him what transmutation looked like in the real world.

So he worked hard constructing the largest and most effective natural history correspondence network he ever attempted, possibly one of the largest and most efficient of the era. Although Hooker knew a great deal about marine zoology, and Henslow and Lyell were always helpful, Darwin intended becoming the hub of a far wider supply of expert zoological information and specimens. Deliberately he set out to re-create something of the geographical spread, the exclusive access to specimens, and the hierarchy of help that he had once enjoyed on the *Beagle*. Owen, Agassiz, and Gray were but a first crucial step towards fulfilling that plan.

He read extensively on invertebrates and wrote to the men in Europe and America he thought likely to assist him. Not many people were working on Crustacea, he found, let alone barnacles. In truth, less than twenty years before, naturalists were quite content to classify barnacles as molluscs until John Vaughan Thomson showed them otherwise: barnacles, Thomson stated, were rather like prawns turned on their heads and cemented to a rock.[12] As Agassiz subsequently pointed out at the British Association, their life cycle and the process of metamorphosis from free-swimming larvae to sessile animals encased in the valves of a shell were virtually unknown. Darwin needed the advice and cooperation of those few experts who were already involved. "Can you aid me in obtaining the loan for me of any specimens?" he wrote to Henri Milne-Edwards at the Paris Muséum d'Histoire Naturelle. Coaxingly, Darwin explained how the British Museum gave him a free rein. "Would it be possible for me to have for examination a single specimen of some of the species figured in the Voyage of the Astrolabe. I am most anxious for the genus Alepas, as it is the only genus which I have not dissected carefully." Darwin listed the other species he particularly wished to see. "I have found a good deal new in the anatomy, & hope & think you will approve of my work. Permit me to say how invaluably useful I have found your work on the Crustacea."[13]

Shamelessly, Darwin threw the same grappling iron out over the Atlantic to Augustus Gould, a Bostonian physician who was an authority on molluscs, and to James Dwight Dana. Unerringly, he hit the most desirable American targets.

Dana's life until then had more or less matched Darwin's in the way he travelled round the world as a civilian geologist on the United States Exploring Expedition under Captain Wilkes, and then took on the role of naturalist when Joseph Couthouy was dismissed from the expedition at Sydney. He was just as inquiring as Darwin, and similarly prolific as a natural history author. After the American ship's return in 1842, he lived modestly at New Haven writing mountainous tomes on the corals, geology, and marine zoology of the voyage, outdoing even Lyell in his devotion to uniformitarianism, and helping his father-in-law, Benjamin Silliman, edit the *American Journal of Arts and Sciences*. Later on, a well-deserved professorship came his way at Yale University. Yet when Darwin wrote to ask if he could have Dana's barnacles, he received a friendly but firm refusal. Not for the first time, Darwin experienced the *frisson* of competition. Dana intended working on the barnacles himself; he was already publishing articles in the United States that Darwin had not seen on metamorphosis and the homologies of parts. More than this, Dana doubted if the American authorities would let specimens go overseas. Underneath lay the fact that Dana—as Darwin knew perfectly well—partly disagreed with Darwin's theory of coral reefs. Dana was the only other naturalist in the English-speaking world sufficiently well travelled and competent in a wide enough field to tackle Darwin's ideas about coral at the same level as Darwin, the only man to provide a modified alternative.

Still, Dana was not unwilling to help. Both he and Augustus Gould struck up a friendly correspondence with Darwin which continued over many years, fortified by the exchange of books and papers and by erudite talk on anatomical and geological points. Dana told Darwin about the natural history work being done in the United States, exchanged news about his own and other geological studies, and freely discussed many of the points Darwin found most puzzling about crustaceans. In return, whenever Darwin could he complimented Dana on his work. "I have not for some years been so much pleased, as I have just been by reading your most able discussion on coral reefs.—I thank you most sincerely for the very honourable mention you make of me. . . . You will see in next number of Geolog. Journal that Sir C. Lyell has read your volcanic chapters & he was *very much* interested by them."[14]

Darwin turned also to British naval captains, travelling naturalists, and the men stationed around the empire. He wrote to Captain King in Australia about the barnacles King had collected on the first *Beagle* voyage and was given permission to use these as he wished. He approached James Clark Ross, Hooker's former captain on the Antarctic survey, who was shortly to go out searching in the Arctic Circle for the lost Franklin expedition. Ross said he would collect some interesting Arctic species for him. Peter Sutherland, a medical surgeon on previous Arctic voyages, gave him a good Arctic collection as well.

Closer to home, Darwin persuaded Hugh Cuming, the much-travelled conchologist, to put valuable foreign material at his disposal. He engineered introductions to a whole range of less well known but no less expert figures like Samuel Stutchbury in Bristol and James Scott Bowerbank, a fellow member of the Geological Society council with Darwin. Specialising in sponges and invertebrate fossils, Bowerbank was just the kind of contact man Darwin valued the most. Solidly prosperous in business, with his money sunk into a privately owned distillery, Bowerbank followed geology and marine zoology avidly, using his sound commercial sense to run one or two small, independent scientific publishing companies and finding himself much in demand as secretary or treasurer to a series of learned societies. Bowerbank put Darwin in touch with numerous local collectors and investigators he would never otherwise have heard of. Most important, Bowerbank suggested that the Ray Society, the most prominent publishing society he was involved with, might produce Darwin's resulting monograph. Like all the Ray Society's publications, this one would be self-financed by annual subscriptions from the members. Darwin accepted with alacrity. No commercial publisher, he recognised, would contemplate the risk of bringing out a book on such an oddly obscure topic as barnacles.

When Darwin decided that he would do fossil barnacles as well for the sake of completeness, Bowerbank came up trumps with the Palaeontographical Society, another publishing society under his general sway. This second society, Bowerbank assured him, was keen to take whatever Darwin offered on terms similar to those of the Ray Society. Darwin consequently sifted through his fossil friends and sent out feelers again. William Lonsdale, Cuming, Bowerbank, the two Sowerby brothers, George Robert Waterhouse, and Samuel Pickworth Woodward were palaeontologists he already knew, and could ask for help—which he did, several times over. Not long afterwards the trail took him to Robert Fitch, one of the greatest if least-known collectors of fossil barnacles in Britain. "Yours is incomparably the finest collection in the world of fossil Secondary Cirripedia," murmured Darwin appreciatively before asking if he could borrow it, lock, stock, and barrel. Since Fitch was a man of fairly humble origins, a pharmacist in Norwich, he was impressed by these unlooked-for compliments, and allowed Darwin to dismember his collection. Later on, when Fitch asked a trifle impatiently about his specimens, Darwin was quick to smooth things over. The course of natural history expertise was often tiresome: "It is most provoking to me to reflect that I have detained so many specimens so long from their owners, some I am ashamed to say for twice as long as I have had yours. I do hope you will let Mr S. [James de Carle Sowerby] keep the specimens till he has completed the engravings—so important has your collection been to me, that the withdrawal would quite destroy my monograph."[15]

Looking overseas, Darwin also wrote for fossil barnacles to Alcide d'Orbigny, his French competitor in South America during the *Beagle* voyage, who was now occupying a comfortable professorial chair at the Muséum d'Histoire Naturelle. He wrote again to the American triumvirate of Agassiz, Dana, and Gould; to Wilhelm Dunker and Professors Roemer and Philippi in Germany; to Joseph Bosquet in Holland; to Professor Forchammer in Denmark (whom he had met and liked at Southampton); and to Forchammer's acquaintance Sven Loven, professor of natural history at the Stockholm museum, whose paper on an unusual barnacle (*Alepas squalicola*) Mary Lyell bravely translated out of Swedish for him.

Most important of all, he wrote to Johannes Japetus Steenstrup in Copenhagen. Steenstrup was professor of zoology at Copenhagen University, the same institution where Forchammer taught geology, and the author of one of the most important books of the century on the reproduction of invertebrate animals. Referring predominantly to the life cycles of polyps and jellyfish, Steenstrup pointed out that there was what he called an alternation of generations: a sequence of births in which adult individuals produced offspring totally unlike themselves, not strictly larvae since they underwent a kind of reproductive process, which in turn produced a form like the adult again. Steenstrup visualised the intermediate generation as something like a sexless nursing mother—a female generation in which the sex organs had been aborted in order to issue the next, properly sexual, adultlike form.[16] Darwin was naturally intrigued by this work as soon as it was translated into English in 1845. "I assure you I consider receiving even a letter from the author of the volume on Alternate Generations a pleasure & honour," he declared, genuinely impressed. It was the beginning of a long and courteous relationship conducted entirely by letter. To the end of his life, Darwin regretted that Steenstrup could not bring himself to believe in evolution.

Darwin's list of correspondents grew larger and larger. In 1849, at the Birmingham meeting of the British Association, he listened to a paper sent in by Albany Hancock, a capable zoologist from Newcastle, announcing the discovery of a new barnacle that drilled holes in rocks. Hancock was not present at the meeting to hear Darwin's impromptu speech afterwards in which he suggested Hancock's barnacle was rather like his own Arthrobalanus, which similarly bored into mollusc shells. Darwin was startled to hear Hancock's proposal that an entirely new taxonomic order (Cryptosomata) should be created for this single rock-excavating species, the justification being that it was so very different from any known crustacean. Darwin was not averse to making the new order because he too saw the necessity of creating a separate niche for Arthrobalanus. But he was anxious about how to locate these aberrant forms in a meaningful classification scheme.[17] The situation prompted him to write to Hancock without an introduction—almost unheard of in his circle. Yet he was unlikely to find another naturalist with problems so much the same as his own and one, moreover, who possessed such an interesting new species. For these reasons, Darwin carefully avoided treading on Hancock's intellectual toes, feeling that he could hardly barge in and stake out his territory as he had done with Gray. "I have no sort of pretension to claim any favour from you, but if you could at any time spare me one or two specimens *in the shell,* preserved in spirits, it would be the most material kindness.—I would pledge my honour not to publish anything so as to interfere with any further researches you might choose to make on the species."[18] He thought Hancock misunderstood the boring process.

Scores of letters later, the two men continued to disagree about the way these two barnacles, and another one of the genus *Lithotrya,* dug out their burrows, Darwin opting for serrated edges on the valves of the shell, and Hancock standing firm on the barnacle's ability to secrete some kind of rock-dissolving fluid. But they were friends too.

And so it went on. Letters and specimens went in and out from Down in every post. Being dead made little difference—Darwin dearly wanted to see one unusual fossil specimen in a collection owned by the late Frederick Dixon, and pestered Owen to fix it for him with Dixon's widow. But rather than go to Worthing to look at it, as Owen arranged, Darwin hoped Mrs. Dixon might save him the trouble and send it to him in the post. She demurred. Undeterred, and undeniably lazy, Darwin happened to know that the artist James de Carle Sowerby was engraving some of Dixon's pictures for posthumous publication: "If you can with any honesty, do purloin a proof-sheet of Mr Dixon's plate with Cirripeds for me," he asked Sowerby in 1850.

He even contacted Syms Covington again, his former manservant and assistant on the *Beagle.* After leaving Darwin's employment at the end of 1838, Covington had emigrated to Twofold Bay in New South Wales, where he had acquired a smallholding, wife, and family. Despite the passing years, the old master-servant relationship surfaced inexorably. "I am now employed on a large volume describing the anatomy and all the species of barnacles from all over the world," wrote Darwin calmly. "I do not know whether you live near the sea, but if so I should be very glad if you would collect for me any that adhere (small and large) to the coast rocks or to shells or to corals thrown up by gales, and send them to me without cleaning out the animals, and taking care of the bases. You will remember that barnacles are conical little shells, with a sort of four valved lid on top. There are others with long flexible footstalk, fixed to floating objects, and sometimes cast on shore. I should be very glad of any specimens, but do not give yourself much trouble about them."[19]

The next year Covington sent him a parcel full of unusual species. Darwin was delighted; and then greatly amused when he saw the old newspapers which Covington had used for wrapping. There, in the Australian broadsheets, were the names of his former shipmate John Clement Wickham, who had emigrated in 1842, and William MacLeay, from the Zoological Society, who had gone in 1839. In an instant he was back on the *Beagle* with Wickham asking about hot coffee and eying Darwin's stones on the deck. It all seemed so very long ago. Sentimentally, he assured Covington that he was always interested to hear how he was doing.

IV

Bit by bit, as the barnacle months went by, Darwin fell ill again, so much so that he afterwards claimed that out of his many years' work on the group he lost nearly two of them from sickness. "Unusually unwell," he wrote at the end of 1848, "swimming head, depression, trembling, many bad attacks of sickness." The symptoms continued into 1849. "Health very bad with much sickness & failure of power. Worked on all well days."[20]

As always his stomach was the immediate cause of the trouble. He felt nauseated, sometimes being reduced to actual vomiting or retching. One trip to London, for instance, unsettled him enough to bring on a night of vomiting. Oh for the good old Cambridge days when he had no such thing as a stomach, he cried piteously to Henslow. Now it was nothing except "incessant sickness, tremulous hands and swimming head." The only solution was to live the life of a hermit.

Not surprisingly, Darwin also used the word "stomach" as a euphemism for other rebellious parts of his digestive tract. He was coy about what really happened. Eventually he shyly confessed to Fox that part of his problem was painful, churning bouts of wind: "all excitement & fatigue brings on such dreadful flatulence that in fact I can go nowhere."[21] That was why he liked to stay in his own room waiting patiently until his body behaved more politely. That was why he retired after meals when they entertained company at Down. The situation was, of course, much more embarrassing when he stayed in friends' or relatives' houses. How could he tell Hooker the real reason for needing private accommodation during British Association meetings? In 1847 he was forced to come clean: "the Magdalen Hall rooms will do capitally," he advised his solicitous friend; only as long as "I can have my meals to myself & a room to be by myself in, for as you know, my odious stomach requires that."

He had trouble with his bowels too, frequently suffering from constipation, and vulnerable to the obsession with regularity that stalked most Victorians. He quickly slipped into the habit of taking a purgative, the old-fashioned "physic" of Dr. Darwin's day, whenever it looked as if he might need it. Moreover, he developed crops of boils (the "old evil") in what he called perfectly devilish attacks, often on his backside, making it impossible to sit upright. He may have used the word "boils" as another catch-all phrase for piles and eczema as well. For days at a stretch these painful skin conditions forced him to lie on a sofa, where he crossly wrote letters to Hooker and Lyell in pencil. When such debilitating signs of weakness arrived in a batch, he felt terribly dejected. His body was virtually taking over. Erasmus noticed the change as much as anyone. "Charles passed thro' on Sunday," he told

Fanny Wedgwood, "looking more exhausted & miserable than ever I saw him."

This time around, however, Darwin also acknowledged the fragile state of his nerves. As Emma had realised long before, his health was "always affected by his mind."[22] Intuitively, she recognised the way a person's body indicates it is time to slow down. After his buoyant start, Darwin's barnacle work appeared to be getting him down. Perhaps his anatomical discoveries pointed towards too much additional labour: he was not particularly keen to contemplate another lifetime of minutely detailed endeavour, not when his larger work on evolution remained unfinished. He was too careful, too cautious, to do anything by halves, and this now looked like a truly difficult taxonomic enterprise. "The barnacles will put off my species book for rather a long period," he lamented to a friendly neighbour, Edward Cresy. "What zeal you have to care about my poor barnacles, at which most of my friends laugh."[23]

Darwin's ambitions may well have been stressfully at odds with will-power. Or perhaps the toxic preservative on the specimens he used—sometimes arsenic, sometimes alcohol—was an accumulative, aggravating physical factor. Certainly, the calomel (mercurous chloride) that he took, and had taken, in huge doses over the years must have been eating away at his nervous system, reducing his resistance to disease and making him unduly sensitive. His digestive problems similarly suggest some intestinal disorder of a chronic recurrent nature. All these would have flared up under emotionally stressful circumstances. Just as likely, although less obviously, anxiety over his species theories probably reemerged along with the possibility of data lurking among his Cirripedia. Instead of allowing him to relax, the barnacle work reintroduced any number of demanding philosophical problems. Whichever way he turned, it seemed, his evolutionary ideas were not going to let him go.

The roots of Darwin's immediate depression nevertheless lay elsewhere. He was intensely concerned about his father, who was gradually sinking towards his end. Darwin was sadly resigned to the inevitable. But he felt guilty about not doing more to help his sisters in looking after their difficult patient—guilty because he did not want to help either. The doctor had been frail for several years by then, his growing weaknesses all the more pitiful in relation to his large, outwardly robust body. He lived in a wheelchair and spent his days in the hothouse wheezing out orders to Susan and Catherine. Gout and old age had left their indelible marks. Yet neither of his sons took any part in nursing Dr. Darwin. Erasmus hardly ever went to The Mount, preferring to spirit his sisters away in turn for a few days' entertainment in London. When he did go he made such fun of the arrangements that the womenfolk found him exasperating. "I am going to kill one of these weeks by going to Shrewsbury on Monday where at all events I shall not have to go up to Bedford Place to a small tea party," he told Fanny Wedgwood. Visits conducted in that kind of spirit were not very helpful. Erasmus had made a speciality of never being a particularly loving or dutiful son.

Of the brothers, it was Charles who had more difficulty in accepting his father's declining powers, though he too was reluctant to visit more than once or twice a year. Although Dr. Darwin's mind was as sharp as ever, he could not talk much—he was very short of breath because of his great size—and depended on Catherine and Susan as never before. In fact, the two sisters did little else except minister to their father. The changes made Darwin melancholy when he visited Shrewsbury in February 1847. His trip in October was just as bad.[24]

When Darwin went back again for two weeks in May 1848, the doctor seemed pretty well, he thought. Susan and Catherine had nursed him carefully through the winter. During this visit, the last time that Darwin saw him alive, Dr. Darwin spoke about his coming death with remarkable frankness. "He thought with care he might live a good time longer," Darwin wrote mournfully to Emma; "& that when he dyed it would probably be suddenly which was best. Thrice over he has said that he was very comfortable, which was so much more than I expected. Catherine has been having wretched nights, but her spirits appear to me as good as used formerly to be."

But soon the underlying gloom got to him. "Oh Mammy I do long to be with you & under your protection for then I feel safe."[25] He went on to say in another letter he thought his father's health was rapidly breaking up.

The end when it came was quick, too quick for Darwin to get to Shrewsbury from Down even if he had wished to. "He is perfectly collected and placid in his mind in every way," wrote Catherine on 12 November 1848, though "his feebleness is excessive." The sisters were going to wheel him into the hothouse, as he still seemed to enjoy this the most. He died peacefully the next day with his servants, Mark and Thurger, on either side and Susan sitting close.

When Darwin received the news he felt puzzlingly dead himself: he did not know what to do. He was not distraught. Rather, his grief came as a heavy sense of regret, a saddened acknowledgement of absence. For one short moment his entire support system fell away. Ever since he'd become a father himself, he had understood his own father much better than before; and for the last ten years or so he had made the most of the doctor's company. He was old enough to appreciate Dr. Darwin's astute judgements, capable of giving way graciously to his eccentricities and of respecting his opinions. He was also grateful. Dr. Darwin had provided him with a safety net, a financial and medical cushion, as well as a fund of good sense and practical advice. Since Darwin's marriage—since the *Beagle* days—he had received unstinting fatherly support: "you were so beloved by him," said Catherine. All this was gone. His link to the chain of the past was irrevocably broken. He felt sad and ill, too ill to move. Erasmus would go straight to Shrewsbury for the funeral. He would have to follow on afterwards alone.

Whatever happened next is not certain. Darwin definitely stayed at Down for a few days before setting out for Shrewsbury, waiting for Emma to return from a visit to her sister's, and he definitely passed through Erasmus's house in London the day before the funeral. He may have missed his Midlands train or been delayed. Either way, he arrived in Shrewsbury after the cortège had left the family home for the church of St. Chad's.

According to Erasmus, Darwin therefore remained at The Mount with their sister Marianne Parker, who was too upset to attend the burial service. "Charles did not arrive till too late," Erasmus wrote to Fanny. Only he, Dr. Parker, and the Parker boys represented the male side of the family at the funeral.[26] Later on, Darwin stated that it was his ill health which had prevented him from attending, in the sense of delaying his journey: "I was at the time so unwell that I was unable to travel which added to my misery." There is no particular reason to believe he deliberately avoided the occasion, although he was probably relieved at the outcome. No one really wants to go to a funeral. But he expressed great sorrow to Hooker and to Fox in after years that he was not there to mark his father's formal exit from the world. "Though it is only a ceremony I felt deeply grieved at this deprivation."[27]

Then came the will: not necessarily a trial but still an ordeal to be got through as best they might. Dr. Darwin had carefully arranged his affairs a few years beforehand, in 1845 and '46, making the fairest possible distribution of his farmlands, mortgage profits, and railway shares among the children, mostly in the form of trust funds, marriage settlements, and other secure investments. That was the year that the brothers and sisters discovered that young Robert Parker, Marianne's oldest boy, had conceived the impossible idea that Dr. Darwin was going to give everything to him: that the oldest grandson would get it all. Dr. Darwin quickly disabused him of this notion. Only the balance of his estate was left to divide up after his death: one quarter to each of the boys and an eighth to the girls, plus the house and its contents to Susan and Catherine for as long as they stayed unmarried. Darwin and Erasmus were to split Dr. Darwin's money-broking exercises down the middle, Darwin taking on the Owen mortgage for £20,000 and the Powis (Lord Clive) interest, while Erasmus juggled uneasily with the rest. In the end Darwin inherited £51,712 over and above the funds already placed in trust for him, a few thousand pounds less than his brother.[28] Tenderly, he thought how judicious his father had been, how well he had looked after them. Gratitude and admiration ran in and out of his regret ever after.

V

But he was still ill. After his father's death, Darwin developed a welter of distressing symptoms. His most common complaints were giddiness, nausea, retching, vomiting, boils, wakeful nights, headaches, and the secret attacks of flatulence. Thoroughly disheartened in January 1849, he began to keep a health diary in which he made brief daily entries. This, he thought, would help doctors analyse and treat his condition.[29] As always, unpleasant things seemed more controllable if he turned them into writing. Lying on the sofa with this health diary in his hands, he plaintively invented symbols to indicate the range of his unwellness, dredging out of his memory a meteorological system formerly in use on the *Beagle* which employed mathematical plus signs and underlines for degrees of emphasis. Darwin was nothing if not methodical about his illnesses. Then he capitulated to words, trying to standardise his fluctuating condition (invariably "poorly") with a set of qualifiers—"very," "rather," "quite," "not quite," "almost very." Occasionally he varied it with "bad," "baddish," and so on. He put mornings on one side of the page, nights on the other, with wind, boils, and headaches making their appearance as appropriate along with the underlines or dashes now transmuted into signs of wellness. At the end of each month he diligently counted up the number of double dashes to see how his weeks had been: the more dashes the better. March to July hardly mustered any dashes at all. August was not too bad with seven, September worse with only three.

Like others in his sorry situation, Darwin turned first to the professionals and sought out high-level traditional medical advice from his cousin the London doctor and writer Henry Holland, as well as consulting the local practitioner and apothecary in Down village, and Sir Benjamin Brodie on occasion. He paid for a medical consultation with Holland early in January 1849. "My stomach fails so often & so suddenly," he told Owen round about then, "that I am never certain of an appointment." He was franker with his old friend William Darwin Fox. "I was very glad to get your note. I have often been thinking of writing to you, but all the autumn & winter I have been much dispirited & inclined to do nothing but what I was forced to."

After Dr. Darwin died, Darwin placed himself entirely in the hands of Henry Holland and began reading Holland's medical books with that special blend of horrified fascination that runs through everyone's psyche. Darwin's smattering of medical knowledge did him a disservice here, since he could easily imagine he had every disease Holland described. Dr. Holland was a firm believer in gout, caused as he thought by toxic materials in the blood, and in inherited disabilities, many of them relating to the blood also. "Supressed gout" could very well induce disorders of the digestive system, he said; and once the first fit of gout appeared, many chronic dyspeptic symptoms were relieved. Glumly Darwin marked up his copy of Holland's *Medical Notes* with morbid certainty. Dr. Darwin's violent attacks of gout were still fresh in his memory.[30]

As his ill-health intensified, and Holland failed to provide a remedy, Darwin turned to solicit sympathy and medical advice from friends and relatives who suffered from similar Victorian maladies. One particular piece of information started haunting him—why not try the water cure? This form of treatment had exploded onto the British medical scene during the 1840s and was much more than a simple revival of the spa culture relished by earlier English society.[31] There were no card tables or genteel dances in gilded Assembly Rooms for Victorian water patients. Instead, its voluntary victims undertook an energetic regime of cold showers, wet wraps, steam baths, strict diets, and long walks in the fresh air, all intended to stimulate a sluggish circulation and draw out debilitating toxins from the internal organs and blood. The new establishments were also highly institutionalised. They were self-contained residential units, like the developing public schools, hospitals, lunatic asylums, and workhouses of the era, and propounded a proselytising doctrine of inner cleanliness and self-regulated therapy: health farms for the nineteenth century, though much more vigorous than anything devised before or after. The idea appealed to Darwin more and more. At least he would be taking active measures against his "accursed stomach."

He succumbed after hearing from Fox. "Thank you very much for your information about the water cure," he wrote to him in February 1849.

> I cannot make up my mind; I dislike the thoughts of it much—I know I shall be very uncomfortable there.... Can you tell me (& I shd be much obliged sometime for an answer) whether either [of] your cases was dyspepsia, though Dr. Holland does not consider my case quite that, but nearer to suppressed gout. He says he never saw such a case, & will not take [it] on him to recommend the water cure.—I must get Gully's book.[32]

Fox, who was just as eager or just as desperate as Darwin to sample new medical treatments, had already been to Malvern to try Dr. Gully's thriving water establishment. As Darwin remarked, it was not customary or even necessary for sufferers to be advised to go by an orthodox practitioner. The water cure took the lead in popularising the flourishing range of alternative therapies that came to typify Victorian medicine: not quite out on the limits of the social fringe along with purveyors of snake oil and hair restoratives, water-cure proprietors nonetheless made capital out of their ability to offer very different medical therapeutics while still bowing to orthodox beliefs and to traditional doctor-patient relationships.[33] Many of the early water doctors, for example, were professionally qualified. They were furthermore willing to treat all kinds of nervous complaints that would previously have been the stock in trade of private nursing homes and asylums; and a great part of their sudden popularity was probably due to the introduction of legal requirements that any patient voluntarily admitting himself to a psychiatric home must be certified by a doctor. Someone like Alfred Tennyson, who took himself to a private mental asylum for recuperation on several occasions during the 1840s, was, after the Asylums Bill went through Parliament, loath to have himself certified insane. He started going to water-cure establishments instead.[34] Nor did water doctors wish to scare off cultivated or fashionable upper-class patients with mere nerves or stomachs. On the contrary, they cultivated them assiduously. Early Victorian establishments like Dr. Gully's and Dr. Wilson's at Malvern expressly catered for the ruling sections of society: people rich enough to pay for private treatment, the professional or independently wealthy classes, overworked intellectuals, dowager duchesses, the high-strung poets and authors of nineteenth-century Britain. These proprietors saw a niche in the medical market and were amply rewarded by the popularity that followed.[35]

James Manby Gully, for instance, was a doctor with a conventional medical background who set up a hydrotherapy establishment in a private house in Malvern in 1842, just a few months after his friend James Wilson purchased a large hotel for the same purpose. Within a few short years, their system became an extraordinary social phenomenon noisily discussed in *Punch* and other prominent journals. "Life at the cold brandy-and-water cure," joked Douglas Jerrold in *Punch,* soon put everyone to rights: four or five glasses of the prescribed remedy had a most "felicitous effect."[36] And all through the 1840s a steady stream of literary London passed through Malvern's watery doors. Tennyson tried Gully's cure after hearing of it from Henry Hallam, Arthur Hallam's surviving brother; Charles Dickens and his wife, Kate, heard from Douglas Jerrold; Jerrold heard from Edward Bulwer Lytton; Lytton met Dr. Wilson at an evening party; and Dickens told Wilkie Collins. Over in Cheyne Row, Thomas and Jane Carlyle were enthusiastic converts. With a grapevine like this, Gully and Wilson hardly needed to advertise.[37]

Fox encouraged Darwin to read Gully's book, and he did so. Using Gully's discreet price lists in the back and the wide variety of case histories supplied in an appendix ("each and every one improved"), Darwin diagnosed his own condition, costed out the expenses and possible length of stay, rejected his plan of visiting Ramsgate for sea-bathing with the family, and ultimately announced that he had "resolved to go this early summer and spend two months at Malvern & see whether there is any truth in Gully and the water cure: regular doctors cannot check my incessant vomiting at all."[38]

However, two months was a long time away from Emma. Valiantly, she agreed to go with him, uprooting the entire family from Down. "It is a great trouble taking all the household," she told Fox resignedly; "but we think he could not give Dr Gully's treatment a fair trial under 6 weeks or 2 months & that would be too long to leave the children, even with their Aunts. We both feel very hopeful that it will be of some use to Charles tho' we do not venture to hope a cure. This has been a disheartening winter with respect to his health." Leaving home for so long as a family group was unprecedented. Six-year-old Henrietta remembered for the rest of her life the exact place in the road coming up from the village where she was told this "tremendous news," and subsequently recalled the happiness of playing in the streams in the fields behind Malvern. Down had no streams, she said sadly. Eventually, the whole entourage, including Parslow, the babies, their maids, Miss Thorley the governess, and all, arrived in Malvern in March 1849 ready for a prolonged visit. They stayed for nearly three months, until 30 June.

Darwin rented one of the large villas along the Worcester Road, called The Lodge, and attended Gully's establishment as an out-patient. Most visitors usually lived in, where their treatment could be closely supervised, although Gully courted famous individuals such as Tennyson and Carlyle by inviting them as personal guests in his own home.[39] For Darwin, there were obvious advantages in a private house over that sort of communal living. He hated anything approximating either a school or a hotel. In The Lodge he could also retain several privileges that institutional residents relinquished, such as seven-o'clock start to the day rather than being up at five, a less Draconian diet, and, to his eyes, the very real advantage of not having to make conversation with all the other patients over dinner. He could sometimes manage a little snuff-taking in the privacy of his own lodgings, although this was eventually disallowed. The family routine continued sufficiently unchanged to include social visits to The Lodge by Susan Darwin and by Hensleigh and Fanny Wedgwood. There was some talk that Darwin's younger sister, Catherine, might come and join him for therapy, since she was slow to regain her usual spirits after Dr. Darwin's death. This way, despite putting himself under Gully's jurisdiction, Darwin retained an element of personal choice in following the cure. He was more or less in charge of his overall therapy.

Gully's regime was based on the idea that all chronic disorders were caused by a faulty supply of blood to the internal organs. His use of water was equally distinctive. Some years before the heyday of "muscular Christianity" and the ethos of cleanliness enforced in Victorian institutions, he believed water was most effective applied cold, and mostly externally. At Malvern the dose came in a number of ways, principally as cold showers and baths, but also through a wide variety of esoteric techniques such as wet-sheet packing and wrapping, steam baths, friction, and rubbing, some of which were developed personally by the Malvern doctors.[40] These external treatments were reinforced by a strict routine of early rising, a multitude of walks on the Malvern Hills, a little plain food, and spring water to drink. Everything was designed to fulfil Gully's spartan promise of "pure air, pure water, and dietic rule."

Darwin loved it. At last someone was ready to sympathise over his symptoms—to take him seriously. After paying for his initial consultation (the cost of a whole week's treatment, he reported in disbelief to Fox), Darwin found Gully gratifyingly puzzled by his case but agreeing that nervous dyspepsia was the culprit. Darwin was working too hard. "The close application of the mind to any one subject," Gully stated in his book, "whether it be abstruse or superficial . . . ranks among the frequent causes of nervous dyspepsia. . . . Intellectual labour and moral anxiety each or con-jointly keep up the derangement of other parts."[41] His analysis was simple: badly balanced digestive organs irritated the brain and spinal cord and these in turn affected the stomach. As Darwin put it, he thought "my head or top of spinal chord cause of mischief."[42]

At last there was something positive to do. All the sluicings and rubbings suited him perfectly, a sign that his condition was being dealt with, almost literally washed and wrung out of him. If Gully had told him to rest, he would have been disappointed. He wanted action. Nor would he have dedicated himself so unashamedly to treatment if it had merely involved lying around reading. He would have felt guilty spending so much time and money being ill. But at Malvern, the therapy was totally demanding, filling each and every day with a succession of suitably exhausting procedures. The air of vigorous intervention appealed to him. Furthermore, although he never admitted it, he liked the attention. Gully was pleasantly concerned about his symptoms, his correspondents wanted to know how he was getting along, even Emma, he thought defiantly, must see how a real doctor dictated intensive remedial action. He often suspected that Emma thought his illnesses were pure hypochondria, blithely unaware that the suspicion itself was a characteristic feature of hypochondria. "At present," he wrote to Hooker with high satisfaction, "I am heated by Spirit lamp till I stream with perspiration, & am then suddenly rubbed violently with towels dripping with cold water: have two cold feet-baths, & wear a wet compress all day on my stomach." However absurd it sounded, "I feel certain that the Water cure is no quackery."

Darwin's therapy soon moved into a routine of regular showers, baths, and the application of various forms of sheets and compresses. Rather than let some unknown medical servant touch him, Darwin insisted that Parslow learn the necessary tricks—the wrapping and unwrapping of his naked body and the hearty rubbings were not things he was prepared to hand over to a stranger. What with the baths, the walks—seven miles a day, up and down the Beacon—and the diet, he was turning into a mere walking and eating machine, he bragged to Fox. Where Dickens found the purposeful atmosphere too much to take, Darwin contentedly believed he was improving.

In the end, he put on weight, felt free of nausea for thirty days in succession, and relaxed so far that he felt indolent and stagnant—"I have ceased to think even of Barnacles!" Compulsively counting up the double dashes in his health diary, he saw a general drift towards "well, nearly," and by June he was spry enough to recollect how much money it was costing him—Gully must be making an immense fortune, he grumbled. Emma became pregnant again, another sure sign of his recovery. Idly, he began looking for beetles on the top of Malvern Hills. "The water cure is assuredly a grand discovery," he cried to Fox. "How sorry I am I did not hear of it, or rather that I was not somehow compelled to try it some five or six years ago."[43]

VI

Returning to Down at the end of June, Darwin methodically reorganised his life around the therapeutic routine dictated by this salutary experience. He grasped eagerly the idea of a rigid timetable which, if it did not exactly keep him healthy, would help him do as much as he could. Gully gave him a comprehensive outline of treatments that could be performed at home and recommended a suitable interval before making another visit to Malvern. Cautiously, Gully also held out the prospect of a permanent cure.

Darwin therefore built himself a shower house down by the garden well which his son George considered something like a diminutive church steeple, and which was in daily use for about five years with Parslow in attendance as bathman.[44] The children, said Henrietta, used to stand outside listening to his groans. "About noon every day he used to take a douche even in the coldest weather," wrote George later on. "I remember well one bitter cold day with the snow covering everything waiting about outside until he had finished & that he came out almost blue with cold & we trotted away at a good brisk pace over the snow to the Sandwalk."[45]

Darwin also followed Gully's dietary rules to the best of the household's ability. Emma's recipe book shows a succession of bland, nursery-style puddings and milk dishes from then on, interspersed with instructions for the ubiquitous "beef tea"; and Darwin's account books display a similar tilt towards regular purchases of potash (soda) water, some of which arrived at

Down in gallon flasks and was probably used for bathing rather than drinking. Acting on Gully's instructions, Emma regulated Darwin's sweet tooth by restricting his intake of sugary puddings and cakes—becoming, her beleaguered husband thought, unnecessarily schoolmarmy about it. This sacrifice was a hard one, since he had loved sweet things ever since his boyhood. "It was unlucky that so many Drs forbade him sweet things," said his son Francis sympathetically. "He often said that the meat of dinner was very dull and the sweets the only part worth." At least he did not have to give up his passion for exotic fruit; and with the surreptitious help of his children sometimes managed to get sugary figs and dates past Emma's watchful eyes. As soon as his friend Hooker heard about this tiresome ban, he started sending bananas gathered from the palm trees at Kew Gardens, going against all civil service rules as he did so: Darwin used to tell the children that questions were being asked in Parliament about where the good bananas went.[46]

As Gully also recommended, he started rising early in the morning, sometimes as early as five o'clock in the summertime. He bought a horse to exercise on and took up a regular routine of several turns on foot around the sandwalk at the bottom of his garden at predetermined intervals during the day, giving up the idea of seven Malvern miles but still counting the number of circuits by knocking a pebble off a pile. The correct number of pebbles made for a satisfactory daily total.

In this way, Darwin channelled his life into a careful management of time. He restricted his family activities just as severely. He would appear in the drawing room only when the specified hour came around, first to read his post, then later on to read the newspaper, and at the end of the day to take tea and listen to Emma playing the piano or reading a story: the older children used to claim they could set the hall clock by the creak of his study door opening.

None of these were particularly unpleasant restrictions to Darwin: they merely gave medical justification to the general withdrawal he was already sliding towards. Far harder was limiting his working time to something he could realistically manage. But he settled down with only a brief sigh of resignation to Dr. Gully's recommended limit of two and a half hours of intense mental activity per day. For, as he informed Fox, "with respect to myself I believe I am going on very well." Writing to Henslow at the same time, he said the water cure "has answered to a considerable extent: my sickness much checked and considerable strength gained." Within the month he was sending some barnacles to Sir John Herschel and telling him how Gully worked "an astonishingly renovating action on my health."[47] Over and over he told anyone who would listen how, only a few weeks beforehand, he would have called the process complete quackery.

Over the next year or two, Darwin kept in touch with Gully, returning to Malvern for brief treatments in September 1849 and June 1850. He got used to his friends laughing about the water cure and shamefacedly enjoyed the satirical literature pouring out from the popular presses. Even Fox, well into his valetudinarian middle years, teased him that any remedy will cure any malady. Grudgingly Darwin conceded that Gully's penchant for fashionable clients and his marked weakness for remedies like homeopathy and mesmerism put him at the cranky end of medicine. During Darwin's first visit, Gully insisted he take homeopathic medicines, which were thought to work by treating each disease with infinitely small quantities of substances producing the same symptoms as the disease; and Darwin obediently swallowed his dose three times a day "without an atom of faith." It was a sad flaw, Darwin thought, in his "beloved Dr Gully" that he believed in everything. "When his [Gully's] daughter was very ill, he had a clairvoyante girl to report on internal changes, a mesmerist to put her to sleep, a homeopathist, viz. Dr Chapman, & himself as hydropathist!" The girl recovered, he said in surprise.

Gully pressed Darwin to try clairvoyance in his turn. There was a woman clairvoyante living at Malvern reputed to be able to see inside people and discover the real nature of their ailments. According to family anecdote, Darwin at last consented on condition that he be allowed to test the clairvoyante's powers for himself. He put a banknote in a sealed envelope. George told the rest of the story:

> After being introduced to the lady he said "I have heard a great deal of your powers of reading concealed writings & I should like to have evidence myself: now in this envelope there is a banknote—if you will read the number I shall be happy to present it to you." The clairvoyante answered scornfully "I have a maidservant at home who can do that." But she had her revenge for on proceeding to the diagnosis of my father's illness, she gave a most appalling picture of the horrors which she saw in his inside.[48]

Gleefully, Darwin retold this experiment at dinner parties for years to come.

By 1850, however, it was not Darwin who felt ill. On the contrary, he thought Gully had put him almost completely right. From 1850 to 1855, when Darwin ultimately gave up his health diary as an unneeded piece of paper, he considered himself very well. These years of carrying out the water cure at home were full of double dashes and encouraging exclamations.

It was his eldest daughter, Anne, who was persistently unwell. All three of the girls—Anne, Henrietta, and three-year-old Elizabeth—had been ill in 1849 with scarlet fever, and Anne never fully regained her health afterwards. In October 1850 they resumed the plan of going for a brief therapeutic holiday in Ramsgate—at that time the most popular seaside town on the south coast, with long sandy beaches and entertainments on the pier, much favoured by convalescents living close to London. Anne was then nine years old, the apple of her proud father's eye, his favourite child, he confessed to Fox. More than any of the other children she treated him with a spontaneous affection that touched him deeply; she liked to smooth his hair and pat his clothes into shape, and was by nature self-absorbedly neat and tidy, cutting out delicate bits of paper to put away in her workbox, threading ribbons, and sewing small things for her dolls and make-believe worlds—her treasures, she called them. He had been charmed by this punctilious neatness ever since he first recorded it for his diary of observations on children: at fourteen months old, he said admiringly, it was curious to see "how neatly Annie takes hold in proper way of pens pencil & keys." William could not handle anything so neatly as Annie did—"often in exact manner of grown up person."[49] Darwin hoped the sea air would blow away her general malaise. But Ramsgate proved an ineffective answer. Emma took her up to London to see Henry Holland in November.

The winter passed drearily for her watchful parents: "she inherits I fear with grief, my wretched digestion," Darwin told Fox. She still seemed no better when the spring came round again; and in March 1851, just after her tenth birthday, Darwin became anxious enough to suggest a few weeks at Malvern for her. What worked for him might work for another member of the family, and Gully often treated children. As soon as the decision was made, he acted. A few days later, off he set for Malvern, taking Anne, plus her devoted nurse, Brodie, and Catherine Thorley, the girls' governess, and the next youngest daughter, Henrietta, to keep Anne company. He intended leaving them there together for up to a month so that Anne could take the cure under Dr. Gully's care. Emma was pregnant yet again and could not go for that length of time. Since she was expecting the baby in May, she stayed at home with the remaining children—all except William, who had just started as a boarding boy at Rugby School.

Yet these well-meaning intentions quickly escalated into tragedy. Soon after Darwin left the little group on their own, Anne developed a bilious fever. When her condition deteriorated, Gully naturally sent for Darwin. He was back at Malvern in the middle of April, powerlessly watching her fever intensify. "She looks very ill," he wrote to Emma on arrival, although "her face lighted up & she certainly knew me.—She has not had wine but several spoonfuls of broth & ordinary physic of camphor & ammonia." Already the two distressed parents were fighting off the unthinkable. "Dr Gully is most confident there is strong hope," Darwin said reassuringly. "I implore you do not think of coming here."[50]

Their anxious letters flew back and forth. Darwin sent daily bulletins, sometimes twice-daily ones if the news changed or he found an opportunity to discuss Anne's condition again with Gully. Gully was kindness itself, he reported, sleeping at their rented house during the first particularly bad night, ready to take her pulse at any moment, and ordering conventional nursing to replace water therapy. Yet there was nothing for them to do except dose her with emetics and spoon-feed gruel or other restoratives. Darwin confessed to Emma in his next letter that Gully had not expected her to last the night—"today he says she is no worse, & at present (12) this is the best which can be said." His fear leaped off the page:

> Your note made me cry much—but I must not give way & can avoid doing so by not thinking about her. It is now from hour to hour a struggle between life & death. God only knows the issue. She has been very quiet all morning but vomited badly at 6 A.M. which, however bad, shows she has more vital force than during two previous days. Sometimes Dr G. exclaims she will get through the struggle; then, I see, he doubts.—Oh my own it is very bitter indeed.[51]

After he had seen the bright green fluid Anne brought up, her prostration seemed to Darwin like "an exaggerated one of my Maer illness."

Emma hated the thought of Darwin being on his own during this ordeal and quickly got Fanny Wedgwood to go to Malvern to share some of the burden. She felt bad enough herself not being there: sending Fanny was a relief in a way. "Poor sweet child," she said sadly. "I feel quite unnatural sometimes in being able to talk of other things." What were they going to do for vital information over the weekend when the post office was closed?

In the event, Darwin fired off a telegram to Erasmus giving him the kind of peremptory instructions that only a family in crisis resorts to. Send a man from London to Sydenham station, he urgently requested, and thence in a fly to Down to say that "Annie has rallied." The danger was much less imminent, he thought. And Fanny Wedgwood had arrived.

He sent a letter too, just to make sure, direct to Emma. Fanny was a great comfort to have around, he said in that note, and busy organising him. Sensibly, she insisted on putting Henrietta onto a coach to go to Caroline and Jos Wedgwood's house (where all Fanny's children were staying), accompanied by one of Fanny's maids—actually crossing on the road with a maid sent by Emma with the same idea of getting her out of Malvern. Aged seven, Henrietta was not really sure what was going on. As for Anne herself, all trace of fever had gone. Dr. Gully hoped she was turning the corner. "An hour ago I was foolish with delight," said Darwin helplessly; "& pictured her to myself making custards (whirling round) as, I think, she called them."

Two days later she died. The tranquillity they so gratefully welcomed was not the peace of recovery but the gradual release of her hold on life. Emma had just finished writing an optimistic note to Darwin listing some of the foods Anne might soon be able to manage when the next letter from Malvern arrived.

> I pray God Fanny's note may have prepared you. She went to her final sleep most tranquilly, most sweetly at 12 oclock today. Our poor dear dear child has had a very short life but I trust happy, & God only knows what miseries might have been in store for her. She expired without a sigh. How desolate it makes one to think of her frank cordial manners. I am so thankful for the daguerrotype. I cannot remember ever seeing the dear child naughty. God bless her. We must be more & more to each other my dear wife.—Do what you can to bear up & think how invariably kind & tender you have been to her.—I am in bed not very well with my stomach. When I shall return I cannot yet say.

But Darwin could not see it through to the end. Fanny told him to go home to Emma, who would need him as much as he needed her, a reasoning with which he sadly agreed. He started out for Down towards the end of the next day, leaving Fanny with Brodie and Miss Thorley, and with the welcome company of Hensleigh Wedgwood, who arrived to help with the funeral arrangements. The fortnight had been too much of a knife's edge for him. He wanted to be with his wife, wanted to believe she was right in saying that "we shall be much less miserable together." Besides, as Fanny accurately predicted, Emma needed to go through it all step by step with him in person. "It is some sort of consolation," Darwin informed Fanny gratefully when he got back to Down, "to weep bitterly together.... Poor Emma is very firm, but is of course repeatedly overwhelmed with grief. I owe it to you that I am here."[52]

Once he was safe at home, Darwin too was repeatedly overwhelmed. His feelings were intensely different from those when his father died. He was not inclined to accept the death of his child calmly. "We have lost the joy of the household, and the solace of our old age," he raged bitterly. "Oh that she could now know how deeply, how tenderly we do still & shall ever love her dear joyous face."[53]

Everyone, moreover, expected him to be ill. Emma in particular was afraid that the anxiety might injure his health. Yet though ill enough at Malvern, exhausted and sick for a day immediately after Anne died, he showed no tendency to retire to bed with stomach problems at Down. He stayed outwardly calm, even businesslike. Death was something that needed organising ability. He decided there was to be no memorial in Malvern churchyard, no angels scooping up a childish figure, other than a headstone inscribed "A

dear and good child"; nothing at the Down village church either. He got
Erasmus to put an announcement in the papers and paid what was owing to
Dr. Gully, and then the expenses of the funeral.

Impassively, he watched Anne's nurse, Brodie, extravagantly mourning,
almost losing her senses, Henrietta said afterwards, and agreed that it was
best if she left the family service. Quietly, he arranged to provide her with an
annual pension for the rest of her life. And he wrote kindly to Mrs. Thorley,
to whom Catherine Thorley had retired for a few weeks to grieve in private,
saying how kind the governess had been to nurse Anne so devotedly. He
only broke down when writing to Fox, a man who had also lost a child. "She
was my favourite," he cried. "Her cordiality, openness, buoyant joyousness
& strong affection made her most loveable. Poor dear little soul."

One slight consolation lingered in his mind: if she had survived she might
well have experienced a life of continued, miserable ill health similar to his
own. Deep in his heart he suspected she had died of something akin to his
own condition, maybe something that ran in the family. Thoughts of his
mother's death surely surfaced to scourge him. He had hardly seen a dead
person since standing reluctantly at Susanna Darwin's bedside as an eight-
year-old, and those he had seen at medical school and during the *Beagle*
voyage had filled him with despair. Death came so suddenly, so violently.
The dragged-out unwellness before taking Anne to Malvern, the green
vomit, the stomach trouble: all these hit him where it frightened him the
most. Yet Gully's death certificate was circumspect, declaring the cause of
death as "bilious fever with typhoid character."[54] No water doctor, however,
would publicly acknowledge the possibility of a death from typhoid in his
sanatorium when his reputation stood or fell on the purity of local springs
and waters. What had she died of? "My bug-bear is hereditary weakness," he
agonised to Fox. Darwin could not cope with the thought that his own frail
bloodline, her inherited vulnerability to stomach disorders, might be a direct
cause of her death.

During the next day or two he exorcised some of his grief by writing a
tender memorial of Anne, describing her chief characteristics.[55] The words
echoed his letter to Fox: he remembered her joyousness and her affectionate
nature, her pirouettes in front of him on the garden path, the day she dressed
up in Emma's clothes, the stolen pinch of snuff for him, her hand slipping
into his. Without thinking, he called her a little angel. During the last illness,
her conduct was "in simple truth angelic."

There lay the real pain. Darwin did not believe in angels. He could not
draw any solace from the idea of an afterlife or salvation. Emma at least
believed Anne had gone to heaven. This was what she told the other children
too, no doubt excusably, but with some sad results. Henrietta, for one,

became heartbreakingly muddled up: the effect of Anne's death was as acute for her as for her parents, though it took a different form. If all the angels are men, she asked Emma in a very distressed way, where do the women go? She worried for months afterwards that she was not good enough, not as good as Anne, to go to heaven herself. "I used to be a very naughty girl when Annie was alive, do you think God will forgive me?" she repeated. She thought she would go to hell otherwise.[56] Emma's notes about these worries unconsciously reveal the intense pressures Henrietta felt herself under, and the same strong feelings came out years later in Henrietta's autobiography. The maids, she remembered, told her how Annie was much superior to her, especially in sweetness of disposition.[57] Almost inevitably, the sharp-tempered little girl reacted against so much grief given to the one dead sister. "Do you think I have done anything wrong today?" she whispered at bedtime. "I will try to help you as much as I can," said Emma. "But you are always with somebody," came the reply. "Do you think you shall come to heaven with me?" she asked again. Emma hoped she might, and they would have Anne there as well. But Henrietta did not want Anne: she wanted baby Georgy instead. It seems clear that Henrietta's most lasting emotion from this experience was a complex mix of grief, fear, and resentment.

No doubt whatever Emma said or did it would have turned out the wrong thing in the child's eyes: such is the frequent fate of mothers. Her well-meaning attempts to draw out the pain probably served their purpose, as far as they went. Darwin, however, found it hard to talk. After the first bursts of mourning were over, the two barely spoke of Anne again. Darwin wrote his feelings down, intensely private as was his custom. Emma put aside some tiny pieces of crochet work and a lock of her daughter's hair. The silence was deafening.

In fact, religion was already creating a thin but impenetrable barrier between them of the kind that married couples rarely acknowledge but regularly confront on a daily basis. This death was the formal beginning of Darwin's conscious dissociation from believing in the traditional figure of God.[58] The doctrines of the Bible that Emma took comfort in were hurdles he could not jump, not even after the exalted feelings of the *Beagle* years, not even with an overwhelming desire to believe in an afterlife for Anne, or his affection for Emma, or his residual, fading hope that it might all be true. Bleakness swept in. The gradual numbing of his religious feelings over the decades, the scatalogical revellings of his notebooks, and the godless world of natural selection he was even then still creating came implacably face to face with the emptiness of bereavement. Over the following months, Darwin became more certain, more fixed in his scepticism. Little by little, his theological doubts turned into conviction.

VII

After this, Darwin turned back to barnacles with a heavy heart, reentering his familiar working routines with a new kind of grimness—a hard edge of determination that helped him carry on where other men might have abandoned their studies. His work provided a different kind of refuge now. He saw how barnacles filled the time that might otherwise be spent fruitlessly yearning, how they pushed out other, more unwelcome thoughts. He began working furiously, harder than ever before. Blindly, he stuck to Gully's prescribed two hours. But he made sure the other parts of the day were not wasted either. He refused to count his scientific reading as part of the two hours, for example, nor the time spent writing long scientific letters. Sundays ran along exactly the same programme. If he relaxed for a moment, too many unhappy feelings pressed in.

Even the keenest grief could not go on forever. Though deadened, he was stoic by nature. In 1851, the same year that Anne died, he successfully completed a volume about fossil barnacles, publishing it through the Palaeontographical Society as arranged with Bowerbank, and a volume about living barnacles for the Ray Society. Three years later he put the finishing touches to second, follow-up volumes for each society.[59] It seemed best to him to separate the Lepadidae, or stalked barnacles, from the more familiar sessile Balanidae in each set of publications. In fact, he believed the two great divisions had diverged early from each other in evolutionary history, and, if one reads between the lines, his taxonomic arrangement was steeped in ideas derived from his theory of evolution. His written descriptions and the manner in which he skilfully grouped species into clusters that resembled each other would have been impossible for him without the idea of real blood relationships existing between them. Yet not a word was officially revealed. As he had come to recognise, his view made sense of the living world in a way few other naturalists could have grasped at that period. Even so, it did not materially alter the existing framework of structural relationships described by generations of nonevolutionary workers. Darwin wanted to be judged as a contributor to high-level taxonomic natural history, not as another sensational Mr. Vestiges.

Outside the home, that is. Fondly he recorded how the children teased him about his lavish descriptions. One larval cirripede possessed "six pairs of beautifully constructed natatory legs, a pair of magnificent compound eyes, and extremely complex antennae." He sounded like an advertisement.[60]

Other diversions eased into view. In July 1851 the family went *en masse* to Erasmus's new house in Park Street for a week to visit the Great Exhibition in Joseph Paxton's glittering Crystal Palace, erected in Hyde Park. All the world's trades and manufactures were gathered together in this great glass cathedral dedicated to Victorian things—a "most gorgeous sight," sighed Lord Macaulay, "I cannot think that the Caesars ever exhibited a more splendid spectacle."[61] The Darwins, like thousands and thousands of other visitors, wandered up and down the aisles mesmerised by the diversity, the technology, the ornamental magnificence of the exhibits: from Metallurgy to Horticulture, taking in Chemical Manufactures, Vitreous Ceramic Manufactures, Textiles, Organic Manufactures, Engineering and Machinery, Architecture, Fine Arts, Music, and Agriculture on the way, including a "bachelor's shirt of peculiar construction without buttons," a model of the docks at Liverpool complete with sixteen hundred fully rigged ships, a garden seat made out of coal for Osborn House, and a stuffed elk from the zoological museum at Turin. It was a jolly week, Emma thought, even with Horace, the recent baby, to hand. Born just three weeks after Anne died, he would, everyone hoped, ease Emma's sorrow. She did enjoy Horace more than she had expected. Yet a new baby can never obliterate the gap left by a dead child. Horace's first summer was overshadowed by Emma's memories as much as Henrietta's. The phantasmagoria of the Crystal Palace may have helped.

By contrast, Erasmus was already quite a habitué of the Great Exhibition, extravagantly hiring three cabs to convey the Wedgwood children there in June, and another three for the Darwins when they came. He was always ready to act the indulgent uncle and ply the youngsters with "sweet cakes and ices." Writing to Fanny Wedgwood, he explained how he had "done" the last of her young ladies at the Crystal Palace, "and all but killed myself over a French sewing machine which puts the needle thro' and thro' just like one of your Christian Socialist friends." Just as indulgently, he listened to his other Wedgwood relatives complaining about Queen Victoria's failing to stop at the Wedgwood stand in the western wing, where the manufactures and industrial products of Britain were displayed. Actually, there was no reason why the stand should have been selected: for the past half-century the Wedgwood company had been trading merely on its reputation and marketing the same well-known pieces, while Minton, Spode, Worcester, and Doulton had all produced new items in keeping with diversifying mid-Victorian tastes. Stolid Frank Wedgwood, Emma and Hensleigh's nearest-older brother, ran the business with no concessions to changing fashion and consequently could have offered little immediate appeal to the eager young queen. The Darwins made the most of their trip to town, taking the children also to the zoological gardens (as a fellow of the Zoological Society, Darwin was entitled to go when the zoo was closed to the public) and the "Polytechnic Conjurers" on Regent Street. All the heat and activity gave Darwin such a bad headache he went home quite his old self.

He had time too to resume his close friendship with Joseph Hooker, who was just back from an arduous plant-collecting expedition in India and brought his bride, Frances Henslow, to Down for a visit. Hooker's botanical friendship with Henslow was pleasantly cemented by his taking Henslow's eldest daughter as a suitably prepared scientific wife, and she had patiently waited for four years while he was off hunting rhododendrons. The Darwins had thought they perceived a flirtation at a picnic after a British Association meeting at Oxford.

Darwin and Hooker's affection for each other was just as strong as before. Now Hooker could tell Darwin about how incongruous it had been to read letters up on top of the Himalayas, how he was thrown into a Nepalese prison with Andrew Campbell, how Mrs. Campbell smuggled one of her fruitcakes to them along a line of helpful sherpas, and about Hugh Falconer's work as a scholar-at-large in Calcutta.[62] More at ease than before with the assembled Darwins, and proud of his freshly acquired set of patriarchal whiskers, Hooker amused the smallest children by waggling shaggy eyebrows behind his spectacles. "I have hardly known any man more lovable than Hooker," Darwin said genially. And he was pleased to hear of Falconer's marvellous fossil finds in the Siwalik hills. Later on he made sure Falconer came with Hooker for a weekend at Down—for the "jaw," as Falconer graphically put it.

Hooker, Darwin heard sympathetically, was looking for a job that would make proper use of his botanical skills while applying for Admiralty money to write up his researches. "Shall I give up botany and stand for Koenig's place at B. Mus?" the younger man asked wistfully. But he plugged away at the government bodies most concerned with science and eventually landed a temporary appointment as an assistant to his father at Kew Gardens—an ideal, though poorly paid, solution and one that all members of his family had hoped for. Under Sir William's capable hands the gardens were already the centre of the empire's botanical and economic aspirations, the hub of the British colonial plantation system.[63] There was no better place for Hooker to settle—and no better place for Darwin to have a friend.

During 1851, Darwin also met Thomas Henry Huxley, the man whose life ultimately interlocked with his in the long evolutionary story. Yet Huxley scared Darwin a little bit at first. He was acerbic, sharply critical, well read, fluent in German, and very brilliant: all the visibly intellectual qualities that Darwin sheepishly eschewed. He was also young and patently ambitious, erupting onto the London scene after spending four years pent up as a surgeon-naturalist on H.M.S. *Rattlesnake,* and like Hooker resentfully biding his time in a succession of inadequately paid, relatively menial natural history positions.[64] He wanted to make a big impression in the scientific world, and fast. If nothing else, he had left the girl he wanted to marry behind in Sydney and could not bring her to Britain to become his wife until he had some kind of settled future. Huxley, like Hooker, was one of a new breed of self-supporting professional scientists emerging uncertainly in London—he had no family money behind him, no opportunity to live as an independent gentleman-specialist like Darwin.

Huxley's first move in attacking the citadel of metropolitan science was to fire a deliberate shot through the debates inspired by Steenstrup's work on reproduction. Boldly, he sent a copy of his researches to Darwin. Before long, the two of them were deep in a detailed correspondence about barnacles, sea-urchins, archetypes, and embryology. "I shd have thought," Darwin puzzled after reading another one of Huxley's illuminating papers, "that the archetype was always in some degree embryonic." Huxley's mercurial thrusts and sallies forced him to think harder than he had ever thought before about some of the most fundamental assumptions of nineteenth-century natural science.

But the warmth really came only after Darwin published his barnacle books. By then Huxley was well known as the writer of important anatomical essays, an irrepressible fellow of the Royal Society, and the recipient of a Royal Medal in 1852. At the time he was temporarily employed as a lecturer in natural history at the Government School of Mines in Jermyn Street. His knowledge of the work of continental naturalists encouraged Darwin to ask his help in forwarding presentation copies of *Living Cirripedia* and *Fossil Cirripedia* to the various figures best placed to appreciate his research. It also became clear that Huxley was just the man to review his books in the British press—just the man, Darwin thought anxiously, whom he would most like to impress. Since so much of Darwin's other work indirectly hinged on how his barnacle studies were received by experts, and since so few experts had in the event reviewed it, he deliberately set out on some tactical self-advancement. "It is very indelicate of me to say so," he wrote to Huxley in 1853, "but it would give me *great* pleasure to see my work reviewed by any one so capable as you of praising anything which might deserve praise, and criticising the errors which no doubt it contains."[65] Huxley ended up discussing Darwin's work in his lectures and praising it highly in the published version of these during 1856.

By then Huxley had also become a close friend of Hooker's, a man nearer his own age with whom he enjoyed a lifelong rapport in scientific, philosophical, and personal affairs. Darwin naturally saw Huxley in a different light as Huxley laughed and joked with Hooker at meetings of the Royal Society, drawing caricatures of scientific bores in his notebook before standing up to make some bravura remark; and he capitulated entirely when Huxley went on to lash a new edition of the *Vestiges* in a review published in 1854.[66] Huxley raged against the idea of transmutation. Yet he did so in such an intelligent way that Darwin felt he had found an ally of sorts. "The way you handle a great professor [Richard Owen] is really exquisite & inimitable. I have been extremely interested on other parts & to my mind it is *incomparably* the best review I have read on the *Vestiges.*" Darwin went on to admit he thought Huxley was rather hard on the poor author. Surely transmutation was not as bad as all that? "But I am perhaps no fair judge for I am almost as unorthodox about species as the Vestiges itself, though I hope not *quite* so unphilosophical."[67] He wanted this clever man on his side just as much as Huxley wanted Darwin's blessing on the other.

Other colleagues drew closer as well: George Waterhouse from the British Museum, an ally from the *Zoology* of the *Beagle* days, and the only entomologist whom Darwin really respected, possibly because his talents also spread to mammalian comparative anatomy and palaeontology as well; Edward Forbes of the Geological Survey, who died unexpectedly in 1854, just as he took over the chair of natural history at Edinburgh from Robert Jameson; Thomas Vernon Wollaston, the entomologist with strong views about species; Hewett Cottrell Watson, the irascible botanist who always argued with Forbes and believed in phrenology and transmutation; and Charles James Fox Bunbury, a good botanist mostly interested in fossil ferns, who married Frances Horner in 1844 and came to feature largely in Lyell's family circle.

As for Lyell, he was securely fixed in a methodical cycle of London and Scotland, interspersed with his usual continental tour with Mary Lyell in the summer—no more extended trips to America for the time being. Darwin liked seeing him regularly for breakfast and various council meetings of the learned societies of which they were both members. The Lyells were considerably grander now, since Lyell had received a knighthood in 1848 and still relished the memory of sitting next to Prince Albert at an official scientific dinner and his trip to Balmoral to meet the queen. Of his generation, only Roderick Murchison and Henry De la Beche were geological knights, and they were the directors of government bodies; whereas Lyell, Darwin proudly thought, was rewarded for "public estimation." However, that did not stop Darwin smiling when Erasmus observed that Lyell's attendance at the queen's ball, combined with the prince's speech about lodging houses, proved that the court was determined to encourage the lower orders. "I shd like to repeat this to the Lyells," Darwin chuckled privately to Emma.

He thoroughly enjoyed seeing these friends in London, at scientific meetings, at Lyell's evening parties, or in the tranquil air of the country. Old friends and old enthusiasms made life much easier for him. And all his old interest in the politics of science slowly rekindled. He had always liked the furtive letters, the private talk at dinners, the canvassing for medals and committee members that went on in the Royal Society and the Geological Society: an interest that was not just confined to the sense of power which came with being an influential man, but also coloured by his increasing desire to push the subjects he loved most in the right direction and to reward the men producing what he considered the best work of the era. He and Lyell would often discuss the work of younger geologists with the Royal Society's medals or the Geological Society's awards in mind, and they threw themselves vigorously into the labyrinthine system of nominations and votes. One of Darwin's nominations began with a strong private recommendation to Hooker, who was on the Royal Society committee for natural historical subjects in 1854. "I have been reading lately Westwood's Modern Class. of insects, & I want you, who take an active share in scientific business, to bear Westwood in mind whenever a turn comes for a zoological Royal medal. I think he must feel that years of hard work & of careful observation & of dissection have not been much recognised by the men of science of this country." Despite Darwin thinking that Albany Hancock was comparatively "a higher class of labourer," as he told Huxley (who was also on the committee), Hancock had not done as much for the general advancement of British science as Westwood.[68] Such private routes of influence worked best for Darwin: it was often a struggle, he thought peevishly, to get natural history topics past the batteries of medical men wanting to reward physiologists and anatomists, or through the serried ranks of Cambridge-trained physicists and astronomers. In the end, Darwin himself nominated Westwood in 1855, providing a formal citation of his merits. With Huxley and Hooker carefully orchestrating the Royal Society's committee that year, Westwood received his award shortly afterwards.

In turn, Darwin was thrilled when his own barnacle work won him a Royal Medal in 1853, even before his monographs were fully published. Hooker broke the good news.

> The R.S. have voted you the Royal Medal for Natural Science—*all along of the barnacles!!!* I am most intensely delighted, infinitely more than you can be ... for you must know that I neither proposed you, nor seconded you, *nor voted for you*—I was base, perfide—Portlock proposed you for the Coral Islands & Lepadidae, Bell followed seconding on the Lepadidae alone, & then followed such a shout of paeans for the Barnacles that you would have [smiled] to hear.[69]

Hooker's confession of disloyalty perversely made it all the nicer for Darwin: he was pleased in a way he had never yet been pleased, his feelings for his friend and his delight at his own success inextricably mingled. "Amongst my letters received this morning, I opened first one from Col. Sabine: the contents certainly surprised me very much, but, though the letter was a *very kind one,* somehow, I cared very little indeed for the announcement it contained. I then opened yours, & such is the effect of warmth, friendship & kindness from one that is loved, that the very same fact told as you told it, made me glow with pleasure till my heart throbbed. Believe me I shall not soon forget the pleasure of your letter. Such hearty affectionate sympathy is worth more than all the medals that ever were or will be coined. Again my dear Hooker I thank you."[70]

Something of the same pleasure—and his pleasure in giving comparable recognition to other naturalists—shone through again when Darwin joined the influential Philosophical Club of the Royal Society a few months later. "I begin to think that dissipation, high-living, with lots of claret is what I want, & what I had during the last visit." This exclusive dining club virtually ran British science by fixing decisions behind the scenes—many of which extended far beyond the purview of the Royal Society. In 1848, for instance, the assembled diners took on the government itself, signing a memorial advocating stronger university reform. Out of the 224 signatures, 133 came from Cambridge men, including Henslow, Thackeray, Matthew Arnold, and Romilly. Charles Darwin and Erasmus (as a long-term member of University College's governing body) added their names just as readily.[71]

But he was more than relieved when the barnacles came to a definite end in September 1854. For several months before then, maybe almost a year, he had longed to return to some more direct work on species—the barnacles raised so many interesting possibilities that he fretted impatiently to get the last proof sheet out of the house. Eventually, on 9 September, he wrote in his journal:

> Finished packing up all my Cirripedes, preparing fossil balanidae, distributing copies of my work &c. &c. &c. I have yet a few proofs for Fossil Balanidae for Pal. Soc. to complete, perhaps a week more work. Began Oct 1, 1846. On Oct 1 it will be 8 years since I began! but then I have lost 1 or 2 years by illness.[72]

The day's entry closed with the words "Began sorting notes for species theory."

SHIP ON THE DOWNS

ITH this cry of relief echoing pleasantly in his ears, Darwin flung himself into a whole series of new schemes and projects, every kind of experimental inquiry: anything, in truth, that was different from barnacles and proof sheets. At last he felt freed from his leash. At last he had no other obligations diverting him from transmutation. He looked forward eagerly to having enough time to get real, practical answers to the questions that still danced in his head. Why, there were things in his notebooks he had never yet investigated fully, he thought to himself. Moreover, his barnacles had shown him—as no amount of reading or thinking could have done—the sheer impact of looking at organisms directly: where he had once met nature face to face on the *Beagle* voyage and gratefully observed its variety, he now appreciated the importance of rolling up his sleeves and getting right into it. He appreciated the incalculable advantage of manipulating natural phenomena to squeeze out the answers he fervently desired. The long anatomical years convinced him that the only way forward was to gather up as much factual information about species as he could.

Everything told him so: facts, facts, facts. From the time of his first setting out on the *Beagle,* he had taught himself how to look and how to interpret, and these very basic attributes now came to lie at the heart of his working life. Ever since his geological blunder over the shelves of Glen Roy he felt edgy about too much unsubstantiated speculation—and this from a man irrevocably wedded to speculation. The drama surrounding the publication of *Vestiges* served as another, frighteningly relevant warning. *Vestiges'* transmutationary arguments were pretty much the same as Darwin's, drawing on embryology, classification, and the fossil record. What would protect him from the same kind of vicious assault except the quality of his research? Moreover, Victorian science in general was shifting to an emphasis on "facts" above all else. Natural philosophers believed they approached a truer understanding of nature through the collection of facts, the collation of great sequences of observations in fields like astronomy, geomagnetism, meteorology, and the study of the tides, the analysis of life insurance tables, bills of mortality, population censuses, and so on. Give us statistics, they cried: numbers, facts, and figures. Efficiently, the institutional, hierarchical, colonial structure of British science responded.[1] Raw information flooded in from every corner of the world, piling up in London's learned societies and in government corridors, all waiting to be processed, as it were, by those authorities who felt themselves best equipped to do so. Of course, the difficult relationships between facts and theories often vexed them, and men such as Whewell and Herschel laid out schemes which served as contemporary guides to scientific reasoning.[2] Defining and constructing "facts" were not easy tasks either. And people like Darwin and Lyell carried on speculating regardless. But the public ethos—the image—of Victorian science glorified the empirical. Facts, Darwin recognised, were his only appropriate route towards establishing his theory of transmutation. Now, he delightedly thought, was the moment to get them. All his previous joy in making practical observations burst out into a thoroughgoing commitment to detailed experimental studies. Purposefully, he emerged from the mourning and the tedious work of the previous years to reappear as one of the most original experimental scientists of the Victorian era.

II

Yet in putting the barnacle work behind him so readily, Darwin did not forget the important messages he had deciphered so laboriously during those eight long years. One message in particular ran unceasingly through his mind. His close anatomical study had forced him to modify the way he actually thought about nature. At one level, certainly the most powerful, grandest level of all, he became sure that evolution had taken place. His barnacles showed him what transmutation could look like. Bit by bit, each apparently trivial adaptation in living structure accumulated, one after another, until animals became so distinct from their parents and cousins that they could be called a different species. Some barnacles had evolved to squat on rock surfaces, others to attach themselves to the ground by stalks. They had all emerged from a single unknown ancestral crustacean. This recognition of constant, accumulative change, pulled as it was out of Darwin's minutely detailed investigations, reassured him in its down-to-earth specificity. He was no longer afraid of admitting that transmutation must have taken place.

Indeed, he allowed himself an easy familiarity with the natural world, taking unsophisticated pleasure in thinking of himself as part of a living chain with animals, happily anthropomorphising the finer feelings of dogs and horses, and embracing the animal inside himself. His sense of God had virtually disappeared along with his daughter Anne. Man was nothing to him now except a more developed animal.

At another level, Darwin's theories of transmutation firmed up and changed. He knew now that all animals and plants were once-hermaphroditic organisms which had diverged over eons of time into two sexes. He knew that this process of divergence was governed by a need in nature to avoid continued self-fertilisation: that the whole point of having two sexes was to ensure sexual reproduction, a mingling of the qualities and characteristics of two individuals to bring about the birth of a third. He knew that Owen's and Milne-Edwards's ideas about the archetype and anatomical resemblances between organisms were absolutely correct, except that he understood these relationships as truly evolutionary ones rather than the manifestation of an idealised, abstract plan for nature. He knew further that parts of an animal's structure could become modified and change their function, something he could hardly overlook after tracing the various ins and outs of barnacle anatomy. All these features of the natural world were adaptations, he thought, to changing modes of life, brought about by the selection of favourable variations. Insofar as there was evidence confirming this, he thought he could discern a gradual sequence of adaptive changes in successive barnacle species which linked the "earliest" or most primitive, ancestral state with the most advanced forms that his researches disclosed. Unobtrusively stuck to their rocks, lodged inside stones or shells, or adhering to pieces of driftwood, his barnacles therefore spoke to him of a world filled with intricately minute evolutionary transformations.

But there had always been some continuing uncertainty in his mind about variation. Why did animals and plants vary, and how? It was all very well believing in his own theory—any proud father would see the best side of his growing child. The problem was how to make sure others would believe it, or at least grasp something of the explanatory power which he felt his ideas offered. The question of variation lingered deep in the centre of his work, unresolved and unanswered.

Above all else, it was Darwin's barnacles that showed him the way forward.

What the barnacles revealed was that every single detail, every single valve of the shell or mouthpart, varied in some way or another. Nothing was constant. Everything was fluid. "You ask what effect studying species has had on my variation theories," Darwin mused at one point to Hooker:

I have been struck (& probably unfairly from the class) with the variability of every part in some slight degree of every species: when the same organ is *rigorously* compared in many individuals I always find some slight variability, & consequently that the diagnosis of species from minute differences is always dangerous. I had thought the same parts of the same species more resembled than they do, anyhow in Cirripedia, objects cast in the same mould. Systematic work wd be easy were it not for this confounded variation, which, however, is pleasant to me as a speculatist though odious to me as a systematist.[3]

However poorly expressed, the thought represented a fundamental change.

Darwin had originally thought that animal and plant forms were more or less stable unless unsettled by some alteration in their circumstances, and in his essay of 1844 he drew a precise analogy between the effects of changes in the natural environment which threw living communities into different competitive relationships, and the effects of domestication on the reproductive system of farmyard animals and plants.[4]

In fact, he based his entire essay of 1844 on a close parallel between reproduction in the wild and under domestication. Transmutation, he had proposed, came about as a result of chance and change, and depended on intimate links between geology and biology; everything he ever expressed interest in during the *Beagle* voyage or while excitedly dashing off his species notebooks fused together into one tightly woven scheme. In that evolutionary essay of 1844 he envisaged an island or an archipelago already peopled with aboriginal species or occasional accidental migrants, rather like the Galápagos Islands or the Keeling Islands. Since domesticated organisms often sported or produced very varied offspring (which Darwin thought was an inevitable consequence of bringing them under mankind's sway), he suggested that wild species were similarly affected when dislocated or subjected to alterations in their conditions of existence. Gradual geological changes like elevation or subsidence, for instance, would upset the "constitution of some of the insular species" and stimulate variations in the offspring. In particular, geological elevation would reveal landscapes previously unoccupied by terrestrial living beings and provide local species with dramatically new environments and conditions. Here, Darwin hazarded, they would vary unchecked. Natural selection would go to work, preserving favourable variations and weeding out the unfit. Prolonged isolation on an islet, coupled with the fact that such regions generally had only a few species to fill all the available spaces, would lead to the production of new, diversified species. For these reasons, "an island would be a far more fertile source, as far as we can judge, of new specific forms than a continent."[5] The Galápagos archipelago was obviously uppermost in his mind. An original importation of organisms such as South American finches or iguanas might well have varied at random and be driven by natural selection to adapt themselves to those "places" left free in nature.

There was more than this to Darwin's essay of 1844. All the years spent travelling and working in London libraries were not wasted. Applying his knowledge of the processes by which large continents came into existence, he went on to argue that continual volcanic activity would lead to more and more islands being produced in an area such as the Galápagos. Eventually, the islands would join together into a single landmass, probably characterised by a line of hills or mountains surrounded by intermediary low-lying regions, something like the Falkland Islands or Mauritius perhaps, or, on a larger scale, like the tail end of South America, where the promontories and straits of Tierra del Fuego, if pushed up out of the sea, could easily look like Chile—Chile with its wall of mountain peaks, central valley, high inland passes, and surrounding flatlands. During this hypothetical geological process, Darwin thought animals and plants native to each island would have the chance to expand their geographical range and mix with new associates: the flora and fauna would intermingle until such a time as partial subsidence separated the irregular landmass into a set of islands once more. The consequences of these alterations in land levels were plain: species would be jumbled into new associations and brought into new relationships with their peers; the conditions of their existence would be upset and they would vary and change; selection and evolution would proceed apace. Rising land therefore encouraged speciation, he stated, and fully elevated land dispersal. Subsiding land, on the other hand, tended to make species extinct (at least locally), because the process removed many different kinds of habitat at the very time it was hardest for animals and plants to migrate elsewhere. Alpine plants, for example, would find nowhere else to go if the tops of mountains subsided into warmer air zones and would speedily die.

If this process of oscillation was repeated enough times—and Darwin made the point there and elsewhere that elevation and subsidence did go on and on in just such a fashion—then all the multifarious relations between the species of different countries could more or less be explained. Speaking generally, the crust of the earth went up and down, converting islands into continents and vice versa, while animals and plants evolved or migrated according to their location on an island or united landmass: with successive changes of level, species altered their form, dispersed, and became extinct. Darwin revealed an intense and very unusual appreciation of the dynamic flux of life in writing so cogently about life forms that adapted, moved, or died, superimposed on the equally dynamic movements of the earth.

Though inadequately buttressed with practical examples, as he sadly acknowledged from the start, and lacking any considered analysis of the history of one group of islands which might substantiate some of his points, Darwin's essay of 1844 was a magnificent tour de force. In one firm stroke he poured all his early endeavours into a single explanatory system linking the present with the past.

Still, as he also recognised, his scheme presented a number of problems. It depended in no uncertain manner on Lyell's concept of a constantly moving earth. Darwin needed Lyell's movements of the earth's crust to provide alterations in physical topography: only these alterations, he thought, were sufficient to "unsettle" the constitution of existing wild species and encourage them to vary. The internal reproductive mould, as it were, had to be broken by definite changes in the external physical or social environment before the organism would sport, as he put it, and before natural selection could go to work.

But after seeing the infinite, apparently spontaneous variation of barnacles, Darwin was obliged to reformulate his ideas. Variation, he saw in surprise, was a natural consequence of reproduction. It happened all the time. He did not need to dream up any "unsettling" causes. He did not have to put Lyell's constantly fluctuating earth at the heart of his theory.

III

Excitedly, Darwin acknowledged the major significance of this altered perspective. He needed to think again about domestic animals, about breeding and all aspects of the reproductive process, about hybridisation, fertilisation, embryology, and sexual differences, all the old questions tumbling together in a different light; and about geological change, animal and plant distribution, and the permanence of type. He possessed a strong working theory, he had an essay already written, he was convinced in his own heart that the basic premise of evolution was true. Yet this unexpected opportunity to explore it once again to its very edges made him catch his breath in anticipation. He had almost forgotten how natural selection was one of the most dazzling, most stimulating of all biological theories: the theory that drove him along in a fever of excitement through the notebook years and sustained him in some of his darkest moments. From the bottom of his soul he wanted to get it absolutely right.

So after packing away his barnacles, Darwin turned to pick up the unravelling threads of his essay.

In good Darwinian fashion, he started with the most basic aspect he could find. How far could he go if he withdrew his emphasis on Lyell's fluctuating land levels? His theory of species constantly mixing, changing, and separating according to the local topography might well be jeopardised. The question also raised important issues in relation to the general geographical distribution of animals and plants, a topic which he believed could be explained only by assuming ancestral connections between living beings.

Actually, Darwin was always fascinated by the way animals and plants got themselves around the globe, often thinking of it as a game of chess with the earth as a giant chessboard. Animal and plant distribution hinged on a range of unknown contingencies, just as in chess, all of which had to be considered when working out the history of their movements. Right from his earliest descriptions of possible evolutionary processes, he believed these geographical arrangements and the power of dispersal were integral parts of what he thought about the changing world, and the elevation and subsidence of interconnecting land played a critical role in determining distribution patterns. But what if the land stayed still? Would animals and plants continue to move around and vary?

Darwin set out to demonstrate that living beings can travel much further under their own devices than most naturalists allowed. Going back to his experiences on the Galápagos Islands, he vividly recalled the way he thought the animals and plants were like Robinson Crusoe's flotsam and jetsam, cast away on their oceanic refuges by a combination of fate and their own inbuilt manoeuvrability. There was no possibility of a land bridge formerly connecting Ecuador and the Galápagos, he reasoned; no possibility of one of Lyell's tracts of land rising up out of the ocean as a temporary highway for these living beings to march over. It was much too far, and there was no hint of any corroborative geological evidence. The Galápagos animals and plants must have travelled from South America under their own power.

Extemporising from this, Darwin decided that most bridges of land that might once have linked islands with continental landmasses, and that were submerged in the modern era, were not intellectually necessary. His friends Edward Forbes, who tried to explain why one particular slug lived only in Spain and southern Ireland, and Thomas Wollaston, who puzzled over identical species of insects appearing in Madeira and Africa, both relied on hypothetical former land bridges which subsequently sank beneath the waves to explain animal distribution.[6] Slugs and beetles, they argued, thus expanded their range by natural means while also keeping their feet dry. Forbes, always the great romantic of nineteenth-century natural history, went on to christen his proposed land bridge Atlantis, paying homage to Plato and the scientific philosopher Francis Bacon simultaneously. But Darwin believed they overlooked another possibility. He insisted that distribution patterns were mostly the result of the sheer dispersive powers of the organisms themselves.

Yet how to show the ability of a slug to shift for itself? Impetuously, Darwin began a series of experiments on seeds and animal larvae that blossomed into a project preoccupying him for several years. He kept the seeds of many different plants, some of them specially chosen with Hooker's advice because they lived on islands, in saltwater tanks and bottles in his cellars at Down, hoping to prove they could survive a number of weeks being whirled around the oceans of the globe and then, when thrown up on some foreign shore, successfully germinate. The work involved daily checks, careful record-keeping, and a great deal of methodical planting out and counting. Down House—and the shed in the garden that he co-opted for the purpose—became an experimental laboratory with a decidedly eccentric, rural atmosphere.[7] Darwin was in his element. "To my surprise," he happily wrote to Hooker, "I found that out of 87 kinds, 64 germinated after an immersion of 28 days, and a few survived an immersion of 137 days."

It took him some time to notice that his seeds usually sank to the bottom of the jars of water. Unfortunately, this did not say much for their chances at sea. Resourcefully, he reconsidered: despite his enthusiasm for facts, he was not a man to let a few contrary ones stand in his way. Dehydrated seeds, he discovered, did float for a time, not so many days as before but enough for Darwin's argument. Off on the scent once more, he promptly recreated the circumstances in which "floods might wash down plants or branches, and these might be dried on the banks, and then by a fresh rise in the stream be washed into the sea." He dried stalks of plants laden with nuts or fruit and recorded their survival in seawater. Hazelnuts, for instance, floated for ninety days, asparagus seeds for thirty-two, both successfully germinating at the end of their ordeal. Darwin used this information to compute, with the aid of Johnston's *Physical Atlas*, the distance over which seeds might travel. Assuming an average rate of thirty-three miles a day for the Atlantic currents, seeds floating for about twenty-eight days would be carried across 924 miles of sea.

Marooned behind his desk at Kew, Hooker was unconvinced. Where, he inquired cynically, were all the seaside colonies of hazel trees and asparagus spears that this conclusion would suggest? "It is I think high time [to] throw overboard laying much stress on the subject of the migration of seeds, except in the cases of land we know to have been recently formed, or, from devastating causes, to be recently clothed with vegetation."[8] This kind of opposition was just what Darwin relished the most. "Fighting a battle with you always clears my mind wonderfully," he said. Boyishly, both men let their competitive spirits flare. Soon Darwin's children were asking gleefully after the seeds, "Did we beat Dr. Hooker?"

I may just mention that the seeds mentioned in my former note have all germinated after 14 days immersion, *except* the cabbages all dead, & the radishes have had their germination delayed & several I think dead; cress still all most vigorous—French spinach, oats, barley, canary-seed, borage, beet have all germinated after 7 days immersion.—It is quite surprising that the radishes shd have grown, for the salt-water was putrid to an extent which I cd not have thought credible had I not smelt it myself, as was the water with the cabbage seeds.[9]

When cress and lettuce seeds germinated after twenty-one days' immersion, Hooker admitted defeat. You are a good man, Darwin reported back promptly, to confess that you expected the crop would be killed in a week, for this "gives me a nice little triumph."

Darwin went on to include other more uncertain means of transport in his investigations. "If you knew some of the experiments (if they may so be called) which I am trying," he confessed candidly to Hooker, "you would have a good right to sneer for they are so *absurd* even in *my* opinion that I dare not tell you." Seeds and animal larvae, for instance, might travel attached to the feet or feathers of birds, or inside their digestive tracts. Gingerly, he hung a pair of duck's feet, neatly severed at the elbow, in an aquarium stocked with freshwater snails to "represent those of a bird sleeping in a natural pond." The children gave a fascinated squirm before helping him count the snails clinging to the feet when Darwin waved them in the air to imitate flying. These resilient molluscs survived in damp air for a period of twelve to twenty hours, and the family's collective imagination soared: "in this length of time a duck or heron might fly at least six or seven hundred miles, and would be sure to alight on a pool or rivulet, if blown across sea to an oceanic island or to any other distant point." Darwin tried to repeat the success with land snails, except they disobligingly failed to lay any eggs for him, "so that I have not at all profited by my scheme"; he also experimented with duckweed, correctly thinking it would be carried from pond to pond on birds' feet.

Not long afterwards, Darwin sent Parslow out with a shotgun to fell partridges after a heavy rainfall in order to count the seeds in the mud sticking to their feet. You would have no idea, he chuckled to Hooker, how many there are. That same February, as he watched an old beech tree being cut down in the village, he wondered if there were any seeds lying dormant under the roots. Carefully, he grubbed up a handful of earth (seventy-seven years old, he told his son William, according to the tree rings inside the trunk) to pick out and grow as many seeds as he could. On other occasions, he would leap from Aunt Sarah's carriage on the road to Westerham or Maidstone if he saw a likely-looking ditch and scoop up handfuls of mud to take home to investigate for the same purpose. It was good fun as well as science. Francis Darwin, aged eight, concocted elaborate scenarios for his father: "Why shd not a bird be killed (by hawk, lightning, apoplexy, hail &c)

with seeds in crop, & it would swim." No sooner said than done, reported Darwin. "A pigeon has floated for 30 days in salt water with seeds in crop & they have grown splendidly."[10]

There was no end to variations on this theme. Taking advantage of a family excursion to the London zoo in 1854, Darwin tried feeding the goldfish with one of his special mixtures of salted seeds. To his disappointment the fish spat it out. But after looking long and hopefully into the pond he thought he could detect them hesitating over onion seed. None of the other fish in the gardens would take any of his proffered morsels. Undaunted, he made inquiries among his relatives and discovered that anglers sometimes used cracked wheat as bait for barbel. So he got James Tennant, the keeper of the zoo aquarium, to spend some time each week trying wheat on this species of fish, with some modest success. In truth, neither Tennant nor his barbels were in any position to argue. Tennant, like the other zoo employees, were paid servants of the Zoological Society, and since Darwin was a fellow of the society he could ask any of the keepers to carry out research projects with every expectation of assent. The animals themselves had ostensibly been collected and displayed solely for the fellows' edification. The society opened the gardens to the public at weekends only because it needed the money.[11]

On another trip to the zoo, Darwin surreptitiously fed small carcasses stuffed with seeds to oceangoing birds. He had spent the week beforehand analysing owl droppings to establish how many seeds might retain their vitality after passing through the guts of animals. He was surprised, and then pleased, at his results, which showed seeds positively thrived under these circumstances. Even Hooker was interested, and he suggested that Darwin send this information to the Linnean Society. The zoo's hawks, Darwin reported back, behaved like gentlemen and cast up pellets with lots of seeds in them. "We have thus an effective means of distribution of any seed eaten by birds, for Hawks and Owls are often blown far out to sea: I am trying whether the seeds will germinate."[12]

At about the same time he asked his nephew Edmund Langton to have a go at the fish in the Langton family pond. "Will you tell your papa," Edmund wrote to Francis in 1856, "that I have tried the experiments with all the seeds."

The minnows only took a very little Dutch clover and spit it out again, and the Prussian carp took one anthoxanthum seed and spit it out again, but it was a rather cold day so I will try again.[13]

Not wanting to admit defeat, in the end Darwin decided that fish full of seeds were probably swallowed by birds and contributed to plant distribution only indirectly. "I find fish will greedily eat seeds of aquatic grasses & that millet seed put into fish & given to Stork & then voided will germinate. So this is the nursery rhyme of this is the stick that beat the pig &c. &c.," he told Hooker.

Nevertheless, towards the middle of 1856 his experiments had taken him so far that he felt entirely justified in criticising Lyell's and Forbes's exclusive emphasis on land bridges. It was the last straw, he thought, when even cautious, pedantic Hooker invented a giant Antarctic continent to explain the similarities between isolated southern floras. He wrote hotly to Lyell about how Lyell's scientific friends were elevating and submerging huge sections of the earth's crust with unscholarly abandon—forgetting in his indignation just how much he too based his geology on exactly the same Lyellian movements.

> Here poor Forbes made a continent to North America and another (or the same) to the Gulf weed; Hooker makes one from New Zealand to South America and round the world to Kerguelen Land. Here is Wollaston speaking of Madeira and Porto Santo as the sure and certain witnesses of a former continent. . . . If you do not stop this, if there be a lower region for the punishment of geologists, I believe, my great master, you will go there.[14]

He was just as touchy in letters to Hooker. Where was the geological evidence for connections between ocean islands and faraway landmasses? "I must try & cease being rabid & try to feel humble, & allow you all to make continents as easily as a cook does pancakes."[15] But he did not fool anyone, least of all Hooker. Crossly, he continued to believe that no one except himself really understood just how readily animals and plants could disperse themselves over the globe.

In so doing, he provided himself with a good strong alternative to Lyell's elevation and subsidence argument. Slowly but surely he started dissociating himself from some of the ideas that had been so pivotal in first grasping the nettle of evolution.

IV

Not long afterwards, Darwin added domestic birds to his researches. Remembering the doves and pigeons kept by his father at The Mount, and following the advice of his ornithological friend William Yarrell, he began keeping ornamental pigeons and a few specialist chickens at Down to study the variations between breeds. This too was a direct result of his barnacle discoveries. Since there was little need now for him to emphasise the effects of "unsettling" causes in the production of individual variations, he naturally wondered what, if anything, did characterise variation as a process. When did individual variations emerge in embryological development, for instance, and were they more obvious in some animals and plants than in others?

There were many interesting breeds of pigeon to choose from, and at one point Darwin possessed some sixteen different kinds and eight or nine types of fowl, nearly ninety birds in total. In the same way as he threw himself completely into working on seeds, he flung himself into this new investigation with eager abandon. Darwin loved his pigeons, getting Isaac Laslett, the carpenter in Down village, to build them a proper aviary divided into pens. He spent hours reading self-help manuals and books by breeders to make sure he was doing the right thing and visiting shows and exhibitions to see what was available. He found it very entertaining hobnobbing with breeding experts and trying to exude an air of practical knowledge as he leaned over cages full of absurdly ruffled feathers. The esoteric world of pigeon fanciers seemed to him delightfully fresh and curious.

Yet the "fancy" was an art form with which Darwin was not familiar. He needed to be tutored before he could see the minute differences in shape that breeders and judges identified.[16] Just as when he was working on barnacles, he had to get his eye in. When his eye came, he was thrilled with the sense of recognition. The minute variations which set a potential pigeon champion apart from a more ordinary specimen were of exactly the same order as variations in barnacles—small but noticeable, constituting the essential raw material on which selection acted. Through studying what the breeders, judges, and exhibitors were after, and the way they bred up particular strains to fulfil those characteristics, Darwin could almost watch the process of artificial selection taking place and draw useful parallels with what he surmised were evolutionary connections between wild organisms in general. However, Darwin did not attempt to produce show breeds himself. He did not try any artificial selection among his own birds. Instead, he made himself alive to the whole range of breeders' problems and aspirations, learning to see as they saw in the same way as he once trained his eyes to see the geological world as Lyell did. When he talked about the "hidden hand" of selection thereafter, he almost always visualised a pigeon breeder picking a favoured bird out of one cage and putting it with another bird, also chosen for its favourable attributes. He could not help but anthropomorphise natural selection into a mating ceremony deftly engineered by a wise, all-seeing, and sensible English gentleman. Conceived primarily as a metaphor, and exceptionally helpful in that role, Darwin's usage of the idea of "natural" selection nonetheless became hopelessly and unavoidably entangled with anthropomorphic overtones. These were to give him and generations of readers many serious problems in later years.[17]

As his experience with pigeons increased, Darwin realised that fanciers believed each breed was more or less specifically distinct, probably originating in several wild stocks. Most university-trained anatomists and taxonomists, on the other hand, himself included, thought they derived from a single common ancestor, the rock pigeon.

Without a second thought, Darwin decided the fanciers were wrong. He was not interested in their theories of origin. His primary aim in keeping pigeons was to pursue an intensive programme of embryological comparisons to demonstrate that each and every one of the fifteen or sixteen breeds of pigeon revealed traces of common descent: that their embryology and maturation from chick to adult revealed that all the breeds ultimately derived from the wild rock dove.[18] If he could show such a process of divergence from one ancestral form, he felt he would be justified in saying the same kind of divergence took place in the real world. His entire analogy between artificial and natural selection ultimately rested on giving the birds' growth and development his closest attention.

This interest in pigeons led Darwin into unusual places and towards unusual men. Bernard Brent, who was a leading fancier and prolific contributor to the *Cottage Gardener*, was "a very queer little fish," Darwin told his son William. William, by then aged fourteen and at Rugby School, showed a great deal of interest in his father's practical researches and collected butterflies himself. "I am getting on splendidly with my pigeons," his father wrote cheerfully one spring term, "and the other day had a present of Trumpeters, Nuns, & Turbits; & when last in London, I visited a jolly old Brewer, who keeps 300 or 400 most beautiful pigeons & he gave me a pair of pale brown, quite small German pouters: I am building a new house for my tumblers so as to fly them in summer."[19] William was old enough also to share some of Darwin's social awareness. After one dinner at a fanciers' meeting, Darwin reported that Mr. Brent handed him a clay pipe, saying "Here is your pipe" as if it were a matter of course that he should smoke. "Another odd little man (N.B. all pigeon fanciers are little men I begin to think) showed me a wretched little Polish hen, which he said he would not sell for £50 & hoped to make £200 by her, as she had a black top-knot. I am going to bring a lot more pigeons back with me on Saturday, for it is a noble & majestic pursuit, & beats moths [and] butterflies, whatever you may say to the contrary."[20]

The same breezy gentleman's air swept through a letter to Huxley. "I have found it very important associating with fanciers & breeders:"

For instance I sat one evening in a gin-palace in the Borough amongst a set of pigeon-fanciers,—when it was hinted that Mr Bult had crossed his Powters with Runts to gain size; & if you had seen the solemn, the

mysterious & awful shakes of the head which all the fanciers gave at this
scandalous proceeding, you would have recognised how little crossing has
had to do with improving breeds, & how dangerous for endless generations the process was.—All this was brought home far more vividly than
by pages of mere statements &c.[21]

Of course, Darwin exaggerated for comic effect: writing to the quick-
witted Huxley always put him on the *qui vive.* The social realm of pigeon
fanciers was not solely one of cloth caps, pipes, and dirty boots, or even gin.
Darwin's Cambridge contemporary Robert Pulleine was a famous exhibitor
and poultry judge as well as a vicar, and the majority of men Darwin came
into contact with at shows or through his correspondence were profoundly
respectable householders from the middling classes, many of them authors
of textbooks about bird breeding or contributors to the popular journals
which sprang up to cater for their interest.[22] Even Queen Victoria sent her
pigeons to competitions.

But it was a world Darwin at first knew very little about. Making contact
with William Tegetmeir was a most important step forward.[23] Tegetmeir
knew practically everyone on the pigeon and poultry circuit, from the
parsons and country gentlemen who enjoyed breeding and exhibiting their
birds at the highest levels right down to the aficionados of lesser rank who
owned just one or two choice specimens. Tegetmeir fell somewhere in
between these two extremes on the social scale: he was a journalist, and
poultry editor of the *Field,* who kept pigeons and poultry in his home at
Wood Green, a suburb of London. He was also a fellow of the Zoological
Society, the author of several scientific papers, and an acquaintance of
William Yarrell's. In his spare time he was secretary of a grandly named
pigeon club, the Philoperisteron Society, which, with its long Greek label,
gave off a distinctly exclusive aura—a club for aspiring gentlemen as well as
bird-lovers.

When Darwin got in touch with him through Yarrell, Tegetmeir was
decidedly impressed. For the next decade or more, he diligently kept Darwin
informed about what was going on in the show world, provided birds from
his own collection, arranged for Darwin to receive special specimens from
people he knew, and answered every conceivable question as best he could,
all the time delicately dropping hints about his intimacy with Darwin in
public letters to the *Cottage Gardener* and *Gardener's Chronicle,* until at last
he plucked up courage to invite Darwin for a visit. The visit was a great
success, both of them thought afterwards, although Darwin was careful to
correct any impression that they might be thought of as "working *together.*"
Tegetmeir was aware of the advantages of associating with a well-known
figure like Darwin, just as Darwin was mindful of Tegetmeir's usefulness as a

middleman. Tegetmeir wanted Darwin as much as Darwin needed him.

It was easy for the rest of the family to empathise with this side of his researches. Darwin's enthusiasm for pigeons was infectious. "I hope Lady Lyell & yourself will remember whenever you want a little rest & have time how very glad we shd be to see you here," he wrote to Lyell one day. "I will show you my pigeons! which is the greatest treat, in my opinion, which can be offered to human beings." From the age of about ten, Henrietta Darwin was also entranced. "I can still recall their different characteristics: a cross old fantail who in taking food from my hand liked to give a good peck & hurt me if he could. The pouter pigeon was good natured but not clever, and I remember a hen Jacobin which I considered rather feeble minded."[24] Unfortunately, Henrietta's pet cat took to killing the pigeons and was destroyed without her knowledge. Resentment against her parents for this act ran undiminished, along with the other resentments about her sister Anne, for the rest of her life.

After this, Darwin reduced the livestock to more manageable proportions. As an alternative, and as his pigeon researches ballooned out in other directions, he asked Tegetmeir, then Fox, and then various cousins, friends, and uncles, for dead birds which he could study and turn into skeletons. "If you had any breed of poultry pure, I wd beg a chicken with exact age stated about a week or fortnight old to be sent in box by post," he wrote to Fox. Politely, Darwin offered to pay the postage. "Indeed I shd be very glad to have a nestling common pigeon sent, for I mean to make skeletons, & have already just begun comparing wild & tame ducks, & I think the results rather curious."[25] He did not like killing the birds himself. And the process of boiling away the flesh for the bones was unpleasant. After three desperate weeks with Parslow and a disgusting, bubbling cauldron, he called for the help of his Shropshire friend Thomas Eyton.

> As you have had such great experience in making skeletons, will you be so kind as to take the trouble to give me some pieces of information. . . . when I took the body out of the water, the smell was so dreadful that it made me retch awfully. Now I was told that if I hung the body of a bird or small quadruped up in the air & allowed the flesh to decay off, & the whole to get dry, that I could boil the mummy in water with caustic soda, & so get it nearly clean, but not white, with very little smell. What do you think of this plan? And pray tell me how do you get the bones moderately clean, when you take the skeleton out, with some small fragments of putrid flesh still adhering. It really is most dreadful work.—Lastly do you pluck your birds?[26]

Eventually both Darwin's and Parslow's noses rebelled and he started sending specimens out to have the skeletons properly prepared.

V

Darwin cheerfully referred to these occupations as "odds & ends with which I am amusing myself." From chickens and pigeons, he moved easily to ducks, dogs, rabbits, and turkeys. "Shd an old wild Turkey ever die please remember me," he beseeched Fox. "I do not care for baby turkey. Nor for a mastiff, very many thanks for your offer.—I have puppies of bull-dogs & greyhound in salt, & I have had carthorse & race horse young colts carefully measured." But, of course, these researches were far more than odds and ends. They provided the concrete detail that Darwin's contemporaries ultimately found so persuasive. He sought information about vestigial stripes on the legs of horses and donkeys, about the skeletons of pigs, about the wildness of domestic geese, and about the origins of the ancient white cattle of Chillingham Park. In every area he hunted out an expert who would either supply the answers directly or act as a sounding board for his researches: Brent and Tegetmeir for pigeons, Edmund Dixon for ducks, John Davy for fish (a keen fisherman, like his brother Humphry Davy), Edward Blyth in Calcutta for Indian birds and miscellaneous information of all descriptions, Mrs. Teresa Whitby for silkworms, his great-aunt Holland for songbirds, a Swedish botanical friend of Hooker's for native fiord ponies, and always, always Fox in his "Noah's ark" at his rectory in Cheshire.

Darwin did not neglect plants, either. How many seeds usually lay dormant in a patch of earth, he wondered, not growing until a vacancy appeared in the turf above? Framing a practical question out of his theories of competition, he commissioned the governess Catherine Thorley in her off-duty hours to guard a small plot of grass, cleared for action, and count the number of seedlings that grew. She marked each seedling as it appeared, to see, as Darwin put it, "at what time of life they suffer most." With young Leonard in tow, Miss Thorley also helped Darwin collect representative samples of the plants in the Down fields, comparing wasteland with cultivated grassland. "We shall want a bit of help in naming puzzlers," Darwin declared to Hooker: "how dreadfully difficult it is to name plants." One day Leonard, aged five and fast turning into the family comedian, laid a blade of grass of a kind neither his father nor Miss Thorley had seen before beside a dinner plate, remarking, "I are an extraordinary grass-finder."

Darwin's interest in variation naturally led him towards the work of plant hybridisers, particularly the magisterial studies by Joseph Kolreuter and Karl von Gärtner which seemed to suggest that cross-breeding plants resulted in different levels of fertility in the offspring. Darwin purchased copies of their books from Hippolyte Baillière, a bookseller in London who specialised in continental scientific texts. He found the German language stiff going, however, and had to battle with every word, a dictionary constantly beside him. He used to complain that even native German speakers could not decide the meaning of a word without the context. The children—eventually fluent linguists themselves—remembered how he would come into the drawing room in the evening with a basket full of dictionaries, putting it down with a groan. He once boasted to Hooker that he had begun German. "Ah my dear fellow that's nothing," retorted Hooker. "I've begun it many times."[27] And on another celebrated occasion he asked Hooker, "Where is this place Wien where so many books are published?"

Still, the scholarly data which emerged was well worth it. In part to test Gärtner's views, Darwin began a series of crossing experiments with more than thirty varieties of garden peas. It was not so much the decrease in fertility that interested him as the increase of mutual sterility: this bore on the general problem of how varieties could keep themselves distinct in nature. John Cattell, a florist and nurseryman at Westerham, supplied seeds and helped him with relevant information, soon supported by Darwin's expanding network of seedsmen and gardeners. Hooker, as could be expected, was more than useful here: located at Kew Gardens, he knew practically every seedsman there was to know in horticultural Britain, and a good few in Paris and Berlin besides. If Hooker's contacts failed, Darwin could always rely on Hooker himself to send seeds or living plants direct from the gardens. Funnily enough, even Hooker was ignorant about the actual extent of cross-fertilisation in the plant kingdom. Darwin's researches depended critically on information gleaned from practical gardeners. They mostly agreed with Darwin that there were no hard and fast rules to crossing.

He also undertook experiments relating to the ultimate origin of variations, trying to break the constitution of plants by growing them under coloured glass domes as advised by the chemist Robert Hunt, or by feeding them with over-rich manure. Not many of his plants responded the way he wanted, giving rise to a frustrated cry to Fox that "all nature is perverse and will not do as I wish it." Eventually Darwin gave the coloured glass as a toy to Leonard. Yet he could hardly restrain his excitement when some forget-me-nots sent by Henslow obligingly produced deformed buds and leaves after heavy doses of fresh cow dung.

Most significant, he began working on plant fertilisation, another of the crucial pillars on which he would ultimately rest his theory of evolution. Darwin's barnacles showed him how individual organisms—even hermaphrodite individuals—must occasionally join with another to reproduce. It was unlikely, he thought, that continual self-fertilisation took place, either in plants or in animals. Echoing the prejudices of any fierce Victorian physician, he developed a prurient abhorrence of the idea of self-fertilisation, almost as if it were an act of self-pollution. In this, Darwin was running against the tide of contemporary scientific opinion. Nearly everyone he knew believed in the widespread incidence of self-fertilisation, even capable botanists like Hooker. Huxley nodded his head when asked about it in marine invertebrates. But Huxley at least made a note to investigate the question: "Darwin—an eternal hermaphrodite" he scribbled casually in his notebook and then spent the next four or five years teasing his friend about the unwitting slur. But Darwin's theories of variation needed sexuality. Without sexual reproduction he had no mechanism for the spontaneous appearance of variations in the offspring; without variations there was no possibility of selection or of transmutation. Sexual relations between plants, and between animals, and between humans, were the essential footing to his version of evolution.

In this respect, garden peas and beans proved Darwin's greatest problem. Their open-fronted flowers seemed to invite wind or insect pollination, and yet there was none of the ad hoc mixing of breeds and varieties that usually arose from such a process: sweet peas, beans, and snapdragons, for example, resolutely remained true to type even when mixed up in rows in a vegetable plot. Several specialist nurserymen told him so, and his own planting experiments confirmed it. Darwin consequently spent many contented mornings in his kitchen garden imitating the action of bees landing on the petals of scarlet kidney beans, watching the curling inner pistil bend down to rub the back of his proffered paintbrush and noting how the honey or nectar was placed so that the bee invariably alighted on the correct side. He threw himself into this delicate masquerade with abandon, identifying almost completely with the different personalities and preferences of hive bees and humble-bees (bumblebees)—some neatly cutting slits in the base of the flower to get at the nectar, others utilizing a hole made by a previous visitor. London bees were much cleverer than country bees, he concluded, after watching some working the flower borders at the zoo. Country bees were much more easily deceived. If Darwin removed the lower petals from a lobelia planted at Down, they thought it was withered and went on their way without looking for nectar or fertilising the waiting flower.

Watching him bending solicitously over his flowers, she said, Emma got the feeling that Darwin would have liked to be a bee above all other species. Working among his plant pots and vegetables, he was as happy as he had ever been, pushing his sticks and bits of coloured rag into the ground next to great rafts of gauze netting, the upturned bell jars, and a forest of metal labels marking individual plants with his complicated hieroglyphics; and he and the children placidly enjoyed checking specimens one by one during daily strolls. Once, after several days of careful observation, Darwin stationed each child at a strategic point along the route he thought humble-bees took.

When the bees arrived at his plants he gently dusted them with flour; everyone was to shout out where they flew so he could find out the number of plants a single bee might conceivably visit.[28] He was so interested in the outcome that he forgot to give the cook her kitchen flour-shaker back. Another time, when the family was at Maer, he tried to trick bees with artificial flowers from Emma's bonnet. Dressing the flowers with fresh leaves, he carefully stuck them into the flower border and waited. It was a child who perceived, across the entire length of the garden, that they were unnatural artifices. "From Mamma's cap," he said, which was true. "He immediately also spied a drop of honey, as large as a pin's head, which I had put at bottom of each flower."[29]

The fertilisation processes of garden broom (*Cytisus*), laburnums, lobelias, salvias, mimulus, stachys, and wallflowers all came under the same ardent scrutiny: every one differently adapted for insect visits. Darwin's *Lobelia fulgens,* for instance, was never visited by bees and never set seed unless he played the part of an insect for it, whereas the ordinary blue lobelia was frequently surrounded by bees and did set seed. "I mention this," he said to a new friend, the American botanist Asa Gray, "because there are such beautiful contrivances to prevent the stigma ever getting its own pollen; which seems only explicable on the doctrine of the advantage of crosses." No wonder the toddler Leonard said, when going to look at a flower, "I've a fact to do."

In the event, Darwin devised countless delicate experiments to show the mutual adaptations between insects and garden plants which enabled each flower to receive pollen from another flower rather than from itself. He gave himself up to unreserved admiration of the ways in which nature produced its variety. It was a particular pleasure to turn his garden, and all the secret thoughts of a green, rural England that had helped him survive the *Beagle* years, into the all-embracing appreciation of diversity his theories required. God was in the details, William Paley had said—and so was natural selection. He read widely, he collected useful bits and pieces in case he needed them for an experiment, he fired off inquiries to every conceivable authority he could find, he persuaded any number of neighbours, nurserymen, and relatives to make observations for him, he sent questions to the letter pages of journals like the *Gardeners' Chronicle,* and he inveigled the staff of the Zoological Society of London, the British Museum, and Kew Gardens to carry out further researches—sometimes of quite a demanding nature. Even the swarm of children whom Henslow taught in Hitcham provided Darwin with information at his request.

Do you think the most able of your little girls would like to collect for me a packet of seeds of such plants as grow near Hitcham, I paying, say 3d for each packet: it would put a few shillings into their pockets and would be an *enormous* advantage to me, for I grudge the time to collect the seeds, more especially as I have to learn the plants! The experiment seems worth trying; what do you think? Should you object to offering this reward or payment to your little girls? You would have to select the most conscientious ones, that I might not get wrong seeds.[30]

He used his household without compunction too. Miss Thorley, Parslow, Jones the stablehand, Brooks the gardener, Henry Hemmings (Aunt Sarah Wedgwood's servant), and a constant procession of children, along with his nieces and nephews, all contributed in some significant way to these exercises.

If Darwin had become a barnacle during previous years, he now turned his house into the *Beagle:* a self-contained, self-regulating scientific ship methodically ploughing onwards through the waves outside. Safely isolated from the usual concerns of the world, he could pursue his own interests and explore his own lines of inquiry, interacting with other men and women only when he wanted to, gathering the information he required through the conveniently impersonal medium of letters and books. Alone in his cabin—the study at Down—he could get on with his thoughts in peace. He could use his undoubted charm and his position in society to good effect just as he had all those years before: almost as if he were on the *Beagle* again, sailing into some unknown port, where people felt it a natural consequence of English life that he should ask and that they should do.

Moreover, Emma ran the ship efficiently, very like FitzRoy or Wickham, providing food and company when he needed it and keeping out of the way otherwise: her role was to make his life as easy as possible. In addition, her strong opinions about some aspects of his work secretly reminded him of the way FitzRoy had behaved. He had to watch his tongue again, cautiously skirting the topics it was best to avoid. Running around below were the staff and his children, rather like the crew and midshipmen, always available to help with his inquiries. The patriarchal hierarchy of the house ensured that his requests were heeded. Further afield, friends like Erasmus, Hooker, Fox, and Henslow were kept busy doing jobs for him—buying books, checking references, killing chickens, sending plants, writing letters on his behalf. And the uneasy compromise he had at last achieved with his failing health kept him to a rigid timetable, a good imitation of the fixed ship's hours he had come to welcome on the *Beagle.*

Both Darwin's personality and his position as head of the household therefore worked materially to his advantage in recreating the environment in which he felt best. The *Beagle* years were when he had felt most productive, readiest to grasp how nature worked; and they had continued into his time as a bachelor in London, when he first tumbled into transmutationary theory.

The *Beagle* made him what he was. Nearly twenty years later at Down, he decisively—reassuringly—pulled it back into existence.

Appropriately enough, Darwin welcomed the thought of Robert FitzRoy's visiting this tightly organised, shipshape community. He was glad to see FitzRoy once more, this time in his drawing room at Down. By then an admiral, but generally disappointed in life, FitzRoy was passing through the area on his way back to London from Sevenoaks and came to call, bringing with him his second wife and his son, a pale boy of eighteen.[31] Cordial as ever, Darwin easily forgot their former differences over the *Journal of Researches* and their diverging viewpoints on slavery and geology. He inquired eagerly about the political state of New Zealand and the careers of Sulivan, Stokes, Wickham, and Bynoe. It was a successful reunion so far as the two men were concerned—their last friendly exchange, in fact. Emma was less certain. "Papa was much awestruck with the honour," she said to William, "& the Admiral was very gracious and friendly. Mrs FitzRoy is a cold dry stick & I could not find a word to say to her. Papa says she is a *remarkably* nice woman (because she laughed at his jokes I say)."[32]

VI

The children clearly felt a strong sense of solidarity with their parents, encouraged by Emma and Darwin at every turn. Their lives were closely integrated into Darwin's. They always had to fit into his routines. This does not mean to say that they were obliged to conform to the image of quiet Victorian children. On the contrary, they clattered round the house noisily, inventing games that involved sliding down the stairs on a board made for them by Parslow, and darted in and out of Darwin's study in search of the necessary equipment of childhood, a ruler, a pair of scissors, a piece of drawing paper, or a sticking plaster. Henrietta had singing lessons ("a good screech") and piano lessons; William and George practised indoor cricket. Left-over souvenirs from the *Beagle* voyage mysteriously found their way into the boys' hands: George remembered flinging Darwin's *bolas* around the lawn at Down, and using South American gaucho stirrups and spurs on the rocking horse. Bone arrow-heads from Tierra del Fuego came to a similar end. William played with the Australian boomerang unsuccessfully until his father came out to show him how it was done. Dismayed, they both watched it turn and land in a cucumber frame: the only time William ever saw gloomy old Brooks the gardener laugh outright.[33]

Darwin tolerated these interruptions perfectly well. Occasionally he would play with the youngest ones. Francis remembered as a very young child putting his hands inside Darwin's shirt and how "he would growl like a bear." His body was very hairy, said Francis.

We all took especial pleasure in the games he played with us; there used to be one called Taglioni [after the ballet dancer] in which the child stood on one of his knees held by one hand & balanced; he used also to play at "by the licklap of me, have . . . " or whatever it is. But I don't think he romped much with us, I suppose his health would stop that. He used sometimes to tell us stories which were considered specially delightful for their rarity. The way he brought us up is shown by the story of Leo on the sofa, which my father was fond of telling; it being forbidden to jump on the sofa for the sake of the springs, my father came in & found Leo dancing about & said "Oh Lenny Lenny it is against all rules" to which Leo [said] "Then I think you'd better go out of the room."[34]

The same air of freedom featured in another of Darwin's stories about Leonard when he was about six years old, and was recorded in Darwin's book of observations on the children. The later pages of this book were dominated by Leonard's funny sayings which amused his parents greatly and also served Darwin as a precise documentation of a child's increasing self-awareness and mental associations. Such information eventually made its way into his evolutionary writings. "Lenny lying on my lap, coolly said 'Well you old ass' & being very slightly shocked, remarked 'Really, I did not mean to spurt that out.' "

The boys' expressive language sometimes worried their governesses— "the devil take it," or "I wish to God," they used to say, which were turns of phrase clearly picked up from Darwin. One governess complained to Emma's sister Elizabeth that the children used "very bad language, so bad that she hardly liked to repeat it." On being asked if she would like to write it down, she plucked up courage and said it was "By George." The combined family shrieked with laughter at this unnecessary stuffiness.

But it also seems plain that the children wished for rather more of Darwin's attention than they usually received. Francis remembered how Darwin would occasionally run a hand over his hair as he paused behind his chair: and as a full-grown man he longed for his father to do it again. Darwin's ever-pressing work, if they did but admit it, took him away from them, despite their mutual strolls to the vegetable garden and the help with rags and sticks. In the way that children do, they knew Darwin's work was central to the family routine. Their recollections of childhood make that obvious. Yet they were uncomprehending accomplices—mere minions in some unknown parental project. And Darwin was honest about finding his obligations to the children demanding: sometimes sentimental, sometimes exasperated. Once when he was away at Shrewsbury he admitted that "absence makes me very much in love with my own dear three chickens." Otherwise, it was a different story. "In the morning I was baddish, & did hardly any work & was as much overcome by my children, as ever Bishop Coplestone was with Duck. But the children have been very good all day, & I have grown a good deal better this afternoon, & had a good romp with Baby—I see, however, very little of the Blesseds."[35]

Moreover, the children had few friends outside the family. No village children came to call, no schoolfriends came to stay. Indeed, the Wedgwood and Darwin families were notoriously clannish, not liking or seeking company any further than their relations. Emma was worse than Darwin in this regard: she mustered only one or two female friends outside the family, and these dated from her Staffordshire childhood. She always looked instead to the female Wedgwoods—her aunts, her sisters, and her brother's wives—and made sure that the other people her own children knew best were her Wedgwood nephews and nieces. It was a restricted upbringing in this sense, one that Henrietta Darwin later regretted. Henrietta confided how awkward it made her: "we led an intensely quiet life seeing practically nothing of our neighbours. This was a misfortune. I think if my mother had been more socially inclined, in spite of my father's ill-health, it might have been to a certain extent avoided. It led to my feeling myself to be a kind of outcast & being shy & ill at ease when in company. But the cousins were many & delightful—the animals also many & delightful."[36]

As might be expected, the household included a governess for the girls. The first one, Miss Thorley of Malvern days, was none too successful as a teacher, though devoted to the family. She was succeeded by her younger sister Emily, whom Henrietta liked much better. It must be said that Emma was not very good at choosing these ladies; she always succumbed to hard-luck stories and, as Henrietta later claimed, was a magnet for volatile and frequently unstable women. Miss Pugh lapsed into madness (she sat at meals with tears pouring down her cheeks) and entered an asylum, with her annual holiday regularly paid for by the Darwin family as a kind of goodwill gesture. Madame Grut lasted only a few weeks before her strong personality clashed with Darwin's: she resigned before he could pluck up courage to sack her. Miss Ludwig, a great beauty by all accounts, was appreciated by the boys, especially Horace as he turned eleven or twelve and developed a romantic crush for her, and by Darwin, who got her to translate German texts, but not by Henrietta: "she taught us no German & not much of anything else." Henrietta had little kind to say about these women's efforts at education. "My mother took very little trouble about our education, and I was frankly bored with schoolroom lessons and schoolroom life. My aim was to escape as soon as possible either to look after some of my many pet animals, or to get a quiet corner to read. I cannot remember playing much with my juniors, unless there was an exciting group of cousins, girls & boys,

& some older than me. The Hensleigh Wedgwoods & Edmund Langton were our greatest friends."

Darwin was similarly relaxed over his daughters' education, failing to look ahead with any of the advanced views about women's position in life that Fanny Wedgwood and his brother Erasmus entertained. Henrietta and Elizabeth were not taught any science or mathematics, for example, beyond some rudimentary botany; their lessons were principally geography, music, singing, and languages. Yet Fanny and Erasmus were closely involved with the foundation of Bedford Ladies College, and Erasmus was a governor of the college for many years, acting as a spirited proponent for women's education, and, furthermore, sincerely believing in what he said. Later on, Henrietta naturally gravitated to his welcoming intellectual circle. Elizabeth (Lizzie or Bessy), the next daughter, suffered rather more from her lack of education. She seems to have had some minor childhood handicap, possibly a slight cerebral palsy which made her clumsy and, as a youngster, late to speak and write properly.[38] There is no evidence confirming Henrietta's opinion that she was retarded. On the contrary, her letters reveal how painfully alive she was to the quick repartee bouncing around Erasmus's drawing room. When she paid a visit there, or when she went to the Hensleigh Wedgwoods, she said she felt very much out of place.

Darwin's placid air seeped out towards the servants also. Parslow was as devoted to the family as Miss Thorley was. "He was a very social, nice sort of gentleman," the butler said, "very joking and jolly indeed; a good husband and a good father and a most excellent master. Even his footmen used to stay with him as long as five years. They would rather stay with him than take a higher salary somewhere else. The cook came there while young and stayed till his death—nearly thirty years."[39] Parslow could have said the same about himself. He stayed with the Darwins, nursing his lumbago and his bad back, for nearly thirty-five years, until he was eventually pensioned off in a cottage in Down village, where the grown-up Darwins went to visit him. In the interval he married a local woman and had a quantity of children: Emma was forever telling William in her letters that Mrs. Parslow had "got" another baby. It was also in the nature of things that the closeness between the two men—master and manservant—rested on an ignorance of their real aims in life. Parslow was loyally uncomprehending of his employer's occupations. "The gardener used to bring plants into his room often of a morning, and he used to tie bits of cotton to them, and try to make them do things," he said.

As far as Francis could remember, Darwin was angry with the servants only once, and that stuck in his memory precisely because it was rare. The culprit was Brooks, the head gardener, who was overheard scolding Lettington, an under-gardener and also his son-in-law. "Get out of the room," shouted Darwin when he interviewed him about this lapse afterwards, "you ought to be ashamed of yourself." Francis scuttled upstairs lest some of the fury fall on him next. No doubt he exaggerated the harmony of the household in retrospect, especially since Darwin was often indignant with Mrs. Evans for bad cooking and scolded Parslow over his slackness with the kitchen economy. Darwin thought Emma's innate untidiness made her too easy-going with the household generally.

Of course, the question of education was different for sons. Darwin made sure the boys were sent to a private tutor from about the age of seven, and then to a small prep school run by Henry Wharton, vicar of Mitcham in Surrey, before moving on to senior schools, and eventually Cambridge University. Their local tutor was the Reverend George Varenne Reed, vicar of Hayes village, very near to Down: the boys would ride over in twos and threes nearly every morning.[40] Reed taught as much of the physical and mathematical sciences as he could manage, and when George Darwin first started, his father recorded how he had already begun optics with him at home. As Darwin's relationship with Reed expanded through Francis and Leonard, he took the opportunity of begging a few plant specimens—"P.S.," Darwin would write at the end of some complicated instruction about Leonard's homework, "Can you give me an offset or cutting of your carrion-smelling Arum—I find I cannot purchase it at Cattell's & I want one for an experiment."

After close consideration of the bad effects of "the old stereotyped stupid classical education," Darwin nevertheless decided to send William to Rugby School, which Hensleigh Wedgwood's oldest boy attended, instead of to the innovative Bruce Castle School in Tottenham, which Fox recommended. Bruce Castle was a continuation of the Hazlewood School, founded by Rowland Hill (of the penny post) and his brothers to provide a self-governing body of boys with the best in modern languages and science. Anxiously reliving his own schooldays, Darwin could not endure "to think of sending my boys to waste 7 or 8 years in making miserable Latin verses."[41] He thought he could already see the dulling effects of constant prep-school grammar on William's once-lively mind. But, as he sadly said to Fox, he did not have the courage of his convictions. There was so much novelty in the Bruce Castle system that they were afraid to try the experiment.[42] Off William went to Rugby, where Darwin gradually saw his worst fears confirmed.

He did not make the same mistake twice. The remaining boys, in their turn, were sent to Clapham Grammar School, a scientific school run by the Reverend Charles Pritchard, afterwards professor of astronomy at Oxford University. Pritchard presided over this school, specially founded for him in

1834, very successfully, drawing in the sons of several famous scientists, including those of John Herschel, George Airy, and William Rowan Hamilton, as well as Darwin. His own activities ranged more widely than mere schoolwork; he contributed papers to the Astronomical Society, investigated early photographic processes, and attended British Association meetings, where he often preached the concluding sermon and became known as the Association's chaplain. At Clapham he ran a small observatory—to which George Darwin attributed his lifelong love for astronomy—and one of the finest specialist ferneries of the Victorian era. Still, despite all these progressive advantages, Darwin was "frightened by having heard that it was rather a rough school"—a snobbism repeated by Henrietta in her autobiography when she claimed the other boys were "not of their own position in life & the moral tone was not good." But John Herschel assured Darwin that the situation was otherwise. In the end, Darwin was happy with what Pritchard did for his sons: "I think favourably of it," he told Fox, and promised to find out if the fees were reduced for clergymen's sons, something that Fox was evidently hoping.

Darwin, moreover, liked his sons to show a passionate interest in their hobbies and did everything he could to encourage them—sometimes encouraging them excessively and then not understanding why their enthusiasm drifted away. He revelled in William's interest in butterflies, and then in botany, and then photography, buying him equipment for all these passing pleasures and trying to stimulate him to take each one further than his son appears to have desired. It seems that William never quite managed to live up to his father's impossibly high expectations.

George was different in his ability to concentrate intently on the things which caught his fancy. From his earliest days, he was interested in knights and castles, compiling laboriously detailed drawings of men in armour and gaily decked horses charging at each other. Some of these coloured drawings were so beguiling that Emma and Darwin put them away as a keepsake, and Darwin fanned George's ardour by borrowing illustrated books on heraldry and suchlike from the London Library.

George sometimes wrote stories to match his pictures. One elaborate tale was "The fairies of the mountain," written on the back of his father's cast-off paper, in this case the back of Darwin's notes about natural selection in pigeons and a few pages relating to barnacles. In one of those quirks of family history, these are the only working notes about barnacles left to posterity, kept for their childish artistry rather than for any intrinsic scientific interest. Furthermore, George's story unconsciously reflected the world of Down House and the routines of his father's work just as much as did Leonard's jokes and clever remarks. When George's fairies (in reality, gnomes) looked inside a flower, they saw faces which smiled at them benignly. When they came up against a wicked dwarf, their response was salutary: first they had tea, then one "cut a hole in the dwarf's stomach & he stuffed it full of wool & then he went away."[43]

The day that he read this, Darwin must have thought that his second son was very like what he had been as a boy.

VII

This inward-looking life made the family almost entirely self-contained and self-sustaining in their ship on the Kentish downs. Darwin and Emma drew together with the children, their relatives, and their staff into a single close-knit unit, hardly needing anyone else and hardly interested in anyone else.

Darwin's work was similarly focussed inwards, at least in the sense that he was preoccupied with gathering information and easing it into the schemes that constantly filled his mind. All scientific arguments have to pass through this kind of intensely private, internal process once or twice in their development, and Darwin's theories were no different.

But towards the end of 1855 and the beginning of 1856 he started looking outwards again, testing the waters in relation to his evolutionary views. He told Charles Bunbury, Lyell's brother-in-law, something of his opinions when they met in London and was pleased to see that he did not seem overly shocked. He read and reread as many transmutationary texts as he could find, deliberately trying to gauge what kind of response his own work would receive. Most significant, he studied a paper by the naturalist Alfred Russel Wallace. It had been strongly recommended to him by Lyell, who thought it covered the same kind of issues that Darwin was trying to resolve. Then, rather worryingly, the same paper was recommended for a second time by his voluminous correspondent in Calcutta, Edward Blyth.[44] "What think you of Wallace's paper in the Ann M.N.H.? Good! Upon the whole!" Blyth wrote. "Wallace has, I think put the matter well; and according to his theory, the various domestic races of animals have been fairly developed into species."[45]

Darwin saw that Wallace certainly addressed the problem of the relationships between closely allied species and that he tried to show how geographical distribution would provide the key for understanding these; but he made a note to himself that this text otherwise contained "nothing very new." The two men had met briefly once, although it is not clear exactly when—either before Wallace set off on a collecting expedition to the River Amazon in 1848, or before he made a similar expedition to the Malay Archipelago in 1854. The possibility of evolutionary undertones in Wallace's work was obvious to Darwin. Yet "it all seems creation with him ... it is all creation ...

put generation for creation & I quite agree." Usually so alert to the different ways of seeing nature, Darwin blindly stared straight past the implications in Wallace's words. Though looking outwards, he was not prepared to see the possibility that someone else might be hesitantly circling around before arriving at the same theory. His own work, not Wallace's, was primary.

Late in April 1856, Darwin invited Thomas Wollaston and Hooker and Huxley and their wives to come to Down for a weekend and, for the men, some extended scientific discussions. The Hookers came for a few extra days beforehand so that Darwin could pump Hooker on botanical problems—always a rash move, as Mrs. Hooker was beginning to realise. Several weeks after this visit, Hooker was still patiently writing out answers to Darwin's stream of bizarrely complicated questions. Still, the Darwins intended to make the visit an occasion. Hewett Cottrell Watson, the avant-garde phrenologist and botanist, was also invited but could not come. They further invited young John Lubbock (son of mathematical Sir John) to come over from High Elms on Saturday night to dine with them: though only twenty-two years old, Lubbock was already a partner in his father's banking concern and a promising naturalist whom Darwin enjoyed encouraging. Secretly, he may have seen in Lubbock some of the ability in natural science that was missing in William. Lubbock told a nice story about his first introduction to Darwin, as a boy aged about eight. Sir John told him of the prospect of a great piece of news. Was he to have a pony? the boy wondered. "No, it was that Charles Darwin was coming to live at Down." A few years further on, Darwin persuaded Sir John to buy Lubbock a microscope and encouraged him to dissect and draw invertebrates, and his first scientific paper was a description of a crustacean from Darwin's collection, politely named *Labiodocera darwinii*.[46] Darwin also liked the looks of Lubbock's pretty wife, Ellen, who played up to his middle-aged attentions in a sprightly way.

Over the weekend, the men let their maverick spirits run wild. Darwin was beginning to feel a need for frankness. And the talk was certainly frank. Huxley was full of marvellous transcendental theories which linked each and every organism together in a metaphysical plan. He was sceptical of any established authority, and forever snapping at the heels of bishops and doctors of divinity. He held no truck with Agassiz's theories of abstract archetypes; he lambasted Owen's understanding of reproduction by parthenogenesis and the alternation of generations. By that time, in fact, Huxley was squaring up for a lifetime of bitter fighting with Owen—fighting on the personal front, on the professional front, and, most damaging for them both, in the public arena, anywhere Huxley could get at him. "He is not referable to any 'archetype' of the human mind with which I am acquainted," Huxley spat in 1852.[47] Distilling the reasons for this hatred is not easy. Apart from competing with Owen for supremacy in the natural-historical world, Huxley came to see his rival as representing all the cant and hypocrisies of British life which restrained him and the advancement of his increasingly positivist interpretation of science. Apes, brains, fossils, jellyfish, natural theology: Huxley was prepared to tackle Owen in every conceivable field. What was more, he lashed out at him when reviewing *Vestiges* in 1854. "By heavens," wrote Darwin, "how the blood must have gushed into the capillaries when a certain great man (whom with all his faults I cannot help liking) read it."[48]

Huxley had plenty to say. So did Wollaston. Though appearing to his friends to be one of the soberest of entomologists, a diligent collector and methodical cataloguer whose talents in that area were so marked that he went to the British Museum every day to catalogue his own gift of Madeiran insects, Wollaston had unconventional theories about creation. These had not been uppermost in Darwin's mind when he first struck up a correspondence with Wollaston the year before. Darwin was keen merely to find out as much as he could about island populations and about the odd wingless insects Wollaston had collected on Madeira. The insects were not really wingless, however. What intrigued both Wollaston and Darwin was that some of them possessed wings uselessly trapped under fused outer cases— they were flightless rather than wingless. What kind of advantage did this give them? wondered Darwin. How could variation and natural selection bring this curious situation about?

Early in 1856, Wollaston began writing a monograph titled *Variation of Species,* which was published later that year. Like Huxley, he was bursting with ideas and counter-ideas and seemed prepared to go further towards limited transmutation in nature than either Darwin expected or someone like Huxley would allow. In his book, Wollaston claimed there were a few island species ("exceptions") which appeared to be derived from other species on the neighbouring landmass—they arrived on an island and changed.[49] But the vast majority of species, he argued, could not—and did not—change beyond the boundaries imposed on them by the Creator. This book was dedicated to Darwin, "whose researches in various parts of the world have added so much to our knowledge of zoological geography." When Darwin read it, he was sure Wollaston would eventually accept his own transmutationary view. "I have heard Unitarianism called a feather-bed to catch a falling Christian," he laughed at him; "and I think you are now on just such a feather-bed, but I believe you will fall much lower & lower."[50] In the event, his cheerful guess backfired. Wollaston became one of Darwin's fiercest critics on both religious and scientific grounds, and one of the most effective.

In his turn, Hooker was more or less favourably disposed to Darwin's theories, although he was not completely familiar with the full depth and scope of the researches that backed them up. He had walked with Darwin step by step for so many years that he was not surprised by anything now. He respected Darwin's intellect as much as Darwin appreciated his specialist knowledge. "I so value your letters," Darwin once said, "that after a heavy batch as of late, I feel that I have been extravagant & have drawn too much money & shall therefore have to stint myself on another occasion."[51] Just as valuable to Darwin was Hooker's long-lasting personal support. If he could get Hooker's approval, Darwin would feel much more confident about the possibility of persuading any number of hostile critics.

With friends like these, transmutation naturally dominated the conversation at Down. Even though no one made notes at the time, it seems they talked about the wavering dividing line between species—if two or more species were discovered to be a single one, where did that leave current definitions of species as aboriginally created forms? Darwin's work on barnacles, Huxley's work on the alternation of generations, Hooker's tendency to lump plant species together where others split them into smaller groups, and Wollaston's catalogue of insects all reinforced the idea that species were much more variable than usually supposed. Perhaps they had no limits at all?

Hearing about the party afterwards, Lyell marvelled at the men's intellectual recklessness. "All four of them ran a tilt against species farther than I believe they are deliberately prepared to go," he reported to Bunbury. He did not like the way they fed off each other's daring, a bad omen for maintaining scientific rationality. Moreover, "I cannot easily see how they can go so far, and not embrace the whole Lamarckian doctrine." To Darwin, he wrote uneasily, "I hear that when you & Hooker & Huxley & Wollaston got together you made light of all species & grew more & more unorthodox."[52]

Safe in London, Bunbury reassured Lyell. He was sure Darwin would not maintain that a moss could be changed into a magnolia, or an oyster into an alderman.

Unfortunately, as Lyell recognised, that was precisely what Darwin would maintain. He too had been to Down for an illuminating weekend earlier in April. During that weekend visit, Darwin had taken the opportunity to explain the theory of natural selection to him in full, not mincing his words about apes and orangs, showing Lyell his pigeon results, and describing how geographical distribution patterns could be explained by assuming common descent. Reluctantly Lyell agreed that Darwin's pigeons and his seed-salting experiments were very striking. "With Darwin," he wrote hesitantly in his scientific journal on 16 April.

> On the formation of species by natural selection. . . . When the conditions
> alter, those individuals which vary so as to adapt them to new circumstances,

flourish & survive while the others are cut off. The varieties extirpated are even more persecuted & annihilated by organic than inorganic causes. The struggle for existence against other species is more serious than against changes of climate & physical geography. The extinction of species has been always going on. . . . The young pigeons are more of the normal type than the old of each variety. Embryology therefore leads to the opinion that you get nearer the type in going nearer to the foetal archetype & in like manner in Time we may get back nearer to the archetype of each genus & family & class.

To him it looked horribly as if Darwin had a case. But what of the dignity of man? he cried. Darwin's theory "brings man into the same system of progressive evolution on which developed the orang out of an oyster."[53]

Lyell, in short, was simultaneously appalled and impressed. It was the first time he had heard the entire range of Darwin's ideas and fully digested their implications. Though he recoiled from admitting the possibility of any form of evolution, and subsequently penned anguished notes in his journal about the soul of man and his place in nature, he courageously recognised that his friend had more to say than either Lamarck or *Vestiges*. He went away thoughtfully mulling it over. And though he never managed to accept everything Darwin was to propose, he wrote promptly to Down House to suggest that Darwin should publish—if not the whole of it, at least some small fragment, "pigeons if you please." He was worried that Darwin would be forestalled. In particular, Alfred Russel Wallace's extraordinary paper remained fresh in his mind. "Out with the theory & let it take date—& be cited—& understood."

Characteristically, Darwin demurred. He hardly knew what to think, he replied in May. The task seemed too daunting on every score. He would have to abandon his old essay and start again.

To give a fair sketch would be absolutely impossible, for every proposition requires such an array of facts. If I were to do anything it could only refer to the main agency of change, selection—& perhaps point out a very few of the leading features which countenance such a view, & some few of the difficulties. . . . I rather hate the idea of writing for priority, yet I certainly shd be vexed if any one were to publish my doctrines before me. Anyhow I thank you heartily for your sympathy.[54]

VIII

Darwin's protests were almost second nature by now. He had got into the habit of letting it be known that he was working on some large project on species without really coming to grips with the inevitability of putting it before the public. It was far easier to carry on collecting facts, to keep busy, to say the work was unfinished, than it was to stop. If he stopped he would feel obliged to present it. Underneath, there ran the incessant fear of being judged, the fear of other people's outrage.

More than fear. Darwin understood that such difficult and controversial concepts could not be sold by facts alone. He knew that he had to make a convincing case. His facts were better and more numerous than he had ever hoped when he first opened his transmutationary notebooks. They would be critical in persuading readers to see things his own way.

But he also faced the arduous task of reorienting the way Victorians looked at nature. He had to show them that their generally received ideas about a benevolent, nearly perfect natural world, in which insects and seeds were designed to feed birds and birds to feed cats, and beauty was given to things for a purpose, were wrong—that the idea of a loving God who created all living things and brought men and women into existence was at the very least a fable. The world that Sedgwick and Henslow cherished, the world steeped in moral meaning which helped mankind seek out higher goals in life, was not Darwin's. Darwin's view of nature was dark—black. At its most basic level his theory required a stunning readjustment of intellectual and emotional focus. Where most men and women generally believed in some kind of design in nature—some kind of plan and order—and felt a deep-seated, mostly inexpressible belief that their existence had meaning, Darwin wanted them to see all life as empty of any divine purpose. As he conceded, the furore over *Vestiges* made this easier than it might have been. But it had taken him five long years travelling round the world and many anxious years afterwards to come to that conclusion. Even then he could still see the pleasure in finding a higher purpose in nature—the scent of the wild thyme, the sense of space out on the Welsh mountains, the fecundity of the jungle, his coral polyps, his seeds, his flowers, and the industrious bees in Down House garden. Without thinking, he humbly appreciated the wonders of life. He knew how hard it was to abandon such a view.

Yet for natural selection to work, the world must be full of competitors and governed entirely by chance. The pleasant outward face of nature was precisely that—only an outward face. Underneath was perpetual struggle, species against species, individual against individual. Life was ruled by death, as Malthus taught him. Heavy destruction was the key to reproductive success. All the theological meaning was thus stripped out by Darwin and replaced by the concept of competition. All the *telos,* the purpose, on which natural theologians based their ideas of perfect adaptation was redirected into Malthusian—Darwinian—struggle. What most people saw as God-given design he saw as mere adaptations to circumstance, adaptations that were meaningless except for the way in which they helped an animal or plant to survive. Much of this was perhaps familiar to a nation immersed in competitive affairs: Darwin had transformed the generalised entrepreneurial ethos of English life into a biological theory which, in turn, derived much of its support from these all-pervasive cultural commitments. The theory of natural selection could only have emerged out of the competitive context of Victorian England, and Darwin could only have hit upon it by thinking of the living world as a financial balance sheet and of life itself as chance. He could have been born a Fuegian. His daughter Anne might have lived. There was no ulterior purpose in it anywhere. In a sense he was becoming his own William Paley, the great natural theology authority of his Cambridge days, whose respect and delight for nature was echoed wholeheartedly by Darwin, but a William Paley who reinterpreted all the myriad contrivances of the living world as an inevitable consequence of chance and change. Now Darwin firmly drove the idea of God out of nature. As he was the first to recognise, his theory bleakly signalled the death of Adam.

To see nature like this required courage. Any book Darwin produced would need to be carefully constructed, sensitive to the great demands he was making of his readers, alive to their sensibilities, judicious in its choice of evidence. Helplessly, he told Lyell he was not sure if he could do it.

Yet the idea took root. Off he went to consult Hooker, and then to London to talk it over properly with Lyell. In his heart he was ready. Twenty years of thought were waiting to be expressed, more if he included the *Beagle* voyage. However reluctantly, he sensed his journey coming to an end.

By 14 May he was convinced. He would write a book. "Began by Lyell's advice writing species sketch," he recorded solemnly in his journal.

"I am like Croesus overwhelmed with my riches in facts," he told Fox soon afterwards, "& I mean to make my book as perfect as ever I can."

He planned to call it *Natural Selection.*

Acknowledgements

There was a time when I thought this book should perhaps be called *Darwin: Another Biography*. Several important new studies have been published since I began working in 1989, and I would like to acknowledge their stimulus, both intellectually and as a spur to getting on with mine: we all seem to have perceived a need at approximately the same time. My greatest debt, however, is to Charles Elliott of Knopf for commissioning the work in the first place. His long-continued help and careful counsel have made all the difference. I would also like to thank Michael Neve for help offered over as many years: his advice has been warmly appreciated.

Many people have helped in other ways. I particularly thank George Pember Darwin for allowing me to quote from Darwin manuscripts at Cambridge University Library and elsewhere. Richard Darwin Keynes and Ursula Mommens kindly gave permission to use their collections of family material; and William Mostyn Owen graciously helped my researches. The Wedgwood Company, Barlaston, granted permission for me to quote from the Wedgwood family archives at Keele University; and Miss Gaye Blake Roberts was very helpful on all occasions. The Syndics of Cambridge University Press kindly allowed me to print extracts from *The Correspondence of Charles Darwin,* and the Wellcome Institute Library generously assisted with books, journals, and archival material from its fine collection. I am especially indebted to the Trustees of the Wellcome Trust; to Eric Freeman, the Institute's librarian; and to Bill Bynum, the most erudite and considerate of colleagues. I am also pleased to acknowledge invaluable assistance from the British Library, the Natural History Museum, Edinburgh University Library, Keele University Library, the Royal Society, the Geological Society, the Hydrographic Office, and the Public Record Office; from the

Mitchell Library, Sydney, and the British Geological Survey; and from the Shrewsbury Local Studies Centre and the National Maritime Museum.

I could hardly have continued without the great resources of Cambridge University Library, especially the Darwin collection housed in the manuscript department. Dr. Patrick Zutshi, Adam Perkins, Peter Gautrey (previously in charge of the Darwin archive at Cambridge), Godfrey Waller, and the Manuscript Room staff gave me every possible assistance. I must have used every other department in the library at least once, including the Oriental section and Music. Everyone invariably dealt with my inquiries efficiently and kindly. I gratefully acknowledge permission from the Syndics of the University Library to use and quote from their collections.

A special acknowledgement is due to Frederick Burkhardt and the late Sydney Smith, friends and colleagues for many years on *The Correspondence of Charles Darwin*. A great deal of what I write ultimately derives from the time I spent working on this correspondence project: one volume a year for eight years took me right into the heart of the Darwin family and nineteenth-century science. Without their enthusiasm for Darwin the complete edition of his letters would never have begun and we all would be much the poorer. I thank them and Stephen Pocock, Marsha Richmond, Peter Saunders, and Anne Secord, former members of the Darwin correspondence project; and Anne Burkhardt, Joy Harvey, Heidi Bradshaw, Sarah Benton, Hedy Franks, Perry O'Donovan, and Jon Topham, the present members, for their long-continued help and support. Alan Crowden, at Cambridge University Press, has been just as helpful.

Similarly, Solene Morris of Down House Museum, Kent, deserves my grateful thanks. She gave me her time as well as access to the museum's marvellous collection. Many individual friends and scholars also contributed materially to my researches. My colleagues at the Wellcome Institute for the History of Medicine all helped in different ways: Bill Bynum, Ann Dally, Christopher Lawrence, Roy Porter, Michael Neve, John Symons, and Andrew Wear on the one hand, and Sally Bragg, Andrew Foley, Chris Carter, Lyn Dobson, and Jo Lane on the other. The institute's students over the years clarified my ideas, and the library staff have always been more than helpful. Dr. Jean Alexander, Gerard Crombie, Martin Phillips, Nick Browne, Anthony Carr, Dr. Barbara Wedgwood, and William Schupbach have been extremely kind in helping me gather illustrations. John Thackray, Hugh Torrens, James Secord, Desmond King-Hele, Sandra Herbert, Mario DiGregorio, Nick Gill, Harriet Ritvo, and Ann Shteir generously shared their knowledge of nineteenth-century natural history with me. Melvin Rosenthal and Paul Schnee at Knopf provided essential assistance in the later stages of production. And other colleagues have unwittingly said the right things at crucial moments. To them, and to the many authors whose works I have used in composing this book, I extend my hearty thanks. Without their careful scholarship to draw on I would not have contemplated writing a life of Darwin and am only sorry that the stylistic requirements of a biography make it impracticable to discuss their researches in detail.

Last but not least, Bill Bynum, Joy Harvey, Jonathan Hodge, and Michael Neve valiantly read the manuscript. I am very grateful for their comments.

Notes

These notes have been kept as brief as possible and supply only the source of material used in the text. It has proved impossible to mention all the detailed studies produced by recent Darwin scholars, or more general accounts of Victorian science and society. But I warmly acknowledge the remarkable body of work built up over the years. Without it I would hardly have been able to proceed.

Books and articles mentioned in the notes are cited in author-date form, and a full listing of these is in the Bibliography. Some items are abbreviated as short titles, e.g., *Correspondence, Journal,* etc. The full reference is given below. These are also listed alphabetically in the Bibliography, once under the short title and again under the author's or editor's name.

Darwin's books, papers, letters, and manuscripts are, for the most part, kept in the Manuscripts Room, University Library, Cambridge. The collection is subdivided in various ways, each with its own handlist or catalogue, available in the Manuscripts Room. For clarity I have called this the "Darwin Collection." The abbreviation "DAR" is the prefix for manuscript call-numbers. Where other material from the University Library is cited, I have tried to make the distinction clear.

Abbreviations

Autobiography: Nora Barlow, ed. 1958. *The Autobiography of Charles Darwin, 1809–1882, with original omissions restored.* London: Collins.

Collected papers: Paul H. Barrett, ed. 1977. *The collected papers of Charles Darwin.* 2 vols. Chicago: University of Chicago Press.

Coral reefs: Charles Darwin. 1842. *The structure and distribution of coral reefs.* Part 1 of *The geology of the voyage of the* Beagle. London. 1842–46.

Correspondence: F. H. Burkhardt, S. Smith, et al., eds. 1983–94. *The correspondence of Charles Darwin.* Vols. 1–9 (1821–61). Cambridge: Cambridge University Press.

DAR: Darwin manuscript collection, University Library, Cambridge.

Diary: R. D. Keynes, ed. 1988. *Charles Darwin's* Beagle *diary.* Cambridge: Cambridge University Press.

Emma Darwin: H. E. Litchfield, ed. 1904. *Emma Darwin, wife of Charles Darwin: a century of family letters.* 2 vols. Cambridge: privately printed.

Fossil Cirripedia: Charles Darwin. 1851–54a. *A monograph of the fossil Lepadidae.* London, 1851. *A monograph of the fossil Balanidae and Verrucidae.* London. 1854.

Journal: Gavin De Beer, ed. 1959. Darwin's Journal. *Bulletin of the British Museum (Natural History) Historical Series* 2: 1–21.

Journal of researches: Charles Darwin. 1839. *Journal of researches into the geology and natural history of the various countries visited by H.M.S.* Beagle. London.

Life and letters: Francis Darwin, ed. 1887. *The life and letters of Charles Darwin.* 3 vols. London.

Living Cirripedia: Charles Darwin. 1851–54b. *A monograph of the sub-class Cirripedia.* Vol. 1. *The Lepadidae.* London 1851. Vol. 2. *The Balanidae.* London. 1854.

More letters: Francis Darwin and A. C. Seward, eds. 1903. *More letters of Charles Darwin: a record of his work in a series of hitherto unpublished letters.* 2 vols. London: John Murray.

Narrative: Robert FitzRoy. 1839. *Narrative of the surveying voyages of H.M.S.* Adventure and Beagle, *between the years 1826 and 1836.* Vol. 1. *Proceedings of the first expedition, 1826–30, under the command of Captain P. P. King.* Edited by Robert FitzRoy. Vol. 2. *Proceedings of the second expedition, 1831–36, under the command of Captain R. FitzRoy.* Vol. 3. *Journal and remarks, 1832–36.* By Charles Darwin. 4 vols. London.

Natural selection: R. C. Stauffer, ed. 1975. *Charles Darwin's* Natural Selection, *being the second part of his big species book written from 1856 to 1858.* Cambridge: Cambridge University Press.

Notebooks: P. H. Barrett et al., eds. 1987. *Charles Darwin's notebooks, 1836–44: geology, transmutation of species, metaphysical inquiries.* London: British Museum (Natural History) and Cambridge University Press.

Origin of species: Charles Darwin. 1859. *On the origin of species by means of natural selection, or the preservation of favoured races in the struggle for life.* London.

South America: Charles Darwin. 1846. *Geological observations on South America.* Part 3 of *The geology of the voyage of the* Beagle. London. 1842–46.

Volcanic islands: Charles Darwin. 1844. *Geological observations on the volcanic islands visited during the voyage of H.M.S.* Beagle. Part 2 of *The geology of the voyage of the* Beagle. London. 1842–46.

Zoology: Charles Darwin, ed. 1838–43. *The zoology of the voyage of H.M.S.* Beagle *under the command of Captain FitzRoy.* Part 1. *Fossil mammalia.* By Richard Owen. Part 2. *Mammalia.* By George Robert Waterhouse. Part 3. *Birds.* By John Gould. Part 4. *Fish.* By Leonard Jenyns. Part 5. *Reptiles.* By Thomas Bell. 3 or 5 volumes. London.

INTRODUCTION

1. The manuscript of Darwin's autobiography is in the Darwin Collection, Cambridge University Library, DAR 27, and has been published in part in *Life and letters* 1:26–107, and in full in *Autobiography* (Barlow 1958). The problems in understanding its nature are discussed in Gruber and Barrett 1974, Brent 1981, Rosenberg 1989, and particularly Colp 1985.

2. A comprehensive list of studies would be very long. Notable biographies are Irvine 1955, Eiseley 1958, Stone 1980, and Brent 1981. More recent works are Croft 1989, Bowlby 1990, Bowler 1990, and Desmond and Moore 1992. General accounts of the history of evolutionary theory are given in Greene 1959, Haber 1959, Bowler 1984 and 1989, and Young 1985. Specialist book-length studies relating to Darwin's scientific work and its context can be found in Ghiselin 1969, Gillespie 1979, Ruse 1979, Ospovat 1981, Chapman ed. 1982, Oldroyd and Langham 1983, and Kohn ed. 1985. Darwin's life is also reflected in his extensive corre-

spondence, which is currently being published in full by Burkhardt, Smith, et al. 1983–94 (*Correspondence*). However, Francis Darwin's editions of his father's letters, *Life and letters* and *More letters* were put together with an appreciation of Darwin's scientific work often missing in Victorian memorials.

3. "Life" written in 1838, DAR 91:56–62, transcribed in *More letters* 1:1–5 and *Correspondence* 2:438–41; and *Autobiography,* p. 141.
4. *Life and letters* 3:238.
5. *Correspondence* vols. 1–9 (Burkhardt and Smith et al. 1983–94).

CHAPTER 1: BOBBY

1. Discussed in different ways in Landes 1969, Perkin 1969, Summerson 1978, McKendrick, Brewer, and Plumb 1982, Mathias 1983, Berg 1985, and More 1989.
2. Historians commonly spell Mrs. Darwin's first name "Susannah." However, the entry for her baptism in the parish registers gives it as "Susanna" (Staffordshire Parish Registers Society, Burslem, vol. 2:289). Her husband and father called her Susan; and this is how she appears on her tombstone. The diminutive "Sukey" was a childhood name.
3. Annan 1955, Thackray 1974.
4. Thompson 1963. See also Meteyard 1865–66.
5. Account books, Robert Waring Darwin collection, Cambridge University Library, Manuscripts Room, DAR 227; and a further account book in the Manuscript collection at Down House Museum, Kent. Permission to cite these manuscripts is by courtesy of the Syndics of Cambridge University Library and the Natural History Museum (Down House).
6. McKendrick 1982 and Reilly 1992.
7. Brewer 1982. See also Perkin 1969, Mantoux 1983, and Mathias 1983.
8. Telford 1838, Trinder 1973.
9. Dr. Darwin's medical income ranged

from £1,822 in 1796–97, the first year in his account book, to an upper level of £3,000, reached twice during the following twenty-year period. The usual amount was between £2,000 and £2,500.
10. DAR 227, box 6, letter dated 1793.
11. R. W. Darwin's account book, Down House Museum. The Cambridge collection (DAR 227, box 2) indicates that in 1845 Dr. Darwin lent a total of £84,049. Information on the estate of Josiah Wedgwood II is in DAR 227, box 1.
12. DAR 112 (ser. 2):94. Also cited in Oswald 1982.
13. DAR 112 (ser. 2):41.
14. DAR 99:205.
15. *Autobiography,* p. 22.
16. "Life. Written August 1838," DAR 91:56–62, transcribed in *More letters* 1:1–5 and *Correspondence* 2: 438–41.
17. Private collection. I am very grateful to Mrs. U. Mommens for access to this material.
18. Private collection.
19. See also Beer 1983.
20. R. W. Darwin 1787 and E. Darwin 1791.
21. Private collection.
22. "Life," *Correspondence* 2:440.
23. Brookes 1763, vols. 4 and 5. These books are in the Darwin Collection, Cambridge University Library; a catalogue of Darwin's books is given in Rutherford 1908 and *Darwin library: list of books received in the University Library Cambridge. March–May 1961* (Cambridge: Cambridge University Library). A full listing is in DiGregorio and Gill eds. 1990.
24. See particularly Hubble 1953, Eiseley 1958, and Colp 1984.
25. *Emma Darwin* 1:81.
26. Bessy Galton, later Mrs. Wheler, in Pearson 1914–30, vol. 1, p. 51.
27. *Correspondence* 1:212.
28. DAR 112:117.
29. Keele University, Wedgwood/Mosley Archive. By courtesy of the Trustees of the Wedgwood Museum, Stoke-on-Trent, Staffs.

30. Keele University, Wedgwood/Mosley Archive.
31. "Life," *Correspondence* 2:439.
32. *Autobiography,* p. 22.
33. "Life," *Correspondence* 2:439.
34. *Autobiography,* p. 24.
35. Colp 1987 and Bowlby 1989, pp. 53–62.
36. DAR 112 (ser. 2):94–98.
37. Keele University, Wedgwood/Mosley Archive.
38. DAR 153, letter dated 20 September 1881.
39. DAR 112 (ser. 2):41.
40. Cowburn ed. 1964. Information on boys at Shrewsbury School comes from Auden 1909.
41. *Autobiography,* pp. 27–28.
42. The atlas is in the Public Library and Art Gallery, Shrewsbury, formerly Shrewsbury School. Darwin's copy of Butler 1818 is in the Darwin Collection, Cambridge University Library.
43. S. Butler ed. 1896, vol. 1, p. 164.
44. DAR 112 (ser. 2):42.
45. DAR 112 (ser. 2):101–2.
46. DAR 99:201.
47. *Correspondence* 1:9.
48. DAR 112:111–13.
49. DAR 112:10.
50. *Autobiography,* p. 43.
51. *Autobiography,* p. 42.
52. Private collection.
53. J. Egerton 1990, p. 61. Erasmus Darwin sat for two portraits by Wright of Derby, the first possibly a gift from Wright c. 1770, the second commissioned by a stepson, Sacheveral Pole, in 1792–93. See M. Keynes 1994.
54. *Correspondence* 1:12.
55. Wedgwood and Wedgwood 1980, p. 83. See also Golinski 1992.
56. Schweber 1985.
57. *Autobiography,* pp. 45–46.
58. *Correspondence* 1:558.
59. "De spectris seu imaginibus ocularibus coloratis exhibens," 1785, printed in English in 1786 in the *Philosophical Transactions of the Royal Society* as "New experiments on the ocular spectra of light and colours."
60. *Correspondence* 1:17.

CHAPTER 2: FROM MEDICINE...

1. Chitnis 1986, Lenman 1981, and Phillipson 1981. General surveys of Scottish medicine are given in Anderson and Simpson 1976 and Comrie 1932.
2. Seward 1804, Krause 1879, King-Hele 1977, and McNeil 1987. See also Hassler 1973.
3. Porter 1989 and Hassler 1973.
4. Krause 1879, p. 69. See also Hunter and Macalpine 1969.
5. Primary sources are Lamarck 1801, 1802, and 1809. Studies of Lamarck are given in Burkhardt 1977, Jordanova 1984, and Corsi 1988a.
6. McNeil 1987. See also King-Hele 1986, and Porter 1989, pp. 59–60.
7. McNeil 1986, and Browne 1989.
8. Bewell 1989.
9. King-Hele 1981, p. 200.
10. E. Darwin 1803, canto 1, lines 294–314.
11. Shelley 1818, author's introduction.
12. Krause 1879, p. 102.
13. Cunningham ed. 1857–59, vol. 9, p. 179.
14. *Edinburgh Review* 2 (1803):499–501; Seward 1804, p. 92.
15. King-Hele 1986, p. 100.
16. Schofield 1963; also discussed in McNeil 1987.
17. Seward 1804. The letter in which Erasmus Darwin described Mary Howard's symptoms and death is reprinted by Nora Barlow in her edition of Darwin's autobiography (*Autobiography,* pp. 223–25). For Erasmus Darwin's gout, see E. Darwin 1794–96, vol. 2, pp. 452–53, and Krause 1879, p. 1.
18. E. Darwin 1803, canto 2, lines 244, 246. The point is discussed in Browne 1989 and Schiebinger 1991.
19. Morgan 1936–37 and Shepperson 1961.
20. C. Darwin [1758–78] 1780, edited by Erasmus Darwin, which includes a "Life of the author," pp. 127–35; and an anonymous *Elegy on the much lamented death of a most ingenious young gentleman, who lately died in*

the College at Edinburgh, where he was a student (Birmingham, Coventry, and Lichfield, 1778).

21. Dr. Darwin's certificate of attendance at Hunter's school is in DAR 227, box 7. I thank Dr. Helen Brock for dating this for me. The Edinburgh University archive of matriculations confirms that R. W. Darwin signed on for courses in all three sessions from 1784 to 1787.
22. *Autobiography*, p. 30.
23. R. W. Darwin [1766–1848] 1789. See also Posner 1975.
24. Seward 1804, p. 407.
25. Krause 1879, p. 36.
26. Krause 1879, p. 76.
27. DAR 210:6.
28. *Autobiography*, pp. 47–48.
29. *Correspondence* 1:19.
30. Neve ed. 1985, p. 77. See also Donaldson 1983.
31. *Correspondence* 1:18. Lothian Street was on the site now occupied by an extension of the Royal Scottish Museum.
32. Horn 1967. Edinburgh medical students are discussed in Rosner 1991.
33. P. Allen 1987. The society was founded in 1820.
34. *Correspondence* 1:35, 30.
35. *St. James's Gazette*, 16 February 1888, pp. 5–6, and 17 February 1888, p. 7.
36. A. Grant 1884, Horn 1967, and Donaldson 1983. For the medical school, see Morrell 1970 and 1972, and Lawrence 1988.
37. Browne 1992.
38. Lawrence 1988, p. 263.
39. Most recently discussed in Brooke 1991. See also Thomas 1983.
40. Tempkin 1963, Ackerknecht 1967, Figlio 1976, and Lesch 1984.
41. Jacyna 1983.
42. *Edinburgh Medical Journal* 24 (1825):363.
43. Appel 1987. See also Russell 1916, Rehbock 1983, and Outram 1986.
44. A. Desmond 1984a and 1984b, and Richards 1989.
45. Cooter 1984. Shapin 1975 and

Cantor 1975 discuss the Edinburgh debate.
46. Christison 1885–86, vol. 1, p. 60.
47. Ashworth 1935 and Morgan 1936–37. Darwin's registration cards are split between the Edinburgh University archives and the Darwin manuscripts in Cambridge University Library, DAR 5.
48. *Correspondence* 1:25.
49. *Lancet* 1 (1828–29):391–94, and Horn 1967, p. 109. See, however, Wright-St. Clair 1964, pp. 115–16, which asserts this story is apocryphal.
50. *Autobiography*, p. 47.
51. DAR 5:16–19.
52. *University Squib*, 9 January 1833, p. 7.
53. MacGregor 1884, R. Richardson 1981, and Edwards 1981.
54. Lonsdale 1870, Rae 1964, and Richards 1989.
55. Browne 1992.
56. Monro 1831.
57. Shapin 1975 and 1979.
58. DAR 5:16.
59. Monro 1829.
60. Monro 1827.
61. *Autobiography*, p. 47.
62. *Correspondence* 1:37.
63. DAR 5:3–4.
64. *Autobiography*, p. 47.

CHAPTER 3: ... TO SEAWEEDS

1. DAR 129.
2. *Correspondence* 1:29. Edmonstone is discussed in Freeman 1978.
3. *Autobiography*, p. 51.
4. Morrell 1972, p. 54.
5. Anderson and Simpson 1978, p. 38.
6. Schweber 1985, Secord 1991a.
7. Browne 1992.
8. DAR 5:6–10.
9. *Correspondence* 1:44.
10. Wedgwood and Wedgwood 1980.
11. *Autobiography*, p. 46.
12. Darwin's admission card to Jameson's lectures is in DAR 5:44. See also Ashworth 1934.
13. Chitnis 1970, Secord 1991a.
14. Corning ed. 1930, vol. 1, p. 9.

15. Ritchie 1956.
16. DAR 112 (ser. 2):43.
17. Wellcome Institute for the History of Medicine, Archives, MS 3388. By courtesy of the Wellcome Institute Library, London.
18. Quoted from Secord 1991a. I am grateful to Dr. James Secord for providing a copy of manuscript materials from Thomas Hope's papers.
19. See particularly Greene 1982 and Laudan 1987.
20. Darwin's copy of Jameson 1821, p. 300, in the Darwin Collection, Cambridge University Library. It seems unlikely that Darwin learned quite as much from this as Secord 1991a suggests.
21. Cuvier 1813. Darwin's copy of the fifth edition (1827) is in the Darwin Collection, Cambridge University Library.
22. *Autobiography,* p. 52.
23. Minutes of the Plinian Society, Edinburgh University Archives, MS Dc.2.53. Permission to cite these manuscripts is by courtesy of Edinburgh University Library. The society is discussed by Gruber and Barrett 1974, Desmond and Moore 1992, and Sloan 1985. That Jameson played no active role in the foundation and continuing activities of the society is indicated by his remarks to the Royal Commission of 1826 and a passage in a student journal: the society was instituted in January 1823 by "some young gentlemen, students at the university, who had a mutual taste for natural history, national antiquities, and the physical sciences in general" (*Lapsus Linguae,* 14 January 1824, p. 13). This journal, and its successors, carried brief reports of the society's meetings. See also Elliott 1870, pp. 16–17.
24. Guthrie 1952.
25. *Cheilead or University coterie* 9 (December 1826):107.
26. Ashworth 1934, p. 102.
27. Ashworth 1934 and, in part, Sloan 1985.
28. Quoted from A. Desmond 1984a.
29. *Lancet* (1850) 2:686–95.
30. A. Desmond 1984a.
31. A. Desmond 1989.
32. Scull 1991.
33. See A. Grant 1883, Ashworth 1934, A. Desmond 1984a, and Gruber and Barrett 1974. It seems overly dramatic to assert, as the latter two studies do, that the society as a whole reflected an outright materialistic philosophy.
34. *Autobiography,* p. 48; Shepperson 1961, p. 28.
35. DAR 5:28–39.
36. Hodge 1985 and Sloan 1985.
37. A. Desmond 1984a. Alternatively, it has been proposed (Secord 1991b) that Robert Jameson may have been the author. Despite the material produced as evidence in the latter case, it seems more likely that this came from some third party, not directly from Jameson's pen.
38. Sloan 1985, pp. 75–80, and A. Desmond 1984b.
39. DAR 118, transcribed in *Collected papers* 2:288. The remarks seem to have been written about a month after the event.
40. *Autobiography,* p. 49.
41. A. Desmond 1984a, p. 196.
42. A. Desmond 1984b.
43. F. Egerton 1976, p. 455. Darwin's notes on Lamarck 1801, dating from this period, are in DAR 5:28.
44. Private collection.
45. A. Desmond 1984a, p. 213.
46. E. Darwin 1794–96, vol. 1, p. 505.
47. DAR 227. See also Thomas Thomson's review of Seward 1804, in which Seward appended an apology of sorts, *Edinburgh Review* 4 (1804):236–37.
48. Abernethy 1822, vol. 2, pp. 14, 59–60.
49. J. Fleming 1822, vol. 1, p. 21.
50. J. Fleming 1822, vol. 1, p. xiii.
51. Jacyna 1983.
52. Barclay 1822, p. 148.
53. Jesperson 1948–49.
54. *Memoirs of the Wernerian Natural History Society* 6 (1826–31):564.
55. R. Grant 1827a and 1827b, p. 161. In the 1850s, Darwin's contribution

to one of these papers was acknowledged in a biographical sketch about Grant, *Lancet* (1850) 2:693.

56. Balfour 1865.

57. DAR 118 and *Collected papers* 2:288–89. My account explains the discrepancy in dates, since Darwin read his paper to the Plinian Society on 27 March and wrote out his discovery on 20 April 1827.

CHAPTER 4: "AN IDLE SPORTING MAN"

1. *Autobiography,* pp. 28, 56.

2. *Autobiography,* p. 57. For an analysis of the country clergyman in Britain during this period, see Addison 1947 and Colloms 1977.

3. Winstanley 1955, p. 151, Garland 1980, and Becher 1986.

4. DAR 112:56.

5. Peile 1900 and Shipley 1909.

6. *Life and letters* 1:165.

7. *Life and letters* 1:113.

8. *Correspondence* 1:109.

9. *Autobiography,* p. 59.

10. *Correspondence* 1:89.

11. *Correspondence* 1:113.

12. *Correspondence* 1:58.

13. *Correspondence* 1:79.

14. *Correspondence* 1:56–57.

15. *Correspondence* 1:58–59.

16. *Autobiography,* pp. 62–63.

17. *Autobiography,* p. 62.

18. D. E. Allen 1978, Barber 1980.

19. D. E. Allen 1978, p. 153.

20. DAR 112:67–68.

21. Quoted from D. E. Allen 1978, p. 153.

22. DAR 112 (ser. 2):17.

23. *Correspondence* 1:89.

24. DAR 112 (ser. 2):61–62.

25. DAR 112 (ser. 2):108.

26. *Correspondence* 1:71, 80, and 81.

27. *Autobiography,* p. 61. See also Manier 1978, p. 165, and Colp 1985, p. 391.

28. *Life and Letters* 1:167.

29. DAR 112 (ser. 2):57–76.

30. *Autobiography,* p. 62.

31. DAR 112:111.

32. *Life and letters* 1:168.

33. *Correspondence* 1:65.

34. *Correspondence* 1:122.

35. American Philosophical Society Archives, 425, reprinted in *Correspondence* 1:123, n. 1.

36. *Correspondence* 1:123.

37. Mabberley 1985.

38. Butler, Nuttall, and Brown 1986.

39. Coddington 1830.

40. Pearson 1914–30, vol. 1, p. 51.

41. Darwin's "notes on shooting" are in DAR 91:1–3. Shooting in upper-class circles is discussed in MacKenzie 1988.

42. *Autobiography,* p. 44.

43. Darwin's beetle collecting list is in DAR 118.

44. *Autobiography,* p. 54.

45. *Autobiography,* p. 56, referring to a passage in the third book of Horace's *Odes: Iustum et tenacem propositi virum/Non civium ardor prava iubentium,/Non vultus instantis tyranni/mente quatit solida,* "Neither fellow citizens feverishly clamouring for what is wrong, nor the presence of a threatening tyrant, can shake the rocklike soul of a just man, firm in purpose."

46. *Correspondence* 1:384.

47. First noticed in Brent 1981.

48. I thank Anthony Carr, of the Local Studies Centre, Shrewsbury, and Mr. W. Mostyn Owen, for information about Fanny Owen. The baptismal register lists her as born in 1808. In the 1851 census returns held in the Shropshire archives, her age was given as forty-one instead of forty-three.

49. *Emma Darwin* 1:308.

50. *Correspondence* 1:48.

51. For an alternative view, see Desmond and Moore 1992.

52. *Emma Darwin* 1:309.

53. See *Correspondence* 1:61, 325, 430.

54. *Autobiography,* p. 68.

CHAPTER 5: THE PROFESSORS

1. Winstanley 1955, pp. 32–41.

2. Thomas Maquire's series of portraits

(known as the Ipswich portraits) were done in 1849–51.

3. P. Allen 1987.
4. Cambridge University Library, University Archives, O.XIV.261.
5. Russell-Gebbett 1977.
6. Winstanley 1955 and Speakman 1982. Sedgwick's list of students for 1815 and 1816 is in Cambridge University Library, Add MS 3144.
7. Clark and Hughes 1890, vol. 1, pp. 152–65, and Winstanley 1955, pp. 183–84.
8. Jenyns 1862, p. 35.
9. A. R. Hall 1969.
10. Jenyns 1862, p. 54. Darwin's recollections of Henslow were printed in Jenyns 1862, pp. 51–55.
11. Babington 1897.
12. Cambridge University Library, Cambridge collection, Cam.d.828.4. See also Walters 1981 and Sloan 1986.
13. Henslow 1833, reviewing Augustin de Candolle, *Physiologie végétale,* 3 vols. Paris 1832.
14. In the absence of any student notes taken during lectures, the content of Henslow's course has been reconstructed from printed syllabi of 1828 and 1833, his own writings of the 1830s, and the recollections given in Jenyns 1862, pp. 37–42. Many of the same themes are addressed in Sloan 1986.
15. Russell-Gebbett 1977, p. 19.
16. Babington 1887.
17. Jenyns 1862, pp. 49–51.
18. Russell-Gebbett 1977, p. 19.
19. Sloan 1986. See also Mabberley 1985.
20. DAR 118, transcribed in *Collected papers* 2:290.
21. For Grant's and Henslow's views on the plant-animal distinction, see Sloan 1985.
22. *Autobiography,* p. 66.
23. Jenyns 1862, p. 51.
24. Romilly 1967, p. 137.
25. Jenyns 1862, p. 51.
26. Whewell 1845b.
27. Garland 1980.
28. Sedgwick 1831, p. 207. See also Bartholomew 1976 and Brooke 1979 and 1991.

29. *Life and letters* 1:171.
30. DAR 112 (ser. 2):120.
31. DAR 112 (ser. 2):118.
32. DAR 112 (ser. 2):95–96.
33. Babington 1897, p. lxviii.
34. Jenyns 1862, p. 11.
35. *Autobiography,* p. 68.
36. Babington 1897, p. 13. See also D. E. Allen 1978.
37. *Correspondence* 1:125–26.
38. DAR 112 (ser. 2):111.
39. Humboldt 1817–29, vol. 1. Humboldt's impact on the British imagination is described in Brock 1993. See also Nicolson 1990.
40. *Correspondence* 1:125.
41. Cambridge University Library, Add MS 7652.III.H2. Biographical accounts of Sedgwick are given in Clark and Hughes 1890 and Speakman 1982.
42. Clark and Hughes 1890, vol. 1, p. 515.
43. *Autobiography,* p. 60. On the basis of reminiscences collected after Darwin's death (DAR 112), Secord 1991a states that Darwin did attend. It seems more feasible, however, that Darwin's recollections in old age were more reliable than those of his equally elderly friends.
44. Printed notices and announcements relating to Sedgwick's courses are in Cambridge University Library, University Archives, CUR 39.17.1–2.
45. *Journal,* p. 6.
46. DAR 112:56.
47. DAR 112:94.
48. Speakman 1982, p. 87.
49. Secord 1986.
50. North 1928, Eyles 1972, and Rudwick 1976a.
51. Cambridge University Library, Add MS 8176:150.
52. C. Lyell 1830–33. See Bartholomew 1979 and Wilson 1974.
53. Clark and Hughes 1890, vol. 1, p. 380.
54. Geological notes in DAR 5 (ser 2): 1–15. The tour is discussed in Barrett 1974 and Secord 1991a.
55. Cambridge University Library, Map Room, C.35.82.16.

56. DAR 112 (ser. 2):7, and *Autobiography*, p. 69.
57. *Correspondence* 1:238, 308.
58. Cambridge University Library, Add MS 7652.III.H2.
59. Secord 1991a.

CHAPTER 6:
THE CAMBRIDGE NETWORK

1. *Autobiography*, pp. 70–71.
2. *Emma Darwin* 1:141 n.
3. *Correspondence* 1:129.
4. *Correspondence* 1:129.
5. Mellersh 1968.
6. See particularly, Friendly 1977 and Bonnett 1968.
7. The history of these changes is given in *Narrative*, vols. 1 and 2. For FitzRoy's remarks, see Cambridge University Library, Add MS 8853/38.
8. FitzRoy's letters about the Fuegians and his attempts to accommodate them in London are printed in *Narrative* 2:1–13 and 4 (Appendix): 89–96.
9. Webster 1938, Graham and Humphreys 1962, and Graham 1965.
10. Portlock 1858, p. li.
11. The reform movements are discussed in Miller 1983, MacLeod 1983, M. B. Hall 1984, and Gleason 1991.
12. W. F. Cannon 1978, pp. 22–72. See also Schweber 1981.
13. *Correspondence* 1:127, 136.
14. *Correspondence* 1:127.
15. Jenyns 1889, p. 51.
16. *Correspondence* 1:139.
17. *Correspondence* 1:128, n. 3.
18. *Diary*, p. 3.
19. *Correspondence* 1:131.
20. *Correspondence* 1:132.
21. Keele University, Wedgwood/Mosley Archive, 222.
22. *Correspondence* 1:133.
23. *Correspondence* 1:133–34.
24. *Correspondence* 1:151.
25. *Correspondence* 1:135.
26. *Correspondence* 1:162.
27. *Correspondence* 1:148.
28. *Correspondence* 1:169.
29. *Autobiography*, p. 72.

30. *Correspondence* 1:147.
31. *Correspondence* 1:143.
32. Friendly 1977, p. 112.
33. *Correspondence* 1:146.
34. *Correspondence* 1:145.
35. *Correspondence* 1:140, 141.
36. *Correspondence* 1:141.
37. *Correspondence* 1:142.
38. *Correspondence* 1:142.
39. *Correspondence* 1:143, n. 1.
40. *Correspondence* 1:145.
41. Darwin's anomalous position is discussed in J. Gruber 1969 and Burstyn 1975.
42. *Correspondence* 1:146.
43. *Autobiography*, p. 72.
44. *Correspondence* 1:146.
45. *Correspondence* 1:161.

CHAPTER 7: NEW HORIZONS

1. *Diary*, transcribed in R. D. Keynes 1988, pp. 17–18.
2. *Narrative* 2:44. Selections from FitzRoy's volume are reprinted in Stanbury 1977.
3. *Narrative* 2:44.
4. *Diary*, p. 18.
5. F. Darwin 1912, 548.
6. *Diary*, p. 12.
7. *Correspondence* 1:175.
8. *Correspondence* 1:179.
9. *Beagle* logbook, Public Record Office, Kew, ADM 51/3055.
10. *Narrative* 2:22.
11. *Correspondence* 1:176–77.
12. The ship's book collection is listed in *Correspondence* 1:553–66.
13. *Diary*, p. 63.
14. *Correspondence* 1:177.
15. *Correspondence* 1:180.
16. Wedgwood and Wedgwood 1980, p. 214.
17. F. Darwin 1912, p. 547.
18. *Autobiography*, p. 74.
19. *Autobiography*, pp. 79–80.
20. *Diary*, pp. 8, 9.
21. *Correspondence* 1:185–86.
22. *Correspondence* 1:174.
23. *Correspondence* 1:509.
24. *Correspondence* 1:182–83.
25. *Correspondence* 1:181.

26. Darwin's copy of Humboldt (Humboldt 1817–29) is a mixed edition in 6 volumes, 1819–29. It is in the Darwin Collection, Cambridge University Library.
27. *Diary,* p. 19.
28. *Diary,* p. 20.
29. *Correspondence* 1:497.
30. *Correspondence* 1:491.
31. *Life and letters* 1:224.
32. F. Darwin 1912, 548.
33. Friendly 1977, p. 146.
34. Graham 1965. See also MacLeod 1982 and Browne 1993.
35. Webster 1938, Graham and Humphreys 1962, and Kaufman 1951. The political underpinnings of the Admiralty's policy at this time are described in Basalla 1963.
36. Basalla 1963, p. 46.
37. *Diary,* p. 23.
38. Discussed in S. Herbert 1991 and Secord 1991a.
39. S. Herbert 1991. See also Judd 1909.
40. *Autobiography,* p. 81.
41. See particularly Hooykaas 1963, Davies 1969, Rudwick 1970 and Rudwick's introduction to C. Lyell 1830–33, Wilson 1972, and Bartholomew 1973, 1976, and 1979.
42. These books are in the Darwin Collection, Cambridge University Library.
43. Described in Bartholomew 1976 and Corsi 1978.
44. Rudwick 1970.
45. Edinburgh University Archives, Jameson to John Murray, 18 February 1832.
46. R. Porter 1976.
47. *Autobiography,* pp. 77, 101.
48. *Correspondence* 3:55.
49. *Correspondence* 1:205.
50. *Correspondence* 1:202.

CHAPTER 8:
LOSS AND NO LOSS

1. *Correspondence* 1:202.
2. *Diary,* p. 37.
3. DAR 106/7.
4. DAR 112:74.
5. *Correspondence* 1:203.

6. DAR 32 to 38. Darwin's field notebooks are at Down House Museum, Kent. Other miscellaneous notes on *Beagle* specimens are in DAR 29. For a complete listing of the manuscripts and extant specimens, see D. Porter 1985.
7. DAR 30, 31.
8. Darwin's diary has been transcribed in Barlow 1933 and R. D. Keynes 1988. My references are taken from the latter.
9. McKendrick 1982.
10. E. Darwin 1791, canto ii, 425–28.
11. Walvin 1982.
12. *Correspondence* 1:302.
13. *Diary,* p. 45.
14. *Autobiography,* p. 74.
15. *Diary,* p. 45.
16. *Correspondence* 1:199.
17. Stenton 1976.
18. *Correspondence* 1:193–94.
19. *Correspondence* 1:220.
20. *Correspondence* 1:176.
21. McCormick 1884, vol. 1, p. 16.
22. *Correspondence* 1:238.
23. Keevil, Lloyd, and Coulter 1957–63, vol. 4, pp. 69–80. See also Keevil 1943, J. Gruber 1969, and Burstyn 1975.
24. *Narrative* 2:56.
25. McCormick 1884, vol. 1, p. 218.
26. McCormick 1884, vol. 1, pp. 217–18.
27. Quoted from J. Gruber 1969, p. 274.
28. Altick 1978, Barber 1980.
29. Briggs 1988.
30. *Correspondence* 1:149.
31. D. E. Allen 1985.
32. I am grateful to Dr. Nicolas Rupke for this point. See also Rupke 1994.
33. Friendly 1977, pp. 242–43.
34. McCormick 1884, vol. 1, p. 219.
35. *Correspondence* 1:225, 238.

CHAPTER 9: NATURALIST ON
THE *BEAGLE*

1. *Diary,* p. 42. See also Paradis 1981, Pagden 1992, and Stepan 1993. The contrast between this delight in scenery and Darwin's later 'deadened'

feelings is discussed in D. Fleming 1960.

2. Earle 1832.
3. *Autobiography,* p. 91.
4. *Diary,* p. 79.
5. Browne and Neve eds. 1989, p. 63.
6. *Diary,* p. 70.
7. *Correspondence* 1:237–38.
8. *Correspondence* 1:251.
9. *Correspondence* 1:293.
10. "Brief descriptions of several terrestrial Planariae, and of some remarkable marine species, with an account of their habits." *Annals and Magazine of Natural History* 14 (1844): 241–51; *Collected papers* 1:182–93.
11. *Correspondence* 1:247.
12. *Diary,* p. 22.
13. *Diary,* p. 89.
14. *Diary,* p. 91.
15. F. Darwin 1912, p. 548.
16. *Diary,* p. 180.
17. *Correspondence* 1:352. See also the introduction to Browne and Neve eds. 1989.
18. *Diary,* p. 156.
19. *Diary,* p. 104.
20. Cambridge University Library, Add MS 8853/43.
21. *Correspondence* 1:276.
22. *Narrative* 2:106–7.
23. Secord 1991a.
24. Bory de Saint Vincent et al. eds. 1822–31, vol. 10, p. 309. The article on *Megatherium* was written by Constant Prévost.
25. *Correspondence* 1:368.
26. R. Desmond 1977, Sulivan 1896, and Keevil 1949.
27. Sulloway 1982c.
28. C. H. Smith 1840, p. 214; *Natural selection,* p. 487.
29. Syms Covington's *Beagle* diary, MS, Linnean Society of New South Wales Collection, Mitchell Library, Sydney. See p. 53.
30. *Correspondence* 1:464–65.
31. *Diary,* p. 44.
32. *Correspondence* 1:392.
33. *Diary,* p. 160.
34. F. Darwin 1912, p. 548.
35. *Gardeners' Chronicle,* 3 October 1846, p. 661.
36. *Autobiography,* p. 79.
37. *Diary,* p. 114. See also Sheets-Pyenson 1988.
38. Sheets-Pyenson 1988, p. 86.
39. *Correspondence* 1:463.
40. MacKenzie 1988, Walvin 1987, and Browne 1993.
41. *Diary,* p. 111.

CHAPTER 10: ALMOST
ANOTHER SPECIES OF MAN

1. *Narrative* 4 (Appendix):142–47. The corpse is mentioned in William Clift's diaries, Royal College of Surgeons of London, Archives.
2. Altick 1978, Visram 1986.
3. *Narrative* 2:6.
4. H. Cannon ed. 1959, p. 197.
5. *Narrative* 4 (Appendix):149.
6. H. Cannon ed. 1959, p. 197.
7. H. Cannon ed. 1959, p. 198.
8. Hamond diary (private collection).
9. *Narrative* 2:205.
10. *Narrative* 2:10.
11. *Narrative* 2:10. See also Stock 1899 and Prochaska 1988.
12. *Descent of man,* vol. 1, p. 232.
13. *Diary,* p. 134.
14. *Correspondence* 1:316.
15. Warrack 1976.
16. *Autobiography,* p. 80.
17. *Diary,* p. 139.
18. *Diary,* p. 125.
19. *Narrative* 2:121–22.
20. Browne and Neve eds. 1989, p. 172.
21. *Correspondence* 1:303.
22. Stocking ed. 1973, p. xlv, and Stocking 1987.
23. Described in Stepan 1982, Stocking 1987, and Harvey 1993. For Knox, see Richards 1989; for Linnaeus, see Broberg 1983.
24. Walvin 1982 and 1987.
25. McKendrick 1982 and McNeil 1986.
26. Fladeland 1984.
27. *Narrative* 2:217.
28. *Diary,* p. 240.
29. *Diary,* pp. 275–76.
30. Summarised in Bowler 1989. See also Bury 1920 and Houghton 1957.

31. Cooter 1984.
32. *Diary,* p. 223.
33. H. E. Gruber 1981, p. 185.
34. *Diary,* p. 137.
35. *Diary,* p. 137.
36. H. Cannon ed. 1959, p. 208.
37. *Diary,* p. 133.
38. *British Baptist Reporter,* September 1859, pp. 293–94.
39. *Diary,* pp. 141–42.

CHAPTER 11:
"UN GRAND GALOPEADOR"

1. *Correspondence* 1:330. Detailed accounts of Rosas are given in Cady 1929 and Lynch 1981.
2. Browne and Neve eds. 1989, pp. 73–74.
3. *Diary,* p. 99.
4. *Diary,* p. 171.
5. *Diary,* p. 171.
6. Browne and Neve eds. 1989, pp. 85–86.
7. *Correspondence* 1:331.
8. *Diary,* p. 186.
9. *Correspondence* 1:326.
10. C. Lyell 1830–33. Darwin's copy, signed by him "M: Video Novemr 1832," is in the Darwin Collection, Cambridge University Library.
11. Rudwick 1978 and McCartney 1976. Darwin's geology during the voyage is discussed in S. Herbert 1991.
12. Browne and Neve eds. 1989, p. 97.
13. Quoted from S. Herbert 1986, p. 122.
14. *Correspondence* 1:379.
15. *Correspondence* 1:335–36.
16. *Diary,* p. 154.
17. *Diary,* p. 202.
18. *Correspondence* 1:342, 343.
19. *Correspondence* 1:353–54.
20. *Correspondence* 1:352.
21. *Diary,* p. 209.
22. *Narrative* 2:320.
23. *Diary,* p. 212, n. 1.
24. *Correspondence* 1:280.
25. Browne and Neve eds. 1989, p. 107.
26. *Diary,* p. 223.
27. *Narrative* 2:324, and Cambridge University Library, Add MS 8853/43.
28. Hamond diary (private collection).

29. DAR 112:97.
30. FitzRoy 1837, p. 122.
31. Darwin's correspondence makes it clear he received a box containing books from Henslow at the Falkland Islands, in which the third volume of C. Lyell 1830–33 probably arrived. See *Correspondence* 1:391, 399.
32. *Narrative* 2:657–82, reprinted in Browne and Neve eds. 1989, pp. 400–24.
33. D. C. Allen 1949, Rappaport 1978, and Browne 1983.
34. Henslow 1823.
35. On genesis and geology generally, see Gillispie 1959.
36. Browne and Neve eds. 1989, pp. 402–3.
37. FitzRoy 1837, p. 115.
38. *Correspondence* 1:379.
39. *Correspondence* 1:399.
40. *Diary,* p. 243.

CHAPTER 12: A NEW MISTRESS

1. *Diary,* p. 250.
2. *Correspondence* 1:405.
3. *Correspondence* 1:397.
4. *Diary,* p. 251. Darwin's geology in the Cordillera is described in S. Herbert 1991 and Rhodes 1991.
5. *Correspondence* 1:406–7.
6. Discussed by R. D. Keynes in his edition of Darwin's diary, *Diary,* p. 263 n.1.
7. F. Darwin 1912, p. 548. Darwin's possible contact with Chagas' disease is described in Adler 1959, Woodruff 1965, and Colp 1977.
8. *Correspondence* 1:411.
9. *Correspondence* 1:418.
10. *Autobiography,* p. 75.
11. F. Darwin 1912, p. 548.
12. *Diary,* p. 280.
13. *Correspondence* 1:430–31, 475–81.
14. *Diary,* p. 292.
15. Covington diary. Linnean Society of New South Wales Collection, Mitchell Library, Sydney.
16. *Diary,* p. 295.
17. *Narrative* 2:418.

18. *Diary,* p. 302.
19. DAR 42:17.
20. C. Lyell 1836, pp. 374–75, and referred to again in C. Lyell 1837a, p. 505.
21. *Nautical Magazine* 5 (1836):137–44, 357–61. The papers eventually came back to FitzRoy, who passed them on to Darwin to use for his post-*Beagle* writings on volcanic action in Chile. The material is in DAR 42: 17–22.
22. *Diary,* p. 300.
23. *Correspondence* 1:436.
24. *Diary,* p. 297.
25. The creative interaction between field-work and theory is discussed in Rudwick 1985, Secord 1986, and Oldroyd 1990.
26. *Diary,* p. 309. The last sentence was subsequently deleted.
27. *Correspondence* 1:442, 443.
28. *Correspondence* 1:445–46.
29. *Correspondence* 1:232.
30. *Correspondence* 1:447, 444.
31. *Correspondence* 1:447–48.

CHAPTER 13: ISLANDS

1. Byron 1826.
2. *Correspondence* 1:461.
3. *Correspondence* 1:460.
4. C. Lyell 1830–33, vol. 2, pp. 62–63, 103–4.
5. C. Lyell 1830–33, vol. 2, pp. 1–17. See also Bartholomew 1973 and 1979, and Corsi 1978.
6. Hickman 1985, and Steadman and Zousmer 1988.
7. *Diary,* p. 353.
8. *Diary,* p. 356.
9. Hickman 1985, pp. 52–54.
10. See also Beer 1989.
11. *Diary,* p. 356.
12. Displayed at the Linnean Society of London.
13. Sulloway 1982a and 1982b.
14. Quoted from the second edition (1845) of Darwin's published *Journal of researches,* H. Cannon ed. 1959, p. 379. The same sentiments were expressed in the first edition, though

less clearly (Browne and Neve eds. 1989, p. 287).
15. Dupetit-Thouars 1840–44, vol. 2, p. 284.
16. DAR 31.2:341–42.
17. Kotzebue 1830. William Ellis, the South Sea Island missionary, refuted Kotzebue's claims in Ellis 1831. Both Kotzebue's and Ellis's earlier book (Ellis 1829) were in the *Beagle* library (*Correspondence* 1:560, 561).
18. Gunson 1978, pp. 31–41.
19. The European fascination with South Seas exploration is described in Veit 1972 and B. Smith 1985.
20. *Diary,* p. 366.
21. *Diary,* pp. 372, 375.
22. Lovett 1899, vol. 1, pp. 117–325.
23. *Diary,* p. 367.
24. *Narrative* 2:545.
25. *Narrative* 2:511, 523. See also *Collected papers* 1:23.
26. *Diary,* p. 377.
27. *Correspondence* 1:472.
28. Gunson 1978, Hilliard 1978, and Wilson 1980.
29. Stock 1899. Mission activity is also described in Ramsden 1936 and Owens 1974.
30. Earle 1832.
31. *Diary,* pp. 381–87.
32. *Correspondence* 1:472.
33. *Diary,* p. 384.
34. *Diary,* p. 384, 385.
35. Mellersh 1968, pp. 197–235. FitzRoy attempted to justify his actions in a substantial work published after his return, FitzRoy 1846.
36. *Narrative* 2:601–4.
37. *Diary,* p. 390.
38. *Diary,* p. 389.
39. *Correspondence* 1:482.
40. Lindsay 1968.
41. *Diary,* p. 403. See also Hodge 1982 and 1990.
42. Branagan 1985.
43. *Correspondence* 1:490.
44. *Correspondence* 1:391.
45. *Athenaeum,* 24 December 1831, pp. 834–35.
46. *Correspondence* 1:495.
47. Darwin's first remarks on coral reefs, drawn up on the coast of South

America in 1835, are in DAR 41:1–
22. A full analysis is given in Judd
1909, Stoddart 1976, and S. Herbert
1991. See also *Correspondence* 1:
567–71.
48. *Autobiography,* pp. 98–99.
49. *Diary,* p. 418.

CHAPTER 14:
HOMEWARD BOUND

1. See particularly Gillispie 1959, Greene
1959, and Ospovat 1981.
2. Moore 1985. Country parsons are
discussed in Addison 1947 and
Colloms 1977.
3. *Correspondence* 1:259.
4. *Correspondence* 1:254.
5. Bartholomew 1979 and Porter 1976.
6. *Correspondence* 1:311, 312.
7. Darwin's religion is discussed in
Mandelbaum 1958, Gillespie 1979,
Brown 1986, Moore 1989, and Kohn
1989. Other studies are listed in
Moore 1989.
8. See particularly W. F. Cannon 1960,
Hooykaas 1963, and Chadwick 1975.
9. DAR 112:54.
10. *Correspondence* 1:493.
11. *Diary,* p. 427.
12. *Autobiography,* p. 107.
13. Evans et al. 1969, Buttman 1970.
14. Evans et al. 1969, pp. 242–43.
15. W. F. Cannon 1961. See also K. M.
Lyell 1881, vol. 2, pp. 5, 9–13.
16. Groves 1948–58, vol. 1. Other useful sources are Clinton 1937 and Ross
1986. See also Rainger 1980.
17. Reprinted in *Collected papers* 1:19–
38.
18. *Correspondence* 1:483.
19. *Correspondence* 1:490.
20. *Correspondence* 1:432.
21. *Correspondence* 1:460.
22. *Correspondence* 1:495.
23. *Correspondence* 1:489.
24. *Correspondence* 1:498.
25. C. Darwin 1835a. Darwin's copy is
in DAR 135(6), reprinted in *Collected
papers* 1:3–16.
26. C. Darwin 1835b, also reprinted in
Collected papers 1:16–19.

27. K. M. Lyell 1881, vol. 1, pp. 460–61.
28. Hydrographic Office, Taunton, Beaufort correspondence, L-244, letter
dated 15 December 1835.
29. Clark and Hughes 1890, vol. 1,
p. 380.
30. *Correspondence* 1:496. See also
S. Herbert 1991.
31. *Autobiography,* p. 82.
32. Barlow 1963, p. 262. See also
Sulloway 1983.
33. *More Letters* 1:367.

CHAPTER 15: PARADISE LOST

1. *Correspondence* 1:516, 517.
2. *Correspondence* 1:523.
3. *Correspondence* 1:531.
4. Freeman 1977. See also H. E. Gruber
1994 for a discussion of similar
points.
5. *Correspondence* 1:532.
6. *Correspondence* 1:514.
7. Clift and Parish 1832. Owen's descriptions of Darwin's fossil mammals were
given in R. Owen 1838–40.
8. *Correspondence* 1:518.
9. The presentation of the Wollaston
Medal is described in R. S. Owen
1894, vol. 1, pp. 19–22, and
*Proceedings of the Geological Society
of London* 2 (1838):621–22. Though
Owen believed he had discovered this
general principle, both Darwin and
Woodbine Parish made claims to it as
well. See Clift and Parish 1832, and
Darwin's *Journal of researches,* Browne
and Neve eds. 1989, pp. 162–63. The
point is further discussed in Browne
1983, pp. 98–99.
10. Rachootin 1985.
11. Owen's 1837 Hunterian lectures are
transcribed in Sloan 1992. See also
Rupke 1994.
12. R. S. Owen 1894, vol. 1, p. 108.
13. C. Lyell 1837a, pp. 510–11, and
Correspondence 2:4.
14. *Notebooks,* RN 129.
15. *Journal,* pp. 163–66.
16. *Correspondence* 2:2, 7.
17. Romilly 1976, p. 110.
18. *Correspondence* 2:4.

19. Wilson 1972, p. 449.
20. Wilson 1972, p. 441.
21. *Autobiography,* p. 100.
22. Ward 1926.
23. *Correspondence* 2:8. Darwin's cultural circle is described in Manier 1978.
24. Carlyle 1881, vol. 2, pp. 207–8. See also Kaplan 1983.
25. *Correspondence* 1:518.
26. *Correspondence* 1:524.
27. Martineau 1877 and Arbuckle 1983.
28. Horner 1890, vol. 1, p. 337.
29. *Correspondence* 2:36.
30. *Correspondence* 1:531.
31. *Correspondence* 1:509.
32. A. Desmond 1985a.
33. Gould 1837a, pp. 4–7. Darwin gave a brief talk on the finches' habits on 10 May 1837, *Proceedings of the Zoological Society of London* 5 (1837):49; *Collected papers* 1:40–41.
34. *Correspondence* 2:80, 98.
35. Sulloway 1982a, 1982b, and 1982c.
36. Gould 1837b, pp. 35–36.
37. Discussed by MacLeod 1965, Brooke 1977, A. Desmond 1985b, and Richards 1987.
38. *Notebooks,* RN.
39. These have been transcribed in *Notebooks* with a full introduction and bibliography. Analyses of Darwin's earliest and changing theories of transmutation are further given in Grinnell 1974, Kohn 1980, and Ospovat 1981. See also Rudwick 1982 for a discussion of the relations between Darwin's public life and his private thoughts.
40. Darwin visited Shrewsbury from around 26 June to 6 July 1837 (*Journal,* p. 7, and *Correspondence* 2:29). "In July," he wrote in his journal, "opened first notebook on Transmutation of species."
41. *Notebooks,* B1.
42. *Correspondence* 2:32.
43. *Notebooks,* B15, D23.
44. *Notebooks,* B44.
45. C. Lyell 1837b, vol. 2, p. 442. Darwin's annotated copy is in the Darwin Collection, Cambridge University Library.
46. DAR 119 and DAR 128. Darwin's

lists of books to read, and books read, with identifications, are transcribed in *Correspondence* 4:434–573. Annotations made on the books he owned are discussed in S. Smith 1960 and in Di Gregorio and Gill 1990. For Darwin's life in literary London, see *Autobiography,* pp. 82, 102–14, and Manier 1978.
47. Browne 1993.
48. *Correspondence* 2:16.
49. *Correspondence* 2:34.
50. *Correspondence* 2:57–59.

CHAPTER 16: "A THEORY BY WHICH TO WORK"

1. The history of the Geological Society is given in Woodward 1907. For an account of élite British geology during this period, see Rudwick 1985.
2. Rhodes 1991.
3. *Correspondence* 2:47.
4. *Notebooks,* B214, 207, 252.
5. Wedgwood and Wedgwood 1980 and Arbuckle 1983.
6. Keele University, Wedgwood/Mosley Archive, 157.
7. *Correspondence* 7 (Supplement):468.
8. DAR 210.10, printed in *Correspondence* 2:443–44.
9. C. Lyell 1837b, vol. 4, pp. 18–19, where Glen Roy is mentioned by Lyell as similar to the shelves at Coquimbo. Darwin's annotated copy is in the Darwin Collection, Cambridge University Library. The debate over Glen Roy is analysed in Rudwick 1974.
10. *Diary,* pp. 331–34. See also Browne and Neve eds. 1989, pp. 261–62.
11. *Correspondence* 2:80.
12. *Correspondence* 2:80.
13. Some of Darwin's geological notes made during this trip are in DAR 5. Others are in a notebook labelled "Glen Roy" (DAR 130), transcribed in *Notebooks.*
14. See Rudwick 1974.
15. *Autobiography,* p. 95.
16. DAR 210.10, transcribed in *Correspondence* 2:444–45.
17. *Emma Darwin* 1:418.

18. *Autobiography,* p. 84. Darwin's paper was printed as "Observations on the parallel roads of Glen Roy," *Philosophical Transactions of the Royal Society of London* 1839, pp. 39–81; *Collected papers* 1:89–137.
19. C. Lyell 1838, p. vii.
20. Transcribed and published in De Beer 1959 (*Journal*).
21. Lists of the books Darwin read, and intended reading, are in DAR 119 and 128, transcribed in *Correspondence* 4:434–573.
22. *Notebooks,* OUN25.
23. *Correspondence* 2:107.
24. See particularly S. Herbert 1974 and 1977, and Gruber and Barrett 1974.
25. Darwin's "Life" written in 1838 (DAR 91:56–62), is transcribed in *Correspondence* 2:438–42. It is discussed in Colp 1980.
26. *Notebooks,* M153.
27. Browne 1985.
28. *Notebooks,* C166.
29. *Notebooks,* C217.
30. *Notebooks,* M143–4.
31. Keele University, Wedgwood/Mosley Archive, 157.
32. Schweber 1977.
33. *Notebooks,* D107–17 referring to R. Owen 1837. See also Kohn 1980 and Sloan 1992.
34. Martineau 1877, vol. 1, pp. 209, 328.
35. James 1979 and *Emma Darwin* 1:335.
36. C. Lyell 1830–33, vol. 2, p. 131. See Schweber 1977 and 1980, Kohn 1980, Ospovat 1981, and Young 1985.
37. Malthus 1798.
38. James 1979.
39. *Notebooks,* OUN29–30.
40. Malthus 1830. I thank Dr. Joy Harvey for bringing this point to my attention.
41. *Notebooks,* D135. The intellectual context is described by F. Egerton 1968 and 1970a.
42. From the many texts about the impact of Malthus on Darwin's thinking, see particularly Limoges 1970, S. Herbert 1971, Bowler 1976a, Schweber 1977, Kohn 1980, Ospovat 1981, Hodge 1985 and 1990, and Young 1985.

43. *Notebooks,* D135.
44. The role of artificial selection in Darwin's pre-Malthusian thinking has been played down of late. See, however, Limoges 1970, Herbert 1971, Ruse 1975b, and Schweber 1977. Darwin's dependence on this analogy is discussed in Young 1985.
45. Russell 1986 and Ritvo 1987.
46. *Notebooks,* MAC28v, 167r.
47. *Notebooks,* E71.
48. Briggs 1990.
49. These events are described in *Emma Darwin* 1:418–20.
50. *Correspondence* 2:115.
51. Shropshire County Record Office, 1011/box 358. See also *Correspondence* 2:119.
52. *Correspondence* 2:117.
53. *Emma Darwin* 1:419, 420.
54. *Correspondence* 2:120.
55. *Correspondence* 2:166.
56. *Emma Darwin* 1:350.
57. Quoted from Kohn 1989, p. 226.
58. *Emma Darwin* 1:347.
59. *Notebooks,* E63, 65.

CHAPTER 17: MACAW COTTAGE

1. The wedding is described in *Emma Darwin* 1:441–42. Emma Darwin's married life is described in Healey 1986.
2. Census return 1841, Public Record Office, London.
3. *Correspondence* 2:151.
4. *Correspondence* 2:166.
5. *Correspondence* 2:157.
6. *Correspondence* 2:166.
7. *Emma Darwin* 1:447.
8. George Richmond's account books, Lister 1981, p. 156.
9. *Emma Darwin* 1:449.
10. Darwin's account books are in Down House Museum.
11. *Emma Darwin* 1:458–59.
12. *Correspondence* 2:161–62. The paper is reprinted in *Collected papers* 1: 87–137.
13. *Correspondence* 2:125.
14. *Correspondence* 2:140.
15. Mantell 1940, p. 143.

16. *Proceedings of the meetings of the Royal Society of London* 4 (1837–40):122, 127–29.

17. Royal Society Archives, Referees reports, RR.1.46. I am grateful to the Royal Society of London for permission to cite this manuscript.

18. *Correspondence* 2:236.

19. William Herbert's work is analysed in Guimond 1967 and Traub 1970. See also W. Herbert 1837.

20. The text of the questionnaire is given in De Beer 1968, and is discussed by Freeman and Gautrey 1969.

21. DAR 210.10, printed in *Correspondence* 2:171–72. This letter is written on the same type of paper as Darwin's earlier "notes on marriage" (DAR 210.10), watermarked "W. Warren 1837," giving rise to assertions that Darwin's notes on marriage are on Maer Hall stationery and therefore were written at Maer during his August visit just before proposing to Emma. Apart from the fact that Darwin's "notes on marriage" are on paper torn off from a folio, and Emma's letter is on quarto writing paper, there seems every reason to believe that the paper was Darwin's stationery, and that Emma simply used a piece of it when writing, later on, to her new husband.

22. *Correspondence* 2:172.

23. Another letter apparently inviting Alphonse de Candolle to the same dinner is misdated by the editors of *Correspondence; see Correspondence* 2:193. The latter occasion took place later in the year, including Henslow for a second time.

24. *Emma Darwin* 1:461.

25. *Correspondence* 2:236.

26. *Correspondence* 2:54.

27. These books are in the Rare Books collection, Cambridge University Library.

28. *Correspondence* 2:197, 200.

29. *Narrative* 2:657–82, reprinted in Browne and Neve eds. 1989, pp. 400–24.

30. *Correspondence* 2:236.

31. No list of presentation copies seems

to have survived. See, however, *Correspondence* 2:198–214 for some of the letters of acknowledgement Darwin received.

32. *Correspondence* 2:218–22, 425–29.

33. *Correspondence* 2:237–38.

34. Henslow 1837 and 1838.

35. *Quarterly Review* 65 (1839):194–234.

36. *Edinburgh Review* 69 (1839):467–93.

37. *United Services Journal* (1841) pt 2:165–69.

38. *Athenaeum,* 1 June 1839, pp. 403–5, and 15 June 1839, pp. 446–49. Darwin's work was discussed on pp. 446, 449.

39. *Autobiography,* p. 116.

40. *Correspondence* 2:68 (probably not dated 1838, as given, but 1839), and 195.

41. These instructions were reprinted in *Athenaeum,* 17 August 1839, 611–20.

42. L. Huxley ed. 1918, vol. 1, pp. 41–53, 66.

43. *Correspondence* 2:214.

44. MacLeod 1981, Morrell and Thackray 1981.

45. *Report of the 9th meeting of the British Association for the Advancement of Science held at Birmingham in August 1839* (London, 1840), pp. viii–xiii.

46. See Rainger 1980 and Morrell and Thackray 1981, p. 284 for the background to this movement.

47. Kass and Kass 1988, pp. 392–93.

48. *Notebooks,* T81. Darwin's copy of Prichard 1836 is in the Darwin Collection, Cambridge University Library.

CHAPTER 18: MAN OF PROPERTY

1. *Correspondence* 2:234–35.

2. *Correspondence* 2:270.

3. *Correspondence* 4:160, 303.

4. *Correspondence* 5:197.

5. *Emma Darwin* 2:9, 10.

6. DAR 210.17, transcribed in *Correspondence* 2:410–33.

7. *Correspondence* 2:269.

8. _Correspondence_ 2:254, and Colvin ed. 1971, pp. 571–72.
9. Holland 1839.
10. _Correspondence_ 2:262.
11. _Correspondence_ 2:399.
12. _Correspondence_ 2:193.
13. DAR 242, August 1840; see also _Emma Darwin_ 2:249.
14. _Emma Darwin_ 2:142.
15. _Correspondence_ 4:183.
16. _Autobiography,_ p. 53.
17. L. Agassiz 1840. See also Lurie 1960, Hansen 1970, Rudwick 1974, and Rupke 1983.
18. C. Lyell 1840, Buckland 1840.
19. Murchison 1839, ch. 39.
20. _Correspondence_ 2:285.
21. _Correspondence_ 2:387.
22. _Correspondence_ 2:298.
23. _Correspondence_ 2:305.
24. _Correspondence_ 2:299.
25. _Autobiography,_ p. 98.
26. _Journal,_ p. 10.
27. Darwin's sketch of 1842 is in DAR 6, and is transcribed in F. Darwin 1909.
28. Ruse 1975a.
29. F. Darwin 1909, p. 6.
30. Kohn 1989.
31. L. Agassiz 1840, p. 332; and Buckland 1840, p. 333.
32. _Correspondence_ 2:322. Darwin refers to Buckland 1841, a paper on Welsh glacial phenomena delivered to the Geological Society in December 1841.
33. See particularly, Howarth 1933 and Atkins 1974.
34. _Emma Darwin_ 2:44.
35. Keele University, Wedgwood/Mosley Archive, 157.
36. Atkins 1974 and Moore 1985.
37. DAR 7. The copy made for Darwin is in DAR 113. The essay is reprinted in F. Darwin 1909.
38. Several of these names were subsequently deleted or changed by Darwin. William Lonsdale and Richard Owen were deleted; question marks were added to Henslow's name; and an extra remark about Hooker was inserted, "Dr Hooker ' would be _very_ good." These changes

were probably made on several occasions.
39. _Correspondence_ 3:43–44.

CHAPTER 19: FORESTALLED BUT FOREWARNED

1. Keele University, Wedgwood/Mosley Archive, 157.
2. A. Desmond 1984a, 1984b.
3. Russell-Gebbett 1977.
4. Rudwick 1985.
5. MacLeod 1965, Richards 1987, and Rupke 1994.
6. A. Desmond 1985b.
7. See Sloan 1992 and Rupke 1993.
8. Di Gregorio 1987.
9. Rehbock 1983 and Mills 1984.
10. Browne 1983, pp. 117–27.
11. See L. Huxley 1918 and Allan 1967.
12. _Correspondence_ 3:2. See also Colp 1986.
13. _Correspondence_ 3:54.
14. _Correspondence_ 3:331.
15. _Correspondence_ 3:56–57.
16. _Correspondence_ 3:170.
17. _Correspondence_ 3:51–52, 64.
18. Rudwick 1982 discusses this point in relation to the period before Darwin moved to Down.
19. _Correspondence_ 3:67–68.
20. Altick 1957 and Feather 1988. See also Browne 1992.
21. Millhauser 1959 and Secord 1989.
22. Secord 1989.
23. Millhauser 1959.
24. See [Chambers] 1844.
25. Quinarianism is discussed in S. Smith 1960, Ospovat 1981, and A. Desmond 1985a.
26. DAR 205.5: 108, dated November 1844.
27. _Correspondence_ 3:103, mistakenly attributed to Darwin in F. Egerton 1970b.
28. _Correspondence_ 3:108.
29. See Millhauser 1959, p. 33, and Cooter 1984, p. 120.
30. Millhauser 1959, p. 118.
31. _Lancet,_ 23 November 1844, pp. 265–66.

32. *Examiner,* 9 November 1844, pp. 707–9.
33. *Spectator,* 9 November 1844, pp. 1072–73.
34. Whewell 1845a.
35. *Correspondence* 3:184.
36. Presidential address. *Report of the 15th meeting of the British Association for the Advancement of Science held at Cambridge* (London, 1845), pp. xlii–xliii.
37. *Correspondence* 3:181.
38. *Correspondence* 3:158.
39. Murray 1919.
40. *Correspondence* 3:197.
41. See H. Cannon ed. 1959.
42. H. Cannon ed. 1959, pp. 194–206.
43. H. Cannon ed. 1959, p. 363.
44. H. Cannon ed. 1959, p. 365.
45. [Sedgwick] 1845. See also F. Egerton 1970b, Brooke 1977, and Yeo 1989.
46. Clark and Hughes 1890, vol. 2, pp. 83–84.
47. See Brooke 1977.
48. *Correspondence* 3:258.
49. *Correspondence* 3:289.
50. *Correspondence* 3:250–51.
51. *Correspondence* 3:253.
52. DAR 31.1:305–8.
53. *Correspondence* 3:363.

CHAPTER 20: DYING BY INCHES

1. Jordan 1922, vol. 1, p. 273.
2. R. S. Owen 1894, vol. 1, p. 292.
3. Very little work has been done on Darwin's barnacle researches, but see Crowson 1958, Ghiselin 1969, Winsor 1969b, and Gunther 1979. A summary of his methods and conclusions is given in *Correspondence* 4: 388–409. A general account of invertebrate researches in this period is given by Winsor 1969a.
4. See Gunther 1975, Stearn 1981, and *Correspondence* 7 (Supplement): 471.
5. *Correspondence* 4:128.
6. *Correspondence* 4:253.
7. *Correspondence* 4:140.
8. *Correspondence* 4:140.

9. *Correspondence* 4:156.
10. *Correspondence* 4:162–63.
11. Lurie 1960, p. 296.
12. Thomson 1828–34.
13. *Correspondence* 4:164. Darwin read Milne-Edwards 1844, a paper on classification in the *Annales des Sciences Naturelles,* in December 1846. See *Correspondence* 4:472 and Limoges 1971.
14. *Correspondence* 4:286, 314.
15. *Correspondence* 4:365.
16. Steenstrup 1845. Ideas about sexual reproduction and the need for two sexes in nature are discussed in Churchill 1979 and Farley 1982.
17. Darwin's comments were reported in *Athenaeum,* 22 September 1849, p. 966, and are reprinted in *Collected papers* 1:250–51.
18. *Correspondence* 4:254.
19. *Correspondence* 4:230.
20. *Journal,* p. 12.
21. *Correspondence* 4:100.
22. *Emma Darwin* 2:142.
23. *Correspondence* 4:135–36.
24. *Correspondence* 4:92.
25. *Correspondence* 4:147.
26. Wedgwood and Wedgwood 1980, p. 249, and Keele University, Wedgwood/Mosley Archive, 157.
27. *Correspondence* 4:227, and *Correspondence* 5:9.
28. R. W. Darwin's probate, Keele University, Wedgwood/Mosley Archive, 238.
29. Darwin's health diary, covering the years 1849–55, is in Down House Museum. It is discussed in Foster 1965 and Colp 1977.
30. Darwin's annotated copy of Holland 1839 is in the Darwin Collection, Cambridge University Library.
31. See Metcalfe 1906, Turner 1967, Price 1981, and R. Porter 1990.
32. *Correspondence* 4:209.
33. Cooter 1988.
34. Martin 1980, Jenkins 1974.
35. Turner 1967, pp. 163–91. See also Browne 1990.
36. *Punch, or the London Charivari* (1846) 11:243–44.
37. See Browne 1990.

38. *Correspondence* 4:150, 219.
39. Jenkins 1974 and Turner, pp. 174–75.
40. The treatments are fully described in Gully 1846, pp. 564–627.
41. Gully 1846, p. 85.
42. *Correspondence* 4:225.
43. *Correspondence* 4:234, 246.
44. *Life and letters* 1:131.
45. DAR 112:9–49.
46. Francis Darwin's recollections, DAR 140(3):14.
47. *Correspondence* 4:234, 235, 239.
48. DAR 112:49.
49. DAR 210.17, transcribed in *Correspondence* 4:411–33. See p. 423.
50. *Correspondence* 5:13.
51. *Correspondence* 5:14.
52. *Correspondence* 5:28.
53. *Correspondence* 5:542. See also Colp 1987 and Moore 1989.
54. Public Record Office, London, death certificate issued at Upton upon Severn, 29 April 1851.
55. DAR 210.13, published in Colp 1987 and *Correspondence* 5:540–42.
56. *Correspondence* 5:542–43.
57. DAR 246. I am grateful to Prof. R. D. Keynes for permission to cite from Henrietta Litchfield's papers.
58. Moore 1989. See also Glisermann 1975 and Kohn 1989.
59. C. Darwin 1851–54a and 1851–54b (*Fossil Cirripedia* and *Living Cirripedia*).
60. *Life and letters* 1:155.
61. Briggs 1979 and 1990.
62. Hooker's life and work is discussed in L. Huxley 1918 and Allan 1977.
63. Brockway 1979.
64. For different accounts of Huxley's life and work, see L. Huxley 1900, Irvine 1955, Paradis 1978, A. Desmond 1982, and Di Gregorio 1984.
65. *Correspondence* 5:130.
66. T. H. Huxley 1854. See also Schwartz 1990.
67. *Correspondence* 5:212–13. See also Darwin's annotated copy of the sixth edition of *Vestiges* (1847) in the Darwin Collection, Cambridge University Library.
68. *Correspondence* 5:215, 296.
69. *Correspondence* 5:165.
70. *Correspondence* 5:166.
71. For the Philosophical Club, see Bonney 1919. For the memorial about university reform, see Winstanley 1955, p. 210.
72. *Journal,* p. 13.

CHAPTER 21:
SHIP ON THE DOWNS

1. W. F. Cannon 1978.
2. See particularly Ruse 1975a and 1979, and Yeo 1979.
3. *Correspondence* 4:344.
4. F. Darwin 1909. See also Kottler 1978.
5. F. Darwin 1909.
6. Browne 1983, pp. 132–34, 200–2.
7. See Atkins 1974 and Allan 1977.
8. *Correspondence* 3:13.
9. *Correspondence* 5:308.
10. *Correspondence* 6:305.
11. Scherren 1905 and A. Desmond 1985a.
12. *Correspondence* 6:248, 250.
13. DAR 205.2 (Letters).
14. *Correspondence* 6:143–44.
15. *Correspondence* 6:147.
16. Secord 1981.
17. See particularly Young 1985.
18. Bartley 1992.
19. *Correspondence* 6:45.
20. *Correspondence* 5:509.
21. *Correspondence* 7:405.
22. Secord 1981, on the other hand, believes the breeders were mostly artisans.
23. E. W. Richardson 1916 and Bartley 1992.
24. DAR 246.
25. *Correspondence* 5:288.
26. *Correspondence* 5:508.
27. DAR 149(3).
28. Freeman 1968.
29. *Correspondence* 4:423.
30. *Correspondence* 5:365.
31. Mellersh 1968. FitzRoy's subsequent career at the Meteorological Office is discussed in Burton 1986.
32. DAR 219, box 1.
33. DAR 112 (ser. 2):12.
34. DAR 149(3).

35. *Correspondence* 3:132.
36. DAR 246.
37. DAR 246.
38. Elizabeth Darwin's letters are in DAR 219, box 1. I thank Joy Harvey for making her transcripts of them available.
39. Jordan 1922, vol. 1, p. 273.
40. Moore 1977.
41. *Correspondence* 4:354.
42. *Correspondence* 4:362, and *Correspondence* 5:83.
43. DAR 185/110.
44. Wallace 1855. Darwin's annotated copy of this article, with a separate page of notes, is in the Darwin Collection, Cambridge University Library.
45. See *Correspondence* 5:519.
46. Howarth 1933 and Hutchinson 1914.
47. A. Desmond 1982.
48. *Correspondence* 5:213.
49. Wollaston 1856.
50. *Correspondence* 6:134.
51. *Correspondence* 6:281.
52. *Correspondence* 6:89.
53. Wilson 1970, pp. 52–55, 87.
54. *Correspondence* 6:100.

Bibliography

Ackerknecht, E. H. 1967. *Medicine at the Paris Hospital, 1794–1848.* Baltimore: Johns Hopkins Press.

Addison, W. 1947. *The English country parson.* London: J. M. Dent.

Adler, S. W. 1959. Darwin's illness. *Nature* 184:1102–3.

Agassiz, E. C. 1885. *Louis Agassiz: his life and correspondence.* 2 vols. London.

Agassiz, Louis. 1840. Glaciers and the evidence of their having once existed in Scotland, Ireland and England. *Proceedings of the Geological Society of London* 3 (1838–43):327–32.

Allan, Mea. 1967. *The Hookers of Kew, 1785–1911.* London: Michael Joseph.

———. 1977. *Darwin and his flowers: the key to natural selection.* London: Faber & Faber.

Allen, D. C. 1949. *The legend of Noah: Renaissance rationalism in art, science and letters.* Urbana: Illinois University Press.

Allen, David Elliston. 1978. *The naturalist in Britain: a social history.* Harmondsworth: Pelican Books.

———. 1985. The early professionals in British natural history. In Alwynne Wheeler and James H. Price, eds. *From Linnaeus to Darwin: commentaries on the history of biology and geology.* London: Society for the History of Natural History.

Allen, Peter. 1987. *The Cambridge Apostles: the early years.* Cambridge: Cambridge University Press.

Altick, Richard. 1957. *The English common reader: a social history of the mass reading public, 1800–1900.* Chicago: University of Chicago Press.

———. 1978. *The shows of London.* Cambridge, Mass.: Belknap Press of Harvard University Press.

Anderson, R.G.W., and A. Simpson, eds. 1976. *The early years of the Edinburgh medical school.* Edinburgh: Royal Scottish Museum.

Annan, N. G. 1955. The intellectual aristocracy. In J. H. Plumb, ed. *Studies in social history: a tribute to G. M. Trevelyan.* London: Longmans, Green & Co.

Appel, Toby A. 1987. *The Cuvier–Geoffroy debate: French biology in the decades before Darwin.* Oxford: Oxford University Press.

Arbuckle, E. S., ed. 1983. *Harriet Martineau's letters to Fanny Wedgwood.* Stanford, Calif.: Stanford University Press.

Armstrong, Patrick. 1992. *Darwin's desolate islands: a naturalist in the Falklands, 1833 and 1834.* Chippenham, Wilts: Picton Publishing.

Ashworth, J. H. 1935. Charles Darwin as a student in Edinburgh, 1825–1827.

Proceedings of the Royal Society of Edinburgh 55 (1934–35):97–112.

Atkins, Hedley. 1974. *Down, the home of the Darwins: the story of a house and the people who lived there.* London: Royal College of Surgeons of England.

Auden, J. E., ed. 1909. *Shrewsbury School register, 1734–1908.* Oswestry, Shropshire: Woodall, Minshall, Thomas & Co.

Autobiography: see Barlow, Nora, ed. 1958.

Babington, Charles Cardale. 1887. *The Cambridge Ray Club.* Cambridge.

———. 1897. *Memorials, journal and botanical correspondence.* Cambridge.

Balfour, J. H. 1865. *Biography of John Coldstream.* London.

Barber, Lynn. 1980. *The heyday of natural history, 1820–1870.* London: Jonathan Cape.

Barclay, John. 1822. *An inquiry into the opinions ancient and modern concerning life and organization.* Edinburgh.

Barlow, Nora, ed. 1933. *Diary of the voyage of H.M.S. Beagle.* Cambridge: Cambridge University Press. Reprint. New York: Kraus Reprint Co., 1969.

———. 1958. *The Autobiography of Charles Darwin, 1809–1882, with original omissions restored.* London: Collins.

———. 1963. Darwin's ornithological notes. *Bulletin of the British Museum (Natural History) Historical Series* 2: 201–78.

Barrett, Paul H. 1974. The Sedgwick–Darwin geologic tour of North Wales. *Proceedings of the American Philosophical Society* 118:146–164.

———, ed. 1977. *The collected papers of Charles Darwin.* 2 vols. Chicago: University of Chicago Press.

Barrett, Paul H., P. J. Gautrey, S. Herbert, D. Kohn, and S. Smith, eds. 1987. *Charles Darwin's notebooks, 1836–1844: geology, transmutation of species, metaphysical inquiries.* London: British Museum (Natural History) and Cambridge University Press.

Bartholomew, Michael. 1973. Lyell and evolution: an account of Lyell's response to the prospect of an evolutionary ancestry for man. *British Journal for the History of Science* 6: 261–303.

———. 1976. The non-progress of non-progression: two responses to Lyell's doctrine. *British Journal for the History of Science* 9:166–74.

———. 1979. The singularity of Lyell. *History of Science* 7:276–93.

Bartley, Mary M. 1992. Darwin and domestication: studies on inheritance. *Journal of the History of Biology* 25: 307–33.

Basalla, George. 1963. The voyage of the Beagle without Darwin. *Mariner's Mirror* 49:42–48.

Becher, Harvey H. 1986. Voluntary science in nineteenth-century Cambridge University to the 1850s. *British Journal for the History of Science* 19:57–87.

Beer, Gillian. 1983. *Darwin's plots: evolutionary narrative in Darwin, George Eliot and nineteenth-century fiction.* London and Boston: Routledge & Kegan Paul.

———. 1986. The face of nature: anthropomorphic elements in Darwin's style. In L. Jordanova, ed. *The languages of nature: critical essays on science and literature.* London: Free Association Books.

———. 1989. Discourses of the island. In Frederick Amrine, ed. *Literature and science as modes of expression.* Dordrecht: Kluwer Academic Publishers.

Bell, Charles. 1806. *Essays on the anatomy of expression in painting.* London.

Bell, Thomas. 1842–43. *Reptiles.* Part 5 of Charles Darwin, ed. *The zoology of the voyage of H.M.S. Beagle.* London, 1838–43.

Berg, Maxine. 1985. *The age of manufactures: industry, innovation and work in Britain, 1700–1820.* London: Fontana.

Bewell, Alan. 1987. Jacobin plants: botany as social theory in the 1790s. *Wordsworth Circle,* pp. 132–39.

Bonnett, Stanley. 1968. *The price of Admiralty: an indictment of the Royal Navy, 1805–1966.* London: Robert Hale.

Bonney, T. G. 1919. *Annals of the Philo-*

sophical Club of the Royal Society. London: Macmillan.

Bory de St. Vincent, Jean Baptiste, et al., eds. 1822–31. *Dictionnaire classique d'histoire naturelle.* 17 vols. Paris.

Bourne, W.R.P. 1992. FitzRoy's foxes and Darwin's finches. *Archives of Natural History* 19:29–371.

Bowlby, John. 1990. *Charles Darwin: a biography.* London: Hutchinson.

Bowler, Peter J. 1974. Darwin's changing concepts of variation. *Journal of the History of Medicine and the Allied Sciences* 29:196–212.

———. 1976a. Malthus, Darwin, and the concept of struggle. *Journal of the History of Ideas* 37:631–50.

———. 1976b. *Fossils and progress: palaeontology and the idea of progressive evolution in the nineteenth century.* New York: Science History Publications.

———. 1984. *Evolution: the history of an idea.* Berkeley, Calif.: University of California Press.

———. 1989. *The invention of progress: the Victorians and the past.* Oxford: Basil Blackwell.

———. 1990. *Charles Darwin: the man and his influence.* (Blackwell Scientific Biographies.) Oxford: Blackwell.

Branagan, David. 1985. Philip Parker King: colonial anchor man. In Alwynne Wheeler and James H. Price, eds. *From Linnaeus to Darwin: commentaries on the history of biology and geology.* London: Society for the History of Natural History.

Brent, Peter. 1981. *Charles Darwin: "a man of enlarged curiosity."* London: Heinemann.

Brewer, John. 1982. Commercialization and politics. In Neil McKendrick, John Brewer, and J. H. Plumb, *The birth of a consumer society: the commercialization of eighteenth-century England.* London: Europa Publications.

Briggs, Asa. 1965. *Victorian people. A reassessment of persons and themes, 1851–67.* Harmondsworth: Penguin Books.

———. 1979. *Iron Bridge to Crystal Palace: impact and images of the Industrial Revolution.* London: Thames and Hudson in collaboration with the Ironbridge Gorge Museum Trust.

———. 1990. *Victorian things.* Harmondsworth: Penguin Books.

Broberg, Gunnar. 1983. Homo Sapiens: Linnaeus's classification of man. In Tore Frangsmyr, ed. *Linnaeus: the man and his work.* Berkeley, Calif.: University of California Press.

Brock, W. H. 1993. Humboldt and the British: a note on the character of British science. *Annals of Science* 50:365–72.

Brockway, Lucille. 1979. *Science and colonial expansion: the role of the British Royal Botanic Garden.* (Studies in Social Discontinuity.) New York: Academic Press.

Brooke, John Hedley. 1977. Richard Owen, William Whewell, and the "Vestiges." *British Journal for the History of Science* 35:132–45.

———. 1979. The natural theology of the geologists: some theological strata. In Roy Porter and Ludmilla Jordanova, eds. *Images of the earth: essays in the history of the environmental sciences.* Chalfont St. Giles: British Society for the History of Science, Monograph 1.

———. 1985. The relations between Darwin's science and his religion. In John Durant, ed. *Darwinism and divinity.* Oxford: Basil Blackwell.

———. 1991. *Science and religion: some historical perspectives.* Cambridge: Cambridge University Press.

Brookes, Richard. 1763. *The natural history of insects, with their properties and uses in medicine.* Vol. 4 of *A new and accurate system of natural history.* 6 vols. London.

———. 1793. *The natural history of waters, earths, stones, fossils, and minerals with their virtues, properties, and medicinal uses.* Vol. 5 of *A new and accurate system of natural history.* 6 vols. London.

Brown, Frank B. 1986. The evolution of Darwin's theism. *Journal of the History of Biology* 19:1–45. Also published as *The evolution of Darwin's religious views.* Macon, Ga.: Mercer University Press.

Browne, Janet. 1983. *The secular ark: stud-*

ies in the history of biogeography. New Haven: Yale University Press.

———. 1985. Darwin and the expression of the emotions. In David Kohn, ed. *The Darwinian heritage.* Princeton, N.J.: Princeton University Press in association with Nova Pacifica.

———. 1989. Botany for gentlemen: Erasmus Darwin and *The Loves of the Plants. Isis* 80:593–621.

———. 1990. Spas and sensibilities: Darwin at Malvern. In R. S. Porter, ed. *The medical history of waters and spas.* (*Medical History,* Supplement 10.) London: Wellcome Institute for the History of Medicine.

———. 1992. Squibs and snobs: science in humorous British undergraduate magazines around 1830. *History of Science* 30:165–97.

———. 1993. A science of empire: British biogeography before Darwin. *Revue d'histoire de Science* 45:453–75.

———. 1995. Botany in the boudoir: the Banksian context. In Peter Reill and David Miller, eds. *Visions of empire: voyages, botany and representations of nature.* Cambridge: Cambridge University Press.

Browne, Janet, and Michael Neve, eds. 1989. *Voyage of the* Beagle: *Charles Darwin's Journal of researches.* Edited with an introduction. Harmondsworth: Penguin Books.

Buckland, William. 1840. Memoir on the evidences of glaciers in Scotland and the north of England. *Proceedings of the Geological Society of London* 3 (1838–43):332–37, 345–48.

———. 1841. On the glacial-diluvial phenomena in Snowdonia and the adjacent parts of North Wales. *Proceedings of the Geological Society of London* 3 (1838–43):579–84.

Burkhardt, F. H., S. Smith, et al., eds. 1983–94. *The correspondence of Charles Darwin.* Vols. 1–9 (1821–61). Cambridge: Cambridge University Press.

Burkhardt, Richard W. 1977. *The spirit of system: Lamarck and evolutionary*

biology. Cambridge, Mass.: Harvard University Press.

Burstyn, H. L. 1975. If Darwin wasn't the Beagle's naturalist, why was he on board? *British Journal for the History of Science* 8:62–69.

Burton, Jim. 1986. Robert FitzRoy and the early history of the Meteorological Office. *British Journal for the History of Science* 19:147–76.

Bury, J. B. 1920. *The idea of progress: an inquiry into its origin and growth.* Reprinted. New York: Dover, 1955.

Butler, Samuel. 1818. *A sketch of modern and ancient geography for the use of schools.* 4th ed. London.

Butler, Samuel, ed. 1896. *The life and letters of Dr. Samuel Butler.* By his grandson, Samuel Butler. 2 vols. London.

Butler, Stella, R. H. Nuttall, and Olivia Brown. 1986. *The social history of the microscope.* Cambridge: Whipple Museum of the History of Science.

Buttman, G. 1970. *The shadow of the telescope: a biography of John Herschel.* Translated by B.E.J. Pagel. Edited by D. S. Evans. New York: Charles Scribner's Sons.

Byron, George Anson. 1826. *Voyage of H.M.S.* Blonde *to the Sandwich Islands, in the years 1824–25.* London.

Cady, J. F. 1929. *Foreign intervention in the Río de la Plata, 1838–50: a study of French, British and American policy in relation to the dictator, J. M. Rosas.* Philadelphia: University of Philadelphia Press.

Cannon, H. G., ed. 1959. *The voyage of the* Beagle. Reprint of the 2d ed. of Charles Darwin's *Journal of researches* (1845). London: J. M. Dent.

Cannon, W. F. [S. F.]. 1960. The problem of miracles in the 1830s. *Victorian Studies* 4:5–32.

———. 1961. The impact of uniformitarianism: two letters from John Herschel to Charles Lyell, 1836–1837. *Proceedings of the American Philosophical Society* 105:301–14.

———. 1976. Charles Lyell, radical actualism

and theory. *British Journal for the History of Science* 9:104–20.

——. 1978. *Science in culture: the early Victorian period.* New York: Science History Publications.

Cantor, G. N. 1975. Phrenological knowledge in early nineteenth century Edinburgh: an historical discussion. *Annals of Science* 32:195–218.

Carlyle, Thomas. 1881. *Reminiscences.* Edited by James Froude. 2 vols. London.

Chadwick, Owen. 1975. *The secularization of the European mind in the nineteenth century.* Cambridge: Cambridge University Press.

[Chambers, Robert.] 1844. *Vestiges of the natural history of creation.* London. Reprinted with an introduction by J. A. Secord. Chicago: University of Chicago Press, 1994.

Chapman, Roger, ed. 1982. *Charles Darwin 1809–1882: a centennial commemorative.* Wellington, New Zealand: Nova Pacifica.

Chitnis, Anand C. 1970. The University of Edinburgh's natural history museum and the Huttonian-Wernerian debate. *Annals of Science* 26:85–94.

——. 1986. *The Scottish enlightenment and early Victorian English society.* London: Croom Helm.

Christison, Robert. 1885–86. *The life of Sir Robert Christison, Bart.* Edited by his sons. 2 vols. Edinburgh and London.

Churchill, F. B. 1979. Sex and the single organism: biological theories of sexuality in mid-nineteenth century. *Studies in the History of Biology* 3: 139–77.

Clark, J. W., and T. M. Hughes. 1890. *The life and letters of the reverend Adam Sedgwick.* 2 vols. London.

Clift, William, and Woodbine Parish. 1832. An account of the discovery of portions of three skeletons of the Megatherium in the province of Buenos Ayres. *Proceedings of the Geological Society of London* 1 (1826–33):403–4.

Clinton, D. K. 1937. *The South-African melting-pot: a vindication of mission-*
ary policy, 1799–1836. London: Longmans.

Coddington, Henry. 1830. On the improvement of the microscope. *Transactions of the Cambridge Philosophical Society* 3:421–28.

Coleman, William. 1971. *Biology in the nineteenth century: problems of form, function, and transmutation.* New York: John Wiley.

Collected papers: see Barrett, P. H., ed. 1977.

Colloms, Brenda. 1977. *Victorian country parsons.* Lincoln, Neb.: University of Nebraska Press.

Colp, Ralph. 1977. *To be an invalid: the illness of Charles Darwin.* Chicago: University of Chicago Press.

——. 1980. "I was born a naturalist": Charles Darwin's 1838 notes about himself. *Journal of the History of Medicine* 35:8–39.

——. 1984. The pre-Beagle misery of Charles Darwin. *Psychohistory Review* 13:4–15.

——. 1986. Confessing a murder: Darwin's first revelations about transmutation. *Isis* 77:9–32.

——. 1987. Charles Darwin's "insufferable grief." *Free Associations* 9:6–44.

Comrie, John D. 1932. *History of Scottish medicine.* 2 vols. London: Wellcome History of Medicine Museum.

Cooter, Roger. 1984. *The cultural meaning of popular science: phrenology and the organisation of consent in nineteenth century Britain.* Cambridge: Cambridge University Press.

——, ed. 1988. *Studies in the history of alternative medicine.* London: Macmillan.

Coral reefs: see Darwin, Charles. 1842.

Corning, Howard. ed. 1930. *John James Audubon: letters,* 1826–40. 2 vols. Boston: The Club of Odd Volumes.

Correspondence. See Burkhardt, F. H., S. Smith, et al., eds. 1983–94.

Corsi, Pietro. 1978. The importance of French transformist ideas for the second volume of Lyell's *Principles of geology. British Journal for the History of Science* 11:221–44.

——. 1988a. *The age of Lamarck: evolutionary theories in France, 1790–1830.* Translated by Jonathan Mandelbaum. Berkeley, Calif.: University of California Press.

——. 1988b. *Science and religion: Baden Powell and the Anglican debate, 1820–1860.* Cambridge: Cambridge University Press.

Cowburn, Philip, ed. 1964. *A Salopian anthology: some impressions of Shrewsbury School during four centuries.* London: Macmillan.

Croft, L. R. 1989. *The life and death of Charles Darwin.* Chorley: Elmwood.

Crouzet, François. 1985. *The first industrialists: the problems of origins.* Cambridge: Cambridge University Press.

Crowson, R. A. 1958. Darwin and classification. In S. A. Barnett, *A century of Darwin.* Cambridge: Cambridge University Press.

Cunningham, Peter, ed. 1857–59. *The letters of Horace Walpole.* 9 vols. London.

Cuvier, Georges. 1813. *Essay on the theory of the earth.* Translated by Robert Jameson. Edinburgh and London.

Darwin, Charles [1758–78]. 1780. *Experiments establishing a criterion between mucilaginous and purulent matter.* Lichfield.

Darwin, Charles. 1835a. Extracts from letters addressed to Professor Henslow. Cambridge: Privately printed for the Cambridge Philosophical Society.

——. 1835b. Geological notes made during a survey of the east and west coasts of South America. *Proceedings of the Geological Society of London* 2 (1833–38):210–12.

——, ed. 1838–43. *The zoology of the voyage of H.M.S. Beagle under the command of Captain FitzRoy.* Part 1. *Fossil mammalia.* By Richard Owen. Part 2. *Mammalia.* By George Robert Waterhouse. Part 3. *Birds.* By John Gould. Part 4. *Fish.* By Leonard Jenyns. Part 5. *Reptiles.* By Thomas Bell. 3 or 5 volumes. London.

——. 1839. *Journal of researches into the geology and natural history of the various countries visited by H.M.S. Beagle.* London.

——. 1842. The structure and distribution of coral reefs. Part 1 of *The geology of the voyage of the Beagle.* London, 1842–46.

——. 1844. *Geological observations on the volcanic islands visited during the voyage of H.M.S. Beagle.* Part 2 of *The geology of the voyage of the Beagle.* London, 1842–46.

——. 1846. *Geological observations on South America.* Part 3 of *The geology of the voyage of the Beagle.* London, 1842–46.

——. 1851–54a. *A monograph of the subclass Cirripedia.* Vol. 1. *The Lepadidae.* London, 1851. Vol. 2. *The Balanidae.* London, 1854.

——. 1851–54b. *A monograph of the fossil Lepadidae.* London, 1851. *A monograph of the fossil Balanidae and Verrucidae.* London, 1854.

——. 1859. *On the origin of species by means of natural selection, or the preservation of favoured races in the struggle for life.* London. Reprinted with an introduction by J. W. Burrow. Harmondsworth: Penguin Books.

——. 1872. *The descent of man.* 2 vols. London. Reprinted with an introduction by J. T. Bonner and R. M. May. Princeton, N.J.: Princeton University Press, 1981.

Darwin, Erasmus [1731–1802]. 1789. *The loves of the plants, a poem with philosophical notes.* Part 2 of *The botanic garden.* Lichfield.

——. 1791. *The economy of vegetation.* Part 1 of *The botanic garden.* London.

——. 1794–96. *Zoonomia; or the laws of organic life.* 2 vols. London.

——. 1803. *Temple of nature; or the origin of society. A poem with philosophical notes.* London.

Darwin, Francis. 1912. FitzRoy and Darwin, 1831–36. *Nature* 88:547–48.

——, ed. 1887. *The life and letters of Charles Darwin.* 3 vols. London.

——. 1909. *The foundations of the "Origin of Species": two essays written in 1842 and 1844 by Charles Darwin.*

Cambridge: Cambridge University Press.

Darwin, Francis, and A. C. Seward, eds. 1903. *More letters of Charles Darwin: a record of his work in a series of hitherto unpublished letters.* 2 vols. London: John Murray.

Darwin, Robert Waring [1724–1816]. 1787. *Principia botanica: or, a concise and easy introduction to the sexual botany of Linnaeus.* Newark.

Darwin, Robert Waring (of Shrewsbury) [1766–1848]. 1789. *An appeal to the faculty, concerning the case of Mrs. Houlston.* Shrewsbury.

Davies, G.L.H. 1969. *The earth in decay: a history of British geomorphology, 1578–1878.* London: MacDonald Technical and Scientific.

De Beer, Gavin, ed. 1959. Darwin's Journal. *Bulletin of the British Museum (Natural History) Historical Series* 2:1–21.

——. 1968. *Questions about the breeding of animals.* By Charles Darwin. Facsimile edition. Sherborn Fund Facsimile 3. London: Society for the Bibliography of Natural History.

Descent of man: see Darwin, Charles. 1872.

Desmond, Adrian. 1982. *Archetypes and ancestors: palaeontology in Victorian London, 1850–1875.* London: Blond & Briggs.

——. 1984a. Robert E. Grant: the social predicament of a pre-Darwinian transmutationist. *Journal of the History of Biology* 17:189–223.

——. 1984b. Robert E. Grant's later views on organic development: the Swiney lectures on "Palaeozoology," 1853–1857. *Archives of Natural History* 11: 395–413.

——. 1985a. The making of institutional zoology in London, 1822–1836. *History of Science* 23:153–85, 223–50.

——. 1985b. Richard Owen's reaction to transmutation in the 1830s. *British Journal for the History of Science.* 18: 25–50.

——. 1989. *The politics of evolution: morphology, medicine and reform in radical London.* Chicago: University of Chicago Press.

Desmond, Adrian, and James R. Moore. 1992. *Darwin.* London: Michael Joseph.

Desmond, Ray. 1977. *Dictionary of British and Irish botanists and horticulturists.* 3d ed. London: Taylor & Francis.

Di Gregorio, Mario. 1984. *T. H. Huxley's place in natural science.* New Haven: Yale University Press.

——, and Nick Gill, eds. 1990. *Charles Darwin's Marginalia.* Vol. 1. New York: Garland.

Diary: see Barlow, Nora, ed., and Keynes, R. D., ed. 1988.

Donaldson, Gordon, ed. 1983. *Four centuries of Edinburgh University life, 1583–1983.* Edinburgh: Edinburgh University Press.

Dupetit-Thouars, Abel. 1840–44. *Voyage de la Vénus.* 10 vols. *Relation.* 4 vols. Paris.

Dunmore, John. 1965–69. *French explorers in the Pacific.* 2 vols. Oxford: Clarendon Press.

Earle, Augustus. 1832. *Narrative of a nine months' residence in New Zealand and Journal of a residence in Tristan da Cunha.* Edited by E. H. McCormick. Oxford: Clarendon Press, 1966.

Edwards, Owen Dudley. 1981. *Burke and Hare.* Edinburgh: Polygon Books.

Egerton, F. N. 1968. Studies of animal population from Lamarck to Darwin. *Journal of the History of Biology* 1: 255–59.

——. 1970a. Humboldt, Darwin and population. *Journal of the History of Biology* 3:326–60.

——. 1970b. Refutation and conjecture: Darwin's response to Sedgwick's attack on Chambers. *Studies in History and Philosophy of Science* 1: 176–83.

——. 1976. Darwin's early reading of Lamarck. *Isis* 67:452–56.

Egerton, Judy. 1990. *Wright of Derby.* London: Tate Gallery.

Eiseley, Loren. 1958. *Darwin's century:*

evolution and the men who discovered it. New York: Doubleday.

——. 1979. *Darwin and the mysterious Mr. X.* London, Toronto, Melbourne: J. M. Dent.

Elliot, Walter. 1870. Opening address. *Transactions of the Botanical Society of Edinburgh* 2:1–42.

Ellis, William. 1829. *Polynesian researches, during a residence of nearly six years on the South Sea Islands.* London.

——. 1831. *A vindication of the South Seas missions from the misrepresentations of Otto von Kotzebue.* London.

Emma Darwin: see Litchfield, H. E., ed. 1904.

Evans, D. S., et al., eds. 1969. *Herschel at the Cape: diaries and correspondence of Sir John Herschel, 1834–38.* Austin, Texas: University of Texas Press.

Eyles, V. A. 1972. Mineralogical maps as forerunners of modern geological maps. *Cartographic Journal* 9:133–35.

Farley, John. 1982. *Gametes and spores: ideas about sexual reproduction, 1750–1914.* Baltimore: Johns Hopkins University Press.

Feather, John. 1988. *A history of British publishing.* London: Routledge.

Figlio, Karl. 1976. The metaphor of organisation: an historiographic perspective on the bio-medical sciences of the early nineteenth century. *History of Science* 14:17–53.

Finlayson, C. P., and S. M. Simpson. 1982. The history of the library, 1710–1837. In Jean R. Guild and Alexander Law, eds. *Edinburgh University Library, 1580–1980: a collection of historical essays.* Edinburgh: Edinburgh University Library.

FitzRoy, Robert. 1836. Sketch of the surveying voyages of H.M.S. *Adventure* and *Beagle*, 1825–1836. *Journal of the Royal Geographical Society of London* 6:311–43.

——. 1837. Extracts from the diary of an attempt to ascend the River Santa Cruz, in Patagonia, with the boats of H.M.S. *Beagle* [Read 8 May 1837.] *Journal of the Royal Geographical Society of London* 7:114–26.

——. 1839. *Narrative of the surveying voy-*

ages of H.M.S. Adventure *and* Beagle, between the years 1826 and 1836. Vol. 1. *Proceedings of the first expedition, 1826–30, under the command of Captain P. P. King.* Edited by Robert FitzRoy. Vol. 2. *Proceedings of the second expedition, 1831–36, under the command of Captain R. FitzRoy.* Vol. 3. *Journal and remarks, 1832–36.* By Charles Darwin. 4 vols. London.

——. 1846. *Remarks on New Zealand.* London.

Fladeland, Betty. 1984. *Abolitionists and working-class problems in the age of industrialization.* Baton Rouge: Louisiana State University Press.

Fleming, Donald. 1960. Charles Darwin, the anaesthetic man. *Victorian Studies* 4:219–36.

Fleming, John. 1822. *The philosophy of zoology, or a general view of the structure, functions and classification of animals.* 2 vols. Edinburgh.

Fossil cirripedia: See Darwin, Charles. 1851–54a.

Foster, W. D. 1965. A contribution to the problem of Darwin's ill-health. *Bulletin of the History of Medicine* 39:476–78.

Freeman, R. B. 1968. Charles Darwin on the routes of male humble bees. *Bulletin of the British Museum (Natural History) Historical Series* 3:177–89.

——. 1977. *The works of Charles Darwin: an annotated bibliographical handlist.* 2d ed. Folkestone: Dawson.

——. 1978–79. Darwin's negro bird-stuffer. *Notes and Records of the Royal Society of London* 33:83–86.

Freeman, R. B., and P. J. Gautrey. 1969. Darwin's "Questions about the breeding of animals." *Journal of the Society of the Bibliography of Natural History* 5:220–25.

Friendly, Alfred. 1977. *Beaufort of the Admiralty: the life of Sir Francis Beaufort, 1774–1857.* London: Hutchinson.

Garland, Martha McMackin. 1980. *Cambridge before Darwin: the ideal of a liberal education, 1800–1860.* Cambridge: Cambridge University Press.

Ghiselin, Michael. 1969. *The triumph of*

the Darwinian method. Berkeley, Calif.: University of California Press.

Gillespie, Neal C. 1979. *Charles Darwin and the problem of creation.* Chicago: University of Chicago Press.

Gillispie, Charles Coulston. 1959. *Genesis and geology: the impact of scientific discoveries on scientific beliefs in the decades before Darwin.* New York: Harper & Row.

Gleason, Mary Louise. 1991. *The Royal Society of London: years of reform, 1827–1847.* New York: Garland.

Glisermann, S. 1975. Early Victorian science writers and Tennyson's *In Memoriam. Victorian Studies* 18: 277–308, 437–59.

Golinski, Jan. 1992. *Science as public culture: chemistry and enlightenment in Britain, 1760–1820.* Cambridge: Cambridge University Press.

Good, Rankine. 1954. The life of the shawl. *Lancet,* 9 January 1954, 106–7.

Gosden, P.H.J.H. 1973. *Self-help: voluntary associations in the nineteenth century.* London: Batsford.

Gould, John. 1837a. Remarks on a group of ground finches from Mr. Darwin's collection. *Proceedings of the Zoological Society of London* 5:4–7.

———. 1837b. On a new Rhea (R. Darwinii). *Proceedings of the Zoological Society of London* 5:35–36.

———. 1838–41. *Birds.* Part 3 of Charles Darwin, ed. *The zoology of the voyage of H.M.S. Beagle.* London, 1838–43.

Graham, G. S. 1965. *The politics of naval supremacy: studies in British maritime ascendancy.* Cambridge: Cambridge University Press.

Graham, G. S., and R. A. Humphreys, eds. 1962. *The Navy and South America, 1807–23.* London: Navy Records Society.

Grant, Alexander. 1884. *The story of the University of Edinburgh during its first three hundred years.* 2 vols. Edinburgh and London.

[Grant, Robert.] 1826. Observations on the nature and importance of geology. *Edinburgh New Philosophical Journal* 1:293–302.

Grant, Robert. 1827a. Observations on the structure and nature of the Flustrae. *Edinburgh New Philosophical Journal* 3:107–18, 337–42.

———. 1827b. Notice regarding the ova of the *Pontobdella muricata. Edinburgh Journal of Science* 7:160–62.

[———.] 1850. Biographical sketch of Robert Edmond Grant, M.B. *Lancet* (2):686–95.

Greenacre, Phyllis. 1963. *The quest for the father: a study of the Darwin-Butler controversy as a contribution to the understanding of the creative individual.* New York: International Universities Press.

Greene, John C. 1959. *The death of Adam: evolution and its impact on Western thought.* Iowa: Iowa State University Press.

Greene, M. T. 1982. *Geology in the nineteenth century: changing views of a changing world.* Ithaca: Cornell University Press.

Grinnell, George. 1974. The rise and fall of Darwin's first theory of transmutation. *Journal of the History of Biology* 7:259–73.

Groves, C. P. 1948–58. *The planting of Christianity in Africa.* London: Lutterworth.

Gruber, H. E. 1981. *Darwin on man: a psychological study of scientific creativity.* 2d ed. Chicago: University of Chicago Press.

Gruber, H. E. 1994. On reliving the *Wanderjahr:* the many voyages of the *Beagle. Journal of Adult Development* 1:47–69.

Gruber, H. E., and P. H. Barrett. 1974. *Darwin on man: a psychological study of scientific creativity.* 2d ed. New York: E. P. Dutton. London: Wildwood House.

Gruber, H. E., and V. Gruber. 1962. The eye of reason: Darwin's development during the *Beagle* voyage. *Isis* 53: 186–200.

Gruber, J. W. 1969. Who was the *Beagle's* naturalist? *British Journal of the History of Science* 4:266–82.

Guimond, Alice. 1967. The honorable and very reverend William Herbert, amaryllis hybridizer and amateur botanist. (Ph.D. thesis, University of Wisconsin, 1966.) Dissertation Abstracts 28:1022a.

Gully, James Manby. 1846. *The water cure in chronic disease.* London.

Gunning, Henry. 1854. *Reminiscences of the university, town, and county of Cambridge from the year 1780.* 2 vols. London.

Gunson, Niel. 1978. *Messengers of grace: evangelical missionaries in the South Seas, 1797–1860.* Oxford, Melbourne: Oxford University Press.

Günther, A. E. 1975. *A century of zoology at the British Museum through the lives of two keepers, 1815–1914.* Folkestone, Kent: Dawson & Sons.

———. 1979. J. E. Gray, Charles Darwin and the Cirripedes, 1846–1851. *Notes and Records of the Royal Society of London* 34:53–63.

Guthrie, Douglas. 1952. *History of the Royal Medical Society, 1737–1937.* Edinburgh: Edinburgh University Press.

Haber, Francis C. 1959. *The age of the world: Moses to Darwin.* Baltimore: Johns Hopkins Press.

Hall, A. Rupert. 1969. *The Cambridge Philosophical Society, 1819–1969.* Cambridge: Cambridge Philosophical Society.

Hall, Marie Boas. 1984. *All scientists now: the Royal Society in the nineteenth century.* Cambridge: Cambridge University Press.

Hanson, B. 1970. The early history of glacial theory in British geology. *Journal of Glaciology* 9:135–41.

Harvey, Joy. 1993. Types and races: the politics of colonialism and anthropology in the nineteenth century. In A. Lafuente, A. Elena, and M. L. Ortega, eds. *Mundialización de la ciencia y cultura nacional.* Madrid: Doce Calles.

Hassler, D. M. 1973. *The comedian as the letter D: Erasmus Darwin's comic materialism.* The Hague: Martinus Nijhoff.

Healey, Edna. 1986. *Wives of fame: Mary Livingstone, Jenny Marx, Emma Darwin.* London: Sidgwick & Jackson.

Henslow, John Stevens. 1823. On the deluge. *Annals of Philosophy* 2d ser. 6:344–48.

———. 1833. Review of *Physiologie vegetale . . .*, by Auguste Pyramus de Candolle (Paris, 1832). *Foreign Quarterly Review* 11:334–82.

———. 1837. Description of two new species of *Opuntia. Magazine of zoology and botany* 1:466–69.

———. 1838. Florula Keelingensis: an account of the native plants of the Keeling islands. *Annals of Natural History* 1:337–47.

Herbert, Sandra. 1971. Darwin, Malthus and selection. *Journal of the History of Biology* 4:209–17.

———. 1974. The place of man in the development of Darwin's theory of transmutation. Part 1. To July 1837. *Journal of the History of Biology* 7:217–58.

———. 1977. The place of man in the development of Darwin's theory of transmutation. Part 2. *Journal of the History of Biology* 10:155–227.

———. 1986. Darwin as a geologist. *Scientific American* 254, no. 5:116–123.

———. 1991. Charles Darwin as a prospective geological author. *British Journal for the History of Science* 24:159–92.

Herbert, William. 1837. *Amaryllidaceae.* London.

Herschel, J.F.W. 1830. *Preliminary discourse on the study of natural philosophy.* London.

Hickman, John. 1985. *The enchanted islands: the Galápagos discovered.* Oswestry, Shropshire: Anthony Nelson.

Hilliard, David. 1978. *God's gentlemen: a history of the Melanesian mission, 1849–1942.* St. Lucia: University of Queensland Press.

Hinde, Wendy. 1981. *Castlereagh.* London: Collins.

Hodge, M.J.S. 1982. Darwin and the laws of the animate part of the terrestrial system (1835–1837): on the Lyellian origins of his zoonomical explanatory program. *Studies in the History of Biology* 7:1–106.

———. 1985. Darwin as a lifelong generation theorist. In David Kohn, ed. *The*

Darwinian heritage. Princeton, N.J.: Princeton University Press in association with Nova Pacifica.

——. 1989. Generation and the origin of species (1837–1937): a historiographical suggestion. *British Journal for the History of Science* 22:267–81.

——. 1990. Darwin studies at work: a reexamination of three decisive years (1835–37). In T. H. Levere and W. R. Shea, eds. *Nature, experiment and the sciences*. Dordrecht: Kluwer Academic Publishers.

Hodge, M.J.S., and David Kohn. 1985. The immediate origins of natural selection. In David Kohn, ed. *The Darwinian heritage*. Princeton: Princeton University Press in association with Nova Pacifica.

Hole, C. 1896. *The early history of the Church Missionary Society*. London.

Holland, Henry. 1839. *Medical notes and reflections*. London.

——. 1872. *Recollections of past life*. London.

Hooker, J. D. 1844–47. *Flora Antarctica*. Part 1 of *The botany of the Antarctic voyage of H.M.S.* Discovery *Ships* Erebus *and* Terror *in the years 1839–1843*. 2 vols. London.

——. 1847a. An enumeration of the plants of the Galápagos Archipelago. *Transactions of the Linnean Society of London (Botany)* 20:163–233.

——. 1847b. On the vegetation of the Galápagos Archipelago as compared with that of some other tropical islands. *Transactions of the Linnean Society of London (Botany)* 20:235–62.

Hooykaas, R. 1963. *Natural law and divine miracle: the principle of uniformity in geology, biology and theology*. Leiden: Brill.

Horn, D. B. 1967. *A short history of the University of Edinburgh, 1556–1889*. Edinburgh: University of Edinburgh Press.

Houghton, Walter E. 1957. *The Victorian frame of mind, 1830–1870*. New Haven: Yale University Press.

Howarth, O.J.R., and E. K. Howarth. 1933.

A history of Darwin's parish, Downe, Kent. Southampton: Russell & Co.

Hubble, Douglas. 1953. The life of the shawl. *Lancet*, 26 December 1953, pp. 1351–54.

Humboldt, Alexander Friedrich von. 1814–29. *Personal narrative of travels to the equinoctial regions of the new continent during the years 1799–1804*. Translated by Helen Maria Williams. 7 vols. London. Facsimile reprint in 6 vols. New York: Ams Press Inc., 1966.

Hunter, Richard, and Ida MacAlpine. 1969. *George III and the mad business*. London: Allen Lane.

Hutchinson, H. G. 1914. *Life of Sir John Lubbock, Lord Avebury*. 2 vols. London: Macmillan.

Huxley, Leonard, ed. 1900. *The life and letters of Thomas Henry Huxley*. 2 vols. London: Macmillan.

——. 1918. *Life and letters of Sir Joseph Dalton Hooker*. 2 vols. London: John Murray.

Huxley, T. H. 1854. Review of *Vestiges of the natural history of creation*. (10th ed., 1853.) *British and Foreign Medico-Chirurgical Review* n.s. 13: 425–39.

Inkster, Ian, ed. 1985. *The steam intellect societies: essays on culture, education and industry, c. 1820–1914*. Nottingham: University of Nottingham.

Inkster, Ian, and J. B. Morrell, eds. 1983. *Metropolis and province: science in British culture, 1780–1850*. London: Hutchinson.

Irvine, William. 1955. *Apes, angels, and Victorians: the story of Darwin, Huxley, and evolution*. New York, London, Toronto: McGraw-Hill.

Jacyna, L. S. 1983. Immanence or transcendence: theories of life and organization in Britain, 1790–1835. *Isis* 74: 311–29.

James, Patricia. 1979. *Population Malthus; his life and times*. London: Routledge & Kegan Paul.

Jameson, Laurence. 1854. Biographical memoir of the late Professor Jameson. *Edinburgh New Philosophical Journal* 57:1–49.

Jameson, Robert. 1821. *Manual of Mineralogy.* Edinburgh.

Jenkins, Elizabeth. 1974. *Tennyson and Dr. Gully.* Tennyson Society Occasional Papers 3. Lincoln: Tennyson Society.

Jenyns [Blomefield], Leonard. 1840–42. *Fish.* Part 4 of Charles Darwin, ed. *The zoology of the voyage of H.M.S.* Beagle. London, 1838–43.

——. 1862. *Memoir of Professor Henslow.* Cambridge.

——. 1889. *Chapters in my life.* Reprint with additions. Bath.

Jesperson, P. H. 1948–9. Charles Darwin and Dr. Grant. *Lychnos,* pp. 159–67.

Jordanova, Ludmilla. *Lamarck.* Oxford: Oxford University Press.

Journal: see De Beer, Gavin, ed. 1959.

Journal of researches: see Darwin, Charles. 1839; and Browne and Neve eds. 1989.

Journal of researches. 2d ed.: see Darwin, Charles. 1845; and H. G. Cannon ed. 1959.

Judd, J. W. 1909. Darwin and geology. In A. C. Seward, ed. *Darwin and modern science.* Cambridge: Cambridge University Press.

Kaplan, Fred. 1983. *Thomas Carlyle: a biography.* Cambridge: Cambridge University Press.

Kass, A., and E. H. Kass. 1988. *Perfecting the world: the life and times of Dr. Thomas Hodgkin, 1798–1866.* Boston: Harcourt Brace Jovanovich.

Kaufmann, William W. 1951. *British policy and the independence of Latin America, 1804–1828.* New Haven: Yale University Press.

Keevil, J. J. 1943. Robert McCormick, R.N., the stormy petrel of naval medicine. *Journal of the Royal Naval Medical Service* 29:36–62.

——. 1949. Benjamin Bynoe, surgeon of H.M.S. *Beagle. Journal of the History of Medicine* 4:90–111.

Keevil, J. J., C. Lloyd, and J. L. S. Coulter. 1957–63. *Medicine and the Navy, 1220–1900.* 4 vols. Edinburgh and London: E. and S. Livingstone.

Keynes, Milo. 1994. Portraits of Dr. Erasmus Darwin, F.R.S., by Joseph Wright, James Rawlinson, and William Coffee. *Notes and Records of the Royal Society* 48:69–84.

Keynes, R. D., ed. 1988. *Charles Darwin's Beagle diary.* Cambridge: Cambridge University Press.

King-Hele, Desmond. 1977. *Doctor of revolution: the life and genius of Erasmus Darwin.* London: Faber & Faber.

——, ed. 1981. *The letters of Erasmus Darwin.* Cambridge: Cambridge University Press.

——. 1986. *Erasmus Darwin and the Romantic poets.* London: Macmillan.

Kirby, W., and W. Spence. 1818–26. *An introduction to entomology.* 4 vols. London.

Kohn, David. 1980. Theories to work by: rejected theories, reproduction, and Darwin's path to natural selection. *Studies in the History of Biology* 4:67–170.

——, ed. 1985. *The Darwinian heritage.* Princeton, N.J.: Princeton University Press in association with Nova Pacifica.

——. 1989. Darwin's ambiguity: the secularization of biological meaning. *British Journal for the History of Science* 22:215–40.

Kottler, Malcolm. 1978. Charles Darwin's biological species concept and theory of geographic speciation. *Annals of Science* 35:275–97.

Kotzebue, Otto von. 1830. *A new voyage round the world in the years 1823, 24, 25, and 26.* 2 vols. London.

Krause, Ernst L. 1879. *Erasmus Darwin.* Translated from the German by W. S. Dallas. With a preliminary notice by C. Darwin. London.

——. 1887. *The life of E. Darwin.* By C. Darwin. 2d ed. London.

Lamarck. 1801. *Système des animaux sans vertèbres, ou tableau général ... precédé du discours d'ouverture du cours de zoologie, donné dans le Muséum national d'Histoire Naturelle.* Paris.

——. 1802. *Recherches sur l'organisation des corps vivans ... precédé du discours d'ouverture du cours de zoologie, donné dans le Muséum national d'Histoire Naturelle.* Paris.

——. 1809. *Philosophie zoologique, ou*

exposition des considérations relatives à l'histoire naturelle des animaux. Paris.

———. 1815–22. *Histoire naturelle des animaux sans vertèbres.* 7 vols. Paris.

Landes, David. 1969. *The unbound Prometheus: technological change and industrial development in Western Europe from 1750 to the present.* Cambridge: Cambridge University Press.

Laudan, Rachel. 1987. *From mineralogy to geology: the foundations of a science, 1650–1830.* Chicago: University of Chicago Press.

Lawrence, Christopher. 1988. The Edinburgh medical school and the end of the "Old thing," 1790–1830. *History of Universities* 7:259–86.

Lenman, Bruce. 1981. *Integration, enlightenment and industrialisation, Scotland 1746–1832.* London: Edward Arnold.

Lesch, J. 1984. *Science and medicine in France: the emergence of experimental physiology 1790–1855.* Cambridge, Mass.: Harvard University Press.

Life and letters: see Darwin, Francis, ed. 1883.

Limoges, Camille. 1970. *La sélection naturelle: étude sur la première constitution d'un concept (1837–1859).* Paris: Presses Universitaires de France.

———. 1971. Darwin, Milne-Edwards et le principe de divergence. *Actes du XIIe congrès internationale d'histoire de science* 8:111–15.

Lindsay, Lionel. 1968. *Conrad Martens: the man and his art.* Rev. ed. Sydney, Australia: Angus & Robertson.

Lister, Raymond. 1981. *George Richmond: a critical biography.* London: Robin Garton.

Litchfield, H. E., ed. 1904. *Emma Darwin, wife of Charles Darwin: a century of family letters.* 2 vols. Cambridge: privately printed.

Living Cirripedia: See Darwin, Charles. 1851–54b.

Lonsdale, Henry. 1870. *A sketch of the life and writings of Robert Knox.* London.

Lovett, R. 1899. *The history of the London Missionary Society.* 2 vols. London.

Lurie, E. 1960. *Louis Agassiz: a life in science.* Chicago: University of Chicago Press.

Lyell, Charles. 1830–33. *Principles of geology, being an attempt to explain the former changes of the earth's surface, by reference to causes now in operation.* Facsimile reprint with an introduction by M.J.S. Rudwick. 3 vols. Chicago: University of Chicago Press, 1991.

———. 1836. Presidential address. *Proceedings of the Geological Society of London* 2 (1833–38):357–90.

———. 1837a. Presidential address. *Proceedings of the Geological Society of London* 2 (1833–38):479–523.

———. 1837b. *Principles of geology.* 5th ed. 4 vols. London.

———. 1838. *Elements of geology.* London.

———. 1840. On the geological evidence of the former existence of glaciers in Forfarshire. *Proceedings of the Geological Society of London* 3 (1838–43): 337–45.

Lyell, K. M., ed. 1890. *Memoir of Leonard Horner.* 2 vols. London.

———. 1881. *The life, letters, and journals of Sir Charles Lyell.* 2 vols. London.

Lynch, John. 1981. *Argentine dictator: Juan Manuel de Rosas, 1829–1852.* Oxford: Clarendon Press.

Mabberley, David. 1985. *Jupiter Botanicus: Robert Brown of the British Museum.* London: British Museum (Natural History).

MacGregor, George. 1884. *The history of Burke and Hare and of the resurrectionist times.* Glasgow and London.

MacKenzie, John. 1988. *The empire of nature: hunting, conservation and British imperialism.* Manchester: Manchester University Press.

MacLeod, Roy M. 1965. Evolutionism and Richard Owen, 1830–1868: an episode in Darwin's century. *Isis* 56: 259–80.

———. 1982. On visiting the "moving metropolis": reflections on the architecture of imperial science. *Historical Records of Australian Science* 5:1–16.

———. 1983. Whigs and savants: reflections on the reform movement in the Royal Society, 1830–48. In Ian Inkster and

Jack Morrell, eds. *Metropolis and province: science in British culture, 1780–1850.* London: Hutchinson.

MacLeod, R., and P. Collins, eds. 1981. *The parliament of science: the British Association for the Advancement of Science.* Norwood, Middlesex: Science Reviews.

Malthus, Thomas Robert. 1798. *An essay on the principle of population.* Edited with an introduction by Antony Flew. Harmondsworth: Penguin Books, 1970.

Manier, Edward. 1978. *The young Darwin and his cultural circle: A study of influences which helped shape the language and logic of the first drafts of the theory of natural selection.* Dordrecht: Reidel.

Mantell, G. A. 1940. *Journal . . . covering the years 1818–1852.* Edited by E. C. Curwen. London: Oxford University Press.

Mantoux, Paul. 1983. *The Industrial Revolution in the eighteenth century: an outline of the beginnings of the modern factory system in England.* Rev. ed. Chicago: University of Chicago Press.

Martin, Robert B. 1980. *Tennyson: the unquiet heart.* Oxford: Clarendon Press.

Martineau, Harriet. 1877. *Autobiography.* With memorials by Maria Weston Chapman. 3 vols. London.

Mathias, Peter. 1983. *The first industrial nation: an economic history of Britain, 1700–1914.* 2d ed. London: Methuen.

McCartney, P. J. 1976. Charles Lyell and G. B. Brocchi: a study in comparative historiography. *British Journal for the History of Science* 9:175–89.

McCormick, Robert. 1884. *Voyages of discovery in the Arctic and Antarctic seas, and round the world.* 2 vols. London.

McKendrick, Neil. 1961. Josiah Wedgwood and factory discipline. *Historical Journal* 4:30–55.

———. 1982. Josiah Wedgwood and the commercialization of the Potteries. In Neil McKendrick, John Brewer, and J. H. Plumb, eds. *The birth of a consumer society: the commercialization of eighteenth-century England.*

London: Europe Publications. pp. 100–145.

McKendrick, Neil, John Brewer, and J. H. Plumb. 1982. *The birth of a consumer society: the commercialization of eighteenth-century England.* London: Europa Publications.

McNeil, Maureen. 1986. The scientific muse: the poetry of Erasmus Darwin. In L. J. Jordanova, ed. *The languages of nature: critical essays on science and literature.* London: Free Association Books.

———. 1987. *Under the banner of science: Erasmus Darwin and his age.* Manchester: Manchester University Press.

Mellersh, H. E. L. 1968. *FitzRoy of the Beagle.* London: Rupert Hart-Davis.

Metcalfe, Richard. 1906. *The rise and progress of hydropathy in England and Scotland.* London: Simpkin, Marshall, Hamilton, Kent & Co.

Meteyard, Eliza. 1865–66. *The life of Josiah Wedgwood.* 2 vols. London.

Miller, David P. 1983. Between hostile camps: Sir Humphrey Davy's presidency of the Royal Society of London. *British Journal for the History of Science* 16:1–47.

Millhauser, Milton. 1959. *Just before Darwin: Robert Chambers and "Vestiges."* Middletown, Conn.: Wesleyan University Press.

Mills, Eric. 1984. A view of Edward Forbes, naturalist. *Archives of Natural History* 11:365–93.

Milne-Edwards, Henri. 1844. Considerations sur quelques principes relatifs a la classification naturelle des animaux. *Annales des Sciences* 3d ser. 1:65–99.

Monro, Alexander. 1827. *The morbid anatomy of the brain. Vol. 1. Hydrocephalus.* Edinburgh.

———. 1829. *Descriptive catalogue of the anatomical museum of the University of Edinburgh.* Edinburgh.

———. 1831. *The anatomy of the brain: with some observations on its functions.* Edinburgh.

Moore, James R. 1977. On the education of Darwin's sons: the correspondence between Charles Darwin and the Reverend G. V. Reed, 1857–1864. *Notes and Records of the Royal Society of London* 32:51–70.

———. 1985. Darwin of Down: the evolutionist as squarson-naturalist. In David Kohn, ed. *The Darwinian heritage.* Princeton, N.J.: Princeton University Press in association with Nova Pacifica.

———. 1989. Of love and death: why Darwin "gave up Christianity." In James Moore, ed. *History, humanity and evolution: essays for John C. Greene.* Cambridge: Cambridge University Press.

More, Charles. 1989. *The industrial age: economy and society in Britain, 1750–1985.* London: Longman.

More letters: see Darwin, Francis, and A. C. Seward, eds. 1903.

Morgan, Alexander. 1936–37. The Darwins as students of medicine in Edinburgh. *University of Edinburgh Journal* 8:221–26.

Morrell, J. B. 1970. The University of Edinburgh in the late eighteenth century: its scientific eminence and academic structure. *Isis* 62: 158–71.

———. 1972. Science and Scottish university reform: Edinburgh in 1826. *British Journal for the History of Science* 6: 39–56.

Morrell, J. B., and Arnold Thackray. 1981. *Gentlemen of science: early years of the British Association for the Advancement of Science.* Oxford: Oxford University Press.

Murchison, Roderick Impey. 1839. *The Silurian system.* London.

Murray, John. 1919. *John Murray III, 1808–1892: a brief memoir.* London: John Murray.

Narrative: see FitzRoy, Robert. 1839.

Natural selection: see Stauffer, R. C., ed. 1975.

Neve, Michael, ed. 1985. *Liber Amoris, or the new Pygmalion.* By William Hazlitt. London: Hogarth Press.

Nicolson, Malcolm. 1990. Alexander von Humboldt and the geography of vegetation. In Andrew Cunningham and Nicholas Jardine, eds. *Romanticism and*

the sciences. Cambridge: Cambridge University Press.

North, F. J. 1928. *Geological maps: their history and development, with special reference to Wales.* Cardiff: National Museum of Wales.

Notebooks: see Barrett, P. H., et al., eds. 1987.

Oldroyd, David. 1990. *The Highlands Controversy: constructing geological knowledge through fieldwork in nineteenth-century Britain.* Chicago: University of Chicago Press.

Oldroyd, David, and I. Langham. 1983. *The wider domain of evolutionary thought.* Dordrecht: Reidel.

Origin of species: see Darwin, Charles. 1859.

Ospovat, Dov. 1981. *The development of Darwin's theory: natural history, natural theology, and natural selection, 1838–1859.* Cambridge: Cambridge University Press.

Oswald, Philip. 1982. Charles Darwin: Shropshire years, 1810–31. *Bulletin of the Shropshire Conservation Trust* no. 53.

Outram, Dorinda. 1984. *Georges Cuvier: vocation, science and authority in post-revolutionary France.* Manchester: Manchester University Press.

———. 1986. Uncertain legislator: Georges Cuvier's laws of nature in their intellectual context. *Journal of the History of Biology* 19:323–68.

Owen, Richard. 1837. *Observations on certain parts of the animal oeconomy.* By John Hunter. With notes by Richard Owen. London.

———. 1838–40. *Fossil mammalia.* Part 1 of Charles Darwin, ed. *The zoology of the voyage of H.M.S. Beagle.* London, 1838–43.

Owen, R. S., ed. 1894. *The life of Richard Owen.* 2 vols. London.

Owens, J.M.R. 1974. *Prophets in the wilderness: the Wesleyan mission to New Zealand, 1819–1827.* Oxford: Oxford University Press.

Pagden, Anthony. 1993. *European encounters with the New World: from Renaissance to Romanticism.* New Haven: Yale University Press.

Paradis, James G. 1978. *T.H. Huxley: man's place in nature.* Lincoln, Nebraska: University of Nebraska Press.

———. 1981. Darwin and landscape. In James Paradis and Thomas Postlewait, eds. *Victorian science and Victorian values: literary perspectives.* New York: New York Academy of Sciences.

Pearson, Karl, ed. 1914–30. *The life, letters, and labours of Francis Galton.* 4 vols. Cambridge: Cambridge University Press.

Peile, John. 1900. *Christ's College.* University of Cambridge College Histories. London: F. Robinson.

Perkin, Harold. 1969. *The origins of modern English society, 1780–1880!.* London: Routledge & Kegan Paul.

Phillipson, Nicholas. 1981. The Scottish enlightenment. In Roy Porter and Mikulas Teich, eds. *The enlightenment in national context.* Cambridge: Cambridge University Press.

Porter, Duncan. 1985. The *Beagle* collector and his collections. In David Kohn, ed. *The Darwinian heritage.* Princeton, N.J.: Princeton University Press in association with Nova Pacifica.

Porter, Roy S. 1976. Charles Lyell and the principles of the history of geology. *British Journal for the History of Science* 9:91–103.

———. 1989. Erasmus Darwin: doctor of evolution? In James Moore, ed. *History, humanity and evolution: essays for John C. Greene.* Cambridge: Cambridge University Press.

———, ed. 1990. *The medical history of waters and spas.* (Medical History. Supplement 10.) London: Wellcome Institute for the History of Medicine.

Portlock, 1858. Presidential address. *Proceedings of the Geological Society of London* 14:xxiv–clxiii.

Posner, E. 1975. William Withering versus the Darwins. *History of Medicine* 6: 51–57.

Prete, F. R. 1990. The conundrum of the honey bees: one impediment to the publication of Darwin's theory. *Journal of the History of Biology* 23:271–90.

Price, Robin. 1981. Hydrotherapy in England, 1840–70. *Medical History* 25:269–80.

Prichard, James Cowles. 1836. *Researches into the physical history of mankind.* 3d ed. 5 vols. London.

Prochaska, F. K. 1988. *The voluntary impulse: philanthropy in modern Britain.* London: Faber & Faber.

Rachootin, S. P. 1985. Owen and Darwin reading a fossil: *Macrauchenia* in a bony light. In David Kohn, ed. *The Darwinian heritage.* Princeton: Princeton University Press in association with Nova Pacifica.

Rae, Isobel F. 1964. *Knox, the anatomist.* Edinburgh: Oliver & Boyd.

Rainger, Ronald. 1980. Philanthropy and science in the 1830s: the British and Foreign Aborigines' Protection Society. *Man* 15:702–17.

Ramsden, Eric. 1936. *Marsden and the missions: prelude to Waitangi.* Sydney: Angus & Robertson.

Rappaport, Rhoda. 1978. Geology and orthodoxy: the case of Noah's flood in eighteenth-century thought. *British Journal for the History of Science* 11: 1–18.

Rehbock, Philip F. 1983. *The philosophical naturalists: themes in early nineteenth century British biology.* Madison: University of Wisconsin Press.

Reilly, Robin. 1992. *Josiah Wedgwood.* London: Macmillan.

Rhodes, F.H.T. 1991. Darwin's search for a theory of the earth: symmetry, simplicity and speculation. *British Journal of the History of Science* 24:193–229.

Richards, Evelleen. 1987. A question of property rights: Richard Owen's evolutionism reassessed. *British Journal for the History of Science* 20:129–72.

———. 1989. The "moral anatomy" of Robert Knox: the interplay between biological and social thought in Victorian scientific naturalism. *Journal of the History of Biology* 22:373–436.

Richardson, E. W. 1916. *A veteran naturalist: being the life and work of W. B. Tegetmeier.* London: Witherby.

Richardson, Ruth. 1981. *Death, dissection and the destitute.* London: Routledge & Kegan Paul.

Ritchie, James. 1956. A double centenary: two notable naturalists, Robert Jameson and Edward Forbes. *Proceedings of the Royal Society of Edinburgh* Section B (Biology) 46:29–58.

Ritvo, Harriet. 1987. *The animal estate: the English and other creatures in the Victorian age.* Cambridge, Mass.: Harvard University Press.

———. 1990. New presbyter or old priest? Reconsidering zoological taxonomy in Britain, 1750–1840. *History of Human Sciences* 3:259–76.

Romilly, Joseph. 1967. *Romilly's Cambridge diary, 1832–42.* Selected passages . . . chosen, introduced and annotated by J.P.T. Bury. Cambridge: Cambridge University Press.

Rosenberg, J. D. 1989. Mr. Darwin collects himself. In L. S. Lockridge, J. Maynard, and D. D. Stone, eds. *Nineteenth-century lives: essays presented to Jerome Hamilton Buckley.* Cambridge: Cambridge University Press.

Rosner, Lisa. 1991. *Medical education in the age of improvement: Edinburgh students and apprentices, 1760–1826.* Edinburgh: Edinburgh University Press.

Ross, Andrew. 1986. *John Philip (1775–1851): missions, race and politics in South Africa.* Aberdeen: Aberdeen University Press.

Rothblatt, Sheldon. 1981. *Revolution of the dons.* Cambridge: Cambridge University Press.

Rudwick, M.J.S. 1970. The strategy of Lyell's *Principles of geology. Isis* 61:4–33.

———. 1974. Darwin and Glen Roy: a "great failure" in scientific method? *Studies in the History and Philosophy of Science* 5:97–185.

———. 1976a. The emergence of a visual language for geological science, 1760–1840. *History of Science* 14:149–95.

———. 1976b. *The meaning of fossils: episodes in the history of palaeontology.* 2d ed. New York: Science History Publications.

———. 1978. Lyell's dream of a statistical palaentology. *Palaeontology* 21:22–44.

———. 1982. Charles Darwin in London: the integration of public and private science. *Isis* 73:186–206.

———. 1985. *The great Devonian controversy: the shaping of scientific knowledge by gentlemanly specialists.* Chicago: University of Chicago Press.

Rupke, Nicolaas A. 1983. *The great chain of history: William Buckland and the English school of geology, 1814–1849.* Oxford: Clarendon Press.

———. 1993. Richard Owen's vertebrate archetype. *Isis* 84:231–51.

———. 1994. *Richard Owen, Victorian naturalist.* New Haven: Yale University Press.

Ruse, Michael. 1975a. Darwin's debt to philosophy: an examination of the influence of the philosophical ideas of J. F. W. Herschel and W. Whewell on the development of Charles Darwin's theory of evolution. *Studies in the History and Philosophy of Science.* 6:159–81.

———. 1975b. Charles Darwin and artificial selection. *Journal of the History of Ideas* 36:339–50.

———. 1979. *The Darwinian revolution: science red in tooth and claw.* Chicago: Chicago University Press.

Russell, E. S. 1916. *Form and function: a contribution to the history of animal morphology.* London: John Murray.

Russell, N. 1986. *Like engend'ring like: heredity and animal breeding in early modern England.* Cambridge: Cambridge University Press.

Russell-Gebbett, J. 1977. *Henslow of Hitcham: botanist, educationalist and clergyman.* Lavenham, Suffolk: Terence Dalton.

Rutherford, H. W. 1908. *Catalogue of the library of Charles Darwin now in the Botany School, Cambridge.* Cambridge: Cambridge University Press.

Scherren, Henry. 1905. *The Zoological Society of London: a sketch of its foundation and development.* London: Cassell.

Schiebinger, Londa. 1991. The private life of plants: sexual politics in Carl Linnaeus and Erasmus Darwin. In Marina Benjamin, ed. *Science and sensibility: gender and scientific enquiry, 1780–1945.* Oxford: Basil Blackwell.

Schofield, R. E. 1963. *The Lunar Society*

of Birmingham. Oxford: Oxford University Press.

Schwartz, Joel. 1990. Darwin, Wallace, and Huxley, and *Vestiges of the natural history of creation. Journal of the History of Biology* 23:127–53.

Schweber, S. S. 1977. The origin of the *Origin* revisited. *Journal of the History of Biology* 10:229–316.

———. 1980. Darwin and the political economists: divergence of character. *Journal of the History of Biology* 13: 195–289.

———. 1981. Scientists as intellectuals: the early Victorians. In James Paradis and Thomas Postlewait, eds. *Victorian science and Victorian values: literary perspectives.* New York: New York Academy of Sciences.

———. 1985. The wider British context in Darwin's theorizing. In David Kohn, ed. *The Darwinian heritage.* Princeton: Princeton University Press in association with Nova Pacifica.

Scull, Andrew, ed. 1991. *The asylum as utopia: W. A. F. Browne and the mid-nineteenth century consolidation of psychiatry.* Reprint edition of W.A.F. Browne, *What asylums were, are, and ought to be* (1837). London: Tavistock & Routledge.

Secord, James A. 1981. Nature's fancy: Charles Darwin and the breeding of pigeons. *Isis* 72:163–86.

———. 1986. *Controversy in Victorian geology: the Cambrian–Silurian dispute.* Princeton, N.J.: Princeton University Press.

———. 1989. Behind the veil: Robert Chambers and *Vestiges.* In James Moore, ed. *History, humanity and evolution: essays for John C. Greene.* Cambridge: Cambridge University Press.

———. 1991a. The discovery of a vocation: Darwin's early geology. *British Journal for the History of Science* 24:133–57.

———. 1991b. Edinburgh Lamarckians: Robert Jameson and Robert E. Grant. *Journal of the History of Biology* 24: 1–18.

Sedgwick, Adam. 1831. Presidential address. *Proceedings of the Geological Society of London* 1 (1826–33):281–316.

[———.] 1845. Review of *Vestiges of the natural history of creation. Edinburgh Review* 165:1–85.

Seward, A. C., ed. 1909. *Darwin and Modern Science: essays in commemoration of the centenary.* Cambridge: Cambridge University Press.

Seward, Anna. 1804. *Memoirs of the life of Dr. Darwin, chiefly during his residence at Lichfield.* London.

Shapin, Steven. 1975. Phrenological knowledge and the social structure of early nineteenth century Edinburgh. *Annals of Science* 32:245–56.

———. 1979. The politics of observation: cerebral anatomy and social interests in the Edinburgh phrenology disputes. In Roy Wallis, ed. *On the margins of science: the social reconstruction of rejected knowledge.* Keele: University of Keele.

Sheets-Pyenson, Susan. 1988. *Cathedrals of science: the development of colonial natural history museums during the late nineteenth century.* Kingston and Montreal: McGill–Queen's University Press.

Shelley, Mary Wollstonecraft. 1818. *Frankenstein: or the modern Prometheus.* London.

Shepperson, George. 1961. The intellectual background of Charles Darwin's student years at Edinburgh. In Michael Banton, ed. *Darwinism and society: a centenary symposium.* London: Tavistock Publications; Chicago: Quadrangle Books.

Shipley, A. E. 1909. Charles Darwin at the Universities: Edinburgh-Cambridge. In Darwin centenary number. *Christ's College Magazine* 23 (1908–9): 187–244.

Sloan, Phillip. 1985. Darwin's invertebrate programme, 1826–1836: preconditions for transformism. In David Kohn, ed. *The Darwinian heritage.* Princeton: Princeton University Press in association with Nova Pacifica.

———. 1986. Darwin, vital matter, and the transformism of species. *Journal of the History of Biology.* 19:369–445.

———, ed. 1992. *The Hunterian lectures in*

comparative anatomy, May–June 1837. By Richard Owen. Chicago: University of Chicago Press.

Smith, Bernard. 1985. *European vision and the South Pacific.* 2d ed. London: Yale University Press.

Smith, C. H. 1839–40. *The natural history of dogs.* 2 vols. London.

Smith, Sydney. 1960. The origin of the *Origin* as discerned from Charles Darwin's notebooks and his annotations in the books he read between 1837 and 1842. *Advancement of Science* 16:391–401.

South America: See Darwin, Charles. 1846.

Speakman, Colin. 1982. *Adam Sedgwick, geologist and dalesman, 1785–1873. A biography in twelve themes.* London and Cambridge: Broad Oak Press.

Stanbury, David, ed. 1977. *A narrative of the voyage of the* Beagle . . . *by Robert FitzRoy, R.N., together with . . . additional material from the diary and letters of Charles Darwin.* London: Folio Society.

Stauffer, R. C., ed. 1975. *Charles Darwin's* Natural Selection, *being the second part of his big species book written from 1856 to 1858.* Cambridge: Cambridge University Press.

Steadman, David W., and Steven Zousmer. 1988. *Galápagos: discovery on Darwin's islands.* Shrewsbury: Airlife Publishing; Washington, D.C.: Smithsonian Institution Press.

Stearn, William T. 1981. *The Natural History Museum at South Kensington. A history of the British Museum (Natural History) 1753–1980.* London: Heinemann in association with the British Museum (Natural History).

Stecher, R. M. 1961. The Darwin-Innes letters: the correspondence of an evolutionist with his vicar, 1848–1884. *Annals of Science* 17:201–58.

Steenstrup, J.J.S. 1845. *On the alternation of generations.* Translated by George Busk. London.

Stenton, Michael, ed. 1976. *Who's who of British members of Parliament.* Vol. 1, 1832–85. Hassocks, Sussex: Harvester Press.

Stepan, Nancy. 1982. *The idea of race in*

science: Great Britain, 1800–1960. London: Macmillan in association with St. Anthony's College, Oxford.

——. 1993. Tropical nature as a way of writing. In A. Lafuente, A. Elena, and M. L. Ortega, eds. *Mundialización de la ciencia y cultura nacional.* Madrid: Doce Calles.

Stephens, J. F. 1827–46. *Illustrations of British entomology.* 12 vols. London.

Stock, Eugene. 1899. *The history of the Church Missionary Society: its environment, its men and its work.* 2 vols. London.

Stocking, George, ed. 1973. *Researches into the physical history of man.* By James Cowles Prichard. Edited with an introductory essay. Chicago: University of Chicago Press.

——. 1987. *Victorian anthropology.* London and New York: Macmillan.

Stoddart, D. R. 1976. Darwin, Lyell, and the geological significance of coral reefs. *British Journal for the History of Science* 11:199–218.

Sulivan, H. N., ed. 1896. *Life and letters of the late Admiral Sir Bartholomew Sulivan.* London.

Sulloway, Frank. 1979. Geographical isolation in Darwin's thinking: the vicissitudes of a crucial idea. *Studies in the History of Biology* 3:23–65.

——. 1982a. Darwin and his finches: the evolution of a legend. *Journal of the History of Biology* 15:1–53.

——. 1982b. Darwin's conversion: the *Beagle* voyage and its aftermath. *Journal of the History of Biology* 15:325–96.

——. 1982c. The *Beagle* collections of Darwin's finches (Geospizinae). *Bulletin of the British Museum (Natural History) Zoology Series* 43:49–94.

——. 1983. Further remarks on Darwin's spelling habits and the dating of *Beagle* voyage manuscripts. *Journal of the History of Biology* 16:361–90.

Summerson, John. 1978. *Georgian London.* 2d ed. Harmondsworth: Peregrine Books.

Telford, Thomas. 1838. *Life.* Edited by John Rickman. 2 vols. London.

Temkin, Owsei. 1963. Basic science, medicine, and the Romantic era. *Bul-*

letin of the History of Medicine 37: 97–129.

Thackray, A. 1974. Natural knowledge in cultural context: the Manchester model. *American Historical Review* 79: 672–709.

Thomas, Keith. 1983. *Man and the natural world: changing attitudes in England, 1500–1800.* London: Allen Lane.

Thomson, Keith Stewart. 1975. H.M.S. *Beagle, 1820–1870. American Scientist* 63:664–72.

Thomson, John Vaughan. 1828–34. *Zoological researches and illustrations.* Facsimile edition with an introduction by Alwyne Wheeler. Sherborn Fund Facsimile 2. London: Society for the Bibliography of Natural History.

Thompson, F.M.L. 1963. *English landed society in the nineteenth century.* London: Routledge & Kegan Paul.

Traub, H. P. 1970. *William Herbert's "Amaryllidaceae" and related works.* Lehre: Cramer.

Trinder, B. 1981. *The Industrial revolution in Shropshire.* 2d ed. London: Phillimore.

Turner, E. S. 1967. *Taking the cure.* London: Michael Joseph.

Veit, Walter, ed. 1972. *Captain James Cook: image and impact. South Sea discoveries and the world of letters.* Melbourne: Hawthorne.

Visram, Rozina. 1986. *Ayahs, lascars and princes: the story of Indians in Britain, 1700–1947.* London: Pluto Press.

Volcanic islands: see Darwin, Charles. 1844.

Wallace, Alfred Russel. 1855. On the law which has regulated the introduction of new species. *Annals and Magazine of Natural History* 2d ser. 16:184–96.

Walters, S. M. 1981. *The shaping of Cambridge botany.* Cambridge: Cambridge University Press.

Walvin, James. 1982. The propaganda of anti-slavery. In James Walvin, ed. *Slavery and British society, 1776–1846.* London: Macmillan.

——. 1987. Symbols of moral superiority: slavery, sport and the changing order. In J. A. Mangan and James Walvin, eds. *Manliness and morality: middle-*

class masculinity in Britain and America, 1800–1940. New York: St. Martin's Press.

Ward, Thomas Humphry. 1926. *History of the Athenaeum, 1824–1925.* London: Athenaeum Club.

Warrack, J. H. 1976. *Carl Maria von Weber.* 2d ed. Cambridge: Cambridge University Press.

Waterhouse, George Robert. 1838–39. *Mammalia.* Part 2 of Charles Darwin, ed. *The zoology of the voyage of H.M.S. Beagle.* London, 1838–43.

Webster, C. K., ed. 1938. *Britain and the independence of Latin America. 1812–30: select documents.* 2 vols. London: Oxford University Press for the Ibero-American Institute.

Wedgwood, Barbara, and Hensleigh Wedgwood. 1980. *The Wedgwood circle, 1730–1897: four generations of a family and their friends.* London: Studio Vista.

Whewell, William. 1837. *History of the inductive sciences, from the earliest to the present times.* 3 vols. London.

——. 1840. *The philosophy of the inductive sciences, founded upon their history.* 2 vols. London.

——. 1845a. *Indications of the creator.* London.

——. 1845b. *Of a liberal education in general, and with particular reference to the leading studies of the University of Cambridge.* London.

Wilson, James. 1980. *A missionary voyage to the Southern Pacific Ocean, 1776–1798.* Introduced by Irmgard Moschner. New York, Washington, London: Frederick A. Praeger.

Wilson, Leonard G., ed. 1970. *Sir Charles Lyell's scientific journals of the species question.* New Haven: Yale University Press.

——. 1972. *Charles Lyell. The years to 1841: the revolution in geology.* New Haven: Yale University Press.

Winsor, M. P. 1969a. *Starfish, jellyfish and the order of life: issues in nineteenth-century science.* New Haven: Yale University Press.

——. 1969b. Barnacle larvae in the nineteenth century: a case-study in taxonomic theory. *Journal of the History of Medicine and Allied Sciences* 24: 294–309.

Winstanley, D. A. 1955. *Early Victorian Cambridge*. Reprint edition. Cambridge: Cambridge University Press.

Wolff, R. L. 1977. *Gains and losses: novels of faith and doubt in Victorian England*. New York: Garland.

Wollaston, Thomas Vernon. 1856. *On the variation of species, with special reference to the Insecta*. London.

Woodruff, A. W. 1965. Darwin's health in relation to his voyage to South America. *British Medical Journal* pt 1:745–50.

Woodward, H. B. 1907. *The history of the Geological Society of London*. London: Geological Society.

Wright-St. Clair, R. E. 1964. *Doctors Monro. A medical saga*. London: Wellcome Historical Medical Library.

Yeo, Richard. 1979. William Whewell, natural theology and the philosophy of science in mid-nineteenth century Britain. *Annals of Science* 36:493–516.

———. 1989. Science and intellectual authority in mid-nineteenth-century Britain: Robert Chambers and *Vestiges*. In Patrick Brantlinger, ed. *Energy and entropy: science and culture in Victorian Britain*. Bloomington, Ind.: Indiana University Press.

Young, Robert M. 1985. *Darwin's metaphor: nature's place in Victorian culture*. Cambridge: Cambridge University Press.

Zoology: see Darwin, Charles, ed. 1838–43.

Index

Abercrombie, John, 366, 384
Abernethy, John, 54, 85
Aborigines, 314, 421
Académie des Sciences (Paris), 53
Adventure (ship), 146, 147
Agassiz, Louis, 431–3, 440, 441, 450, 476, 480–2, 484
Ainsworth, William, 74, 78, 80
Airy, George Biddle, 127, 535
Albert, Prince, 448, 508
Alison, Robert Edward, 276
Alison, William Pulteney, 61, 62
Amici, Giovanni, 125
anatomy: comparative, 53, 76; of plants, 124–5; traditional courses in, 55–9
Andes, 227, 232, 270, 271, 274, 277, 280, 289, 291–3, 308, 317, 318, 338, 418, 431
Anglican Church, *see* Church of England
animals: African, 328; Australian, 315; *Beagle* specimens of, 226, 230, 231, 349; behavior of, 383; domestic, 409–10; geographical distribution of, 353, 517; of Galápagos, 297, 299–305; *see also* birds; fossils; zoology
Anning, Mary, 102
anthropology, 265–6, 421–2
Apostles (Cambridge society), 93, 118
Argentina, 217–19, 254–8; *see also* Bahía Blanca; Buenos Aires
Arkwright, Richard, 5, 9
Ash, Edward John, 94

Athenaeum Club, 366, 384, 395, 405, 408, 445, 473
Audubon, John James, 69, 70, 75
Austen, Jane, 3, 5, 47, 167
Australia, 181, 311, 314–16, 371, 419, 486

Babbage, Charles, 127–8, 150, 329, 354, 385, 390, 404, 420, 428
Babington, Charles Cardale, 121, 124, 132, 134
Bahia, 196–9, 211, 213, 245
Bahía Blanca (Argentina), 218–19, 223, 227, 254, 256–8, 260, 266, 267
Banks, Joseph, 42, 181, 241, 307, 308
Bantu tribesmen, 330
Barclay, John, 51, 54, 56–8, 75, 76, 85
barnacles, 471–2, 475–88, 496, 497, 504, 509, 510, 512–14, 516, 527, 530, 536, 540
Barnes, Francis, 119
Beagle expedition, 96, 114, 130, 132, 141, 142, 149, 167–340, 351, 361, 365, 390, 397, 413, 438, 475, 482, 486, 511, 514, 543; in Argentina, 217–19, 223, 232–3, 254–8, 260–4; artist of, 199, 265, 326–7; in Australia, 314–16; in Brazil, 196–201, 254; Beaufort's plans for, 151; in Cape Verde Islands, 183–6, 189–91; CD invited to join, 145–6, 149–61; in Chile, 227, 275–95;